Ozawa Ichirō and Japanese Politics

Ozawa Ichirō was the axis on which Japanese politics turned for more than two decades. He helped to reshape the electoral system, political funding rules, the evolution of the party system, the nature of executive government, the roles and powers of bureaucrats, and the conduct of parliamentary and policymaking processes. Admired and reviled in almost equal measure, Ozawa has been the most debated and yet least understood politician in Japan, with little agreement to be found amongst the many who have debated his patent political assets and palpable political flaws.

This book examines the political goals, behaviour, methods and practices of Ozawa Ichirō, and in doing so, provides fascinating insights into the inner workings of Japanese politics. It explores Ozawa's paradoxical and conflicting contributions in terms of two contrasting models of 'old' and 'new' politics. Indeed, therein lies the problem of understanding the 'real' Ozawa: he remains a practitioner of old politics despite his rhetorical agenda of change to bring about new politics. In seeking to unravel the Ozawa enigma, Aurelia George Mulgan reveals his primary motivations, to establish whether he sought power primarily to enact reforms, or, whether his reform goals simply disguised power-seeking objectives. This volume seeks to illuminate Ozawa's true character as a politician, and untangle the complex elements of old and new politics that he represents.

Through an in-depth study of Ozawa and his political activities, this book shows how the Japanese political system works at the micro level of individual politicians, political relationships and systems. As such it will be of huge interest to students and scholars of Japanese politics, Asian politics and political systems.

Aurelia George Mulgan is Professor in the School of Humanities and Social Sciences at the University of New South Wales, Australia

Nissan Institute/Routledge Japanese Studies
Series Editors:
Roger Goodman, Nissan Professor of Modern Japanese Studies, University of Oxford, Fellow, St Antony's College
J.A.A. Stockwin, formerly Nissan Professor of Modern Japanese Studies and former Director of the Nissan Institute of Japanese Studies, University of Oxford, Emeritus Fellow, St Antony's College

Other titles in the series:

The Myth of Japanese Uniqueness
Peter Dale

The Emperor's Adviser
Saionji Kinmochi and pre-war Japanese politics
Lesley Connors

A History of Japanese Economic Thought
Tessa Morris-Suzuki

The Establishment of the Japanese Constitutional System
Junji Banno, translated by J.A.A. Stockwin

Industrial Relations in Japan
The peripheral workforce
Norma Chalmers

Banking Policy in Japan
American efforts at reform during the Occupation
William M. Tsutsui

Educational Reform in Japan
Leonard Schoppa

How the Japanese Learn to Work
Second edition
Ronald P. Dore and Mari Sako

Japanese Economic Development
Theory and practice
Second edition
Penelope Francks

Japan and Protection
The growth of protectionist sentiment and the Japanese response
Syed Javed Maswood

The Soil, by Nagatsuka Takashi
A portrait of rural life in Meiji Japan
Translated and with an introduction by Ann Waswo

Biotechnology in Japan
Malcolm Brock

Britain's Educational Reform
A comparison with Japan
Michael Howarth

Language and the Modern State
The reform of written Japanese
Nanette Twine

Industrial Harmony in Modern Japan
The intervention of a tradition
W. Dean Kinzley

Japanese Science Fiction
A view of a changing society
Robert Matthew

The Japanese Numbers Game
The use and understanding of numbers in modern Japan
Thomas Crump

Ideology and Practice in Modern Japan
Edited by Roger Goodman and Kirsten Refsing

Technology and Industrial Development in Pre-war Japan
Mitsubishi Nagasaki Shipyard, 1884–1934
Yukiko Fukasaku

Japan's Early Parliaments, 1890–1905
Structure, issues and trends
Andrew Fraser, R.H.P. Mason and Philip Mitchell

Japan's Foreign Aid Challenge
Policy reform and aid leadership
Alan Rix

Emperor Hirohito and Shôwa Japan
A political biography
Stephen S. Large

Japan: Beyond the End of History
David Williams

Ceremony and Ritual in Japan
Religious practices in an industrialized society
Edited by Jan van Bremen and D.P. Martinez

The Fantastic in Modern Japanese Literature
The subversion of modernity
Susan J. Napier

Militarization and Demilitarization in Contemporary Japan
Glenn D. Hook

Growing a Japanese Science City
Communication in scientific research
James W. Dearing

Architecture and Authority in Japan
William H. Coaldrake

Women's Gidayû and the Japanese Theatre Tradition
A. Kimi Coaldrake

Democracy in Post-war Japan
Maruyama Masao and the search for autonomy
Rikki Kersten

Treacherous Women of Imperial Japan
Patriarchal fictions, patricidal fantasies
Hélène Bowen Raddeker

Japanese-German Business Relations
Co-operation and rivalry in the inter-war period
Akira Kudô

Japan, Race and Equality
The Racial Equality Proposal of 1919
Naoko Shimazu

Japan, Internationalism and the UN
Ronald Dore

Life in a Japanese Women's College
Learning to be ladylike
Brian J. McVeigh

On The Margins of Japanese Society
Volunteers and the welfare of the urban underclass
Carolyn S. Stevens

The Dynamics of Japan's Relations with Africa
South Africa, Tanzania and Nigeria
Kweku Ampiah

The Right to Life in Japan
Noel Williams

The Nature of the Japanese State
Rationality and rituality
Brian J. McVeigh

Society and the State in Inter-war Japan
Edited by Elise K. Tipton

Japanese-Soviet/Russian Relations since 1945
A difficult peace
Kimie Hara

Interpreting History in Sino-Japanese Relations
A case study in political decision making
Caroline Rose

Endō Shūsaku
A literature of reconciliation
Mark B. Williams

Green Politics in Japan
Lam Peng-Er

The Japanese High School
Silence and resistance
Shoko Yoneyama

Engineers in Japan and Britain
Education, training and employment
Kevin McCormick

The Politics of Agriculture in Japan
Aurelia George Mulgan

Opposition Politics in Japan
Strategies under a one-party dominant regime
Stephen Johnson

The Changing Face of Japanese Retail
Working in a chain store
Louella Matsunaga

Japan and East Asian Regionalism
Edited by S Javed Maswood

Globalizing Japan
Ethnography of the Japanese presence in America, Asia and Europe
Edited by Harumi Befu and Sylvie Guichard-Anguis

Japan at Play
The ludic and logic of power
Edited by Joy Hendry and Massimo Raveri

The Making of Urban Japan
Cities and planning from Edo to the twenty-first century
André Sorensen

Public Policy and Economic Competition in Japan
Change and continuity in antimonopoly policy, 1973–1995
Michael L. Beeman

Men and Masculinities in Contemporary Japan
Dislocating the Salaryman Doxa
Edited by James E. Roberson and Nobue Suzuki

The Voluntary and Non-Profit Sector in Japan
The challenge of change
Edited by Stephen P. Osborne

Japan's Security Relations with China
From balancing to bandwagoning
Reinhard Drifte

Understanding Japanese Society
Third edition
Joy Hendry

Japanese Electoral Politics
Creating a new party system
Edited by Steven R. Reed

The Japanese-Soviet Neutrality Pact
A diplomatic history, 1941–1945
Boris Slavinsky translated by Geoffrey Jukes

Academic Nationalism in China and Japan
Framed by concepts of nature, culture and the universal
Margaret Sleeboom

The Race to Commercialize Biotechnology
Molecules, markets and the state in the United States and Japan
Steve W Collins

Institutions, Incentives and Electoral Participation in Japan
Cross-level and cross-national perspectives
Yusaku Horiuchi

Japan's Interventionist State
The role of the MAFF
Aurelia George Mulgan

Japan's Sea Lane Security, 1940–2004
'A matter of life and death'?
Euan Graham

The Changing Japanese Political System
The Liberal Democratic Party and the Ministry of Finance
Harumi Hori

Japan's Agricultural Policy Regime
Aurelia George Mulgan

Cold War Frontiers in the Asia-Pacific
Divided territories in the San Francisco System
Kimie Hara

Living Cities in Japan
Citizens' movements, Machizukuri and local environments
Andre Sorensen and Carolin Funck

Resolving the Russo-Japanese Territorial Dispute
Hokkaido–Sakhalin relations
Brad Williams

Modern Japan
A social and political history
Second edition
Elise K Tipton

The Transformation of the Japanese Left
From old socialists to new democrats
Sarah Hyde

Social Class in Contemporary Japan
Edited by Hiroshi Ishida and David H. Slater

The US–Japan Alliance
Balancing soft and hard power in East Asia
Edited by David Arase and Tsuneo Akaha

Party Politics and Decentralization in Japan and France
When the Opposition governs
Koichi Nakano

The Buraku Issue and Modern Japan
The career of Matsumoto Jiichiro
Ian Neary

Labor Migration from China to Japan
International students, transnational migrants
Gracia Liu-Farrer

Policy Entrepreneurship and Elections in Japan
A political biography of Ozawa Ichirō
Takashi Oka

Japan's Postwar
Edited by Michael Lucken, Anne Bayard-Sakai and Emmanuel Lozerand
Translated by J. A. A. Stockwin

An Emerging Non-Regular Labour Force in Japan
The dignity of dispatched workers
Huiyan Fu

A Sociology of Japanese Youth
From returnees to NEETs
Edited by Roger Goodman, Yuki Imoto and Tuukka Toivonen

Natural Disaster and Nuclear Crisis in Japan
Response and recovery after Japan's 3/11
Edited by Jeff Kingston

Urban Spaces in Japan
Edited by Christoph Brumann and Evelyn Schulz

Understanding Japanese Society
Fourth edition
Joy Hendry

Japan's Emerging Youth Policy
Getting young adults back to work
Tuukka Toivonen

The Organisational Dynamics of University Reform in Japan
International inside out
Jeremy Breaden

Schoolgirls, Money and Rebellion in Japan
Sharon Kinsella

Social Inequality in Japan
Sawako Shirahase

The Great Transformation of Japanese Capitalism
Edited by Sébastien Lechevalier
Translated by J. A. A. Stockwin

Neighborhood Associations and Local Governance in Japan
Robert Pekkanen, Yutaka Tsujinaka and Hidehiro Yamamoto
Translated by Leslie Tkach-Kawasaki

Japan's International Fisheries Policy
Law, diplomacy and policy governing resource security
Roger Smith

Japan's Modern History
A new political narrative
Junji Banno
Translated by J. A. A. Stockwin

Configurations of Family in Contemporary Japan
Edited by Tomoko Aoyama, Laura Dales and Romit Dasgupta

Ozawa Ichirō and Japanese Politics
Old versus new
Aurelia George Mulgan

Ozawa Ichirō and Japanese Politics
Old versus new

Aurelia George Mulgan

LONDON AND NEW YORK

First published 2015
by Routledge
2 Park Square, Milton Park, Abingdon, Oxon OX14 4RN

and by Routledge
711 Third Avenue, New York, NY 10017

Routledge is an imprint of the Taylor & Francis Group, an informa business

© 2015 Aurelia George Mulgan

The right of Aurelia George Mulgan to be identified as author of this work has been asserted by her in accordance with sections 77 and 78 of the Copyright, Designs and Patents Act 1988.

All rights reserved. No part of this book may be reprinted or reproduced or utilised in any form or by any electronic, mechanical, or other means, now known or hereafter invented, including photocopying and recording, or in any information storage or retrieval system, without permission in writing from the publishers.

Trademark notice: Product or corporate names may be trademarks or registered trademarks, and are used only for identification and explanation without intent to infringe.

British Library Cataloguing in Publication Data
A catalogue record for this book is available from the British Library

Library of Congress Cataloging in Publication Data
Mulgan, Aurelia George.
Ozawa Ichiro and Japanese politics : old versus new / Aurelia George Mulgan.
    pages cm. – (The Nissan Institute/Routledge Japanese studies)
    Includes bibliographical references and index.
1. Ozawa, Ichiro, 1942- 2. Japan–Politics and government–1989- 3. Politicians–Japan–Biography. I. Title.
    DS890.O93M85 2014
    952.04'8092–dc23
                    2014012397

ISBN: 978-1-138-77834-4 (hbk)
ISBN: 978-1-315-77205-9 (ebk)

Typeset in Baskerville
by Taylor & Francis Books

Contents

List of tables		xii
General editors' preface		xiii
Acknowledgements		xv
1	Introduction: the politician Ozawa Ichirō, and his political significance	1
2	New politics and policies	12
3	Old politics	58
4	Old policies	129
5	The Ozawa dictatorship	174
6	*Datsu* Ozawa	220
7	Ozawa *redux*?	270
8	Conclusion: Ozawa, visionary or villain?	286
	Bibliography	295
	Index	320

Table

1.1 The Ozawa models of old and new politics 5

General editors' preface

Few politicians have had a greater impact upon the politics and political system of Japan since the early 1990s than Ozawa Ichirō. Yet he never became prime minister, and rarely held significant posts in the cabinet. Even so, he was the central figure in the construction of two governments that challenged the long hegemony of the Liberal Democratic Party (LDP), otherwise in power continuously from its formation in 1955. The first was the eight-party coalition that held the reins of government for about nine months in 1993–94, under Prime Minister Hosokawa Morihiro, initiating major electoral system reform. The second was the government based on the Democratic Party of Japan (DPJ), which won a clear majority in general elections of August 2009 and remained in power until it was defeated in the general elections of December 2012. The 2009 elections are particularly significant in that for the first time in Japanese post-war political history, a single opposition party won a convincing victory over the LDP, thus creating (or so it seemed at the time) a two-party system on the British model. The British political system, indeed, was the model to which Ozawa made most frequent reference.

Ozawa was the prime mover in the formation of the Hosokawa coalition government in 1993, and many observers agree that his cobbling together of so many disparate political forces into a government that excluded the mighty LDP was a *tour de force* of outstanding audacity. It may be seen as a political tragedy that the coalition government lasted for such a short time, since it had the potential to transform the system from a single-party monopoly into one based on democratic competition. Ozawa's second success, in 2009, was a logical extension of the first, in that for the first time the main opposition party replaced the LDP in government. However, once again, for complex reasons, the experiment ended in failure.

The personality and career of Ozawa have fascinated more observers than those of almost any other Japanese politician. This is confirmed, indeed, by the fact that this book by Aurelia George Mulgan is the second in this series to assess Ozawa's career. The first, by Takashi Oka, is entitled *Policy Entrepreneurship and Elections in Japan: A Political Biography of Ozawa Ichirō*, published in 2011. The vortex of controversy that has surrounded Ozawa over many years is graphically illustrated by the fact that these two authors subject him to contrasting evaluations. Whereas Takashi Oka (writing when the DPJ government still seemed likely to succeed) focuses principally, though not wholly, on his entrepreneurship and radical plans for root and branch reform of the Japanese political system, Aurelia George Mulgan, while fully acknowledging the far-sighted radicalism of his political vision, especially in the 1990s, also probes in depth Ozawa's entrenched patterns of political behaviour, concluding that these had the long-term effect of undermining the reformist policies that he espoused.

This book is organised around the concepts of 'new politics' and 'old politics'. Ozawa's new politics was his vision of a radically reformed and rationalised system of governance, so eloquently set out in his book *Blueprint for a New Japan*, published in 1994, whereas the meaning of old politics was his factional, autocratic and destabilising behaviour, including the habit of forming and dissolving political parties to suit his constant power plays. The author believes that while his radicalism in the 1990s was based on rigorous neo-liberal principles, in the new millennium it had become tainted by opportunistic appeals to sectional interests. In a shocking indictment, she argues that much of the instability that led to the failure of the DPJ government between 2009 and 2012 (for which Ozawa had worked so long to bring about) was caused mainly by self-interested manoeuvring on the part of Ozawa and his tight-knit faction – in effect a party within a party. In this interpretation Ozawa's political trajectory reads like a Shakespearean tragedy, of a talented leader and outstanding visionary whose career is blighted by entrenched behavioural flaws, leading in the end not to glory, but to obloquy and eventual irrelevance.

Analyses of Japanese politics have been an important part of the Nissan Institute/Routledge Japanese Studies Series, since we regard issues of democracy and governance as central to the health of Japanese society. This is the fourth book that Professor George Mulgan has written for the series, and we thank her for her contribution.

Arthur Stockwin
Roger Goodman

Acknowledgements

This book could not have been written without the superlative assistance that I received from Yong Suk Koh, whose dedication, exactitude and hard work contributed so much to generating the information that went into it. We spent many an enjoyable afternoon drinking tea, eating cakes and cracking jokes in front of NHK News 7. I would also like to thank the Australian Research Council and their award of a Discovery Project Grant that funded much of this assistance. Jo Muggleton from the School of Humanities and Social Sciences, UNSW Canberra, with her usual competence and willingness, ensured that all the funding flowed like a smooth river. Her positive and affectionate encouragement is sorely missed. Key Japanese contacts, who either knew Ozawa personally or had dealings with him, were very helpful in providing valuable insights into his political methods, funding sources and support structures. Others who furnished stimulation and inspiration along the way, for which I am very grateful, were Arthur Stockwin, Rick Katz, Michael Cucek, Brian Woodall, Justin Wang, Jeff Kingston, Bill Grimes and Miyoko Asai. Thanks should also go to Routledge for continuing to show confidence in my work and for their professionalism. As ever, I owe so much to my husband Richard, who not only acted as a politically literate sounding board, sympathetic ear and editorial adviser, but who also compiled the index as he has done for all my books. I dedicate this volume to Jasper who is now singing with the angels.

Canberra
July 2014

1 Introduction

The politician Ozawa Ichirō, and his political significance

Ozawa Ichirō was the axis on which Japanese politics turned for more than two decades. Until the triumphant return of the Liberal Democratic Party (LDP) to office in December 2012, he was a prime mover and shaker in the political world, a larger-than-life figure whose presence could not be ignored even when he disappeared from public view. Admired and reviled in almost equal measure, Ozawa has been the most debated and yet least understood politician in Japan. Little agreement can be found amongst the many who have debated his patent political assets and palpable political flaws.

Ozawa's political persona and influence on the conduct of politics in Japan make for a complex story. The dominant image he projects is that of the quintessential political boss or power broker, controlling people, votes and key party resources as well as important decisions of state from behind closed doors. Hence, his attracting of the classic label 'shadow shogun' (*yamishōgun*), a concept that reaches back into Japan's feudal past when military dictators, or shoguns, wielded the real political power by manipulating emperors from behind the scenes. In its modern incarnation, 'shadow shogun' depicts both a preference for backroom dealings and an ability to exert considerable power and even control over governments without occupying any formal government office. It certainly encapsulates key aspects of the way in which Ozawa practises politics.

Understanding Ozawa, however, and his impact on Japanese politics requires deeper analysis than simply resorting to labels from the Japanese vernacular.[1] Ozawa presents a paradox: an old-school backroom fixer from the LDP who set out to reform many aspects of Japanese politics, particularly entrenched power structures and political institutions, but without discarding his old political habits.

The key to understanding Ozawa lies in the concepts of 'old' and 'new' politics. Ozawa was a politician who preached 'new' politics and was the most important political reformer of his generation. However, in the way he conducted himself as a politician, he remained the embodiment of the unreformed 'old' political system.

Ozawa's contribution: new rules, old practices

Ozawa had a unique role in shaping not only political developments in Japan, but also the nature of politics itself. His influence was 'systemic', extending beyond the 'who' and 'what' of politics to the 'how' – to the rules of the game and thus to how the Japanese political system actually functions. Ozawa achieved this by acting as an architect of political system change. He contributed substantially to the major modifications and adjustments in the Japanese political system from the early 1990s onwards, not least by formulating prescriptions for political reform. He devoted energy to placing proposals for systemic reform in the public arena and on to the policy agenda of governments. He was unequalled amongst Japanese politicians for articulating and then implementing plans for wide-ranging reform of Japan's political institutions. In this way, he helped to reshape the electoral system, political funding rules, the evolution of the party system, the nature of executive government, the roles and powers of bureaucrats, and the conduct of parliamentary and policymaking processes. Ozawa not only possessed a reforming vision but also played a pivotal role in achieving significant change in line with that vision.

Ozawa deserves comparison with former Prime Minister Koizumi Junichirō in this regard. The key difference between the two was the nature and rationale of their respective contributions to political reform. Koizumi certainly changed the way politics and policymaking were conducted in a number of important ways, but his primary agenda was economic structural reform, not the structural transformation of Japanese politics. Moreover, in pursuing his quest for economic structural reform, he relied primarily on exploiting to the full existing political mechanisms and powers rather than attempting to change them by enacting systemic reforms.[2] His view of political reform was instrumentalist: it was a means to an end. Even his much-vaunted goal of 'destroying the LDP', which he continued to lead rather than founding a new party based on neo-liberal principles, was a threat to the old guard in the party to support his reforms or else.

Ozawa, who also shared Koizumi's goal of destroying the LDP (by leaving it first, in contrast to Koizumi), set out to make alterations to Japan's political structure beyond any contemplated by Koizumi. Like Koizumi, Ozawa also had an agenda for neo-liberal economic reform such as deregulation, privatisation, and tax and trade policy reform. However, these were transient goals to which he failed to dedicate himself as policy priorities, unlike Koizumi, for whom they remained long-held ambitions. Other reforms that Ozawa espoused related to social policy and even fundamental attitudinal changes to what one might call Japan's political culture, which Koizumi did not pursue at all. Nevertheless, Ozawa's economic and social policy reforms remained largely declaratory goals and statements of good intentions rather than concrete policy objectives. Although they amply demonstrated his economic reform credentials in the early 1990s, his economic policy standpoint changed dramatically over time. As a reformer, he was primarily dedicated to changing the structure of power in the political system and how politics was conducted rather than the content of government policy and the economic and social principles underpinning it.

If Ozawa's unique moulding influence on Japanese politics stemmed from his role as an architect of political system change, it also derived from the impact of his *modus operandi* on other politicians and on political institutions and processes. Beyond his role in catalysing a series of political reforms, Ozawa's own political behaviour, style, methods, practices and choices had a wide-ranging influence on many aspects of Japanese politics including the nature of political leadership, policymaking structures and processes, election campaigning and vote mobilisation, the activities of intra-party groups, political fundraising and deal making, and clientelistic connections between the political and construction worlds. In these and other areas, Ozawa was frequently a force for political regression rather than political reform: re-energising and restoring power to intra-party factions; strengthening the role of key party executives in allocating government patronage; undermining ministerial prerogatives and the power of the cabinet in policymaking; conducting 'politics behind closed doors' (*misshitsu seiji*); exploiting government-funded public works as a tradable political commodity; practising 'money-intensive politics';[3] and allocating budgetary largesse for short-term political and electoral gain – to name a few. Ozawa was, therefore, pivotal in entrenching some of the Japanese political system's singular pathologies, particularly those inherited from the era of LDP governance under former Prime Minister Tanaka Kakuei.

Ozawa thus played a dual and contradictory role: he was both an agent of political reform and an agent of path dependence in Japanese politics.[4] These contradictory aspects of Ozawa's character and contribution make him a subject worthy of further analysis and explanation. They may help to explain why, despite many systemic changes to Japanese political institutions, political behaviours have not yet fully adjusted to these changes and some old pre-reform patterns are still in evidence.

Models of 'old' and 'new' politics

This book encapsulates Ozawa's paradoxical and conflicting contributions in terms of two contrasting models of 'old' and 'new' politics. He embodied these models by advocating, pursuing and assisting in the implementation of new politics goals, while, at the same time, continuing to conduct old politics, particularly in the way in which he built and exercised his power. In some cases, he simply transferred old habits to a new set of institutional arrangements and political contexts, even using old politics methods to achieve new politics goals. Hence, operating within new politics systems did not necessarily lead to changes in Ozawa's political style and behaviour. Nor did it allow the new institutions to become fully embedded and functioning in the way they were originally intended. In this respect, Ozawa appears not to have honoured the intent of his own reforms and, in some ways, even to have betrayed it. Despite his rhetoric and contribution to political system change, he remained the same old Ozawa, unreconstructed and unrepentant in his attachment to old ways and approaches. He contributed to political system change, but he himself did not change as a politician.

Understanding Ozawa therefore requires an appreciation of how he practised old politics while acting as a change maker to bring about new politics. He represents a genuine enigma in his peculiar combination of mutually contradictory roles and methods. To some extent, these contradictions are captured in oxymoronic epithets such as 'creative destroyer', 'disruptive reformer', 'heretic authoritarian', and 'radical conservative'. However, not even these epithets provide a definitive understanding of the man as a political actor. Ozawa confounds analysts who cannot agree on his true character or motivations. On the one hand, his stated goals and demonstrated commitment were patently for political reform. In other respects, his unchanged conduct as a politician suggested that he remained locked in an old politics paradigm. The problem of understanding the 'real' Ozawa thus arises because he remained a practitioner of old politics despite his rhetorical agenda of change to bring about new politics. At times this manifested as a profound disjunction between what Ozawa said and what he did.

At the heart of the Ozawa enigma is, therefore, a fundamental question about Ozawa's primary motivations and whether he was a genuine political reformer. Was he a reformer by conviction or by strategic choice? Was he an authentic political reformer whose ambition was to use his power and position in order to bring change to what he has denounced as ossified and dysfunctional aspects of the Japanese political system? In short, did he seek power primarily to enact reforms? Or, were his reform goals simply disguised power-seeking objectives? Was he a supreme political manipulator who cynically used the cause of reform for his own narrow political ends? Did his stated goals obscure his real goals? Was his prior ambition consistently to wield untrammelled political power? In short, which were the ends and which were the means? Ozawa's actions could so often be interpreted or explained in different ways – in terms of either power seeking or reform seeking, or even a mixture of both. This book seeks to illuminate Ozawa's true motivations and character, and untangle the complex elements of old and new politics that he represents.

How are 'old' and 'new' politics to be defined? Table 1.1 outlines in a systematic and contrastive way the conceptual paradigms that are relevant to this study of Ozawa. They are generalised constructs of political system attributes distilled from Ozawa's political reform programme and his actual conduct as a politician. The 'new' model of politics is encapsulated in Ozawa-inspired reforms, in his writings and statements, and in his stated goals for reform of the political system. They encompass the systemic attributes designed by Ozawa to produce a new kind of politics in Japan and his aspirations for a reformed polity.[5]

Counterposed to the 'new' model is the 'old' model of politics, which can be discerned in Ozawa's actions, methods and *modus operandi*. It is essentially the paradigm of politics that was in evidence during the almost uninterrupted rule of the LDP from 1955 until 2009. At its core, it embodies the political style and practices of Tanaka Kakuei, Ozawa's mentor and the original shadow shogun of post-war Japanese politics. Ozawa has continued the Tanaka 'line' in many aspects of his politics. Like Tanaka also, Ozawa represents 'a particular figure as a type or pattern [that captures] the essence of an age'.[6] Ozawa is important to understanding Japanese politics from the late 1980s until the early 2010s, just as Tanaka was the key to understanding Japanese politics in the 1970s and 1980s.

Actors and political institutions

In terms of social science methodology, the theoretical premise of this work is that individuals influence the way in which political institutions work in any given

Table 1.1 The Ozawa models of old and new politics

	Old politics	New politics
Party system	Fluid system with major-minor parties and transient party loyalties leading to coalitions, amalgamations and splits, and nominal party policy competition	Two-party system with two major (government and opposition) parties competing in terms of policies and regularly alternating in government
Electoral system	Willingness to work within multi-member district system	Single-member districts; equal representation across electoral districts
Electoral competition	Candidate-centred elections	Party-centred elections; manifesto-driven, issue-oriented elections with real policy competition between candidates from different political parties
Policy bias	Rural-regional policy bias particularly in public works	Balanced distribution of benefits to urban-rural dwellers/producers and consumers; public-interest, reform-oriented policies
Vote mobilisation strategies	Personalised party leader/secretary-general-directed election campaigns	Centralised party-directed election campaigns
	Reliance on pork-barrel promises (particularly of public works), catering to local, clientelistic and sectional interests; promises of political patronage and particularistic benefits to individuals and companies, and specific policy benefits to interest groups	Appeals to broad categories of voters through distributive 'from concrete to people' policies, and internet and door-to-door campaigning permitted
	Cultivation of candidate-centred personal votes relying on politicians' local election offices, leader-provided campaign resources and candidates' support organisations (including *kōenkai*) representing a network of personal supporters and political support groups enlisted as campaigners and vote and fund mobilisers, especially from construction companies	Cultivation of broad voter appeal and party- and policy-centred votes through election manifestos

Table 1.1 (continued)

	Old politics	New politics
Political funding	• Money-driven politics reliant on corporate and organisational funding, including hidden money flows to individual politicians ('money for favours' and 'illicit contributions') leading to political corruption and financial scandals, including violations of the Political Funds Control Law • Decentralised distribution of funding to individual politicians by faction leaders and secretary-general with hidden faction-building objectives	• Transparent public funding for political parties; funds centrally allocated to party organisations, not to individual politicians; abolition of/restrictions on private funding from companies, organisations and individuals (incl. to individual politicians) • Centralised distribution of party funding to individual politicians by party executive
Party organisational and power structures	• A personalised, faction-based, leader-follower, power-seeking group • Party membership primarily based on personal loyalty and receipt of patronage • Policy settings decided by party leader • Weak party policy discipline and legislative cohesion • Diet members' election offices and support groups (kōenkai) substitute for regional organisations; weak mass membership base • Predominance of informal power structures, factions (habatsu) based on patron–client relations, and political boss rule; prevalence of inter-factional strife • Personnel decisions, including candidate pre-selection and appointments to senior party positions, and resource distribution made by party leader/secretary-general • Primacy of personal and factional loyalty over party loyalty; political relationships built on dispensing patronage and reciprocal obligation	• A political organisation seeking power in order to implement a policy programme agreed amongst its membership • Party membership based on shared policy preferences and ideological principles • Policy settings decided by party executive with input from Diet membership • Strong party discipline and legislative cohesion • Strong regional organisations and grassroots party branches • Predominance of formal power structures – party executive, incl. president and secretary-general, committees and councils • Personnel decisions, including candidate pre-selection and appointments to senior party positions, and resource distribution centralised in party executive • Primacy of party loyalty over personal and faction/group loyalty

Table 1.1 (continued)

	Old politics	New politics
Political leadership and policy-making	• System of centralised leadership by a political strongman/'actual power holder(s)' (*jitsuryokusha*) operating behind the scenes and acting as king maker • Disjunction between actual power holders and formal power holders; policymaking power wielded informally by secretary-general and *ad hoc* decision-making structures; reliance on factional numbers to wield intra-party and intra-government power • Dual structure of power with official power holders and 'actual power holder(s)'; weak government accountability; poor public communication • Weak prime minister and cabinet manipulated from behind the scenes and unable to take the policy initiative • Ministers and parliamentary vice-ministers, etc. weak relative to ruling party and actual power-holders • Party a separate policymaking institution intervening in policymaking via the secretary-general's office, displacing bureaucrats and formal party policy committees and informal groups (*zoku*); party and actual power holders' political and electoral interests prioritised	• Political leadership primarily exercised through institutional power; system of collective cabinet-centred leadership led by a strengthened Kantei • Conjunction of formal and informal authority; policymaking power centralised in formal positions of prime minister and cabinet; prime minister-/minister-led party and bureaucracy • Single structure of official power holders with strong, accountable government; good public communication • Strong prime minister and cabinet taking the policy initiative and responsibility for government decision making • Strong sub-cabinet support structures for ministers including senior vice-ministers and parliamentary secretaries; large numbers of ruling party politicians incorporated into government in sub-cabinet positions; politician-led bureaucracy • Integration of ruling party and cabinet to exclude bureaucracy; party and bureaucracy non-participants in policymaking as separate institutions and subordinated to prime minister and cabinet; party and bureaucratic influence displaced by cabinet/ministerial (i.e. political) leadership
Proceedings of the legislature	• Diet displaced as primary arena for policy discussion and government accountability • Little participation of actual power holders in Diet proceedings, policy debates and question time	• Ministers and parliamentary vice-ministers/senior vice-ministers (not bureaucrats) answer for government policy in Diet; bureaucrats excluded from Diet deliberations • Strong policy debates in Diet; Diet politicians able to question the prime minister in question time

Table 1.1 (continued)

	Old politics	New politics
State administrative and fiscal structure	• Exploitation of centralised fiscal and administrative systems for political ends	• Abolition of centralised bureaucratic system; fiscal and administrative decentralisation with budgetary authority shared between central and local governments
Budget allocations	• Allocations distorted by electoral objectives and politically strategic distributive goals	• Distribution based on broad policy principles including rational economic and fiscal principles

historical, political and cultural setting, how these institutions evolve and develop, and why particular political conventions, norms and practices persist. While institutions clearly shape the behaviour of political actors through path dependence and other mechanisms, at the same time they are themselves significantly influenced by these actors. In the technical language, institutions are not simply an exogenous given because the rules that constitute them are 'provided by the players themselves'.[7]

From this perspective, an institutional account of Japanese politics – an outline of its principal structures, conventions, norms and rules – cannot fully explain how Japanese politics works, nor how it has changed over time. It is necessary also to take account of the shaping role of individual political actors, particularly political leaders and other powerful political figures who may set out to alter various aspects of how a political system operates. These are individuals whose behaviours mould both structured and unstructured institutions, and the way these institutions change and evolve in particular national settings.

This approach therefore rejects institutional determinism, which argues that both political behaviour and policy outcomes are influenced by their institutional settings. In short, not everything is structural; some may be individual.[8] The approach also rejects electoral determinism, which explains the nature of party systems simply by reference to electoral system factors. Electoral rules cannot fully account for the way in which Japanese political parties form and operate, and how the party system is organised and develops.[9] Both institutional and electoral explanations ignore the role of individual politicians as independent variables – in explaining, for example, how particular policymaking and electoral systems function, or how parties organise themselves.

However, rather than focusing on the shaping role of groups or actors or general categories of actors, this book is concerned with one particular political actor – Ozawa Ichirō. Ozawa had a formative influence on Japanese politics for the two major reasons noted earlier. First, he was a principal player in the drama of political reform in Japan. He was proactive in his quest to change Japanese politics and the way key institutions – party, electoral and policymaking – operated. Second, many aspects of the way in which he conducted politics displayed old political patterns that continued to influence political processes and behaviours and deflected the direction of political reform. In this respect, whilst laying claim to the creation of a system of new politics, Ozawa remained a prominent exemplar of old politics. He was a study in contrasts, a contradictory figure whose significance in Japanese politics cannot be overstated. The book is thus a systematic empirical analysis of a politician who played a pivotal role in shaping Japanese politics in the late 20th and early 21st centuries by wielding pivotal influence over how the Japanese political system functioned and how particular political institutions worked. The account it provides is not simply the story of Ozawa's role in helping to mould particular policies or election outcomes, although these topics are included in the span of the work.

The book is also more than a study of one politician, albeit an extremely important one. It aspires to be a treatise on Japanese politics. It is hoped that

10 *Introduction*

understanding Ozawa through the lens of 'old' and 'new' politics will enhance readers' understanding of Japanese politics as a whole. For this reason, the book is not a political biography of Ozawa, a number of which have been published in recent decades.[10] It is a study of Ozawa in the context of Japanese politics in a way designed to illuminate both.

The book also seeks to make available in English Ozawa's written and spoken words (both public and private), as well as a diverse range of commentary on Ozawa originally published in Japanese. The aim is to bring these sources into the international discourse on Ozawa and Japanese politics. In particular, the book provides extensive coverage of Ozawa's activities after the Democratic Party of Japan (DPJ) came to power in 2009 with the aim of presenting readers with a clear picture of how his words and deeds were viewed, explained and interpreted not only by media commentators but also by Japanese political scientists, political critics, other politicians (including former prime ministers), previous employees of Ozawa, and Diet and party officials.

A wide range of commentary has been deliberately explored in order to counter the argument frequently made by Ozawa's supporters that criticism of him 'just reflects media bias' and should, therefore, be dismissed. It is certainly true that Ozawa's relationship with the mass media has generally been one of (mutual) hostility. As with many of Ozawa's former allies and close aides, journalists have abandoned him and few newspapers like him.[11] Ozawa attacks them as part of the structure of vested interests that he himself tried to change.[12] However, when large numbers of those who have known Ozawa and who have worked with him over the years point not only to his strengths but also to his weaknesses, and when astute and well-informed analysts, authors and commentators make considered assessments and evaluations of his behaviour, then these deserve a wider airing and need to be taken into account in forming an overall judgement about him, including his wider significance and contribution to Japanese politics.

Perhaps hardest of all for Ozawa to accept is that he is hardly considered worthy of public comment any more, given plummeting public interest in his affairs since the LDP returned to power in December 2012. His fall from grace was rapid and precipitous. In 2010 he was at the pinnacle of power, running a newly elected DPJ government, having ousted the ruling LDP after 54 years (1955–2009) of almost uninterrupted rule. Today he is an 'empty ruin'[13] on the periphery of Japanese politics. Even shorthand labels such as 'shadow shogun' have made him an outlier in contemporary political affairs, which have moved on from Ozawa politics.

Notes

1 Other labels in a similar vein, all of which have been used to describe Ozawa, are: *fikusā* ('backroom fixer'), *seikai no ōmono* ('political heavyweight') and *jitsuryokusha* ('actual power holder' or 'wielder of real power'), as well as more traditional terms such as *kage no kenryokusha* ('a powerful or influential person in the shadows'), *kagemusha*

('wire-puller'), *kugutsushi* ('puppeteer'), and *kuromaku* ('shadowy string puller' – literally 'puppet master pulling the strings and controlling politics from backstage').
2 George Mulgan, *Japan's Failed Revolution*, pp. 178–83.
3 McCall Rosenbluth and Thies, for example, refer to 'money-intensive electoral politics'. See McCall Rosenbluth and Thies, *Japan Transformed*, p. x.
4 According to Page, 'path dependence means that current and future states, actions, or decisions depend on the path of previous states, actions, or decisions'. See Page, 'Path Dependence', p. 88.
5 In this respect, the typology of 'new' politics differs from other paradigms of majoritarian politics, which are derived from actual practice, rather than aspiration, e.g. Lijphart, *Democracies*.
6 Nishibe, 'Tanaka Kakuei', p. 67.
7 Shepsle, 'Rational Choice Institutionalism', p. 25. See also Aldrich, *Why Parties?*, p. 6; and Krauss and Pekkanen, *The Rise and Fall of Japan's LDP*, p. 2.
8 These mutually distinct explanatory variables have also been represented as 'structure' (the role of institutional structures) versus 'agency' (the role of human agents). As Gaunder writes in her study of Ozawa's role in political reform, 'Structuralists assert that events and processes are the result of structures which individuals have no influence over. In contrast, voluntarists posit that the choices and actions of individuals are what in fact determine the course of events'. Gaunder, 'Reform Leadership', p. 174.
9 See also Krauss and Pekkanen, *The Rise and Fall of Japan's LDP*, p. 2.
10 The most recent is Oka, *Policy Entrepreneurship*, but earlier examples in Japanese (in order of publication with the most recent first) include Hayano, *Ozawa Ichirō Tanken*; Okuno, *Ozawa Ichirō Hasha no Rirekisho*; Watanabe, *Ano Hito*; and Oda, *Ozawa Ichirō Zenjinzō*. In addition to the political bibliographies of Ozawa, many books have been written that focus on aspects of Ozawa's politics, including (in order of publication with the most recent first): Hirano, *Shinsetsu!*; Suzuki, *Saigo no Ozawa Ichirō*; Ishikawa, *Akutō*; Matsuda, *Kakuei ni Narenakatta Otoko*; Watanabe, *Ozawa Ichirō Kirawareru Densetsu*; Matsuda, *Ozawa Ichirō, Kyoshoku no Shihaisha*; Hirano, *Ozawa Ichirō to no Nijūnen*; Kuji and Yokota, *Seiji ga Yugameru Kōkyō Jigyō*; Kuji, *Ozawa Ichirō – Sono 'Kyōfu Shihai'*; Kaieda, *Boku ga Ozawa (Seiji) o Kirai*; Ise, *Ozawa Ichirō no Wanryoku*; Hanaoka,'*Ozawa Shintō*' *wa Nani o Mezasu ka?!*; Satō, *Ozawa Ichirō no Himitsu*; Itagaki, *Heisei Dōran*; and Kikuchi, *Ozawa Ichirō no Seiji Bōryaku*.
11 Endō, *Shōhi Sareru Kenryokusha*, p. 95.
12 For an extensive elaboration of this argument, see Hashimoto, 'Minshutō zen daihyō Ozawa Ichirō', pp. 374–79.
13 Abiru, 'Minshutō "A kyū senpan" hōtei', pp. 44–45.

2 New politics and policies

As a proponent of new politics, Ozawa was a visionary in his quest to change Japan, to change the way its political system worked and to revamp Japan's place in the world. Ozawa not only made a singular contribution to the debate about how Japan should change, but was also the main driving force behind many of those changes. He shared with former British Prime Minister Winston Churchill a strong sense of historical destiny,[1] believing it was his mission to reform post-war Japanese politics.[2] As a path breaker seeking to make radical changes to existing political institutions, he appeared to many as a revolutionary,[3] but Ozawa preferred to cast himself as a reformer.[4]

Certainly, amongst LDP politicians in the late 1980s and early 1990s, Ozawa was the most prominent advocate of reform.[5] In 1993, he published a new grand design for the Japanese nation entitled *Nihon Kaizō Keikaku*, which was republished in English as *Blueprint for a New Japan: The Rethinking of a Nation* in 1994 (hereafter *Blueprint*). It represented the first comprehensive articulation of Ozawa's proposals for wide-ranging political, economic and social reform.

Internationally it became best known for the idea that Japan should become a 'normal nation' (*futsū no kuni*), which meant expanding its international contributions, including greater security cooperation with the United States and actively participating in the building of a new international order.[6] *Blueprint* also provided a comprehensive analysis of Japan's domestic political, economic and social ills, and offered a vast array of recommendations for reform. 'Book I', entitled 'The Urgency of Political Reform', presented the case for structural transformation of Japanese politics. In Ozawa's view, 'Every aspect of politics has become entrenched and limited'.[7] 'Book III', on 'The Five Freedoms', argued the case for sweeping social and economic change.[8]

Ozawa's view was that none of the problems rooted in the political system would change unless the system itself was changed.[9] His theories of reform did not just call for radical adjustments at the policy level; they sought to achieve institutional reorganisation – in other words, 'changes to the basic frameworks of society, politics, administration and the economy'.[10] Ozawa outlined his approach in the Diet, declaring, 'What is important in carrying out major reforms to the nation is to have a clear vision of the grand design and the goal, to present specific visions of the future to the people in a way that is easy to understand, and to then implement [the various reforms] as part of one comprehensive policy on that basis'.[11]

Blueprint was followed in 2006 by the publication of *Ozawashugi*, or *Ozawa-ism*, which, Ozawa claimed, included all of his theories and ideas as a politician advocating Japan's 'self-reform'.[12] Ozawa had already launched an 'Ozawa Ichirō Political School' (Ozawa Ichirō Seiji Juku) in 2001 in order to transmit his philosophy, principles and theories on leadership and reform to young, aspiring politicians. Thereafter, the school held annual conventions not only for future political leaders but also for Diet members, including his political followers.[13] Taken together, Ozawa's many interviews, statements, essays, books and political school established his reputation as the most prominent political reformer of his time.

The Ozawa reforms

While *Blueprint* made Ozawa famous in domestic political circles and amongst well-informed Japan observers internationally, he had been contemplating and advocating political reform on and off for some time. Distilled to their essence, his core ideas embraced the notion that Japan should modernise its party system, effect fundamental changes to policymaking institutions and power structures, and accomplish a series of radical changes in economic and social policy.

Modernising the party system

Modernising the party system combined a broad-ranging and inter-related set of goals that focused on transformative reform of the LDP – later regime change, electoral reform and reform of so-called 'money politics'. For Ozawa modernising the party system was also important for improving the quality of political leadership.

Transformative reform of the LDP

In 1972, just before the LDP leadership election that made Tanaka Kakuei prime minister, Ozawa wrote a 400-page essay entitled *A Theory of Conservative Party Reform (Hoshu Seitō no Taishitsu Kaizen Ron)*, and also collaborated with other LDP politicians in producing *Ideas for Reforming the LDP – An Examination of Tomorrow's Conservative Administration (Jimintō Kaizōan – Asu no Hoshu Seiken o Kangaeru)*, a book published by *Yomiuri Shinbun* in September 1972.[14]

In his contribution, Ozawa wrote that a number of problems needed to be addressed in order to reform the LDP. On the list were factions centring more on interests and personal relationships than on policies, underdeveloped party regional organisations that were overly dependent on individual Diet members' personal support groups (*kōenkai*), a Diet member-centred party that was distant from the general public, seniority-based promotions to minister, bureaucrats' superiority in policymaking matched by Diet members' lack of policy study, and the party's collusion with financial circles (*zaikai*) in relation to political funding.[15]

Ozawa then proposed three concrete ideas for reforming the LDP: increasing the number of party members to 1 million in order to create a financial base for the party through membership fees as well as having members directly elect the party president;[16] turning to the public for political funds in order to shake free of dependence on donations from *zaikai*; and reorganising the various divisions in the LDP's Policy Affairs Research Council (PARC) away from alignment with the ministries, and in line with function and issue in order to overcome dependence on bureaucrats. Ozawa wrote, 'Why are we accepting the current situation where the tail is wagging the dog – where Diet members, who are in charge of law making, take orders from bureaucrats who are in charge of the administration?'[17] He also proposed the creation of a think tank consisting of scholars and specialists from private companies to assist in strengthening the party's policymaking capabilities.[18]

When Ozawa became LDP secretary-general in the Kaifu Toshiki administration of 1989–91, following the Recruit scandal and the fall of the Takeshita Noboru government, he said to his close confidante and adviser Hirano Sadao:

> I want transformative reform of the party, and I want a political system that can deal with global society after the Cold War. Only doing things that look good in the public eye, such as political ethics and regulating political funds, isn't enough. We need to reform the electoral system fundamentally and change the awareness of the people and politicians so that we can conduct politics that is centred on parties and policies.[19]

He had observed the LDP's chronic inability to deliver serious policy reforms, particularly in times of crisis, both domestic and international, or when placed under pressure to act by the United States. He was particularly frustrated by his own government's abortive attempt to implement proposals for electoral reform as well as its inadequate response to the Gulf War, including the strong resistance of LDP-led politics to the dispatch of the Self-Defence Forces (SDF) overseas.[20] In January 1991 Ozawa declared: 'politics has to be able to respond properly in order for Japan to survive peacefully and prosperously in international society.'[21] He belonged to the so-called 'national interest group' of reform advocates,[22] who argued that political reform was indispensable because of 'the need to establish "powerful politics" that could respond to [diplomatic] crises'.[23]

After Ozawa resigned as secretary-general in April 1991, he actively pushed for constitutional reform to permit the SDF to be dispatched overseas, and further developed his arguments for political reform.[24] His declared objective was 'to provide a stage on which Japanese politics can actually hold proper debates and respond properly in the face of the historic turmoil being experienced around the world'.[25] These ideas ultimately found expression in his multi-faceted long-term vision for remodelling the state in *Blueprint*.

Regime change

On the cusp of his departure from the LDP in 1992–93, Ozawa developed the idea that regime change – booting the LDP out of office – was necessary if political reform were to take place. Even though the LDP had itself presented goals for reform,[26] he questioned whether it could reform itself or its style of governance, insisting that overthrowing and breaking up the LDP was a precondition for reform.[27] Many years later he wrote in *Ozawashugi*:

> Some may think 'why did Ozawa try to destroy the solid LDP regime when he was a member of the party?' However, my actions were a result of my desperation, as I thought, 'If we do not reform the political framework now, there is no hope for Japan's future'. It was precisely because I was close to the centre of political power that I started to feel the sense of impending crisis that we cannot continue on like this. There were quite a few members who agreed with me in the LDP. However, not everyone had the courage to let go of their vested interests. As I expected, movements against our reform began, and I finally decided to leave the LDP.[28]

Regime change meant interrupting the uniform one-party dominant trajectory of the LDP from 1955 onwards. As Ozawa saw it, 'one-party government is a distorted form of democracy because there is no meaningful competition in such a system'.[29] His proclaimed goal was to establish a two-party system (*nidai seitōsei*) following a change of regime because, 'If one power group remains in government of a country for too long, then that country's politics will be doomed for certain. The LDP had been in control of the reins of power for far too long'.[30]

Ozawa's contribution was catalytic if not decisive in helping to bring down the LDP in both 1993 and 2009, and hence he must be considered one of the primary architects of regime change in Japan. Former Japan Communist Party (JCP) policy chief and Upper House Diet member Fudesaka Hideyo claimed, 'If Ozawa has charisma, it is because he overthrew LDP administrations twice and achieved regime change…' 'Koizumi Junichirō declared, "I will destroy the LDP if they oppose reforms", and received the people's applause, but there is no doubt that Ozawa Ichirō was the one that truly delivered a devastating blow to the LDP.'[31]

In June 1993, the no-confidence motion in the Miyazawa Kiichi government passed because it was supported by 39 rebels from the LDP, mainly from the group organised by Ozawa and Hata Tsutomu (the Hata-Ozawa faction), with Ozawa playing a key role in the success of the motion. Voting against the government as a member of the ruling party was 'a "forbidden move" that completely turned the political situation around'.[32]

At the time, the 'LDP' for Ozawa meant the political forces within the LDP, chiefly in the Takeshita faction (Keiseikai), which were arrayed against him.[33] Although the party had been in government since 1955, power within the party had been effectively monopolised by one faction for more than a decade – the lineage of power passed down from the Tanaka faction to the Takeshita faction.[34] Keiseikai's dominance in the party translated into a wider monopoly of political power in the government. It was this monopoly that Ozawa broke when he split the faction in two and finally left the LDP in mid-1993, thus destroying the political structure led by the Takeshita faction.[35]

Ozawa then set about replacing the LDP as the ruling party. Six days after Prime Minister Miyazawa dissolved the Lower House, the Hata-Ozawa group, having left the LDP, formed the Renewal Party, or RP (Shinseitō). With the backing of his new party, Ozawa worked hard behind the scenes to form a coalition to replace the LDP's one-party government. By August 1993 he had engineered the coalition of eight non-LDP parties led by Prime Minister Hosokawa Morihiro, which included Hosokawa's Japan New Party, or JNP (Nihon Shintō).[36] Ozawa had earlier established close ties to key individuals in both the Japan Socialist Party, or JSP (Nihon Shakaitō)[37] and Kōmeitō, on which he later drew to construct the new coalition administration. It was a political amalgam that ranged philosophically from socialists on the left to non-LDP conservative parties on the right, but it was Ozawa's skills as a behind-the-scenes power broker and his canny political instincts that made it possible.[38] He brought all the parties together 'in the blink of an eye',[39] outwitting the LDP when it was still in shock from its failure to win a majority in the July Lower House election.[40]

The final piece of the puzzle was the consent of Hosokawa, who was reluctant to contemplate a link-up with Ozawa's RP.[41] Ozawa had been in touch with Hosokawa ever since the Hata-Ozawa faction began strongly advocating political reform, and both had originated from the Tanaka faction.[42] Ozawa had decided fairly early on that the head of the coalition should be Hosokawa and he had apparently obtained the agreement of Kōmeitō secretary-general, Ichikawa Yūichi, to install him as prime minister. Ichikawa had previous links with Ozawa, guaranteeing him money and votes when Ozawa was leaving the LDP.[43] In fact, the scenario for the new coalition government was written by Ozawa, Ichikawa and the chairman of the Japanese Trade Union Confederation (Rengō), Yamagishi Akira.[44] Ozawa's relationship with Yamagishi had entered a honeymoon period after Ozawa approached him in the spring of 1993.[45] Securing the JSP's participation in the coalition proved the biggest obstacle, but it was overcome with the assistance of Yamagishi, who persuaded the JSP led by Chairman Yamahana Sadao to support Hosokawa becoming prime minister. Hosokawa's agreement with the scenario was won when Ozawa offered him the position, saying, 'It would be best if you became prime minister'.[46]

Orchestrating the Hosokawa prime ministership was said to be 'the most brilliant moment in Ozawa's life'.[47] He was to deploy the same skills to put Hata into the prime ministership in 1994, following Hosokawa's resignation that spring,[48] although he had earlier led Hata to believe that he would be prime minister in the first post-LDP administration.[49]

Twenty-two years later, Ozawa's attainment of the DPJ leadership in April 2006 breathed new life into the party and strengthened its position as the alternative government. Ozawa remained singularly focused on removing the LDP from office, successively hounding the Abe, Fukuda and Aso governments to hold a Lower House election. In adopting a confrontational stance in the divided Diet following the 2007 Upper House election, he was a major force in promoting real party competition between the LDP and DPJ. His refusal to cooperate with the established norms of deal-making politics was a major reason behind Prime Minister Abe Shinzō's resignation in September 2007.

In 2009, building on the DPJ's great victory in the Upper House election of 2007, which he masterminded, Ozawa helped to engineer the DPJ's stunning victory in the Lower House election, thus cementing the LDP's apparent demise as Japan's predominant ruling party. He had successfully transformed the DPJ into an effective fighting force capable of taking over government.[50] At a gathering of the DPJ faithful in March 2009, Ozawa told the assembled audience that bringing down the LDP was his 'lifetime dream and my last task as a politician'.[51] He then became a major figure in organising the DPJ's coalition with the People's New Party, or PNP (Kokumin Shintō) and the Social Democratic Party, or SDP (Shamintō).

Electoral reform

Ozawa's commitment to reshaping the electoral system, and specifically to the creation of single-member districts, could be traced back to the beginning of his career in 1969.[52] In this respect, Ozawa assumed the mantle of his father, Ozawa Saeki, who had been examining the single-seat constituency system since the early 1950s.[53]

In 1980, Ozawa contributed an article to the book on his father entitled *Ningen Ozawa Saeki* (*The Man Ozawa Saeki*). He touched on his father's efforts to implement electoral reform and then identified what he saw as the basic problems in the existing multi-member constituency system. He wrote:

> Under the multiple-seat constituency system, candidates from the same party inevitably have to fight against each other. In particular, the majority party needs to use up most of their energy on this internal strife...I think that the introduction of the single-seat constituency system is the only way we can eliminate this hindrance and realise party-oriented elections.[54]

Ozawa also elaborated on the relationship between the single-seat constituency system and the possibility of a more competitive system of party politics developing:

> It's true that in the first one or two elections [after introducing the single-seat constituency system] the LDP would secure the vast majority of seats, but it is hard to imagine that situation would continue for long...[A] national party that can meet the people's demands would most certainly develop. When that happens, the LDP would be put in a tougher situation than they face now – right now they only have to deal with opposition parties that have no incentive to take the reins of government.[55]

These ideas were those he pursued as LDP secretary-general in the Kaifu administration nine years later.[56] He constantly urged the prime minister to carry out electoral reform and attempted to influence deliberations of the Election System Advisory Council (Senkyo Seido Shingikai) by persuading its chairman to his point of view.[57] Ozawa proposed that the LDP's Upper and Lower House members realise a 'political reform outline' (*seiji kaikaku taikō*) that included reform to the Lower House electoral system. However, he was met with opposition from LDP members, particularly from the Takeshita faction to which he belonged. His opponents argued that there was no need for reforms that could lead to the LDP losing power.[58] According to Hirano, Ozawa's attempts to effect these changes caused him to be disliked and mistrusted, provoking an anti-Ozawa network within the LDP across factional boundaries.[59]

Ozawa then articulated his comprehensive vision for electoral reform in *Blueprint*, devoting an entire chapter to 'The Advantages of Creating Small Electoral Districts'.[60] He reiterated earlier criticisms of multi-member constituencies and linked the shortcomings in the electoral system directly to the issue of regime change in providing 'the important underpinning of the LDP's "perennial rule" [and]…the stagnation of Japanese politics'.[61] Multi-seat districts also gave rise to 'money-politics' problems.[62] Hence, electoral reform was necessary for both 'countering the high cost of national politics and eventually terminating the LDP's single-party rule'.[63] The LDP was entrenched in the Lower House multi-member districts through its strong *kōenkai* networks, which meant that there was little chance of the LDP losing its overwhelming power.[64] In contrast, the single-member district system was 'conducive to a change of administration'.[65]

Ozawa preferred the single-seat constituency system to either proportional representation (PR) or a combination of PR and single-member districts, declaring in *Blueprint* that he did 'not necessarily support a combined proportional representation and single-seat district electoral system. The "combination" proposal is essentially a version of proportional representation: it will simply drag the principles that underlie the current multi-seat system into the new system'.[66] PR also hindered Japan's political dynamism and produced a system of 'unanimous accord' and 'unanimous agreement', in which 'it takes too long to reach decisions'.[67]

Ozawa intuitively realised that electoral reform would have far-reaching effects on the structure of governance.[68] Converting the Lower House electoral system from multi-member to single-member districts would ultimately produce two dominant parties, majority rule and easier transfers of power.[69] It would also require voters to choose only one representative to express their political will clearly. As he explained:

> Candidates from the ruling and opposition parties are elected together in the same constituency in the multi-seat constituency system, so the voters deal with both sides half-heartedly and they do not have to have a proper opinion…If we introduce the single-seat constituency system, [politics will] gradually change into a two-party system. Candidates have to clearly indicate their intentions. Voters can only choose one candidate or the other.[70]

Britain was consistently Ozawa's model for electoral reform and the idea of two major parties alternating in government. As he stated, 'In Britain, alternation in government has been the rule continuously, but in Japan it has not yet taken a firm hold…I want a parliamentary system under which it is possible for rotation in power to take root in Japan'.[71] The inception of single-member districts would permit 'electoral competition among parties, rather than among LDP factions'.[72] He rejected traditional LDP theories of reforming the party by dissolving the factions and increasing the transparency of political funding, as he thought these touched on just petty details. They 'did not break out of the old framework of consensus-oriented politics founded on the multi-seat constituency system, but instead reinforced the existing framework'.[73]

Ozawa also recommended that politicians' *kōenkai* should be reorganised into local party branches that would decide which candidates to field.[74] With the eradication of *kōenkai*, the role of factions in elections would be eliminated. As he explained, 'With elections managed by the parties, the kinds of factional abuses we have seen in the LDP are likely to be corrected in the process'.[75] He proposed that election campaign activities should be handed over to the parties in their entirety as part of a system that replaced candidate-centred campaigns with 'Policy-Centred, Party-Directed Election Campaigns' (see Table 1.1).[76] As he reasoned, 'In multi-member electoral districts where several candidates from the same party run for election, it becomes a battle for service (*sābisu kasen*) and a battle of slander (*chūshō kasen*) rather than a contest in which policy debates take centre stage. Therefore, we should have single-member districts'.[77] Under the new system, 'parties will compete with each other based on policies rather than on financial advantage',[78] and will be 'forced to present their approaches to the problems of the day. This is an election as it was meant to be'.[79]

The larger goal of issue-oriented election campaigns was the emergence of a system of competitive party politics based on policy differences. Ozawa criticised the existing role of politics as 'just to distribute the budget amongst the Japanese while taking into consideration what the opposition parties have to say…There is no need for political opinions or policies…'.[80] He 'bemoaned the absence of true competition between the LDP and its chief rival, the Japan Socialist Party'.[81] In particular, he condemned the JSP for making under-the-table deals with the LDP in order to profit financially and to share power,[82] calling it 'total collusion politics (*sōdangō seiji*)'.[83] As he later wrote in *Ozawashugi*:

> It is often said that the history of Japanese politics after the war was a history of conflict between the Liberal Democratic Party and Japan Socialist Party, but this is not true. While they acted as though they were in conflict with each other, in actual fact they were very cooperative under the surface…[I]n Japan everything was decided through the collusion between the Liberal Democratic Party and Japan Socialist Party…The Liberal Democratic Party and Japan Socialist Party had a tacit agreement that they would treat very difficult political issues as taboos and not discuss them, or made ambiguous agreements to postpone finalising these issues…So in reality, serious policy debates were not held at all, and a period where politics was non-existent continued for a long time.[84]

Ozawa's plan was to form a new conservative party to compete with the LDP by integrating and weeding out the smaller parties in elections under the single-member district system.[85] He was disillusioned with the JSP's potential to play the role of alternative ruling party and envisaged two conservative parties competing against each other in a conservative two-party (*hoshu nidai seitō*) system.

Electoral reform would also rectify the malapportionment between urban and rural electorates, thus correcting the rural-regional policy bias endemic in LDP rule and empowering urban consumers and salaried workers, who comprised the new urban middle class (see Table 1.1).[86] Ozawa calculated that electoral reform would allow the ruling party to tap into a new and growing support base in the cities, freeing it from its traditional stronghold amongst rural dwellers and small business operators.[87] Electoral reform thus offered a way to liberate the LDP from its dependence on special interests that blocked reform across a range of spheres. Unlike his fellow LDP politicians, Ozawa did not want to tie himself to vested interests.[88] He sought to broaden the appeal of the conservatives to a much wider electorate of unaffiliated, largely urban middle-class voters who were the fastest expanding group within Japan's political economy and who did not benefit directly from the LDP's traditional distributive policy package.

Electoral reform thus had direct implications for economic policy. Without electoral reform to undermine the decentralised and fragmented power structure within the ruling party in which factions and *kōenkai* played a key role, and without replacing it with a more centralised structure that was better insulated from the pressures of traditional economic sectors, the ruling party would not be able to secure the necessary autonomy to pursue the national interest in economic policy.[89] In his sights were organisations such as the agricultural cooperatives and small shop owners who prevented the government from realising economic reforms in the national interest. Essential to these reforms was the need to centralise power to the party and dissolve the *kōenkai* and factions that worked to decentralise power.[90] In Ozawa's view, the LDP's practice of delivering benefits and protection to supporting interest groups prevented governments from undertaking economic reforms and responding to international pressures (see Table 1.1).[91]

In *Ozawashugi*, Ozawa continued to outline a national vision in which the politics of spoils distribution and protectionism could no longer block change:

> Throughout the post-war era, politics was preoccupied with wealth redistribution, and true politics was not practised. Under such circumstances, it was only natural that true politicians were not born…The reason why I left the LDP in June 1993 was because I desperately wanted to reform this conventional style of politics…I started to feel that the LDP's political methods were reaching their limit.[92]

Attempts to engineer electoral reform during the Miyazawa administration of 1991–93 were unsuccessful despite the support of Hata as chairman of the LDP's Electoral System Research Council and that of young reformers in the party.[93] It was at that point that Ozawa decided to leave the LDP because he found internal reform impossible. As he explained in the DPJ's 2007 election manifesto, reform became contingent on regime change: 'I tried to bring about political reform, centring on the introduction of single-seat constituencies. But what awaited me was a huge up-swelling of opposition from within, that is from inside the LDP. Upon seeing this, I made up my mind...I left the LDP.'[94] He put together the coalition of non-government parties in order to destroy the LDP 'from the outside'.[95]

The 'spirit of the "political reform outline" was [finally] realised during the non-LDP Hosokawa coalition administration'.[96] In January 1994, the Hosokawa government passed electoral reform legislation centring on the introduction of single-member districts in the Lower House. Much of the drive and credit for the passage of the laws could be attributed to Ozawa, who played a crucial role in coordinating with other key party leaders in the ruling coalition.[97] Ozawa was said to expect only one thing of Hosokawa – to 'implement the small electoral district system'.[98] In fact it was Ozawa's attachment to this system that prevented the proposed reforms from being further amended. Hosokawa records in his diary that Ozawa stuck to the original plan of an electoral district system with small district areas with 300 seats and PR areas with 200 seats, and strongly resisted attempts by others in the coalition government, particularly the smaller parties, either to resist electoral reform altogether or to raise the ratio of PR seats to single-member seats.[99]

Moreover, because passage of the legislation required a political compromise that produced a mixed system of 300 single-member districts and 200 members elected by PR, this was not satisfactory to Ozawa, who consistently aimed to reduce the size of the PR element of the system, whilst acknowledging that PR ameliorated the faults of the single-seat system to some extent.[100] In 1996, Ozawa also turned his attention to the Upper House, arguing that the number of seats should be reduced to 200 and the PR constituency should be abolished.[101]

Ozawa retained his long-term ambition to strive for a pure single-member district system in the Lower House. He later claimed to have 'realised'[102] the reduction in Lower House PR seats from 200 to 180 in 2000. He did this by threatening to take his Liberal Party, or LP (Jiyūtō) out of the LDP-LP-New Kōmeitō coalition.[103] His original plan was to cut the number of Lower House members by 50 PR seats.[104] The LDP and LP jointly submitted a bill to this effect in 2000. However, the bill was ultimately unsuccessful because of opposition from the New Kōmeitō, more than half of whose Lower House seats were elected through PR.

In the 2007 DPJ manifesto, Ozawa proposed a further cut in the number of PR seats in the Lower House from 180 to 100.[105] The same election promise was made in the 2009 DPJ manifesto, which pledged to reduce the number of PR seats in the Lower House by 80. It was designed to increase the likelihood of having 'elections that can make a change of government possible',[106] and thus to enhance the possibility of a two-party system becoming firmly established.

This ambition was initially advanced by the formation of the New Frontier Party, or NFP (Shinshintō) in December 1994. The NFP represented an amalgam of the remaining remnants of the Hosokawa-led coalition government minus the JSP, which had joined hands with the LDP and New Party Harbinger, or NPH (Shintō Sakigake) to form the new government. Ozawa had taken the next step on his journey towards creating a two-party system, which required the establishment of a party that was large and strong enough to take on the LDP and replace it in government. Ozawa thought the birth of the NFP had enormous significance in this and other respects:

> For one thing, the 1955 system, in which the perpetual party in power and the perpetual opposition parties were connected behind the scenes, was at least changed by the New Frontier Party into a sound relationship between the party in power and the opposition parties in which backroom meetings didn't happen. The New Frontier Party put the parliamentary government system on a normal rule-based footing, and this was greatly important.[107]

Another reason was the party's policy manifesto entitled 'Japan Reconstruction Declaration' (*Nihon Saikōchiku Senden*).[108] According to Ozawa, compared with the LDP, which had 'simple documents written by bureaucrats, real politics needed things like principles and from those principles, frank discussion of systematic policy'.[109]

Even though Ozawa was later to prove not only the 'creator' but also the 'destroyer' of the NFP, political analyst, former LDP political staffer and later head of the DPJ's secretariat Itō Atsuo argued that this was all part of Ozawa's grand plan to establish a conservative two-party structure. He 'dissolved the NFP to abandon the people who were going to hinder his efforts'.[110] Ozawa himself justified the split in terms of the difficulties caused by the refusal of the Kōmei faction in the NFP to disband properly and thus to assimilate into the NFP. This had serious implications for the existence of the party, particularly in fighting the 1998 Upper House election. Ozawa also claimed that the split was at Kōmei's request.[111] Moreover, despite the rupture, he still thought that establishing the NFP was an important step in the evolution of a two-party system in Japan.

The inauguration of the DPJ administration in 2009 was even more significant in this respect, although Ozawa later became disillusioned with the DPJ's failure 'to become strong enough to create his vision of a true two-party system for Japan following more than 50 years of rule by the Liberal Democrats'.[112] In his view, even though the DPJ had finally become the ruling party, it was unable to consolidate a strong two-party system because the DPJ and LDP had not completely shifted their awareness as the ruling and opposition parties and 'politicians' minds had not completely adapted to the two-party system'.[113] As he observed, 'my hope was for the LDP to be reborn and the DPJ also to improve through friendly rivalry, so it is extremely unfortunate that the DPJ administration that I built after much effort was unable to carry out reforms and was instead swallowed up by the old regime'.[114]

The DPJ's failure to become the major alternative ruling party in Ozawa's view justified his creation of a new political grouping or 'study group' (*benkyōkai*) called the 'New Policy Research Group' (Atarashii Seisaku Kenkyūkai, or Shinseiken),[115] which was formed by his supporters inside the DPJ in late December 2011. His ambition was reportedly to use it as part of the preparation for rebuilding the two major-party system through political realignment.[116] Ozawa was pleased with electoral system reform insofar as it had produced a situation where 'the ruling party could be replaced by a rival party if it didn't carry out good politics'.[117] He also retained the objective of cutting the number of Diet seats, adding proposals for examining a different electoral system for the Upper House and for reform of the way the Upper and Lower Houses functioned as well as prefectural assembly electoral systems.

Reform of 'money politics'

Ozawa made a series of proposals relating to political funding reform. He had first referred to the 'problem' of 'collusion with financial circles in relation to political funding'[118] in his 1972 essay, and proposed that parties should turn to the public for political funds 'in order to shake free of dependence on financial circles'.[119] In his election bulletin for the 1976 Lower House election, he called for a ban on political donations and for the provision of political funds from the national treasury.[120] He justified this stance in his 1980 tribute to his father in *The Man Ozawa Saeki*, writing:

> The biggest problem in today's politics is elections that cost a lot of money. Furthermore, we see corruption in relation to political funds, and politicians' ethics are being called into question. The LDP is also being required to make an active response to this issue and is currently working on reforming the Political Funds Control Law and the Public Offices Election Law through the Electoral System Research Council. However, these debates do not touch on...the fundamental way political funds ought to be managed. They merely cover up the [basic] problems by working on petty details.[121]

He advocated a complete ban on private donations to politicians and political parties and transferring the financial burden to the people as a whole, with funds coming from the government (see Table 1.1). As he reiterated:

> The evil of political donations lies in the establishment of collusive relationships caused by donations from specific individuals or corporations, which then lead to politics itself being distorted...I think that we should adopt a system where political donations are completely banned, and instead individual politicians and political parties are paid...from the national treasury...If this money will solve the various problems relating to political funds and realise the complete purification of politics, then this is the best plan that we can adopt.[122]

When he was LDP secretary-general in 1989–91, Ozawa raised the issue of abolishing all donations from companies and organisations.[123] However, because the LDP's factions could not be sustained without these donations, he was met with strong opposition from within the ruling party and the issue was not taken up for public discussion. Ozawa unsuccessfully broached the issue again in his newly created political reform group, Reform Forum 21, after the Keiseikai split, and later in the NFP.[124]

Ozawa also discussed the problem of 'money politics' in *Blueprint*, where he referred to the unclear flow of large amounts of political funds and because of that, voters' concerns that policy decisions would be distorted by money and politicians might amass large personal fortunes. He acknowledged that the succession of scandals involving political funds had heightened the people's distrust of politics to the point where it was shaking the foundations of Japan's parliamentary democracy.[125] He claimed that under the existing system, politicians had 'no way of proving their innocence even if they wanted to. Since the people's distrust is so deep-rooted, they do not believe the politicians' explanations'.[126]

As a way to disperse the people's distrust, Ozawa advocated that, first, income and expenditure of political funds should be made completely transparent, which would deter wrongdoing by politicians and leave the people with 'no scope to harbour any distrust'.[127] Second, political donations from companies and organisations to political parties should be limited and banned in the case of individual politicians.[128] Third, the electoral system itself should be changed because it engendered money politics. Under the multi-seat district system, politics was driven by expensive competition between factions.[129] Because individual candidates representing different factions competed to provide personal services to voters, it led to an enormous amount of money being used in elections. The confrontation between candidates from the same party in the same constituency was, therefore, responsible for not only factional conflict at the centre of the party but also for money-driven politics and political corruption.

To compensate politicians for the cost of political activities, Ozawa envisaged public funding of political parties amounting to as much as ¥100 billion annually, which was 'inexpensive compared to the cost of…repeated political scandals, political stalemates, and public distrust'.[130] Former NFP Secretary-General Yonezawa Takashi recalled: 'When he was drunk, Ozawa said things like this regarding political party subsidies: "I've been in the LDP for a long time, but if I wanted to become prime minister I'd need to tiptoe on the border of legal and illegal, and people (such as secretaries) die…That's why we need political party subsidies".'[131]

The 1994 electoral reform laws included provisions for government subsidies to political parties under the Political Parties Subsidy Law (*Seitō Joseihō*), where a party of five or more people could receive subsidies from the government to cover operational expenses. The quantity of funding would be determined by the number of seats party members held in both houses of the Diet, but approximately one third of the cost of party activities would be covered by taxpayer funds.

As part of the political funding reforms, the number of personal fundraising groups that each politician could legally possess was restricted, and quantitative and time limits were placed on the amount that corporations and other organisations could contribute to individual politicians or their personal fundraising groups. Political donations from these sources were restricted to a maximum of ¥500,000 per annum, with a total ban after five years.[132] From 1 January 2000, individual Diet members were permitted to receive a maximum of ¥1.5 million in donations from individuals, as well as unrestricted funding from party sources, to which organisations and companies were allowed (and encouraged) to donate. Penalties for violating the new measures were also introduced.

Because of the Matsuoka Toshikatsu political expenses scandal, which came to a head with his suicide in May 2007,[133] Ozawa incorporated into the DPJ's 2007 manifesto a provision for greater transparency of office expenses, including the filing of receipts covering all expenses higher than ¥10,000.[134] He also challenged Prime Minister Abe Shinzō on the issue in the Diet, criticising him for not ordering an investigation of the issue and 'taking refuge in the defects of the current political funds system'.[135] Ozawa offered to disclose receipts and other relevant documents from his own office in order to dispel any rumours about his own very high office expenses.

In March 2009, following the arrest of Ōkubo Takanori, Ozawa's state-funded secretary and chief accountant of his political fund management organisation, Rikuzankai, on suspicion of violating the Political Funds Control Law, or PFCL (*Seiji Shikin Kiseihō*),[136] Ozawa proposed that all donations from companies and organisations, including political groups, should be banned as well as pressing for the modernisation of campaign laws to lift the ban on the use of the internet and door-to-door campaigning (see Table 1.1). At a press conference, he said, 'We cannot categorise (companies) based on (whether or not the companies receive contracts for) public works. We need to prohibit donations from companies and organisations completely. The prohibition would be pointless unless it is thorough. If [the DPJ] comes to power we will fundamentally change the way political funds work'.[137] On 9 April 2009, the DPJ set out a policy of completely abolishing corporate contributions over a three-year transition period (a provision that was included in the DPJ's 2009 manifesto), while on 28 April, Ozawa even suggested an 'immediate prohibition' on corporate contributions.[138]

Party modernisation and political leadership

For Ozawa, modernising the party system also served the larger purpose of empowering Japan's political leaders. In his view, promoting competition between two alternative ruling parties on the basis of competing policy programmes would enable them to draw on a stronger electoral mandate when in office, which would in turn underpin effective policy leadership.[139] As he argued in *Blueprint*, 'we must have a government that takes responsibility for a fixed period of time, for clearly defined powers and policies'.[140] He sought to create a government with a strong mandate to undertake new policies across a range of spheres including economic, trade, defence and foreign policy. Having two clear party options would enable voters to reject unsatisfactory governments and thus strengthen the legitimacy of the political system as well as underpin the authority of national political leaders both domestically and internationally.[141]

If Ozawa had a grand vision for Japan, it was to raise his country's international standing by encouraging the development of more policy-focused leadership and engendering political leaders who could guide Japan to play a larger role in international political and security affairs.[142] Ozawa wanted to create domestic political conditions that were conducive to Japan playing such a role. It needed a political system that could respond clearly, flexibly and rapidly to international events. A two-party system would facilitate such decision making because it could 'decide between black and white instantly'.[143]

The long-term impact of the Ozawa-inspired reforms on Japan's party system was profound. Both regime change and electoral reform helped to restructure the political system into an embryonic two-party system. Indeed, it was electoral reform that laid the basis for competition between two major parties, and hence for the regime change that took place in 2009.[144] As an individual politician, Ozawa arguably contributed more than any other politician to bringing about change to these aspects of the Japanese polity.

Institutional reform

In *Blueprint* Ozawa argued strongly for institutional reform, presenting ideas for strengthening the leadership of the prime minister, for integrating the ruling party and the cabinet, for a 'politician-led bureaucracy'[145] and for transferring power from central to local government (see Table 1.1).[146] These proposals were designed to effect a fundamental transformation of the institutions of governance, policymaking processes and power structures.

Bolstering the Prime Minister's Official Residence

At the very crux of Ozawa's vision for political reform was the concept of strengthening prime ministerial leadership so that the prime minister could 'lead both in form and in substance' (see Table 1.1).[147] He was frustrated with the practice of consensus decision making and the weakness of the prime minister and prime minister's office in policymaking.[148]

Ozawa made very specific recommendations for expanding the Prime Minister's Official Residence (Kantei), including the provision of systematic support in areas such as policy advice and coordination. Although his actual proposals were not taken up, amongst central government reforms enacted in 1999, when Ozawa's LP was in coalition with Prime Minister Obuchi Keizō's LDP, were a number of reforms that honoured the basic thrust of Ozawa's recommendations, if not his precise formulations. These related primarily to enhancing the administrative leadership of the prime minister, expanding his powers of policy initiation, and providing him with a much larger personal staff and formal, organisational support structures.

Integrating the ruling party and the cabinet

In Ozawa's view, strengthening the leadership of the prime minister, providing a single line of accountability and speeding up the process of policymaking also required integration of the ruling party and the cabinet. As he wrote in *Blueprint*, under the existing system, the government consisted of:

> two parts: the executive branch and the ruling party. Since each carries out its own policy coordination, the policy process is not only complex but takes far too long. If decision making is handled in two places, the cabinet cannot be held strictly accountable. There is no way of ensuring responsible politics...It is the elected parliament, and the cabinet selected by that parliament, that must take responsibility for politics.[149]

Much later Ozawa recalled that under the 1955 system the relationship between the government and ruling party was rivalrous:

> As such, when the ruling party and government had to negotiate – on the price of rice, for example – they argued with each other when they should have discussed the matter as allies. During the days of the LDP administration – the 1955 system – LDP members saw government – the bureaucratic structure – as the 'authorities' [*okami*]. The government and ruling party did not work together as one, but instead put on performances where the ruling party 'won' things from the government.[150]

Ozawa's prescription for institutional reform included 'bringing the ruling party's main posts into the cabinet',[151] including that of secretary-general, establishing the party's policymaking offices under the cabinet and drawing 150–160 backbenchers into the ministries in sub-ministerial positions, thus ridding Japan of the division between the government executive and the ruling party (see Table 1.1). As he reasoned:

> ruling-party politicians who are not in the cabinet today behave as if they are altogether outside the government. Policy is drafted in two separate channels: the bureaucratic line and the ruling party's Policy Affairs Research Council...The locus of responsibility thus remains ambiguous...The locus of responsibility would be clarified and the policy process would become more comprehensible if the politicians, who today are only unofficially affiliated with policy areas – the co-called 'policy-tribe' (zoku giin) Diet members who have strong ties to particular ministries – were instead given public authority, assigned formal positions in those ministries, and instructed to participate in drafting policies.[152]

Once again, Ozawa's model was Britain, 'the prototypical parliamentary-cabinet government',[153] in which executive and legislative power merged in the cabinet. Making the cabinet the core of government decision making would give Japanese politics a clear centre, which Ozawa regarded as lacking.[154] As he reasoned, Japan's 'lack of leadership in politics...[caused by] extreme diffusion of power...divided between the party and the government'[155] gave rise to periodic paralysis and "The Politics of Indecision'",[156] which was all too clearly on display during the Gulf War of 1990–91.

When running for the leadership of the NFP in December 1995, Ozawa again advocated the need for integrating the ruling party and the cabinet, including the introduction of senior vice-ministers, parliamentary secretaries and special advisers to the prime minister. This proposal was on a list of structural reforms in political, administrative, economic and social systems that Ozawa compiled for the election and which he committed himself to undertake based on a ten-year plan and on track by 2000.[157] Taken largely from *Blueprint*, Ozawa drew up the list as a set of basic policies for the NFP, entitled 'Japan Reconstruction Declaration' (*Nihon Saikōchiku Dengen*). It remained the basis of Ozawa's policies in later years, including the LP's 'Scenario for Japan's Revival' (*Nihon Saikō e no Shinario*) and the DPJ's core principles after its amalgamation with the LP.[158]

The DPJ's 2009 policy manifesto also pledged to shift 'From a two-track system in which policy-making proceeds in parallel in government and in the ruling party, to a unitary system of Cabinet-centered policy-making'.[159] When the DPJ administration was launched in September 2009, Ozawa insisted that the DPJ's Policy Research Council, or PRC (Seisaku Chōsakai) be disbanded. He saw its destruction as necessary to eliminate the party as a separate policymaking institution, which undercut the principle of cabinet centralism (see Table 1.1). In opposition, the DPJ had focused its high-level policy deliberations in a so-called 'Next Cabinet' rather than in its PRC.

The dual structure of party-government power really troubled Ozawa. He was not opposed to *zoku giin* as such, merely their location in the party and not in the government. His view was that they should be 'assigned formal positions in the ministries, and instructed to participate in drafting policies'.[160] In *Ozawashugi*, he wrote:

> some *zoku giin* today influence the administration from outside the government when they are just members of the ruling party. This is the problem. I repeat again: authority must come with responsibility. Although it is a basic rule of democracy that if one is to utilise power then one must take responsibility for the result, *zoku giin* have influence over policy decisions without having official positions or authority…However, such problems can be resolved by including these *zoku giin* in the government sector. If specialist Diet members clarify their responsibility and participate in the administration, more knowledge can be gathered. Isn't this what you could call real talent recruitment?[161]

Ozawa also viewed the division between the ruling party and the government as contributing to the maintenance of bureaucratic power (see Table 1.1). As he observed in *Ozawashugi*:

> In Japan, the government and the ruling party form a dual structure…Furthermore, policy adjustment between the government and ruling party does not have any substance any more. Officially, it appears as though the ruling

party opposes the government's idea, and the government considers the ruling party's opposition. However, the aim of this is to hide the fact that 'everything is left for the bureaucrats to deal with'. My belief is that the 'unification of the government and the ruling party' is essential to prevent this harmful effect…There is no question that the relationship between the government and ruling party must be changed in order to shake free of bureaucratic leadership and make Japan a real 'democratic country'.[162]

He urged the need to shift policy- and budget-making authority back to the cabinet in order to curtail bureaucratic power, unite the party around its policy manifesto and enable the government to speak with one voice. He again looked to the British model where policymaking was centralised in the cabinet, which 'in turn treats the bureaucracy as a body of obedient servants'.[163] He was convinced of the need for budget flexibility under cabinet leadership rather than merely retaining the traditional LDP system of budget formulation whereby the proposed allocations of the ministries were simply added up year after year and there was no order of policy priorities. He wanted subsidies and policy-based spending to be prioritised and all unnecessary expenditures abolished.[164]

A politician-led bureaucracy

Subordinating the bureaucracy to political leadership was an enduring theme in Ozawa's proposed reforms. When first elected in 1969 at the young age of 27, he made a public promise to 'abolish bureaucratic politics' and 'restore decision making to the politicians' in his election bulletin.[165] He also attacked bureaucratic power in *Ideas for Reforming the LDP*, and suggested some ideas for restoring the balance of power between politicians and bureaucrats. Although he was still a member of the LDP, he realised that the party needed to change its structure and processes so that political decisions could be made by politicians rather than by bureaucrats. Taking power away from the bureaucrats was his job and the definition of political leadership.[166]

In 1991 when secretary-general in the Kaifu administration, he set about reorganising the PARC's divisions in order to strengthen the LDP's policymaking and research functions and reduce dependence on bureaucrats.[167] After the Hosokawa administration was established in 1993, Ozawa declared that policy must be formed under the leadership of politicians.[168] He led the discussions on introducing a new and expanded system of vice-ministers to replace the existing system of parliamentary vice-ministers as a means of demonstrating that members of the government, not the bureaucracy, were in charge (see Table 1.1). Concrete proposals for the creation of new positions for politicians within the ministries were, however, stymied by opposition from within the coalition.[169]

Having returned to the opposition ranks, Ozawa continued to demand these reforms as NFP secretary-general. They were included on his list of structural reforms for the party leadership election in December 1995 and in the NFP's pledge in the 1996 election campaign. This was his first general election as NFP leader and he promised to 'eliminate dependence on bureaucrats, and realize a political regime in which politicians bear full responsibility'.[170] In 1997, the NFP together with the newly established DPJ submitted a bill to the Diet to introduce a new system of vice-ministers, but the ruling LDP refused to support it. The legislation proposed that the existing system of parliamentary vice-ministers be abolished and replaced with a new system in which two senior vice-ministers and no more than six parliamentary secretaries together with one political assistant be appointed to each ministry.[171] Ozawa disparaged the Hashimoto Ryūtaro administration at the time as:

> a bureaucratic government…Their system is not one in which politicians make decisions and take responsibility for their implementation…[T]he aim of Mr. Hashimoto's administrative reform is changing the names of the ministries. The nature of true political reform is removing bureaucrats' authority by abolishing regulations. The Hashimoto administration has not really understood that point at all from the start.[172]

It was not until 1999 that Ozawa's plans were realised. When he brought his LP into the coalition with the LDP in January 1999, he was the force behind reform of the system of parliamentary vice-ministers and their replacement with an expanded system of senior vice-ministers and parliamentary secretaries (see Table 1.1). This reform was one of nine items in the LP-LDP policy agreement setting up the coalition between the two parties.[173] It entailed the replacement of the existing system of parliamentary vice-ministers with 22 senior vice-ministers and 26 parliamentary secretaries, with senior vice-ministers given the elevated status of confirmation by the Emperor, just like the prime minister and ministers. This reform enabled the senior vice-ministers literally to speak on behalf of their ministers on the floor of the Diet.[174]

According to Ozawa's former private secretary, Ishikawa Tomohiro, Ozawa saw the new system as the driving force behind the abolition of bureaucratic leadership over policies.[175] For the LP, changing the structure of power was more important than changing policy.[176] As LP leader, Ozawa told the Diet, 'we cannot build a new country today on the foundation of the centralised bureaucratic system that has existed from the Meiji Era…and the structure of collusion between politicians and bureaucrats that was born under the LDP's politics'.[177] He proposed a Basic Law on Establishing Politics Led by the People (*Kokumin Shudō Seiji Kakuritsu Kihonhō*), which would limit direct contact between bureaucrats and Diet members, and a Cabinet Legislation Bureau Abolition Law (*Naikaku Hōseikyoku Haishihō*), which would ban bureaucrats' involvement in Diet deliberations on various bills and take back national politics from the hands of bureaucrats (see Table 1.1).[178] These were among Ozawa's Eleven Basic Laws for Remodelling Japan (*Nihon Isshin 11 Kihon Hōan*), which he presented as '"the blueprint for a new nation" but…[which] he actually wanted to say were the "New Nihon Kaizō Keikaku"'.[179] He submitted them to the Diet just before the LP's merger with the DPJ was decided in 2003.

Ozawa emphasised the importance of further reforms along these lines in *Ozawashugi*, arguing that in these respects Japan still needed to learn from the United Kingdom:

> In Japan, government party members who can enter the cabinet are limited to ministers, and senior vice-ministers and parliamentary secretaries were established based on the Liberal Party's claims – and they only have limited power. In the UK, in addition to cabinet ministers, there are posts called ministers of state outside the cabinet, parliamentary vice-ministers and assistant parliamentary vice-ministers etc., and including these members, the number of government party politicians who enter the government and deal with actual administrative work reaches more than 100…In practice, these members have their own roles, answer questions as members of the government, participate in debates and are involved in making decisions within the government. Because politicians with authority and responsibility are directly involved in administration, bureaucrats are prevented from becoming 'pseudo-politicians' in the United Kingdom. The bureaucrats, on the other hand, are…prohibited from coming into contact with politicians and almost excessively avoid becoming involved in politics…By actually participating in government…politicians can experience the realities of administration and get to know problems of current systems and legislation through which they can broaden their view…Under the current system in Japan, young Diet members and newcomers rarely have the chance to get to know the reality of administration since members who can participate in the government sector are limited.[180]

This view underlay Ozawa's insistence that teams of politicians be sent into government agencies to place them under political control (see Table 1.1). Ozawa inserted into the 2009 DPJ manifesto a proposal to install 100 or more Diet members from the DPJ into the ministries and agencies as ministers, senior vice-ministers, parliamentary secretaries and ministerial assistants.[181] Even after the earlier reforms, there had only been 70 Diet members holding the sub-cabinet posts of senior vice-minister and parliamentary secretary but they had rarely been involved in government decision making.

When the DPJ won government in 2009, Ozawa described the election victory as one in which 'we were given the reins of government by appealing to the people that we will change our politics from being led by the bureaucrats [*kanryō shudō*] to one that is led by the politicians, led by the people [*seijika shudō, kokumin shudō*]'.[182] For him, this was his first real opportunity to curb the power of the bureaucracy by subordinating it to the authority of politicians elected to government.

A system was immediately installed whereby each ministry was allocated three layers of political 'executives in charge of policy affairs' (*seimu sanyaku*), consisting of the minister, senior vice-ministers and parliamentary secretaries who were tasked with a central role in policymaking, policy coordination and decision making. The following January a heads of government and party meeting discussed how to beef up the government's leadership capacity by increasing the number of senior vice-ministers, parliamentary secretaries and ministerial assistants. The government side said that they wanted to expand the number of Diet members entering the government mainly in order to strengthen the function of the cabinet.[183] The meeting agreed to lift the number of Diet members entering the government by 15 from the existing 73. The new posts would include additional senior vice-ministers and parliamentary secretaries. The reforms would make politicians clearly responsible for the management of the ministries.[184] An Ozawa-sponsored bill was submitted to the Diet, which implemented the increase in the number of senior vice-ministers and parliamentary secretaries in May 2010.

The abolition of the PRC was also designed to allow cabinet ministers, senior vice-ministers and parliamentary secretaries to exercise policy leadership not only in name but also in practice. With the unification of the ruling party and the cabinet, the practice of the ruling party conducting 'prior examination and approval' (*jizen shinsa • shōnin*) of government policy and legislation ceased. Ozawa envisaged a division of labour whereby policy decisions would be centralised in the political executive, while all other political issues relating to the organisation of the party, elections and Diet affairs would be dealt with by the secretary-general's office.[185]

The creation of 'policy councils in each ministry' (*kakushō seisaku kaigi*), also at Ozawa's instigation, served to displace both the bureaucracy and the ruling party as separate power centres in the policymaking process (see Table 1.1). In September 2009, Ozawa sent a notice to all DPJ members, which outlined the new policymaking system between the government and ruling party. It stated: 'Functions of the "next cabinet" (the DPJ's shadow cabinet in opposition) and the DPJ's Policy Research Council are to be fully transferred to the government (cabinet)'.[186] He also outlined the structure of the new ministry policy councils. They would be government bodies comprising senior vice-ministers and parliamentary secretaries. They would draw their membership from ruling party Diet members in the Upper and Lower House standing committees corresponding to each ministry. Other ruling party members could also participate.[187] The government side would explain their policy plans to the policy councils while members could exchange opinions and make policy proposals, but the councils would have no policymaking power.[188] The councils would provide non-cabinet parliamentary members of the ruling party with a venue in which to develop their policy skills and understanding in lieu of the normal training ground in the PRC, but importantly, within the ministries, not in the party. Moreover, DPJ politicians could not become involved in the policy process apart from attending the ministry policy councils.[189]

Under the new system, the 'ministerial team' (*daijin chīmu*) consisting of the minister, senior vice-ministers and parliamentary secretaries would formulate policy plans and the cabinet would make policy decisions.[190] As Ozawa later elaborated, 'Policy decisions relating to general administration will be made by the government whilst listening to everyone's opinions in the ministry policy councils... This is only natural considering the essence of the parliamentary cabinet system'.[191]

The new structure was also designed to build political leadership by politicians, who would draft, coordinate and determine policy within each ministry as part of the assertion of policy leadership over the bureaucracy.

The DPJ's subsequent failure to accomplish this goal became a constant irritant to Ozawa, who insisted that politicians should have the courage of their convictions. He declared:

> I think each person [in the government] should…have the guts to make up their mind…Since [this is] a democracy, politicians must reach decisions [on issues]. Ministers, or whoever it might be, people who [are responsible] should be able to say 'I have reached this conclusion'…If [the leader] does not make a decision and if they do not think along the lines of 'I have to decide and I have responsibility', then public servants won't follow us.[192]

He condemned Prime Minister Kan Naoto's handling of the triple disasters of March 2011 and their aftermath, accusing the Kan administration of being worse than the LDP in succumbing to the power of the bureaucracy, observing, 'the government is just riding on the bureaucratic system, and we are even criticised that it is worse than when the LDP was in power'.[193] He attributed the declining support for the DPJ to the government's failure to continue his line of bureaucrat bashing under which he had led the party to power, saying '"I expected the DPJ to be more serious and almost brutally honest" in breaking the co-dependent relationship between politicians and bureaucrats'.[194] He went on:

> we ended up being severely criticised for being even worse than before. Why is this so? In politics led by the people and politicians, the people, that is to say the politicians who represent the people, have to take the responsibility for deciding on and executing administrative policies. Otherwise, 'politics led by the people and politicians' become mere words…If the politicians say, 'I'll take responsibility, so you people do things this way', then the bureaucrats will follow, unless what the politician is saying is ridiculous. But if the politicians say, 'I'm not responsible, you decided to do that, we entrusted you with this matter', then our assertions become total lies…[At the moment] everything depends on the bureaucratic system, and bureaucratic control reaches all aspects of the people's lives. I think that breaking away from this bureaucratic control and for the people to choose politicians who can make such daring actions are one of the basic aspects of democracy. I think that is also a form of major reform towards politics led by the people.[195]

In a New Year interview in 2012, Ozawa made a plea for politicians with political ideals and vision without which they would only be able to do what the bureaucrats told them and would become spokespersons for the bureaucracy. He criticised the cohort of DPJ members as not having the knowledge or courage to take responsibility for policies and for only doing what the bureaucrats told them.[196]

For Ozawa, the goal of curtailing the power of the bureaucracy and putting politicians in charge required a change in Japan's political culture. He questioned whether Japan was really a democratic country because of the extent of bureaucratic power over the entire nation. He wanted greater awareness amongst the people that they were sovereign and that deference towards authority (*okami ishiki*)[197] was the biggest reason for the bureaucrats maintaining their power.[198] His desire was to 'change society into one that values "individuals' sense of values" and…[where] individual people's decisions determine the course of politics'.[199]

In *Ozawashugi* Ozawa linked the two themes of individualism and leadership under the heading of 'Breaking free from "deference to authority"'.[200] He wrote:

> When we think about 'what politics is', the relationship between politics and bureaucrats is an important issue to consider. The concept of 'faith in bureaucrats' has long been established amongst the people in Japan. Politicians in Nagata-chō are not to be trusted, because they are always struggling for power and practising money politics. On the other hand, bureaucrats in Kasumigaseki are elites who graduated from Tokyo University and are people of integrity. It would be much safer if these bureaucrats support the country. This is generally what the 'faith in bureaucrats' means. However… the fact that politics has been run by bureaucrats and not by politicians in Japan, a 'democratic' country, is itself abnormal.[201]

As Ozawa saw it, a key flaw in the exercise of political power by bureaucrats was their lack of accountability – their refusal to take responsibility for their actions. Politicians, on the other hand, were chosen as the people's representatives and were, therefore, 'eligible to deal with politics. This is the principle and rule of democracy'.[202] He condemned the fact that in Japan, not even the prime minister could dismiss bureaucrats who were supposed to be his subordinates. Far from it, even when ministers criticised bureaucrats, they were blackballed. He cited the example of Tanaka Makiko as minister of foreign affairs during the Koizumi administration.[203] He also thought the saying, 'All power tends to corrupt and absolute power corrupts absolutely', aptly described the Japanese bureaucratic system.[204]

Ozawa depicted the July 2010 Upper House election as 'the final war' for state reform, making the point in an election campaign speech that, 'It is not easy to change centralised authoritarian rule and control by the bureaucracy, which have lasted since the Meiji era. If the DPJ does not secure a majority in the Upper and Lower Houses, it will be impossible to defeat such an old-style system. The Upper House election will be the final war'.[205] When later campaigning for the DPJ leadership in September 2010, Ozawa explained that he 'threw his hat into the ring in the strong belief that a system should be created where politicians decide the policies and budgets'.[206] He advocated 'leadership by politicians…[saying] I can definitely achieve this and I'm aware of my responsibilities and my duties, and I will achieve this as though my life depended upon it'.[207]

The concept of fundamentally changing the structure of the state under political leadership was also an important facet of the philosophy of the Ozawa-led party in the making for the post-DPJ period – Shinseiken. He developed this theme through the medium of Shinseiken's website, insisting that the transition from the politics of bureaucratic leadership to the people's leadership and the politics of political leadership had not taken root in Japan under the DPJ.[208]

Reforms to Diet processes

For Ozawa, Diet reforms were also necessary to reduce bureaucratic power and he consistently paired his proposed reforms to the political executive with reforms to Diet processes and procedures. In *Blueprint*, he broached the subject of abolishing the longstanding tradition of bureaucrats answering questions on behalf of ministers in the Diet. In his view, cabinet ministers and parliamentary vice-ministers, not bureaucrats, should reply to Diet questions (see Table 1.1), because politicians had 'ultimate responsibility for decision making'.[209]

In October 1993, as secretary-general of the RP, Ozawa announced a basic plan for abolishing the government committee member system (*seifu iin seido*),[210] the official term given to the practice of senior bureaucrats, usually bureaux directors-general, answering questions in the Diet on behalf of ministers. This system had been seen as undermining Diet members' ability to gain policy experience and as passing over the task of policy formulation largely to bureaucrats.

In 1996, as NFP leader, Ozawa's antipathy towards the bureaucracy and his desire to establish strong leadership by politicians were again manifested in a call for bureaucrats to be banned from answering questions in the Diet in lieu of ministers. In 1997, work towards the formulation of a bill to that effect was advanced in the NFP,[211] and then in November 1997 the bill, which also promised to introduce the revamped vice-ministers system, was submitted to the Diet.

In the following year when, as LP leader, Ozawa was negotiating with Prime Minister Obuchi on forming the coalition with the LDP, abolishing the *seifu iin seido* was again on the list of demands for political reform to be incorporated into the policy agreement between the two parties. Other items included the establishment of the new vice-ministers system and a Diet committee in which the prime minister and opposition party leaders could debate fundamental policies of the state instead of individual bills. The Law to Revitalise Diet Deliberations and to Establish a Policymaking System under Political Leadership (Diet Revitalisation Law, or *Kokkai Shingi Kasseikahō*), which was subsequently passed in July 1999, eliminated the government committee member system although bureaucrats were still permitted to attend Diet committee hearings if invited as so-called 'reference witnesses' (*seifu sankōnin*). They could answer questions on detailed and technical matters relating to government administration where it was inappropriate for ministers and vice-ministers to do so.[212]

When asked why he had rejoined the LDP in coalition and what the point was of the five years he had spent away from the party, Ozawa answered:

36 *New politics and policies*

> I left the party because I saw that it was impossible for the LDP to carry out such reforms. My leaving the LDP was not pointless, as the LDP and government have now become able to accept policies including the abolition of the government committee member system, which leads to breaking down the bureaucrats' rule over the Diet.[213]

The legislation also established the new system of senior vice-ministers and parliamentary secretaries, and set up a National Basic Policy Committee (Kokka Kihon Seisaku Iinkai).[214] Held as a joint meeting of both Lower and Upper House committees, it was designed to act as a forum for weekly debates between the prime minister and opposition parties leaders (*tōshu tōron*), and to allow Diet members the opportunity to question the prime minister with questions on notice, and to ask follow-up questions without notice along the lines of the British system of Prime Minister's Questions (see Table 1.1). Ozawa claimed that the reforms that entailed expelling bureaucrats from Diet interpellations and having Diet members debate policy with each other were 'epoch-making'.[215] No longer could politicians hide behind bureaucrats; they had to figure policies out for themselves.

Two further demands made by Ozawa were a reduction in the total number of ministers from 20 to 17, and over the longer term to 14, and cutting the size of the central bureaucracy by 25 per cent over ten years.[216] The former was partially achieved with a cut in the number of ministers in the Obuchi cabinet from 20 to 18, while the latter was put off for the indefinite future.[217]

Having passed the first bill on revitalising Diet deliberations, Ozawa continued to advocate Diet reform. In *Ozawashugi*, he was very critical of what he regarded as retrograde developments under the Koizumi administration:

> During the coalition between the LDP and the Liberal Party, I realised the 'abolition of government committee members'. I did this in order to shake ourselves free from bureaucratic dependency by making ministers and senior vice-ministers answer questions in the Diet and by making politicians take responsibility for their own policies. However, this system has been emasculated under the LDP government. Prime Minister Koizumi himself has said that 'specialised issues should be answered by bureaucrats'. Even when ministers and senior vice-ministers answer questions in the Diet, they do not speak with their own words and beliefs but instead just read essays written by the bureaucrats. It is impossible to shake free from bureaucratic politics like this.[218]

Ozawa continued to take the credit for having accomplished the Diet reforms of 1999 in the 2007 DPJ election manifesto, which he wrote. He referred to 'the abolition of the system of having government bureaucrats speak in Diet debates instead of ministers, [and] initiating Prime Minister's Question Time'.[219] These were designed to 'complete the introduction of a series of British-style parliamentary systems'.[220]

Ozawa took parliamentary reforms a step further in the DPJ's 'Index 2009', which stated that only Diet members were to engage in Diet committee discussions, although sub-committees of these committees could convene hearings at which the opinions of national government employees or private citizens could be presented. He later outlined his intention to amend the Diet law further to end the practice of allowing bureaucrats to give replies on behalf of cabinet ministers in Diet committee deliberations as reference witnesses. The practice was particularly prevalent with respect to the content of legislation drafted by the bureaucrats, who subsequently answered questions about it during Diet committee deliberations. Ozawa emphasised, 'The overthrow of bureaucratic rule must start with the Diet. I would like to see the Diet become a venue where politicians can pursue discussions'.[221]

Ozawa was appointed as head of the DPJ's Political Reform Promotion Headquarters (Seiji Kaikaku Suishin Honbu).[222] He instructed close associates to draft another Diet reform bill, which was submitted to the Lower House in May 2010 with his name on the top of the list of sponsors. He had 'strong feelings' about the legislation,[223] which banned bureaucrats from answering questions in the Diet and increased the number of senior vice-ministers and parliamentary secretaries. It was submitted without waiting for mediation by the chairman of the Lower House between the ruling and opposition parties who opposed the bill.

Specifically, the legislation banned the director-general of the Cabinet Legislation Bureau (CLB) and the director-general of the International Legal Affairs Bureau (formerly Treaties Bureau) of the Ministry of Foreign Affairs (MOFA) from answering questions in the Diet. This was a far more significant development than appeared at first sight. The CLB director-general, not the Supreme Court, had traditionally had the final say in interpreting the constitution, including Article 9, the peace clause, while the director-general of the Treaties Bureau had previously had responsibility for interpreting the US–Japan Security Treaty and thus a primary role in managing the US–Japan alliance. The upshot of these Diet reforms was that the cabinet would have the final say on constitutional matters, particularly covering controversial issues such as Japan's participation in collective defence, and the major role of maintaining the US–Japan Security Treaty would be transferred from MOFA to Diet politicians. Ozawa set out deliberately to engineer these reforms, given, it is said, his bad history with the CLB going back to 1990–91, when the bureau's director-general effectively blocked a Japanese military contribution to the Gulf War.[224] At the time, this stymied Ozawa's hopes for the SDF to participate in collective security operations in the Gulf under United Nations (UN) auspices.

Shinseiken's Policy Vision subsequently took up the theme of fortifying the Diet against the predations of the bureaucracy. It argued strongly for strengthening supervision of the administration and the investigative abilities of the Diet in order to 'secure independence from the government and exercise investigative powers with binding power over the administration'.[225] Ozawa continued to see these as integral to changing the balance of power between politicians and bureaucrats. In addition, Shinseiken proposed measures to 'stimulate, enrich and optimise deliberations by Diet members'[226] by eliminating the CLB director-general from the position of the government's special assistant and abolishing the government reference witness system.[227] Also included on the list of reforms were proposals to buttress the cabinet's role in Diet deliberations and the investigative abilities of the Diet under the rubric of 'strengthening supervision of the administration', including the prosecutorial use of power.[228]

Decentralisation

Transferring fiscal and administrative power from central to local government under the rubric of 'decentralisation' (see Table 1.1) was another perennial theme in Ozawa's plan for curtailing the powers of the central bureaucracy, although his specific recommendations for how it should be achieved changed over time. In *Blueprint*, he called for power, except where really necessary, to be 'transferred from the national to the local governments'.[229] He wrote, 'Anything that does not absolutely require intervention from the central government should be transferred over to local governments'.[230] He put his mind to how to reverse the concentration of administrative and fiscal power in the central government and its ministries, and 'how to create a system in which the local governments take the lead and the center provides the support'.[231] Decentralisation, in his view, should involve the wholesale transfer of both fiscal authority and revenue sources from the central government to local governments, which would, at the same time, help to eliminate the vested interests of the Kasumigaseki ministries and revive the economy. Ozawa thought that it was vital to 'reform "concession-driven politics" (*riken seiji*) led by bureaucrats'.[232]

The fundamental principle guiding the new system of central-local government would be one where 'local areas have the authority and bear the responsibility for all domestic affairs except those that require a unified national policy'.[233] The system itself would consist of a two-tier framework, with local government consisting of 300 self-governing units called 'municipalities', or 'cities', replacing the current city-town-village system, although it was not clear under this plan how the prefectures would be dealt with. A former newspaper journalist who was reportedly working as Ozawa's 'brain' on *Nihon Kaizō Keikaku*, recalled that Ozawa 'deliberately did not write about them [i.e. mention the prefectures]'.[234]

Decentralising power was a key item on the list of structural reforms that Ozawa compiled for the December 1995 NFP leadership election and which reappeared in Ozawa's 'Eleven Basic Laws for Remodelling Japan', which he formulated while in the LP. Three of the laws, including the Basic Law on Establishing Local Autonomy (*Chihō Jichi Kakuritsu Kihonhō*), which would restrict national administration to areas such as diplomacy, defence, basic social security, etc., and entrust local governments with funding sources and authority for other matters, with the nation divided into 300 cities, were included in the DPJ's 2003 election manifesto.[235] Ozawa revised this idea further prior to the 2009 election, aligning his thinking more closely with the LDP-Keidanren concept of decentralisation. This proposed a system of regional states (*dōshūsei*), under which the 47 prefectures would be abolished and replaced with broader regional bodies possessing wider fiscal and administrative powers.

Ozawa revisited the decentralisation theme yet again in his September 2010 bid for the DPJ leadership,[236] arguing that the only way to revive the nation was to engineer 'a wholesale transfer of both authority and revenue sources from Tokyo's Kasumigaseki administrative district to local governments'.[237] He suggested that wasteful spending could be eliminated and funds freed up for necessary government expenditure if the system of government subsidies to municipalities were replaced by a so-called 'lump-sum grant system' (*ikkatsu kōfukin seido*), which had been canvassed as a fiscal structural reform in the 2009 DPJ manifesto. Under the new system, conditional subsidies for specific uses paid to local governments would be abolished and replaced by a single block grant that would increase regional government bodies' discretionary spending powers. Ozawa also stressed the point that revenues could be found by paying subsidies to local governments as lump-sum grants, thereby reducing waste.[238] He quoted local leaders who offered the reassurance that they could make do with 50 per cent of existing subsidies if they could use all the funds freely.[239]

As part of his promised commitment if elected DPJ leader, Ozawa also pledged to increase the share of tax revenues for local governments from the existing 40 per cent to 50 per cent in line with demands from prefectural governors. Under this system, the central government would reduce their subsidies to local governments while boosting local governments' tax receipts and taxation power.[240] This would be another way of curbing the power of central government bureaucrats, including abolishing the branch offices of the central ministries. At the same time, handing money and authority to local governments would allow for greater flexibility in the delivery of services, such as social welfare. In addition, Ozawa proposed to transfer control over expressway construction to the prefectures as the centrepiece of his policy of placing importance on the regions.

Ozawa raised the issue of decentralisation again after the March 2011 earthquake and tsunami disaster, arguing that 'We can make changes to various systems, including the way our country is governed, to make the change from centralisation to decentralisation of power, if we dare to do so. It is a perfect chance, our greatest opportunity to realise our advocacy'.[241] He elaborated his ideas in more detail in a 2012 New Year interview:

> We should give money to regional governments and tell them to make roads, bridges and dykes as they wish…We should not have to get the bureaucrats in the central government to assess each and every project and provide subsidies. Instead, we should allow the regional governments to use their own budgets based on their own ideas. In that way, we can achieve regional sovereignty, which in turn will stimulate regional economies. If the regional governments think for themselves and formulate their own budgets, this will significantly speed up the process of the projects and they can use the necessary budget to have regional companies work on them. We will be able to eliminate waste in the central and regional governments, which will increase efficiency.[242]

Ozawa also revisited the decentralisation theme during the Noda Yoshihiko administration as an alternative to raising the consumption tax,[243] claiming that he had tried to convert the state's governing structure to decentralisation when he was secretary-general in the Hatoyama administration.[244] The phrase 'convert the state's governing structure' (tōji kikō no tenkan) was significant insofar as its usage closely coincided with the phrase used by the newly elected Osaka mayor, Hashimoto Tōru, with whom Ozawa was considering some kind of political alliance at the time.[245] Ozawa expressed support for Hashimoto's goal of promoting decentralisation, saying that his 'goal of creating a new system is "the same as mine"'.[246] He praised the 2011 campaign manifesto of Hashimoto's local political party, the Osaka Restoration Association (Ōsaka Ishin no Kai), saying, 'I agree with the party's assertion that a government system that can make decisions and take responsibility should be created. I also agree with the idea of destroying the old structure and creating a new system'.[247] He declared that 'decentralisation of power to local governments' was one of the DPJ's starting points and insisted that this was not an argument made exclusively by Hashimoto but was something that he had also asserted 'in a loud voice [which was why] he was hated by many bureaucrats'.[248] In his 2012 New Year interview he added:

> Osaka City Mayor Hashimoto Tōru's way of thinking is similar to mine. I think that he wants to destroy the old system, in other words, the established bureaucratic structure and governing structure, because otherwise we cannot conduct politics that is truly for the people. I agree with that idea. That is what the DPJ had been advocating – in a sense, he stole our thunder.[249]

Shinseiken later adopted the idea of regional sovereignty as an important policy principle involving the transfer of powers to conduct public works and projects, as well as the function of and power to collect taxes and determine tax rates to local governments. It advocated giving discretionary powers to local governments over half of the public investment that would form the foundation of 'additional economic measures' of about ¥20 trillion per annum for five consecutive years that it was proposing as a means to 'shake free of deflation and increase income by 1.5 times'.[250] Shinseiken also linked these regional sovereignty reforms to reform of Kasumigaseki, namely the central government bureaucracy, in order to change their mindset and to achieve political leadership to carry out the reforms.[251] After the DPJ's demise was cemented in the 2012 and 2013 elections, Ozawa's harsh verdict on its accomplishments reflected what he regarded as its failures in this and other areas of institutional reform. As he told an interviewer, 'The ideas that we will…shift from centralised power to decentralised power formed the foundation of all policies, but they were lost'.[252]

Social and economic reforms

In Ozawa's thinking, transformation of Japan's political structure should be complemented by policy reforms in the economic and social spheres. In 'Book III' of *Blueprint* on 'The Five Freedoms', he called for 'Freedom from Ageism and Sexism',[253] devoting an entire chapter to 'the contributions of senior citizens', 'senior citizens in the workplace' and 'providing pensions to housewives'.[254] While not a social radical, Ozawa espoused the view that women should have freedom and equality, and he consistently recruited female candidates to stand as election candidates. This approach proved spectacularly successful in the 2009 Lower House election.[255]

The economic reforms that Ozawa advocated in *Blueprint* were essentially neo-liberal: deregulation, privatisation, tax cuts, the imposition of fiscal discipline and trade liberalisation. He proposed reductions in income, residential and corporate taxes[256] while advocating an increase in the consumption tax from 3 to 10 per cent. He was pivotal in negotiating the introduction of the consumption tax in January 1989 during the period when he served as deputy chief cabinet secretary, from December 1987 until June 1989, in the Takeshita administration.[257] He wrote, 'Democracy is premised on the people's ability to stand on their own two feet'.[258]

Later, during the Hosokawa administration, Ozawa pressured the prime minister into accepting a proposal for a 'national welfare tax' (*kokumin fukushizei*), which would effectively raise the consumption tax from 3 per cent to 7 per cent.[259] The rationale behind it originated in the 'Five Freedoms' concept in *Blueprint*, and involved using the consumption tax to fund basic social security.[260] When the idea was opposed by Chief Cabinet Secretary Takemura Masayoshi, who was the leader of the NPH, Ozawa suggested to Hosokawa that he eject Takemura from the cabinet.[261] The Ministry of Finance (MOF) had approached Ozawa as the key person in the tax reform process because he believed in 'healthy government finances with a balanced budget'.[262] Takemura, on the other hand, was considered unacceptable to the MOF because he had called for a tax reduction first.[263]

With respect to deregulation, *Blueprint* revealed Ozawa's penchant for abolishing 'excess regulations…[with] only the minimum number of rules necessary to govern economic and social activity'.[264] Deregulation figured as one of the 'Five Freedoms'. It entailed the abolition of 'anachronistic and meaningless rules… [and] allowing individuals and companies more freedom'.[265] Ozawa referred to the '[m]eaningless regulations [that] tie up our lives in issues related to transport, finance, distribution, and land use',[266] and argued for the immediate introduction of deregulation.[267] The NFP under Ozawa's leadership subsequently adopted deregulation as one of its major policy themes.

At the inauguration of the LP, Ozawa continued in the same vein, saying:

> Talking about the economy, we should remove all regulations. Then, we should make the minimum fundamental rules and then let it be free. From now on, we should make a society where people can freely enter new fields with their individual creativity and ideas. For that purpose, we should abolish the regulations established by the bureaucrats. We have to shift that power to the private sphere.[268]

Amongst his 'Eleven Basic Laws for Remodelling Japan' in 2003, Ozawa included a Basic Law on Establishing a Market Economy (*Shijo Keizai Kakuritsu Kihonhō*), which would replace regulations on particular business activities with general rules to strengthen markets.[269]

Privatising public corporations was another item on Ozawa's list, in order 'to utilize the knowledge and ideas of the private sector'.[270] Part of the Hosokawa government's proposed administrative reforms included discussion between Hosokawa and Ozawa about the possibility of privatising special public corporations such as the Housing and Urban Development Corporation.[271] Later when standing for the NFP leadership in 1995, Ozawa espoused a policy of abolishing all special public corporations within five years.[272] Such a platform clearly placed Ozawa in the category of a small-government, neo-conservative Rinchō-ist.[273] The NFP was widely depicted at the time as representing this style of 'reformist' party. Ozawa's proposed Basic Law on Organising Government-Affiliated Corporations (*Tokushu Hōjintō Seiri Kihonhō*) incorporated the abolition and privatisation of government-affiliated corporations, authorised corporations other than the Bank of Japan and independent administrative institutions within three years as a general rule.[274]

Also in line with Rinchō-ist thinking was Ozawa's advocacy of measures to promote self-help and heighten fiscal discipline.[275] Before the NFP leadership election in December 1995, Ozawa gathered together the members of his support group and said he would stand for the leadership providing that they all agreed to approve his specific list of policies and political ideas, including a comprehensive agenda of tax reform. On the list was 'Rebuilding the economy and society', where he wrote, 'taking into consideration the current economic conditions, I will cancel the consumption tax rise (to 5 per cent) scheduled to take place in fiscal 1997, and will establish a law so that the tax rate will rise to 6 per cent five years after enactment, and then to 10 per cent ten years after enactment'.[276] This would mean leaving the consumption tax rate at 3 per cent for five years then raising it to 6 per cent, and after ten years increasing it to 10 per cent.[277]

Ishikawa attributed Ozawa's about-face on the consumption tax rise to his desire 'to improve the economy after seeing the severe economic conditions that Japan was experiencing'.[278] The short-term economic gains from temporarily freezing the consumption tax would give way to the long-term pain of consumption tax rises as the economy recovered. At the same time, what the government would take in consumption tax increases it would give back in tax cuts in other areas. As explained by DPJ Diet member Kaieda Banri, Ozawa based his reasoning on the fact that Japan's consumption tax rate was the lowest amongst the 24 advanced industrial economies in the Organisation for Economic Co-operation and Development (OECD). Therefore, raising the consumption tax from 3 to 10 per cent would place Japan between the European countries and the United States. At the same time, income and residence taxes could be halved.[279]

As well as lowering income and residence taxes, Ozawa also proposed abolishing the land-value tax, real estate acquisition tax and registration licence tax.[280] Altogether the tax cuts amounted to ¥60 trillion.[281] In addition, Ozawa committed himself to ¥1 trillion in annual public investment in new technologies and industries, and a reduction in the effective rate of corporation tax from the existing 50 per cent to 45 per cent, which would bring it closer to international standards.[282]

The NFP's manifesto for the 1996 Lower House election continued some of these themes. Ozawa renewed his pledge to keep the consumption tax at 3 per cent while offering a 'gigantic tax cut of ¥18 trillion'.[283] This was based on halving income and residential taxes as well as a large cut in the corporate tax. In the Diet, Ozawa stated that he was motivated by the desire to move to a 'system that allows the people to decide how they use their income...[and] to revive the economy, as increasing disposable income would result in increased individual consumption'.[284]

In the transition from the NFP to the LP, Ozawa became even more of a market liberal. The LP policy platform called for a lowering of the consumption tax, then at 5 per cent, back to 3 per cent. It also proposed a Market Law (*Shijohō*) that would abolish restrictions on the market as well as halving income tax and municipal tax rates.[285] When interviewed at the launching of the new party, Ozawa said:

> I have...called for the halving of income and municipal taxes for many years. I think taxes are too high in Japan...What I am saying is that we should cast off regulated society and strip away restrictions...We should create a society that is freer and where individuals are more independent...We should reduce the amount of people's income that is taken forcefully.[286]

The policy agreement that Ozawa negotiated before joining the coalition with the LDP in January 1999 ran along similar lines, with a demand for a ¥10 million tax cut in income, residential and other taxes, and a lowering of the effective corporate tax rate to 40 per cent.[287] At the same time, Ozawa dropped his previous insistence on the consumption tax being reduced to 3 per cent or even lower.[288] What he got from Obuchi was a ¥3.3 trillion addition to ¥6 trillion in tax cuts for fiscal 1999. Ten years later, Ozawa committed the DPJ to cutting the corporate tax rate for small and medium-sized enterprises in the DPJ's 2009 election manifesto.[289]

Ozawa brought a similar neo-liberal mindset to his understanding of trade policy. In *Blueprint*, he argued the need for Japan to adopt 'a new economic diplomacy'[290] and for a sector-by-sector review from the perspective of the Japanese consumer as 'part of economic reform toward opening our markets'.[291] He called for Japan aggressively to open its markets and for establishing the World Trade Organization (WTO).[292] He wrote that Japan must act 'by opening its domestic market to the outside world and significantly reducing government interference in businesses. By working toward a classically liberal market economy...Japan would...be in a stronger position to promote the creation of a WTO'.[293] Ozawa wanted the 1986–94 General Agreement on Tariffs and Trade (GATT) Uruguay Round negotiations to succeed, urging Japan 'to aggressively work towards a successful conclusion of the Uruguay Round of GATT, and to play a leadership role in maintaining and expanding the principle of free trade'.[294]

Ozawa's pronouncements on trade certainly impressed many business and opinion leaders, including the chairman of Keidanren at the time, Hiraiwa Gaishi.[295] Ozawa had already put neo-liberal principles into practice, personally negotiating trade agreements with the US Administration when he was deputy chief cabinet secretary in the Takeshita administration,[296] and taking the politically risky decision with Prime Minister Hosokawa to sign on to the Uruguay Round Agreement on Agriculture (URAA). Ozawa visited Europe in the autumn of 1993, holding secret negotiations with Ministry of Agriculture, Forestry and Fisheries (MAFF) bureaucrats who were there to argue Japan's position in the negotiations. His aim was to hasten the agreement on agricultural trade liberalisation.[297] Hosokawa and Ozawa were both determined that Japan had to open its rice market in the face of resistance from the opposition LDP's agricultural *zoku gin* and their own coalition partner, the JSP.[298] Hosokawa felt that he would have to solve this problem and Ozawa was determined no matter what.[299] They agreed between themselves who should have the job of securing agreement from the JSP to market-opening concessions on rice.[300]

Ozawa later explained the reasons for his insistence on trade liberalisation in *Ozawashugi*, where he professed support for the principles of liberal economics and market opening, 'if trade partners want a truly free trade'.[301] His justification was that 'the benefits of liberalisation are far greater than the costs of sustaining agricultural protection'.[302] He also argued the case for 100 per cent food self-sufficiency, even in the absence of import tariffs.[303] He regarded Japanese agricultural products as enjoying a degree of natural protection because of their quality and safety. This would enable them to stand up to competition from cheaper imports.[304] He later admitted that he was viewed as an enemy by the agricultural cooperative organisation (JA) and by the MAFF because of his views. In his judgement, only JA and the MAFF would have problems as a result of agricultural import liberalisation, because they would lose their vested interests.[305]

The manifesto for the 2007 Upper House election, which Ozawa faced as party leader, offered the assurance that Japan would 'manage to maintain and expand domestic production of agricultural products, and at the same time promote the WTO trade liberalisation negotiations and the conclusion of Free Trade Agreements with different countries'.[306] The introduction of an 'individual farm household income compensation system would ensure that sufficient food would be produced and farmers' incomes and the rural environment would be maintained'.[307]

In the 2009 DPJ manifesto, Ozawa again displayed his market-opening philosophy by inserting a proposal that a free trade agreement (FTA) with the United States should be concluded. As he explained just before the election in August 2009, 'imported products would be cheaper than domestic products, but people can choose good quality products. If market prices become lower than production costs, the gap would be subsidised. It would be good for consumers and producers'.[308] He told the press in Kimotsuki township in Kagoshima Prefecture, 'I am suggesting the introduction of an individual household income compensation system for farmers. Securing a food self-sufficiency system and free trade do not contradict each other'.[309]

Ozawa got angry with JA for criticising the statement in the DPJ's electoral manifesto about 'concluding a Free Trade Agreement between Japan and the United States',[310] and for demanding that this statement be amended to read 'promote negotiations'.[311] When he was questioned about the issue of 'concluding' the FTA, Ozawa did not attempt to hide his irritation, saying, 'organisations, including JA, in Tokyo have been bureaucratised as all they are concerned about is the protection of vested interests. There is no need to listen to them'.[312] He also attacked the DPJ executive (party leader Hatoyama Yukio and deputy leader Kan) for capitulating to pressure from JA by changing the word 'conclusion' of a Japan-US FTA to 'promotion'. Ozawa included 'JA reform' on the list of campaign pledges of his new party going into the 2013 Upper House election.[313]

In the debate with Prime Minister Kan in the September 2010 DPJ leadership election, Ozawa declared, 'We should actively sign free trade agreements. The biggest reason for opposing this was because if we signed FTAs, agriculture and fisheries, our primary industries, would not be able to continue. However, we introduced the individual household income compensation system keeping this in mind'.[314] When Prime Minister Kan later declared a proactive policy on signing economic partnership agreements (EPAs) and talked about examining Japan's possible participation in the Trans-Pacific Strategic Economic Partnership (TPP), Ozawa again revealed his support for free trade in an interview with Nico Nico Douga on 3 October 2011. He said, 'I am an advocate of free trade. And Japan is the country that has received the most benefits from trade liberalisation. So I [fundamentally] agree with Japan's participation in the TPP...[We've been] guided by [the fact that] Japan's life has depended on trade liberalisation. It is no problem to set our trade liberalisation goals in that direction'.[315]

Consistent with Ozawa's neo-liberal mindset was his philosophical individualism and his conviction that 'the individual had to be progressively freed from the tyranny of the group'.[316] He advanced the idea that Japan should become 'a society that truly values the individual',[317] saying that 'the liberation of the individual is the most important task facing Japan's political leadership today'.[318] He called for liberating the Japanese people from their social and political shackles, revisiting this theme in his speech at the inauguration of the LP in January 1998, linking his party to the Freedom and People's Rights movement of the early Meiji period.[319]

The formation of the LP seemed to underline Ozawa's commitment to individualism and to the liberal economic and social values he expressed in *Blueprint*. The LP's policies emphasised individual independence and were contained in a paper entitled 'Urgent Policies for Reform without Taboos', which Ozawa distributed at the birth of his new party.[320] The LP's rallying cry for an 'open, fair and free society' was contained in its manifesto.[321] According to this view, 'free, fair and open' should be the basic principle of economic activities, with 'free' meaning stopping bureaucrats from excessively interfering in the private sector and individuals' domains, 'fair' referring to guaranteeing fair competition based on fair rules, and 'open' referring to abolishing regulations and allowing everyone to participate in competition.[322]

Ozawa railed against the kind of democracy in which the people left politics up to their representatives (*omakase minshushugi*). He wrote in *Blueprint*: 'The Japanese people still lack the prerequisite for democracy, and even though American-style "post-war democracy" was introduced into Japan, democracy has not truly taken root up to this day…We should create independent individuals that have their own sense of values and can act based on their own judgement.'[323] He wanted to carry out reform towards this kind of democracy and to create a society that was more supportive of reform.

Another of Ozawa's pet grievances was how Japan's consensus society stifled reform. He 'was strongly opposed to the village society-style of harmonious politics…which was governance in order not to change anything'.[324] He was quoted as saying:

> I worked under people who were typical of those whose lives were based on a Japanese consensus where people always found a middle ground. Tanaka, Kanemaru and Takeshita were all very talented at doing so. In that sense, I have fully mastered the Japanese consensus. However, I believe that we cannot continue to act based on this consensus. In that sense, the LDP itself is an example of how not to behave.[325]

In *Blueprint* he 'asserted the need to shake free of "consensus politics (irresponsible politics)" and shift to "a regime where people that were democratically given a mandate by the people can make decisions and bear responsibility"'.[326] In his view, 'There was no scope for the idea of self-responsibility to be established (in the Japanese style of democracy)'.[327] It was a distortion caused by 'Japanese consensus society', for example, that prevented the prevailing conservative politics from implementing rice liberalisation or dispatching the SDF to participate in international peacekeeping 'because it was too preoccupied with achieving consensus with opposition parties and the people'.[328] He 'realised that he would not be able to keep up with the changing times with such traditional political methods'.[329] As he wrote in *Ozawashugi*:

> A more serious problem is that Japanese society is a consensus society that traditionally does not accept the existence of leaders…In such a society, a small number of prominent leaders leading the society and groups is not welcome. 'The nail that sticks out gets hammered down' – that is Japan. As long as we have this kind of cultural foundation, we cannot expect drastic reforms to take place. No matter how important or urgent the reform might be, there will always be people who will lose their vested interests. Reform where everyone profits is impossible. This is why in a consensus society, reforms are always either watered down or completely crushed.[330]

Ozawa described Japanese society as one of back scratching and cosy relationships, and claimed that the Japanese people needed to get rid of their dependence on the government to build an independent society and survive in international society as an independent nation. In order to build such a society, the Japanese people needed to shake free of bureaucrats and realise politics led by the people, which became one of Ozawa's favourite mantras.[331] In Ozawa's mind, changing Japan's political culture and reforming its political structures were mutually reinforcing.

Conclusion

Ozawa's published writings and myriad statements about reform identified him as the loudest and most consistent advocate of political system change in Japan. What marked him out from other Japanese political reformers and allies such as Hata was that he could see what needed to be done and he made great efforts to develop a comprehensive case for reform by publicly presenting his wide-ranging ideas systematically and coherently. These ideas bespoke his vision and ambitions for the structural transformation of Japanese politics and systems of governance. *Blueprint*, which outlined a systematic programme of reform and associated policy changes, stands as his most far-reaching and comprehensive manifesto for transforming the Japanese nation. It also showed off his credentials as an economic and social reformer. More than a decade later Ozawa published *Ozawashugi*, which updated and amplified many of the themes in *Blueprint*.

Ozawa's legacy can also be seen in the actual changes that he helped to engineer. From the early 1990s onwards, both in government and in opposition, he promoted a multi-faceted programme of reform that ultimately effected some fundamental changes to Japan's political structures and rules of the game. His aims and achievements can be perceived in terms of overturning the existing political order in order to install new political institutions and conventions. This meant rejecting the accepted way of doing things, which had become entrenched under LDP rule. As Ozawa explained, initially he hoped to change the system from the inside, but when the LDP resisted reform, he realised he had to do it from the outside. He had to refashion himself as a 'disruptive reformer'[332] in order to rid the system of the LDP's style of politics. After that, the LDP was fairly and squarely in his sights: he would have to bring the LDP down to achieve reform. In so doing, he was instrumental in terminating the ageing one-party predominant system through regime change. As Hirano Sadao saw it, he was 'the last successor to former Prime Minister Yoshida Shigeru. Ozawa…successfully achieved Yoshida's broken dream of constitutional government, "a democracy with regime change"'.[333]

Electoral reform was perhaps Ozawa's singular achievement, the means for him to realise his prior goal of introducing a system of alternating two-party politics and the key to a number of other changes in the political system.[334] Ozawa also contributed to reform of the institutions of executive governance and thus helped to buttress the cabinet as an executive decision-making body as well as enhancing the exercise of policy leadership by politicians, not only vis-à-vis the bureaucracy but also within the Diet. Ozawa's overall assessment of the LDP-LP coalition's policy agreement that largely followed these ideas and accomplished many of these changes was that it was a '"bloodless revolution"…The LDP has already completed its mission as a conservative party. The…items [in the policy agreement] would never have been proposed from within the LDP. It is best to change and contain [the LDP] from the outside'.[335]

The call for reform remained one of Ozawa's trademarks. Some ideas he continued to pursue in many different political contexts, such as decentralisation, unification of the government and ruling party, the primacy of politicians over bureaucrats, and conversion to a wholly single-member district electoral system in the Lower House. These were structural reform goals to which Ozawa demonstrated consistent attachment down the years. He also emphasised that there was 'little time left'.[336]

Ozawa's record as a reformer is not without serious blemishes, however. While his contribution to political system change in Japan went well beyond assessments of him as someone who 'bungled chances at key moments to control the reconstruction of the Japanese polity',[337] his elaboration of principle and his plea for further reforms were not necessarily always prioritised or fully realised in practice. Nor were Ozawa-inspired political reforms necessarily institutionalised by becoming embedded in new political norms, conventions and practices that he necessarily followed himself. Not only were his reforms only partially realised in some cases, but as will become more evident, some reforms were also subverted by how he conducted himself as a politician. In short, there was a lack of consistency between theory and practice. These issues raise the question whether Ozawa was primarily an agent of change in Japanese politics or a force for regression.

Notes

1 Ozawa's former private secretary, Ishikawa Tomohiro, compared Ozawa to Winston Churchill and also to *Kinnikuman* (Muscleman), a character in Japanese *manga* comic books. See Ishikawa, *Akutō*, pp. 164–76, 203–11.
2 Watanabe writes that Ozawa had 'a strong sense of mission that he became a politician in order to reform post-war politics'. Watanabe, *Ano Hito*, p. 160.
3 Uchida, '"Ozawa Ichirō"', p. 125.
4 Ozawa stated, 'I cannot say that I am a revolutionary, but I am an advocate of reforms and cannot be easily satisfied with the establishment'. Quoted in Watanabe, *Ano Hito*, p. 108. See also Chapter 5.
5 Watanabe, *Seiji Kaikaku to Kenpō Kaisei*, p. 31.
6 Ozawa, *Blueprint*, pp. 91–112. This book only focuses on Ozawa's plans for domestic reform.
7 Ibid., p. 64.
8 See pp. 151–208.
9 Watanabe, *Ano Hito*, p. 260.
10 Ibid., p. 250.
11 Watanabe, *Ozawa Ichirō Kirawareru Densetsu*, p. 267.
12 Ozawa, *Ozawashugi*, pp. 4, 6.
13 For more details about the establishment and activities of the school, see also Watanabe, *Ozawa Ichirō Kirawareru Densetsu*, pp. 256–57.
14 Watanabe, *Ano Hito*, p. 139.

15 Ibid., p. 140. See also below.
16 When LDP secretary-general in 1991, Ozawa successfully introduced the latter system into the election of the LDP president. Ibid., p. 144.
17 Ibid., p. 142.
18 Ibid., p. 142. *Blueprint* itself was the product of Ozawa's privately sponsored research activities. He never fully explained his own contribution relative to those of others who included scholars, bureaucrats and businessmen.
19 Hirano, *Ozawa Ichirō to no Nijūnen*, pp. 26–27.
20 Watanabe, *Seiji Kaikaku to Kenpō Kaisei*, p. 31.
21 Ibid., p. 28, quoting from Ozawa Ichirō in *Voice*, January 1991, p. 62.
22 There was also a 'cleansing politics group', but these were not groups in the formal sense. See Watanabe, *Seiji Kaikaku to Kenpō Kaisei*, p. 413.
23 Ibid., p. 415.
24 Ibid., p. 31.
25 Quoted in Suganuma, 'Ozawa Ichirō kanjichō jidai', p. 30.
26 See below and also Chapter 3.
27 Oka, *Policy Entrepreneurship*, pp. 144, 186, fn. 62.
28 Ozawa, *Ozawashugi*, p. 70.
29 Nonoyama, '"Bunretsu senkyo"', www.fsight.jp/article/5617.
30 'Ichiro Ozawa, President, the Democratic Party of Japan', in *Manifesto*, p. 2.
31 Fudesaka, 'Kenryoku tōsō', jbpress.ismedia.jp/articles/-/35958.
32 '"Kan nuki renritsu"', in *Bungei Shunjū*, gekkan.bunshun.jp/articles/-/241.
33 See Chapter 3.
34 Watanabe, *Ano Hito*, p. 7.
35 See also Chapter 3.
36 As Curtis points out, Ozawa was instrumental in keeping the LDP out of the eight-party coalition. Curtis, *The Logic of Japanese Politics*, pp. 111–14.
37 One of these was Akamatsu Hirotaka, JSP secretary-general, who became minister of agriculture, forestry and fisheries in the Hatoyama government, and who remained a loyal supporter of Ozawa's within the DPJ. See also Chapters 3, 4 and 5.
38 Iinuma, 'Referendum on Ozawa', p. 8. Ozawa declared the day after the 1993 election, '"I'm disappearing"…heading to the secrecy of a hotel suite to cut the deals necessary to form an administration'. Schlesinger, *Shadow Shoguns*, p. 271.
39 Tahara, 'Kenbōjussū', www.nikkeibp.co.jp/article/column/20120627/314051/.
40 Ibid.
41 Two months earlier he had reputedly 'dismissed the prospect of a linkage with Ozawa as "suicide"'. Schlesinger, *Shadow Shoguns*, p. 271.
42 Kaieda, *Boku ga Ozawa (Seiji) o Kirai*, p. 76.
43 Satō, *Ozawa Ichirō no Himitsu*, p. 226. In 1983–85, Ozawa served for two terms as chairman of the Lower House Steering Committee, where he formed a strong relationship with opposition party leaders such as Ichikawa. As secretaries-general in the LDP and Kōmeitō, respectively, the two meddled in Tokyo gubernatorial politics in the early 1990s, when Ozawa plotted to 'take down Suzuki', the incumbent governor. As a result, they became known as the 'Ichi-Ichi duo'. Their relationship became even stronger with the formation of the New Frontier Party (NFP). See Kaieda, *Boku ga Ozawa (Seiji) o Kirai*, pp. 35–39. See also below, and Chapters 3 and 5.
44 Satō, *Ozawa Ichirō no Himitsu*, p. 226. He wrote, 'It is said that Sōka Gakkai's Ichikawa and Rengō's Yamagishi recommended that Ozawa run away from the LDP as they would give him money and votes' (p. 127). Ichikawa, as the former chief of staff of the Sōka Gakkai, was a confidante of Sōka Gakkai President Daisaku Ikeda (p. 226). Ichikawa became secretary-general of the Kōmeitō after first being elected to the Lower House in 1976.
45 Kaieda, *Boku ga Ozawa (Seiji) o Kirai*, p. 79. Uchida wrote that 'Ozawa and Yamagishi secretly met in February 1993, and agreed that political reform and political

realignment should be the two major factors…Ozawa sat Yamagishi down in the seat of honour, while he himself went down on his knees at the foot of the table and pleaded, "I will achieve political reform even if that means splitting the LDP. I want you to lead the Socialist Party [to cooperate with me]". Yamagishi promised full cooperation. They did more than simply reach an agreement – the two men established a rapport with each other, and their meeting was later compared to the Satsuma and Chōshū Alliance [which overthrew the Tokugawa Shogunate] at the end of the Edo era'. Uchida, '"Ozawa Ichirō"', p. 119. See also Oka, *Policy Entrepreneurship*, p. 61, and Chapters 3 and 5.

46 Kaieda, *Boku ga Ozawa (Seiji) o Kirai*, p. 78.
47 Iokibe Makoto quoted in Oka, *Policy Entrepreneurship*, p. 70.
48 Ozawa later regretted not doing everything in his power to prevent Hosokawa's resignation. In his view, the government could have continued for another year if Hosokawa had not suddenly decided to resign, which Ozawa never expected.
49 Tahara, 'Kenbōjussū o megurasu Ozawa Ichirō', www.nikkeibp.co.jp/article/column/20120627/314051/.
50 Futami, 'Ozawa "Seikatsu no Tō"', www.the-journal.jp/contents/futami/2013/01/post_46.html.
51 'Waiting in the Wings', in *Newsweek*, www.newsweek.com/2009/03/27/waiting-in-the-wings.html.
52 Oka, *Policy Entrepreneurship*, p. 46. See also Chapter 5.
53 Watanabe, *Ano Hito*, p. 111.
54 Ibid., p. 255, quoting from the article Ozawa contributed to *Ningen Ozawa Saeki*.
55 Ibid., pp. 255–56, quoting from the article Ozawa contributed to *Ningen Ozawa Saeki*.
56 Watanabe, *Ano Hito*, p. 144.
57 Ōtake, 'Seiji kaikaku o mezashita', p. 22.
58 See Hirano's comments in Kaneki, 'Ozawa Ichirō', 11 July 2013, www.data-max.co.jp/2013/07/11/post_16454_kmk_1.html.
59 Watanabe, *Ano Hito*, p. 159. See also Chapter 3.
60 See pp. 62–75.
61 Hoshi, 'Left Behind by the Reform Bandwagon', p. 2.
62 Ozawa, *Blueprint*, pp. 62–66.
63 Mizuguchi, 'Political Reform', p. 254.
64 Ibid.
65 '(Intabyū) Shōhizei to seikai saihen', in *Asahi Shinbun*, p. 17.
66 Ozawa, *Blueprint*, pp. 67–68.
67 Ibid., p. 66.
68 Iinuma, 'Referendum on Ozawa', p. 8.
69 Ozawa, *Blueprint*, p. 66.
70 Quoted in Yakushiji, 'Kako no hatsugen', 20 July 2010, astand.asahi.com/magazine/wrpolitics/2012071900005.html?iref=webronza.
71 Oka cites the *Asahi Shinbun* of 11 May 2010 for this comment. See *Policy Entrepreneurship*, p. 179, fn. 1.
72 Iinuma, 'Referendum on Ozawa', p. 8.
73 Watanabe, *Ano Hito*, p. 260.
74 Ozawa, *Blueprint*, pp. 70, 71.
75 Ibid., p. 72.
76 Ibid., p. 70.
77 Quoted in Nonoyama, '"Bunretsu senkyo"', www.fsight.jp/article/5617.
78 Ozawa, *Blueprint*, p. 72.
79 Ibid., p. 66.
80 'Wareware wa naze kaikaku o mezasu ka', in *Bungei Shunjū*, p. 145.
81 Oka, *Policy Entrepreneurship*, p. 57.
82 Ibid., p. 48.

83 Watanabe, *Seiji Kaikaku to Kenpō Kaisei*, p. 38. According to Kuji, 'collusion politics' (*dangō seiji*) that involved both the ruling and opposition parties was initiated by Tanaka Kakuei. Kuji, *Ozawa Ichirō – Sono 'Kyōfu Shihai'*, p. 27.
84 Ozawa, *Ozawashugi*, pp. 62, 63, 64. In 1992, he had said that if the JSP could 'cut off their leftists and we can share a common foundation in regard to matters like security, diplomacy and education, than I would support getting the LDP involved with the JSP'. Kuji, *Ozawa Ichirō – Sono 'Kyōfu Shihai'*, p. 29.
85 Satō, *Ozawa Ichirō no Himitsu*, p. 227.
86 Just before the formation of the NFP in 1994 Ozawa said, 'From now on we should show consideration towards the middle-class workers. Improving the lives of these people will not only give rise to increased demand, but will also lead to the sound development of democracy'. Quoted in Hirano, *Ozawa Ichirō to no Nijūnen*, p. 127.
87 Ōtake, 'Seiji kaikaku', p. 21; Ōtake, 'Forces for Political Reform', p. 286.
88 Etō, 'Why I Back Ozawa Ichirō', p. 20.
89 Ōtake, 'Forces for Political Reform', p. 285. Ozawa also argued that 'without drastic reforms, Japan would not be able to fulfil its international responsibilities' (p. 283).
90 Ōtake, 'Seiji kaikaku', p. 21.
91 Ibid., p. 18.
92 Ozawa, *Ozawashugi*, pp. 67–68.
93 Ōtake, 'Seiji kaikaku', p. 22.
94 'Ichiro Ozawa, President, the Democratic Party of Japan', in *Manifesto*, p. 2.
95 Iinuma, 'Referendum on Ozawa', p. 8. See also Chapter 3.
96 Hirano Sadao quoted in Kaneki, 'Ozawa Ichirō', www.data-max.co.jp/2013/07/11/post_16454_kmk_1.html.
97 Oka, *Policy Entrepreneurship*, pp. 4, 46.
98 Satō, *Ozawa Ichirō no Himitsu*, p. 227.
99 Hosokawa, *Naishōroku*, pp. 133–34 *et passim*.
100 Oka, *Policy Entrepreneurship*, p. 47.
101 Hirano, *Ozawa Ichirō to no Nijūnen*, p. 226. Ozawa largely bypassed issues of Upper House reform in *Blueprint*, although he did suggest that the 'Upper House election system must also be thoroughly reformed' (p. 72).
102 See 'Political History 2. Toward the Era of a Two-party System', in *Manifesto*, p. 6.
103 In late 1999, Watanabe reports that Ozawa 'was angered by the fact that the LDP was not working seriously on the bill regarding the reduction of seats in the Diet... and became determined to leave the coalition. He had even prepared a statement for his party's secession...On seeing Ozawa's attitude, the LDP hastily proposed a compromise to pass the bill for reducing Diet seats'. Watanabe, *Ozawa Ichirō Kirawareru Densetsu*, p. 17. See also the detailed account in Reed, 'Realignment', pp. 48–52.
104 When he was negotiating to join the coalition in 1998, one of his demands was for a cut in the number of Diet members in both houses by 50 each. Oka, *Policy Entrepreneurship*, p. 94.
105 See 'Reducing the Number of Diet Members', in *Manifesto*, p. 54. This proposal was carried over to the 2009 manifesto.
106 Ibid.
107 Quoted in 'Hitsuyō na no wa hassō no tankan da', in *Shūkan Shinchō*, p. 135.
108 This also became part of the LP's policy platform.
109 'Hitsuyō na no wa hassō no tankan da', in *Shūkan Shinchō*, p. 135.
110 Itō, *Seitō Hōkai*, p. 128. See also Chapter 3.
111 'Hitsuyō na no wa hassō no tankan da', in *Shūkan Shinchō* p. 134. See also Chapter 5.
112 Hayashi and Sekiguchi, 'WSJ: Ozawa Challenges Kan', e.nikkei.com/e/ac/tnks/Nni20110527D27JF067htm.
113 'Seiken kōtai de mezashita koto to wa nan datta no ka – Hijō jitai ni okeru kiki kanri', shinseiken.jp/pdf/H240313.pdf. See also Chapter 6.

114 Matsuda, 'Tokushū waido', mainichi.jp/feature/news/20130410dde012010084000c.html.
115 See also Chapters 3 and 6.
116 Suzuki, *Saigo no Ozawa Ichirō*, pp. 181–183.
117 Matsuda, 'Tokushū waido', mainichi.jp/feature/news/20130410dde012010084000c.html.
118 Watanabe, *Ano Hito*, p. 140.
119 Ibid.
120 Yakushiji, 'Kako no hatsugen', 20 July 2010, astand.asahi.com/magazine/wrpolitics/2012071900005.html?iref=webronza.
121 Ozawa, quoted in Watanabe, *Ano Hito*, pp. 254–55.
122 Quoted in Matsuda, *Kakuei ni Narenakatta Otoko*, p. 171.
123 In fact, Watanabe reports that Ozawa had been advocating the abolition of donations from companies and organisations and the provision of political funds from public expenditure as part of political reform since he was in his thirties. *Ozawa Ichirō Kirawareru Densetsu*, p. 85.
124 Ibid., p. 49. See also Chapter 3.
125 Matsuda, *Ozawa Ichirō Kyoshoku no Shihaisha*, p. 65.
126 Quoted in Watanabe, *Ozawa Ichirō Kirawareru Densetsu*, p. 50.
127 Quoted in Matsuda, *Ozawa Ichirō Kyoshoku no Shihaisha*, p. 65.
128 Quoted in Watanabe, *Ozawa Ichirō Kirawareru Densetsu*, p. 50. See also Ozawa, *Blueprint*, p. 69.
129 Itō, '"Seiji kaikaku no kishu"', tukamoto-office.seesaa.net/article/141084654.html.
130 Ozawa, *Blueprint*, p. 69.
131 Matsuda, *Kakuei ni Narenakatta Otoko*, p. 206.
132 See also below and Chapter 3.
133 See George Mulgan, 'The Perils of Japanese Politics', pp. 183–208.
134 'Government and the Bureaucracy', in *Manifesto*, p. 53.
135 Ito, 'Ozawa Challenges Abe', www.japantimes.co.jp/cgi-bin/nn20070130a.html.
136 This law was once described by Satō as 'a bucket without a bottom'. *Ozawa Ichirō no Himitsu*, p. 89. See also Chapter 3.
137 Quoted in Matsuda, *Ozawa Ichirō Kyoshoku no Shihaisha*, p. 66.
138 Nonoyama, 'Seiji kaikaku', www.fsight.jp/article/4959. See also Chapter 3.
139 Reed, Mori McElwain and Shimizu, 'Preface', p. viii.
140 Ozawa, *Blueprint*, p. 29.
141 Gaunder, *Political Reform*, p. 83.
142 Ibid., pp. 92, 93.
143 Kaieda, *Boku ga Ozawa (Seiji) o Kirai*, p. 227.
144 Iinuma, 'Referendum on Ozawa', p. 8.
145 Ozawa, *Blueprint*, p. 58.
146 Ibid., p. 54.
147 Ibid., p. 46.
148 Endō, *Shōhi Sareru Kenryokusha*, p. 63. See also Chapter 5.
149 Ozawa, *Blueprint*, p. 56.
150 'Seiken kōtai de mezashita koto to wa nan datta no ka – Hijō jitai ni okeru kiki kanri', shinseiken.jp/pdf/H240313.pdf.
151 Ozawa, *Blueprint*, p. 56.
152 Ibid., pp. 59–60.
153 Ibid., p. 55.
154 As he wrote, 'The government itself is scattered among many institutions and interests. Its ministries and agencies are discrete entities. No overarching institution exists to coordinate and control the whole. The cabinet, of course, technically plays this role, but it has never actually been expected to do so and has therefore never developed the necessary procedures...Japan's political framework is a strong

parliamentary-cabinet system in name only. Numerous problems result. The cabinet meeting – nominally Japan's supreme decision making body – is an empty institution'. Ibid., p. 24.
155 Ibid., p. 23.
156 Ibid., p. 41.
157 Watanabe, *Ozawa Ichirō Kirawareru Densetsu*, p. 229. Other key items on the list included tax reforms, establishment of a unit for United Nations policing, safety nets, decentralising power and restructuring government ministries and agencies. See also below.
158 Ibid., p. 230.
159 'The Vision of Government in a Hatoyama Administration', p. 4.
160 Ozawa, *Blueprint*, p. 60.
161 Ozawa, *Ozawashugi*, pp. 106–7.
162 Ibid., pp. 104, 108.
163 Martin, 'Ozawa Girds for Major Diet Reform', www.japantimes.co.jp/cgi-bin/nn20100107f1.html.
164 '(Intabyū) Shōhizei to seikai saihen', p. 17.
165 Yakushiji, 'Kako no hatsugen', astand.asahi.com/magazine/wrpolitics/2012071900 005.html?iref=webronza.
166 Tazaki, Yamaguchi and Azumi, 'Ozawa Ichirō wa Nihon o dō shiyō to iu no ka', p. 41.
167 Watanabe, *Ano Hito*, p. 144.
168 Satō, *Ozawa Ichirō no Himitsu*, p. 219.
169 For details, see Takenaka, 'Introducing Junior Ministers', pp. 932–33.
170 Oka, *Policy Entrepreneurship*, p. 85.
171 Takenaka, 'Introducing Junior Ministers', p. 933.
172 'Hitsuyō na no wa hassō no tankan da', in *Shūkan Shinchō*, p. 138.
173 See also below.
174 Oka, *Policy Entrepreneurship*, p. 94. Takenaka's figures are slightly different for senior vice-ministers (26) and parliamentary secretaries (27). 'Introducing Junior Ministers', p. 934.
175 Ishikawa, *Akutō*, pp. 196–97.
176 Personal interview with *Asahi Shinbun* journalist, 9 December 2011.
177 Watanabe, *Ozawa Ichirō Kirawareru Densetsu*, p. 267.
178 Ibid., p. 267.
179 Ibid., p. 271. See also below.
180 Ozawa, *Ozawashugi*, pp. 102–4, 105.
181 'Policy 1' in the 2009 DPJ manifesto states: 'We will place a hundred or more Diet members in government posts such as minister, senior vice minister, parliamentary secretary (these three forming the top three positions), and ministerial assistant. With the minister, senior vice minister, parliamentary secretary playing a central role, politicians will take the lead in drafting, coordinating and deciding policy'. 'Five Policies', p. 4.
182 'Ozawa Ichirō x Kareru van Worufuren kōkai tōronkai', live.nicovideo.jp/watch/lv57454701.
183 *NHK News 7*, 11 January 2010.
184 Takayasu, 'Kokka Senryaku Kyoku', pp. 140–7.
185 Sugiyama, 'Saidai no atsuryoku dantai', business.nikkeibp.co.jp/article/topics/20091210/211447/. See also Chapter 4.
186 Ishikawa, 'Seifu yotō no seisaku', blog.canpan.info/ishikawa/archive/471.
187 Ibid.
188 Ibid.
189 Kamikubo, '"Ozawa shihai"', diamond.jp/articles/-/3752.
190 Ishikawa, 'Seifu yotō no seisaku', blog.canpan.info/ishikawa/archive/471.

191 Minshutō, 'Seifu yotō no seisaku kettei shisutemu', www.dpj.or.jp/article/17082/政府 与党の政策決定システム「各省政策会議」を改めて説明%E3%80%80小沢幹事長、輿石幹事長職務代行.
192 *Hatena Diary*, d.hatena.ne.jp/kojitaken/20101113/1289625937.
193 'Ozawa Ichirō x Kareru van Worufuren kōkai tōronkai', live.nicovideo.jp/watch/lv57454701.
194 Hayashi and Sekiguchi, 'WSJ: Ozawa Challenges Kan', e.nikkei.com/e/ac/tnks/Nni20110527D27JF067htm.
195 'Ozawa Ichirō x Kareru van Worufuren kōkai tōronkai', live.nicovideo.jp/watch/lv57454701.
196 'Ozawa Ichirō shinshun intabyū', in *Nikkan Gendai*, p. 429.
197 *Okami* means 'honourable superiors', and is a colloquial term used to refer to government officials in the days when officials ruled and the common people were their subjects. *Okami ishiki* means 'consciousness of superiors'.
198 Ozawa, *Ozawashugi*, p. 108. See also Chapter 4.
199 Watanabe, *Ano Hito*, p. 216.
200 Ozawa, *Ozawashugi*, p. 89.
201 Ibid., pp. 90–91.
202 Ibid., p. 92.
203 Ibid., p. 94.
204 Ibid., p. 96.
205 Satō, 'Izumo no Ozawa', web.archive.org/web/20100609015014/http://seiji.yahoo.co.jp/column/article/detail/20100531-01-0101.html.
206 Martin and Takahara, 'Kan, Ozawa Kick Off DPJ Poll Race', www.japantimes.co.jp/cgi-bin/nn20100902a1.html. The *Nikkei* quoted Ozawa as saying that 'the DPJ must redouble its efforts to wrest control from the country's powerful bureaucracy in managing taxpayers' money and formulating policies'. 'Kan Wins', e.nikkei.com/e/ac/TNKS/Nni20100914D14NY736.htm.
207 *NHK News 7*, 13 September 2010. This was a comment that Ozawa had made in the past. When he stood for the NFP leadership in 1995, he said that he would 'give his life for the country'. Hirano, *Ozawa Ichirō to no Nijūnen*, p. 156.
208 'Seiken kōtai de mezashita koto wa nan datta no ka', shinseiken.jp/pdf/H240228.pdf.
209 Ozawa, *Blueprint*, p. 58.
210 'Kokkai kaikaku', www.shugiin.go.jp/itdb_annai.nsf/html/statics/ugoki/h11ugoki/h11/h11kaika.htm?OpenDocument.
211 Ibid.
212 'Kokkai kaikaku', www.shugiin.go.jp/itdb_annai.nsf/html/statics/ugoki/h11ugoki/h11/h11kaika.htm?OpenDocument.
213 Quoted in Watanabe, *Ozawa Ichirō Kirawareru Densetsu*, p. 232.
214 'Kokkai kaikaku', www.shugiin.go.jp/itdb_annai.nsf/html/statics/ugoki/h11ugoki/h11/h11kaika.htm?OpenDocument.
215 Oka, *Policy Entrepreneurship*, p. 95.
216 Watanabe, *Ozawa Ichirō Kirawareru Densetsu*, p. 180.
217 Oka, *Policy Entrepreneurship*, p. 94.
218 Ozawa, *Ozawashugi*, pp. 97–98, 100.
219 'Political History 2. Toward the Era of a Two-party System', p. 6.
220 Kamikubo, '"Ozawa shihai"', diamond.jp/articles/-/3752.
221 'Ozawa kanjichō', in *Tōkyō Shinbun*, p. 2.
222 Watanabe and Fujita, 'Kokkai kaikaku', www.asahi.com/seikenkotai2009/TKY201005140634.html.
223 Ibid.
224 Samuels, 'Politics', www.jpri.org/publications/workingpapers/wp99.html.

225 Atarashii Seisaku Kenkyūkai, 'Shinseiken "Rippōfu no arikata"', shinseiken.jp/pdf/rippougaiyou.pdf.
226 Ibid.
227 Ibid.
228 Ibid. See also Chapter 3.
229 Ozawa, *Blueprint*, p. 12.
230 Ibid., p. 29.
231 Ibid., p. 77.
232 Hirano Sadao quoted in Kaneki, 'Ozawa Ichirō', www.data-max.co.jp/2013/07/09/post_16454_kmk_1.html. In fact *riken* can be granted by both politicians and bureaucrats. They are 'rights' or 'concessions' that generate benefits/profits (e.g. government contracts) for individuals, companies, etc., and which are secured by colluding with those who hold positions (i.e. politicians and bureaucrats), enabling them to grant such concessions. Politicians and bureaucrats also benefit from *riken* insofar as they are rewarded by the recipients of the benefits with, for example, political funds and *amakudari* positions in the private sector, respectively. See also Chapters 3, 4 and 5.
233 Ozawa, *Blueprint*, p. 77.
234 Ishikawa, *Akutō*, p. 136.
235 Ibid., p. 177.
236 See also Chapter 4.
237 'Editorial: Decentralization Debate', *Asahi Shinbun*, doshusei.wordpress.com/2010/09/07/editorialdecentralisationdebat/.
238 Osawa, 'Japan's Kan Takes on Rival', online.wsj.com/article/SB10001424052748703417104575473480826754628.html.
239 Sakai and Hisada, 'Minshutō daihyōsen', mainichi.jp/select/seiji/news/20100907ddm008010143000c.html. See also Chapter 4.
240 'Ozawa, Kan Both Vow Local Power', in *Japan Times*, www.japantimes.co.jp/cgi-bin/nn20100910a4.html.
241 'Ozawa Ichirō x Kareru van Worufuren kōkai tōronkai', live.nicovideo.jp/watch/lv57454701.
242 'Ozawa Ichirō shinshun intabyū', in *Nikkan Gendai*, pp. 425–26.
243 See also below.
244 'Noda to Ozawa ga idomu "Roshian rūretto"', in *Bungei Shunjū*, gekkan.bunshun.jp/articles/-/332.
245 Ibid. See also Chapter 6.
246 'Ozawa Says to Oppose Bills', e.nikkei.com/e/ac/TNKS/Nni20120204D04JF528.htm?NS-query=Ichiro%20Ozawa.
247 'Zōzei kaisan', in *Asahi Shinbun*, p. 1.
248 'Ozawa-shi, shōhizei zōzei hōan ni aratamete hantai shimesu', www.asahi.com/politics/update/0512/TKY201205120364.html.
249 'Ozawa Ichirō shinshun intabyū', in *Nikkan Gendai*, p. 427.
250 Atarashii Seisaku Kenkyūkai, 'Keiki taisaku', shinseiken.jp/pdf/keikityuukan.pdf.
251 Atarashii Seisaku Kenkyūkai, '"Kuni no tōchi"', shinseiken.jp/pdf/kunityuukan.pdf.
252 Matsuda, 'Tokushū waido', mainichi.jp/feature/news/20130410dde012010084000c.html.
253 Ozawa, *Blueprint*, p. 8.
254 Ibid., pp. 187–96.
255 Oka, *Policy Entrepreneurship*, p. 9.
256 He advocated halving income and residential taxes. He also wrote in *Blueprint*, 'we must reduce the corporate tax to the lowest levels in the world' (p. 177).
257 See also Chapter 4.
258 Hirata, 'DPJ Must Take Care', e.nikkei.com/e/ac/20091102/TNW/Nni20091102OP2KIND1.htm.

259 See also Chapters 4 and 5.
260 Watanabe, *Ozawa Ichirō Kirawareru Densetsu*, p. 271.
261 Oka, *Policy Entrepreneurship*, p. 79. See also Chapter 5.
262 Shinoda, 'Ozawa Ichirō as an Actor', p. 54, quoting Ishihara, *Kan Kaku Aru Beshi* [*The Way Bureaucrats Should Be*], p. 59. See also Chapters 4 and 5.
263 Shinoda, 'Ozawa Ichirō as an Actor', p. 54.
264 Ozawa, *Blueprint*, p. 12.
265 Ibid., p. 157.
266 Ibid., p. 198.
267 Ibid., p. 198.
268 'Hitsuyō na no wa hasso no tankan da', in *Shūkan Shinchō*, p. 137.
269 Watanabe, *Ozawa Ichirō Kirawareru Densetsu*, p. 269.
270 Ozawa, *Blueprint*, p. 202.
271 Hosokawa, *Naishōroku*, p. 193.
272 Hirano, *Ozawa Ichirō to no Nijūnen*, p. 155.
273 Otake, 'Forces for Political Reform', pp. 284, 293.
274 Watanabe, *Ozawa Ichirō Kirawareru Densetsu*, p. 268.
275 Hirata, 'DPJ Must Take Care', e.nikkei.com/e/ac/20091102/TNW/Nni20091102 OP2KIND1.htm.
276 Kaieda, *Boku ga Ozawa (Seiji) o Kirai*, p. 194.
277 Hirano, *Ozawa Ichirō to no Nijūnen*, p. 155. See also Chapter 3.
278 Ishikawa, *Akutō*, p. 208.
279 Kaieda, *Boku ga Ozawa (Seiji) o Kirai*, pp. 191–92.
280 Hirano, *Ozawa Ichirō to no Nijūnen*, p. 155.
281 Kaieda, *Boku ga Ozawa (Seiji) o Kirai*, p. 194.
282 Ibid., p. 194; Hirano, *Ozawa Ichirō to no Nijūnen*, p. 224.
283 Oka, *Policy Entrepreneurship*, p. 85.
284 Quoted in Watanabe, *Ozawa Ichirō Kirawareru Densetsu*, p. 266.
285 'Hitsuyō na no wa hasso no tankan da', in *Shūkan Shinchō*, p. 136.
286 Ibid., p. 137.
287 Watanabe, *Ozawa Ichirō Kirawareru Densetsu*, p. 181.
288 Oka, *Policy Entrepreneurship*, p. 93.
289 'Employment and the Economy', www.dpj.or.jp/english/manifesto/manifesto2009.pdf, p. 16.
290 Ozawa, *Blueprint*, p. 124.
291 Ibid., p. 124.
292 Ibid., p. 7.
293 Ibid., p. 127.
294 Shinoda, 'Ozawa Ichirō as an Actor', pp. 139, 146.
295 Ibid., p. 52. See also Chapter 3.
296 Oka, *Policy Entrepreneurship*, p. 45.
297 *The Independent* in the United Kingdom reported that 'Ichiro Ozawa visited Europe in October to conduct top-secret negotiations for a compromise agreement that would lead to the liberalisation of Japan's rice market'. Quoted in Kuji and Yokota, *Seiji ga Yugameru Kōkyō*, p. 134.
298 Shinoda, 'Ozawa Ichirō as an Actor', p. 52, quoting Ishihara, *Kan Kaku Aru Beshi*, p. 54.
299 Hosokawa, *Naishōroku*, p. 226.
300 Ibid., p. 193.
301 Ozawa, *Ozawashugi*, p. 32.
302 Ibid., p. 32.
303 Yamashita, 'TPP seikyoku', astand.asahi.com/magazine/wrbusiness/2010121300015.html?iref=webronza.
304 Ozawa, *Ozawashugi*, pp. 33–34.
305 Ibid., p. 35.

306 Quoted in Ichimura, 'Ozawa Ichirō', business.nikkeibp.co.jp/article/topics/20111109/223726/.
307 Quoted in ibid.
308 Satō, 'Izumo no Ozawa', web.archive.org/web/20100609015014/http://seiji.yahoo.co.jp/column/article/detail/20100531-01-0101.html.
309 Ichimura, 'Ozawa Ichirō', business.nikkeibp.co.jp/article/topics/20111109/223726/.
310 Ichinokuchi, 'Minshutō', www.fsight.jp/article/5241.
311 Ibid.
312 Ibid.
313 Seikatsu no tō, www.seikatsu1.jp/political_policy.
314 *NHK News 7*, 10 September 2010. See also Chapter 4.
315 *Hatena Diary*, d.hatena.ne.jp/kojitaken/20101113/1289625937. See also Chapter 4 and Chapter 7.
316 Oka, *Policy Entrepreneurship*, p. 8. It is debateable whether Oka's view (and that of American commentators such as Henry Kissinger and Senator John D. Rockefeller IV) that Ozawa's goal to make Japan a so-called 'normal nation' (*Policy Entrepreneurship*, p. 1) and to effect radical political, economic and social reforms were all primarily derivative of his core philosophy of individualism is correct. Ozawa himself does not consistently make this link either analytically or philosophically. He discusses extensively the nature of the reforms that he desires as a subject in their own right, just as he does the changes to Japan's defence and foreign policies, which he saw as integral to Japan's becoming a 'normal nation'. These discussions took up the bulk of *Blueprint* (pp. 19–150).
317 Ozawa, *Blueprint*, p. 157.
318 Ibid., p. 156.
319 Oka, *Policy Entrepreneurship*, p. 87.
320 Ibid., p. 89.
321 Ibid., p. 88.
322 Watanabe, *Ozawa Ichirō Kirawareru Densetsu*, p. 272.
323 Quoted in Hirano, *Shinsetsu!*, p. 27.
324 Tazaki, Yamaguchi and Azumi, 'Ozawa Ichirō wa Nihon o dō shiyō to iu no ka', p. 41.
325 Yakushiji, 'Kako no hatsugen', astand.asahi.com/magazine/wrpolitics/2012071900005.html?iref=webronza.
326 Endō, *Shōhi Sareru Kenryokusha*, p. 89. See also Chapter 5.
327 Ibid., p. 101.
328 Watanabe, *Seiji Kaikaku to Kenpō Kaisei*, p. 47.
329 Yakushiji, 'Kako no hatsugen', astand.asahi.com/magazine/wrpolitics/2012071900005.html?iref=webronza.
330 Ozawa, *Ozawashugi*, pp. 74, 75.
331 Watanabe, *Ozawa Ichirō Kirawareru Densetsu*, p. 38.
332 Iinuma, 'Referendum on Ozawa', p. 8. See also Chapter 3.
333 Quoted in Kaneki, 'Ozawa Ichirō', www.data-max.co.jp/2013/07/11/post_16454_kmk_1.html.
334 For Oka, Ozawa's motive in changing the electoral law 'was to reduce and eventually to end the LDP's single-party dominance of political power'. *Policy Entrepreneurship*, p. 4. This suggests that Ozawa's prior goal was not electoral reform but getting rid of the LDP.
335 Watanabe, *Ozawa Ichirō Kirawareru Densetsu*, p. 232.
336 Ozawa, *Ozawashugi*, p. 71.
337 Samuels, *Machiavelli's Children*, p. 326.

3 Old politics

While unmatched in his reform ideas and a principal in the political drama that brought unprecedented change to a political system in long-term stasis, Ozawa's own political style and practices remained very much enmeshed in the system that he was formally committed to transforming. In fact, a profound disjunction and even a direct contradiction could often be discerned between what Ozawa advocated and how he acted. His political values, methods, priorities, connections and career history, and indeed his political *modus operandi* in general, were the absolute antithesis of reform. He was literally two-faced: one pro-reform and the other anti-reform. He preached the language of new politics whilst persistently practising old politics. Nowhere was the apparent conflict in Ozawa's political persona more apparent than in relation to his pursuit of political reform in the early 1990s.

Reform versus political strategy

The sequence of events leading to Ozawa's departure from the LDP in 1993 suggests that he took up the cause of reform when and if it suited his political purposes at the time. In particular, he used reform as a political weapon in a power struggle within his own party. It became a tool of his extreme anti-mainstream factional strategy. Having been defeated in a contest for control of the Takeshita faction, which arose as a result of the Tokyo Sagawa Kyūbin scandal in 1992, he found himself removed from the centre of power. He then seized on reform as the means to restore his political fortunes.

The politician at the centre of the Sagawa Kyūbin scandal, former Deputy Prime Minister Kanemaru Shin, who was LDP vice-president and chairman of the Keiseikai, resigned from the Diet in October 1992, leaving the Takeshita faction without its supreme leader and godfather, triggering a struggle to replace him. It quickly became apparent that Ozawa, as acting chairman and heir apparent, wanted to step into Kanemaru's shoes. He went to the Kantei to see Prime Minister Miyazawa to hand over Kanemaru's letter of resignation, which was viewed by many as an attempt to seize the position of Keiseikai chairman, provoking internal conflict within the faction. Kanemaru preferred Ozawa, who was younger than the other members of the Keiseikai's so-called 'seven magistrates' (*nanabugyō*), as his successor.[1] The majority of the Keiseikai did not support the appointment, but they did not oppose Kanemaru's choice. As Kaieda wrote, 'This old monster of the LDP, Kanemaru, supported Ozawa too much...there must have been many people who envied him for being favoured when he was so much younger than them'.[2] Ozawa showed 'almost *yakuza*-like loyalty towards Kanemaru'.[3] He was even called 'Kanemaru's toady'.[4]

Personal antipathy towards Ozawa, not differences in policies, became the main divisive force in the Keiseikai. The succession issue divided the faction into supporters of Obuchi, who formed a group of 67 Diet members, and those of Ozawa and Hata, with 44 members (35 from the Lower House and nine from the Upper House).[5] It was a 'pure power struggle that had nothing to do with political arguments. At the root of it all was personal antipathy towards Ozawa'.[6]

In the circumstances, Ozawa 'suddenly found himself with greatly reduced prospects'.[7] He realised that his chances of ascending to the leadership of the LDP were dim, with a truncated support group of only 44 members compared to the Mitsuzuka faction with 75, the Miyazawa faction with 73, the Watanabe faction with 68, and now 67 aligned with Obuchi.[8] It was at this point that Ozawa, reading the writing on the wall, began to call openly for political reform, launching in October 1992 a new 'study group' called Reform (Kaikaku) Forum 21 organised around the theme of electoral and political funding reform.

In an interview with *Bungei Shunjū* in October 1992, Ozawa for the first time used the word 'conservatives' or 'Old Guard' (*shukyūha*) to describe his opponents in the LDP, while positioning himself as a 'reformist' (*kaikakuha*).[9] The confrontation between them came to represent the two sides of an intense power struggle between the Ozawa and anti-Ozawa forces.[10] At the popular level, the distinction also appealed to those in the mass media and elsewhere who were hoping for political reform. In this project, Ozawa used Hata as the credible 'face' of reform.

When Obuchi was installed as the replacement chairman of the Keiseikai, not Ozawa, Ozawa and his supporters refused to accept it. The split in the faction was formalised with the official launching of Reform Forum 21 in December 1992 on the same day as the general assembly of the Keiseikai selected Obuchi as its new president. A total of 44 Diet members joined, while 66 remained in the Keiseikai that supported Obuchi.[11] The forum's policy platform entitled 'We Want to Change This Country's Politics Now' adopted political reform, including eliminating the multi-seat system, as its official goal.

With the Takeshita faction rent asunder, Prime Minister Miyazawa Kiichi decided to reshuffle his cabinet in December 1992. Unlike his first cabinet, which was compiled under the heavy influence of the Takeshita faction including Ozawa, the prime minister freely chose cabinet members and party executives.[12] In particular, he appointed the leader of the anti-Ozawa movement in the party and a member of the Obuchi group, Kajiyama Seiroku, to the position of secretary-general.[13] Ozawa pressed Miyazawa to replace Kajiyama as the price of his cooperation but Miyazawa wanted to underline the power shift within the party and the Takeshita faction's newly weakened position. More importantly, he wanted to repay Ozawa for his earlier humiliation in the formation of his first cabinet in October 1991 when, as acting chairman of the Keiseikai and at

Kanemaru's behest, Ozawa had pre-emptorily taken on the role of kingmaker like Tanaka.[14] He had interviewed the three candidates for prime minister (Miyazawa, Watanabe Michio and Mitsuzuka Hiroshi) in order to decide whom the faction should back.

Once Miyazawa had chosen his second cabinet, other factions then aligned with Miyazawa to reinforce the containment of Ozawa's political influence.[15] In this hostile political environment, Ozawa saw a campaign for reform as the means to defeat anti-Ozawa forces in the LDP, although publicly he rejected the power struggle explanation for his defection. He preferred instead to describe it as a struggle over political ideals in which reformers were pitted against defenders of the status quo.[16] Others, however, including Obuchi and Hatoyama Yukio, claimed that Ozawa only adopted reform as a means to advance his own position and to hide the real reason for why he left the LDP.[17]

Ozawa's loud call for reform was reinforced by further revelations of Kanemaru's misdeeds, resulting in his arrest in March 1993 after the discovery of vast quantities of assets including stock certificates and gold ingots stashed away in his house and offices. This followed earlier revelations that Takeshita had secured his ascension to the prime ministership by negotiating with a *yakuza* group. An outraged public, sick and tired of five years of political scandals starting with the Recruit scandal in 1988, demanded reform.[18]

Ozawa cannily caught this wave as various proposals for electoral, funding and administrative reform were being debated. He published *Blueprint* in late May 1993 and began attracting widespread public attention by saying 'now is the time for reform in politics'. However, the timing suggested that he was reacting to the political situation in which he found himself after Kanemaru, his main protector, came under threat of indictment. When Kanemaru was arrested, Ozawa, who relied on him, became uneasy and anxious, so he needed, more than ever, to deflect criticism and portray himself as a reformer. Indeed, it was the members of the former Takeshita faction who suffered the greatest direct damage from the Sagawa Kyūbin scandal and who had, therefore, the greatest need to polish their image as reformers.[19] Reinventing himself as a reformer was a clever tactical move by Ozawa.[20]

However, there were high levels of cynicism about Ozawa's motives, particularly given his political associations and pedigree, which undermined his image and credibility as a reformer.[21] In fact, Ozawa was considered in the eyes of many to have been a major beneficiary of the corrupt system that he was now condemning.[22] These contradictions constantly overshadowed his actions. Itō Atsuo, who had worked in the LDP's Secretariat when Tanaka was prime minister, and who, from 1989, was the LDP's Political Reform Secretariat's assistant chief investigator in charge of compiling the party's political reform outline, revealed, 'I do not remember hearing Ozawa say anything about the principle of political reform. However, as his actions later on proved, there is no doubt that Ozawa was aiming to "use" political reform, change the political system and completely realign political circles'.[23]

The Hata faction presented itself as ready to act if the prime minister were not enthusiastic about reform. When it threatened to leave the party, Miyazawa decided to block the move by sponsoring a party decision to press on with the LDP's original set of political reform bills,[24] which Ozawa himself had promoted, but which had no chance of passing the Diet.[25] In proposing 500 single-member districts for the Lower House, the March 1993 Miyazawa bill offered no concessions to the smaller parties in the opposition, which held a majority in the Upper House. By May, Ozawa himself had helped to work out a compromise proposal, which offered a combination of single-member districts and PR seats, which had better political prospects. It was rejected by anti-Ozawa politicians in the LDP, however, because of their reluctance to reward him with success. It was at this point that Kajiyama declared that the LDP would delay electoral reform, precipitating the opposition's no-confidence motion in the Miyazawa cabinet. The motion was joined by the Hata group including Ozawa, who left the LDP. A total of 39 LDP Lower House Diet members voted for the motion, including 34 from the Hata group.[26]

Six days after the Lower House was dissolved by Prime Minister Miyazawa, the Hata faction formed the Renewal Party in June 1993, with 36 Lower House members who had left the LDP after the no-confidence vote. The move put greater distance between the Hata group and Kanemaru, who was due to face trial in July 1993. The group was able to refocus public attention by concentrating on the call for political reform. It paid off handsomely in the July 1993 Lower House election with gains for the RP, which increased its numbers to 55. The formation of the coalition government encompassing LDP remnants, new parties and existing opposition parties was where ultimately the confrontation of Ozawa vs. anti-Ozawa in the LDP ended up, decisively changing the axis of conflict in Japanese politics into reform vs. anti-reform, driven by Ozawa's ideas and actions.[27]

Ozawa made sure that the appointment of JNP leader Hosokawa as prime minister would serve to cement his new party's reform image.[28] Nevertheless, writing at the time, journalist and Tanaka biographer Tachibana Takashi derided the RP's reform slogan and commented in the *Asahi Shinbun* on 24 June 1993 that it was '"absolutely ridiculous" for former members of the Keiseikai to speak of political reform'.[29]

The way in which Ozawa handled the break-up of the Keiseikai and the formation of the RP and its eventual electoral victory using the slogan of reform certainly suggests that improving his prospects for taking power was an important motivator of his leaving the LDP. He had lost out in a power struggle in the Takeshita faction, which meant that he was deprived of his position of influence over the party and the government.[30] In fact, he was 'completely encircled by an anti-Ozawa net'.[31] Secretary-General Kajiyama and Minister of Construction Nakamura Shirō, who was linked to the Kajiyama group, took over Ozawa's only vested interest in construction,[32] which sidelined him even further. This meant Ozawa lost both money and power.[33] Ozawa's behaviour in the situation in which he found himself points to an inability to tolerate a dramatic loss of power, being relegated to an anti-mainstream faction, poor immediate prospects for leadership of the party and a hiatus in his ambitious career trajectory.

Pursuing reform held out the prospect of bringing down the Miyazawa government and cementing a coalition of anti-LDP political groupings as a potential alternative government in which Ozawa could play a pivotal role. A power struggle was thus disguised as a split over policy, with Hata and Ozawa able to position themselves advantageously as the vanguard of reform. Even Ozawa acknowledged in *Blueprint* that in the LDP, 'serious matters of policy tend to become little more than tools in factional haggling, as was all too evident in the recent struggle over political reforms'.[34]

Moreover, a new coalition government of smaller parties actually reduced the prospect of Ozawa's template for electoral reform centring on the single-member district system being implemented. It was the LDP under Prime Minister Miyazawa that was proposing to replace all existing multi-member constituencies with 500 single-member districts in the Lower House,[35] precisely the kind of electoral reform that Ozawa had advanced in *Blueprint*, where he explicitly rejected the 'combination' proposal of single-member and PR seats in the Lower House. If he had been truly in favour of electoral reform as a necessary condition for creating a two-party system, he would have remained in the LDP and fought for this system from inside the ruling party.

Instead, Ozawa crafted the compromise proposal that made major modifications to the plan for single-member districts in order to secure the support of minor parties.[36] The electoral reform legislation submitted to the Diet in September 1993 by the Hosokawa administration envisaged a Lower House made up of 250 single-member district seats and 250 PR seats. It clearly undercut the potential for the new electoral system to produce a two-party system. In January, the draft legislation that was finally passed with 300 single-member districts and 200 PR seats offered the minor parties 50 fewer seats than the original Hosokawa government legislation. It was another compromise proposal worked out between Hosokawa and LDP President Kōno Yōhei, in which, quite clearly, the LDP was able to extract concessions in favour of major parties at the expense of minor parties, such as those in the Hosokawa-led eight-party coalition.[37] On this occasion, it was the LDP that was pushing a reform plan closer to Ozawa's own.

Ozawa's close association with corrupt LDP faction bosses and persistent rumours of his direct involvement in dubious funding practices also gave the lie to his professed desire to clean up Japanese politics by enacting electoral reform.[38] He was seen as intimately connected to the kind of corrupt practices that the electoral reform legislation was aiming to eliminate.[39] Others opposed the 1994 electoral reform bills simply because they distrusted and disliked Ozawa.[40] Personal enmity towards Ozawa, distrust of his motives and a rejection of his style of politics were thus in the mix of motivations prompting many Diet members to oppose the 1994 electoral reform legislation.[41]

Old party modes

Although Ozawa sought to modernise the party system, the historical record of his treatment of political parties and his behaviour within them suggests that he conceived of party organisations principally as instruments of personal power seeking rather than as groups with shared political ideals seeking to gain office in order to implement an agreed policy programme (see Table 1.1). Between 1993 and 2003, as Ozawa made his journey into the DPJ, he helped to form and then dissolve the RP, the NFP and the LP, which first allied with the LDP and then merged with the DPJ. Over this period, Ozawa was almost constantly manoeuvring for party realignment in a way that paid little heed to existing party loyalties and party identification based on common policy preferences and ideological standpoints. All told, Ozawa belonged to five different parties in ten years.

For Ozawa angling to get back into power, political realignment was constantly on the agenda. On the hunt for followers, he showed little respect for the party affiliations of others. In the lead-up to the formation of the NFP in December 1994, for example, he was scouting for likely candidates for a consolidation of the parties that had found themselves bundled into opposition after the LDP-NPH-JSP coalition took over from the Hata-led coalition. At the time, Ozawa, who was still in the RP, organised to hold informal get-togethers with JNP members although it was unheard of for the secretary-general of one party to meet rank-and-file members of another. He justified his action by telling the JNP politicians, 'Now that we have single-seat constituencies, we all have to get together. Otherwise we won't be able to win'.[42] When subsequently laying the groundwork for the LP's link-up with the LDP, Ozawa assiduously entertained potential LDP supporters, following the same strategy of inducement to facilitate a process of party realignment.

Ozawa later dissolved the LP and was asked his thoughts regarding its extinction. He responded bluntly, 'Parties are just tools to realise my purposes, so I do not have any deep emotion at the break-up of the Liberal Party'.[43] If a party no longer served his purpose he discarded it 'without hesitation'.[44] His earlier break-up of the NFP was symptomatic of this mindset. Ozawa split the NFP after only three years because he was reportedly getting sick of it given the constant level of conflict amongst its members.[45] In an interview in January 1998, just after the party broke up, he said:

> I find [lots of things ridiculous] these days, but in the case of the New Frontier Party we used energy in dealing with problems within the party. Because our enemy was the LDP administration, we should have firstly focused on defeating them. But somehow [we got caught up in our own battles]...I got sick of it.[46]

However, it was not just that the 'walls that existed between the old political parties [that made up the NFP] never disappeared'.[47] Ozawa was himself the major cause of discord within the party, particularly as a result of various arbitrary personnel decisions that caused strife between Ozawa and Hata, and a rift with the Sōka Gakkai. Moreover, given its massive size, Ozawa was less keen on keeping the NFP going because he could not control it. He also ran foul of those who opposed his idea of forming a *hoho rengo* (conservative-to-conservative coalition) with the LDP. He was much happier to act as one of the select few who formed the LP.[48] In 1997 he plotted with Kamei Shizuka to establish just such a *hoho rengo*, which ultimately paved the way for the LDP-LP agreement to form a coalition in November 1998.[49]

Ozawa's reputation as a 'destroyer' (*kowashiya*) derived largely from the ease with which he formed then discarded political parties at regular intervals.[50] Kaifu traced this penchant of Ozawa's to a personality defect, which first became evident in the early 1990s when he first split and then brought down the LDP, followed by his dissolution of the RP and the NFP. Although Ozawa led the 'new party boom' and achieved regime change, whenever he felt his existential value decreasing he would wreck things, repeating this pattern time after time.[51]

Parties were expendable because Ozawa was always able to leave a party and take some, if not most, of his supporters with him. Hence the greater weight he attached to factions.[52] Ozawa also preferred factions because members completely obeyed the leader, whereas political parties were based on much looser cooperation and sometimes members did not follow instructions from the top. Ozawa was not able to tolerate such relationships.[53]

Over time, it became increasingly apparent that Ozawa-allied party groupings exemplified the more traditional leader-follower type of political party, rather than the modern programmatic type where party cohesion is underpinned by shared policy preferences and values (see Table 1.1). Parties that Ozawa led became smaller and more personalised, in which the primary basis of party organisation was clearly personal loyalty to Ozawa, albeit sometimes disguised by an overlay of shared policy positions. These groupings were essentially parties of Ozawa's followers and, as their leader, Ozawa was primarily a power seeker rather than a policy protagonist.

Even Ozawa's 'first' party, the RP, was faction-based given that its core was originally formed from members with factional links that had been established in the Takeshita faction.[54] Young former ex-Takeshita faction members were also the most concerned about their electoral prospects at a time when a strong electoral backlash was expected from the public at the polls because of the frequent money-politics scandals in which leading LDP figures had been involved.[55]

The RP's unity was not based on ideological conviction like the NPH, for instance, which was solidly founded on the goal of achieving political reforms.[56] The members of the Hata-Ozawa faction who followed Ozawa and Hata out of the LDP in 1993 in fact formed two distinct sub-groups made up of the loyalty-motivated Ozawa group and the more reform-minded Hata group.[57] For Ozawa's followers, the receipt of patronage, especially for former junior LDP members who owed him their seats, was the most important factor.[58] The LDP's finances had suffered when the economic bubble burst and so there was no money to induce members to stay in the party.[59] By sticking with Ozawa, they stood to gain from a continuing flow of benefits as long as he was in the ruling party. Distributing concessions (*riken*) and posts became extremely important in Ozawa's leadership of the RP.[60]

Later, when the NFP was dissolved and Ozawa formed the LP, loyalty to Ozawa as party head became paramount. The LP was little more than the 'Ozawa'ist rump'[61] of the NFP, or more accurately 'Ozawa's party', or his personal fiefdom. Although Ozawa described the 54 who turned up for the LP's inaugural convention in January 1998 as 'a good turn-out',[62] he and his supporters had hoped that around 100 members of the NFP could be persuaded to join. The much smaller group were those 'who were prepared to obey him completely'.[63]

The trend towards more personalised and privatised parties belied Ozawa's stated goal of 'creating a two-party system based on policy differences'.[64] He left the LDP with a view to injecting more ideological coherence into inter-party competition, yet he consistently failed to realign Japanese politics along these lines because of the personalised and faction-based nature of the parties that he led himself (see Table 1.1). He also remained open to coalition deals that undercut his commitment to creating an era of two-party politics.[65] At one time he was hoping for an LDP-NFP coalition,[66] then as LP leader, he linked up with the LDP in January 1999 to form a coalition (*Jiji renritsu*) only a year after the LP itself was formed. Voters had been given the hope of a two-party system but Ozawa was eager to regain power. He left the alliance of opposition parties, reversing his earlier position when the LP had cooperated with the DPJ to impose a financial reform plan on the LDP after the DPJ-led opposition gained a majority in the Upper House.

Ozawa even put pressure on Prime Minister Obuchi to allow him to rejoin his old party.[67] The question this immediately raised was why Ozawa would want to rejoin his old party if his aim were to establish a bipartisan system of competitive party politics.[68] His wish to ally with and even return to the LDP also conflicted with his commitment to regime change in order to effect systemic political reforms. This was reflected in his oft-repeated statement, 'You cannot expect real reform from the LDP. The only way to get reform is through an alternation in power'.[69]

Later, when Ozawa pulled the LP out of the coalition in April 2000, his band of Liberals became a small group in search of a more permanent home. It was only when the DPJ looked as though it had good prospects in the 2003 Lower House election that Ozawa decided to merge his LP with it.[70] The DPJ was not Ozawa's party, although he tried to force it into this mould, settling in the short term for a triumvirate with Hatoyama and Kan. Then as head of the DPJ, Ozawa, citing 'lack of power',[71] agreed to consider the possibility of a 'grand coalition' between the DPJ and the LDP in November 2007 when invited to do so by Prime Minister Fukuda Yasuo, who was trying to find a way around the 'twisted Diet' at the time. 'It does not matter which woman you sleep with' was the way Ozawa rationalised his position.[72] It was only the objections of Ozawa's DPJ colleagues that prevented this grand coalition from coming into being.

For Ozawa the crucial criterion appeared to be whether he could secure a position from where he could control any given administration rather than what the ruling party stood for or what its fundamental policy objectives were. Political parties were merely a means for Ozawa 'to capture political power for himself'.[73]

After regime change in the 2009 election and the establishment of an embryonic two-party system, the question remained whether the DPJ would remain Ozawa's permanent home or merely a flag of convenience for as long as it suited his political purposes.[74] His instrumentalist attitude towards political parties and record of ephemeral party loyalties suggested that he might leave the DPJ if he could see personal political advantage in doing so. The first steps in this direction were taken in December 2011, when Ozawa established his new 'study group', Shinseiken, within the DPJ.

Shinseiken was a new Ozawa party in the making with the aim of launching Ozawa into the prime ministership. First, its title – New Politics Research Group – implied that it wanted to promote Ozawa as prime minister and establish a 'new administration' (also pronounced *shinseiken*).[75] Second, its eight sectional committees covering such topics as nuclear energy, state governance, crisis management, national security and the tax system could provide input into the manifesto of a new party as well as into the platform of a candidate in the next DPJ presidential election. Third, Shinseiken's website was focused on Ozawa and made no mention of the DPJ, although it had appropriated as its own the DPJ's 2009 manifesto slogan originally crafted by Ozawa as DPJ leader: 'putting the people's lives first'. Fourth, the group had an organisational structure modelled along political party lines, including a chairman (Ozawa), secretary-general, deputy secretaries-general, secretariat head, executives and advisers. Finally, it outlined its own policy 'vision' presented as three issues and eight themes.

Shinseiken was thus a 'party' of Ozawa's followers in the DPJ and a sixth 'party-in-waiting' should Ozawa decide to leave the ruling party or should he be expelled. In this respect, it was his passport out of the DPJ. In the meantime, it bound his followers more closely to him and could be used as an instrument of his personal power against the Noda administration. In this respect, Shinseiken was a quintessential old politics 'party' – a political grouping primarily designed to serve the power-seeking aims of its leader, despite its overlay of shared policy objectives. While it noisily opposed the Noda government's proposal to raise the consumption tax, first and foremost it was united by Ozawa-centred factional loyalties.

When a core group of 49 Ozawa followers finally joined him in splitting from the DPJ in July 2012 to form People's Life First, or PLF (Kokumin no Seikatsu ga Daiichi) under the banner of opposition to the Noda government's consumption tax hike,[76] he was accused of undermining the very concept of a political party and replacing it with the idea of a party as simply a power-seeking group (see Table 1.1).[77] The picture was further complicated by Ozawa's later transition through the Tomorrow Party of Japan, or TPJ (Nihon Mirai no Tō), into the People's Life Party, or PLP (Seikatsu no Tō) in January 2013.[78] This made a total of eight parties to which Ozawa had belonged since 1993 and the fifth that he had personally launched over the same period.

Leaving the major party of government and creating a succession of minor political groupings in the Diet patently conflicted with Ozawa's professed goal of creating a two-party system despite his accusation that the three-party (DPJ-LDP-New Kōmeitō) coalition that had steered the consumption tax legislation through the Diet 'denied two-party politics'.[79] Certainly, with the defection of Ozawa and his followers from the DPJ, the structure of politics, where the primary axis of party confrontation was between the two major parties (DPJ and LDP), began to change into a more pronounced major plus minor party configuration (see Table 1.1).

Ozawa's actions over the years thus raise serious doubts about whether he conceived of political parties primarily as groups of politicians with a common political purpose grounded in shared policy principles. In fact, his record suggests that he viewed them as personal groups clustered around a boss-leader, blurring the distinction between faction and party, and as temporary arrangements for political and electoral convenience, where party loyalty and policy discipline were secondary considerations if they figured at all.

The attributes of Ozawa-led parties thus posed a fundamental question about what the process of party formation, dissolution, alignment and realignment was about for Ozawa: for gaining power, or for gaining power with a purpose, that is, to put an agreed policy programme into action? Over time, it became clear that the main rationale for the seemingly endless process of party destruction and creation was to restore Ozawa to the position of 'main player' in any particular party setting.

Old factional modes

Similar gaps between 'theory' and 'practice' were evident in Ozawa's treatment of factions. For a Japanese Diet member who championed a switch from multi-member to single-member districts in the Lower House in order to rid the LDP of internally divisive factional politics and prevent elections from being factional contests, Ozawa built a group of personal followers inside the DPJ that looked remarkably like an old-style LDP faction. It was characterised by high levels of organisational unity and strong personal loyalty to Ozawa. It also sought to exercise influence over policymaking and party and government appointments by taking advantage of strength in numbers (see Table 1.1).[80]

What really distinguished the Ozawa group from the rest in the DPJ was not only its size but also its strict internal hierarchy, its military-like discipline and its firm basis in the distribution of patronage.[81] Ozawa was clearly the 'boss-leader' (*oyakata*); there was a small group of trusted executives but members were clearly 'subordinates'. It was a top-down, hierarchical grouping where the members' political careers were largely determined by how they were evaluated by the leader and where the basic organising principle was patron-client[82] relations (see Table 1.1).[83] Ozawa dispensed patronage to members while they reciprocated in the form of obedience and fealty to the 'boss'. In such a faction, rising up the ranks depended on demonstrations of loyalty rather than on innate talent and political capabilities.[84] Ozawa's followers were variously referred to as the Ozawa 'faction' (*habatsu*), the Ozawa 'bloc', the Ozawa 'group' (*guruppu*) and the Ozawa 'children'. Other DPJ groups mobilised to back particular candidates in party presidential elections, but they were more loosely organised than the Ozawa group, and even in party leadership elections their votes were fluid.[85]

Building the Ozawa faction

As soon as he joined the DPJ, Ozawa set about forming a faction within the party in order to assert his presence and influence. The first sign of Ozawa-led factional manoeuvring was evident in January 2004 when at least ten of Ozawa's followers, including those who had previously been in the LP, launched a faction called the 'Small Government Research Group', reflecting Ozawa's neo-liberal Rinchō-ist standpoint at the time. Ostensibly a policy-centred rather than deal-making group, even in those early days after the LP-DPJ amalgamation, it intensified power struggles within the party because Ozawa was at the time critical of DPJ leader Kan Naoto.[86] It was a harbinger of things to come, particularly Ozawa's involvement of his followers in policy disputes with the DPJ leadership as 'cover' for a bid for power.[87]

Ozawa's main goal was to form a body of personal followers in the DPJ following the Tanaka principle that 'numbers are power'[88] and employing the same methods that he had used when he was Kanemaru's protégé in the Takeshita faction. As deputy chairman of the Keiseikai, and as Kanemaru's choice to take over leadership of the faction, Ozawa was responsible for recruiting new candidates and for providing them with electoral endorsement, campaign funds and organisational support, as well as valuable contacts in the political, bureaucratic and business worlds, and sponsorship to positions in the government and party. Many of the recipients of Ozawa's patronage felt obligated to him for helping them win office, enabling him to create a group of loyal supporters in the LDP.

In the DPJ, Ozawa continued to operate according to the same factional logic, recruiting new members in each election (in 2004, 2005, 2007 and 2009) and making them obligated to him for his support. The size of the Ozawa group after the 2007 House of Councillors election was around 50[89] and consisted mainly of members who had been elected once or twice. That number swelled to around 150 after the 2009 Lower House election, which amounted to about one third of the DPJ's Diet membership.[90] The DPJ's factional structure had clearly shifted 'towards a one-faction-dominant structure'.[91]

Almost all of the new members in Ozawa's group were first-term Diet members. He had personally invited many of the 114 new DPJ candidates standing for single-member districts to run for election.[92] His *seiji juku* also played a role as a recruitment tool.[93] Those handpicked by Ozawa acknowledged the assistance that he had rendered them during the campaign in terms of teaching them how to campaign.[94] As an indefatigable campaigner himself, Ozawa was happy to impart the lessons learned from his vast experience of fighting elections. He even provided direct campaign assistance in the electoral districts of those he recruited and coached into Diet seats. This involved the provision of campaign workers and advisers from amongst his Diet secretaries. About 20 of Ozawa's staff, the so-called 'army corps of secretaries' (*hisho gundan*), conducted thorough grassroots door-to-door election campaigns across the country.[95] Their approach was to 'divide the entire country into blocks with the election campaign in each block taken care of by a responsible secretary, including researching information in each area and so on'.[96]

Most importantly, however, Ozawa's faction-building success relied on the distribution of generous election funds. On 21 July, 27 July and 17 August 2009, Rikuzankai[97] distributed a total of ¥449 million to 91 DPJ candidates in the election.[98] The amounts ranged from ¥2 million to ¥20 million per candidate. Of the 91 candidates funded by Ozawa, 88 were successful.[99] The money was handed over in cash by Ozawa's policy secretary in either a Tokyo hotel or at the Rikuzankai office. The funds were designated in Rikuzankai's income and expenditure report as 'election donations'.[100] The policy secretary was quoted by one recipient as saying, 'We'll count on you in the future when it comes to a showdown',[101] indicating that Ozawa was making a financial down-payment on the recipient's future loyalty to the Ozawa faction.

Deploying funds and secretaries as tools gave rise to 'the more than 100 Ozawa children as a result'.[102] The term 'children' aptly captured the dual elements of dependence and control that characterised Ozawa's relations with this group of younger Diet members, who found it difficult to operate independently of his influence and who looked up to him as their mentor.

Despite the relatively junior status of many of its members, Ozawa's group was thus fashioned into an instrument of his personal influence within the DPJ and enabled him to reign over by far the largest political 'power group' within the party.[103] Its strength was not only in numbers but also in members' loyalty to Ozawa, with their primary allegiance to their patron rather than to the party. Moreover, the new recruits were beholden to Ozawa not only for their seats, an obligation that engendered strong loyalty, but also for ongoing guidance as they navigated the political world. This was the big difference between the Ozawa 'children' and the Koizumi 'children'. Although both groups were made up of rookies, Ozawa 'took care of his children after they were elected, watching every move they made and educating them as well, practising the kind of mentoring characteristic of LDP factions in the past'.[104]

The size of Ozawa's group prompted some concern in the DPJ about his growing influence as these junior members flooded into the Ozawa faction. Its size and discipline potentially enabled him to use it not only in intra-party elections but also in matters relating to Diet affairs, policymaking and legislation. His faction also provided protection, making punishing Ozawa for any misdemeanours or action against the party leadership difficult.

Ozawa wanted to use the 2010 Upper House election to recruit even more factional followers. His push to run two DPJ candidates in the multi-seat prefectural constituencies, which he justified in terms of securing a majority of seats in the election for the DPJ, was also designed to increase the number of his 'children'. He delivered speeches mainly in those electorates where his hand-picked first-time candidates were running, departing from the party leadership's priorities on backing incumbent Upper House members who were seeking another term. The political funding records for 2010 showed that Rikuzankai distributed ¥125 million to new faces in this election.[105]

Much of the anger that Ozawa vented during his campaign against Prime Minister Kan's abrupt proposal for raising the consumption tax was likely due to the potential impact of this proposal not only on the DPJ's chances of victory but also on the chances of his personally selected candidates winning in their districts. Ozawa was aware that smaller increases in his group size could possibly alter his chances of regaining the party leadership in the September 2010 presidential election. His faction-building rationale also helped to explain his devotion to winning elections as well as the dominance of electoral considerations in his policy interventions.[106]

Exploiting positions in the party executive

In building his faction within the DPJ, Ozawa was able to call on not only his own political funds, but also on the considerable powers and largesse at the disposal of party executives, in particular those of the party president and secretary-general, positions that Ozawa held at crucial times in the DPJ's trajectory to power and during its first nine months in office. Ozawa exploited to the full the control over party funds and electoral endorsements that his party offices bestowed. In total, he distributed ¥22.9 billion in party subsidies provided to the DPJ in 2007–08. Moreover, it was put to good use not only in winning elections but also in expanding the size of his group.

As the 2009 election approached, secretaries and other staff members from the Ozawa office visited constituencies in which the DPJ's new candidates were standing. Just as with the distribution of his own political funds, the recruits were given a brown envelope containing money, with the words 'This is from Ozawa'.[107] Inside the envelope were election funds provided by the party. Accompanying the money was the query, 'Would you like to join the group Isshinkai?[108] If you join us, we will give you guidance in the election'.[109] Once the candidate signed the application to join Isshinkai, the Ozawa office dispatched a secretary to assist the candidate.

It was also suspected that Ozawa used '"whether or not [the candidate] would enter the Ozawa group after being elected" and "whether [the candidate] was pro- or anti-Ozawa" as the standard for deciding whether to give official endorsement to candidates and how much money he should use on them'.[110] In short, Ozawa was ruthlessly self-interested in his decisions on party endorsements and funding. Yet, this behaviour ran directly counter to the view he originally expounded in *Blueprint*, where he argued against the idea that the party executive should be given the power to choose candidates for electoral endorsement, saying that this should be the job of local party branches.[111] He even pointed out the disadvantage of the change from a multi-seat, faction-centred system to a single-seat, party-centred system, claiming that 'there is a risk of authority being concentrated amongst the party executives, leading to oligarchic control'.[112] Ozawa was, therefore, well aware of how reform of the electoral system had boosted the powers of the party executive.[113] He himself elaborated:

> The most significant grounds on which those opposing the single-seat constituency system base their arguments are that if the single-seat constituency system driven by political parties is introduced, the leader, secretary-general and executives will come to hold despotic authority and they can arbitrarily decide the candidates. However, it is natural that the party's power as an organisation strengthens when it becomes party-driven instead of being

individual-driven. It is also natural that everyone follows the organisation's decision.[114]

He said the same thing in 1995, when he remarked, 'elections will be conducted by the party, and necessarily, the initiative will be exercised by headquarters' leaders who control party funds. They will decide what candidates to run and their ranking on the proportional representation list'.[115]

In fact, there was a direct connection between Ozawa's promotion of the single-seat district system and the greater control he could exert over party members, particularly from the position of secretary-general, because of the greater risks that candidates faced under the new system. Only a few influential DPJ Diet members were not scared of rebelling against his authority[116] because of his 'power to endorse' and 'power to distribute funds'.[117] Kaieda described the difference between the power of the secretary-general under the old multimember district system and his power under the new single-member district system as being 'as different as a mouse to an elephant, or a cockroach to a sperm whale'.[118] Effectively what happened was that the party executives replaced the factions' powers in relation to funding and endorsement.[119]

Kobayashi Kōki, who won a Lower House seat from the Tokyo PR bloc in 2009 and who revealed that he had not received any party subsidies, said:

> For Mr. Ozawa, a Diet member who wins a seat in the proportional representation constituency may as well be a 'scarecrow'…We only won because the party put us on their list, and we can be replaced if need be in the next election…It is a big lie to say that subsidies to political parties are a clean system. It is a terrible system because far more than ¥10 billion deposited by the people is completely centralised by the party and arranged by some of its executives. It is not a problem if the money is fairly distributed but it can be a serious problem if it is done by some people of the party in line with their disposition. Because of this, all lawmakers have to crawl to a person in the position of power. This is the reality of the subsidies to political parties.[120]

Of all the powers Ozawa acquired, the power of the party purse was the greatest. Under his stewardship, the flow of DPJ party funds became highly centralised and lacked transparency, which Prime Minister Kan alluded to in his call for these funds to be allocated openly when he listed his policies for the June 2010 DPJ presidential election.[121] In fact, Kan and his supporters 'rounded up party votes by warning that Ozawa should not get his hands on that money'.[122]

When Ozawa stepped down as secretary-general in June 2010, he wanted someone close to him selected as his successor because the new appointee would be entrusted with the party's funds, including the subsidies over which Ozawa wished to retain control for future use. Ozawa had in mind the upcoming Upper House election campaign.[123] Failing in this desire, Ozawa spent only two minutes on the handover of business to his successor Edano Yukio, who was known for having distanced himself from Ozawa.[124]

In early December 2010, speaking before reporters at the Kantei, Kan again emphasised that he wanted the allocation of DPJ funds to be transparent in order to stop a secretary-general like Ozawa from single-handedly wielding money power within the party. The new secretary-general in the second Kan administration, Okada Katsuya, did things differently from Ozawa. He was more transparent in his allocation of party funds and also introduced a system whereby these funds were subject to external auditing in order to secure their transparent distribution.

The Ozawa faction in action

In 2009–10, at around 150 members, the Ozawa group constituted the biggest factional bloc within the DPJ (approximately one third of the DPJ's Diet membership). In total there were nine groups in the DPJ, including the Ozawa group, Hatoyama group, Kan group, etc.

The members of the Ozawa bloc were distributed across several sub-groups. Isshinkai[125] comprised Ozawa's supporters amongst second- to fourth-term Lower House members. It met once a week and was a political organisation registered with the Ministry of Internal Affairs and Communications (MIAC). It consisted mainly of ex-members of the LDP and previous Ozawa-led parties. Amongst its members were politicians with close personal ties to Ozawa such as former secretaries or graduates of Ozawa's *seji juku*.[126] The former LP group consisted of a small number of ex-LP affiliates. It was originally established in 2003. Another group consisted of some 20 Upper House members, who were first elected in 2007 and who met on an irregular basis.[127] There were also regular meetings of Ozawa-affiliated Upper House members who used to belong to the LP.[128] Another small group of Ozawa supporters from the Upper House, called the 'Thursday Club' (Mokuyōkai), was formed on 11 November 2010. Its chairman was Tanaka Naoki, husband of Tanaka Makiko.

Ozawa's followers amongst first-termers were initially members of the so-called Isshinkai Club (Isshinkai Kurabu),[129] but this was reorganised into a new, more strongly united group called Hokushinkai on 25 November 2010. Ozawa assumed the post of supreme adviser. A total of 43 DPJ Diet members attended its first meeting and of these 43 members, 24, or more than half, had received campaign funds from Ozawa prior to the 2009 general election. For Ozawa, the formation of the group was a direct dividend from his private distribution of election funds.[130] Hokushinkai's membership soon expanded to 53, which represented more than a third of the total number of first-term Lower House members, including the so-called Ozawa 'girls' – women whom Ozawa had sponsored and supported as first-time candidates in the 2009 Lower House election.

The dispersion of Ozawa's followers across different groups was deliberate so as not to cause alarm among other party members. The unification of Isshinkai and Isshinkai Kurabu, for example, was contemplated and rejected for that reason. Over time, however, Ozawa's followers were consolidated into three groups: Isshinkai, Hokushinkai and a group of Upper House members.

Within his own faction, Ozawa held court like a feudal overlord and had high expectations of members subordinating themselves to him as if it were the natural order of things. Bound together in a tight relationship of reciprocal exchange, the group had the capacity to operate as a bloc in multiple political and policy arenas. After Ozawa resigned as secretary-general in June 2010, his power base within the DPJ was largely personal rather than deriving from any official position that he held.[131]

Certainly the Ozawa group's rock-solid unity ensured that his wishes strongly influenced the outcome of any DPJ presidential race.[132] Apart from giving Ozawa the power to act as kingmaker by backing his preferred choice as candidate for president,[133] his group also furnished him with a launch-pad from which to run for DPJ president himself, or even to take his group as a bloc out of the party.[134] The Ozawa group had first acted in perfect unison to put Hatoyama into the top job in May 2009, with members giving their unanimous support to Hatoyama on Ozawa's instructions.[135]

Later, when Hatoyama decided to resign in June 2010, Isshinkai desperately cast around for an alternative candidate to Kan to take over as party leader and prime minister. Senior Isshinkai officials tried unsuccessfully to persuade a number of candidates, including Tanaka Makiko, to run, in the hope of finding a candidate behind whom the group could unite.[136] In fact, Tanaka and other Ozawa loyalists had tried to persuade Ozawa himself to stand. In particular, some of the younger members of his group pressed him to run against Kan, saying that they wanted to see *oyakata* become prime minister.[137] Ozawa, however, was reluctant to declare his candidacy.

Other possibilities were MIAC Minister in the Hatoyama cabinet Haraguchi Kazuhiro, and Kaieda Banri, neither of whom was willing to stand. The Ozawa faction still made preparations to put up their own candidate but were unable to nominate anyone except for Tarutoko Shinji, so they did not bother to consolidate their group's support for him by requiring all members to back him.[138] Ozawa said that he did not know much about Tarutoko but to the Ozawa group, Tarutoko's chief advantage was that he was not Kan. Although not an official candidate of the Ozawa group, some senior members worked hard to drum-up support for him right up until the election. However, Isshinkai allowed members a free vote because they could not reach a consensus on backing Tarutoko, with many actually preferring Kan as a replacement for Hatoyama. This show of independence angered Ozawa considerably. He declared, 'Why? That's ridiculous! Voting [by group members] should never be discretionary, but instead we must act [in the party election] resolutely for a favorable outcome in the run-up to our party's presidential election in September'.[139] Tarutoko won 129 votes in the election while Kan secured 291 votes, 'a wider margin than anyone had anticipated'.[140]

Ozawa reiterated the view that the real battle would come in September, suggesting that either he would run himself or he would put up another candidate with his group's backing. The voters would not be just Diet members but also other DPJ members and supporters who registered their names in the party and who paid membership fees. Ozawa still stood a chance of demonstrating his power in this system because of the time and effort he had earlier invested in travelling all around the country as secretary-general, collecting many DPJ members and supporters as his allies.[141] The Ozawa bloc then started gathering votes in preparation for the election.

Ozawa consulted widely before finally deciding to stand as a candidate, conducting 'secretive one-on-one *kaidan* with one or two influential MPs per day'.[142] The matter was then intensively discussed with his Diet supporters. Ozawa's position was that he would consider running in the race providing that he could garner support from DPJ Diet members outside his own group, including those in the Hatoyama group and former members of the JSP and Democratic Socialist Party, or DSP (Minshatō). Finally Ozawa met with Hatoyama, who said that if Ozawa decided to run he would support him, so Ozawa decided to contest the leadership.

Ozawa ran his campaign like a real faction boss, mobilising his cohorts in machine-politics fashion. He assembled Isshinkai executives – Lower House Diet members Suzuki Katsumasa and former LP member Matsuki Kenkō – in his private office in the city. He then requested cooperation from DPJ 'strong men' – Lower House Speaker Yokomichi Takahiro and Upper House President Nishioka Takeo – by telephone. Nishioka had known Ozawa ever since they had worked together in the LDP more than 20 years previously, when Nishioka was the chairman of the Executive Council and Ozawa was the secretary-general.[143] Ozawa also had friendly relations with Yokomichi.

Ozawa's next move was to confer with former Prime Minister Hata and secure his support. He then requested cooperation from the members of each of the Hatoyama, former JSP and Hata groups, and from the group that used to belong to the DSP.[144] The leading members of the 'Ozawa camp' who gathered to declare their backing for his bid were long-time ally former JSP Secretary-General Akamatsu Hirotaka, close confidante Hirano Sadao who was a former official of the Lower House Secretariat and later member of the Upper House, Kaieda, deputy chairman of the DPJ's Diet Affairs Committee and key Ozawa supporter Mitsui Wakio, and head of the DPJ in the Upper House Koshiishi Azuma.

Ozawa's vote-gathering method amongst non-faction members focused on collecting votes by mobilising personal connections and major organisations affiliated with the DPJ. He made one-on-one visits to all DPJ Diet members asking for their support, and met with Tsuge Yoshifumi, head of the National Association of Commissioned Postmasters (Zenkoku Tokutei Yubinkyokuchōkai, or Zentoku), requesting that his organisation use its wide network to back his bid for the leadership post.[145] He also talked to the head of Rengō, Koga Nobuaki, to ask for the cooperation of the DPJ's largest support group.[146] In addition, he visited the Japan Dental Association (Nihon Shika Ishikai) to request its support.

Even though Kan proved victorious in the election (the overall vote was 721 and 491 points, respectively, an overall difference of 230 points, which was huge), the gap was much smaller amongst DPJ Diet members. There were 206 votes for Kan (or 412 points with each politician's vote counting for two points) and 200 votes for Ozawa, or 400 points, revealing that the party was effectively split down the middle into pro- and anti-Ozawa camps. The numbers suggested that the Ozawa group largely managed to hold firm as well as acquiring additional supporters from at least the Hatoyama group (with 60 members) because of Hatoyama's pledge that he would offer his cooperation.

The contrast between Ozawa's performance amongst DPJ Diet politicians and the levels of support he received from regional assembly members and rank-and-file DPJ members and supporters could not have been more stark. Kan won 249 out of 300 points gained from local party members and supporters (with Ozawa winning only 51), and 60 out of the 100 points from regional assembly members (with Ozawa winning 40).

The disparity between Ozawa's relatively high level of support from DPJ Diet members and his relatively low level of support amongst the wider party membership had a number of possible causes. First, it appeared to reflect the rank-and-file's negative assessment of his standing amongst the general public, following revelations of his suspect financial dealings. This was confirmed by public opinion polls. A *Nikkei* poll showed that 73 per cent wanted Kan to remain as prime minister, compared with a meagre 17 per cent who preferred an Ozawa win.[147]

Second, Ozawa's lacklustre performance in the wider party may also have reflected his inability to bind the much larger number of ordinary party members and supporters with ties of loyalty and obligation based on patronage. Amongst the Diet members who voted for Ozawa were those who had won tight races in the 2009 elections, with Ozawa's support proving the decisive factor in their victories. Ozawa was heard to comment to his close associates during the campaign, 'I trust Diet members',[148] indicating that he was sure of beating Kan in the Diet member's vote even if the party member/supporters' vote and local assembly vote went Kan's way.

Kan Nobuko, the prime minister's wife, offered an anecdotal view on which Diet members were more likely to support Ozawa. She said, 'The strange thing is that Diet members seem to distance themselves from Ozawa as they become elected for more terms, but first-term Diet members seem to like Ozawa. However, a company with only a CEO and rank-and-file employees won't last long'.[149] Moreover, not every single one of Ozawa's 'children' necessarily fell into line in the leadership election. One who had been dubbed an 'Ozawa girl', Yamao Shiori, defected from the ranks of his supporters explaining 'I'm nobody's girl'.[150]

Old money politics (kinken seiji)

Although Ozawa's big political ideas included proposals for reform of money politics, in reality his power base rested primarily on abundant financial resources. He conducted old money politics in three different ways. First, he was a 'money-power politician' (*kinken seijika*)[151] in the sense that he used money as a tool for expanding his political power. Indeed, money was the key element in the patronage that he dispensed to his followers and gave Ozawa's factions and political parties the solidity they possessed, enabling him to utilise them as instruments in his political forays and power plays.

Second, given that such a political fiefdom could only be sustained by the continuing inflow of funds, Ozawa honed his skills as a fundraiser and amassed large quantities of funds for political use. According to Itō Atsuo, who had seen many politicians in both government and opposition over the years, no politician was more enthusiastic about building up financial assets than Ozawa.[152] He excelled at raising funds,[153] which helped to account for how someone from Iwate, one of Japan's poorest prefectures, could become so rich.[154]

In the 1990 Lower House election campaign alone, Ozawa was said to have collected about ¥20 billion in political contributions.[155] In 1996 he was the Diet member with the highest income from *kōenkai*-related parties and with the greatest ability to collect funds through this channel.[156] His political funding reports also supplied evidence of his prowess at fundraising. After the DPJ's election victory in 2009, the 2008 report showed that Rikuzankai raised the most money for any politician in either the DPJ or LDP – ¥163.03 million, up 60 per cent on the previous year. This compared with Prime Minister Kan, whose reported funding total was ¥12.15 million, most of it from individual donations.[157] Similarly, when MIAC released the political funding report for 2009, Rikuzankai was again the front runner, with an income totalling ¥912.82 million, which was over ¥600 million more than the second place getter.[158] In 2010, Rikuzankai once more topped the list of recipients with ¥328.63 million in political donations, compared with Prime Minister Noda who received a mere ¥30.17 million.[159] In 2011, Ozawa again emerged the front runner, collecting ¥258.6 million through related organisations, including Rikuzankai.[160] A total of ¥161.9 million came in the form of donations from individuals, which was triple the amount received in 2010.[161] As PLF-PLP leader, Ozawa also raised more funds than any other Diet member in 2012, raking in ¥359.08 million, more than any other Diet member including Prime Minister Abe.[162]

Ozawa's substantial financial resources enabled him to open his *seiji juku*, expand the number of his followers into a formidable faction, deploy his secretaries around the country, win elections and control parties.[163] In fact, his large cohort of secretaries was one of the biggest drains on his purse. They manned his offices in the Diet members' building in Tokyo and in his constituency in Iwate Prefecture, as well as his research offices, etc. Of his secretaries, three were publicly funded, but all the rest were privately employed and were, therefore, paid out of Ozawa's own pocket. He provided living quarters to go with the job, purchasing a dormitory for them as well as apartment units, and a house and land.[164] Initially secretaries resided in Ozawa's home in Tokyo for a few years, where they acquired general knowledge including etiquette.[165] Some graduated to being full secretaries and were trained to work anywhere on any task such as handling petitions and gathering material for policies, with electoral activities the most important.[166]

Rikuzankai was at the top of the pyramid of Ozawa's money-gathering system.[167] One of its main legal sources of funding was party subsidies paid to the Iwate (4) DPJ party chapter, of which Ozawa was the leader, receiving approximately ¥707 million from this source between 1995 and 2008, including some corporate donations.[168] The Iwate party chapter began donating money to Rikuzankai beginning in 2001, when it was no longer legal for corporations to make donations directly to individual politicians' political funding organisations.[169]

Another legal source of funding was Ozawa's political organisation, the Ozawa Ichirō Seikei Kenkyūkai (Ozawa Ichirō Politics and Economics Research Association), the main activity of which was to hold fundraising parties. It held three to four parties each year called the Ozawa Ichirō Seikei Forum, with each party ticket costing ¥20,000.[170] It collected a total of around ¥1.02 billion between 2000 and 2008 from the sale of party tickets (as a form of corporate donation). Of this, Rikuzankai received about ¥360 million.[171] Rikuzankai and the Ozawa Ichirō Seikei Kenkyūkai were located in the same apartment unit in Akasaka as Ozawa's state-funded secretary, Ōkubo Takanori, who performed the dual roles of Rikuzankai's chief accountant and the Seikei Kenkyūkai's representative. The Seikei Kenkyūkai also donated funds to the Ozawa Ichirō Tokyo *kōenkai*, which was located in the same apartment. The Tokyo *kōenkai* also made donations to and received donations from Rikuzankai. Ōkubo was Tokyo *kōenkai* representative as well. What these arrangements amounted to was a complex flow of funds in the same room.[172] Whatever route they took, they ultimately ended up as Ozawa's political funds.

The question is whether the donations that Ozawa received from companies, organisations and individuals included 'money for favours', known in Japanese as *uragane* (lit. 'money for bribery') or 'illicit contributions' (*ura kenkin*) (see Table 1.1). Certainly Ozawa was continually associated with 'dubious political funding practices'[173] from his old LDP days. Political corruption of this kind was very much linked to the role of individual politicians as patronage brokers who could deliver specific policy favours to clients by virtue of the strong political influence they wielded over government decisions, including over public works. Although Ozawa was never convicted of this sort of political corruption, he was certainly accused of it.[174]

Third, scandal about 'politics and money' (*seiji to kane*) was the handmaiden of money-power politics, *uragane* and *ura kenkin* in Ozawa's political life (see Table 1.1). *Seiji to kane* involves matters relating to legal requirements to report funding sources and flows accurately, thus raising questions of compliance with the PFCL. It represents a more technical form of financial irregularity, which is a different beast from *kinken seiji*.[175] Nevertheless, it can also bring in wider issues of illegal funding such as 'money for favours', which often lie behind misdemeanours in relation to the law. Violations of the Political Parties Subsidy Law and the Public Office Election Law (*Kōshoku Senkyohō*), which regulate matters relating to money flows, are other areas encompassed by *seiji to kane*.

Ozawa has been tainted by several episodes of this type of money politics, particularly with respect to the disposition of party subsidies as well as by questionable activities in relation to the appropriation of factional funds and donations from companies. Indeed, the two major sources of funding for Ozawa appeared to be money from political parties, which Ozawa acquired each time he destroyed a party and created a new one, and donations from construction contractors.

Many informed observers have felt that, given the many 'incidents' to which Ozawa has been linked, he never got his just deserts. Not only was he one of the beneficiaries of donations from Recruit,[176] but he was also one of the so-called 'dirty dozen' – the 12 politicians whom the head of Sagawa Kyūbin's Tokyo subsidiary, Watanabe Hiroyasu, identified as having received a total of ¥2.23 billion from the company in 1989 and 1991.[177] In fact, one of the main reasons why Ozawa left the LDP in 1993 was to avoid questioning over the Sagawa Kyūbin issue.[178]

At the time, those who made promises of money and votes included leaders from business, trade unions and the Sōka Gakkai.[179] Hiraiwa Gaishi, chairman of the Federation of Economic Organisations (Keidanren), reportedly donated ¥5 billion to Ozawa for the 1993 elections (in addition to the ¥10 billion that he donated to the LDP). Hiraiwa was also the chairman of an Ozawa *kōenkai*.[180]

Even the Hosokawa administration, which partly resulted from public disgust with corrupt politicians, and which was supposedly a 'political reform cabinet' (*seiji kaikaku naikaku*), was not very enthusiastic about solving the general contractors' corruption scandal (*zenekon oshoku jiken*) of 1993.[181] The administration postponed summoning people with connections to the general contractors as well as politicians suspected of involvement, including Ozawa.[182]

While Ozawa escaped formal indictment for political funding violations until January 2011,[183] he was questioned in connection with investigations into possible illegal activity. In one incident relating to the Sagawa Kyūbin affair, he was identified by witnesses as a party to the discussions where illegal deals were allegedly struck involving Kanemaru and the Sagawa Kyūbin trucking company. Ozawa's description of his role at this meeting in the course of Diet testimony was that his job 'was "to refill the others' glasses and empty the ashtrays." He insisted, "I did not participate in the discussion"'.[184]

Although Ozawa managed to come through the Sagawa Kyūbin scandal unscathed, facts later surfaced about what happened to ¥1.3 billion in Keiseikai funds on the day that the Takeshita faction split, suggesting that they were unilaterally appropriated by Ozawa. Obuchi faction member Nonaka Hiromu, one of Ozawa's 'mortal enemies',[185] revealed, 'When the Keiseikai was divided, he [Ozawa] took money from the faction's safe before any of us knew. I didn't know he would go as far as that. We must have been too trusting'.[186] In perfect timing with the 'pillage', Ozawa began purchasing real estate using Rikuzankai's political funds. The suspicion was that the ¥1.3 billion funded these purchases with the aim of making 'hidden money' public, that is, money laundering.[187]

The LDP's campaign position on Ozawa in the 1993 elections was that he was 'as dirty as any of them and, even worse, that he was a traitor too'.[188] Ozawa and Hata had benefited from Tanaka and Kanemaru's 'dirty money', but Ozawa acted as if he were not connected to it and talked about political reform in terms of introducing single-seat constituencies and party subsidies funded by taxpayers as if that would stamp out corruption.[189]

Also like Kanemaru, Ozawa's main source of funds was the construction industry.[190] He did nothing to reform construction-based political financing. In fact, he adopted a defiant attitude in an interview with *Iwate Nippō* in early 1992, asking, 'What is wrong with receiving electoral support and funds from general contractors during elections?'[191] He later reasoned in his 1996 book *Kataru*, 'Firstly, most politicians receive donations and other forms of funds as well as electoral support from construction companies and general contractors. Why is that considered unconditionally evil?...[R]eceiving support for elections has been normal until now'.[192] With Kanemaru's arrest, Ozawa thought that the public prosecutors had broken their understanding with politicians about the *tatemae* and *honne* of the PFCL.[193] He did not think that politicians should have to observe the absolute letter of the law and therefore no individual politician should be prosecuted for apparent violation of it. In his view, the prosecutors had enforced the regulations in a way that exceeded the scope of traditional practice.[194]

Ozawa later watered down the Hosokawa administration's political subsidy reforms. The original proposal was for ¥60 billion in state subsidies to be paid to political parties in exchange for a ban on companies and organisations contributing donations to politicians. However, Ozawa phoned Hosokawa to say that the party subsidy 'needed to be reduced to ¥40 billion ...[because] ¥500 per head of population will be too high [as a subsidy]'.[195]

In the end, total subsidies to political parties were cut to ¥30 billion and companies and organisations could still donate to individual politicians for five years. For those who expected that public subsidies would eliminate shady connections between construction companies and politicians, it was a disappointment. When the loophole was due to expire, the LDP-LP coalition replaced it with another one in 1999 allowing political parties (both headquarters and branches) and political funding groups (*seiji shikin dantai*) designated by political parties, to receive donations from corporations and organisations.

Rorting party subsidies

The reality was that party subsidies become just another 'wallet' that supported Ozawa,[196] although they were officially established on the pretext of prohibiting donations from companies and organisations. After the passage of the Political Parties Subsidy Law in 1994, Ozawa was in charge of subsidies in the NFP, LP and DPJ as virtually the most powerful figure in these respective parties. It meant that he controlled close to ¥100 billion in public funds in the 15 years after the law was passed.[197]

One of the major flaws in the new system related to the disposition of subsidies when a party split. Under the Political Parties Subsidy Law, when a party breaks up, it is treated as a case of either 'secession' or 'division'. In the case of secession, because the members are leaving the party of their own free will, there is no 'distribution of assets'. However, when it is a case of division, a distribution of assets is undertaken in some way or another.

When the NFP was disbanded, it split into six separate parties, which, under the law, was treated as a 'division', and what was left of the party's political subsidies was distributed amongst the six parties. However, how much was paid in total to each party was unknown because there were no legal rules about how to apportion amounts.[198] Moreover, in a celebrated case of secession – when Hata broke away from the NFP and formed the Sun Party, or SP (Taiyōtō) in 1996,[199] the Hata side requested that the Ozawa side treat it as a case of 'division of the party', and asked for a share of the party subsidy provided to the NFP. Ozawa, however, flatly refused.[200] Ozawa treated the Conservative Party (Hoshutō) in the same manner (as a secession) and refused to share the LP's subsidy.[201]

Another flaw in the new system was lack of accountability over what happened to party subsidies when a party was dissolved. As Itō explains:

> The law specifies that when a party is dissolved, the Ministry of Internal Affairs and Communications can order the party to return any amount of money that was not used [from the political party subsidy]. However, if the order is not issued, it is legal for the party not to return the money…[S]ince the political party subsidy is a fund that is supplied to political parties, from the perspective of morality, the money should be returned when the party is dissolved. However, Ozawa seems to have made this enormous amount of money his own.[202]

In fact, money disappeared every time Ozawa's parties were dissolved.[203] By establishing and disbanding political parties, Ozawa was able to transfer enormous amounts of subsidies (i.e. taxpayers' money) – his so-called 'hidden wallet'[204] – into his own fund management organisation. He used his thorough knowledge of the Political Parties Subsidy Law to suck up huge sums of money.[205] For example, when he dissolved the RP and LP, 'he transferred about ¥2.2 billion in total, which was almost all of the remaining funds those parties had, into two political organisations with which he had a strong relationship'.[206] These were the Reform Forum 21 and the Reform People's Council (Kaikaku Kokumin Kaigi).[207]

Reform Forum 21 was established in February 1993 by the policy group of the same name headed by Ozawa. When the RP was set up, the Forum continued to operate as one of Ozawa's political organisations. On the dissolution of the RP in December 1994, it received ¥925.26 million in funds from the party.[208] As of 2008, it still had some ¥690 million in funds.[209] On 21 July 2009, after the Lower House had been dissolved prior to the August general election, Reform Forum 21 donated ¥370 million to the local DPJ chapter headed by Ozawa in Iwate (4). On 22 July, the DPJ prefectural branch handed the money on to Rikuzankai.[210] Receipt of the ¥370 million enabled Rikuzankai to repay a loan for the same amount that Ozawa had made to it two days earlier.[211] The ¥370 million went towards the ¥449 million that Rikuzankai gave to the 91 DPJ candidates standing in the election.

One month before the July 2010 Upper House poll, Reform Forum 21 donated ¥100 million to the DPJ chapter in Iwate (4) and then on to Rikuzankai, this time on the same day.[212] Later in October 2010, Seizankai, another political organisation headed by Ozawa,[213] donated ¥95.88 million to the DPJ Iwate (4) branch.[214] Two weeks later the same amount was transferred to Rikuzankai.[215]

The Reform People's Council was originally established in October 1994 as a political funding organisation (*seiji shikin dantai*) for the RP and later played the same role for the NFP and LP. It regularly channelled funds to Rikuzankai, annually donating between ¥5 million and ¥35.5 million between 1997 and 2001.[216] In September 2003, when the LP was dissolved in the process of amalgamating with the DPJ, the council received around ¥1.36 billion, 'which was more than 85 per cent of the LP's remaining funds balance',[217] including approximately ¥561 million in party subsidies.[218] It 'took maximum advantage of the "legal loophole" that exempts a party from returning party subsidies to the national treasury if its balance is zero by the day the party is dissolved'.[219]

After the LP was disbanded, the Reform People's Council changed its legal status from a party's political funding organisation to 'other political organisation' (*sono ta no seiji dantai*). It thus became just another 'one of Ozawa's money bags'[220] according to the person in charge of accounting in Ozawa's office from 1999 to 2001.

Both Reform Forum 21 and the Reform People's Council thus acted as receptacles for political funds that were left over when political parties were dissolved. The two organisations had the same treasurer, address and phone number.[221] The Reform People's Council also served as a source of funds for Ozawa's *seiji juku* according to the political funding report for 2008[222] and donated ¥5 million to Isshinkai.[223]

The disposition of funds at the dissolution of the LP also drew in finance minister in the Hatoyama administration, Fujii Hirohisa, as a possible conduit for the funds later transferred to one of Ozawa's political organisations. When Fujii resigned in January 2010, there was speculation that he did so for fear of being questioned in the Diet about money issues during his term as secretary-general of the LP.[224] In particular, he was concerned that he would face questioning about how the sum of ¥1.5 billion was used after the LP was dissolved.[225] LP reports on the use of political funds in 2002 stated that it paid Fujii ¥1,520,900,000 in total – ¥979 million in July 2002 and ¥541.9 million in December. The money reputedly went to his political fund management body. Fujii himself, however, did not know anything about it.[226] Although ostensibly given to Fujii, it may have been used by Ozawa,[227] with one report suggesting that the funds were transferred to one of Ozawa's political organisations.[228] This was not, strictly speaking, illegal but the bulk of the funds would have come from party subsidies, a system that Ozawa and others supposedly established for the purpose of political reform. The loophole in the system allowed party leaders to distribute the funds at their own discretion once they were granted.[229]

Questions were also raised about whether Ozawa used the 'pilfered party subsidies'[230] to buy real estate. The purchases were made using Rikuzankai's 'office expenses', but Ozawa's name was listed as the owner of all the properties.[231] He bought the dormitory for his secretaries using ¥365.87 million in 2005. It was located in Ozawa's own expensive residential area in Fukazawa. Why he had to build a new dormitory for his secretaries when he had already bought them a luxurious house for ¥300 million in his wife's name and Rikuzankai already owned 12 properties, including apartment units, was not clear. Real estate seemed to be one of Rikuzankai's main businesses.[232] Between 1994 and 2007, it purchased 14 properties for a total value of more than ¥1.05 billion.[233] Ozawa unsuccessfully sued a journalist and the weekly magazine *Shūkan Gendai* for defamation when they published an article claiming that he was using Rikuzankai to build up assets.[234] His secretaries admitted that it was 'Ozawa's hobby to purchase properties'.[235] Nonaka, Ozawa's enemy, declared:

> I have never seen a politician like Ozawa. The money he used to build up an enormous amount of assets like land and apartment units were political funds, right? Those political funds include the people's tax money (in the form of political party subsidies). He used tax money to build up assets for himself (i.e. in his name)...He's someone that repeatedly made and broke political parties...What did he do with the money that was left in the Renewal Party when he moved...to the New Frontier Party? I heard that he didn't take the Liberal Party's money (political funds including the party subsidy) (to the DPJ) when the Liberal Party joined the DPJ either. He hasn't revealed where the money disappeared to, has he?...He's pocketing [the money] just because it's not stipulated in the law [that what he is doing is illegal]. The same can be said for his political funds. The law doesn't prohibit using political funds to buy lots of properties. But that doesn't mean that politicians should be allowed to buy a whole lot of properties and build up assets by taking advantage of the flaws in the law. Most importantly, the political funds include the people's tax money (in the form of party subsidies)...I'm going to repeat myself again but he is using the people's tax money (to build up assets). He is the biggest 'miser' I know. Even if it were part of his political activities, why did he have to buy so many expensive apartment units and build a dorm for his secretaries in the best residential district in Tokyo? Can we really say that this is good use of tax money?[236]

Yet another political funding loophole that Ozawa exploited was 'expenditure for organisational measures' (*soshiki taisakuhi*), an item in the broader category of 'expenditure for organisational activities' (*soshiki katsudōhi*) in the PFCL. Although politicians are legally entitled to receive funds for these purposes under the law, this particular loophole enabled Ozawa to use vast sums in an unaccountable fashion.[237] Diet politicians are not required to provide any explanation of what the money has been spent on, merely a handwritten receipt for the amount they have received, without additional details. So, by transferring party money to individual politicians, the need to declare what it has been used for is unnecessary. In this way, a party can legally use money as it pleases without further explanation.[238]

Ozawa's method of making the use of funds secret in the name of 'expenditure for organisational measures' became possible after the amendment of the PFCL enacted on his initiative in 1994, which abolished the 'holding money system' (*hoyūkin seido*) that required a Diet politician who received funds to declare how they were used.[239] When he was in the NFP-LP, for example, he channelled a total of ¥7,657,670,000 to five politicians: Yonezawa Takashi (¥410,920,000 in 1996), Nishioka Takeo (¥2,989,040,000 in 1996 and 1997) and Natano Shigeto (¥108,000,000 in 1996 and 1997) of the NFP, Noda Takeshi (¥1,013,480,000 in 1998) and Fujii Hirohisa of the LP (¥3,136,230,000 in the period from 1999 to September 2003).[240]

The question mark hanging over these sums was whether the funds allocated in the name of 'expenditure for organisational measures' was actually handed to the politicians named as the recipients. Some of them claimed to have no knowledge of having received any such funds. If the 'expenditure for organisational measures' during Ozawa's NFP-LP period is added to the ¥2,288,200,000 during Ozawa's tenure as DPJ leader and secretary-general, it amounts to ¥9,945,770,000, a huge amount of money in unaccounted-for funds.[241] It meant that the gargantuan sum of nearly ¥10 billion passed through Ozawa's hands in this category of expenditure.[242]

Furthermore, DPJ documents and an audit of DPJ finances published in late 2010 revealed that between January 2007 and May 2010, Ozawa's close associates benefited from ¥3.7 billion in 'expenses'.[243] The audit was ordered by Ozawa's successor as secretary-general, Edano, and by Komiyama Yōko, the DPJ's Finance Committee chairwoman, both opponents of Ozawa. The job of receiving the funds in question and issuing receipts was done by Yamaoka Kenji, perhaps Ozawa's closest confidante in the DPJ, and by Upper House Diet member Satō Taisuke (who retired in the July 2010 election) as successive chairmen of the DPJ's Finance Committee. Making up almost half of the 'expenses' was the sum of ¥1.6 billion drawn by Yamaoka in December 2006 through to January 2007 'for unspecified "measures for organizations and corporations"'.[244] There was a strong suspicion that the funds were 'under-the-table' money because there were no proper accounts kept.

Another report disclosed that between September 2006 and April 2008, a total of ¥1,703,100,000 was paid to Yamaoka in 15 instalments as 'expenditure for organisational measures', with most of the payments made while Yamaoka was chairman of the DPJ's Finance Committee.[245] It was only after Ozawa was re-elected as DPJ leader in an extraordinary party meeting in September 2006 that he established the post of Financial Committee chairman and appointed Yamaoka to the position. On the same day, the first payment of ¥68 million in 'expenditure for organisational measures' was made.[246] Similarly, between March and September 2008, a total of ¥530 million was given in five instalments to Satō. Between 2006 and 2008, a total of ¥2,233,100,000 was paid to the two chairmen.[247] Later investigations revealed no such large financial flows in Yamaoka's or Satō's fund management organisations, political organisations or party chapters.[248] The suspicion was that the funds were rerouted into Ozawa's own political funds. The page on the DPJ website where the political funds income and expenditure reports were published disappeared when Ozawa became leader.

In Prime Minister Kan's view, revelations of this sort made it even more imperative to 'change the money-drenched aspects of [Japanese] political culture'.[249] He signed off on a contract with an auditing company to check the party headquarters' finances before he resigned as prime minister in 2011. One of the key elements of the contract was not to allow non-transparent expenses such as *soshiki taisakuhi*. Because of the contract, Ozawa's group was prevented from shifting funds around as they liked.[250]

Plundering the public works industry

Throughout his political career, Ozawa used construction companies involved in public works as his primary source of external (non-party, non-government) funding. His ties to other industries including the major manufacturers, their industry associations and other rent-seeking interest groups were much weaker.[251] Political income and expenditure records for the DPJ's Iwate (4) chapter showed that in the three years from 2005 until 2007, Ozawa officially received a total of ¥38.13 million from construction-related sources.[252]

Ozawa's preference for construction industry funds was not only inherited from his political mentors and reflected his family connections,[253] but was also influenced by the nature of his constituency/ies in Iwate Prefecture. Located in rural Japan, Iwate was a priority recipient of government-funded public works.[254] Moreover, in prefectures such as Iwate with low prefectural income, public works construction was a very important industry.[255]

Despite his advocacy of political funding reform, the substantial cuts to public works allocations under successive governments from 2001 onwards and the slogan 'from concrete to people' in the DPJ's 2009 manifesto, Ozawa remained the quintessential patronage broker in Japan's 'construction state' (*doken kokka*). He was widely viewed as 'a typical pork-barrelling type of politician [*rieki yūdōgata no seijika*]',[256] who 'took care of the local area', reflecting the phenomenon of 'public works distorted by politics'.[257]

Ozawa also went a lot further than most other politicians in harnessing the construction industry as the organisational basis of his election campaigns in Iwate as well as in the Tohoku region more broadly (see Table 1.1). He took advantage of the industry's high mobilisation capacities, enabling it to mount 'construction-based election campaigns' (*doken senkyo*) and 'general contractor-based election campaigns' (*zenekon senkyo*).[258] In Iwate alone, there were more than 5,000 construction-related companies employing approximately 72,000 workers. This meant that whether or not a party or politician gained the support of this sector helped to determine the result of all the elections in the prefecture.[259] Under Ozawa's influence, *zenekon senkyo* became the norm.[260]

The first time Ozawa conducted a construction industry-based campaign was in the Mizusawa mayoral election of 1984. He was determined to overcome the personal setback he had suffered in the December 1983 Lower House election. In the mayoral election, the Ozawa camp mobilised a former Ministry of Construction (MOC) administrative vice-minister-turned-Upper House member, Inoue Takashi, former MOC bureaucrats and general contractors to lend their support to an executive of a local construction company. They promised that they would bring large-scale projects back to the region based on their strong pipeline to the central government. Ozawa's *kōenkai* ran around gathering votes as well. In the end, the Ozawa-backed candidate won the election using a prototype of the *doken senkyo* and *zenekon senkyo*.[261]

After the Mizusawa 1984 mayoral election, this prototype was developed further and construction companies began to operate in Ozawa's election campaigns in a more systematic fashion. First, Ozawa exerted political influence on bureaucrats in order to bring public works back to his district[262] and to influence which companies would be permitted to bid for projects and which ones would be selected as the successful contractor. This meant acting as the 'voice of heaven' (*ten no koe*) in the bid-rigging (*dangō*) system of allocating contracts.

Second, Ozawa systematically sought votes, funds and other forms of electoral support from construction companies in exchange for his patronage. The Ozawa office in Iwate conducted *doken senkyo* and *zenekon senkyo*, which involved wholesale mobilisation of general contractors and other construction companies as a 'shadow' election structure. The office would directly pressure construction companies to deliver votes, funds and campaign assistance not only to Ozawa himself but also to his favoured candidates, including for local government office. The support was delivered in a highly organised, top-down fashion under the leadership of the *zenekon*, which, according to a former member of Ozawa's campaign staff, 'built the Ozawa Kingdom [*Ozawa Ōkoku*]',[263] a term that reflected Ozawa's power and standing in regional affairs. In their entirety, the connections between Ozawa and the construction industry formed a labyrinthine web of interpersonal connections, groups, influence peddling, illegal political contributions, corruption and collusion, including bid rigging.

Someone who understood these connections better than anyone else apart from Ozawa himself was Takahashi Yoshinobu, his first public secretary for more than 20 years, who was the key intermediary between Ozawa and the construction industry. Later falling out with Ozawa for unknown reasons,[264] he recounted:

> He [Ozawa] talks about fine things like 'true democracy' and 'the people's lives come first', but in actuality he created Diet members who were at his beck and call based on votes gathered through general contractor-based elections. He obtained power and money in this way, and became powerful as a politician.[265]

After Ozawa left the LDP and formed a succession of new parties in the 1990s, he really began to organise *zenekon senkyo* on a grand scale.[266] A former member of Ozawa's campaign staff disclosed that he was able to manipulate general contractors after becoming LDP secretary-general in 1989, but he 'started general contractor-based elections from 1993'.[267] Takahashi himself wrote:

> [I]n the general election in 1993, Ozawa ordered me to 'make thorough use of general contractors'. This order was where it all began. In this election Ozawa obtained 50,000 more votes than in the previous general election, gaining 142,451 votes in Iwate (2), and won an overwhelming victory…

Given this victory, Ozawa became convinced that general contractors were the tools that he could use to win elections.[268]

Various observers provided details of how Ozawa conducted the *zenekon senkyo* in the July 1993 Lower House election.[269] In addition to contesting his own seat for the RP, Ozawa was backing Kudō Kentarō in Iwate (1). A *zenekon* source related how 60 major general contractors in the prefecture formed a 'hidden election measures group' (*ura sentai*) to back Kudō. Kajima Construction's Morioka City branch manager[270] was in charge,[271] and they mobilised people from their Tohoku and Morioka branches.[272] Ozawa and Kajima allegedly had a 'deep relationship'.[273]

In a press conference in November 1992, Ozawa had earlier acknowledged that 'Kajima…provides financial assistance to some [of our] organisations'.[274] Before the general contractors' corruption scandal broke in 1993, in which the incumbent governors of Miyagi and Ibaraki were arrested, there were reports that Ozawa had been receiving ¥10 million a year in 'hidden donations' (*ura kenkin*) from Kajima – ¥5 million at the Bon Festival in August and another ¥5 million at the end of the year.[275] None of Ozawa's political organisations recorded anything from Kajima in their political funds income and expenditure reports at the time. When he was asked to explain this, Ozawa refused to do so, saying, '(Publicising the breakdown) is not a legal requirement'.[276] He also ignored demands to summon him to the Diet as a sworn witness. However, Takahashi revealed:

> Ozawa directly received ¥5 million from the general contractor Kajima. Not only did he lie to the people, but he also ordered me to go to the prosecutors office in place of him to attend to their questioning…[Ozawa] said 'the transfer (of money) was not done by my own hand', but that is not true. The truth is this: [Ozawa] ordered me, who knew nothing, to be questioned by the prosecutors. The night before…Ozawa told me in strong words, 'Takahashi, think of them as your parents' foes. You understand? Your parents' foes', and demanded that I be determined.[277]

In the 1993 Lower House election, the general contractor-based election machine was mobilised as a pyramid structure involving all of the general contractors that supported Ozawa. The branch heads and sales department managers of the major general contractors went to Ozawa's election office in Mizusawa to lead the campaign.[278] Executives from more than 20 *zenekon* including Kajima also formed a separate hidden election campaign headquarters (*ura no sentai honbu*). From there they allocated votes to local construction companies, subcontractors and sub-subcontractors. They ordered them as well as agricultural cooperatives, commercial and industrial associations and neighbourhood associations to submit lists of *kōenkai* members and to conduct exhaustive phone call and door-to-door tactics using those lists to ask voters to vote for the candidates in question (Ozawa and Kudō).[279]

The construction industry was ideal as a working unit in elections because they had a vertical structure of prime contractors, subcontractors and sub-subcontractors, which could be easily mobilised from the top down.[280] If they wanted work, it was impossible for local construction companies to reject requests for support made by general contractors who were the primary contractors on large-scale works.[281]

In the election itself, Ozawa won twice the number of votes as the second-ranked candidate (140,000 as the top candidate in the constituency), even though he did not set foot in his hometown throughout the campaign.[282] Even Kudō, who was not expected to do well, came third in Iwate (1) and was elected to the Lower House. Kudō himself publicly acknowledged that he had received support and donations from general contractors.[283]

After he left the LDP, Ozawa successfully transferred the construction industry as the financial and electoral base of the LDP first to the RP and then to the NFP in Iwate. He conducted a full-scale general contractor-based election campaign in the April 1995 Iwate Prefecture gubernatorial election, supporting former MOC bureaucrat Masuda Hiroya as candidate for governor. Masuda was attractive to Ozawa because, as an opposition member for the first time in his political career, Ozawa was unable directly to interfere in the central government budget. Ozawa and his allies in the NFP calculated that, 'We can do anything as long as we secure the post of governor',[284] meaning that if they could establish a foothold in the prefectural government office, they would be able to maintain their influence on public works.[285] Ozawa was desperate to establish a regime of public works patronage based on local government starting from the governor's position. More than 40 per cent of the public works projects undertaken in Iwate were either funded solely by the prefectural government or were mainly conducted by the prefectural government with central government subsidies, which was much higher than the national average.[286]

The election marked the beginning of the wholesale conversion of Iwate from the 'LDP Kingdom' to the 'Shinshintō Kingdom'.[287] It displayed key elements of Ozawa-style *doken senkyo* and *zenekon senkyo*.[288] In the style of a 'pressuring election' (*shimetsuke senkyo*), the Ozawa office sent a letter to construction companies requesting support for Masuda and the submission of signatures (of supporters) with the implied threat that if the companies did not cooperate, they would face various forms of discrimination in terms of work.[289] *Zenekon* executives were then instructed to bring executives from their affiliated companies to the election office, where they were asked to mobilise support for Masuda amongst their employees, relatives and acquaintances. A congratulatory advertisement in a newspaper after the election listed the names of 460 major construction companies in the prefecture.[290] Immediately after the election, Masuda went to Tokyo to request budgets for 37 public projects, 44 per cent of which involved the MOC.[291] One of Ozawa's secretaries also became Governor Masuda's secretary, thus stationing an NFP affiliate in a key post in the prefectural bureaucracy.

Construction company executives seeking public works contracts were also required to make obligatory rounds of both government offices and Ozawa's offices in Mizusawa City, Morioka City and Tokyo. In Iwate, bureaucrats in the prefectural construction division questioned them as to whether they had paid a courtesy visit to the Ozawa office. MOC officials asked them the same question. At both levels of government, bureaucrats openly acknowledged that paying respects to the Ozawa office was necessary in order to receive orders for public works.[292]

The Ozawa office influenced the allocation of construction contracts through its exercise of the 'voice of heaven'. If a construction company were nominated to bid for a project as a result of its visits to administrative offices, it would discuss its bid with other nominated construction contractors beforehand under the pretext of a 'research meeting' or 'workshop'. At this meeting, one of the companies would say, 'We have gained Mr. Ozawa's approval over this construction work'.[293] Other construction contractors would then confirm this with Ozawa's secretary to check whether it were true. When the secretary said 'yes', this became the 'voice of heaven' and the order was made to the first construction company.[294] One construction executive related how:

> Ozawa's secretary...rings the nomination examination committee [*shimei shinsa iinkai*][295] and says, 'Don't nominate this construction contractor for this construction work', or, 'Nominate this construction contractor'...I once got angry about the fact that a mere secretary decided (the allocation of public works).[296]

Another link in the chain of connections between Ozawa and the construction industry was his personal relationship with the Don of the construction industry in Iwate and Tohoku, Mochizuki Shigeru, who was chairman of Takaya Construction[297] and a senior member of the Tōshō Club,[298] which was the core of the general contractor-based support structure (*shien soshiki*) for Ozawa. Functioning as an Ozawa *kōenkai*, the club's official goal was to assist Ozawa's political activities. The key link person between the club and Ozawa was Takahashi, who was listed as its 'secretary in charge of liaison'.[299] It was a widely acknowledged amongst people in the construction industry that they could not win contracts unless they helped Ozawa's election, and that they could get more contracts by joining the Tōshō Club.[300]

Mochizuki was also chairman of the Iwate Prefecture Construction Industry Political Federation (Kenseiren). Its membership consisted of approximately 6,500 people involved in construction and related industries in the prefecture.[301] It supported Ozawa when he was in the LDP along with other LDP candidates, but after Ozawa formed the RP, Mochizuki recommended him saying that he wanted to support Ozawa as Japan's representative[302] and served as the RP's Supreme Adviser for Electoral Affairs. In addition, Mochizuki was chairman of Keyaki no Kai, a group of local businesses that provided support for Ozawa in Iwate (1) constituency.[303] The Keyaki no Kai was first established in 1992 when Ozawa was acting leader of Keiseikai. Initially there were around 500 members with the majority of them construction and civil engineering companies that did subcontracting work for major general contractors. It was organised when a call went out to 'make Ozawa Ichirō prime minister'.[304]

When the NFP was established, Mochizuki and Kenseiren began supporting it, trying to bring the local construction industry together as one. In the 1995 gubernatorial election, the Keyaki no Kai pitched in as a powerful force in the campaign, with Mochizuki at the helm and at Ozawa's request. It mobilised members to gather lists of names, including company directors and directors of agricultural cooperatives and chambers of commerce and industry. Everyone on the list was called and asked for electoral support. Mochizuki claimed: 'If I move, the construction industry moves'.[305]

The 1995 Iwate gubernatorial election was followed by the prefectural assembly election, the Upper House election and the Morioka mayoral election. Mochizuki and the Kenseiren led the NFP to victory in all these elections.[306] Construction companies were each assigned to muster a certain number of people in different places to attend meetings, speeches, etc. The numbers were determined by the size of the company.[307] Moreover, it was not just a question of conscripting company employees; it was also about mobilising employees' friends, acquaintances and relatives.[308] What is more, Ozawa's secretary checked the quality of the lists of 'supporters'. If he noticed that a contractor had written the same name multiple times or if the people on the list did not respond well when the secretary rang them, he would complain, threatening a loss of contract opportunities.

After these victories in 1995, the NFP dominated the top posts in the prefectural government as well as the majority of seats in the prefectural assembly,[309] eclipsing the LDP. In the 1996 Lower House election, the tussle between the LDP and NFP over the construction industry as their main support structure in the region went on with Mochizuki and Takaya Construction crucially throwing their weight behind Ozawa and the NFP candidate Tasso Takuya, an unknown former bureaucrat, in Iwate (1).[310] Tasso was previously Ozawa's assistant when he was NFP leader and considered himself one of the 'Ozawa children', winning elections 'based on Ozawa's full support'.[311] Ozawa supported Tasso in the Lower House election in the same way in which he had thrown his support behind Masuda in the 1995 gubernatorial election.[312] While the NFP did not perform well nationally, in Iwate it demonstrated overwhelming power, winning 51 per cent of votes and recording victories for Ozawa and Tasso as well as for the NFP candidate in Iwate (3).

In the 1998 Upper House election, 60 *zenekon* and other companies including medium- and small-scale construction contractors mainly in Iwate, Akita, Miyagi and Kanagawa, which were being handled by the Ozawa office, submitted a total of more than 150,000 names on their lists of supporters.[313] The office ranked each company's degree of contribution (A, B, C, etc.) based on the strength of support provided by the voters on the lists. Even Kanagawa Prefecture was included, despite its location far from Tohoku. Not only were the names of 35,000 voters in Kanagawa submitted, but 37 *zenekon* also stationed approximately 210 employees in Kanagawa for the whole month prior to election day.[314] This support was all because the person running in the election was none other than 'Ozawa-ism follower' Hidaka Takeshi, who later became DPJ deputy secretary-general in the Noda administration.[315] Hidaka was one of Ozawa's former secretaries who had been in charge of administrative work for Rikuzankai before Ishikawa Tomohiro.[316]

According to Takahashi, from about the mid-1990s Ozawa was mostly backing others with construction-based elections:

> [S]ince 1996, Ozawa has not conducted full-scale general contractor-based elections on his own behalf. This is because there is no one in Iwate who could win against Ozawa. Instead, he used general contractors in other elections to create his own protégés. Masuda in the Iwate gubernatorial election in 1995, Tasso Takuya in the general election in 1996, Hidaka Takeshi in the Upper House election in 1998…Whenever we heard that the candidate 'might lose', I went to the local constituency and took command. Masuda and Tasso probably would not have been able to win the election without the general contractors' cooperation; more than 200 people connected to general contractors came and provided electoral support. If we include affiliated companies and subordinate companies, more than 1,000 related companies submitted lists of hundreds of thousands of names and provided electoral support for Ozawa. There was no way the rival candidates would have been able to win…Based on the lists of names we created 'summary sheets' and assessed which lists were useful in the elections. Then, based on that assessment, 'voice of heaven' was issued in relation to the public works.[317]

In the 2000 Lower House election, approximately 60 *zenekon* submitted lists with approximately 21,000 names.[318] They also '"permanently stationed" 80 people [in the Ozawa election office] and mobilised an additional 40 people to make phone calls [to voters] as "cooperating personnel"'.[319] The list of general contractors was contained in a document entitled '2000 LH election Iwate 1st Constituency, individual tally, Tasso'. The reference was to Tasso, now a successful candidate for Ozawa's LP. With Ozawa's backing, Tasso took over the Iwate governorship from Masuda in 2007.

In addition to operating like a giant vote-gathering machine, construction companies provided political funds. One contractor disclosed, 'From the Ozawa office's point of view, contractors have either to contribute to the election campaign or provide funds. If a construction contractor can do neither, then it could be deprived of opportunities to receive contracts'.[320] A former *kōenkai* executive revealed his knowledge of Ozawa's money-gathering system:

> It is tacitly understood in the [construction] industry that Ozawa's office had been demanding various general contractors provide a predetermined amount of money as donations…The amount was determined based on the scale [of the company], but I heard that ten years ago a middle-scale general

contractor had to provide more than ¥20 million per year. General contractors came up with ways to hide these donations; for example, they gave subcontractors extra money in addition to the construction payments so that the subcontractors could use that money to buy party tickets [from Ozawa's office].[321]

The Tōshō Club also played a key intermediary role in securing political funds for Ozawa. Information would be sent to several high-ranking members through Kajima Construction, the leading member, and the high-ranking members would then send the information on to other general contractors to which they were linked. Adding up contributions went in the reverse direction. High-ranking members would first tally up the amount and then Kajima Construction would do the final tally. By keeping a record of these numbers, the various companies' degree of contribution could be monitored. As for party tickets sold through the network, each company would be assigned a purchase quota of about five tickets at the standard price of around ¥20,000 each. Requests for campaign assistance were made in the same way. When companies were short of manpower, they employed part-time workers to do the work at their own expense.[322]

Non-compliance could bring retribution from Kenseiren down on the heads of offending companies. For example, it could deprive the contractor of work by putting pressure on companies that were close to the defecting company by saying that it was about to go bankrupt or that the quality of its work was declining.[323] Several construction companies were crushed in this way. On the other hand, if a company went all-out to provide support in line with the industry's decision, the contractor would enjoy a smooth supply of projects.

Many companies decided not to support the LDP any more under these conditions arguing, 'We won't be able to get any jobs unless we side with the New Frontier Party',[324] and 'You can't get your hands on any works unless you are politically connected'.[325] More than 90 per cent of the construction contractors in the prefecture ended up affiliating themselves with Ozawa, which underpinned the NFP's 'great leap forward'. Some voters called the NFP's style of organisation- and company-based electioneering 'old-fashioned'.[326] Ozawa had clearly done nothing to reform 'construction elections' in spite of his moving ahead with electoral and other reforms during the Hosokawa administration. As far as the construction companies were concerned, 'The LDP and New Frontier Party were no different'.[327] For them, the overriding consideration was to get orders for public works.[328]

Not surprisingly, Ozawa-affiliated companies ended up dominating public works in the prefecture. Member companies of the Tōshō Club and the Toryōkai (a subsidiary organisation of Tōshō Club),[329] and construction contractors affiliated with the NFP almost completely monopolised orders for prefectural or municipal public works in Iwate that were ¥1 billion or more in scale.[330] In particular, Takaya Construction with Mochizuki at the helm became the leading construction company in Iwate by a large margin. In 1994, it accounted for more than 10 per cent of the total construction revenue of the top 100 construction companies in Iwate, with orders from the MOC, prefectural government and municipal governments for all kinds of projects such as dams, roads, bridges, agricultural fields, ports, buildings and repairs.[331]

Another equally important piece of the web linking Ozawa to the construction industry in Iwate was the connection between the Ozawa office and the actual bid rigging conducted by the construction companies themselves. Kajima once again featured heavily.[332] The arrangement was that Kajima would arrange the bid rigging after referring to Ozawa's office (who told them which company should win the bid). The main player was Ozawa's secretary, Takahashi, who had a close connection to Kajima's bid-rigging specialist who was its Tohoku branch deputy head, Kadowaki Kazutsugu, adviser to the Tōshō Club. In practice, Kadowaki acted in partnership with Kajima's sales manager, Itō Shōichirō. Together they were known as the 'Kadowaki-Itō line'.[333] They managed the big-rigging organisation called the Tohoku Construction Industry Council (Tōhoku Kensetsugyō Kyōgikai, or Tōkenkyō), which arranged the winner and loser candidates for large-scale public works contracts before the bidding started.[334]

The reality was that neither general contractors nor construction contractors in Iwate could go against Kajima Construction and Takaya Construction because of Mochizuki's role as chairman of the Tohoku Construction Industry Association and Kenseiren, which controlled the entire prefecture through local construction company executives. Moreover their respective heads (Mochizuki and Deguchi Chōshitsu, who was chief of Kajima's Morioka branch) were senior members of the Tōshō Club. Takahashi was the coordinator and he 'completed the trinity structure that reigned over the construction industry'.[335] According to a *zenekon* executive, Takahashi knew the amount each construction company had contributed. Not surprisingly, construction contractors all went to Ozawa's office in Tokyo to meet Takahashi. A source connected to a general contractor in Morioka explained:

> The amount of donations to be made by general contractors is decided by Ozawa's office. It is impossible for [general contractors] that receive contracts for works in Iwate to object to Ozawa's office. In this relationship, Ozawa is 'superior' and general contractors are 'inferior'. They don't know what kind of abuse they would suffer if they were to disobey Ozawa's office.[336]

The list of public works in Iwate Prefecture provided rich pickings for Ozawa, including the Isawa Dam in Ōshū City, located near his family home in his local electorate of Iwate (4). Although a state government project, it was called the 'Ozawa Dam'[337] in reference to Ozawa's influence over the contracts to construct it. Between 2002 and 2007, 16 out of the 65 companies (other than general contractors) that received contracts for works on the Isawa Dam donated a total of ¥26.25 million to the DPJ's Iwate (4) branch headed by Ozawa, whilst receiving contracts to the value of ¥4.782255 billion.[338] In addition, nine companies that sub-contracted to two of the major general contractors on the project – Kajima Construction and Nishimatsu Construction – donated a total of ¥37.92 million to the Iwate (4) branch.[339]

The possibility of unreported donations to Ozawa from construction companies that received contracts for the dam was first investigated by the Public Prosecutors Office (PPO) in 1993. Ozawa's political funds income and expenditure report for that year revealed that Nittoku Construction, a *zenekon*, had made a ¥1 million donation to Rikuzankai during the 1993 Lower House election.[340] This was the only amount that was officially reported. However, the sum hardly squared with the ranking of Nittoku Construction as a 'special A-grade in construction' on the list of companies qualified to receive contracts for prefectural construction works. This was the highest rank, while B-grade companies were widely acknowledged as having to donate ¥10 million per year.[341] Nittoku Construction was also a 'second-grade' member of the Tōshō Club. Although the Morioka District PPO dropped the case in 1995, questions were raised in the Diet about whether the ¥1 million donation was repayment for the order received to conduct the geological survey for the Isawa Dam, and whether it violated the Public Office Election Law. It was also noted that the value of the contracts that Nittoku Construction received doubled in the year that they made the 'contribution' to Rikuzankai.[342]

It was the Isawa Dam that also acted as the 'glue' between Kajima Construction and Ozawa.[343] Kajima won the bid for constructing the heart of the dam, which involved creating the layer made up of rocks and other material, with a bid of ¥20.349 billion.[344] By the mid-1990s, Kajima Construction was the successful builder of 11 of the 58 large dams in Iwate including the Taki Dam, and had received the contract for the main construction of the Isawa Dam as well as the Hyachine Dam and Sannōkai Dam, which were said to be Ozawa projects.[345]

Suspicion regarding dubious donations to Ozawa from the former president of a *zenekon* (Hazama Corporation)[346] also surfaced in relation to another dam in Iwate Prefecture – the Hinata Dam.[347] The Special Investigation Department (SID) of the Tokyo District PPO found data saying 'Hinata, remuneration, ¥10 million' on a floppy disk confiscated from Hazama Corporation, although the Ozawa side denied any wrongdoing.[348] Ozawa had reportedly been 'compensated' for the fact that his father-in-law's company, Fukuda Gumi, did not win a contract for the dam's construction, which had been decided by Kajiima-led bid rigging.[349] Moreover, three subcontracting companies affiliated to the LDP were suddenly dismissed from dam contracts and were replaced by companies affiliated to Ozawa, suggesting that the Ozawa office had actually intervened in prefectural administration. These companies quickly changed sides and started supporting the NFP.[350]

Ozawa's former secretary Takahashi also testified to the SID that he heard Ozawa's 'voice of heaven' in relation to the construction of the Takō Dam in Ōfunato City, Iwate Prefecture, with a total project cost of approximately ¥32.3 billion.[351] Ozawa insisted that the contract be given to Shimizu Construction via the usual process of bid rigging directed by Kajima.[352] This was borne out in the Takō Dam contracting. Shimizu Construction and joint venture companies including Kumagai Corporation won the general competitive bidding. Furthermore, 'the winning companies each bought ¥20 million worth of tickets to Ozawa's parties for several years as repayment'.[353]

There were many questionable aspects to the classic clientelistic structure that Ozawa had established to generate electoral support and political funding from the construction industry. First, on the Ozawa side, it involved a type of parasitic 'privatisation' (*shibutsuka*) of public works decision making and administration. The JCP accused Ozawa of 'leeching' off public works,[354] meaning that he exploited this policy domain for his own private political gain by intervening in and influencing decisions at several crucial points in the 'plan to implementation' stages of construction projects. In terms of the entry points of his influence, his intervention was particularly salient in two interlinked stages: the decision-making stage in the public works bureaucracy, where companies were nominated or designated to bid for projects; and the stage where contract winners were actually selected, which was directly linked to bid rigging undertaken by general contractors, a process that he also directed.

Second, on the contractors' side, the system was characterised by very high levels of organisation and coordination, with the formation of intermediary groups incorporating construction company executives, including within Ozawa's *kōenkai*, which were designed to facilitate the delivery of funds and votes to Ozawa. A hierarchy of construction companies led by large general contractors at the top rallied lower-ranking *zenekon* and second- and third-tier construction companies, enabling Ozawa partially to subcontract out the tasks of fund and vote mobilisation to his closest *zenekon* allies who acted as his political agents. The whole top-down set-up was authoritarian and even draconian. The Ozawa office closely monitored how well each construction company was performing as a supplier of votes, funds and campaign assistance. The monitoring was necessary in order to determine the level of 'reward' that could be made in terms of selection as a 'nominated' or 'designated' company given the opportunity to join the select circle of public works project bidders, and as a winner of contracts. Many companies were under duress to back Ozawa merely for the privilege of being able to participate in the bidding process and resented the element of compulsion built into the system. One *zenekon* executive 'said in disgust, "a staggering number of people gave electoral support to Ozawa's office. The DPJ's slogan 'from concrete to people' just sounds hollow"'.[355]

Whether from a position in government or in opposition, Ozawa was able cleverly to exploit this system because he had 'captured' the governorships in Iwate plus a significant proportion of municipal mayorships. This was fundamental as no subsidised works could be conducted without the allocation of funds by the prefectural or municipal governments.[356] Iwate Prefecture was the 'Ozawa Kingdom' in the sense that his clientelistic network centring on public works provided the financial and electoral bedrock of his continuing political power.

Subsidiary funding sources

Ozawa's other personal sources of political funding have included horse-racing interests including off-track betting, media companies, the Korean Unification Church (Tōitsu Kyōikai, or the 'Moonies' as they are popularly known),[357] multi-level marketing businesses such as Amway Japan,[358] salaryman loan companies and *pachinko* parlour businesses.

Ozawa is also reported to have connections with *yakuza* through his mentor Kanemaru, 'who was well known for his ties to organised crime',[359] although he does not meet gang members directly.[360] A former construction company executive revealed that one of Ozawa's functions 'is that he is alleged to have the clout to keep the *yakuza* in line, which means that he has the wherewithal to keep them gainfully employed, at the price of occasionally using them to bludgeon his (or his client's) enemies'.[361] Prior to the 2009 election, there were reports of a deal worked out between Japan's biggest crime gang, the Yamaguchi-gumi, and a senior figure in the DPJ for the 40,000 members of the gang to throw their support behind the DPJ in the 2009 election. This was in exchange for an agreement from the senior DPJ figure not to pass a criminal conspiracy law that would have outlawed the *yakuza*.[362] The *yakuza* would not only vote for the DPJ, they would also provide donations, including from 'front' companies as well as contributions from individual employees. The *yakuza* would also furnish inside information on the DPJ's political rivals and use stand-over tactics on any opposition party members who attempted to embarrass the party.[363] Although Ozawa was not named in the story, the implication was that the senior DPJ figure in question was in fact Ozawa.

Paying the price of 'money politics'

The taint of political corruption and money politics followed Ozawa throughout his career, exacting a toll on his political prospects and thwarting his political ambitions. In particular, issues around *seiji to kane* dogged his political career during his attachment to the DPJ and helped to shape his political fortunes in the party. They prevented him from leading the DPJ to victory in August 2009 by forcing him to resign as party leader over a money-politics scandal on 11 May that year. They were also the primary cause of his resignation from the position of DPJ secretary-general in June 2010, as well as a contributory cause of his defeat in the DPJ leadership election against Kan in September 2010.

The possibility that Ozawa's financial dealings might have infringed the PFCL brought him and his office to the attention of the Tokyo District PPO with its proud record of pursuing highly placed politicians.[364] On 3 March 2009, the Tokyo District PPO arrested Ozawa's secretary, Ōkubo, on suspicion of violating the PFCL. On 24 March 2009, Ōkubo was indicted on the charges of receiving illegal donations and falsely reporting them. The corporate donations allegedly came from general contractor Nishimatsu Construction. They were illegal because under the PFCL, corporate donations must not be made to individual politicians, only to political parties or parties' political fund management organisations.

On 12 March, JCP Chairman Shii Kazuo had revealed at a news conference that over the three financial years 2003–06, at least ¥33 million had allegedly been donated to Ozawa through two dummy groups set up by Nishimatsu Construction.[365] Ōkubo, who was Rikuzankai's chief accountant, was said to have reported to the government ¥21 million in donations from the groups in 2003–06 even though he was aware the money was from the company itself.[366] The two groups – the New Political Issues Research Association (Shin Seiji Mondai Kenkyūkai) and the Future Industry Research Association (Mirai Sangyō Kenkyūkai) – were proxies for Nishimatsu Construction. The money was donated from membership fees collected from the company's manager-level employees, but the company actually paid the membership fees by adding them to the employees' bonuses and instructing the groups how to donate the funds. A retired Nishimatsu Construction official headed each of the two political groups. Another source reported that between 2003 and 2006, the two dummy organisations had donated a combined total of ¥46 million to Rikuzankai, the Iwate federation of DPJ chapters and the DPJ Iwate (4) chapter.[367]

Nishimatsu Construction's donations to Ozawa's parties had actually begun in 1994 – first to the RP, then to the NFP and later the LP. Over the 11-year period up to and including 2006, the Ozawa camp as a whole received ¥180 million from the company.[368] Furthermore, between 1996 and 2006, it benefited from ¥28.2 billion in construction contracts in Iwate.[369]

Until Ozawa joined the DPJ in 2003, Nishimatsu's donations to Ozawa's parties were under his direct personal control so they did not present a problem. They were made through the Reform People's Council, which received the money directly from Nishimatsu Construction and one of its dummy groups, the New Political Issues Research Association, until 2002.[370] The problem arose in September 2003 when the LP merged with the DPJ, which reduced Ozawa's control over party funds. Ōkubo then told Nishimatsu Construction to divert its political funding to Rikuzankai to safeguard Ozawa's control.[371] The prosecutors suspected that Rikuzankai had been receiving these funds ever since the LP-DPJ merger, which was illegal. Nishimatsu Construction did not make any donations to the DPJ's political fund management body from the time of the LP's merger with the DPJ.[372] During this period, Ōkubo and the Ozawa office were still organising *zenekon senkyo*, having taken over from Takahashi who had originally established the system and previously served as chief accountant for Rikuzankai like Ōkubo.

Ozawa reacted angrily to Ōkubo's sudden arrest, saying it was 'an unfair use of state power'.[373] Ever since the Kanemaru case, he had been critical of the way in which the public prosecutors arbitrarily used their administrative discretion in enforcing the PFCL in some cases and not in others. He said, '[They] suddenly conducted a criminal investigation when it was a formal violation that has traditionally been settled by correcting [records] and paying a fine'.[374] He followed this up with the comment:

> If people are going to say the reports have been falsified even though I have recorded all inflow and outflow of political funds in my political funds income and expenditure reports in accordance with the Political Funds Control Law, then we have no choice but to immediately abolish and ban all donations from companies and organisations.[375]

Making such a proposal was part of a well-established pattern of presenting ideas for political reform whenever he became involved in political controversies, particularly those involving 'politics and money'.[376]

At the same time, Ozawa argued that all responsibility for handling that money was in the hands of his secretaries, and although he took responsibility for mismanaging them, that was not 'a prosecutable offence'.[377] He declared that he had no idea where the money originated and wouldn't seek to look into it. However, as Takahashi said many times, 'The secretaries follow Ozawa's orders to the smallest detail'.[378]

In reference to Nishimatsu Construction's ¥21 million in illicit donations, former Ozawa aide Kanazawa Kei, who worked under Ozawa's former private secretary Ishikawa (who was in charge of administrative affairs at Rikuzankai and thus responsible for keeping records of all financial transactions), told reporters that 'Ozawa gave orders to "hide files, to get rid of anything that could cause trouble"'.[379] Kanazawa:

> helped to carry out the documents just before the prosecutor's investigation of Ozawa's office. He testified about some of the things that were said at the time, such as 'We escaped by a hair's breadth. If these things had been checked, starting with Ozawa, everyone would have been arrested', '[Money from] Nishimatsu is the smallest portion…'[380]

Ōkubo was arrested along with two ex-Nishimatsu executives (former President Kunisawa Mikio and Manager of the Administrative Department Okazaki Akifumi), on suspicion of creating dummy political organisations and giving instructions to provide illegal donations through these organisations. The executives told investigators that the donations were made to Ozawa in an attempt to win contracts for public works projects in the Tōhoku region.[381] They added, we 'can't believe that Mr. Ozawa…knew nothing about the donations from Nishimatsu… We were afraid of being obstructed by Mr. Ozawa in the Tohoku…region, especially in Iwate Prefecture. We wanted to be awarded contracts for the Isawa Dam construction projects'.[382] According to bidding records for Isawa Dam, Nishimatsu won the bid for the spillway installation works as the primary contractor in March 2006 with a bid of ¥10.0276 billion.[383] Kunisawa testified that he understood this successful bid to be the result of his company's donations to Ozawa.[384] A report in the *Mainichi Shinbun* noted that Nishimatsu's two dummy political organisations had donated a total of ¥180 million to Rikuzankai, the local DPJ Iwate branch and DPJ's Iwate (4) branch on 11 occasions between December 2005 – three months after the official announcement of the spillway installation works – and November 2006.[385]

At Ōkubo's trial in December 2009, the prosecution's opening statement argued that the Ozawa office predetermined which companies would win contracts based on its decisive influence on bid rigging and in return induced construction companies to provide electoral support and donate political funds in exchange for contracts.[386] According to the prosecutors, 'Okubo assumed the role of issuing the "voice from heaven", or an authoritative command, around 2000 in determining the winners of biddings for public works projects financed by local governments'.[387]

The prosecution's opening statement also reported a remark that Ōkubo had made to Nishimatsu's Morioka branch manager immediately after a joint venture involving the company won the bid for pouring the concrete for Isawa Dam's spillway in March 2006. Ōkubo intimidated him for not providing enough electoral support.[388] He said, 'You haven't been cooperative lately. The Isawa Dam that you got the contract for is the Ozawa Dam. Don't forget that, we need you to keep cooperating'.[389] The prosecutors also asserted that Ōkubo held discussions with senior Nishimatsu officials about donations from dummy entities of the company and that they had reached an agreement that Nishimatsu would be the winner of two public works projects in Iwate Prefecture, suggesting that the donations were a reward for receiving the projects.[390] The prosecutors also pointed out that the Reform People's Council was in fact 'a front for donations to Ozawa from general contractors'.[391]

The prosecutors cited affidavits from several construction company executives that described how 'the Ozawa office demanded that these companies make cash donations for elections'.[392] Kunisawa reportedly made a full confession when he was arrested and prosecutors found a written claim made by Ozawa's side asking for donations.[393] Kunisawa claimed that 'Nishimatsu needed (Ozawa's) "heavenly voice"',[394] admitting that his company had created dummy political organisations to make roundabout donations to the Ozawa office in line with its demands. Kunisawa was subsequently convicted of violating the PFCL by making illegal donations to Rikuzankai.

At Ōkubo's trial, the prosecutors also revealed that a computer confiscated from Ozawa's office in Akasaka contained records of the amounts donated by various general contractors, which amounted to ¥600 million between 2000 and 2006. The funds were received from various *zenekon*, including those that had benefited from contracts for the Isawa Dam, such as Kajima Construction, Shimizu Construction, Taisei Construction, Ōbayashi Construction and Tekken Construction.[395] The prosecutors claimed that the Ozawa office had long been acting as the 'voice of heaven' with respect to public works in Tohoku, and general contractors had made political donations to Ozawa in the hope that he would give them the contracts.[396] The SID leaked information that Ōkubo not only approved bid rigging among *zenekon* in the Tohoku area, but was also acting as an intermediary for Kajima Construction, which was directing the bid rigging.

As it turned out, the Ōkubo-Nishimatsu Construction scandal was a short prelude to a wider scandal involving three of Ozawa's former secretaries, which later extended to Ozawa himself. On 15 and 16 January 2010, the Tokyo District PPO arrested Ōkubo as well as DPJ Lower House Diet member Ishikawa, and Ikeda Mitsutomo (Ishikawa's successor as Ozawa's private secretary), for alleged false reporting of funds over a land deal in Tokyo, in violation of the PFCL. Ozawa fulminated against the public prosecutors, charging that the arrests 'cast a shadow over the nation's democracy'[397] and that any misreporting of fund flows was a matter of 'simple mistakes'.[398]

At the centre of the PPO's indictments was the purchase of a plot of land for ¥352 million in Setagaya Ward in Tokyo by Rikuzankai, on 29 October 2004. As secretaries, the three allegedly failed to record the money flows in Ozawa's political fund reports when Rikuzankai allegedly borrowed ¥400 million from Ozawa to buy the land for some ¥352 million, returning the sum in 2007. NHK had earlier reported that just before the land transaction was made, more than ¥400 million was transferred temporarily into the bank accounts of a number of Ozawa's political organisations such as the Ozawa Ichirō Seikei Kenkyūkai. The funds were then transferred to Rikuzankai's bank account straight away. They were not recorded as income and the SID suspected that the funds were used to purchase the land and decided to investigate. They also believed that the funds originated from illegal political donations and the funding reports were falsified in order to obscure the origins of the money.

Rikuzankai responded by explaining that the source of the funds was a loan from a financial institution with a term deposit of ¥400 million as collateral. However, it was suspected that the money for the land purchase was paid before the loan was taken out and that the source of the ¥400 million term deposit was not recorded. Records were then falsified to say that the transaction (the purchase of land) was made the year after the actual transaction.[399]

On 13 January 2010, prosecutors searched the offices of Rikuzankai, Ishikawa and Kajima Construction to gain evidence relating to illegal financial dealings. The public prosecutors were believed to suspect that the unreported ¥400 million included secret donations from one of Kajima's subcontracting companies, Mizutani Construction, a general construction company headquartered in Kuwana City, Mie Prefecture, on a project to build the Isawa Dam. The company's former chairman, Mizutani Isao, testified to prosecutors that, 'In return for getting the subcontract for the Isawa Dam construction, I gave ¥50 million in 2004 and 2005, a total of ¥100 million, to Ozawa's secretaries'.[400] The company had been told by Kajima that it needed Ozawa's consent to become a subcontractor for the works.

Ōkubo admitted when he was arrested that he had received cash from Mizutani Construction.[401] The company simply added the percentage that it said it paid in kickbacks to Ozawa's secretaries on to construction costs in other areas of its business, such as land improvement works as a kind of 'political tax' or payment for Ozawa's 'heavenly voice'. This was known as *jōnōkin* (a tax or 'tithe'),[402] traditionally 3 per cent of the contracted price for dam, road and railway construction, which was funnelled back to politicians as hidden donations (*yami kenkin*).[403] One farm family in Ōshu City (in Ozawa's electorate) reported that Mizutani Construction put a loading on to the cost of laying pipes for irrigation works on their farm, with the money used to pay for Mizutani Construction's bribes to Ozawa, which were paid to his secretary.[404]

Other construction companies linked to Ozawa were also investigated by the public prosecutors, including Shimizu Construction, which annually purchased ¥20 million in tickets to Ozawa's fundraising parties after being selected as one of the leading contractors for the Tako Dam in Iwate. Shimizu was reportedly told by an executive of Kajima, which had rigged the bid in their favour, to visit Ozawa's office after winning the contract. At the office, they were asked to purchase ¥20 million in party tickets annually for several years.[405]

The Tokyo District PPO also investigated a heavy machinery engineering company, Yamazaki Construction, which partially constructed the Isawa Dam, in relation to the land purchase by Rikuzankai. Yamazaki funded Ozawa through various political donation routes from 1995 until 2006. Political funding reports revealed that it had purchased party tickets for the Ozawa Ichirō Seikei Kenkyūkai and donated funds to Ozawa's local district branches for the LP and DPJ, and to the Reform People's Council. In addition, it had donated to Rikuzankai via its Tohoku branch office as well as from its headquarters, and the former president and founder of the company made individual donations. In all, the total donated was ¥22,860,000 distributed through six separate routes.[406] The period of funding overlapped with that of Nishimatsu Construction's dummy fund contributions so it was suspected that the money had been used for a backstairs deal in order to receive orders for the Isawa Dam. In October 2004, Yamazaki Construction secured a subcontract for Isawa Dam construction from Kajima, and in March 2005 obtained a subcontract from Taisei Construction, which received a partial order for dam construction. A former executive of Yamazaki Construction reportedly testified that he provided ¥50 million to Ozawa as thanks for getting subcontracting work on the Isawa Dam. The PPO on 19 January 2010 searched the headquarters of Yamazaki Construction on suspicion of an infringement of the PFCL.[407]

Ozawa's three secretaries were subsequently indicted on charges of misreporting the flow of funds in Rikuzankai's 2004 and 2005 reports and with falsifying the group's 2007 report. Ishikawa and Ōkubo were charged with conspiring not to report for 2004 the ¥352 million that Rikuzankai used to buy the land as well as a ¥400 million loan from Ozawa to Rikuzankai, which was said to have funded the land purchase. Ikeda, who took over from Ishikawa in compiling the fund reports, was charged with falsely declaring ¥352 million in the 2005 report even though no such donation was received, conspiring with Ōkubo and failing to report ¥400 million as expenditure in the 2007 report when that amount was repaid to Ozawa in that year. Ikeda denied the charges. Ōkubo was charged with conspiring to record the ¥352 million outlay in the 2005 report and for not reporting the repayment of the ¥400 million loan to Ozawa in the 2007 report. He was additionally charged with disguising ¥35 million in donations from Nishimatsu as having been received from various political groups.[408]

Ishikawa told prosecutors that the funds to buy the land came from Ozawa's own personal assets, but in fact, there were very complex financial dealings at the heart of the matter, which made prosecutors suspicious. After Rikuzankai borrowed ¥400 million from Ozawa, it put the same amount into a time deposit account at a bank. Then, with the time deposit as collateral, it borrowed ¥400 million in Ozawa's name from the bank to buy the land. This money 'was entered into reports as a loan from Ozawa'.[409] What made the SID suspicious was Ozawa's easy access to such a large sum of money, which looked like an attempt to launder illegal donations.[410]

The zeal with which the PPO pursued Ozawa and his secretaries gave rise to speculation that its actions might have been politically motivated. Ozawa and his supporters were convinced that the PPO had targeted him even while the general public continued to view Ozawa with a high degree of approbation as reflected in opinion polls.[411] Ozawa had never been on good terms with the PPO and was a politician who had vowed to dismantle and reorganise the central bureaucracy of which the PPO was a very important part. The public prosecutors were also anti-DPJ.[412]

The question then arose whether Ozawa was too clever and too familiar with the methods of the public prosecutors ever to be found guilty in a court of law. He was well acquainted with Tanaka's Lockheed scandal, Takeshita's Recruit scandal and Kanemaru's Sagawa Kyūbin scandal and massive tax evasion case. In these scandals, he sometimes acted as the point of contact with the public prosecutors. He also attended every sitting of the court during Tanaka's extended trial for taking bribes from Lockheed, which lasted for 191 sessions over the period 1977–83. He used this experience to learn about the finer points of judicial procedure.[413] When the 1989 Recruit scandal forced the Takeshita cabinet to step down, Ozawa asked, 'Has the Tokyo District Public Prosecutors Office turned into the Kwantung Army?'[414] Similarly, when Kanemaru's hidden donations scandal was exposed in 1992, Ozawa objected, saying the prosecutors' methodology exceeded their discretionary powers.[415]

Because Ozawa officially had no authority to authorise the allocation of public works contracts and because it was unclear whether a construction company had asked Ozawa to facilitate its participation in the construction of Isawa Dam, proving a bribery case against him was going to be difficult. The focus of the SID's investigation thus switched from investigating the source of the ¥400 million for the purchase of the land to Ozawa having conspired with his secretaries to violate the PFCL.

When Ozawa was finally questioned in January 2010 about the source of the ¥400 million he explained that it had originated from funds left over after selling his house and building a new one, and withdrawals from family accounts, which were all kept in his personal office.[416] The problem was that at a press conference in February 2007, he had said that the money had come from 'donations from supporters', later changing this explanation in October 2009 to 'a loan from financial institutions',[417] which 'was borrowed on the security of a ¥400 million term deposit'.[418] Moreover, while the land transaction was completed on the morning of 29 October 2004, the ¥400 million term deposit account and loan on the security of that account were made in the afternoon.[419]

With respect to the income and expenditure report in which the money used to buy the land was not recorded, Ozawa told the public prosecutors that these were acts of his secretaries in which he was not involved. His former secretary, Takahashi, however, attacked Ozawa's credibility on this point and condemned the way that Ozawa left his secretaries to hang out to dry. A former executive of Ozawa's *kōenkai* also argued that Ozawa did not trust others over money matters and would never have left such major transactions to his secretaries.[420] For these reasons he must have noticed the donations from Nishimatsu through its dummy organisations, which it was likely that he tacitly approved.[421]

On 4 February 2010, the public prosecutors decided not to seek criminal charges against Ozawa because of insufficient evidence to convict him as a conspirator. Ozawa welcomed the result, saying that he would carry on as secretary-general. Not only did he refuse to step down from his post, but in February 2010 he also declined to attend the Lower House Deliberative Council on Political Ethics to give an account of himself. The reason he gave was, 'Nothing surpasses the prosecutors' investigation, which has legal power, even the political ethics committee'.[422]

The significance of Ozawa's refusal was that when given the opportunity to honour the very code that he was instrumental in establishing,[423] Ozawa declined. The Political Ethics Deliberation Council had been set up to require politicians under a cloud of suspicion in a financial scandal to provide explanations of their involvement. Ozawa, however, disregarded the rules that he had laid down for other Diet politicians. In fact, Ozawa never took up the many opportunities he had to explain himself fully,[424] particularly to give a satisfactory accounting of Rikuzankai's flawed income and expenditure reports.

A citizen's group, the Association of Those Seeking the Truth (Shinjitsu o Motomeru Kai),[425] called for a review of the PPO's decision and requested that a prosecutorial inquest panel (*kensatsu shinsakai*) reinvestigate Ozawa's suspected involvement in the alleged false reporting by his political fund management body in 2004 and 2005. The establishment of the Tokyo No. 5 Committee for the Inquest of Prosecution, made up of 11 members of the public, followed. On 27 April 2010, the committee unanimously agreed that Ozawa should face charges of violating the PFCL in relation to his fund management body's false reporting of political donations in 2004 and 2005. In the panel's judgment, Ozawa's principal defence – that he did not review the financial statements prepared by the secretaries of his political funds management organisation – was not credible. The members concluded that Ozawa's secretaries would not on their own have cooked up the elaborate scheme to hide the source of ¥400 million in funds and therefore it merited indictment on a charge of conspiracy.

The panel also noted that Ishikawa had 'confessed to prosecutors that he had reported to and consulted with Ozawa before filing a 2004 report in which he allegedly failed to list 400 million yen'.[426] In their view, this was 'direct evidence' of a conspiracy between Ozawa and Ishikawa.[427] The panel described Ozawa as 'an absolute authority' (*zettai kenyokusha*), using this as further grounds for concluding that 'there was no need or reason for the former secretaries to conceal the flow of funds without Ozawa's noticing'.[428] It also 'cited a deposition by Mitsutomo Ikeda…saying that he briefed Ozawa and obtained his endorsement before submitting a 2005 funds report in which the expenditure for the land deal was erroneously entered'.[429]

Despite these arguments, the prosecutors, after considering the panel's decision and opening a new investigation, decided for a second time not to indict Ozawa over the 2004 and 2005 case because of insufficient evidence. This left it to the

No. 5 Committee to make a second decision on whether Ozawa should be charged over the alleged falsification by Rikuzankai of its 2004 and 2005 fund records.

In July 2010, another inquest panel, the Tokyo No. 1 Committee for the Inquest of the Prosecution, concluded that the decision by the prosecutors in February 2010 not to indict Ozawa was 'unjust', and so he should be indicted over his alleged involvement in falsifying Rikuzankai's 2007 report. The panel alleged that Ozawa had been involved in concealing the transfer of the ¥400 million used in the Tokyo land purchase. The panel also found 'credible testimony', including by Mizutani Construction, that Ozawa took part in falsifying the reports, and cited the evidence of Ozawa's secretaries, who acknowledged that they had shown him the funding reports before filing them. Given that the panel's ruling was not binding, prosecutors determined again that Ozawa did not merit indictment for the events of 2007 because of insufficient evidence and closed the case.

However, in October, the No. 5 Committee announced their decision that Ozawa should be indicted for issuing false funding reports in 2004 and 2005, thus overturning earlier decisions by the prosecutors that there was insufficient evidence to warrant Ozawa's indictment. The point on which the judicial panel focused was the testimony made by Ozawa's former secretaries during the investigation that they had reported and discussed the matter with him. As for Ozawa, who was denying any complicity, the judicial panel said it simply could not trust Ozawa's explanation that he had left everything to his secretaries and was not involved at all. This was based on indirect evidence such as his signature on documents connected to the land purchase.[430] With respect to Ozawa's explanation for where the ¥400 million came from, the judicial panel commented, 'we can't possibly trust that. Ozawa explained that it came from his own money, but if that were true, he did not have to borrow the ¥400 million from the bank'.[431] They added, 'for Ozawa to claim that the ¥400 million used for the land purchase came from personal funds while simultaneously claiming the money was borrowed from a bank is "remarkably unreasonable and not credible"'.[432] The panel concluded that there was sufficient evidence to suggest that Ozawa was directly involved in making the false entries in the political fund report and recommended that he be indicted.

The upshot of the No. 5 committee's recommendation was that Ozawa faced mandatory indictment because the panel had determined twice that Ozawa should be indicted even though the PPO had declined to do so for lack of sufficient evidence. Ozawa was subsequently indicted on 31 January 2011. Three court-appointed lawyers acting as designated prosecutors charged him with 'violating the Political Funds Control Law over false reporting of funds by his political funds management body…in connection with a land deal in Tokyo'.[433] The indictment stated that Ozawa had conspired with his three former secretaries not to list ¥400 million he lent to Rikuzankai in its 2004 political funds report and in listing ¥352 million used to purchase a 476-square metre parcel of land in Setagaya Ward in the 2005 funds report, which should have been entered in the 2004 report. The indictment also stated that Ozawa lent the ¥400 million to

Rikuzankai in October 2004 to purchase the land. Ishikawa had allegedly informed Ozawa that he did not intend to enter the ¥400 million in the political funds report for 2004 and Ozawa approved the plan. The money was not listed in the report because Ishikawa 'regarded the money as "derived through political activities, and thus it could not be disclosed"'.[434] Instead, Ishikawa entered the bank loan for the same amount in the report.

In early February 2011, the trial of Ishikawa, Ikeda and Ōkubo began with all defendants pleading 'not guilty' to the charge of inserting false information into Rikuzankai's income and expenditure reports in violation of the PFCL. The trial absorbed the earlier case in which Ōkubo went on trial for receiving hidden donations from Nishimatsu Construction. In their opening statement to the court the prosecutors said that they would demonstrate that the secretaries intentionally did not record the ¥400 million 'because they feared such a large sum would attract attention and eventually reveal that they [Ishikawa and Ōkubo] separately received ¥50 million around the same time from general contractor Mizutani Construction in connection with a dam project in Iwate Prefecture'.[435]

During the proceedings, the prosecutors argued that Ōkubo demanded ¥100 million from Mizutani Construction in return for the Ozawa office accepting it as a subcontractor on the Isawa Dam project,[436] and Ishikawa and Ōkubo each received ¥50 million from the company as *uragane*. The prosecutors repeated that the secretaries had falsified the report in order to hide the huge amount of *uragane* they had received. The prosecutors also charged that the president of Mizutani Construction at the time, Kawamura Hisashi, was given the task of actually handing the money over to Ishikawa and Ōkubo.

In April, former President Kawamura appeared as a witness at the trial. His testimony was pivotal insofar as it was the first time anyone had publicly admitted supplying *ura kenkin* to Ozawa. Kawamura testified that he had given ¥100 million (to Ozawa's secretaries).[437] He said, 'It [the ¥100 million] was requested by Ōkubo Takanori in Ozawa's office in the Lower House Diet members' building. I paid the money later'.[438] He also testified that in the year in which he became president of Mizutani Construction (2003), he continued to meet Ōkubo and to entertain him at restaurants. He recalled that he had identified two specific projects for which he wanted to receive orders but when he met Ōkubo to deal with the subcontracts for the dam construction, he was cautioned (*chūi suru*) for being later than the other construction companies in coming to meet him (i.e. Ōkubo) and so after that, he had started entertaining Ōkubo. Then in September 2004, Ōkubo had requested that he donate ¥100 million and give the amount in two lots of ¥50 million each time the contractor was decided. Kawamura contributed the first lot – ¥50 million – to Ishikawa in paper bags in a hotel in Tokyo on 15 October 2004. The other ¥50 million he gave to Ōkubo around mid-April 2005.[439] In addition, Kawamura revealed that at the end of 2003, he presented Ōkubo with ¥1 million in cash and expensive beef as a year-end gift at Ōkubo's house.[440] He also '"treated Mr. Ōkubo and Ishikawa at a fine restaurant in Tokyo several times", and then "in September 2005 at a hotel in Morioka City, I passed ¥20 million to Mr. Ōkubo as a courtesy for the Lower House election"'.[441] When asked why he went to Ozawa's office as part of his business operations, Kawamura explained, 'The dam is in Ozawa's home area. I had heard that if you were opposed by the powerful Ozawa office, you could not participate in the construction'.[442] He testified that after he gave Ozawa the money, he was able to achieve great results as a subcontractor on the dam construction. He thought that this was due to the Ozawa office's recommendations and the former secretaries' cooperation.[443] Further testimony at the trial from other Mizutani executives supported Kawamura's statements.

Despite these developments, the reliance by the public prosecutors on previous testimony by Ishikawa, Ōkubo and Ikeda as evidence at their trials received a major setback on 30 June 2011 when the presiding judge of the Tokyo District Court, Toishi Ikurō, declared as inadmissible 12 of the 38 depositions made by Ozawa's former secretaries, on the grounds of unlawful questioning.[444] The court lambasted the SID for their investigation, including the questioning of suspects in which both threats and inducements were used.[445]

On the other hand, the Ozawa camp suffered a severe setback on 26 September when all three former secretaries were found guilty of falsifying Rikuzankai's financial reports in 2004, 2005 and 2007 in relation to the purchase of land in Tokyo's Setagaya Ward. Despite the court rejecting many of the depositions that supported the prosecution's claims, it accepted almost all of its assertions, including that the Ozawa office had received ¥100 million as 'hidden donations' from Mizutani Construction, and 'deemed that Ōkubo, Ikeda and Ishikawa conspired over false reporting'.[446] Ōkubo was additionally found guilty of accepting illegal political donations from Nishimatsu Construction.

The court recognised that there were many years of 'adhesion' (*yuchaku*) between Ozawa's office and companies in relation to public works,[447] that general contractors petitioned Ozawa's office's secretary/ies to give them approval as the favoured company in the collusion process,[448] that general contractors had for many years chosen the winners of public works contracts in Iwate and Akita through bid rigging, and that the Ozawa office had exercised a huge influence on that process through the 'voice of heaven' of Ozawa's secretaries. Since 2002–03 Ōkubo had played this 'heavenly' role,[449] asking for large amounts of political donations from construction contractors.[450] The court also accepted that Ōkubo had falsified the financial reports of Rikuzankai and other Ozawa political organisations between 2003 and 2006, disguising ¥35 million in donations from Nishimatsu Construction as those from dummy political organisations set up by the company, which violated the PFCL.[451]

Similarly, the court accepted as reliable Kawamura's evidence that he had provided ¥50 million to Ishikawa and another ¥50 million to Ōkubo for the purpose of winning contracts on the Isawa Dam project. The ruling also acknowledged that Ishikawa had not reported the ¥400 million that Rikuzankai had borrowed from Ozawa when it purchased the block of land in Setagaya Ward in October 2004 in order to conceal the ¥50 million received from Mizutani Construction at around the same time.

The ruling concluded that the collusive relations of the Ozawa office with construction contractors were behind both incidents,[452] and that Ishikawa and others had falsified the records in order to hide the 'adhesion' between Ozawa's office and construction companies.[453] The court relied on objective circumstantial evidence of the complicated fund transfers made by Ishikawa where he divided the ¥400 million borrowed from Ozawa into five different deposits in five different banks and later gathered the money into one deposit. Because Ishikawa had not provided a logical explanation for this, the court judged that it was an act of concealment.[454] The prosecutors, therefore, had proven their case using evidence other than the depositions taken from the three secretaries.

Speculation was rife about whether the guilty verdicts could affect Ozawa's own trial due to begin on 6 October, because he was accused of conspiracy with his former secretaries to make false entries in Rikuzankai's funding reports. The court in the secretaries' trial also rejected as 'untrustworthy' Ozawa's claim during the investigation that the ¥400 million was cash he had on hand.[455]

In their opening statement at the Ozawa trial, the prosecuting lawyers argued that he had lent ¥400 million to Rikuzankai in 2004 for the land purchase, conspiring with Ishikawa and Ōkubo deliberately to omit details of the transaction from Rikuzankai's 2004 funding report. Ozawa and Ōkubo then gave their approval for Ikeda to falsify the funding records by recording the transaction of ¥352 million used to purchase the land in the 2005 report instead of the 2004 report when the purchase was actually made.[456] The prosecution also alleged that when Ikeda reported to Ozawa that he would list the ¥352 million for the land purchase in the political funds report for 2005, Ozawa had given his consent. The prosecutors reasoned that it was 'inconceivable that Ozawa's former secretaries falsified [Rikuzan-kai's political funds report] without permission from Ozawa'.[457]

The prosecuting lawyers further argued that Ozawa provided the ¥400 million to purchase the land while also signing an application to receive a loan from the bank for the same amount, which was unnecessary. In their view, this was proof that Ozawa tried to hide the ¥400 million coming out of his own pocket.[458] Moreover, the fact that Ozawa signed the documents pertaining to the bank loan that was entered in the 2004 report was an important piece of circumstantial evidence that he was a party to the alleged conspiracy.[459] Another piece of circumstantial evidence was the fact that Ishikawa had said in a February 2007 magazine interview that Ozawa had instructed him beforehand to make a false statement in relation to funding for the land transaction.

Amongst the evidence presented by the prosecutors were the depositions made by Ozawa's secretaries under interrogation by the PPO, which Ozawa's defence lawyers argued were inadmissible. A key issue was whether those rejected by the court in the trials of Ōkubo, Ishikawa and Ikeda would be accepted in Ozawa's case. Without them, proving Ozawa's collusion in the false reporting would be difficult.[460]

Ozawa resolutely stuck to his plea of innocence, denying that he conspired with his former secretaries to falsify Rikuzankai's income and expenditure reports in 2004 and 2005. He also read an eight-minute prepared statement to the court, which he turned into a political tirade against the prosecutors, adding that 'conducting an investigation for something as trivial as making errors or inappropriate entries on political fund reports encumbers political activities and violates sovereignty of the people'.[461] He also condemned the timing of the investigation:

> In March 2009, the prosecutors targeted me and started mandatory investigation just before the special general election in which regime change was anticipated. This use of power by the prosecutors could have had an impact on the results of the general election. If something like this can happen, Japan can no longer be called a democratic country.[462]

Following Ozawa's claim that the prosecutors were trying to destroy him politically, his defence team reiterated that the case represented a prosecutorial conspiracy 'to destroy the DPJ and Ozawa's power after he took the reins of the party in 2006'.[463]

More trial sessions followed later in October and in January, February and March 2012. At the 10 January session, Ozawa explained that he was concerned with affairs of state and entrusted everything else to his secretaries. He never checked the income and expenditure reports and never gave any instructions to his secretaries, who never explained anything to him.[464] This was a way of saying 'there were no conspiracies because I left everything up to my secretaries'.[465] Ozawa explained that the ¥400 million for the land purchase had come from his own assets, including money that he had inherited from his parents, royalties from his books and funds that he had saved from his own salary as a Diet member for more than 40 years. The money for the land purchase had been handed over in cash, but this had ended his involvement in the deal. Regarding the fact that he had ¥400 million in cash available he answered, 'I've been keeping cash on hand for a long time. [If I have the cash] I can respond immediately when needed. It's safe to keep it on hand and I don't feel it's that strange'.[466] As for why Ishikawa had divided the ¥400 million into multiple bank accounts allegedly to hide 'dirty money', Ozawa commented, 'I think it is natural for a secretary to make sure that the lawmaker can avert negativity and unfounded, harsh slander'.[467] He categorically rejected the allegation that either he or his former aides had received money from construction companies, including Mizutani Construction and others in the construction industry. He also denied speculation that he had pocketed the political subsidies that were left over when the NFP and LP were dissolved in 1997 and 2003, respectively.

In February, the Tokyo District Court disallowed key depositions from Ozawa's secretaries as evidence on the grounds that the interrogation methods used by the prosecution were 'illegal'. The only deposition accepted as evidence was Ikeda's, in which he stated that he had 'reported the contents of the income and expenditure report for fiscal 2005'[468] to Ozawa. However, Ozawa's defence team argued that this deposition did not prove that the matter in question had been reported to Ozawa, and that Ozawa had given his approval.

In their closing arguments to the trial in March, the prosecuting lawyers explained how the five political organisations relevant to the case (Rikuzankai, Seizankai, Ozawa Ichirō Seikei Kenkyūkai, Ozawa Ichirō Tokyo *kōenkai* and the

DPJ Iwate (4) chapter) were formally separate groups but operated as one. Each specialised in a different form of funding, with Rikuzankai receiving individual donations, the fourth chapter corporate donations and the Seikei Kenkyūkai fundraising party revenue. As for outgoings, Rikuzankai's spending was on real estate, the Seikei Kenkyūkai's on parties and the Tokyo *kōenkai* and Seizankai on personnel expenses and other costs. According to the prosecuting lawyers, Ozawa's personal assets and the assets of the five organisations were separate.[469] Initially, the plan was to scrape up ¥400 million from the five organisations to purchase the block of land for the dormitory, but Ishikawa thought that this might lead to a lack of operating funds in the groups. In the end, Ozawa approved Rikuzankai buying the land and a personal loan in cash from his own funds to do so. The lawyers' account of the fancy financial footwork that followed involving Ozawa's own funds in cash, multiple deposits in Rikuzankai's name in different banks, and a term deposit in Rikuzankai's name and loan for ¥400 million in Ozawa's name diverged substantially from Ozawa's own testimonies in court.

Ozawa's acquittal on 26 April 2012 came as no surprise, given the dearth of evidence to show that he had actually conspired with his secretaries to make false entries in Rikuzankai's political funds report. The court ruling condemned the fact that falsified investigation records created by the Tokyo District PPO were used by the judicial panel to recommend Ozawa's mandatory indictment.

Certainly the PPO deserved to lose the case for lack of hard evidence. If Ozawa had been convicted it would have been largely on the basis of supposition and inference. The court acknowledged that there was circumstantial evidence to suggest that Ozawa had received reports from his secretaries as to how the ¥400 million was handled and that he had approved those reports. Furthermore, the court pointed to Ozawa's different explanations for the source of the funds for the land purchase and his vague accounts on other points. The judgment also stated that his secretaries had not entered the ¥400 million borrowed from Ozawa in the income and expenditure report and had changed the date of the land purchase, thus committing financial irregularities under the PFCL.

The court agreed with the prosecuting lawyers' argument that the secretaries feared that if Rikuzankai's political funding report revealed that ¥400 million had come from Ozawa, it would be widely publicised in the media, which would hurt Ozawa politically. Nevertheless, Ozawa was exonerated from the charge of conspiracy because the court accepted the possibility that he was not informed by his secretaries that the way in which the ¥400 million was handled was illegal, and that he may not have been aware that false entries had been made in Rikuzankai's funding report. So while acknowledging Ozawa's involvement to a certain degree, there was insufficient evidence of deliberate intent on Ozawa's part to make false entries in the political funding reports, and therefore no conspiracy took place between Ozawa and his secretaries.

The court did not accept, however, the argument of the defence that Ozawa entrusted the details of his political funding accounts to his secretaries and had not received any detailed reports from them concerning these financial matters. It stated as 'questionable' Ozawa's claims that he had not seen the relevant Rikuzankai reports even after the matter came to light. Presiding Judge Daizen Fumio condemned Ozawa's stance as inappropriate, given his responsibilities as a Diet politician under the PFCL.

Although Ozawa was found 'not guilty' of conspiracy, residual suspicion of his corrupt behaviour remained as with all previous scandals with which he had been associated. His defence team declared him 'completely innocent' (*kanzen muzai*), but the designated lawyers acting as prosecutors emphasised that he was 'pretty much guilty' (*hobo yūzai*).[470] Even the judge said 'the situation "smelled"'.[471] LDP Secretary-General Ishihara Nobuteru declared that Ozawa was '99 per cent' guilty, while the verdict was called 'grey' by the LDP's Policy Affairs Research Council Chairman Motegi Toshimitsu.[472] Certainly Ozawa was convicted in the court of public opinion.

Encouraged by the fact that the court had accepted almost all of their claims, the prosecuting lawyers decided to appeal the verdict to the Tokyo High Court in spite of intimidating phone calls that they would not be forgiven if they did so.[473] They condemned the lower court ruling for containing irrational points and factual errors and were confident of a successful appeal.

When the time came for the appeal trial, the Tokyo High Court did not approve the examination of witnesses requested by the prosecuting lawyers, nor the submission of new evidence, and therefore it only lasted for one hour.[474] The High Court also reversed the premise of the first verdict that the secretaries had intentionally falsified entries in the reports. Therefore, Ozawa, who was briefed on the reports by his secretaries, would not have been aware of any illegality. Following the ruling, the prosecuting lawyers ruled out appealing the verdict, thus closing another chapter in Ozawa's history of 'money politics'.

The fact that, in the final analysis, there was insufficient evidence to convict Ozawa of conspiring with his secretaries to falsify Rikuzankai's financial records proved neither that these records were not falsified nor that he was not a regular recipient of *uragane* and *ura kenkin* from companies seeking public works contracts. Furthermore, many politicians and other observers were clearly cognizant of the details of other suspect funding flows relating to the break-up of political parties and 'organisational expenses'. This raised questions of Ozawa's probity with respect to the use of taxpayers' funds allocated as party subsidies, let alone his sharing in the costs of public works construction by siphoning off a share of the monies paid by the government for those projects.

The public's verdict

As a politician tainted with money-politics scandals, Ozawa was a distinct liability for the DPJ, undermining its public standing and image as a party of reform. As a result, many ordinary Japanese saw it as just as contaminated by aspects of old politics as the former LDP. In the spring of 2009, the DPJ's support rate dramatically increased when Ozawa relinquished the party leadership over the money-politics issue, which later contributed to the party's great victory in the August

Lower House election. Then in early 2010, the Hatoyama cabinet's approval rating plunged when Ozawa's three secretaries were arrested and the public demanded that he resign as party secretary-general. The Nagasaki gubernatorial election of February 2010 registered a big loss for the DPJ, indicating that it was beginning to pay the electoral price of Ozawa's money-politics scandal.[475]

In the lead-up to the 2010 Upper House election, polls confirmed Ozawa's continuing unpopularity with voters, 70–80 per cent of whom wanted him to step down as DPJ secretary-general.[476] Moreover, 57 per cent said they would take into account Ozawa's fundraising scandal in deciding whom to vote for in the election.[477] Public support for the DPJ then almost doubled when Hatoyama and Ozawa resigned together in June 2010. In the press conference announcing his candidacy for party president, Kan said, 'Ichiro Ozawa has invited the suspicions of the Japanese people. For his own sake, the sake of the party, and the sake of Japanese politics, it would be best for him to be quiet for a while'.[478] This was a directive for Ozawa to remove himself from the political scene.

Kan clearly believed in politics driven by policy debate and public opinion, rather than in politics that were reliant on personal connections cemented by money and the exercise of personal power. Ozawa stood for the 'politics of money and numbers', whereas Kan represented a new style of politics where leadership was based on policy advocacy and demonstrable public leadership skills. His viewpoint echoed that of key members of his administration and party executive consisting of the non-Ozawa club of 'seven magistrates',[479] who formed the core of his leadership group who had largely created the culture of the 'new' DPJ. It valued 'the ability to draft political policy and Diet debates more than power struggles fought through the power of numbers scraped together by driving money and personnel assignments',[480] the kind of political culture represented by Ozawa.

Kan's personal attack on Ozawa's style of politics reflected the views of many of his colleagues in the DPJ, widespread public opinion and the question that many people were asking about whether such a person was suitable to be prime minister.[481] It was important for Kan to stake his claim to a different style of politics and to do so publicly in order to drive his point home. In this respect, the leadership contest between Ozawa and Kan went far beyond policy matters. By criticising Ozawa's style of politics, Kan raised the very important issue of what kind of politics Japan and the DPJ wanted to have: old or new. He talked a lot about 'clean politics' and 'a cabinet that is true to its word'.[482] He declared that one of his major goals was 'to make Japanese politics more open and clean where money does not talk'.[483] In his first speech to the Diet as prime minister, he acknowledged that 'politics and money' had seriously undermined the Hatoyama cabinet and were one of the major reasons for both Hatoyama's and Ozawa's resignations.[484] Nevertheless, the Ozawa-Hatoyama scandals still exacted a price in the July 2010 Upper House elections, with voters clearly disillusioned with the DPJ's ability to project a clean image and offer a new style of politics.

In late August 2010, a *Nikkei Online* poll revealed that 71 per cent of respondents were hoping that Ozawa would not stand in the party leadership election in September, considerably higher than the proportion (54 per cent), who did not approve of the Kan administration.[485] Kan again went on the offensive, commenting on Ozawa's involvement in the money-politics scandal involving the ¥400 million land purchase. He stressed what were once Ozawa's calls – banning corporate donations to political parties and cutting the number of Diet members in Lower House PR seats – as well as making a general appeal for 'clean and open politics', in a clear attempt to differentiate himself from Ozawa.[486] Kan's proposal to ban both companies and groups from making political donations was countered by a rather feeble call from Ozawa to 'make political funding public' (a rather meaningless notion, given that it was already public through the submission of political funding reports).

At the Kan-Ozawa leadership debate hosted by the National Press Club in Tokyo, Kan openly belittled Ozawa for how he conducted politics, saying 'politics that places too much importance on money and numbers [*kane to kazu*] is old politics'.[487] He reiterated the need to emerge from this kind politics, 'citing the Lockheed Scandal involving former Prime Minister Tanaka Kakuei, whom Ozawa looked up to as his mentor. By superimposing Ozawa's political style onto the image of the former Tanaka faction of the LDP, Kan underscored his resolve to build a clean and open DPJ'.[488]

As the polls continued to reveal, the public remained very critical of Ozawa even as they became more critical of the Kan government.[489] The public's view of Ozawa dimmed even more after his mandatory indictment on 31 January 2011, with many people taking the view that he should resign as a Diet member, or at least leave the DPJ voluntarily as his former secretary, Ishikawa Tomohiro, had done, in order to take political responsibility. Regardless of the outcome of any subsequent trial, the mandatory indictment sullied Ozawa's public image, contributing to a widespread public view that he was a 'dirty politician'.[490]

By March 2011, more than three quarters of those canvassed in polls were saying that they approved of the DPJ's suspension of Ozawa's DPJ membership because of his indictment in relation to the political funding scandals, and more than half supported either his expulsion from the party or the DPJ urging him to leave. Even polls taken after Ozawa's acquittal in April 2012 showed high levels of public support for the appeal to the Tokyo High Court and for Ozawa to explain his 'politics and money' issue to the Diet, as well as disapproval of the DPJ's decision to lift Ozawa's suspension from the party. The vast majority of those polled thought that Ozawa had not provided an adequate explanation of the scandal involving Rikuzankai, and that politicians should be charged if there were false statements in their political funds reports.

Conclusion

Many aspects of Ozawa's politics challenge his persona as a genuine reformer of Japan's political structures and practices. The political circumstances under which Ozawa became a flag bearer for electoral reform suggest that he was eager to restore his position of political pre-eminence by using reform as a clarion call to mobilise support for himself and his followers. The background to his split from the Keiseikai, the formation of Reform Forum 21 and finally his departure from the LDP indicate that restoring his power was an important consideration not only in his calculations about what political moves to make but also in his policy choices. At the very least, Ozawa's desire for electoral reform was mixed with motivations relating to the survival and aggrandisement of his own political influence. Although the political circumstances offered an opportunity to launch institutional change, Ozawa was more political opportunist than dedicated reformer. His behaviour in the sequence of events leading up to his break with the LDP and afterwards indicates that ambition to regain and exercise power outweighed idealistic ambition to work for the reform of politics. Pursuing electoral reform was a tactical strategy, not the goal to which he set himself above all else – in short, the means, not the end.

Similarly, Ozawa retained an instrumentalist view of political parties as tools for achieving his own personal political ambitions rather than as the means to unite with like-minded politicians in order to achieve an agreed set of policy goals. Power politics took priority over policy agendas in both the creation and demolition of political parties. They were simply temporary arrangements of convenience, which he made or broke depending on whether they suited his political purposes at the time. In the case of both the NFP and LP, for example, he disbanded them in order to create a more satisfactory vehicle to serve his personal political ambitions. In June 2012, he left the DPJ for the same reason. In Ozawa's conception, political parties were groups held together by personal loyalties within a leader-follower framework. In short, they were factions writ large. The LP, for example, was little more than a collection of pro-Ozawa politicians within a personal power network, while both the RP and LP were essentially factions-turned-political parties, as were the PLF and PLP despite their dramatically shrinking numbers. So while Ozawa repeatedly invoked the discourse of reform and party modernisation, and despite his stated preference for an electoral system that engendered policy-based competition between two major parties rather than intra-party factional competition, his practical preference was for parties that had key faction-like attributes.

As for factions themselves, Ozawa used them as instruments of personal power seeking within parties, including attacking political rivals, just as the 'old' factions had been employed in the LDP. In the DPJ, Ozawa's faction provided an independent power base from which he could engage in intra-party machinations. It was at his disposal for whatever political ends he sought to deploy it. Again, like the 'old' LDP factions, it was constructed on the basis of patron-client relations cemented by generous donations of political funds, particularly in order to recruit new members. In this respect it remained largely a patronage network based on money. Earlier factional experiences had taught Ozawa that big numbers bestowed greater flexibility in manoeuvring in and out of parties, forming new parties and determining who got what position in these political parties. In this respect, Ozawa behaved like 'the last factional politician'.[491]

The details of the many political scandals in which Ozawa was involved, including those brought to light at his own trial and those of his secretaries, revealed that Ozawa remained a practitioner of old money politics. Indeed, with his abundant funds remaining the foundation of his power.[492] Ozawa represented the quintessential money power politician and, in this respect, the epitome of old politics. Ozawa's money power was, in turn, based primarily on the construction industry involved in government-funded public works. He and his office exercised influence at key points in the awarding of construction contracts on public projects, putting construction companies under pressure to provide him with votes, funds and other forms of electoral support in return. Ozawa's 'construction kingdom' (*doken ōkoku*) in Iwate formed a vast network of interpersonal and financial linkages characterised by a very high degree of organisation. It was an entrenched system that was both impervious to and left untouched by the Ozawa-led reforms of the early 1990s. It later came back to haunt him and his secretaries as scandals exposed the 'tip of the iceberg' of his deep and longstanding financial connections to the construction industry.

At the same time, many aspects of the professional conduct of the PPO remained problematic in relation to the Ozawa case and those of his secretaries. Amongst some of the questionable aspects of their investigation were the timing of their pursuit of Ozawa's secretaries, the coercive nature of their questioning and reliance on confessions obtained under duress in the absence of hard evidence, their politically biased investigation methods including a selective focus on Ozawa when Nishimatsu Construction, for example, had well-known connections to a number of LDP politicians including Ministry of Economy, Trade and Industry (METI) minister in the Asō government at the time, Nikai Toshihiro, who remained untouched, and the low-level technical nature of the final charges. A guilty verdict against Ozawa would have had to rely on inference and huge leaps in logic, which would have also eroded the legitimacy of the judicial process. The palpable deficiencies of the PPO, however, were not necessarily 'proof' of Ozawa's innocence. They merely indicated a lack of reliable evidence on which to bring him to book for both corruption and conspiracy.

Inevitably, Ozawa's entanglement in numerous episodes of money politics took its toll even though he was never convicted of committing any offence. Whether or not Ozawa was found innocent or guilty, he was harmed politically, as was the DPJ, so if that were the PPO's real objective, they achieved their goal. Moreover, even though Ozawa consistently denied any misdemeanours relating to illegal funding, it was very difficult for him to wield power while a criminal defendant, which he became in October 2011 when his trial began, and remained until November 2012 when the Tokyo High Court rejected the appeal of the original trial verdict. Ozawa inevitably invested considerable time, energy and funds in fighting his legal battles, which were a source of distraction and restriction on his political options. Nevertheless, a wounded lion can still be dangerous, as Ozawa showed through his almost constant political machinations and manoeuvring, which had a destructive impact on successive DPJ administrations.

Perhaps the most politically significant outcome for Ozawa from his recurrent episodes of scandal was the erosion of his political reputation and standing as a politician amongst 'the people' in whose name he so often claimed to act. He became irrevocably tarnished as the leader of any political party and thus continues to operate without a broader public following beyond his own electorate. This constrains his much-vaunted electoral genius as well as his personal political ambitions.

Notes

1. Ozawa was a member of the so-called 'Seven Magistrates' during Takeshita's heyday along with Hata, Hashimoto, Obuchi, Kajiyama Seiroku, Watanabe Kōzō and Okuda Keiwa. They played an active role in handling practical matters in the Sōseikai, a study group, or 'faction within a faction' established in the Tanaka faction by Ozawa, Takeshita, Kanemaru and others. When the Takeshita faction was formed, Takeshita transferred most of the Tanaka faction members from the Sōseikai to the Keiseikai. Kaieda, *Boku ga Ozawa (Seiji) o Kirai*, p. 53. See also Chapter 5.
2. Ibid., p. 54.
3. Watanabe, *Seiji Kaikaku to Kenpō Kaisei*, p. 32.
4. Kuji, *Ozawa Ichirō – Sono 'Kyōfu Shihai'*, p. 37.
5. Mizuguchi, 'Political Reform', p. 253. Tachibana listed the Obuchi faction as having 62 members. 'Ososugita shūen', p. 100.
6. Ibid., p. 101.
7. Mizuguchi, 'Political Reform', p. 254.
8. Ibid.
9. Watanabe, *Ozawa Ichirō Kirawareru Densetsu*, p. 19.
10. Ibid.
11. Matsuda, *Kakuei ni Narenakatta Otoko*, p. 139.
12. Shinoda, 'Truth Behind LDP's Loss', www.iuj.ac.jp/faculty/tshinoda/ldploss.html.
13. Ibid.
14. Ibid. See also Chapter 5.
15. Ibid.
16. Ozawa, 'My Commitment to Political Reform', p. 8.
17. Obuchi, 'In Defense of the Mainstream', p. 13; Abiru, 'Minshutō "A kyū senpan" hōtei', p. 45.
18. Mizuguchi, 'Political Reform', pp. 246, 252. Ozawa also received large amounts of political funds directly from the so-called 'Iwate Recruit Empire'. Kuji, *Ozawa Ichirō – Sono 'Kyōfu Shihai'*, p. 107.
19. Kōno, '93 nen no seiji hendō', p. 37. See also below.
20. See also Chapter 5.
21. Watanabe, *Seiji Kaikaku to Kenpō Kaisei*, p. 32.
22. Mizuguchi, 'Political Reform', p. 254. See also below.
23. Itō, *Seitō Hōkai*, p. 37.
24. These proposed 500 single-member districts in the Lower House with a plurality voting system. See also below.
25. Not only would the LDP lose its majority in the Lower House with the Hata faction breaking away, but it did not have a majority in the Upper House.
26. Oka, *Policy Entrepreneurship*, p. 63.
27. Watanabe, *Ozawa Ichirō Kirawareru Densetsu*, p. 41.
28. Shinoda, 'Truth Behind LDP's Loss', www.iuj.ac.jp/faculty/tshinoda/ldploss.html.
29. Quoted in Kaifu, *Seiji to Kane*, p. 163.
30. According to Oka, this is also the view of Tazaki Shiro and Itō Atsuo in their books, as well as of Hashimoto Ryūtarō's biographers, Kanō Tadao and Osada Tatsuji. Gerald Curtis is also inclined to this view, whilst acknowledging Ozawa's reformist tendencies. *Policy Entrepreneurship*, p. 155.

Old politics 115

31 Satō, *Ozawa Ichirō no Himitsu*, p. 62.
32 See also below and Chapter 5.
33 Satō, *Ozawa Ichirō no Himitsu*, p. 62.
34 Quoted in Katz, 'Ozawa: Creator and Destroyer', p. 8.
35 This proposal was encapsulated in the Miyazawa bill of March 1993.
36 Gaunder, 'Reform Leadership', p. 185.
37 Oka, *Policy Entrepreneurship*, p. 78.
38 See also below.
39 Christensen, 'Electoral Reforms', p. 595.
40 Ibid., pp. 595–96. Prominent amongst this group were the YKK (Yamasaki Taku, Katō Kōichi and Koizumi Junichirō) who led the movement against the single-seat constituency system. Yamasaki and Katō in particular implemented the strategy of 'containing Ozawa' in the sense of forming an anti-Ozawa network. Watanabe, *Ano Hito*, p. 32. See also Chapter 5.
41 Christensen, 'Electoral Reform', p. 596.
42 Kaieda, *Boku ga Ozawa (Seiji) o Kirai*, p. 22.
43 Itō, 'Dare mo shiranai Minshutō', p. 140.
44 Itō, 'Gisō kenkin', p. 115.
45 Akasaka, '"Posuto Hatoyama"', gekkan.bunshun.jp/articles/-/216. See also Chapter 5.
46 'Hitsuyō na no wa hasso no tankan da', in *Shūkan Shinchō*, p. 135.
47 Itō, *Seitō Hōkai*, p. 127.
48 Uno, 'Ozawa Ichirō-shi ni miru "seijika"', www.fsight.jp/article/11884.
49 Akasaka, '"Posuto Hatoyama"', gekkan.bunshun.jp/articles/-/216.
50 The qualification 'largely' is used in this sentence because Ozawa also had a reputation for forming, then destroying inter-party coalitions.
51 Kaifu, *Seiji to Kane*, pp. 162–63. See also Chapter 5.
52 See below.
53 Itō, 'Dare mo shiranai Minshutō', p. 142.
54 Ōtake, 'Seiji kaikaku o mezashita', pp. 25–26.
55 Otake, 'Forces for Political Reform', p. 287; Kōno, '93 nen no seiji hendō', pp. 38, 39.
56 Ōtake, 'Seiji kaikaku o mezashita', pp. 25–26.
57 Reed and Scheiner, 'Electoral Incentives', p. 474.
58 Ōtake, 'Seiji kaikaku', pp. 23, 32; Gaunder, *Political Reform*, p. 147, fn. 4; Reed and Scheiner, 'Electoral Incentives', p. 487. See also below.
59 Satō, *Ozawa Ichirō no Himitsu*, p. 61.
60 Ōtake, 'Seiji kaikaku', p. 26.
61 Oka, *Policy Entrepreneurship*, p. 87.
62 'Hitsuyō na no wa hasso no tankan da', in *Shūkan Shinchō*, p. 136.
63 Itō, 'Dare mo shiranai Minshutō', p. 142.
64 Katz, 'Ozawa: Creator and Destroyer', p. 9.
65 See also Chapters 5 and 6.
66 Watanabe, *Ozawa Ichirō Kirawareru Densetsu*, p. 24.
67 Katz, 'Ozawa', www.eastasiaforum.org/2010/02/18/ozawa-the-shiva-of-japanese-politics-creator-and-destroyer/. According to Reed and Shimizu, this was never confirmed, although it was widely reported. 'An Overview', p. 16. See also Chapter 5.
68 Saito, 'Pork-barrel Politics', p. 71.
69 Quoted in Reed and Shimizu, 'An Overview', p. 43.
70 The LP joined the DPJ just before the 2003 Lower House election. Watanabe reports that Hatoyama secretly approached Ozawa with the idea of amalgamating the DPJ and LP in November 2002. Watanabe, *Ozawa Ichirō Kirawareru Densetsu*, p. 23.
71 Matsuda, 'Tokushū waido', mainichi.jp/feature/news/20130410dde012010084000c.html. Itō reports that at a press conference following the failed move, Ozawa said,

'the DPJ won't be able to win at the next election, so it is necessary to form a coalition'. Itō, 'Dare mo shiranai Minshutō', p. 144. See also Chapter 5.
72 Yakushiji, 'Kako no hatsugen ni miru Ozawa Ichirō-shi (ge)', astand.asahi.com/magazine/wrpolitics/2012072300010.html.
73 Itō, 'Hatoyama Ozawa jinin!', p. 62.
74 This question is taken up more systematically in Chapter 6.
75 '"Tenka tori miete kita"', sankei.jp.msn.com/politics/news/120426/stt12042614330016-n1.htm. See also Chapter 6.
76 See also Chapter 7.
77 Makabe, 'Ichi keizai gakusha', diamond.jp/articles/-/20960.
78 See also Chapter 7.
79 'Kuzureta nidai seitō sei', *Asahi Shinbun*, digital.asahi.com/articles/TKY201207020574.html?ref=comkiji_txt_end.
80 See also Chapter 5.
81 Patronage dispensed to members included money, electoral support, political funding and positions in the government and in the party. Ozawa provided his own funds to members of his group as well as funds sourced from party coffers. See below.
82 Scott defines the basic pattern of patron-client relations as 'an informal cluster consisting of a power figure who is in a position to give security, inducements, or both, and his personal followers who, in return for such benefits, contribute their loyalty and personal assistance to the patron's designs'. 'Patron-client Politics', p. 92. See also Gaunder, 'Reform Leadership', pp. 183–84, and *Political Reform*, p. 87.
83 See also Chapter 5.
84 Watanabe, *Ano Hito*, p. 65.
85 The groups made up of former Democratic Socialist Party and SDP members were more ideologically motivated than the rest, although the Maehara-Edano group considered itself to be neo-conservative and were united in their anti-Ozawa stance. Schmidt, 'The DPJ and its Factions', p. 10. The DPJ also had many independent members and even expanding vote numbers by gaining factional support did not, therefore, guarantee victory in leadership elections. 'Minshu daihyōsen', www.tokyo-np.co.jp/article/politics/news/CK2011082102000022.html.
86 'Ozawa Followers', www.japantimes.co.jp/cgi-bin/nn20040123a5.html.
87 See Chapter 6.
88 See also Chapter 5.
89 Elsewhere this figure has been put at 42. See table 1 in Schmidt, 'The DPJ and its Factions', p. 4.
90 Ibid.
91 Ibid., p. 3.
92 Yasumoto, 'Ozawa Reaches Goal', www.japantimes.co.jp/text/nn20090831b7.html.
93 Its original political purpose was to recruit new members for the LP. It then morphed into an organisation that played an increasingly important role in recruiting new candidates for the DPJ. Schmidt, 'The DPJ and its Factions', p. 5. Wang also writes that the *seiji juku* 'was repurposed as Ozawa's personal recruitment vehicle'. *Ozawa's Children*, p. 7.
94 Takahara, 'Rookies Hold Crucial DPJ Votes', www.japantimes.co.jp/cgi-bin/nn20100910f1.html.
95 Matsuda and Kaneko, 'Tōnai gurūpu', p. 4. See also below.
96 Itō, 'Dare mo shiranai Minshutō', p. 140.
97 Rikuzankai was formed in 1969, the first year that Ozawa was elected to the Diet. It became Ozawa's political fund management organisation in 1995, following the amendment of the Political Funds Control Law in 1994, which established the political funds management organisation system (*shikin kanri dantai seido*) to replace the existing 'designated group system' (*shitei dantai seido*) and 'holding money system'

(*hoyūkin seido*), which obligated politicians to report their income and expenditure under the law. See also below.
98 Matsuda, *Kakuei ni Narenakatta Otoko*, p. 265. See also below.
99 'Ozawa's Power', www.yomiuri.co.jp/dy/national/T101201005616.htm.
100 '"Nodo kara"', www.yomiuri.co.jp/politics/news/20101130-OYT1T01191.htm?from=top.
101 'Ozawa's Power', www.yomiuri.co.jp/dy/national/T101201005616.htm.
102 Itō, '"Seiji kaikaku no kishu"', tukamoto-office.seesaa.net/article/141084654.html. See also below.
103 Nonoyama, 'Sōsenkyogo', www.fsight.jp/article/5091.
104 Yamazaki, 'Ozawa Ichirō-shi to kenryoku', diamond.jp/articles/-/4929.
105 'Ozawa Earns Biggest Amount', findarticles.com/p/articles/mi_m0XPQ/is_2011_Dec_12/ai_n58504083/.
106 See Chapter 4.
107 Matsuda, *Ozawa Ichirō Kyoshoku no Shihaisha*, p. 238.
108 See below.
109 Matsuda, *Ozawa Ichirō Kyoshoku no Shihaisha*, p. 238.
110 Matsuda, *Kakuei ni Narenakatta Otoko*, p. 198.
111 See p. 70.
112 Quoted in Ishikawa, *Akutō*, p. 199.
113 See also below.
114 Ozawa, 'Seiji kaikaku', p. 186.
115 Quoted in Oka, *Policy Entrepreneurship*, p. 48.
116 Yamazaki, 'Ozawa Ichirō-shi to kenryoku', diamond.jp/articles/-/4929.
117 Kamikubo, 'Kan naikaku', diamond.jp/articles/-/13585.
118 Kaieda, *Boku ga Ozawa (Seiji) o Kirai*, p. 151.
119 Watanabe, *Seiji Kaikaku to Kenpō Kaisei*, p. 421.
120 Quoted in Matsuda, *Kakuei ni Narenakatta Otoko*, pp. 208–9.
121 See also below.
122 'Maehara's Tightrope Strategy', ajw.asahi.com/article//behind_news/AJ201108257452.
123 See also Chapter 6.
124 'Minshu Ozawa-shi', in *Asahi Shinbun*, p. 1.
125 This was originally established in June 2004 for Diet members who were in their first to third terms at the time. It was named after the LP's slogan 'Renewing Japan' (*Nihon Isshin*).
126 Schmidt, 'The DPJ and its Factions', p. 5. See also below.
127 Matsuda and Kaneko, 'Tōnai gurūpu ga habatsu ka?', p. 4.
128 Ishikawa, *Akutō*, p. 186.
129 This was originally formed in 2005 for those DPJ politicians who lost or ran in the 2005 Lower House election in which the party suffered a massive defeat.
130 'Ozawa's Power Built on Cash', www.yomiuri.co.jp/dy/national/T101201005616.htm.
131 See also Chapter 6.
132 Matsuda and Kaneko, 'Tōnai gurūpu ga habatsu ka?', p. 4.
133 See also Chapter 5.
134 Yasumoto, 'Ozawa Reaches Goal', www.japantimes.co.jp/cgi-bin/nn20090831b7.html.
135 Matsuda and Kaneko, 'Tōnai gurūpu ga habatsu ka?', p. 4.
136 See also Chapter 5.
137 'Ozawa Aims to Regain Clout', www.asiaone.com/News/Latest+News/Asia/Story/A1Story20100606-220500.html.
138 Isoyama, 'Can the DPJ Government Recover?', business.nikkeibp.co.jp/article/eng/20100614/214930/.

118 Old politics

139 'Ozawa Aims to Regain Clout', www.asiaone.com/News/Latest+News/Asia/Story/A1Story20100606-220500.html.
140 Isoyama, 'Can the DPJ Government Recover?, business.nikkeibp.co.jp/article/eng/20100614/214930/.
141 '"Bunretsu senkyo"', www.fsight.jp/article/5617.
142 Michael Cucek, email communication, 25 August 2010.
143 '"Kan nuki renritsu"', gekkan.bunshun.jp/articles/-/241.
144 'Ozawa-shi ga Minshutō daihyōsen ni shutsuba hyōmei', www.asahi.com/politics/update/0826/TKY201008260089.html?ref=reca.
145 'Battle Heats Up', www.japantimes.co.jp/cgi-bin/nn20100828a2.html.
146 Ibid.
147 The *Nikkei* referred to the DPJ's general party supporters' apparent dislike of 'Ozawa's high-handed political practices and his scandal-ridden image'. 'Kan Wins', e.nikkei.com/e/ac/TNKS/Nni20100914D14NY736.htm.
148 Gotō, '"Ozawa fūji"', diamond.jp/articles/-/9433.
149 Ishikawa, *Akutō*, p. 161.
150 Takahara, 'Rookies Hold Crucial DPJ Votes', www.japantimes.co.jp/cgi-bin/nn20100910f1.html.
151 *Kinken seiji* is translated variously as 'money politics', 'money-power politics' and 'buying influence'.
152 '"Seiji kaikaku no kishu"', tukamoto-office.seesaa.net/article/141084654.html.
153 Matsuda and Kaneko, 'Tōnai gurūpu ga habatsu ka?', p. 4.
154 'Japan's Ichiro Ozawa', www.economist.com/node/21557788.
155 Yamaguchi, 'An Insider's View', p. 28.
156 Yoshida and Yamamoto, 'Giin o umidasu kosuto', p. 30.
157 'Ozawa Emerges as King', e.nikkei.com/e/ac/20091012/TNW/Nni20091012IS9-FUND2.htm.
158 '"Nodo kara"', www.yomiuri.co.jp/politics/news/20101130-OYT1T01191.htm?from=top.
159 'Ozawa Top Recipient', www.japantoday.com/category/politics/view/ozawa-top-recipient-of-political-funds-for-second-year-in-row.
160 'Nagata-chō kīman', www.zakzak.co.jp/society/politics/news/20121201/plt1212011446002-n1.htm.
161 Ibid.
162 'Ozawa Top Fund Raiser', www.japantimes.co.jp/news/2013/12/07/national/ozawa-top-fund-raiser-in-2012/#.UqQ8reKls-8.
163 Matsuda, *Kakuei ni Narenakatta Otoko*, p. 177.
164 See also below.
165 Watanabe, *Ozawa Ichirō Kirawareru Densetsu*, p. 103.
166 Ibid.
167 The PFCL permits five types of political organisation to receive political donations: party headquarters, local party branches, party fund management organisations, politicians' fund management organisations and 'other political organisations'. See Ministry of Internal Affairs and Communications, 'Seiji Shikin Kanren', www.soumu.go.jp/senkyo/seiji_s/kanpo/shikin/h22_yoshi_111130.html. The JCP calls this last category of organisation a 'general political organisation' (*ippan no seiji dantai*). 'Ozawa-shi kanren seiji dantai', www.jcp.or.jp/akahata/aik09/2010-01-01/2010010123_01_1.html.
168 Matsuda, *Ozawa Ichirō Kyoshoku no Shihaisha*, p. 176.
169 From 1 January 2000, the PFCL banned donations from corporations to individual politicians' fund management groups, only allowing it in the case of parties and their fund management bodies.
170 Matsuda, *Ozawa Ichirō Kyoshoku no Shihaisha*, p. 70.
171 Matsuda, *Kakuei ni Narenakatta Otoko*, p. 176.
172 Matsuda, *Ozawa Ichirō Kyoshoku no Shihaisha*, pp. 73–75.

173 Ishizuka, 'Japan Can't Seem to Shake Off Old Ghost', e.nikkei.com/e/ac/20100222/TNW/Nni20100222OP7DIARY.htm.
174 See below.
175 Nakano, 'Panel Discussion', 2 September 2011.
176 Schlesinger, *Shadow Shoguns*, p. 235.
177 Herzog, *Japan's Pseudo-Democracy*, p. 189.
178 Satō, *Ozawa Ichirō no Himitsu*, p. 62.
179 Kuji reveals that it was an open secret that Ozawa's wife Kazuko was an executive of the Sōka Gakkai's Women's Division. He also reports that President of Sōka Gakkai Ikeda Daisaku provided a vast fortune to Ozawa when he rose in revolt against the LDP and formed the RP. *Ozawa Ichirō – Sono 'Kyōfu Shihai'*, pp. 131, 133. However, Ozawa's primary connection was with Ichikawa Yūichi, the former chief of staff of the Sōka Gakkai, who was a confidante of Ikeda's and who later became secretary-general of the Kōmeitō. Satō, *Ozawa Ichirō no Himitsu*, p. 226.
180 Ibid., p. 127.
181 See also below.
182 Kuji and Yokota, *Seiji ga Yugameru Kōkyō Jigyō*, p. 16. Watanabe reports that questions were raised about Ozawa in relation to this scandal, with Ozawa refuting allegations in the media about his involvement. He refused to hold press conferences for over a month because of what he regarded as inaccurate media reports. *Ozawa Ichirō Kirawareru Densetsu*, p. 55.
183 See below.
184 Bowen, *Japan's Dysfunctional Democracy*, p. 17.
185 Hirano, *Shinsetsu!*, p. 72.
186 Matsuda, *Kakuei ni Narenakatta Otoko*, p. 182.
187 Ibid., p. 238.
188 Hunziker and Kamimura, *Kakuei Tanaka*, www.rcrinc.com/tanaka/ch5-4.html.
189 Matsuda, *Kakuei ni Narenakatta Otoko*, p. 143.
190 Satō, *Ozawa Ichirō no Himitsu*, p. 71. See also below and Chapter 5.
191 Kuji, *Ozawa Ichirō – Sono 'Kyōfu Shihai'*, pp. 48–49. According to Matsuda, Ozawa made this comment on 1 January 1994, saying, 'What is wrong with receiving electoral support and funds (from general contractors)? It is only natural to get them to support us'. *Ozawa Ichirō Kyoshoku no Shihaisha*, p. 42.
192 Quoted in Kuji and Yokota, *Seiji ga Yugameru Kōkyō Jigyō*, pp. 203–4.
193 Watanabe, *Ozawa Ichirō Kirawareru Densetsu*, pp. 81–83.
194 Quoted in ibid., pp. 82–83.
195 Hosokawa, *Naishōroku*, pp. 66–67.
196 Itō, '"Seiji kaikaku no kishu"', tukamoto-office.seesaa.net/article/141084654.html.
197 Matsuda, *Kakuei ni Narenakatta Otoko*, p. 206.
198 Itō, '"Seiji kaikaku no kishu"', tukamoto-office.seesaa.net/article/141084654.html.
199 See also Chapter 5.
200 Itō, '"Seiji kaikaku no kishu"', tukamoto-office.seesaa.net/article/141084654.html.
201 Ibid.
202 Ibid.
203 Ibid.
204 Matsuda, *Kakuei ni Narenakatta Otoko*, p. 144.
205 Ibid., p. 158.
206 Okamoto, 'Shitō!', p. 30.
207 See also Chapter 7.
208 '[Zukai, shakai] Rikuzankai jiken', www.jiji.com/jc/graphics?p=ve_pol_ozawa-rikuzankai20111125j-02-w290.
209 'Ozawa Fund Body', www.japantimes.co.jp/text/nn20101127a9.html. See also below.

210 Jackson, 'What's Taking Ozawa So Long?', the-diplomat.com/tokyo-notes/2010/12/13/whats-taking-ozawa-so-long/.
211 Matsuda, *Kakuei ni Narenakatta Otoko*, p. 265.
212 '[Zukai, shakai] Rikuzankai jiken', www.jiji.com/jc/graphics?p=ve_pol_ozawa-rikuzankai20111125j-02-w290.
213 Its representative was Ōkubo. According to political funds income and expenditure reports, Seizankai received funds from Reform Forum 21 and the Ozawa Ichirō Seikei Kenkyūkai.
214 In December 2010, the DPJ chapter in Iwate (4) led by Ozawa failed to declare ¥74 million in political donations. 'Ozawa-shi no shibu', p. 1.
215 '[Ozawa hikoku ronkoku kyūkei (1)]', sankei.jp.msn.com/affairs/news/120309/trl12030913060004-n3.htm. According to the political funds income and expenditure report for 2006, Reform Forum 21 donated ¥10 million to Seizankai, which channelled ¥10 million to the Ozawa Ichirō Tokyo *kōenkai*, which transferred ¥10 million to Rikuzankai. Abiru, 'Seiji shikin', abirur.iza.ne.jp/blog/day/20070916/.
216 'Ōkubo "Ordered Nishimatsu Fund Switch"', *iStockAnalyst*, 20 March 2009, www.istockanalyst.com/article/viewiStockNews/articleid/3135483.
217 Okamoto, 'Shitō!', p. 30.
218 Matsuda, *Kakuei ni Narenakatta Otoko*, p. 167. See also 'Ozawa-shi kanren seiji dantai', www.jcp.or.jp/akahata/aik09/2010-01-01/2010010123_01_1.html.
219 Matsuda, *Kakuei ni Narenakatta Otoko*, p. 168. The Political Parties Subsidy Law actually states that when a party is dissolved, any remaining subsidies must be returned to the state except if the party empties its account before it is disbanded (p. 164).
220 Okamoto, 'Shitō!', p. 29.
221 'Ozawa-shi kanren seiji dantai', www.jcp.or.jp/akahata/aik09/2010-01-01/2010010123_01_1.html.
222 Matsuda, *Kakuei ni Narenakatta Otoko*, pp. 169–70.
223 'Ozawa-shi kanren seiji dantai', www.jcp.or.jp/akahata/aik09/2010-01-01/2010010123_01_1.html.
224 Itō, '"Seiji kaikaku no kishu"', tukamoto-office.seesaa.net/article/141084654.html.
225 'Seiji shudō', p. 11. The total amount, according to Itō, was ¥1.6 billion, which was recorded in the LP's income and expenditure reports as having been spent on Fujii as an individual – an enormous amount of money. '"Seiji kaikaku no kishu"', tukamoto-office.seesaa.net/article/141084654.html.
226 Matsuda, *Kakuei ni Narenakatta Otoko*, p. 162, 166; Tsutsumi, 'Ozawa Ichirō no "Nihon haijakku"', img.fujisan.co.jp/digital/actibook/2489/1301276354/320545/_SWF_Window.html?uid=16129246&pwd=297050528975611&bid=320545.
227 Itō, '"Seiji kaikaku no kishu"', tukamoto-office.seesaa.net/article/141084654.html.
228 Toshikawa, 'Ozawa Not Out of the Woods', p. 5.
229 Itō, '"Seiji kaikaku no kishu"', tukamoto-office.seesaa.net/article/141084654.html.
230 Tsutsumi, 'Ozawa Ichirō no "Nihon haijakku"', img.fujisan.co.jp/digital/actibook/2489/1301276354/320545/_SWF_Window.html?uid=16129246&pwd=297050528975611&bid=320545.
231 Matsuda, *Ozawa Ichirō Kyoshoku no Shihaisha*, p. 76.
232 Ibid., pp. 118, 119.
233 Figures calculated from the table in ibid., pp. 116–17.
234 Ibid., p. 138.
235 Tsutsumi, 'Ozawa Ichirō no "Nihon haijakku"', img.fujisan.co.jp/digital/actibook/2489/1301276354/320545/_SWF_Window.html?uid=16129246&pwd=297050528975611&bid=320545.
236 Quoted in Matsuda, *Ozawa Ichirō Kyoshoku no Shihaisha*, pp. 111, 114–15, 120.
237 Matsuda, *Kakuei ni Narenakatta Otoko*, p. 199.
238 Ibid., p. 201.
239 Ibid., p. 204.

Old politics 121

240 Ibid., p. 205.
241 Ibid.
242 Ibid., p. 204.
243 Toshikawa, 'Showdown at DPJ Corral', p. 5.
244 Ibid., p. 5.
245 Matsuda, *Kakuei ni Narenakatta Otoko*, p. 199.
246 Ibid., pp. 202, 203.
247 Ibid., p. 202.
248 Ibid., p. 203.
249 Toshikawa, 'Showdown at DPJ Corral', p. 5.
250 '"Hisho yūzai"', p. 14.
251 Oka, *Policy Entrepeneurship*, p. 73. When secretary-general of the LDP in 1989–91, he did, however, demand political donations for the party from Keidanren and from industrial organisations representing the automobile, electrical machinery and financial industries, as well as from the construction industry. Watanabe, *Seiji Kaikaku to Kenpō Kaisei*, p. 411. He reportedly said to Keidanren Chairman Saitō Eishirō, 'We will need ¥30 billion for the next election'. Watanabe, *Ano Hito*, p. 18. As Ozawa recollected, 'Since I was first elected, I had not been associated with anyone in financial circles or economic circles and I was never asked to become associated with anyone, so I was able to make strong requests to financial circles for funds for the party' (ibid.).
252 Matsuda, *Ozawa Ichirō Kyoshoku no Shihaisha*, p. 199.
253 See Chapter 5.
254 Tanaka, 'Japan Politics Seeks New Character', e.nikkei.com/e/ac/20100125/TNW/Nni20100125OP3TANAK.htm. Iwate Prefecture ranked around the middle amongst prefectures in terms of administrative investment (in public works), but had the sixth highest per capita expenditure. Kabashima, *Doken Tengoku Nippon*, p. 47.
255 Ibid., p. 48.
256 Kuji and Yokota, *Seiji ga Yugameru Kōkyō Jigyō*, p. 206.
257 This was the title of Kuji and Yokota's book *Seiji ga Yugameru Kōkyō Jigyō*, which was a compilation of a series of articles the authors published in the magazine *Shūkan Kin'yōbi* (*Weekly Friday*) entitled 'Seiji ga yugameru kōkyō jigyō' ['Public works distorted by politics'] in November 1995–March 1996.
258 Kabashima, *Doken Tengoku Nippon*, p. 24.
259 Ibid., p. 34.
260 Matsuda, *Ozawa Ichirō Kyoshoku no Shihaisha*, p. 64.
261 Kabashima, *Doken Tengoku Nippon*, pp. 27–28.
262 Brian Woodall reports that a MOC official told him 'a story about Ozawa's applying pressure to ensure that a public works project was undertaken in his own district… rather than in that of a rival. The MOC bureaucrat claimed that he deflected the pressure'. Personal communication, 30 July 2013.
263 'Zenekon senkyo Ozawa ryū', nitiban.blog.ocn.ne.jp/blog/ozawa_gigoku.PDF.
264 Takahashi became a DPJ Diet member in 2000–03 but later left the DPJ and joined the LDP. He stood against Ozawa as an LDP candidate for the seat of Iwate (4) in the 2009 Lower House election and lost. See also Chapter 5.
265 Takahashi, 'Ozawa moto hisho', p. 130.
266 Kase, Tanaka and Sawaaki, 'Ozawa ryū zenekon senkyojutsu', www.asahi.com/seiken kotai2009/TKY201001310346.html.
267 'Zenekon senkyo Ozawa ryū', nitiban.blog.ocn.ne.jp/blog/ozawa_gigoku.PDF.
268 Takahashi, 'Ozawa moto hisho', pp. 130–31.
269 See, for example, Matsuda, 'Zenekon marugakae senkyo', gendai.ismedia.jp/articles/-/268.
270 Kajima Construction has been described as one of the five leading general contractors in Japan – also referred to as the 'Big Five' or 'super general contractors' – the others

being Taisei Construction, Shimizu Construction, Ōbayashi Corporation and Takenaka Corporation.
271 Matsuda, 'Zenekon marugakae senkyo', gendai.ismedia.jp/articles/-/268. See also below.
272 Matsuda, *Ozawa Ichirō Kyoshoku no Shihaisha*, p. 42.
273 Kuji, *Ozawa Ichirō – Sono 'Kyōfu Shihai'*, p. 48. See also below.
274 Ibid.
275 Ibid.
276 Matsuda, *Kakuei ni Narenakatta Otoko*, p. 241.
277 Ibid., pp. 241–42.
278 Kuji, *Ozawa Ichirō – Sono 'Kyōfu Shihai'*, p. 43.
279 Ibid., p. 42.
280 Kabashima, *Doken Tengoku Nippon*, p. 24.
281 Matsuda, *Ozawa Ichirō Kyoshoku no Shihaisha*, p. 45.
282 This is an extract from Matsuda Kenya, *Ozawa Ichirō Zen Kenkyū*, in 'Saiaku!', blog. goo.ne.jp/handa3douzo/e/829ba12a41604bec9e2ba2a7a2add57b.
283 Kuji, *Ozawa Ichirō – Sono 'Kyōfu Shihai'*, p. 42.
284 Kuji and Yokota, *Seiji ga Yugameru Kōkyō Jigyō*, p. 23.
285 Ibid., pp. 31–32.
286 Kabashima, *Doken Tengoku Nippon*, p. 78.
287 Kuji and Yokota, *Seiji ga Yugameru Kōkyō Jigyō*, pp. 19–20, 21.
288 Ibid., p. 25.
289 Kuji, *Ozawa Ichirō – Sono 'Kyōfu Shihai'*, p. 73.
290 Ibid., p. 77.
291 Kabashima, *Doken Tengoku Nippon*, p. 87.
292 Kuji and Yokota, *Seiji ga Yugameru Kōkyō Jigyō*, p. 30.
293 Ibid., p. 31.
294 Ibid., p. 31.
295 These committees operate at municipal and prefectural levels. Members are appointed from municipal and prefectural government staff and they select the companies that are allowed to participate in bids for individual projects based on a set of guidelines such as the company's capability to undertake the work, the company's scale and state of management, past and current achievements and contract amounts, etc. The process is only required for projects of a certain scale or larger. These committees therefore decide the list of designated bidders, which, for construction companies, is a vital step towards actually winning contracts. The committees' deliberations are secret.
296 Quoted in Kuji and Yokota, *Seiji ga Yugameru Kōkyō Jigyō*, p. 31.
297 He was also chairman of the Tohoku Construction Industry Association, chairman of the Federation of the Iwate Prefectural Construction Industry Groups and chairman of the Federation of National Construction Industry Groups. Ibid., p. 63.
298 Ibid., p. 60. The Tōshō Club's members were all highly ranked executives (mainly Morioka branch heads) of *zenekon* listed in the first section of the Tokyo Stock Exchange (apart from Takaya Construction). Its chairman was the chief of Kajima Construction's Morioka branch, Deguchi Chōshitsu, its deputy chairman was chief of Shimizu Construction's Morioka branch and its secretary-general was chief of Taisei Construction's Morioka branch. Its nine 'first-grade members' were executives of other general contractors including Mochizuki Shigeru and the chief of the Morioka branch of Ōbayashi Corporation. Another member (Kawashima Michio) was an executive of the Morioka Branch of Nishimatsu Construction, which was later to figure in an Ozawa-related scandal (see below). The group's six 'second-grade' and two 'third-grade' members were also local executives of other general contractors. Ibid., p. 41. Ranked even higher on the list of members than Chairman Deguchi were its two advisers, Kadowaki Kazutsugu (Kajima Construction Tohoku deputy

branch head) and Amata Kōji (Taisei Construction Tohoku Sales Department manager), with Amata being arrested in the general contractors' corruption scandal of 1993. In 1992, before the scandal erupted, the top seven general contractors (in terms of contracts received for projects commissioned by the Iwate prefectural government) were all Tōshō Club members. Kuji, *Ozawa Ichirō – Sono 'Kyōfu Shihai'*, p. 45.
299 Kuji and Yokota, *Seiji ga Yugameru Kōkyō Jigyō*, p. 41. See also below.
300 Kuji, *Ozawa Ichirō – Sono 'Kyōfu Shihai'*, p. 46.
301 Ibid., p. 65.
302 Ibid., p. 65.
303 Kuji and Yokota, *Seiji ga Yugameru Kōkyō Jigyō*, p. 40. As Kabashima described it, the Keyaki no Kai was a group of companies that supported Ozawa as a future candidate for prime minister. Many of its corporate members were involved in the construction industry and desperately wanted to get their hands on the nation's public works budget. Kabashima, *Doken Tengoku Nippon*, p. 75.
304 Matsuda, *Ozawa Ichirō Kyoshoku no Shihaisha*, p. 194.
305 Ibid., p. 196.
306 Kuji and Yokota, *Seiji ga Yugameru Kōkyō Jigyō*, p. 67.
307 Ibid., p. 44.
308 Ibid., p. 46.
309 Ibid., p. 24.
310 Kabashima, *Doken Tengoku Nippon*, p. 35.
311 Matsuda, 'Zenekon marugakae senkyo', gendai.ismedia.jp/articles/-/268.
312 Matsuda, *Ozawa Ichirō Kyoshoku no Shihaisha*, p. 28.
313 Kase, Tanaka and Sawaaki, 'Ozawa ryū zenekon senkyojutsu', www.asahi.com/seiken kotai2009/TKY201001310346.html.
314 Matsuda, 'Zenekon marugakae senkyo', gendai.ismedia.jp/articles/-/268.
315 See also Chapter 6.
316 'Zenekon marugakae senkyo', gendai.ismedia.jp/articles/-/268.
317 Takahashi, 'Ozawa moto hisho', p. 131.
318 Matsuda, 'Zenekon marugakae senkyo', gendai.ismedia.jp/articles/-/268. The figure was 53 general contractors according to another source. 'Zenekon senkyo Ozawa ryū', nitiban.blog.ocn.ne.jp/blog/ozawa_gigoku.PDF.
319 Ibid.
320 Kase, Tanaka and Sawaaki, 'Ozawa ryū zenekon senkyojutsu', www.asahi.com/seiken kotai2009/TKY201001310346.html.
321 Quoted in Matsuda, *Ozawa Ichirō Kyoshoku no Shihaisha*, p. 27.
322 Kuji and Yokota, *Seiji ga Yugameru Kōkyō Jigyō*, pp. 91, 92.
323 Ibid., p. 46.
324 Ibid., p. 47.
325 Ibid., p. 59.
326 Ibid., p. 48.
327 Ibid., p. 67.
328 Ibid., p. 67.
329 As of April 1993, 60 companies were listed as members, which included most of the general contractors listed in the first section of the Tokyo Stock Exchange. When a member of the Toryōkai achieved a higher level of contribution to Ozawa in elections and in other areas, they were upgraded to membership of the Tōshō Club. Kuji, *Ozawa Ichirō – Sono 'Kyōfu Shihai'*, p. 46.
330 Kuji and Yokota, *Seiji ga Yugameru Kōkyō Jigyō*, p. 59.
331 Ibid., p. 66.
332 'Dam Bidders', www.japantimes.co.jp/text/nn20100115a1.html.
333 Kuji and Yokota, *Seiji ga Yugameru Kōkyō Jigyō*, p. 84.
334 Ibid., p. 86.
335 Ibid., p. 90.

336 Quoted in Matsuda, *Ozawa Ichirō Kyoshoku no Shihaisha*, p. 64.
337 '[Yuragu "Ozawa Ōkoku"]', www.iza.ne.jp/news/newsarticle/politics/politicsit/409335/.
338 Matsuda, *Ozawa Ichirō Kyoshoku no Shihaisha*, p. 69.
339 Ibid. See also below.
340 Kuji and Yokota, *Seiji ga Yugameru Kōkyō Jigyō*, p. 72.
341 Ibid.
342 Ibid., pp. 73, 74.
343 Ibid., p. 107.
344 Matsuda, *Ozawa Ichirō Kyoshoku no Shihaisha*, p. 61.
345 Kuji, *Ozawa Ichirō – Sono 'Kyōfu Shihai'*, p. 49.
346 Hazama Corporation is one of the second-tier *zenekon*, along with Nishimatsu Construction. See also below.
347 Hazama was responsible for constructing two large-scale dams in Iwate by the mid-1990s. Kuji, *Ozawa Ichirō – Sono 'Kyōfu Shihai'*, p. 49. One of these was the Hinata Dam (begun in 1981 and completed in 1997).
348 Kuji and Yokota, *Seiji ga Yugameru Kōkyō Jigyō*, p. 104. Kuji independently reported that former Hazama President Kagami testified to the PPO that 'We provided ¥10 million to Ozawa's office in Tokyo for receiving the contract for the Hinata Dam'. *Ozawa Ichirō – Sono 'Kyōfu Shihai'*, p. 51.
349 Kuji and Yokota, *Seiji ga Yugameru Kōkyō Jigyō*, p. 106. See also Chapter 5.
350 Kabashima, *Doken Tengoku Nippon*, p. 97.
351 Takahashi, 'Ozawa moto hisho', p. 131.
352 Ibid., pp. 131–32.
353 Ibid., p. 132. The article cites the *Mainichi Shinbun*, 25 January 2010 as the source of this information.
354 'Zenekon senkyo Ozawa ryū', nitiban.blog.ocn.ne.jp/blog/ozawa_gigoku.PDF.
355 Quoted in ibid.
356 Kabashima, *Doken Tengoku Nippon*, p. 71.
357 The Korean Unification Church seeks a change in government policy to allow votes for foreigners with permanent residence in Japan.
358 Ozawa's henchman, Yamaoka, also received financial support from this industry, which proved so troublesome for him when minister of state for consumer affairs and food safety in Prime Minister Noda's first cabinet in 2011–12. See Chapter 6.
359 Adelstein, 'The Last Yakuza', pp. 68–69.
360 Personal interview, *Asahi Shinbun* journalist, 9 December 2011.
361 Personal communication, former construction company executive, 2 August 2010.
362 Adelstein, 'The Last Yakuza', p. 63.
363 Ibid., p. 68.
364 George Mulgan, 'The Perils of Japanese Politics', pp. 183–208.
365 'LDP and DPJ Must Come Clean', www.japan-press.co.jp/2009/2614/scandal_3.html.
366 'Secretary of DPJ Leader', home.kyodo.co.jp/modules/fatStory/index.php?storyid=426508.
367 Matsuda, *Ozawa Ichirō Kyoshoku no Shihaisha*, p. 17.
368 'Secretary of DPJ Leader', home.kyodo.co.jp/modules/fatStory/index.php?storyid=426508.
369 'Saiaku!', blog.goo.ne.jp/handa3douzo/e/829ba12a41604bec9e2ba2a7a2add57b.
370 'Ōkubo "Ordered Nishimatsu"', www.istockanalyst.com/article/viewiStockNews/articleid/3135483. The amounts, according to this report, were between ¥3.24 million and ¥35.88 million per year.
371 Ibid.
372 Ibid.
373 Watanabe, *Ozawa Ichirō Kirawareru Densetsu*, p. 56.

374 Ibid., p. 85.
375 Ibid., p. 85.
376 Ibid., p. 80.
377 Yamazaki, 'Ozawa Ichirō-shi wa tsugi no soridaijin ni fusawashiku nai', diamond.jp/articles/-/7032.
378 Matsuda, *Kakuei ni Narenakatta Otoko*, p. 244. See also below.
379 Hongo and Martin, 'Ex-Ozawa Secretary', www.japantimes.co.jp/cgi-gin/snn20100116a4.html.
380 Tsutsumi, 'Ozawa Ichirō no "Nihon haijakku"', img.fujisan.co.jp/digital/actibook/2489/1301276354/320545/_SWF_Window.html?uid=16129246&pwd=297050528975611&bid=320545.
381 'Ozawa Tied to Nishimatsu Cash', www.japantimes.co.jp/cgi-bin/nn20090620a1.html.
382 'LDP and DPJ Must Come Clean', www.japan-press.co.jp/2009/2614/scandal_3.html.
383 Matsuda, *Ozawa Ichirō Kyoshoku no Shihaisha*, p. 36.
384 Ibid., p. 37.
385 The *Mainichi* report was dated 2 March 2009. See also Matsuda, *Ozawa Ichirō Kyoshoku no Shihaisha*, p. 64.
386 'Zenekon senkyo Ozawa ryū', nitiban.blog.ocn.ne.jp/blog/ozawa_gigoku.PDF.
387 'Ozawa's Secretary Pleads Not Guilty', www.thefreelibrary.com/2ND+LD%3A+Ozawa's+secretary+pleads+not+guilty+in+Nishimatsu+funds...-a0215718562.
388 'Zenekon senkyo Ozawa ryū', nitiban.blog.ocn.ne.jp/blog/ozawa_gigoku.PDF.
389 Matsuda, 'Zenekon marugakae senkyo', gendai.ismedia.jp/articles/-/268.
390 'Ozawa's Secretary Pleads Not Guilty', www.thefreelibrary.com/2ND+LD%3A+Ozawa's+secretary+pleads+not+guilty+in+Nishimatsu+funds...-a0215718562.
391 Okamoto, 'Shitō!, p. 29.
392 'DPJ is Urged', www.japan-press.co.jp/modules/news/index.php?id=562.
393 'Seiken kōtai senkyo', p. 37.
394 'DPJ is Urged', www.japan-press.co.jp/modules/news/index.php?id=562.
395 'Saiaku!', blog.goo.ne.jp/handa3douzo/e/829ba12a41604bec9e2ba2a7a2add57b.
396 Nagata, 'Ozawa saiban', p. 14.
397 'Ozawa Submits to Questioning', e.nikkei.com/e/ac/20100125/TNW/Nni20100125FP30ZAWA.htm.
398 Ibid.
399 *NHK News 7*, 28 December 2009. See also below.
400 'Mizutani moto kaichō', in *Nikkan Gendai*, p. 120.
401 'Ozawa-shi, moto hisho, gyōsha', www.iza.ne.jp/news/newsarticle/event/crime/394062/.
402 *Jōnōkin* originally referred to the money civilians paid to feudal lords for various purposes like a tax. These days, it is often used to refer to money that lower-ranking *yakuza* pay to their superiors and figuratively in a broader sense to money that people pay to their superiors in any area in order to maintain their positions in that area, etc. The *jōnōkin* system in public works was originally established by Tanaka Kakuei. See also Chapter 5.
403 Tanaka reports that, 'of the money paid to contractors for the work commissioned by the government, around 1–2% was funnelled to the politicians, ending up as just more expensive public works bills for the taxpayer'. 'Japan Politics Seeks New Character', e.nikkei.com/e/ac/20100125/TNW/Nni20100125OP3TANAK.htm.
404 Personal communication with the granddaughter of the farmers in Ōshu City. See also Woodall, *Japan Under Construction*, p. 14.
405 Katz, 'Part 2: Tanaka's Protégé', p. 4.
406 'Yamazaki Kensetsu', www.iza.ne.jp/news/newsarticle/event/crime/417103/.
407 Ibid.

408 'Editorial: Trial of Mr. Ozawa's Aides', www.japantimes.co.jp/cgi-bin/ed20110211a1.html. When Ōkubo was indicted, the amount of illegal donations from Nishimatsu rose from ¥21 million to ¥35 million.
409 Toshikawa, 'Ozawa Not Out of the Woods', p. 4.
410 Ibid., p. 5.
411 Katz, 'Janus-faced DPJ', p. 2. See also below.
412 Satō, 'Shin teikoku shugi', pp. 119–20. Tanaka, 'Seijiteki jiken', www.the-journal.jp/contents/kokkai/2012/05/post_299.html. Hirano, *Shinsetsu!*, p. 82.
413 Oka, *Policy Entrepreneurship*, p. 20.
414 Shima, Kamisawa and Mitsuhashi, 'Ozawa Kanjichō', www.asahi.com/special/ozawa_sikin/TKY201002060200.html.
415 Okamoto, 'Naze "Tōkyō Kōken Kenjichō" wa Ozawa Ichirō o mamotta ka', p. 32.
416 Toshikawa, 'Ozawa Not Out of the Woods', p. 5.
417 'Ozawa Denies Role', injectionmoldes.blogspot.com.au/2012/01/ozawa-denies-role-in-funds-scandal-says.html. NHK reported a similar story, saying that 'Ozawa's explanation for where the ¥400 million came from changed over time: first, political funds; second, a bank loan; and third, money inherited from his father'. *NHK News 7*, 6 October 2011.
418 Matsuda, *Kakuei ni Narenakatta Otoko*, p. 179.
419 Ibid.
420 Matsuda, *Ozawa Ichirō Kyoshoku no Shihaisha*, p. 23.
421 Ibid., p. 24.
422 Matsuda, *Kakuei ni Narenakatta Otoko*, p. 178. See also Chapter 6.
423 In 1985, as LDP chairman of the Lower House Steering Committee, Ozawa took the initiative in developing a code of political ethics and in establishing a Deliberative Council on Political Ethics (Seiji Rinri Shinsakai) in each house of the Diet as the bodies to enforce it. His initiative was partly a response to the shattering of public trust in politics as a result of the Lockheed scandal. The code of political ethics states, 'If suspicion emerges that a lawmaker committed a misdeed that runs counter to political ethics, he must strive to clarify the truth earnestly and make clear where the responsibility rests'. 'When There's Doubt', e.nikkei.com/e/ac/20100201/TNW/Nni200100201OP4SUSPI.htm. Each ethics council consists of 25 members. It has the power to summon a politician to attend its deliberations if more than a third of its members demand it and a majority agree. Alternatively, the member can attend voluntarily. A council meeting may be requested by a Diet member who is under suspicion of involvement in an incident or scandal, or by a member of the council. In contrast to those who appear as sworn witnesses in the Diet, those who appear before the councils cannot be charged with perjury if they lie. Nor is their testimony open to the public. In fact, politicians have often chosen to appear before a council in lieu of testifying before the Diet for these reasons.
424 See also Chapter 6.
425 This was described in the *Asahi Shinbun* of 5 February 2010 as, 'A Tokyo citizens' group composed of administrative scriveners, former journalists and the like…' See Cucek, 'The Dark Side', shisaku.blogspot.com/2010/02/dark-side-of-moon.html.
426 'Prosecutors Question Ozawa's Ex-aide', e.nikkei.com/e/ac/TNKS/Nni20100517D17JF678.htm.
427 'Prosecutors Forced My Confession', www.japantimes.co.jp/text/nn20110118a3.html.
428 *NHK News 7*, 28 April 2010. Ishikawa argued, however, that 'the stance that this figure of "absolute authority" takes is one that says "do what you think is best"', *Akutō*, pp. 106, 107.
429 'Prosecutors Question Ozawa's Ex-aide', e.nikkei.com/e/ac/TNKS/Nni20100517D17JF678.htm.
430 *NHK News 7*, 4 October 2010.

431 Ibid.
432 Toshikawa, 'Rising and Setting Suns', p. 4.
433 'Ozawa Must Take Responsibility', www.asianews.net/home/news.php?sec=3&id=17181.
434 'Ozawa Pleads Not Guilty', www.yomiuri.co.jp/dy/national/T111006005170.htm.
435 Kamiya, 'Ozawa Ex-aides Deny Cooking Funds Books', www.japantimes.co.jp/cgi-bin/nn20110207x1.html.
436 '3 Ex-Ozawa Aides', e.nikkei.com/e/ac/tnks/Nni20110207D07JF092.htm.
437 *NHK News 7*, 28 April 2011.
438 '"Ozawa-shi gawa ni uragane 1 oku en haratta"', sankei.jp.msn.com/affairs/news/110427/trl11042711260003-n1.htm.
439 *NHK News 7*, 28 April 2011.
440 '"Ozawa-shi gawa ni uragane 1 oku en haratta"', sankei.jp.msn.com/affairs/news/110427/trl11042711260003-n1.htm.
441 Okamoto, 'Naze "Tōkyō Kōken Kenjichō" wa Ozawa Ichirō o mamotta ka', p. 31.
442 '"Ozawa-shi gawa ni uragane 1 oku en haratta"', sankei.jp.msn.com/affairs/news/110427/trl11042711260003-n1.htm.
443 *NHK News 7*, 28 April 2011.
444 The depositions that were rejected were 10 records involving Ishikawa and two involving Ikeda and some parts of other statements.
445 *NHK News 7*, 1 July 2011.
446 'Ex-Ozawa Aides', www.yomiuri.co.jp/dy/national/T110926005647.htm.
447 *NHK News 7*, 26 September 2011.
448 Ibid.
449 'Ozawa Bears Heavy Responsibility', mdn.mainichi.jp/perspectives/news/20110927p2a00m0na007000c.html.
450 'Guilty Verdicts', ajw.asahi.com/article/behind_news/politics/AJ2011092712240.
451 'Ozawa Bears Heavy Responsibility', mdn.mainichi.jp/perspectives/news/20110927p2a00m0na007000c.html.
452 Ibid.
453 *NHK News 7*, 26 September 2011.
454 Ibid.
455 'Editorial: Ozawa Still Refusing', www.asahi.com/english/TKY201110070305.html.
456 Kamiya, 'Ozawa Sticks to Innocence Plea', www.japantimes.co.jp/cgi-bin/nn20111007a1.html.
457 'Ozawa Pleads Not Guilty', www.yomiuri.co.jp/dy/national/T111006005170.htm.
458 'Ozawa's Remarks Inconsistent', www.yomiuri.co.jp/dy/national/T111006005909.htm.
459 'Ozawa Pleads Not Guilty', www.yomiuri.co.jp/dy/national/T111006005170.htm.
460 'Ozawa's Remarks Inconsistent', www.yomiuri.co.jp/dy/national/T111006005909.htm.
461 'Editorial: Ozawa Still Refusing', www.asahi.com/english/TKY201110070305.html. By 'sovereignty of the people', terminology often used by Ozawa, he meant 'The people decide the shape of this country, the people choose the administration and the people decide the policies'. Suzuki, *Saigo no Ozawa Ichirō*, p. 26.
462 *NHK News 7*, 6 October 2011.
463 Kamiya, 'Ozawa Sticks to Innocence Plea', www.japantimes.co.jp/cgi-bin/nn20111007a1.html.
464 *NHK News 7*, 11 January 2012.
465 Former Tokyo SID assistant department head speaking on *NHK News 7*, 10 January 2012.
466 *NHK News 7*, 11 January 2012.
467 Kamiya and Ito, 'Onus on Aides', www.japantimes.co.jp/text/nn20120112a4.html.
468 *NHK News 7*, 17 February 2012.

469 '[Ozawa hikoku ronkoku kyūkei (1)]', sankei.jp.msn.com/affairs/news/120309/trl12030913060004-n3.htm.
470 *NHK News 7*, 27 April 2012.
471 Toshikawa, 'Twilight', p. 3.
472 'Ozawa-shi "Noda oroshi" e', sankei.jp.msn.com/politics/news/120426/stt1204261 1120008-n2.htm.
473 'Ozawa Prosecution Mulls Appeal', p. 1. As justification, one of the designated lawyers stated, 'Given that so many of our arguments were accepted, the acquittal is not convincing' (p. 1).
474 The witnesses in this case were two of Ozawa's former secretaries who made depositions when they were questioned after the verdict for the first trial. The depositions included statements such as 'We absolutely had to report to Ozawa'. Negishi, 'Ozawa-shi no kōsoshin', digital.asahi.com/articles/TKY201209260180.html?ref=comkiji_txt_end_kjid_TKY201209260180.
475 Toshikawa, 'Chickens Roosting', p. 3.
476 Toshikawa and Katz, 'Flailing', p 2.
477 'Public Support for Hatoyama', e.nikkei.com/e/ac/TNKS/Nni20100228D28JFF01.htm.
478 Adelstein, 'The Last Yakuza', p. 71.
479 The term 'seven magistrates' was given by Watanabe Kōzō to seven next-generation DPJ leaders. They were (at the time) Minister of Foreign Affairs Okada, DPJ Secretary-General Edano, Chief Cabinet Secretary Sengoku, Chairman of the newly revived PRC Genba Kōichiro, Minister of Finance Noda, Minister of Land, Infrastructure and Transport Maehara, and Chairman of the DPJ Diet Affairs Committee Tarutoko, with Sengoku the organiser and Watanabe their senior adviser. See also Chapter 6.
480 Shimizu, 'Friendship', e.nikkei.com/e/ac/20090720/TNW/Nni20090720FP7DPJ01.htm.
481 Hara, 'Kokumin no akireta shisen', diamond.jp/articles/-/9199.
482 Tanaka, 'Naze meikaku na seisaku nakushite', diamond.jp/articles/-/11355.
483 'Kan Wins', e.nikkei.com/e/ac/TNKS/Nni20100914D14NY736.htm.
484 Prime Minister of Japan and his Cabinet, *Policy Speech*, www.kantei.go.jp/foreign/kan/statement/201006/11syosin_e.html.
485 Hayashi, 'Long, Hot Summer', blogs.wsj.com/japanrealtime/2010/08/24/long-hot-summer-for-kan-ozawa-and-dpj/.
486 *NHK News 7*, 13 September 2010.
487 *NHK News 7*, 2 September 2010.
488 Sudō and Takeshima, 'Minshutō daihyōsen', web.archive.org/web/20100906142028/http://mainichi.jp/select/seiji/minshudaihyousen/hikaku/news/20100903org00m010016000c.html.
489 Tanaka, 'Naze meikaku na seisaku nakushite', diamond.jp/articles/-/11355.
490 'Ichiro Ozawa Headed for Indictment', www.panorientnews.com/en/news.php?k=476.
491 Itō, 'Dare mo shiranai Minshutō', p. 144.
492 Itō, '"Seiji kaikaku no kishu"', tukamoto-office.seesaa.net/article/141084654.html.

4   Old policies

In *Blueprint* Ozawa called for a series of neo-liberal, market-orientated reforms, so-called 'new policies'. However, just as his policy goals took a back seat to power politics when it came to the formation and dissolution of political parties, so politics trumped policy when it came to his agenda for economic reform. Although Ozawa theorised about the need for economic reform on the basis of rational economic principles, in practice, he consistently filtered issues of economic policy through the lens of electoral strategy and personal political advantage rather than economic conviction. Not only did he rethink his standpoint on a range of economic reforms in order to advance his immediate political objectives, but, in some cases, he also demonstrated a willingness to reverse earlier policy positions.

Two catalysing events were significant in this process: first, the Koizumi administration of 2001–06 which made it politically expedient for Ozawa to reject the neo-liberal agenda of economic reform, and second, the merger of Ozawa's LP with the DPJ in 2003. Under Ozawa's tutelage, DPJ policies moved away from the kind of market reforms he espoused in *Blueprint*. He switched his philosophical position on the primary axis of policy confrontation between progressives and conservatives, the big versus small government spectrum defined as 'neo-liberal versus social democratic', with a further breakdown into 'competition versus regulation', and 'fiscal reconstruction versus government spending', making a distinct shift from right to left. Moreover, when given the opportunity to enact a range of economic policy reforms – in coalition with the LDP in 1999–2000 and when the DPJ took power in September 2009 – Ozawa remained curiously passive. In both cases, he was much more concerned about reforming the structure of power, aggrandising his own position in government and subordinating economic policy to political ends.

Viewed in historical perspective, Ozawa displayed his economic reform credentials most clearly when it suited his immediate political purposes. In the early 1990s, he argued the case for economic reform as a means to break down hostile political forces and advance his own political prospects, beginning with his break with the LDP. Equally, Ozawa abandoned economic reform when he envisaged little political gain to be had from proselytising an agenda of economic change. Subsequently, he used economic policy simply as a means of winning votes or catering to special interests in order to solidify his connections with key supporting blocs. In other words, he politicised economic policy following time-honoured LDP principles of promising and doling out pork (*baramaki*) and other selective benefits. Economic policies were used as political tools – as a source of personal political patronage and as electoral strategy – rather than as instruments to restore the Japanese economy to growth as had been former Prime Minister Koizumi's priority. By the time Ozawa was leader of the DPJ, he was back in the big-government, big-spending camp, eagerly engaging in the politically strategic distributive politics typical of the LDP. His retreat from economic reform became particularly pronounced in the DPJ's election manifestos as his policy influence in the party grew. He abandoned his neo-liberal economic goals for the prospect of short-term electoral gain.

When the DPJ finally came to power in 2009, Ozawa was eager to occupy a position of authority over government spending policies, which he saw as the key to winning the 2010 Upper House election. His changed thinking manifested itself in economic and budget policy under the Hatoyama administration. Despite the fact that he was not a member of the government executive, Ozawa ensured that he was in a position to dictate economic policy outcomes by placing himself advantageously in the policy process, bypassing the executive policymaking structures that he ostensibly wanted to strengthen by centralising policymaking power in the cabinet, by expanding executive decision-making institutions and by excluding the ruling party from government policymaking. Ozawa's own conduct thus helped to sabotage the very institutional reforms that he had advocated earlier and which the new DPJ government was endeavouring to implement. As a result, Ozawa's policy imprint was visible across a range of economic policy spheres consequent upon his direct personal intervention during the Hatoyama administration.

The September 2010 leadership contest with Prime Minister Kan further illustrated Ozawa's changed economic thinking and electoral strategies, underlining how far he had departed from his original standpoint on neo-liberal economic reform. This shift was also underscored by the policy positions he adopted under the Kan and Noda governments. While removed from the centre of policymaking, he remained a loud advocate of the DPJ's original 2009 manifesto when it suited his political purposes.

Ozawa's *modus operandi* in which political and electoral opportunism primarily shaped economic policy thus brings his economic reform credentials into question. Not only did his neo-liberal impulse fade over the years, but it also gave way to strident criticism of free market principles and consistent advocacy of populist big-spending policies, including large-scale public works programmes. In his pursuit of a self-serving political calculus, Ozawa consistently neglected the cause of economic reform. He had no convincing answer to the most fundamental policy dilemma facing his country: how a debt-laden government could engineer economic growth whilst mitigating social and economic disparities.

Ozawa's retreat from economic reform

Over time, Ozawa dramatically altered his policy position on market-oriented reforms such as the consumption tax and deregulation. Furthermore, in the agricultural sector, he rewrote the agricultural subsidy manual to outflank the LDP in terms of generosity to farmers. Rather than reflecting a genuine ideological conversion, these policy switches could be largely attributed to a mixture of political opportunism and expediency as Ozawa sought to advance his own political ambitions.

Developing and implementing policy: the pre-DPJ and Hatoyama administration years

The consumption tax

Ozawa's position on the consumption tax was markedly inconsistent. In 1988, after the Takeshita cabinet had decided to introduce the consumption tax, he reportedly said to Futami Nobuaki, former member of the Kōmeitō and NFP, 'The consumption tax is a strongly regressive tax that directly affects small and medium enterprises and mid- to low-income earners'.[1] He then went on to play a pivotal role in the initial introduction of the consumption tax in 1989 under the Takeshita government.

A few years later, during the Hosokawa administration, Ozawa pushed for a 'national welfare tax' of 7 per cent to replace the consumption tax. The proposal, which was described as 'a conspiracy between Ozawa Ichirō and the MOF',[2] was suddenly announced on Ozawa's initiative without any discussion with coalition partners and met with vehement opposition from ruling party executives. At the time in early 1994, Japan had been suffering from a long recession.[3] Although the proposal was withdrawn, it ultimately led to the collapse of the Hosokawa administration, which at the time was at the height of its popularity.[4] Immediately after the cabinet was forced to abandon the proposal, Ozawa said on a TV programme, 'We have to do what we can do before we are faced with a super-ageing society'.[5] While emphasising the need to increase the consumption tax, he rejected media criticism stating, 'Their arguments are all based on emotions, like it was too sudden and they hadn't heard about it'.[6]

Ozawa himself abandoned the idea of increasing the consumption tax from the mid-1990s onwards, even though he appeared, nominally, to retain it. When running for the NFP leadership election in 1995, he declared himself to be a radical politician,[7] pairing several proposals for tax reform, which included a delay in the consumption tax rise, with a plan for massively increased public works spending in the form of an annual investment of ¥1 trillion in each of the five major public works areas.[8] The funds, if necessary, would be raised by government bonds. Kaieda, however, wrote scathingly about Ozawa's scheme, saying:

> He must be joking. Even without the additional issuances, the total value of outstanding government bonds is already at ¥240 trillion. If we were to carry out a ¥13 trillion tax cut and a ¥5 trillion investment in public projects for ten years, this comes to a total of ¥180 trillion. Our debt will come to a total

of ¥400 trillion. With that much debt, we won't be able to carry out financial reconstruction, but rather we will suffer financial collapse. It is simply absurd. How can such policies lead to rebuilding our economy and society? So I want to ask Ozawa this question: isn't it the opposite? From now on, there are going to be more and more elderly people in Japanese society, and accordingly, welfare costs will continue to rise. There is only one way to resolve this issue without relying on issuing government bonds – that is to cut down the costs of public projects.[9]

Kaieda also condemned the self-interested politics behind Ozawa's advocacy of increased public works spending as 'taking sides with general contractors'.[10] In a similar vein, Oka criticised the NFP's policy promises for the 1996 general election, commenting that much of the manifesto sounded like 'pie in the sky'.[11]

Later, in 2007, Ozawa substantially modified the DPJ's manifesto commitment to raise the consumption tax. There was a marked contrast between the 2005 and 2007 manifestos during the Okada and Ozawa presidencies, respectively. Okada's DPJ in 2005 proposed to raise the consumption tax by 3 per cent to fund a new system of unified pension programmes,[12] but Ozawa deleted the proposed tax increase from the 2007 manifesto,[13] which he virtually wrote as DPJ leader. The manifesto gave an explicit assurance that a DPJ government would keep the consumption tax at the existing level, while the DPJ pledged in 2009 not to raise the consumption tax during its first four years in office. The manifesto committed the party to raising the necessary funding to honour its spending promises by reducing wasteful spending and accessing tax money in so-called 'buried treasure' funds. Throughout the Hatoyama administration, Ozawa was adamant that the party should stick to its commitment not to raise the consumption tax.

Agricultural policy

In *Blueprint*, Ozawa argued strongly for agricultural trade liberalisation while at the same time proposing a massive injection of funds into rural areas. On 7 December 1993, the government announced its policy of partially liberalising the rice market. Six days later, on 13 December, the RP set up an Emergency Headquarters for Agriculture and Rural Areas with Ozawa as director. He was entrusted with negotiations on the issue between the government and the ruling party. Hosokawa was, at the time, stressing the need for funding for agricultural infrastructure development. Minister of Foreign Affairs Hata Tsutomu referred to the establishment of new employment opportunities in hilly and mountainous regions rather than income compensation for farmers as a likely policy response to market opening. In other words, government policy was moving in exactly the direction that Ozawa wanted.

Not surprisingly, the budget for agricultural public works expanded in the wake of the GATT URAA. Ozawa and the RP's reign continued until June 1994, and during that six months they laid the groundwork for prioritising agricultural public works, especially agricultural infrastructure development, in budget formulation and the implementation of measures in response to the GATT. The outlay for farmland consolidation (*hojō seibi*) increased in particular. Individual blocks of land of 30 ares were expanded into large 1-hectare blocks, which required even larger amounts of funding as well as general contractors' technical skills and mechanical power. Moreover, farmland consolidation was always accompanied by the development of farm roads and agricultural facilities. This explained why Ozawa was so fixated on farmland consolidation. It created jobs for general contractors as well as 'concessions' (*riken*) to be distributed by politicians.[14] In Iwate there was a group of public works contractors that preferred land consolidation works, including Takaya Construction[15] with its special links to Ozawa.

After joining the DPJ, Ozawa was still calling for new agricultural, forestry and fisheries policies geared to developing regional society as a whole,[16] and arguing against agricultural structural reform policies that aimed to improve economic efficiency through scale expansion. As a result, there was a marked trend away from reform in DPJ agricultural policy. In its 2001 election manifesto, the DPJ had pledged to abolish the rice acreage reduction (*gentan*) scheme and offered limited direct income subsidies to full-time farmers. The same promises were included in the 2003 manifesto. The arrival of Ozawa and his LP, however, produced a dramatic change in policy direction. Prior to the 2004 Upper House election, all farmers were made eligible for direct income support. Similarly, in the 2005 Lower House election, the DPJ offered ¥1 trillion in direct payments to all farm households marketing agricultural products. It also extended this offer to farm households in hilly and mountainous areas and those whose agricultural production activities served environmental protection functions.

Ozawa's political purpose was to outflank the government's scheme, which limited direct income support to so-called agricultural 'bearers'. The combined LDP-MAFF approach amounted to a structural reform policy because it left small farmers out of the loop. In contrast, the DPJ's approach was not a structural reform policy at all because it offered no incentives to small-scale farmers to abandon agriculture and relinquish their land to larger-scale, full-time producers. Its effect would be to prop up as many inefficient, small-scale farmers as the old agricultural price support system.

Ozawa, however, derided the MAFF for its 'stupidity'[17] in prioritising large-scale farmers with direct subsidies and for abandoning small-scale farmers in not making them part of the income compensation scheme. He proposed a deficiency payment scheme where the government would calculate the production costs for major agricultural products and cover the gap for farmers when the market prices for the producers were lower than the production cost, a method that would 'neither harm the principle of a liberalised economy nor abandon small-scale farmers'.[18]

In the 2007 Upper House election the DPJ under Ozawa's leadership reiterated its proposal for direct farm income support, now called the 'individual farm household income compensation scheme', which would directly subsidise the incomes of all commercial farm households, large and small. The party's election

134   Old policies

manifesto also promised to revitalise the forestry and lumber industries, and to promote the fishing industry, including public works. These programmes proved a real vote winner in regional prefectural constituencies. Ozawa had successfully made *baramaki* and 'no tax increases' into policies in order to win the election.[19]

The DPJ's 2009 manifesto promised to expand the direct income support scheme to include more farm products and also the fisheries and forestry sectors. The proposed FTA with the United States that Ozawa inserted into the manifesto only became possible in his mind because farmers would be compensated for price falls with income subsidies. He reasoned that opening agricultural markets and compensating farmers were complementary policies.

However, the question was raised whether the direct subsidy scheme was income compensation for promoting FTAs or whether it was just *baramaki* for the purpose of gathering votes, particularly amongst small-scale, part-time farmers who comprised about 6 per cent of the national electorate.[20]

The DPJ's agricultural policy reversals were the centrepiece of Ozawa's strategy of winning over rural voters, particularly small-scale part-time farmers who constituted the majority of agricultural producers. He realised that ultimately, to win general elections, he needed the votes of part-time farmers.[21] His political intention was to outbid the LDP for the farmers' votes and thus detach the LDP from its traditional agricultural support base. Nor was farm policy the only sector in which Ozawa appeared to discard his reform credentials. Similar trends could be seen in a range of other economic policy sectors.

Deregulation and other market-oriented reforms

Ozawa backtracked on his commitment to deregulation despite his self-proclaimed antipathy towards the bureaucracy and a desire to cut them down to size. The proposals in the DPJ's 2005 manifesto to 'comprehensively review all business regulations'[22] and to 'drastically reduce the size of postal savings and insurance, and allow funds to flow from the public to the private sector',[23] which emphasised market mechanisms, were eliminated from the 2007 manifesto.[24] Similarly, the pledges to 'establish fair and transparent market rules...and...to realise a free market society',[25] to 'enhance the capacity and power of the Fair Trade Commission'[26] and to '[d]rastically reform the Anti-Monopoly Law'[27] vanished. The DPJ promised to triple the budget relating to small and medium-sized enterprises (SMEs) and to re-regulate employment practices affecting non-permanent employees – all geared to winning votes from these sectors.

In the 2009 manifesto, the commitment to a free market society was watered down to merely a promise to develop a fair market environment by strengthening the operations of the Fair Trade Commission.[28] Any reference to deregulation was again absent from the 2009 election platform.[29] In fact, the DPJ committed itself to re-regulating the labour market.[30] It also promised to pay ¥100,000 a month in allowances to job seekers during job training and to cut the corporate tax rate for SMEs.[31] The earlier reference to tax measures to promote investment in stocks and businesses were gone, as were references to restoring fiscal soundness and other fiscal constraints apart from a pledge to 'eradicate wasteful spending of tax money'.[32] Postal privatisation was stopped dead in its tracks, with the DPJ committing itself merely to a 'review' of postal businesses.[33] Putting the brakes on neo-liberal reform such as postal privatisation was reminiscent of the 'old LDP' as was Ozawa's 'loose, fiscal policy based on handouts'.[34] At the very least, Ozawa campaigned along the lines of traditional old-style *baramaki* politics (see Table 1.1).[35]

A genuine conversion or political opportunism?

The question that Ozawa's about-face on neo-liberal economic reform raised is whether it could be attributed to a genuine conversion of his economic beliefs involving a change of doctrinal position and a rejection of competitive free market philosophy. The media referred rather disparagingly to Ozawa's apparent shift from small-government conservative in 1993 to 'socialist' between his original manifesto in *Blueprint* and his leadership of the DPJ in 2006–09.[36]

Ozawa's supporters attributed the change in his view of the role of government and the need for economic liberalisation to what he perceived as the negative consequences of the Koizumi style of neo-liberal reforms, which 'confused freedom with selfishness, and as a result gave rise to a monster in the form of an unequal society that operates based on the law of the jungle'.[37] Ozawa made this statement during the election campaign for the DPJ leadership in 2006, in which he advanced his long-standing principle of 'coexistence' (*kyōsei*), which was about everyone living together under fair rules and responsibilities.[38] When he became DPJ leader in April 2006, he launched the catch phrase 'politics is about livelihoods' (*seiji wa seikatsu de aru*).[39] This evolved into the DPJ's slogan of 'putting people's lives first', which assisted the party ultimately to its 2007 election victory and regime change in 2009.[40] It also formed the basis of social policies such as a child-support scheme[41] and the individual household income compensation scheme for farmers.[42] As DPJ politician Azumi Jun explained:

> with the passing of the Koizumi era, Ozawa's way of thinking…also changed. When he was in the Liberal Party, [he had] a theory of simple and small government. However, during the Koizumi administration, the LDP implemented this [before Ozawa could]. The problems created by small government, such as the ruin of local areas, poverty and unfairness and the timing of when Mr. Ozawa gained control within the DPJ were almost simultaneous. In that sense, Mr. Ozawa made a decision that in order to win power, [he] had to show a clear counterpoint to the small government of the Koizumi era. So then, Mr. Ozawa changed from [a belief in] a self-responsibility society, which he had once held, to [a belief in] the theory of big government.[43]

Ozawa publicly condemned the neo-liberal economic reforms that produced 'greater income differentials, destabilised the life of the poor, and exposed the weakness of Japan's safety net',[44] laying the growing social divide squarely at the door of Koizumi-style economic reforms.[45] He wrote, 'Under the Koizumi government, Japan became a society where "disparities" are prominent',[46] adding, 'Koizumi's reform only brought benefits to certain people while others were made to suffer, so this is nowhere near a real reform'.[47] He denounced Koizumi's advocacy of 'market forces', saying, 'Freedom is not about benefiting only a handful of winners. The DPJ's goal is to realise a society where workers' efforts are rewarded in a fair manner'.[48] He stressed the importance of social safety nets, including for workers.[49]

Despite blaming Koizumi-style policies for his change of position, Ozawa's reversal on neo-liberal reform was really about engineering electoral advantage rather than a genuine conversion of economic principles. He wanted to emphasise the widening economic disparities in Japanese society in order to draw a sharp contrast between DPJ policies and those of the LDP. He saw potential electoral dividends in adopting a strong anti-Koizumi line, which inevitably entailed attacking his economic reforms. He also had ambitions to split the LDP apart, perhaps setting off a new round of political realignment, using the issue of economic reform as an instrument to polarise the party internally and aggravate the discontent within the LDP towards Koizumi.

Ozawa helped to orchestrate the victory of a young, female rookie candidate, Ōta Kazumi, in the by-election for Chiba (7) in April 2006, attacking 'the gap emerging between rich and poor in a hitherto homogeneous middle class'.[50] This was the same month that he assumed the DPJ presidency when he adopted a centre-left approach, wrapping it up in the slogan of 'Putting People's Lives First', which he knew nobody would oppose.[51] The DPJ's earlier advocacy of neo-liberal economic reform was replaced with 'people-first' policies, including commitments to protect jobs and rectify economic disparities.[52] Policies to enhance the social safety net were expanded: the proposal for a child allowance was increased from ¥16,000 yen per child to ¥26,000 yen and the DPJ promised to introduce free high school education. In fact, it was Ozawa who in January 2007 picked up the proposal made years previously by DPJ Diet member Komiyama Yōko for the government to provide ¥16,000 a month to families with children. In Ozawa's hands it became an election ploy as he set about planning the DPJ's Upper House campaign for July of that year. Unlike Komiyama's earlier proposal, however, how to secure the funding for such a programme was not specifically identified.[53] In addition, the 2007 manifesto gave the assurance that all pension benefits due would be paid by the state.

In September 2008 in a policy speech to a DPJ extraordinary party convention, Ozawa argued for revamping the budget by prioritising what was important for the people's lives, which would deliver the necessary financial resources for realising the DPJ's spending policies, with a grand total of ¥22 trillion needed over a projected four-year DPJ administration. Ozawa also reiterated the themes of eliminating waste and cutting expenditures by 10 per cent, but no specific details were spelled out, just a commitment to the principles of 'totally rearranging the budget' and broaching a 'major shift in the financial structure'.[54]

Because Ozawa's electoral strategy was successful in winning votes in the 2007 election, the main provisions of the 2007 manifesto were continued and expanded in 2009. There were further additions to social spending policies such as a promise to pay a minimum ¥70,000 a month old age pension, abolishing the discriminatory health insurance scheme for people aged 75 years and over, and raising the wages of long-term care workers. Ozawa rationalised his approach as 'returning to the original starting point of politics…[that is] caring for people's concerns'.[55]

It could be argued that these and other policy initiatives such as a promise to eliminate highway tolls were designed to revive the economy by putting more money in people's pockets, raising real incomes, narrowing the income gap and stimulating consumption.[56] Hence, they were informed by a fundamental economic growth imperative. It could also be argued that they supplied what was missing from the Koizumi reform agenda, namely the need to provide a stronger social safety net to the disadvantaged. However, in the absence of any elaboration of the economic philosophy underlying them, they could be viewed as simply government handouts to buy votes. As Iinuma commented, 'The policies strongly tilted towards a social democratic model of distribution. But, they were not a policy package backed by conceptual and ideological consistency or by careful study of practicalities. It was rather an expedient policy patchwork for marketing the DPJ to voters who were resentful of former Prime Minister Junichiro Koizumi's market-oriented reforms'.[57]

Moreover, by the time the DPJ government had been in power for several months, it became clear that Ozawa was primarily positioning himself to intervene in areas where he could cater to special interests traditionally cultivated by the LDP. These were policies that essentially focused on a growth strategy reliant on government spending, particularly the allocation of huge sums for public investment in infrastructure and maintaining employment mainly in the construction industry, whilst doing little to revive an economy wallowing in the doldrums.

Establishing a structure of personal policy intervention[58]

Ozawa established a structure of personal policy intervention under the Hatoyama administration, ensuring that he was in a position to use economic policy as political tool for his own ends. In particular, he saw his role in policy-making as an extension of his responsibilities as the DPJ's chief electoral strategist.

When the DPJ came to power, Ozawa's predecessor as DPJ secretary-general, Okada Katsuya, reported to the media that Ozawa well understood that he was outside the government (i.e. cabinet) and therefore would not interfere in day-to-day government decision making on policy. Furthermore, Hatoyama and Ozawa agreed, on Hatoyama's initiative, to keep the DPJ secretary-general out of the cabinet.[59] There would be a division of labour with Hatoyama running the government and Ozawa running the party.[60] Okada also offered the double assurance that the government and party would be unified on policy, meaning that the party would not operate as a separate power structure outside the cabinet and try to influence the cabinet and its ministers.

Ozawa's strong support for the major principle of centralising the government decision-making process in the cabinet was displayed in *Blueprint* and *Ozawashugi*,

138 *Old policies*

as well as in the DPJ's 2009 manifesto and subsequent abolition of the PRC. Under Ozawa's influence, however, the proposal for the move to a centralised cabinet decision-making system effectively became 'a dead letter'.[61] As the former head of the JCP's secretariat, Fudesaka Hideyo, observed:

> [O]nce Ozawa succeeded in taking over the administration, he abolished the Policy Research Council and centralised party decisions to the secretary-general's office on the pretext of the DPJ's policy of 'centralising policy decisions in the government'. This must have been a bolt from the blue for the DPJ's members. Originally, the idea of 'centralising policy decisions in the government' was aimed at eliminating the situation where the status of the party was higher than that of the government [*tōkō seitei*], which was seen under the LDP administration, and at preventing tribe Diet members from being born. However, Ozawa's actions led to the creation of a system where the secretary-general's office had control over all authority…He created the worst 'party high government low [*tōkō seitei*]' system possible. It was only natural that DPJ executives other than those belonging to the Ozawa group developed a crucial sense of distrust in Ozawa.[62]

Ozawa sabotaged his own reforms with the part he played in the Hatoyama administration of 2009–10. He chose not to enter the government formally, with the indictment of Ōkubo in the Nishimatsu Construction case a consideration in this decision. In practice, however, he became a *de facto* member of the government.[63] The reality was that his words and wishes had the power to overrule any policy decision, particularly in the absence of the institutionalisation of the new policymaking system.

As DPJ secretary-general, Ozawa's formal duties included devising the party's electoral strategy, deciding official party endorsements, allocating the party's political funds and managing Diet affairs including the DPJ's parliamentary strategies as well as exercising ultimate power over the selection of the chairpersons of both houses and their standing committees, because the party decided these positions. Hatoyama appointed Ozawa to run the party's campaign for the 2010 Upper House election in order to win a majority in the house and thus put the new DPJ administration on a solid parliamentary footing. He also told Ozawa that he would '"entrust the party's personnel affairs [to him]" so Ozawa came to control all personnel affairs in the party'.[64] In practice, Ozawa's powers extended far beyond formally prescribed duties such as these.[65]

First, he appropriated for himself the powers of the defunct PRC. He had proclaimed that its dissolution was to allow policymaking tasks to be left to the government (ministers, senior vice-ministers and parliamentary secretaries), while ruling party backbenchers could participate in policy discussions through the policy councils in each ministry. In this scenario, the policymaking process within the party was not necessary.[66] According to Ozawa, all policy decisions were to be dealt with by ministers, senior vice-ministers and parliamentary secretaries[67] in line with his vision for centralised policymaking within the cabinet.

Ozawa also advised backbenchers to focus on their own constituencies and on securing re-election. He saw to it that the roughly 140 newly elected DPJ members were overseen by the DPJ's Diet Affairs Committee whose core members were his close aides.[68] He also requested that backbenchers refrain from submitting legislation to the Diet, provoking criticism that this was done to secure 'Ozawa rule' (*Ozawa shihai*).[69] Yet another restriction was the constraint on DPJ Diet members participating in parliamentary leagues (*giren*).

In addition to the abolition of the PRC, these arrangements and restrictions were all means to prevent DPJ members from having any impact on government policy and to restrict their ability to become influential in particular policy domains.[70] The concern was that if ordinary Diet members' actions were limited in this and other ways, Ozawa would have control over a majority of the party.[71] Former supreme adviser to the DPJ Watanabe Kōzō, who distanced himself from Ozawa, described the situation in a lecture in Fukuoka City on the 4 November 2009, saying, 'Even though we have become the government party, only ministers, senior vice-ministers and parliamentary secretaries are busy, and all others are free'.[72] Media critics questioned whether the people had voted for Diet members for them simply to focus on elections and not do their work as Diet members properly.[73]

In particular, questions were raised about the quality of the phalanx of new DPJ Diet members and Ozawa recruits who were described as 'useless' and derided by LDP leader Tanigaki Sadakazu for behaving like 'Hitler Youth' in their unquestioning and enthusiastic endorsement of each utterance of the prime minister during his first policy speech to the Diet. They continued their performance in the Budget Committee, clapping their hands each time the prime minister responded to a question, like puppets controlled from behind the scenes.[74] More experienced politicians condemned them for not even knowing how the Diet functioned, asking whether it were possible for the Diet to function properly in the circumstances.[75] This was nothing like the role that Ozawa had envisaged for backbenchers in *Blueprint* where he saw them not as mere parliamentary and election fodder, but as contributors to the policymaking process through their activities in Diet committees and as appointees to the various ministries in non-cabinet roles such as parliamentary vice-ministers and parliamentary councillors, where they could 'study policy and participate in drafting policy'.[76] Revitalisation of the Diet committee system through the participation of backbenchers was also envisaged under the Hatoyama administration.

Ozawa changed his view, however, requiring DPJ backbenchers to leave the party's input on policy to him as a kind of one-man PRC. He became the lone policy coordinator for the party. Although the DPJ did establish the new system of policy councils within each ministry as a channel for backbenchers to become involved in policymaking, the new approach never really took off, with insufficient numbers of meetings and more influential gatherings taking place elsewhere, largely centring on Ozawa.[77] This focused the party's power over policy in Ozawa's own hands.

Ozawa's centralised management over policy in the party was likened to the kind of iron-fisted control that he had exerted over the RP as secretary-general in

1993–94. At the time this prompted attacks from the young reformers in Sakigake who wanted to protect their individual policy autonomy against party leaders such as Ozawa.[78] Similarly, his disbanding of the DPJ's PRC went against the wishes of many backbenchers, who agitated to re-establish it because they felt excluded from the decision-making process.[79]

Hatoyama had initially sought to retain the PRC as the DPJ's own policy council and to put it under Kan's control. In the end he yielded to Ozawa who wanted to take the more drastic step of disbanding the PRC altogether and shifting its powers to the cabinet. Although Kan objected to the move, Hatoyama sided with Ozawa in overriding him. When the chairman of the LDP's PARC, Ōshima Tadamori, sought to confirm the dissolution of the PRC, Ozawa told him that the PRC was unnecessary because the party would agree with the cabinet and would not contradict the government on policy.[80] The upshot was that Hatoyama ceded control over party affairs to Ozawa, who became virtually the sole channel for party input into policymaking as well as effectively functioning as government whip, keeping DPJ backbenchers firmly behind government legislation before the Diet. The lack of a PRC made the role of a whip necessary because of the need to ensure that party members backed government policy in the absence of a party forum to discuss it and to accommodate individual legislators' concerns.[81]

The second significant grab for power by Ozawa was to allocate sole control over the receipt of petitions from local government leaders, industry groups and others to the secretary-general's office.[82] As Uesugi explains, under the old system:

> the great majority of petitions were submitted to Diet members' offices, particularly to their local offices. They were received by the Diet members' secretary in charge of the constituency, who were familiar with the local situation and who 'had their roots in the local area'…Of these, many petitions…those that were of high importance and which local staff could not deal with were sent to the Tokyo office [of the Diet member]…[T]he secretaries…gathered these petitions and worked on communicating the requests to the various government offices…or sent them around to the Diet members who had strong influence in the related area [*zoku giin*].[83]

On 6 November 2009, Ozawa issued an official edict to DPJ Diet members under the title, 'Regarding Measures for Requests and Petitions', a document that laid out in detail the new rules of how they, as the ruling party of the Hatoyama government, should deal with petitions. According to the new rules, requests from petitioning interest groups and local politicians, previously transmitted through individual Diet members' local and national offices to bureaucrats in the relevant ministries and to *zoku giin* with specialist expertise, connections and influence in the relevant policy sector, would thereafter be channelled through each of the DPJ's prefectural chapters, which would then send them on to the secretary-general's office. The secretary-general's office would then select and arrange petitions to be conveyed to the *seimu sanyaku* in the relevant ministry or agency.

Only petitions transmitted through this route would be accepted; those that did not follow this process would not.[84] Moreover, only those petitions deemed worthy of government action would be handed on to the *seimu sanyaku*. Having received the selected petitions, the *seimu sanyaku* would then instruct the bureaucrats what to do.[85]

In theory, the new system was designed to transfer power over government spending to political leaders and away from both the bureaucracy and *zoku giin*.[86] There would no longer be direct requests to bureaucrats from local assemblies, mayors and others. Instead, there would be integrated instructions from the *seimu sanyaku* and the expectation was that bureaucratic leadership and centralised authoritarian rule would be removed.[87] The only contacts between the localities and Kasumigaseki would henceforth be through the secretary-general's office. Ozawa hoped that under the new system he could reprise the role he played in the newly established Hosokawa administration of 1993 when his aim was to make the bureaucrats obey the new government and have the various budget requests come directly to him.[88]

Likewise, centralising the handling of petitions in the secretary-general's office would advance 'the great cause of getting rid of *zoku giin*'.[89] It would neutralise their influence along with that of the bureaucrats in the distribution of pork-barrel benefits. With respect to the allocation of public works, for example, the mediation of *zoku* would be replaced by the mediation of the whole ruling party.[90] Ozawa also sought to terminate the co-dependent relationship between the *zoku giin* and ministry bureaucrats. He wanted to block direct contact between politicians and bureaucrats, and in particular, to freeze relationships between *zoku giin* with close links to certain interest groups and ministry officials in specific bureaux or departments who oversaw those groups.[91]

According to Ozawa supporter Uesugi, Ozawa thought that the new system would have four principal effects: it would eliminate cosy ties between politicians and bureaucrats and shake free of the politics of guiding benefits to local areas and special interests (*rieki yūdō seiji*); it would stamp out the practice of 'paying homage to bureaucrats in Kasumigaseki' and thus encourage the decentralisation of power; it would contribute to the country's administrative revival and regional administrative reform; and it would establish a system of handling petitions in which transparency and fairness were ensured.[92] For Ozawa these developments would, in turn, have political benefits, such as strengthening the DPJ's prefectural chapters' political activities and organisation, reinforcing policy activities by Diet members, reducing the burdens on each ministry's *seimu sanyaku* and economising on local government's fiscal expenditure.[93] Another positive effect would be substantially to reduce the burden of processing petitions by Diet members' offices and their secretaries.[94] Finally, petitions dealt with through party headquarters would be more likely to become policies (*seisaku*) compared with petitions handled by Diet members' offices, which were more likely to turn into concessionary benefits (*riken*).[95]

In practice, while Ozawa went out of his way to provide an elaborate justification for restructuring the petition system, a number of his latent objectives gradually became more apparent. First, the new system deposed the *zoku*, particularly the construction (*kensetsu*) *zoku*, allowing Ozawa to appropriate for himself the power to allocate pork and other special benefits. In short, the reform boiled down to a power grab by a former prominent member of the *kensetsu zoku*.[96]

Second, Ozawa could use the new system of handling petitions, which always required votes and money as a trade-off, as a political tool in elections, strengthening his power even further.[97] It was not Ozawa's intention to abolish the petitions process itself, merely to monopolise the handling of petitions through his office.

Third, while officially the bureaucrats' role under the old system had been replaced by the *seimu sanyaku*, which shifted power from the bureaucracy to the political executive, it was still the ruling party that would make the key decisions on which petitions would be accepted, while the government would merely put the decisions into practice. In short, the new system centralised powers relating to government resource allocation in the party, which effectively meant Ozawa because he was the most powerful person in it. Ozawa's former secretary, Takahashi Yoshinobu, condemned the change in methodology, saying, 'This level of concentration of power was not even seen in the LDP in the past. It is nothing but democratic centralism'.[98]

Furthermore, the process by which the secretary-general's office received petitions and conveyed some of them to the government was opaque, which meant that the DPJ had failed 'to achieve their original goal of establishing transparent policy decision making, in which it was clear who holds responsibility'.[99] As Yamazaki observed, 'whether or not a petition was accepted was not decided by democratic discussions within the DPJ, but rather it was decided as a result of examination by Secretary-General Ozawa and those around him behind closed doors'.[100] This process lacked transparency, with information monopolised by Ozawa and a few aides in his office.

The 'new' scheme turned out to be just another Ozawa ploy to expand his own power at the expense of those who had traditionally shared in the dispensation of government benefits – namely the *zoku giin* and bureaucrats – particularly with respect to budget allocation and election spending. This was part of a pattern of political behaviour whereby Ozawa's institutional reforms contained hidden agendas that served his own interests. As Nonoyama pointed out:

> Ozawa is said to be 'not interested in individual policies, but is fixated on institutional reforms'...However, political plotting always comes as a set with institutional reforms. Since the inauguration of the Hatoyama administration, Ozawa has been talking big about unification of the government and DPJ, Diet reform and the petition reform, in rapid succession. Publicly, they are all experiments for securing political leadership. However, as can be seen with the example of petition reform, under the surface, there is suspicion of a political struggle.[101]

On top of the functions and powers that Ozawa already exercised as DPJ secretary-general, acquisition of authority over petition management only served to solidify the 'Ozawa Empire'.[102]

Ozawa's policy intervention under the Hatoyama government

During the Hatoyama administration, Ozawa usurped the role of the cabinet and prime minister by intervening directly in routine policymaking, thus undermining the formal policymaking roles and powers of the cabinet and subjecting individual ministers to the exercise of his informal power.[103] The result was a power structure that concentrated policy decisions in the secretary-general and his office (see Table 1.1).[104]

Paradoxically, it was the shift from a decentralised policymaking system, in which there was greater scope for intervention by the bureaucracy and by the party through the PRC, to a more centralised system ostensibly where policymaking power was centralised in the cabinet, which enabled Ozawa to intervene so effectively in the policymaking process. The way Ozawa exercised power promoted a return to the traditional division of power at the heart of government by reinstalling an LDP-style dual structure of party-cabinet government, which blocked the transition to a truly cabinet-centred system, the DPJ's proclaimed goal. In this case, instead of the PRC, it was Ozawa himself who appropriated the power of the party in policymaking in his own hands.

This was certainly not how the Japanese policymaking system was supposed to function according to Ozawa's own prescription for reform in *Blueprint* and to the new rules Ozawa was pivotal in setting. By intervening in key policy areas, Ozawa directly undercut cabinet ministers and therefore the cabinet's functioning as the government's highest policy authority. If Ozawa had seriously believed in converting Japan to a cabinet-centred system, he would have taken a senior role in the cabinet and used that as the proper institutional base for exerting power over policymaking, rather than perpetuating an extra-cabinet role in government decision making as DPJ secretary-general. As it was, he distanced himself from the formal policymaking process in the cabinet, whilst informally intervening behind the scenes at key junctures.

In exercising policy leadership in the Hatoyama administration, Ozawa directly undermined Hatoyama who proved a weak leader, with his inability to control Ozawa exposing the limits of his own leadership in government. Indeed, Ozawa's strong exertion of power and regular interventions in policymaking made it more difficult for the prime minister to make key decisions. The overall impression was that the orchestra had two conductors, with Ozawa controlling the DPJ and the prime minister from behind the scenes.[105] The government became a 'dual-power structure',[106] in which the cabinet 'could not decide on anything without listening to Ozawa's views'.[107] Hatoyama was criticised for his dependence on Ozawa, but it was Hatoyama who allowed Ozawa to operate far outside his job description as secretary-general. Only occasionally did he resist Ozawa's views. For example, Ozawa was shocked at Hatoyama's 'rebellion' when he did not follow the agreed line on the Futenma Air Station in Okinawa, giving prior consideration to the coalition and in particular to SDP leader Fukushima Mizuho's position on the issue. Then when Hatoyama capitulated to the American position and agreed to stick to the 2006 United States-Japan agreement, as well as dismissing Fukushima from her position as minister of state for consumer affairs and food safety, the Ozawa camp quickly moved to draw up a 'Dump Hatoyama' scenario.[108] What is more, Ozawa telephoned to give Fukushima encouragement after her withdrawal from the coalition administration, saying, 'Reason is with you'.[109]

Sometimes Ozawa stepped into a power vacuum, or at least, into an unresolved policy mess, responsibility for which ultimately lay at Hatoyama's door. Hatoyama-led policymaking tended to be chaotic, with cabinet ministers pushing their own barrows and openly attacking each other in public, and cabinet committees, which were supposed to be the centrepiece of the new policymaking system, barely convened. The prime minister often failed to assert his authority over his ministers, and at times there was a complete lack of coordination within the government and between the DPJ and its coalition partners. It was at these junctures that Ozawa's clout was needed to settle things.

Over time, Ozawa became as powerful a figure as Hatoyama in practice, if not more powerful.[110] At crucial moments, he presented his decisions to the Kantei, indicating that he was using Hatoyama as a conduit for his preferred policies and as an instrument of policy control over the government executive. For example, he exercised his power directly and personally to arrange a meeting between China's Vice-President Xi Jinping and the Japanese Emperor at China's request, brooking no opposition to his plan. In a *Jiji* poll taken in December 2009, 71 per cent of respondents named Ozawa as Japan's most influential policymaker, with just 10 per cent naming Prime Minister Hatoyama.[111]

Ozawa directly intervened in government policymaking in several key areas, proclaiming that he was the 'voice of the party' or the 'voice of the people'. Not only was he proactive in pushing his own ideas on policies, but he also acted as a channel for bottom-up pressure from other DPJ backbenchers as well as from interest groups and local politicians. Under Ozawa's tutelage, the DPJ was gradually refashioned into a policy department store along the lines of the old LDP, catering to a range of special interests and large socio-economic groups. This was not a new strategy of Ozawa's. *Blueprint* also bespoke Ozawa's strategy to build a new 'catch-all' party that would cater to a range of social, economic and political interests in order to challenge the LDP.[112]

1 The 2010 budget

When the new administration was looking to generate the necessary fiscal resources for its spending programmes in late 2009, Ozawa played a central role in formulating the fiscal 2010 budget. Immediately after its inauguration, the DPJ-led government decided to shift responsibility for making decisions on budget compilation and on foreign policy from the MOF and the MOFA, to the National Strategy Unit, or NSU (Kokka Senryaku Shitsu) under the prime minister. However, because the NSU took an excessive amount of time to secure the necessary financial resources for measures incorporated in the manifesto, Ozawa stepped in and became directly involved in the decision-making process.[113] He chided Hatoyama, saying, 'Some people have come to doubt the government's ability to exert political leadership in governance'.[114]

In relation to spending requests presented through the new petitions system, Ozawa's office screened thousands of budget requests gathered by the DPJ's local chapters across the nation, then he took the lead in deciding which ones should be shelved and which ones should be taken forward.[115] His absolute authority over petition management enabled him to suppress petitions from those (i.e. Diet members and prefectural party federations) he disliked[116] and, conversely, to direct patronage to his own and his supporters' constituencies.

Ozawa also used the budget process to expand the DPJ's support base.[117] As the sole person ultimately in charge of budget-related petitions, he had the power to urge local government leaders and industry organisations to switch their allegiance to the DPJ.[118] By early December 2009, his office had massed over 300 petitions, which were then prioritised in decision-making meetings in the secretary-general's office.[119] When Ozawa submitted the prioritised list to a meeting of Prime Minister Hatoyama, the cabinet and the DPJ's executive committee, it was called 'a collection of people's voices'.[120] Ozawa explained that the requests were from people across the country rather than from the party, and said that he hoped they would be 'reflected as much as possible in the budget'".[121] There was no doubt, however, that Ozawa ended up making the key decisions on which projects should proceed.[122] Hatoyama initially resisted Ozawa's requests, but in the end accepted most of them.[123]

Ozawa also acted as scrutiniser and prior coordinator in relation to spending requests from the bureaucracy in much the same way as the PARC divisions used to function during successive LDP administrations. In drawing up his priority list of spending programmes, Ozawa trimmed and pruned the extensive enumeration of requests for budgetary appropriations (*gaisan yōkyū*) from the ministries and agencies with a view to crafting a budget without bureaucratic interference.[124]

Ozawa then stepped in and partially displaced the role of the cabinet and the prime minister in relation to the budget. Hatoyama prevaricated about whether he should implement the DPJ's manifesto as he had promised, or maintain discipline over public spending.[125] The cabinet could not reach a consensus on the relative importance of particular items and which measures in the manifesto should be prioritised. Neither Finance Minister Fujii nor Deputy Prime Minister and NSU head Kan stepped into the breach to take the lead in building a cabinet consensus. Order was immediately imposed on this chaotic situation when Ozawa intervened and presented his priority list on 16 December 2009.[126] The Ozawa list became the basis for the budget by default. This had the effect of nullifying budget coordination efforts within the ministries and amongst cabinet ministers as a whole.[127] The 2010 budget was settled by a process of 'Ozawa arbitration [*Ozawa saitei*]'.[128] The scale of Ozawa's intervention was such that it spelled the end of any semblance of coordinated and centralised policy decision making in the cabinet on budget matters, as well as sidelining the NSU. Rather than a dual-power situation in which Ozawa shared equal power with Hatoyama, Ozawa's pivotal role once again confirmed that, in practice, power rested solely with him.[129]

Ozawa's priority spending list had several main features. First, it sought to address the problem of fiscal imbalance by modifying and cutting the DPJ's

146 *Old policies*

campaign promises on child allowances[130] and abolition of the provisional tax rate on gasoline and other road-related taxes respectively, whilst retaining other key elements such as free high school education, income subsidies for farmers and toll-free highways.[131] In other words, it set the priorities for the government's tax reform and other budget policies.[132]

Second, it was compiled on the basis of benefiting particular lobby groups.[133] In this respect, Ozawa's budget was a politicised document geared to the 2010 Upper House election. It sought to expand the DPJ's support base and to induce local government leaders and industry organisations to switch sides from the LDP to the DPJ.[134]

2 Public works allocations

Given his new powers, particularly over the petitions process, Ozawa exercised decisive influence over the public works budget. The DPJ's allocation plan, or *kashotsuke*, which showed how the public works budget was to be distributed around the country for particular construction projects, was drawn up by the Hatoyama administration on the basis of a draft public works budget prepared by the Ministry of Land, Infrastructure and Transport (MLIT) in November 2009. The base public works budget was then modified to reflect the petitions from across the country channelled through Ozawa's office.

When the media put the public works allocation plan under close scrutiny, they concluded that the government was gearing spending to the next Upper House election. More public works funding was allocated to prefectures on which the DPJ placed importance in the election.[135] Key election battlegrounds received the biggest 'political additions' (*seiji kasan*). One in particular – Tottori – was a traditional bastion of support for the LDP where LDP defector Tamura Kōtarō, recruited directly by Ozawa, was standing for the DPJ in the national PR constituency. Other prefectures that benefited were those where Ozawa aimed to win both prefectural constituency seats.[136]

3 Road building

MLIT Minister Maehara Seiji laid down the principle of freezing new construction work on road development in October 2009. In November, prefectural governments were notified that about 150 routes would be candidates for a budget freeze, with the focus on roads that could not be expected to be completed in under three years. In the end, however, only four out of the 200 roads listed for scrapping or major funding cuts ended up being completely abandoned.[137] Small budgetary sums were distributed to almost all routes.[138] As part of its function of centralising the receipt of petitions from all local government bodies, the Ozawa office demanded that funds be restored for these roads.

Ozawa also organised a special road works deal for Tottori, with a view to winning its prefectural constituency seat in the 2010 Upper House election. The carrot Ozawa dangled before voters was allocation of budget funds for the construction of the Sanin Motorway for which residents in both Tottori and Shimane had been angling. In Tottori's case, the budget had been stopped because of the completion of the high-quality Himeji-Tottori road in 2009. As a result, MLIT's budgetary request for roads supervised by the prefecture was 64–79 per cent of the level of the initial budget in the previous fiscal year. When the final budget was announced, however, Tottori received 92 per cent of the previous fiscal year's level. This ratio of budgetary restoration was the highest in the whole country.

According to DPJ Upper House member from Tottori, Kawakami Yoshihiro, Diet members from the DPJ and PNP formed a 'Road Network Promotion Diet Members League' immediately after the road construction budget request (*gaisan yōkyū*) was cut in November 2009. They decided to demand emphasis in budget distribution on nine prefectures – Tottori, Shimane, Yamagata, Fukui, Wakayama, Tokushima, Kōchi, Miyazaki and Ehime – by mobilising Diet members from those prefectures. Kawakami had an interview with Ozawa immediately after the league was set up, saying, 'The Sanin Motorway is necessary. If the budgetary appropriation remains at the requested level, the locals would definitely think they should have supported LDP (to obtain more budget)'.[139] Ozawa agreed to request the necessary funds as 'an important measure for the party'.[140]

4 Agricultural public works

Ozawa also exercised the 'voice of authority'[141] in allocating the budget for agricultural and rural infrastructure projects (so-called 'land improvement').[142] The MAFF initially calculated that a budget of ¥488.9 billion was necessary for these public works (which was inserted into their budget request, or *gaisan yōkyū*), but Ozawa had the final word on the issue. His authoritative remark was that 'we should reduce it by half', and so the appropriation was cut to ¥212.9 billion, which was less than half of the original request in the draft budget and a 63.1 per cent reduction compared with the previous year's appropriation of ¥577.2 billion.[143] The budget priority list from Ozawa included the following item: 'Halve the requested budget of ¥488.9 billion for land improvement, and use this money as a revenue source for the farm income compensation scheme, etc.'[144]

In reality, the land improvement budget fell victim to Ozawa's political goal of destroying the land improvement organisations as electoral support groups for the LDP by curtailing the LDP's ability to use these subsidies to obtain farmers' votes. Over a long period, the subsidies for land improvement had supported LDP candidates because the land improvement budget was directly linked to the construction of farmers' paddy fields, so it was easy to use these subsidies to mobilise farmers' votes.[145] Moreover, the Rural Development Bureau within the MAFF, called 'a ministry within a ministry', not only monopolised these works, but the bureau also distributed the land improvement budget. Traditionally two seats in the Upper House had been 'reserved seats' for Rural Development Bureau technical officials (*gikan*) 'Old Boys' (OBs), standing with the support of the National

148 *Old policies*

Federation of Land Improvement Industry Works Groups (Doseiren). In November 2009, Doseiren made the mistake of deciding to put up Nambu Akihiro, a former head of the MAFF's Kyūshū Agricultural Administration Bureau, as an LDP candidate in the 2010 Upper House election, which made Ozawa angry as it showed that these groups remained loyal to the LDP and thought the DPJ regime would not last long.[146] Ozawa reportedly declared, 'Their political attitude is bad. We cannot fund them in the budget'.[147] His aim was to drive a wedge between the LDP and the land improvement organisations in the 2010 Upper House election.[148]

Minister Akamatsu simply accepted Ozawa's instructions without question, halving the requested budget for land improvement works.[149] This prompted a visit from Nonaka, a former Doseiren chairman, to DPJ headquarters on 21 December 2009, where he requested an audience with Ozawa, which was denied. Nonaka said that the LDP candidates recommended by the land improvement groups would be re-examined and the LDP cancelled Nambu's official endorsement. In spite of Nonaka's capitulation, however, it was too late, and the agricultural public works budget was finalised in the cabinet on 25 December at ¥212.9 billion.[150] Ozawa did not object in principle to public funds being used for land improvement works, merely the LDP using these funds to garner support for its candidates. An added dimension to Ozawa's dispute with Nonaka was the record of historical enmity between the two.[151] As a former construction executive explained, 'Hiromu Nonaka was the big boss of agricultural public works. Cutting the budget in half was just a way to bring Nonaka to his knees and force the construction companies to come to Ozawa begging for work'.[152]

5 *The provisional tax rate on gasoline*

Ozawa was directly responsible for the government's postponement of its 2009 election pledge to abolish or reduce the provisional tax rate on gasoline as well as other road-related taxes in fiscal 2010. His budget intervention was pivotal in maintaining these levies, which generated ¥2.5 trillion annually in funds for central and local government public works programmes. Prime Minister Hatoyama initially said that the provisional tax rate on gasoline would be abandoned but changed his position on the issue as a result of pressure channelled through the Ozawa office.[153] Some reports suggested that Ozawa single-handedly persuaded the prime minister to scrap this campaign promise without Minister of Finance Fujii's agreement.[154] When the prime minister was about to make the decision to lower the tax rate, Ozawa telephoned him and pressed him not to, saying, 'You can't do that'.[155] Former LDP politician and one of the founders of the Sunrise Party of Japan (Tachiagare Nippon) in 2010, Yosano Kaoru, recounted:

> Ozawa visited the prime minister's office and requested that the tax rate be maintained as a 'request from the party'. Hatoyama then changed his mind saying 'the party's request is the people's voice' and obeyed Ozawa's request. I heard that the Ministry of Finance entreated Ozawa to keep the tax rate in

order to preserve a revenue resource, even though the Minister of Finance at the time Fujii said that the tax rate would be revoked.[156]

After going back on his promise in relation to the gasoline tax, Hatoyama was also quoted as saying, 'I will make sure that the public's voices are heard',[157] in a reference to the pressure from Ozawa that his government had sustained on the issue. The matter reportedly precipitated Fujii's sudden departure from the cabinet in January 2010:

> Fujii explained it as a health problem, but that was not the reality. One cause was strife between him and Ozawa…It was…decided to keep the gasoline tax based on 'Ozawa's decision'. Ozawa decided various matters by having direct discussions with various people in the Ministry of Finance, and Fujii thought strongly that he was forced to play the role of a 'clown'.[158]

Ozawa's intervention in the budget was the last straw for Fujii. Because he had played a key role in compiling the budget on the government side, his work was not only sidelined by Ozawa's interference but Fujii would have been in the position of having to defend the government's budget proposals to the Diet, proposals that had been effectively dictated by Ozawa.[159] This was an ironic turn of events given that in the past Fujii was appointed minister of finance in the Hosokawa cabinet in 1993 as a member of the RP and on Ozawa's say-so.

6 Highway tolls

Policymaking on the highway tolls issue showed how pressure from Ozawa could sabotage the cabinet-centred policymaking process, with Ozawa acting as veto player over government policy. The DPJ's election campaign promise to abolish highway tolls was abandoned after a phone call from Ozawa to Hatoyama.[160] Despite the insertion of 'toll-free highways' in the manifesto, Ozawa decided to withdraw the promise from applicability to all highways in Japan.[161] In December 2009, there had been a so-called 'request from the party', namely Ozawa, for the promotion of new highway construction. He was on record as wanting to use the surplus funds generated by road tolls as money for constructing new roads as an electoral ploy for the July 2010 Upper House poll.[162] He had expressed dissatisfaction that road construction was not progressing in regional areas. Such a policy wound back road administrative reforms under Koizumi, which were designed to halt rampant construction of highways for dubious economic benefit. When the DPJ was in opposition, it had criticised the LDP for constructing highways with taxpayer money funnelled to highway operators.[163]

In an about-face, however, Ozawa later directly challenged MLIT Minister Maehara's road toll plan announced on 9 April 2010, which was scheduled for introduction the following June, on the grounds that the new toll regime, which would mean a hike for some users such as truck drivers, would break the DPJ's election pledge to make highways toll-free. The Maehara plan had incorporated the party's (i.e. Ozawa's) earlier request for funding from highway tolls to be channelled to highway construction. It was due to divert about ¥1.4 trillion into road construction and maintenance from funds that had been allocated to expressway operators as money to finance toll discounts.[164] Maehara himself commented, 'The ministry drew up the plan because the DPJ requested that the ministry help build new highways…It is only natural that we need to finance such a plan with some of the money originally earmarked for highway toll discounts… It is contradictory to say that toll hikes are unacceptable after submitting such a request'.[165] He had earlier protested strongly against Ozawa's plan, saying that it 'would be incompatible with DPJ doctrine',[166] but had slowly come round, 'only to be turned into a defender of the plan by Ozawa's last-minute about-face'.[167]

The large number of signatures collected amongst the trucking industry in opposition to Maehara's plan was sufficient to induce Ozawa to change his mind on the issue, saying that 'voters could not understand the reasoning behind the hikes'.[168] He told a meeting of a DPJ prefectural branch in Kagoshima that there would be no way to explain the failure to make expressways toll-free to voters.[169] On this issue, as on so many others, Ozawa saw his role in policymaking as an extension of his responsibilities as the DPJ's chief electoral strategist.

Ozawa organised a meeting of cabinet members and party executives, which resulted in an agreement to review the plan. Watanabe Kōzō pointed out that it was Maehara who was the minister, and therefore he should have the final word on road toll policy.[170] He said, 'Maehara is in the government, so shouldn't his opinion come first?'[171] Ozawa's intervention, however, had undercut Maehara's ministerial authority. Maehara fought back, saying that as a general principle, policies were centralised in the government, so if they revised the new toll plan, they would be overturning this principle.[172] Ozawa retaliated by questioning Maehara's abilities, saying, 'This outcome occurred because he could not overcome the bureaucrats' resistance by persuading them'.[173] Ozawa later met with the chairman of the All-Japan Trucking Association (Zennihon Torakku Kyōkai) in the lead-up to the September 2010 DPJ leadership election, considering the truckers his own personal support group and expecting a reward for his defence of their interests.[174]

7 Postal reform

Minister of Postal Reform in the Hatoyama government Kamei Shizuka secured Ozawa's prior approval for the so-called Kamei-Haraguchi plan for postal reform before its public release in March 2010, suggesting that Ozawa's consent was needed for its advancement as the government plan. Ozawa naturally agreed to the plan because of the concessions made to postal interests, including doubling the maximum deposit in Japan Post savings banks. The proposal was geared to securing the support of the national organisation of commissioned postmasters in the July Upper House election.[175] In backing the Kamei plan, Ozawa sided with Kamei and SDP leader Fukushima against the prime minister, Deputy Prime Minister Kan and Minister of State for National Strategy Sengoku Yoshito in the confrontation over the government's postal policy.[176]

Ozawa later provided guarantees that the postal reform laws would pass the Diet prior to the July 2010 Upper House election. When addressing a meeting of 7,000 commissioned postmasters in Nagoya in May 2010, he promised that the postal reform bills would be passed in the Diet session due to end on 16 June. Kamei said in his greeting to the meeting that 'the secretary-general of the DPJ has promised the passage of the bills during this Diet session. As the minister in charge I am very much encouraged'.[177] At a press conference on the same day as his address, Ozawa claimed that Koizumi's 'fake reforms' had been damaging and needed to be fixed as soon as possible.[178]

Ozawa's treatment of Kamei was reflective of his broader strategy during the Hatoyama administration of going out of his way to consult with the DPJ's coalition partners – the PNP and SDP. He allowed great latitude to their leaders to participate in government policymaking and designed a system whereby the opinions and requests of the DPJ's coalition partners were incorporated into government policy. The privileged position that the PNP and SDP leaders occupied in the DPJ-led coalition was attributable to the importance Ozawa attached to maintaining a stable coalition in order to provide a firm basis from which to battle the LDP in the 2010 Upper House election.[179] For their part, the leaders of both coalition parties were well aware of Ozawa's influence and never failed to get clearance from him and gain his support prior to presenting their own policy proposals.

'Elections first' policy principles

Ozawa was well known for his 'elections first' approach to policymaking. He consistently gave top priority to elections,[180] ranking the needs of election campaigning over any other aspect of policies. He justified his approach by arguing a defence of the people's democratic right to vote in elections, asserting, 'The only time the people can exercise their sovereignty is when they vote. The media are ever ready to criticize us for going out of our way to win elections, but what on earth is wrong with that?'[181] In reality, his greed for power was based on the idea that he could do anything he wanted as long as he could win elections.[182] Unless his party won the election, it could not seize power, or pass legislation or the budget.[183]

After he brought his band of Liberals into the DPJ, he realised that if the newly merged party were to win government, it would need an electoral platform designed to appeal to a broad cross-section of voters. As Koizumi's electoral victory in the 2005 general election illustrated only too well, the DPJ's policy programme had to appeal to floating voters, particularly the expanding group of disaffected voters in the cities, which Ozawa had identified more than a decade earlier in *Blueprint* as a potential source of new-found party support. This group was dissatisfied with the traditional LDP model of narrowly targeted special-interest politics.[184] On the other hand, the DPJ also needed to attract former LDP voters and therefore find a way to win majorities in districts where the party was not strong.[185] Unseating the LDP also meant levering it out of its comfort zones in rural and regional electorates.

152   *Old policies*

Under Ozawa's leadership, the DPJ's 2007 and 2009 manifestos thus combined policies designed to appeal to unaffiliated urban voters with those designed specifically to threaten the LDP's voting base in traditional industries in rural areas of Japan. This explained the particular combination of policies on offer by the party: to broad sections of society, the DPJ offered child allowances, free high school education, pension guarantees and job-seeker assistance; to special interests and rural and regional voters, it offered direct income subsidies to those engaged in farming, forestry and fishing, elimination of highway tolls to reinvigorate local economies, cuts in taxes for SMEs, and a repeal of postal privatisation so that universal postal services across the country could be guaranteed; and to voters everywhere it offered abolition of the provisional tax rate on gasoline and no rise in the consumption tax. In this way, Ozawa's manifestos covered all segments of society. As electoral strategy, his approach proved highly effective. His 'proposed wealth redistribution captured the hearts and minds not only of rural voters, but also of city dwellers displeased at the fraying social safety net'.[186] It was a grand spending programme of gargantuan proportions.

During the Hatoyama administration, Ozawa's various policy interventions became an extension of his predominant role in crafting electoral strategy for the DPJ, in which catering to traditional special interests came to the fore. In particular, his prerogatives in policymaking seemed to be exercised in those areas that could be seen to have a direct impact on the DPJ's performance in the July 2010 Upper House poll. In its campaign pledges, Ozawa strongly advocated honouring the 2009 manifesto and openly objected to the dropping of any of the promises of fiscal largesse, such as paying child allowances in full and abolishing expressway tolls by fiscal 2011.[187] This was despite the fact that Ozawa himself had earlier switched positions on these key manifesto promises. His support for the full payment of child allowances at the promised level of ¥26,000 in 2011 contradicted his earlier suggestion that an income qualification should be introduced for the payment. When he had proposed that the DPJ should break its promise on child allowances and impose income limits on recipients, he had been overridden by Hatoyama. Then there were the issues of the provisional tax rate on gasoline and highway tolls. Ozawa had been instrumental in the Hatoyama administration's abandonment of its promise to abolish the gasoline tax along with other road-related taxes. The government's stance on highway tolls going into the election was similarly riddled with contradictions. On the one hand, it stood by its pledge to make expressways toll-free as a gesture to put more money into the hands of consumers in order to encourage spending. On the other, it continued to support a policy of effectively raising tolls in order to divert funding to highway construction. These key switches in policy were to secure more funding for old-style LDP public works. On balance, Ozawa was once again advocating a broad policy of government handouts in combination with specific benefits for particular sectors and interests.

Such profligacy for electoral purposes at a time when the budget was facing such a large deficit was textbook LDP behaviour. Ozawa was prepared to do anything to crush the LDP in the election and secure a stable majority for the

DPJ in the Upper House, calling it the 'final battle'. Paradoxically, in order to defeat the LDP, the DPJ had to become more like the LDP. Ozawa's shallow electoral opportunism had the effect of slowly turning 'the DPJ into a replica of the LDP'.[188]

However, Ozawa's election campaign strategy was more than just a policy platform to win votes. It was also an anti-LDP organisational strategy, which sought to undermine the longstanding political connection between the LDP and its traditional support groups. The DPJ's Policy Statement, 'Index 2009', for example, which was the original basis of its 2009 election manifesto, took direct aim at the agricultural cooperatives, traditionally a bastion of support for the LDP. The statement included 'reform of JA and others...[in order to] secure the political neutrality of JA and others, and to strive for creating environments in which active establishment of other agricultural organisations may take place'.[189] The clause was later removed from the election manifesto as unnecessarily provocative of JA.[190] Instead, Ozawa settled for the much more effective approach 'joining hands with the farmers directly'[191] by offering them direct income subsidies.

The DPJ also established their own organisation for connecting with farmers, called the Food and Agriculture Revitalisation Council (Shokuryō to Nōgyō Kasseika Kyōgikai), with a view to forming a regional organisation to communicate and diffuse DPJ agricultural policies. Some even envisaged that it might grow up to be 'a second JA'. Ozawa continued to maintain the squeeze on JA by virtually excluding it from access to government. He was very close to MAFF Minister Akamatsu and imposed a policy of isolating it. When the head of National Central Union of Agricultural Cooperatives (Zenkoku Nōgyō Kyōdō Kumiai Chūōkai, or JA-Zenchū) tried to present a petition to Akamatsu and MAFF Senior Vice-Minister Yamada Masahiko, he was denied access and had to accept a meeting with a lower-ranking party functionary – Deputy Secretary-General Hosono Gōshi – who simply stated that he acknowledged their case.[192] JA reforms were also on the agenda for working group talks by the Government Revitalisation Unit, or GRU (Gyōsei Sasshin Kaigi), including tighter inspection of JA's financial businesses and a review of its anti-trust exemption in order to break its economic power. Furthermore, Akamatsu issued an order for them to reform.

By the time of the 2010 Upper House election, JA's political arm, the National Federation of Farmers' Agricultural Policy Campaign Organisations (Zenkoku Nōgyōsha Nōsei Undō Soshiki Renmei, or Zenkoku Nōseiren), had dropped its traditional near-universal support for LDP candidates. Further, the DPJ picked a former chief of JA's youth group, Fujiki Shinya, to stand in the PR segment of the 2010 Upper House election alongside another ex-JA youth group chairman standing for the LDP (Monden Eiji), whom Zenkoku Nōseiren refused to recommend. Fujiki's candidacy signified that Ozawa was prepared to work through JA to secure the farm vote for the DPJ.

Ozawa's organisational strategy in the election targeted not only farmers but also a broad network of special interests such as the heads of post offices, doctors, dentists, truck drivers and small business owners. To these interests, represented by organised pressure groups, he primarily looked for votes. He was not aiming to reduce the power of vested interests that had previously underpinned the LDP but to unwind the connections between the LDP and its support groups with a combination of carrots and sticks.

Another of Ozawa's talents was to understand exactly what kind of benefit each organisation was seeking. For example, he made a direct appeal to Zentoku with his reassurance to members in May 2010 that he would guarantee passage of the postal reform bills in the current Diet session, saying, 'I hope you will continue to support us as usual'.[193] His aim was to pull the estimated 400,000 postal votes in the Upper House election. Ozawa was desperate enough for these votes also to try to engineer a merger of the PNP with the DPJ in early May in talks with Kamei. Kamei rejected the idea, instead proposing electoral cooperation between his party and the DPJ. Immediately after the talks, executives of the DPJ election committee passed to PNP executives a list of requests for election support consisting of 61 people's names. In a press conference on 23 May, the president of Zentoku, Tsuge, indicated support for candidates who were recommended by the PNP.[194] In this way, Zentoku's support for DPJ candidates constituted a 'return' for the hoped-for passage of the bill for postal reform during the current Diet session.[195]

In March 2010, Ozawa also met with the chairman of the Japan Chamber of Commerce and Industry (Nihon Shōkō Kaigisho), Okamura Tadashi, in order to show that the DPJ was sensitive to the interests of SMEs prior to the Upper House election. This was the first official meeting that Ozawa had had with a leader of one of Japan's three major business lobbies, the others being Keidanren and the Japan Association of Corporate Executives, or JACE (Keizai Dōyūkai). At the meeting, Okamura handed Ozawa a list of requests relating to an economic growth strategy for Japan. Ozawa said, 'I understand your requests…We need to make sure that we deal with deflation'.[196] Ozawa was hoping to improve his party's relations with local chambers of commerce and industry right across the nation, given their significance as a major source of votes amongst small business owners.[197]

The Japan Medical Association, or JMA (Nihon Ishikai), the Japan Dental Association and the All-Japan Trucking Association were also brought into the fold in a move devised by Ozawa to poach them from the LDP. The JMA found itself in a similar transitional position to JA – 'escaping from' (*datsu*) the LDP – except that it was even further along the road towards realigning with the DPJ.

In fact, Ozawa was prepared to strike deals with any major interest group in order to expand the DPJ's vote. A secret meeting took place between Ozawa and the former president of Sōka Gakkai, Akiya Einosuke, in February 2010.[198] Speculation swirled about Ozawa's motives, including his calculation that both his and Hatoyama's money-politics scandals would weaken the DPJ in the Upper House poll and so the DPJ might need to govern in coalition, possibly with the New Kōmeitō. At worst, Ozawa might persuade the New Kōmeitō leadership to stop supporting the LDP in Upper House constituencies. As Nonoyama explained:

The DPJ has a plan to put two candidates up in two-seat electoral districts where they will be competing. Ozawa understands that it is not easy to secure two seats, but his idea is that 'when one candidate is supported by the Japanese Trade Union Confederation and the other has a connection with conservative businesses and Sōka Gakkai, the party gains strength and the LDP loses strength'…Of course, if the DPJ cannot secure a majority in the election, it also means the 'insurance' of a new alliance partner.[199]

The division of support amongst organisations certainly made sense at a time when the two-candidate strategy was potentially less viable because of the DPJ's declining poll ratings.[200]

As for Rengō itself, the DPJ's largest organised support group with some 6.8 million members from both public and private sector unions, it did not see eye to eye with Ozawa from time to time. However, Ozawa and Rengō Chairman Takagi Tsuyoshi patched up relations prior to the 2007 elections, and indeed worked hand-in-hand to unite local groups behind the DPJ, which contributed greatly to the party's victory in those elections.[201] Ozawa put a lot of effort into rebuilding the pipeline to Rengō, travelling all over the country to drink with labour union executives.[202] The restored relationship also contributed greatly to the DPJ's electoral victory in 2009. Rengō again featured in Ozawa's 2010 Upper House election strategy because of his promotion of dual DPJ candidacies in some multi-seat prefectural constituencies. He had to do his best to ensure that Rengō played its part in directing votes to specific DPJ candidates in order to maximise the chances of both DPJ contestants winning a seat.

Ultimately, Ozawa's elections-first approach had a divisive and destructive impact on the DPJ. Nowhere was this negative influence more apparent than in the 2010 DPJ leadership contest and the dispute over raising the consumption tax, and to a lesser extent the TPP issue, between Ozawa on the one hand, and the Kan and Noda administrations on the other.

Ozawa's policies in the 2010 DPJ leadership contest

In the contest for leadership of the party in September 2010, the axis of policy confrontation between Ozawa and Kan was essentially whether or not to implement the DPJ's 2009 manifesto in full.[203] At its core, however, the dispute was about government spending.

What Ozawa advocated differed little from his strategy of extending fiscal largesse to a broad cross-section of voting blocs, which he regarded as the key to the DPJ's 2007 and 2009 election victories. He committed himself to fulfilling the promises the party had made when it became government.[204] Kan, on the other hand, was committed to the DPJ's manifesto only if the promises contained therein could be implemented one by one so as to ensure sufficient funding.[205]

Ozawa rationalised his commitment to implementing the 2009 manifesto on the grounds that it was a 'promise to the people'.[206] He proposed to launch the new age pension scheme of ¥70,000 per month and increase the child allowance to ¥26,000 in 2012 (after a rise to ¥20,000 in 2011). These promises were considerably more generous compared with Kan's.[207] The contrast between Ozawa and the cautious and fiscally prudent Kan could not have been greater. The prime minister appeared to share the concerns of many in the DPJ that the 2009 manifesto was an irresponsible *baramaki* document not backed up by available revenue. Kan argued that the future of politics was predicated on fiscal health, hence his emphasis on growth and a budget austerity line, like Koizumi's structural reforms. Viewed in these terms, the options in the leadership contest were between support and opposition to Koizumi's reforms.[208] Others painted the dispute in terms of an efficient society achieved mainly by the market and competition versus a fair society achieved by strengthening regulations on the market.[209]

Ozawa proposed to raise the necessary funds for his spending programmes by completely revamping the government's ¥207 trillion budget, exercising political leadership and cutting wasteful spending. He was enthusiastic about integrating public pension programmes into a uniform system and vowed to abolish all unnecessary projects and programmes without seeking a rise in the consumption tax. He saw the latter as necessary only *in extremis* – he would first make serious efforts to cut wasteful spending and streamline government administration, and only then raise the consumption tax if there were a shortage of funds. While gesturing to fiscal prudence by promising to eliminate government waste, he took no responsibility for the fact that the Hatoyama government had not made much progress in reducing government spending.[210]

Kan said that he would investigate wholesale reform of the taxation system, including the consumption tax, as part of an effort to secure funding for social security over the long term. He advocated the need for a debate on tax and regulatory reform, saying that job creation in new business areas, rather than reliance on public spending were the key ingredients in any revival policy for the Japanese economy. In these respects, Kan's position was much closer to the neo-liberal template. His top priority was the generation of jobs.

As part of its tax reform agenda, the Kan government was looking at lowering the corporate tax rate and offering tax breaks to companies to boost employment, with the aim of generating more jobs in line with its growth strategy. Ozawa, on the other hand, had his own view on tax, disagreeing with business opinion that an effective corporate tax rate of 40 per cent was onerous, and therefore taking issue with the Kan government's proposal. In addition to maintaining the consumption tax at the existing rate of 5 per cent for the rest of the DPJ's four-year term (as stated in the DPJ's manifesto), Ozawa mooted the possibility of reductions in income and property taxes.[211]

On agriculture, Ozawa revealed strong support for the sector, meeting with MAFF Minister Yamada Masahiko and exchanging opinions about agriculture in general. Ozawa said, 'agriculture is agriculture and fisheries are fisheries; we have to protect them; we have to create a system that protects them'.[212] Yamada recounted that he had told Ozawa 'give it your best shot…[adding] I've been working with Ozawa since our days in the Liberal Party and so I don't have to put my thoughts into words. He already understands and I also understand Ozawa's thoughts'.[213]

Ozawa's biggest support-seeking ploy in regional areas, however, was to offer old LDP-style pork-barrel benefits with promises to revive the economy through a fiscal injection into public works, which directly challenged the DPJ manifesto's 'from concrete to people' slogan. His solution to Japan's economic woes was to use orthodox pump-priming methods to bring the economy back to life by pouring funds for public works projects into local areas. He tried to make an old-fashioned, pork-barrel *baramaki* approach look respectable as a macro-economic management strategy that focused on short-term fiscal stimulus. His approach also served his own political interests in general contractor-based politics.

Another question Ozawa's plan raised was whether feeding public works projects to the construction industry had ever sufficiently revived the economy. This form of stimulus had been discredited by previous LDP governments when package after package failed to deliver the promise of sustained economic growth during the 1990s and in 2008–09 following the global financial crisis. Moreover, year after year of general contractor-based politics in the 1970s, 1980s and 1990s had contributed greatly to Japan's enormous public debt, with its threat to long-term growth and stability.

To pay for his proposed spending plans, Ozawa promised to use the full ¥2 trillion in reserve funds immediately, saying, 'Today's recession is very severe so this ¥2 trillion in reserves should be immediately implemented'.[214] Any additional government bonds would be interest-free and non-taxable (with inheritance tax exemption), with even more funds raised by the securitisation of government property.[215] Ozawa said, 'I am thinking of a mechanism to allow prefectural governments to build expressways, as well as using zero-interest bonds to cover the cost'.[216]

In the lead-up to the 14 September poll, Ozawa went campaigning in regional areas, saying that there was a need to mobilise fiscal resources. He visited Utsonomiya City, Tochigi Prefecture, and disparaged Kan in his speech, saying:

> Kan said that there are no funds. That's why he said that we had to put up the consumption tax rate during the Upper House election and it came out of the blue. Isn't that strange? That's too ridiculous. He betrayed the people and that's why the people said 'No' to him. So he got a hiding in the election. As a stimulus measure, we have included ¥2 trillion in reserves in this year's budget, but what the Kan cabinet is saying is that they want to spend half that (¥920 billion). Why won't they use the ¥2 trillion at once? I find it very strange. There's going to be a need for further mobilisation of fiscal resources and this can't be helped. This is the only way we can protect the people's lives.[217]

Those to whom Ozawa appealed were construction company bosses in regional areas who saw him as their saviour in the midst of lean times. One said, 'At a time like this, you don't need the clean guys, you need the guys who can get things done...Ozawa has excelled at getting public works in the countryside. He knows how much rural Japan needs reviving. Most people in the construction industry know he will provide the adrenalin injection quickly'.[218] Ozawa's proposals suggested that he still believed in concrete over people.

Another plan Ozawa advanced was to generate funds for government spending by converting subsidies to local governments into block grants,[219] revisiting his fiscal decentralisation concept and the DPJ's 2009 election manifesto commitment. The central government would put these grants into the hands of local governments instead of allocating them as central government subsidies with strings attached. This would transfer power to local governments at the same time as cutting government expenditure. Local government spokespersons were claiming that they could offer more services by using just 70 per cent of the money they were currently receiving as state subsidies if they could decide themselves where to allocate the money.[220] However, what Ozawa failed to acknowledge was the difficulty of reducing these subsidies by much because such a large proportion of the money transferred to local governments would be taken up with fixed expenditures for health care and social security such as welfare benefits and nursing services, and compulsory education costs, which could not be readily cut, and so the amounts that local governments could freely use would be limited.[221] Ozawa's proposal would not generate sufficient savings unless these mandatory outlays were slashed.[222] It thus made no sense to use a plan to integrate state subsidies into no-strings grants, which was designed to increase the amount that local governments could spend at their own discretion, into a scheme to raise new funds.[223] The DPJ's own experience in formulating the fiscal 2010 budget left little doubt that changing the system of budget allocations or eliminating wasteful spending alone would not generate sufficient funds to finance all its policy proposals.[224]

Another criticism of Ozawa's idea for no-strings-attached block grants to local governments came from Masuda Hiroya, the former Ozawa ally who was elected governor of Iwate Prefecture in 1995 and who later became an LDP cabinet minister after resigning from his gubernatorial position in 2007. Masuda said that Ozawa's 'proposal to provide lump sum money to prefectures, ostensibly with no strings attached, would make project choices subject to covert political connections. "His mind-set is still that from the years of the LDP rule...By having the central government control the money, Ozawa is trying to exert his influence over heads of local governments, as well as local assemblies"'.[225] Masuda had detected the political self-interest embedded in Ozawa's proposal to transfer more power to local governments to fund public works that he had finessed the art of influencing.

Ozawa, however, went on the attack against the inflexibility of the Kan administration's proposed 10 per cent cut in expenditures across the board (excluding social security expenses) in the 2011 budget, saying that there would be no uniform cut under an Ozawa administration. There would be flexible allocation based on need. On the day the election contest was launched, he said, 'We have to make a system where the politicians can make decisions on policies and the budget through their own responsibility'.[226] He declared that an across-the-board cut showed no advancement from the past, arguing, 'It's been decided that there will be an across-the-board ceiling of 10 per cent. This is the way they did it under the LDP and we will only get the same results. I'm concerned that nothing has changed and they're still doing it in the same old way'.[227]

In a later stumping speech, he asserted that the prime minister must decide which specific budgetary items to cut, showing great resolve and political responsibility.[228] This was clearly the role he envisaged for himself. He visited Kochi Prefecture to gain the support of local DPJ assembly members, party members and supporters. He said, 'If the prime minister says I want to do things this way, then nothing is impossible. But why can't he do it in reality? If I am allowed to be in that position with everyone's support then I will keep my promises, putting my political career and in a sense putting my own life on the line'.[229] He continued to hammer the point that the DPJ was merely following the LDP's methodology of budget compilation. His idea was to permit the prime minister to exercise the right of patronage over all discretionary spending in the entire budget, thus allowing wide scope for government spending for political purposes rather than for economic effect.

Ozawa also linked his diatribe against uniform budget cuts to the notion of excessive bureaucratic power. He accused Kan of following a typical MOF budgetary approach in pressing his ministers to cut their 2011 policy-related budget requests by a minimum of 10 per cent, rather than asserting political leadership over policymaking.[230] He declared, 'Kasumigaseki decides everything and administration and budget distribution is done following their menu. Unless we change this system with political leadership, we can't secure fiscal resources. We need to put in all efforts to get rid of waste and make effective use of the people's taxes. The consumption tax will come later'.[231] These comments tied the issue of public spending and budget compilation to the question of leadership by politicians. Ozawa affirmed, 'We must build a system in Japan under which politicians can be responsible for making policies and deciding on budgets by themselves'.[232] In this way, he was attacking the budget-making role of the Budget Bureau in the MOF.[233] As for the bureaucracy itself, Kan promised to cut the cost of the national bureaucracy by 20 per cent and grant basic labour rights to public servants (which Ozawa was also prepared to grant), but he also wanted to reduce their number and convert some into local public servants. Ozawa just repeated his mantra 'don't entrust it to the bureaucracy; politicians should make decisions and implement these decisions'.[234]

On the crucial issue of political funding for politicians, Kan suggested banning companies and groups from donating funds to political groups, and making the allocation of party funds transparent. Ozawa, on the other hand, only committed himself to a vague promise of 'making political funds public' (which, to a large extent, they already were).

Ozawa's policy offerings in the leadership race were also influenced by the organisational backing that he sought. He automatically looked for support from the groups that backed the DPJ such as Rengō, but he once again hooked up

160 *Old policies*

with the head of Zentoku with whom he had built channels for electoral cooperation, committing himself to seeking early passage of the bill to scale back postal privatisation if he became prime minister.[235] In another gesture seeking support in exchange for policy favours, he met with Nakanishi Eiichirō, chairman of the All-Japan Trucking Association. It was only one of eight support groups that Ozawa visited in one day during the leadership campaign.

Ozawa went out of his way to demonstrate to first-term DPJ politicians that he had the support of key organisations. A dinner was organised for a group of first-term Diet members to meet the Zentoku chairman who told them, 'I respect Mr. Ozawa most. I will support the DPJ with all my strength after the leadership election as well'.[236] JMA Chairman Haranaka Katsuyuki also held an informal meeting with first-term lawmakers.

In the end, Ozawa's tactics all came to nought. Despite his mobilisation of an array of political connections and the offer of policy benefits to special interests in addition to the populist appeals that Ozawa had made to broader sections of the public under the slogan of 'putting people's lives first' (*kokumin no seikatsu ga daiichi*), it was Kan, not Ozawa, who claimed victory in the leadership election.

Opposing the Kan and Noda administrations' signature policies

Nowhere was Ozawa's retreat from economic reform more evident than in his tax and trade policies under the Kan and Noda administrations.

The consumption tax

During the 2010 Upper House election campaign, Ozawa had openly campaigned against Prime Minister Kan's proposal to increase the consumption tax and even organised the endorsement and election campaigns of candidates who opposed the consumption tax, such as Kawakami Mitsue in Kyoto Prefecture. This angered a number of Diet members from Kyoto as well as members of the Kyoto branch of the DPJ. The election contest in Kyoto became a proxy war between pro- and anti-Ozawa groups based on the consumption tax issue.[237]

Ozawa, on the other hand, condemned the prime minister for breaking promises to the people.[238] He had clearly forgotten that as DPJ secretary-general, he had pushed the Hatoyama government into retaining the provisional tax on gasoline in the first blatant example of a broken manifesto promise. DPJ Election Campaign Committee Chairman Azumi Jun observed at a press conference, '[Ozawa] made changes to the manifesto through discussion while he was serving as secretary-general. Perhaps he has suffered a slight loss of memory'.[239] Moreover, a source close to Ozawa revealed that he fully intended to change his policy stance on the consumption tax issue if the party achieved a resounding victory in the Upper House election, in order to put public finances back onto a sound footing and take 'all the blame for the policy about-face'.[240] After all, he had already altered his stance on a consumption tax increase because he prioritised politics over policies.[241]

Secretary-General Edano's response to Ozawa's criticism of Prime Minister Kan on the consumption tax rise was to call it 'irresponsible populism'.[242] Ozawa's complaints about Kan's proposal, however, paled into insignificance compared with the campaign he ran against Prime Minister Noda's signature policy goal of increasing the consumption tax increase to 10 per cent by 2015.[243] Ozawa again charged that the prime minister had broken a key promise that the DPJ made in the 2009 election not to raise the consumption tax during the party's first term of office. In a 2012 New Year interview, he stated:

> If [the DPJ's politicians] keep following the bureaucrats' instructions and do not work on reforming the state's governing structure, they will never be able to find fund sources to realise policies that 'put the people's lives first', which is the promise that we made to the people in our manifesto. If they keep doing what the LDP administration has been doing, there will be no excess money. Then, they will come to the point where they have to increase taxes because they can't find any fund sources. However, the people will not allow us simply to increase the consumption tax rate when we haven't carried out any institutional reforms in the four years since the last general election. That is why I am opposed.[244]

In an online programme in February, he 'declared, "I oppose tax hikes without drastic reforms"',[245] in an attempt to paint himself as the grand reformer of yore. He added, 'We have done very little in administrative, financial, and political reform. To ask for a consumption tax increase without having accomplished that would be a betrayal of the public. So I cannot support it'.[246] He continued the same line of reasoning in a newspaper interview, saying, 'the DPJ took the reins of government by promising voters that it would eliminate the wasteful use of tax money by drastically reforming the political and administrative systems, including the governing system. If we raise the consumption tax without making such efforts, we won't be able to obtain support from the public'.[247] In his view, the 'grand reforms for changing the "ruling system" had not yet started, the vision for pension reforms had been forgotten, current reform plans could not be considered "integrated reform" and Japan had yet not recovered from the Great East Japan Earthquake'.[248] In these circumstances, 'Voting for a consumption tax hike…before anything else was unacceptable'.[249]

Although Ozawa claimed that he was not opposed to discussing the consumption tax per se, it was a matter of government priorities – in other words, not hiking the tax before major reforms, improvements in social security and economic rebirth. He offered the standard economic objections to a hike at the time: a slow economy, a high level of deflation, etc. Raising the consumption tax under these circumstances 'would cool consumption and directly hit the lives of the vulnerable, especially midsize and small companies and those in the agriculture, forestry and fisheries industries'.[250] He wanted to increase spending on various restoration and revival projects, calling it a 'growth strategy' that would facilitate fiscal reconstruction down the track. He continued to campaign unremittingly both inside and outside the DPJ against Noda's proposed consumption tax rise, using it as an instrument around which to galvanise his followers.[251]

His more comprehensive blueprint for Japan's economic revival appeared in Shinseiken's policy vision. In it, he proposed massive additional government spending (¥20 trillion a year for five years), consisting mainly of public investment in infrastructure such as water supply and sewerage systems, disaster prevention and mitigation, and renewing the domestic power distribution grid and medical facilities. Funding sources would centre once again on 'hidden treasure' funds and the sale of 'Japan economic restoration bonds', together with reorganisation of the budget through decentralisation and the use of comprehensive special zones.[252] The money would not come from raising the consumption tax.

Trade policy

Another important about-turn was Ozawa's adoption of a more equivocal stance on trade liberalisation. Despite his long-standing avowal of the need for trade reform as an economic liberalisation measure and his advocacy of new FTAs with direct farm income subsidies providing support for farmers facing a more competitive market, he gradually de-emphasised the liberalisation half of this policy. When Prime Minister Kan embraced a pro-active policy on signing FTAs, those close to Ozawa who had agricultural connections saw the income support programme solely as a protective measure and voiced their differences with the administration's 'aggressive policy'[253] on trade liberalisation.

Much of Ozawa's increasing opposition to Kan's trade policy was politically motivated. Ozawa and his group were opposed to everything the Kan government did on principle.[254] They saw the prime minister's trade policy stance as a ready target for their campaign to undercut the government. This was the political context in which the Ozawa group, which had initially been an opening-of-the-country faction, became protectionist.[255] When Prime Minister Kan raised the possibility of examining Japan's participation in the TPP, the Ozawa faction immediately joined the anti-TPP camp[256] and continued their anti-TPP campaign under the Noda administration.[257] Ozawa himself adopted a cautionary stance, which aligned him squarely with the so-called 'cautious' group in the DPJ, which led the opposition to the TPP from within the ruling party and to which many in his group belonged.

Ozawa found a number of hooks on which he could side with the anti-TPP group. For example, although a free trade advocate, he questioned the regional focus of the TPP in contrast to the superior global scope of the WTO.[258] He also supported the idea of a larger multilateral trade liberalisation framework that included China.[259] As one of his group explained, 'Economic partnerships comprising a limited number of countries will divide the world economy into blocs and may cause confrontations among blocs, like those around the time of World War II'.[260] Ozawa further qualified his pro-trade stance with the view that 'we should not sign up [to the TPP] without standing up for our own interests',[261] particularly vis-à-vis the United States.[262] He also made a plea for supporting affected industries, arguing:

> Currently, [the public] is talking only about agriculture, but the TPP includes not only agriculture but also finance, services and everything else. So if the government does not do anything to prepare the domestic system and opens [Japan], there will be chaos. All industries would be seriously damaged. So I don't think we should sign up to the TPP without defending our interests or considering the full gamut [of its implications].[263]

The point that he began to drive home more than ever was the need for safety nets, professing agreement with the fundamental direction of trade liberalisation but arguing that the government should establish safety nets first.[264] According to Ishikawa, Ozawa was concerned that, 'Unlimited free trade will lead to a world where the weak fall prey to the strong, both domestically and multilaterally',[265] a view that reflected strong anti-market thinking. When asked whether individual farm household income support should be a safety net, Ozawa agreed, saying that the same argument was also applicable to fisheries and even normal salaried workers to protect them against unemployment and part-time employment, which had already resulted from deregulation. He argued that the government should establish the necessary safety nets first, then liberalise trade.[266] His approach revealed how far he had left behind the economic reform agenda that he had espoused more than ten years earlier.

Conclusion

Between *Blueprint* and the 2009 Hatoyama administration, Ozawa changed his economic policy goals in key areas, shifting from a principled economic reform stance to sheer political expediency. In *Blueprint*, Ozawa espoused a progressive, neo-liberal, market-orientated perspective, arguing for the need to implement a very broad range of economic reforms. At the time, these were 'new' policies that predated Koizumi by nearly ten years. However, Ozawa's radical shift on economic policy over the years showed how far he had moved away from a neo-liberal agenda.

Most stark is the way in which Ozawa ditched neo-liberal reforms during and after the Koizumi administration, when he sensed which policy space might maximise his own and the DPJ's chances of coming to power. His attachment to market principles retreated because political mileage could be made out of an anti-Koizumi agenda. By the time of the Hatoyama administration, Ozawa was trying to show how much he had 'converted' to social democratic principles, having abandoned the free-market model and his 'small government' LP principles. What he ended up with was a combination of policies to improve social welfare (so-called 'people-first' policies) and 'old' policies offering selective benefits to special interests that used to support the LDP (see Table 1.1). His big-spending 'worry about the budget and how to pay for it later' approach[267] included very generous promises for public works spending redolent of the heyday of the Tanaka-Takeshita faction despite the DPJ's much proclaimed 'from concrete to people' slogan.

Under Ozawa's leadership the DPJ became more and more like the LDP with its predominance of *baramaki* policies offering broad-spectrum handouts to a range of interests including traditional LDP voting blocs. His direct intervention in the economic policymaking process – with respect to the 2010 budget, including the public works budget, the provisional tax rate on gasoline, highway tolls and postal reform – were typical pork-barrel gestures designed to support short-term political and electoral goals, including undermining the LDP in the 2010 Upper House election.

When given his big chance to act as an economic reformer during the Hatoyama administration, Ozawa reduced economic policy to mere political gestures. Across a range of sectors, his policy interventions demonstrated no consistent economic policy approach, let alone economic doctrine, neo-liberal or otherwise. Government economic policy was merely a tool of political and electoral strategy designed to consolidate not only the DPJ's position in the Diet but also his own position of political pre-eminence.

Even Ozawa's 'reform' of the petitions process turned out to be a gesture more to self-interest than to restructuring the political process to produce more accountable government led by the cabinet. Ozawa himself took over the functions of the *zoku* both in relation to the party's policymaking and in dealing with special interest claimants such as local politicians and the leaders of interest groups seeking policy benefits through the petitions process. Whilst preaching the principle of centralising policymaking power to the cabinet, he shamelessly intervened in any policy area that interested him. Even after the Great Eastern Japan Earthquake, what reportedly concerned him the most, given his position on the 'outer' in the Kan administration, was the possibility that all the contracts for reconstruction in Iwate, one of the hardest hit prefectures, would be let without his exercising any influence over them and the huge amount of government spending they would involve.[268]

In habitually reverting to shallow, short-term, politically strategic policy goals, Ozawa's days as an economic and social reformer appeared to be well behind him. Indeed, Ozawa-led opposition to Koizumi-style neo-liberal reforms remained a potential pivot of party realignment involving the Ozawa group and an intra-party group in the LDP in 2010 and 2011. At this time, Ozawa, discontented with his lot in the DPJ and with the '*datsu* Ozawa'[269] course set by the Kan administration,[270] was searching for political options, including leading a realignment of political forces. He retained his anti-economic reform standpoint under the Noda administration when his group campaigned in an open and hostile fashion against both the TPP and consumption tax rise.

Ozawa's policy reversals were symptomatic of his subordination of policies to political ends, which explained the marked inconsistencies and contradictions in his policy advocacy over time. For Ozawa the political situation always came first; it was more important than policies.[271] His former secretary, Takahashi

Yoshinobu, declared, 'We have had enough of Ozawa Ichirō who uses policies as cards that he can play in political situations'.[272] Ozawa did not adopt a uniform ideological standpoint on economic policy because he was prepared to do deals with anyone if it suited his larger goal of building and exercising power. As a result, his policy convictions appeared shallow, transient and malleable, depending on the political circumstances of the moment. What always mattered more to Ozawa was how power was wielded rather than what it was wielded for. Policy principles were a means to an end and could be changed depending on the political situation. Although Ozawa reiterated the importance of 'regime change' in 2009, critics seriously wondered whether he had any vision for what was to follow once 'regime change' had been achieved.[273] Certainly, it did not become clear as the Hatoyama government unfolded.

The only principle that remained consistent in Ozawa's thinking was his desire to use policy measures, including economic policies, for political purposes. Policies were expendable – mere tools of his political calculations. As a result, while laying out various policy principles from time to time, he never hesitated to politicise economic policy in order to enhance prospects for winning elections and thus exploit his power over the distribution of policy benefits to key interests and groups. Nor did he hesitate to use policies as political weapons against his enemies, with his anti-consumption tax hike stance against Kan and Noda being clear examples. As Fudesaka put it, 'if Ozawa's rival says that something is "black", Ozawa says it is "white". If his rival advocates a "tax hike", he says "eliminate wasteful spending". That is all'.[274]

In both the key elections that Ozawa fought in 2010 – the Upper House election in July and the DPJ leadership election in September – he preached the virtues of honouring manifesto promises, whilst his own record of policy intervention during the Hatoyama administration showed that he himself was picking and choosing which pledges he would observe. Similarly, his spending proposals directly challenged any notion of 'from concrete to people'. Some might call these revisions and reversals a form of policy flexibility in line with the changing times. Others might argue that Ozawa's remarkable degree of policy flexibility meant that he never displayed a consistent attachment to any particular policy goal, in contrast to a politician like Koizumi, for example, whose unchanging stance on postal privatisation reflected the degree of his unwavering commitment to a particular reform.

As for political structural reform, another avowed Ozawa goal, the main problem was that the role Ozawa chose for himself in the Hatoyama administration subverted many of the reforms that he had previously advocated.[275] Indeed, the way in which he involved himself in economic policymaking showed how far he had departed from his original model of political system reform. In some areas, Ozawa took over policy leadership from the prime minister and encroached on the functions of cabinet. His constant interventions as a party official on matters of government policy demonstrated that the principle of centralised cabinet decision making was effectively a dead letter. Ozawa successfully installed a system of policymaking that enabled him to exert great personal influence.

In other respects, particularly during the Kan and Noda administrations, Ozawa's political reform vision seemed no longer to be part of a constructive agenda for change, simply an instrument of destructive adversarial politics, or worse, a degeneration into mere banality. This put him at odds with others in his own party, such as Sengoku, Noda and Kan, who were aiming to achieve politics centring on policies, but who were constantly caught up in political strife focussing on Ozawa. 'Putting the people's lives first', the rather meaningless slogan that Ozawa used to attack Noda's plan to increase the consumption tax, and which became the banner under which he formed two new parties to oppose the DPJ, was nothing more than a populist slogan to justify his rebellion using policy arguments.[276] Similarly, references to 'the people' and 'democracy', which regularly popped up in his tired rhetoric about the shortcomings of the political system, were simply terms vague enough to mean anything, but which were, once again, symbolic of Ozawa's populist appeals.

Ozawa condemned the DPJ for not being true to the Ozawa vision in an interview with the *Wall Street Journal* in May 2011, saying, 'The path the DPJ took in reality was different from the path I had in mind...my ultimate vision hasn't changed despite the gap between the reality and the image I had in mind. I want to establish parliamentary democracy in Japan. This goal of mine has not changed at all'.[277] In fact, it was primarily Ozawa himself who compromised parliamentary democracy under the Hatoyama administration, subordinating both the party and the government to his power in the fashion of a dictatorial leader. Being an advocate of reform did not necessarily make him a democrat. As Kaieda sarcastically quipped, 'Even Hitler advocated reform'.[278]

Notes

1. Futami, 'Naze, imadoki Ozawa Ichirō ka', www.the-journal.jp/contents/futami/2012/11/post_44.html.
2. Fudesaka, 'Kenryoku tōsō', jbpress.ismedia.jp/articles/-/35958. See also Chapter 5.
3. Tahara, '"Fukō" na seijika', www.nikkeibp.co.jp/article/column/20120426/307058/.
4. Tanaka, 'Noda shushō', diamond.jp/articles/-/14110.
5. Yakushiji, 'Kako no hatsugen', astand.asahi.com/magazine/wrpolitics/2012072300010.html.
6. Ibid.
7. Kaieda, *Boku ga Ozawa (Seiji) o Kirai*, p. 232.
8. Ibid., p. 194.
9. Ibid., pp. 194–95.
10. Ibid., p. 196.
11. Oka, *Policy Entrepreneurship*, p. 85.
12. The 2005 DPJ manifesto says, 'We will realise a minimum guarantee pension of ¥70,000 per month by introducing a consumption tax specifically for pensions'. The Democratic Party of Japan, 'Realisation of a Safe and Secure Society', in *DPJ Manifesto*, p. 6.
13. Nishida, 'Embattled Parties', e.nikkei.com/e/ac/20090713/TNW/Nni20090713FP6NISID.htm.
14. Kuji and Yokota, *Seiji ga Yugameru Kōkyō Jigyō*, p. 135.
15. Ibid., p. 140.

16 Hirano, *Ozawa Ichirō to no Nijūnen*, p. 225.
17 Ozawa, *Ozawashugi*, p. 36.
18 Ibid., p. 39.
19 Itō, 'Hatoyama Ozawa jinin!', p. 60.
20 Endō, 'TPP wa kiki de wa naku', diamond.jp/articles/-/10068.
21 Kamikubo, 'Saninsen', diamond.jp/articles/-/7423.
22 The Democratic Party of Japan, 'Toward a Transparent and Fair Market Economy', in *DPJ Manifesto*, p. 11.
23 The Democratic Party of Japan, 'Real Postal Reform – From the Public to the Private Sector', in *DPJ Manifesto*, p. 12.
24 Goromaru, '(Minshutō kenkyū 4)', p. 4.
25 The Democratic Party of Japan, 'Toward a Transparent and Fair Market Economy', in *DPJ Manifesto*, pp. 10–11.
26 The Democratic Party of Japan, 'Economy, Regulatory Reform, and Small and Medium-sized Enterprise', in *DPJ Manifesto*, pp. 53–54.
27 Ibid., p. 53.
28 'Provide comprehensive support to SMEs, including adoption of an SME Charter', in *2009 Change of Government*, p. 21.
29 This is despite Oka and Hughes's contention that Ozawa would continue to champion deregulation as a means to curb bureaucratic power. See 'Ozawa as We Knew Him', p. 10.
30 The relevant provision in the manifesto states: 'We will expand regular employment and ban, in principle, the dispatch of temporary workers to manufacturing jobs'. 'Employment and the Economy', in *2009 Change of Government*, p. 17.
31 Ibid., p. 16.
32 '1 The End of Wasteful Spending', in *2009 Change of Government*, p. 1.
33 'Policies to Revitalise the Regions', in *2009 Change of Government*, p. 16.
34 Ito, 'LDP Basks', www.japantimes.co.jp/text/nn20100712a9.html.
35 '"Minshutō kaibō"', sankei.jp.msn.com/politics/situation/090302/stt0903020008000-n1.htm.
36 Ibid.
37 Hirano, *Shinsetsu!*, p. 20.
38 Ibid., pp. 19–21. See also Chapter 7.
39 Watanabe, *Ozawa Ichirō Kirawareru Densetsu*, p. 260.
40 Hirano, *Shinsetsu!*, p. 21.
41 See below.
42 Watanabe, *Ozawa Ichirō Kirawareru Densetsu*, p. 260.
43 Quoted in Tazaki, Yamaguchi and Azumi, 'Ozawa Ichirō wa Nihon o dō shiyō to iu no ka', p. 142.
44 Iinuma, 'Referendum on Ozawa', p. 9.
45 'Koizumi 5 nenkan', web.archive.org/web/20060413172124/http://www.gendai.net/.
46 Ozawa, *Ozawashugi*, p. 54.
47 Ibid., p. 84.
48 'Koizumi 5 nenkan', web.archive.org/web/20060413172124/http://www.gendai.net/.
49 Ozawa, *Ozawashugi*, pp. 54–55, 56.
50 Oka, *Policy Entrepreneurship*, p. 131.
51 Yamaguchi, 'The Failings', www.japanechoweb.jp/diplomacy-politics/jew0110/5. Ozawa first inserted the phraseology of 'Putting People's Lives First' into the front page of the 2007 DPJ election manifesto.
52 See 'The Democratic Party of Japan: Our Three Pledges and Seven Proposals to Achieve Our Policy of "Putting People's Lives First"', in *Manifesto*, p. 7.

53 'Hasty Policy Implementation', e.nikkei.com/e/ac/20100517/TNW/Nni20100517 FP9KARU2.htm.
54 'Inauguration', www.at.emb-japan.go.jp/English/japanbriefarchive.htm.
55 Park, 'Bloodless Revolution', www.globalasia.org/l.php?c=e247.
56 Iinuma, 'Referendum on Ozawa', p. 9.
57 Iinuma, 'Behind the Gridlock', p. 6.
58 See also Chapter 5.
59 Hirano reports that Ozawa had at first believed that he had a tacit agreement with Hatoyama that he would join the cabinet as secretary-general. *Shinsetsu!*, p. 85.
60 Oka, *Policy Entrepreneurship*, p. 138.
61 'Karendā naki Hatoyama Kantei', in *Nihon Keizai Shinbun*, p. 2.
62 Fudesaka, 'Kenryoku tōsō', jbpress.ismedia.jp/articles/-/35958.
63 Nonoyama, 'Sōsenkyogo', www.fsight.jp/article/5091. See also Chapter 5.
64 Tanaka, 'Shinseiken', diamond.jp/articles/-/5774.
65 See also Chapter 5.
66 'Sukōpu: Ozawa rosen no shūsei kasoku', p. 2.
67 Kamikubo, '"Ozawa shihai"', diamond.jp/articles/-/3752.
68 'DPJ Fights', e.nikkei.com/e/ac/TNKS/Nni20100315D12HH383.htm.
69 Kamikubo, '"Ozawa shihai"', diamond.jp/articles/-/3752.
70 Yamazaki, 'Ozawa Ichirō-shi to kenryoku', diamond.jp/articles/-/4929.
71 Kamikubo, '"Ozawa shihai"', diamond.jp/articles/-/3752.
72 Quoted in 'Hatoyama seiken', www.fsight.jp/article/5332.
73 'Hatoyama seiken', www.fsight.jp/article/5332.
74 Ibid.
75 Ibid.
76 Ozawa, *Blueprint*, p. 57.
77 'Small Parties', www.nni.nikkei.co.jp/e/ac/20091228/TNW/Nni20091228FR0CHARG.htm.
78 Otake, 'Forces for Political Reform', p. 282.
79 See also Chapter 5.
80 Shimizu, 'Ozawa Looks to British Example', e.nikkei.com/e/ac/20091012/TNW/NNi10091012FP9OZAWA.htm.
81 Ibid.
82 See also Chapter 5.
83 Uesugi, 'Ozawa kanjichō', diamond.jp/articles/-/1963.
84 Ibid.
85 Nonoyama, 'Ozawa Kanjichō', www.fsight.jp/article/5331.
86 Yamazaki, 'Ozawa Ichirō-shi e no kenryoku ichigenka', diamond.jp/articles/-/5735.
87 Nonoyama, 'Ozawa Kanjichō', www.fsight.jp/article/5331.
88 Satō, *Ozawa Ichirō no Himitsu*, p. 219.
89 Akasaka, '"Posuto Hatoyama"', gekkan.bunshun.jp/articles/-/216. In fact, as argued in Chapter 2, Ozawa was not opposed to *zoku giin* as such, merely the exercise of their influence from outside the government.
90 'Shasetsu: "Kashotsuke" shiryō', mainichi.jp/select/opinion/editorial/news/20100217k0000m070123000c.html.
91 Tanaka, 'New Two-party System', e.nikkei.com/e/ac/20091228/TNW/Nni200912 28OP0TANAK.htm.
92 Uesugi, 'Ozawa kanjichō', diamond.jp/articles/-/1963.
93 Ibid.
94 Ibid.
95 Ibid.
96 See Chapter 5.
97 Akasaka, '"Posuto Hatoyama"', gekkan.bunshun.jp/articles/-/216.
98 Takahashi, 'Ozawa moto hisho', p. 130. See also Chapter 5.

99   Tazaki, Yamaguchi and Azumi, 'Ozawa Ichirō wa Nihon o dō shiyō to iu no ka', p. 134.
100 'Ozawa Ichirō-shi to kenryoku', diamond.jp/articles/-/4929.
101 'Ozawa Kanjichō', www.fsight.jp/article/5331.
102 Nonoyama, 'Ozawa Kanjichō', www.fsight.jp/article/5331.
103 See also Chapter 5.
104 Yamazaki, 'Kan Shinshushō', diamond.jp/articles/-/8377.
105 '(Jijikokukoku) Kan karā', in *Asahi Shinbun*, p. 2.
106 Ibid. See also Chapter 5.
107 'Karendā naki', in *Nihon Keizai Shinbun*, p. 2.
108 Toshikawa, 'Master in his Own House?', p. 4.
109 Yamagishi, 'Ozawa-shi kabau Shamin Fukushima-shi', www.asahi.com/politics/update/0511/TKY201205110140.html.
110 See Chapter 5.
111 Katz, 'Part 2: Tanaka's Protégé', pp. 2–3. See also Chapter 5, fn 45.
112 See, for example, Samuel's argument where he refers to the significance of *Blueprint*, viz., 'He was positioning himself to build a catchall party, the "large tent" that single-member districts would reward with a Diet majority and stable control of the government'. *Machiavelli's Children*, p. 331.
113 Takayasu, 'Kokka Senryaku Kyoku', p. 1.
114 'Pulling Strings', www.nni.nikkei.co.jp/e/ac/20091228/TNW/Nni20091228FR0CHARG.htm.
115 'DPJ Betrays Campaign Pledges', www.nni.nikkei.co.jp/e/ac/20091221/TNW/Nni20091221FR9BUDG1.htm.
116 Nonoyama, 'Ozawa Kanjichō', www.fsight.jp/article/5331.
117 'Parties Brace', e.nikkei.com/e/ac/20100111/TNW/Nni20100125GY1POL00.htm.
118 Ibid.
119 Sugiyama, 'Saidai no atsuryoku dantai', business.nikkeibp.co.jp/article/topics/20091210/211447/.
120 'DPJ Betrays Campaign Pledges', www.nni.nikkei.co.jp/e/ac/20091221/TNW/Nni20091221FR9BUDG1.htm.
121 Ibid.
122 'Parties Brace', e.nikkei.com/e/ac/20100111/TNW/Nni20100111GY1POL00.htm.
123 'Pulling Strings', www.nni.nikkei.co.jp/e/ac/20091228/TNW/Nni20091228FR0CHARG.htm.
124 Cucek, 'Comment', www.eastasiaforum.org/2011/08/14/japanese-leadership-fails-at-post-disaster-reconstuction-test/#more-20887.
125 Oh, 'Jimin no ashimoto', www.fsight.jp/article/5446.
126 Tanaka, 'New Two-party System', www.nni.nikkei.co.jp/e/ac/20091228/TNW/Nni200912280POTANAKlhtm.
127 Ibid.
128 Yamazaki, 'Kan Shinshushō', diamond.jp/articles/-/8377.
129 Tanaka, 'New Two-party System', e.nikkei.com/e/ac/20091228/TNW/Nni20091228OP0TANAK.htm. See also Chapter 5.
130 In this policy, Ozawa was unsuccessful. See also below.
131 See also below.
132 'Pulling Strings', www.nni.nikkei.co.jp/e/ac/20091228/TNW/Nni20091228FR0CHARG.htm.
133 Tanaka, 'New Two-party System', e.nikkei.com/e/ac/20091228/TNW/Nni200912 28OP0TANAK.htm.
134 'Parties Brace', e.nikkei.com/e/ac/20100111/TNW/Nni20100111GY1POL00.htm. See also below.
135 'Public Works Budget', www.nikkei.co.jp/news/seiji/20100212ATFS1101E11022010.html.

170 *Old policies*

136 Ibid.
137 'Govt Cuts', e.nikkei.com/e/fr/tnks/Nni20100326D26JFA17.htm.
138 'Kokudōyosan', www.asahi.com/politics/update/0326/TKY201003260514.html?ref=any.
139 Satō, 'Izumo no Ozawa', web.archive.org/web/20100609015014/http://seiji.yahoo.co.jp/column/article/detail/20100531-01-0101.html.
140 Ibid.
141 'Editorial: Flip-flop on Highway Tolls', www.asahi.com/english/TKY201004230358.html. The phrase *tsuru no hitokoe* is used in Japanese, which literally means the 'final word' or 'a decision made by a figure of authority'.
142 Land improvement works are general public works relating to agriculture such as agricultural land creation, maintenance of agricultural roads, and building dams for agricultural use. The annual budget for land improvement works exceeded ¥1 trillion around 2000. Oh, 'Jimin no ashimoto', www.fsight.jp/article/5446.
143 'Yamada Toshio', in *Nōsei Undō Jānaru*, p. 9.
144 Oh, 'Jimin no ashimoto', www.fsight.jp/article/5446.
145 Satō, 'Izumo no Ozawa', web.archive.org/web/20100609015014/http://seiji.yahoo.co.jp/column/article/detail/20100531-01-0101.html.
146 Oh, 'Jimin no ashimoto', www.fsight.jp/article/5446.
147 Satō, 'Izumo no Ozawa', web.archive.org/web/20100609015014/http://seiji.yahoo.co.jp/column/article/detail/20100531-01-0101.html.
148 Ozawa had used similar covert tactics against LDP support groups before. In April 2006, shortly after becoming leader of the opposition DPJ, he secretly visited the office of the Japan War Bereaved Association after having earlier visited the offices of the Japan Dental Association and the Japan Pharmaceutical Association. These were all influential LDP support groups with which Ozawa had established connections when he was still an influential LDP member. 'Ozawa-shi, Taiketsu shoku zenmen ni', p. 2.
149 Oh, 'Jimin no ashimoto', www.fsight.jp/article/5446.
150 Ibid.
151 See Chapter 5.
152 Personal communication, 24 July 2010.
153 Tanaka, 'New Two-party System', www.nni.nikkei.co.jp/e/ac/20091228/TNW/Nni200912280POTANAKlhtm.
154 'Bad Blood', www.economist.com/world/asia/displayStory.cfm?story_id=15210046.
155 Yamazaki, 'Ozawa Ichirō-shi to kenryoku', diamond.jp/articles/-/4929.
156 Yosano, 'Shintō kessei', p. 140.
157 'DPJ Betrays Campaign Pledges', www.nni.nikkei.co.jp/e/ac/20091221/TNW/Nni20091221FR9BUDG1.htm.
158 'Seiji shudō', in *Liberal Time*, p. 11.
159 'Kan's Story', e.nikkei.com/e/ac/20100111/TNW/Nni20100111FR1FMINS.htm.
160 Katz, 'Janus-faced DPJ', p. 1.
161 Yamazaki, 'Tatakae, daihyōsen!', diamond.jp/articles/-/9238.
162 'Confusion Over Highway Tolls', mdn.mainichi.jp/perspectives/news/20100426p2a00m0na002000c.html.
163 'Editorial: Incoherent Road Policy', www.asahi.com/english/TKY201003110392.html.
164 'Editorial: Flip-flop on Highway Tolls', www.asahi.com/english/TKY201004230358.html.
165 'Ozawa's Argument', e.nikkei.com/e/ac/TNKS/Nni20100423D23SS861.htm.
166 'DPJ Pinned', e.nikkei.com/e/ac/TNW/Nni20100517FP9KARU3.htm.
167 'Sandwiched Hatoyama', e.nikkei.com/e/ac/TNKS/Nni20100422SS769.htm.
168 'DPJ Pinned', e.nikkei.com/e/ac/TNW/Nni20100517FP9KARU3.htm.

169 'Govt Eyes Lowering New Expressway Tariff', e.nikkei.com/e/ac/TNKS/Nni20100423D22JFA26.htm.
170 His words were: 'Maehara is in the government, so shouldn't his opinion come first?' 'Sandwiched Hatoyama', e.nikkei.com/e/ac/tnks/Nni20100423D22JFA26.htm.
171 Ibid.
172 *NHK News 7*, 23 April 2010.
173 Toshikawa, 'Not-so-merry Month', p. 5.
174 See also below.
175 Toshikawa and Katz, 'Flailing', p. 3. See also below.
176 Ibid.
177 'Yūsei kaikaku', www.asahi.com/politics/update/0523/TKY201005230332.html?ref=any.
178 'Yūsei kyōkō', p. 3.
179 'Small Parties', www.nni.nikkei.co.jp/e/ac/20091228/TNW/Nni20091228FR0CHARG.htm.
180 '(Seiron): Keiō daigaku', *Sankei Shinbun*, p. 7.
181 'Editorial: Six Months of Hatoyama', www.asahi.com/english/TKY201003160331.html.
182 Matsuda, 'Zenekon marugakae senkyo', gendai.ismedia.jp/articles/-/268.
183 Ishikawa, *Akutō*, p. 199.
184 Mori McElwain and Reed, 'Japanese Politics', p. 286.
185 Ibid., p. 285.
186 Matsumura, 'Ozawa: Japan's Secret Shogun', www.japantimes.co.jp/cgi-bin/eo20100204a1.html.
187 'DPJ's Ozawa', e.nikkei.com/e/ac/tnks/Nni20100412D12JFN02.htm.
188 Katz, 'LDP Drops', p. 3.
189 Ichinokuchi, 'Minshutō', www.fsight.jp/article/5241.
190 Ibid.
191 Ibid.
192 '"Nokyo" Losing Say', e.nikkei.com/e/ac/20100524/TNW/Nni20100524FT0FARM1.htm.
193 'DPJ Ozawa', in *Asahi Shinbun*, p. 1.
194 'Yūsei kaikaku', www.asahi.com/politics/update/0523/TKY201005230332.html?ref=any.
195 Ibid.
196 'Ozawa, Chamber of Commerce Chief Discuss Growth', e.nikkei.com/e/ac/TNKS/Nni20100311D11JFA20.htm.
197 Ibid.
198 Others who attended the meeting were Chairman of the DPJ Upper House caucus Koshiishi Azuma, and Ichikawa Yūichi, former secretary-general of the Kōmeitō.
199 '"Atta jijitsu ga taisetsu"', www.fsight.jp/article/5598.
200 Election results showed that in all the multi-seat prefectural constituencies, the DPJ vote was remarkably evenly split, except for Tokyo where Renho's vote tally was almost three times that of the other DPJ candidate, Ogawa Toshio.
201 Kaneko and Isogai, '(Minshutō kenkyū 3)', p. 4.
202 Suzuki, *Saigo no Ozawa Ichirō*, p. 66.
203 'Minshutō daihyō senkyo', www.the-journal.jp/contents/kokkai/mb/post_230.html.
204 *NHK News 7*, 1 September 2010.
205 Kamikubo, 'Seijika no "kessa"', diamond.jp/articles/-/9298.
206 'Prime Minister Kan to Remain', www.at.emb-japan.go.jp/English/japanbriefarchive.htm.
207 'Futenma zei zaisei', in *Nihon Keizai Shinbun*, p. 3.
208 'Minshutō daihyō senkyo', www.the-journal.jp/contents/kokkai/mb/post_230.html.
209 Hara, 'Kokumin', diamond.jp/articles/-/9199.

172   Old policies

210 Yamazaki, 'Tatakae, daihyōsen!', diamond.jp/articles/-/9238.
211 Sharp, 'Ozawa-Kan Leadership Finale', the-diplomat.com/tokyo-notes/2010/09/13/ozawa-kan-leadership-finale/.
212 *NHK News 7*, 12 September 2010.
213 Ibid.
214 *NHK News 7*, 10 September 2010.
215 Nonoyama, 'Ozawa-shi shutsuba', www.fsight.jp/article/5740.
216 Sudō and Takeshima, 'Minshutō daihyōsen', web.archive.org/web/20100906142028/http://mainichi.jp/select/seiji/minshudaihyousen/hikaku/news/20100903org00m010016000c.html.
217 Quoted on *NHK News 7*, 7 September 2010.
218 'Japan's Leadership Challenge', www.economist.con/node/16992215?story_id=16992215.
219 Sudō and Takeshima, 'Minshutō daihyōsen', web.archive.org/web/20100906142028/http://mainichi.jp/select/seiji/minshudaihyousen/hikaku/news/20100903org00m010016000c.html.
220 '(Shasetsu) Chiiki shuken ronsō', shasetsu.ps.land.to/index.cgi/event/475/.
221 Sudō and Takeshima, 'Minshutō daihyōsen', web.archive.org/web/20100906142028/http://mainichi.jp/select/seiji/minshudaihyousen/hikaku/news/20100903org00m010016000c.html.
222 'DPJ Election Debate', e.nikkei.com/e/ac/TNW/Nni20100913OP6EDIT1.htm.
223 '(Shasetsu) Chiiki shuken ronsō', shasetsu.ps.land.to/index.cgi/event/475/.
224 'DPJ Election Debate', e.nikkei.com/e/ac/TNW/Nni20100913OP6EDIT1.htm.
225 Katz, 'What's at Stake?', pp. 1–2.
226 *NHK News 7*, 1 September 2010.
227 *NHK News 7*, 2 September 2010.
228 Klein, 'Ozawa's "seiji juku"', ssj.iss.u-tokyo.ac.jp/archives/2010/09/ssj_6334_ozawas.html.
229 Quoted on *NHK News 7*, 5 September 2010.
230 Takahara, 'Rookies Hold Crucial DPJ Votes', www.japantimes.co.jp/cgi-bin/nn20100910f1.html.
231 *NHK News 7*, 1 September 2010.
232 '"Shushō no shishitsu" zessen', in *Asahi Shinbun*, p. 1.
233 Kamikubo, 'Seijika no "kessa"', diamond.jp/articles/-/9298.
234 *NHK News 7*, 1 September 2010.
235 'Battle Heats Up', www.japantimes.co.jp/cgi-bin/nn20100828a2.html.
236 'Minshutō daihyōsen: Soshikigatame hageshiku', p. 2.
237 '(Seiji no genba)', in *Yomiuri Shinbun*, p. 4.
238 'Kan seiken no jūgokagetsu', www.chugoku-np.co.jp/Syasetu/Sh201108270068.html.
239 Ikushima, 'Sukōpu', p. 2.
240 'Ozawa's Indictment', e.nikkei.com/e/ac/tnks/Nni20110201D01HH528.htm.
241 Toshikawa, 'Taxes uber alles', p. 2.
242 'Ozawa Minshu zen kanjichō', in *Mainichi Shinbun*, p. 5.
243 See also Chapter 6.
244 'Ozawa Ichirō shinshun intabyū', in *Nikkan Gendai*, p. 429.
245 Katz, 'It's Leadership, Stupid!', p. 1.
246 Toshikawa, 'Noda's Leadership Style', p. 3.
247 'Zōzei kaisan nara seikai saihen', in *Asahi Shinbun*, p. 1. See also Chapter 6.
248 'Ozawa-shi, saido kaidan', sankei.jp.msn.com/politics/news/120530/plc12053013420011-n1.htm.
249 Quoted in 'Ozawa shintō', www.nikkeibp.co.jp/article/column/20120703/314579/.
250 Ito, 'Ozawa Vows', www.japantimes.co.jp/news/2012/08/02/national/ozawa-vows-new-party-will-dethrone-nodas-dpj/#.UX3U7ODtIqY.

251 See Chapter 6.
252 Atarashii Seisaku Kenkyūkai, 'Keiki taisaku', shinseiken.jp/pdf/keikityuukan.pdf.
253 'Kan Faces Bumps', e.nikkei.com/e/ac/TNKS/Nni20101020D19JFA25.htm.
254 See Chapter 6.
255 Endō, 'TPP wa kiki de wa naku', diamond.jp/articles/-/10068.
256 *Hatena Diary*, d.hatena.ne.jp/kojitaken/20101113/1289625937.
257 See Chapter 6.
258 Ishikawa, *Akutō*, p. 208.
259 Ibid., p. 48.
260 'PM Indicates', www.yomiuri.co.jp/dy/nationa/T111009003175.htm.
261 *Hatena Diary*, d.hatena.ne.jp/kojitaken/20101113/1289625937. See also Chapter 7.
262 '(Intabyū) Shōhizei to seikai saihen', in *Asahi Shinbun*, p. 17.
263 *Hatena Diary*, d.hatena.ne.jp/kojitaken/20101113/1289625937.
264 Ibid. See also Chapter 6.
265 Ishikawa, *Akutō*, p. 49. See also Chapter 7.
266 *Hatena Diary*, d.hatena.ne.jp/kojitaken/20101113/1289625937.
267 As Winkler wrote, 'Ozawa has been extremely flexible when it comes to policy, not to mention ideology...For instance, throughout the 1990s Ozawa kept emphasizing neoliberal reforms...but once his old pals in the LDP decided to execute those neoliberals [sic.] reforms, Ozawa returned to his Tanaka-Takeshita faction roots, in other words spending and worrying about the budget later'. 'About Hatoyama, Ozawa', ssj.iss.u-tokyo.ac.jp/archives/2011/09/ssj_6837_fwd_re.html.
268 'Ozawa Prepares', www.asahi.com/english/TKY201104140127.html.
269 As well as 'escaping from', *datsu* can also mean 'breaking away from', 'removing', 'getting rid of', 'sidelining', 'eliminating' or 'distancing oneself from'.
270 See Chapter 6.
271 Matsuda, *Ozawa Ichirō Kyoshoku no Shihaisha*, p. 132.
272 Quoted in ibid., p. 214.
273 Ibid., p. 132.
274 'Seijika toshite no meimyaku', jbpress.ismedia.jp/articles/-/36052.
275 See also Chapter 5.
276 Andō, 'Seisō no hate', business.nikkeibp.co.jp/article/topics/20120628/233886/?rt=nocnt.
277 'Transcript of Interview', online.wsj.com/article/SB10001424052702304066504576348263512336934.html.
278 Kaieda, *Boku ga Ozawa (Seiji) o Kirai*, p. 79.

5 The Ozawa dictatorship

Amongst the many reasons for Ozawa's continuing prominence in Japanese politics has been his reputation as a political kingpin and 'actual power-holder' (*jitsuryokusha*),[1] regardless of the formal position that he held. His political behaviour over more than 40 years revealed a predisposition for exerting hegemonic control over any party or administration of which he was a part. His preference for wielding personal power did not change even when he became a key figure in the 'new' politics regime inaugurated by the DPJ in 2009. He remained 'unreconstructed' in the sense that he continued to operate as a dominating influence behind the scenes, to demonstrate a dictatorial leadership style and to observe the fundamental precepts of the old Tanaka model of politics. Even when given the best opportunity of his political career finally to perform within political institutions newly strengthened by reform and to consolidate the systemic structural changes to the political system that he had previously advocated, Ozawa instead focused almost exclusively on maximising his own power across the gamut of Diet, party and government affairs. This raises the fundamental question about what truly motivates Ozawa: is it a desire to acquire power in order to restructure the system of Japanese politics or is it an ambition merely to exert political power for its own sake?

Ozawa's dominance over the Hatoyama administration

When Ozawa joined the DPJ, he pledged to adopt a consensual approach and to work cooperatively with other party members.[2] His official position as DPJ secretary-general placed him second in command to President Hatoyama. In practice, Ozawa lived up to descriptions of him as 'the most powerful person in the DPJ' (*Minshutō saidai no jitsuryokusha*)[3] and 'the most influential person in the ruling party' (*yotō no saikō jitsuryokusha*).[4]

Ozawa's claim to pre-eminence in the party was partly based on his relative seniority compared to the vast bulk of the DPJ's Diet members. His Diet career had spanned four decades while the great majority of the ruling party's politicians had been elected fewer than four times, and a huge number were first-term Diet members elected in either 2007 or 2009. His quick assertion of dominance over the party, however, was more than just a question of experience and seniority. As Tanaka Shūsei points out:

Before we knew it, the DPJ had come under 'Ozawa's one-man rule'...I do not know anyone else in Japan's post-war political history whose political force has been as strong as Ozawa's. Former Prime Minister Satō Eisaku and former Prime Minister Tanaka Kakuei also established strong political foundations in the party but both had rivals – former Prime Minister Ikeda Hayato and former Fukuda Takeo respectively – who were on an equal footing with them. However, from this point onwards, the DPJ is virtually going to be under Ozawa's one-man rule. Even those who were displaying anti-Ozawa and non-Ozawa attitudes have waved the white flag.[5]

It was not just the party that Ozawa ruled. By coordinating personnel affairs between the party and government as part of his secretary-general's duties, Ozawa began wielding influence over the people who would be sent into government[6] on the grounds that they 'needed to be in line with the party's personnel matters'.[7] At his behest, the launching of the so-called 'transition team', which was supposed to make various arrangements for the inauguration of the new cabinet, was put on hold. This was a plan that had been worked out when Kan and Okada were DPJ presidents in 2003 and 2005, respectively. The president would pick party executives and cabinet members right after the Lower House election, and as a team, they would coordinate their views in the run-up to the launching of a new administration. However, the plan collapsed when Ozawa said he had not heard of it.[8] Hatoyama then fell into line with Ozawa, handing over the personnel selections to him, so Ozawa took charge not only of filling key party posts but also of building the prime minister's cabinet, 'interviewing' various candidates for ministerial office and making his selections. For example, he appointed his old ally, a politician with 'no interests, no connections and no expertise' to the post of MAFF minister – Akamatsu Hirotaka.[9]

Ozawa subsequently showed his displeasure over prospective appointments to the newly established GRU, which was due to conduct its first round of budget screenings in late 2009. The choice of personnel for the unit became the focus of a behind-the-scenes battle, in which the Hatoyama office wholly capitulated to the Ozawa office.[10] Ozawa objected to new Diet members joining the unit and complained that the selection process had gone ahead 'without the party's knowledge'.[11] Chief Cabinet Secretary Hirano Hirofumi, as Kantei representative, went to Ozawa's office in order to try to settle the matter but returned without any agreement. The selection of GRU personnel was then reviewed. Sugiyama reported one of Sengoku's staff saying, 'This one case gives you an idea of what always happens. Hirano, who is supposed to function as a breakwater, cannot protect Prime Minister Hatoyama. He cannot stop Secretary-General Ozawa'.[12] Although both Sengoku and Hirano avoided serious conflict by apologising to Ozawa,[13] the incident clearly displayed Ozawa's superiority over the government as well as over the management of individual Diet members. It warned DPJ Diet members that any future appointments in the government depended on the secretary-general's approval.[14]

Thereafter, Ozawa consolidated a structure of personal power more elaborate and all-encompassing than any that had existed under LDP rule.[15] He leveraged key sources of power to extend his influence outwards from the party into the government. First was the large number of DPJ Diet members, around 150, at his beck and call.[16] His group was big enough to make even Hatoyama step down as party leader.[17] It enabled him to influence the whole party and even the Diet and cabinet.[18] Second was the formal list of tasks and duties that Ozawa conducted as secretary-general, including official party endorsements and the distribution of the party's money, which he could use, if necessary, to bring recalcitrant DPJ Diet members into line. Third was his commandeering of all policy initiation from the party side, a development that was reinforced by his abolition of the PRC. Because there was no solid decision-making system within the party, Ozawa's 'words had the power to overrule any policy'.[19] Another essential element was his centralisation of the flow of petitions through the secretary-general's office, which meant that he could exercise sway over the allocation of government funds by interfering directly in the budget, displacing not only the *zoku giin* but also ministers, deputy ministers and parliamentary secretaries. Lastly, with respect to the bureaucracy, Ozawa exercised power over the appointment of ex-bureaucrats to particular *amakudari* positions, such as the appointment of Saitō Jirō as head of Japan Post. The appointment violated the DPJ's manifesto commitment to ban *amakudari*, but this could still be threatened in order to bring bureaucrats into line.[20]

Ozawa often used power openly and directly, such as when he interfered in the selection of GRU personnel and as his demands 'from the party' over budget expenditure showed. At other times, he operated behind the scenes taking very few into his confidence and making decisions in a completely opaque style. Those close to him, including his aides, would also surmise his intentions and things would progress as if they were following Ozawa's instructions. The effect was to amplify Ozawa's presence, making it difficult for individual Diet members to know from where he was observing them. It was akin to a chief warden and his prisoners who could be watched 24 hours a day. Ozawa's aides were the wardens.[21] The upshot was that all cabinet members and other DPJ Diet members were always aware of Ozawa's power and tended to act in anticipation of his wishes even without formal instructions.[22]

Over time, Ozawa was widely seen as dominating the Hatoyama administration across the entire spectrum of government and party affairs and as the effective leader of Japan.[23] The government quickly assumed the character of an Ozawa dictatorship with a puppet prime minister. To most people, it was obvious that Hatoyama was under Ozawa's control and could not speak out against him.[24] Kan commented at a DPJ meeting, 'Ozawa is someone who wants to maintain his authority at the maximum possible level at all times. Everything else is just a means to achieve this end. That is the kind of person he is. His criteria for making judgements are not based on policies but on what he needs to do to maximise his political influence. That's all. I didn't know he was this bad'.[25]

Many in the party shared this view and Ozawa became more and more unpopular in DPJ ranks. His iron-fisted rule amounted, according to some, to a suppression of free speech.[26] A mid-level DPJ member in the Lower House remarked, 'there was a general atmosphere that discouraged any discussions'.[27] Another revealed, 'The climate…is strangely oppressive…No one can criticize party chief Ichiro Ozawa. Everyone seems abnormally scared of him. They're so scared of Ozawa, they can't say a thing'.[28] Murakoshi Hirotami, a DPJ Lower House Diet member, who often criticised Ozawa's dictatorial management of the party, became famous after tweeting on social media site Twitter in October 2009 that 'the current DPJ is like North Korea'.[29] Itō also noted that 'some veteran Diet members were complaining behind the scenes, saying, "it is like a concentration camp"'.[30] Even LDP opposition leader Tanigaki Sadakazu made the call, 'It's time to fight Ozawa's dictatorship',[31] asking Prime Minister Hatoyama, 'Are you this nation's true leader, representing the DPJ in both name and reality, or is it an Ozawa dictatorship?'[32]

Deputy Secretary-General Ubukata Yukio, who called for Ozawa to give an account of himself over his money-politics scandal in April 2010,[33] complained that 'In the current DPJ, someone alone keeps a grip on power and funds'.[34] For this he was fired from his position as deputy secretary-general by Senior Deputy Secretary-General Takashima Yoshimitsu, a close associate of Ozawa's, but this decision was overturned by the DPJ executive. Hatoyama intervened, asking Ozawa if Ubukata could be retained and Ozawa assented. He called Ubukata to his office and suggested that they work together again. However, when Ubukata responded with the comment, 'I have something to say too',[35] Ozawa got up and left, saying 'You're a Vice Secretary General so you can talk to me anytime. But right now, I don't have time'.[36] To counter Ozawa, Ubukata formed a group of DPJ backbenchers to press for the re-establishment of the PRC. They had a theory that reviving the PRC was the first step towards participating in policy decisions and generating criticism of Ozawa in the party.[37] As one DPJ lawmaker put it, 'His authoritarian style of party management…changed the DPJ's good features, key among which was a liberal climate where members conducted lively discussions'.[38]

Nevertheless, the party leadership and a large cohort of party Diet members, including some in the anti-Ozawa forces, were reluctant to move against Ozawa in recognition of his political skills, particularly when it came to election strategy, which was identified as his real forte. Ozawa was, for example, the only DPJ politician who laid out a detailed plan for victory in the 2010 Upper House campaign by obtaining information on every electorate.[39] When he also toyed with the idea of collaborating with the New Kōmeitō in the election, the New Kōmeitō leadership officially distanced itself from the DPJ because a majority of its members had a strong allergy to Ozawa, whom they said was 'too dictatorial a politician'.[40]

Ozawa initially planned to win the election with Hatoyama still in the prime minister's position, although if he judged that Hatoyama had become a political liability, he would have been expendable. Deputy Prime Minister Kan was widely considered as Hatoyama's likely successor, but Ozawa had already taken note of the fact that Kan was not a person who would obey his suggestions once in the prime minister's position.[41]

Ozawa surmised correctly. After Ozawa's resignation as DPJ secretary-general and Hatoyama's fall from grace in June 2010, Prime Minister Kan appointed Edano under his control as party secretary-general. This was explicitly to prevent the kind of dual party-government system (*seifu to tō nigen taisei*)[42] or 'dual power structure' (*nijū kenryoku kōzō*) (see Table 1.1) that had emerged under Hatoyama. When Ozawa and Kan later lined up in the contest for the DPJ leadership in September 2010, the leader of Your Party (Minna no Tō), Watanabe Yoshimi, charged that it was the dual power structure that Ozawa had set up under Hatoyama that was preventing leadership by politicians and prolonging the dependence of the policymaking process on bureaucratic input. Watanabe rejected the possibility of supporting Ozawa in a possible coalition to overcome the divided Diet situation, saying, 'Your Party does not need Mr. Ozawa…So we should not give him a hand…Your Party is an "Ozawa-free party"'.[43]

In fact, the situation under the Hatoyama administration was less a dual structure than one where one person appeared to hold all the levers of power. It was like a TV drama where Ozawa combined the roles of producer (who selected the cast and decided budget allocation), screenwriter (who made the policies) and director (who supervised and instructed the actors), while Hatoyama was just the lead actor who could be freely replaced.[44] This view was widely shared by the public. A December 2009 poll revealed that more than two thirds of respondents thought that Ozawa actually ran the Hatoyama cabinet, while only just over 10 per cent thought that the prime minister did so.[45]

Ozawa's reluctance to hold government office

In October 1991 Ozawa turned down an offer that would have almost certainly resulted in his becoming prime minister when Kaifu resigned and when Kanemaru, as chairman of the Takeshita faction, let it be known that he was intending to recommend Ozawa for prime minister. He attempted to persuade him for a whole day.[46] LDP Diet member Nonaka Hiromu also encouraged Ozawa to stand for the post, but Ozawa replied, 'I cannot do it yet. It will take about ten years to be prime minister, including the time required to put my affairs in order'.[47] He declared that he would not run because he did not consider himself an appropriate candidate,[48] asserting, 'I am not fit to be prime minister', and 'I am not confident about my health'.[49] He also said, 'There is no point in being prime minister unless I know what I should do as prime minister and what I can do based on the demands of the times, and have prepared the conditions for realising them'.[50]

Ozawa's reluctance to occupy the top job was also attributed to his prior ambition to realise political reforms, including the installation of single-seat constituencies.[51] As soon as he became LDP secretary-general in 1989, he said, 'If the LDP is going to continue like this, I cannot become prime minister, nor do I want to become one. [Look at] how much money you need to become prime minister. If we leave things as they are, faction leaders are going to be arrested by judicial authorities once every two years. We won't be able to conduct proper politics'.[52]

In Ozawa's political experience, Japanese prime ministers had not traditionally been the supreme power wielders. He regarded the prime minister's position as that of a figurehead who acted for the actual power holders operating behind the scenes (see Table 1.1). He was 'obsessed with being the actual power holder who sets the prime minister in motion'.[53] He 'wanted to be a puppeteer [*kugutsushi*]'.[54]

Ozawa had no ambition to lead by example in line with his own vision for strengthening the prime ministership in *Blueprint* and thus use the position to enact a programme of political and policy reform. Nakasone Yasuhiro set the example in this regard: he wanted to become prime minister and he had a clear policy agenda. He claimed that he would become prime minister one day and had 30 notebooks full of policies that he was going to implement. Ozawa was the complete opposite. He did not want to become prime minister; he was satisfied with 'moving politics'.[55] Ozawa admitted that 'he was more suited to playing a supporting role to the prime minister'.[56] When asked why he declined Kanemaru's offer to become prime minister in 1991, he answered, 'I can become prime minister whenever I want to'.[57] He could also have been prime minister when the Hosokawa coalition was inaugurated, but he preferred to continue an active role behind the scenes.[58] Tahara reported that, 'He once said that he did not want to answer stupid questions from the opposition parties for hours in the Diet'.[59]

In finally vying for the DPJ leadership with Prime Minister Kan in September 2010, Ozawa was merely pursuing the prime ministership as a power-maintenance strategy in an environment of *datsu* Ozawa.[60] He later told an interviewer, 'I do not particularly want to become prime minister...I would be satisfied if someone else took the post. I would be satisfied with being the cheering section'.[61]

Ozawa's reluctance to occupy the top post extended to ministerial positions. Throughout most of his career, in contrast to all other prominent Japanese political leaders, he eschewed ministerial posts (the only cabinet portfolio he held was minister of home affairs in the Nakasone administration in 1985–86). He turned down Takeshita's invitation for him to become minister of finance in 1991. In fact, after being deputy chief cabinet secretary in the Takeshita cabinet in 1987, Ozawa did not occupy any more official posts in government, choosing instead to build his power base 'within the party-political network'[62] and to occupy the post of secretary-general (see Table 1.1). He justified this stance by arguing that it was close to impossible to change the bureaucratic structure simply by being a normal minister.[63]

Ozawa preferred a position where he bore little accountability to the public and to the Diet (see Table 1.1), and where he could scheme without coming out into the open. He explained this away by pointing to his lack of a positive, open communicating style, acknowledging, 'I am not good with words'.[64] As Ōtake observed, he 'lacked the ability to appeal to the people through the mass media'.[65] Ozawa admitted:

> 'What I do not like are inflammatory speeches that include irresponsible lies. I don't like speeches on ceremonial occasions either. I like debates but I don't

like formalities. In that sense I lack an element that is essential to being a politician'. Sure enough, Diet minutes show that Ozawa has only asked questions in the Diet during formal questioning by party leaders in Lower House plenary sessions. He is a rare politician that hardly asks any question in Diet sessions.[66]

Ozawa had a rule of 'not appearing on TV programmes where he had to debate many commentators and politicians'.[67] As DPJ secretary-general in the Hatoyama administration, he avoided public appearances as much as possible, 'saying he was a poor speaker and should concentrate on election campaign planning. Ozawa entrusted his public duties to his deputy, Gōshi Hosono'.[68]

Ozawa was also well known for disliking the mass media just as the media disliked him in return. He first declared war on the media during the Hosokawa administration, refusing to hold press conferences after articles were published in newspapers about his behind-the-scenes negotiations over the rice import issue. He announced to the media, 'Press conferences are my service to you, not my duty'.[69] A few months later, he attacked critical coverage of him as 'black journalism'[70] and unleashed his fury at the press for investigating his money politics, arguing that reformers such as himself were often targeted by the media for slander – the same argument he used to defend himself during his trial. When the media refused to be cowed, he stopped talking to them altogether.[71] The characteristics of his politics lay in four things he did not do: attend meetings, answer the phone, give detailed explanations and reveal his true intentions. The common element in all of these was that he did not discuss matters.[72]

Contradictions between Ozawa's political principles and practice

Ozawa's unwillingness and inability to communicate openly contrasted starkly with the reforms he proposed to modernise the Japanese political system. Following the installation of the Hosokawa administration, he seemed to think he was somehow impervious to the new politics principles of competition and accountability.[73] Similarly, having promoted Diet revitalisation including the introduction of question time as LP leader, he eschewed any opportunities himself formally to debate policy issues in the Diet (see Table 1.1). In fact, he made only rare appearances in question time, preferring always to operate behind the scenes on both policy and political fronts.[74]

The contradiction between theory (*tatemae*) and practice (*honne*) in Ozawa's politics was equally apparent under the new DPJ administration of 2009–10, when he subverted the embryonic institutionalisation of the 'new' official political system by remaining within the 'old' unofficial political system. The DPJ attempted to operationalise many of the changes that Ozawa had originally advocated and initiated, but his own behaviour undermined the reforms that he had played such a pivotal part in introducing, thus betraying his own reform agenda.[75] For example, he argued for the consolidation of power in formal positions of government along constitutional lines, yet he himself sought to exercise broad policy powers without formal institutional authority (see Table 1.1). His intervention in the policymaking process from his position as party secretary-general undermined the cabinet and manifestly obscured the lines of accountability in government. It also flew directly in the face of one of his main political reform goals: integrating the ruling party and cabinet in policymaking (see Table 1.1). Ozawa might have been part of a new government and one of the primary architects of regime change, but his proclivity for running governments from behind the scenes[76] meant that he subverted the intent of the DPJ, which was to make institutions more open to public scrutiny, more accountable and less subject to backroom wheeling and dealing where political leaders were largely unanswerable to the general public.

As the power behind the throne in the Hatoyama administration, Ozawa was merely reverting to form. His long history of leading governments from behind rather than from the front began with the Kaifu administration, which was also managed as though Ozawa were the virtual or *de facto* prime minister.[77] Because of Kaifu's weak power base as a member of the smallest (Komoto) faction, it was Ozawa who became the central political figure in the administration with the support of the Takeshita faction.[78] As secretary-general, his power was greater than the prime minister's. The Kaifu cabinet was often called a 'double government'.[79] In media cartoons at the time, Kaifu was depicted as a monkey with Ozawa as his trainer.[80] Ozawa also commented about Kaifu, 'The best *mikoshi* (portable shrine) to carry is a light and dumb one'.[81]

Like the Kaifu cabinet, the Hosokawa cabinet was also 'remotely controlled' by Ozawa[82] and Hosokawa was a '"remote-control" prime minister'.[83] Although Ozawa held no formal position in the administration, effective leadership was once again perceived to be in his hands.[84] It was as if he had never left the LDP. He constructed a dual power structure that was 'equivalent to that of Keiseikai',[85] concentrating in his own hands all the powers that Keiseikai used to wield in order to form such a structure.[86] Kaifu wrote in his memoirs:

> To be honest, I did not expect Hosokawa, who had just been elected as a Lower House member for the first time, would become prime minister with such rapid strides. Upon his appearance, the media hailed Hosokawa as the new wind in the political world; but in the end former members of the Takeshita faction such as Ozawa were the ones actually running the cabinet.[87]

Hosokawa in fact asked Ozawa to take the job of prime minister but Ozawa refused. They reached an understanding that Ozawa would occupy no formal position in the government, but 'would have great influence...He would be the "shadow shogun" for reform'.[88] However, he went on to seize actual power.[89] When the media criticised him for secretly manoeuvring behind the scenes and creating a dual power structure, Ozawa responded by dismissing such criticism as '"trivia". He said the mission of politics was to "provide the people with security and affluence. If that…can be achieved, it doesn't matter whether the structure is two-layered or four-layered"'.[90]

Ozawa made the cabinet selections including the decision not to appoint any other members of the JNP (other than Hosokawa himself) to a cabinet position.[91] Hosokawa himself recounts that when he was working to form his cabinet, 'A sealed letter [came] from Ozawa. It said: "I have received lists of cabinet member candidates from the JSP, Kōmeitō and DSP. As for the RP, I want the five members whom I agreed to last night to be in the cabinet, and the names are listed in a separate note"'.[92]

In addition to controlling these personnel appointments, Ozawa established 'a new decision-making mechanism outside the cabinet'[93] called the council of ruling party representatives (*yotō daihyōsha kaigi*), consisting of the secretaries-general of each of the coalition parties, including, of course, Ozawa himself.[94] The council operated in parallel to the cabinet and other intra-coalition executive bodies and was, in practice, the most influential policymaking body in the Hosokawa administration (see Table 1.1).[95] It enabled Ozawa to seize control of government decision making and so other coalition party leaders labelled it 'undemocratic'.[96] It acted, for example, as the 'final decision-making organ'[97] in opening the rice market.

Similarly, on the introduction of the proposed national welfare tax Ozawa did not consult with key coalition leaders, the Ministry of Health and Welfare and business leaders, instead devising the policy in secret negotiations with the MOF.[98] When Hosokawa was pressured into accepting the policy and then suddenly announced it without further consultation, the strength of the opposition from within his own coalition forced him to withdraw it. It was a humiliating defeat that hastened the collapse of the coalition.[99] JSP leader Murayama Tomiichi criticised Ozawa's handling of the tax proposal, saying 'a coalition government should be operated in a democratic manner in order to reflect a wider range of opinions. Secretary General Ozawa of the Renewal Party did not understand this at all'.[100]

Ozawa-style democratic dictatorship

It was also during the early 1990s and the break-up of the LDP administration that Ozawa's enemies within the party began to criticise him for acting arbitrarily like a dictator.[101] Reform Forum 21's prospectus, which later became the foundation of the RP, expounded Ozawa's way of doing things and rationalised 'his method of arbitrarily doing things without discussing anything with others'.[102] It advocated:

> 1) from responsive politics [*taiōgata seiji*] to politics with leadership [*shidōgata seiji*]; 2) from politics based on interest coordination [*rigai chōseigata seiji*] to politics based on setting forth ideals [*risō teijigata seiji*]; 3) from politics based on unanimous accord [*zenkai icchigata seiji*] to politics based on majority rule [*tasūketsugata seiji*]; and 4) from politics based on Diet affairs [*kokkai taisakugata seiji*] to politics based on policy debates [*seisaku ronsōgata seiji*].[103]

These points encapsulated Ozawa's 'top-down method of making decisions behind closed doors'.[104] He was known to prefer strong-arm tactics – a technique he cultivated under the guidance of Kanemaru (who was similar) – to quiet persuasion.[105] He was supremely confident in his own ideas and unwilling to brook opposition to them.[106] He advocated the need for completely taking control of the power structure and firmly establishing a system in which he could fulfil his duties even if he were criticised by those around him.[107] He pushed people into complying with his plans and objectives, and he was reluctant to compromise, share power and operate in a system where he did not exercise personal control.

In Ozawa's view, a democratic majority existed for the purpose of enabling political leaders to act decisively to bring about change and reform. Securing a majority would 'let you do anything'.[108] His model was the Meiji Restoration as a 'masculine democracy',[109] which he understood as the practice of 'resolute politics based on determined decisions'.[110] As Watanabe elaborated:

> He was severely frustrated by the fact that the LDP was unable to implement 'necessary' policies even though they always had a majority in the Diet, because they had to take into consideration the opposition parties and public opinion...Ozawa has abandoned the idea that consideration of public opinion and respect for minority opinions are essential driving forces behind the creation of democracy...Ozawa's democracy is simply the practice of 'majority rule', but from there his 'democracy' discourse has been refined further and transformed into meaning simply 'determined decisions', in other words 'centralising power' and 'despotism'.[111]

Ozawa-style democracy made forming a majority group more important than anything else and it did not matter how you achieved it.[112] Having taken the reins of government, he could then impose 'forcible decision-making and policy implementation...In response to...criticisms, he once argued back, "How am I top-down? Democracy is not about not reaching a conclusion"'.[113] He aimed to eliminate the process of prolonged discussions necessary to form a consensus, thus eradicating the Japanese style of consensus decision making, which was too slow and where participants repeatedly made compromises and concessions behind the scenes. If he could win a majority and thus gain power, he could make decisions through majority decision making without wasting a lot of time. He was well known to respect his own abilities above all and to be too impatient to wait for a consensus because he wanted to decide outcomes himself.[114] One of his former recruits offered the observation, 'The problem is that Ozawa is quite clear about what he likes and what he doesn't like. He is not about compromise'.[115]

In that sense, Ozawa rejected Tanaka's way of showing consideration to others and Takeshita's laying the groundwork (*nemawashi*) for decisions. Ozawa arrogantly said, 'Tanaka *sensei* and Takeshita *sensei* were politicians who emphasised interest coordination [*rigai chōseigata seijika*]. I learnt from Tanaka *sensei* as a negative example. Politicians in the future need the power to coordinate plus the power to make decisions'.[116] Even in opposition Ozawa ran political parties as personal fiefdoms and brooked no opposition to his rule. Kano Michihiko, MAFF minister in the Kan and Noda cabinets, stood against Ozawa for the NFP leadership in 1997 because he thought 'it was time to put an end to Ozawa's autocratic rule'.[117] Ozawa dissolved the party only a week later.

Ozawa subsequently wrote in *Ozawashugi*, 'Once the people decide on a leader, they need to be determined to leave things up to the way that leader wants'.[118] Ozawa's idea of how the Ozawa-Fukuda 'grand coalition' of 2007 would have worked if it had ever eventuated revealed his preference for personal rule, his disregard for due political process, and his basic contempt for both the role of the cabinet as a body for exercising policy leadership in government and for the functions of ordinary Diet members as policymakers. Ozawa outlined his:

> cabinet formation plan to Prime Minister Yasuo Fukuda at the time: 'I will become deputy prime minister. I do not mind serving as a minister without portfolio.' He then continued: 'I would like to see a coalition fixed first. If that is fixed, policies can be set at our own discretion. Since we cannot rely on politicians, both sides should appoint a couple of persons other than lawmakers to attend talks.' He proposed leaving his aides to work out policy talks, without trusting LDP lawmakers.[119]

This comment may have been inspired by his view that 'the DPJ is actually "incapable of governing"',[120] but the way he went about trying to organise a secret deal with Fukuda revealed his strong penchant for unilateral action, his unwillingness to consult and his basic contempt for other leaders in his own party behind whose backs he tried to organise this 'grand coalition'. When he approached the LDP with the idea and was asked whether the DPJ would remain united, he responded 'There's no problem. We've won the [Upper House] election, and right now my magic is still working. Our party is full of idiots'.[121] He exploded in anger when met by opposition from within the DPJ, declaring that it showed a lack of confidence in him.[122] He held a press conference to announce his resignation as DPJ leader saying 'The DPJ is still incompetent in various ways'.[123] When asked why the grand coalition never came into being, Fukuda himself said:

> The basic premise for a grand coalition was that Ozawa Ichiro was able to control the Democratic Party of Japan (DPJ). Mr. Ozawa assumed that he could control the party. He was very proud of its substantial victory in the Upper House election. However, he was not able to control it...I obtained agreement from key figures in the party in advance. Mr. Ozawa didn't seem to do that.[124]

Fukuda's renowned skills for coordination and consensus building were clearly not replicated by Ozawa on the DPJ side. The two had completely different political leadership styles. Ozawa was not a consensus seeker, preferring instead to act arbitrarily on his own account without thought to the political views and interests of others. His much-vaunted espousal of social and cultural individualism – what might be called his doctrinaire individualism – and his fevered espousal of the virtues of strong political leadership could be seen as a rationalisation of his own personal leadership style and his ego-driven approach to politics.

When Ozawa campaigned for the DPJ political leadership in September 2010, he contrasted himself with Kan, whom he dismissed as captive of the bureaucracy, in offering to create a system of strong political leadership. What he was offering, however, was leadership by a political strongman (see Table 1.1). He made his pledge respectable by claiming that his offer was no more than fulfilling a commitment to convert to a political system led by politicians (as opposed to bureaucrats) in the 2009 DPJ manifesto. On the other hand, he had already burdened the DPJ with the negative image of his control.[125] For him, 'regime change' meant 'seizing power and twisting the DPJ around his little finger'.[126] He was preoccupied with attacking and defeating those he deemed his enemies, who were people who did not obey him.[127] His overbearing methods often proved counterproductive, eliciting fierce opposition that led to setbacks.[128] Even within his own group, Ozawa avoided debates, used close aides and thoroughly imposed 'a top-down style of communication'.[129] He once said, '(The young) politicians who come from the Matsushita Institute all nag too much. They should just listen to what I say and do as I tell them. It took 25 years for me to be able to state my own opinion'.[130] He made no effort to explain the benefits of his proposals and to persuade his fellow DPJ members and supporters to his point of view. His attitude was one of 'trust me and follow',[131] showing that he had not changed from his early years in the LDP. As secretary-general, his mindset was: 'If there is a decision that needs to be made, I will prioritise making the decision over following democratic procedures and take responsibility for that.'[132] However, as Ozawa's former ally, Hata Tsutomu, commented, 'If a party leader says nothing but "follow me", they will become someone like Hitler'.[133] Similarly, right-wing commentators attacked Ozawa, accusing him of being undemocratic and preferring a Soviet Union-style of 'democratic centralism'.[134] His 'old, follow-me-without-any-questions-style of leadership…[was] in stark contrast with his own "modern" political philosophy'.[135] Former secretary Takahashi observed, 'There is a gap between the ideals of political reform that Ozawa talks about and Ozawa's personality in reality'.[136]

Ozawa's political personality and relationships

Ozawa's personality underpinned his political leadership style. His disposition was depicted as imperious and autocratic, his manner authoritarian and the kind of personal ties he maintained with those around him essentially those of a superior-subordinate, boss-underling, patron-client type.

Again, it was when Ozawa became LDP secretary-general that his personality characteristics became fully evident. The most revealing incident was his 'summoning' of the three candidates for the LDP presidency in 1991 in order to interview them even though he was only deputy chairman of the Takeshita faction at the time and younger than all three candidates. Comments such as "'What is he doing, acting so important...'" "Isn't Ozawa being a little arrogant?" "He's very conceited" were bandied around Nagata-chō and in the media [and] certainly cemented the coercive image of Ozawa'.[137]

The successful creation of the RP was later attributed to the force of Ozawa's personality. According to Itō, 'the Hata faction's decision that led to the formation of the Renewal Party would not have been made without the force of attraction exuded by Ozawa, who still had sufficient "aura" about him at the time, and the expectation that "something will happen if we follow Ozawa"'.[138] Yamaguchi likened Ozawa to 'Oda Nobunaga, the Sengoku Period lord who invaded enemy camps himself under his own banner. Subordinates get dragged in and follow him'.[139]

Later in the NFP, his close aide Koike Yuriko revealed that his 'authoritarian attitude, which was [again] branded as "Hitler-esque", was the subject of criticism within the party from the outset'.[140] A veteran NFP executive commented, 'He doesn't listen to what other people have to say. Everything is about himself'.[141] A former national newspaper executive who had known Ozawa since his LDP days described him as 'the ultimate narcissist'.[142]

One of Ozawa's chief power tools was the fear that he managed to instil in others. Even former LDP-turned-DPJ politician Katō Kōichi, who had drinks with Ozawa, was scared of him.[143] Itō explained the unusual psychology that enabled Ozawa to generate such fear:

> In the past, there were politicians that made you feel 'pressure'. When politicians that make you feel 'pressure' walk towards you in the hallway of the Diet building you feel the need to give way to them, and when you face these politicians you become so nervous that your body becomes stiff...Ozawa back then was the first politician that made me feel 'pressure' in a long time. In particular, during the time between his appointment as LDP secretary-general and the inauguration of the Hosokawa administration, he was even giving off some kind of 'aura'...Ozawa gave off an atmosphere that bewildered his opponents and made them shrink back.[144]

Hosokawa's published diary tells of the difficulties he had in dealing with Ozawa, particularly when Ozawa did not get his own way, precipitating bad moods, sulking, non-attendance at meetings, being uncontactable, 'disappearances',[145] and more generally exhibiting the behaviour of a spoilt child.[146] In late December 1993, Hosokawa complained that because Ozawa would not contact him at all, he had to communicate with him through intermediaries, which consumed a lot of time and energy.[147] One major point of contention was Ozawa's demand for Hosokawa to reshuffle Takemura (with whom Ozawa had a very rivalrous relationship) from his position as chief cabinet secretary because he had criticised Ozawa and complained about his political methods, which Hosokawa refused to do.

Ozawa's forceful side was not leavened by a sense of loyalty and compassion towards others. Unlike Tanaka and Kanemaru, who knew how to manoeuvre people skilfully, including the opposition parties and bureaucrats, Ozawa relied on coercion, calculation and cunning.[148] According to former Minister of Posts and Telecommunications Watanabe Hideo, Ozawa 'categorised people depending on whether or not they were beneficial to him'.[149] Because of his lack of consideration or sense of loyalty and compassion, Ozawa did not inform Hata that his administration was about to become a minority government when the JSP left the coalition in opposition to Ozawa's organisation of a Lower House caucus that excluded it.[150] On the fateful day in 1994 just before the entire cabinet resigned, Hata wanted to contact him but Ozawa had disappeared and was unavailable. He had clearly deserted Hata who was his sworn political friend.[151]

These manoeuvres reflected Ozawa's Machiavellian instincts where political parties and politicians were merely pawns to be moved around on a chessboard regardless of the personal costs to those involved.[152] Koike relates how she 'became mentally and physically exhausted by being twisted around Ozawa's little finger'.[153] Even Tanaka, who threatened and intimidated people into submission, was personally liked by many for being caring and generous. He even showed consideration for his enemies, making sure that his opponents survived. He took pity on them, saying 'He's necessary too'.[154] Ozawa lacked these sentiments. Another key personality difference between Ozawa and Tanaka was that Ozawa did not show any warmth towards the people of his hometown. After his third election, he did not return to his constituency, instead using general contractors to rule the local area and making local construction companies compete with each other to show loyalty to him.[155]

Ozawa's ruthlessness in his quest for power and lack of consideration for others over the years swelled the ranks of his political opponents and those willing to desert him. In times of political strife, 'even his allies and close aides left to join the enemy'.[156] No politician had a stronger predisposition to make enemies than Ozawa. Moreover, once an enemy, there was no going back for Ozawa, whose approach was to crush his political rivals to pieces.[157]

Ozawa ended up in adversarial relationships with a who's who of leading Japanese politicians such as Tanaka, Takeshita, Hashimoto, Kajiyama, Nonaka and Obuchi, as well as key Japanese politicians in the Kōmeitō and NFP, including Ichikawa Yūichi, Hosokawa and Hata.[158] Fujii, once a close Ozawa associate and co-founder of the LP, but who in the end split from him, commented, 'He has eloquently said that he doesn't consult, doesn't explain, and doesn't persuade. With no one to consult with, all he'll have left in the end is sycophants'.[159] By the time of the Kan administration, the impression was that Ozawa's supporters included no people of talent.[160] He always operated in the company of subordinates and associates (some might say 'henchmen' or 'lackeys and flunkeys'), who comprised his large staff of secretaries and some of his followers who were prepared to do his bidding without question, who were prone to demonstrations of loyalty in both word and deed, and who often spoke for him in order to get his message out. Some Ozawa 'devotees' went as far as to accord

Ozawa the status of a cult leader and were little more than an echo of their master's voice, expressing his thoughts and repeating his words like a Greek chorus. They changed their attitudes and opinions to follow their leader's views and moves. Some displayed a kind of blind loyalty, which held that Ozawa could do no wrong, showing their willingness to suspend their own judgement and potentially sacrifice their immediate political interests in order to support Ozawa's position. They were 'complete "believers in the Ozawa religion"'.[161] The nature of Ozawa's followership only served to strengthen his image as an autocrat who ran a boss-subordinate, leader-follower show. He made many followers but no partners.[162]

Ozawa's reputation contrasted with that of Kan, who was surrounded by talented politicians such as Maehara, Okada and Minister of Finance Noda.[163] The only politician who stayed close to Ozawa from the early days back in 1993 was Yamaoka.

Divide and misrule

Within coalitions Ozawa was generally a divisive force, as he was in the Hosokawa coalition, in the NFP (which merged a spectrum of smaller parties) and in the LDP-LP coalition. His record of crafting coalitions and then destroying them was legendary. His high-handedness alienated coalition partners, as it did in the eight-party administration led by Hosokawa. Not only did relations between the JNP and NPH sour over how to deal with him[164] but Ozawa also failed to consult, which excluded the JSP from decision making on key policies.[165] He also fell out with the JSP over policy issues such as security and taxation reform. He was reported as saying, 'If we're going to accept the Japan Socialist Party's policies as they are, I will resign as secretary-general. If we're going to accept Murayama as prime minister, I will leave the Renewal Party...I will go my own way'.[166]

However, it was more than just failure to consult and policy differences that destroyed the coalition. The JSP did not fit easily with Ozawa's grand plan for political realignment in which he hoped to use the RP and Kōmeitō as a lever to absorb the JNP, NPH and right-wingers in the JSP. This meant chopping off the leftists in the JSP and others, and forming a conservative power base against the LDP based on right-wingers in the JSP, his own supporters and the solid system of Sōka Gakkai.[167] By getting rid of the JSP's left-wingers, he was hoping to make the option of joining the Ozawa forces more attractive to potential defectors in the LDP in line with his long-term ambition to destroy his old party.[168] However, in the end, Ozawa rejected his scheme for dividing the JSP's rightists and leftists because they continued to oppose liberalising rice imports and were hysterically opposed to raising tax rates by changing the name of the consumption tax to 'national welfare tax'.[169] He concluded that the coalition 'government would not be able to go anywhere with people like this involved'.[170] His hatred of the JSP also went deep because of their partnership with the LDP in the 1955 system when he wanted to construct a two-party system.[171] So in the end he decided to throw them away in order 'to get rid of trouble'.[172] As for the socialists, it was primarily antipathy towards Ozawa that drove them into the arms of the LDP, with the result that Hata's administration became a minority government, which subsequently fell, and the LDP-Socialist-NPH coalition under Prime Minister Murayama replaced it.

Ozawa came to regret his behaviour in dealing with the JSP under the Hata administration.[173] Many years later he told political journalist Watanabe Kensuke:

> Back then, the Japan Socialist Party would have followed us if we said we would make Murayama prime minister. If we had won the Japan Socialist Party over, even if that meant turning a blind eye to all other problems including the policy talks, maintained the non-LDP coalition administration and kept the LDP as an opposition party for another one to two years, the LDP would have completely disintegrated.[174]

In fact, unknown to Ozawa, the LDP, JSP and Sakigake had been secretly scheming to form a new government. In January 1994, about six months before the coalition finally collapsed, moves to form a coalition between the LDP and JSP were making progress under the surface. A top-secret meeting took place at the Asakusa View Hotel, where it could slip under the political radar. The crucial characteristic of this meeting, was that it was 'one where people who "disliked Ozawa" gathered to plan the establishment of an "anti-Ozawa government"'.[175]

The NFP, which began as an amalgamation of the RP, Kōmeitō, JNP, DSP and the Liberal Reform League (Jiyū Kaikaku Rengō), also had a troubled history. Ozawa had big hopes for the party as a conservative alternative to the LDP and as a giant step towards the creation of a two-party system. However, the NFP got off to a rough start, thanks to Ozawa, based on the way its leader was chosen. When the party was inaugurated, deep-seated discord between Ozawa and Hata immediately surfaced.[176] Hata was leader of the RP, the largest group in the NFP, and so had a claim on the leadership. On the other hand, Ozawa, who was already appointed secretary-general, decided to support Kaifu while avoiding Hata, even though they had once been strong allies. As usual, hard-nosed electoral calculations were behind Ozawa's abandonment of Hata. The Kōmei group supported Kaifu, which would bring in the votes of Sōka Gakkai.[177] Ozawa also pressured groups that supported Hata both publicly and behind the scenes.[178] His actions caused resentment amongst a large number of NFP members, including Hata, and sowed the seeds of the party's eventual collapse.[179]

Others in the NFP also fell out with Ozawa, such as Funada Hajime, who at one time was secretary of state affairs (*seimu kanji*) in the RP, a position that followed the party leader and secretary-general in rank, and which wielded a considerable amount of authority. However, in the transition from the RP to the NFP, Funada was demoted to the post of vice-chairman of the party's organising committee because he was increasingly critical of Ozawa. He moved away from Ozawa after that.[180] Ozawa treated Okuda Keiwa in a similar fashion in the transition from the RP to the NFP because, as chairman of the Lower House Steering Committee, Okuda had good relations with JSP Chairman of the Lower

House Doi Takako, and made fair judgements, which Ozawa seemed not to like.[181] In this way, Ozawa alienated many former supporters.

Kaifu also disclosed his misgivings at becoming the leader of the NFP because of his previous difficulties in relations with Ozawa:

> It was my second time to lock squarely with the 'secretary-general who ran away'…To be honest, by this time I did not consider building a genuinely trusting relationship between us. His past actions as a man who 'heightened expectations only to let people down' had already been inserted into my head. However, people around me raised ardent voices that they 'wanted to form a new, healthy ruling party', and there were also strong opinions to be cautious of Ozawa. 'Mr. Kaifu, please lead our way. We cannot follow Ozawa'…With the determination that I will become the adhesive between Ozawa and those that view him with caution, and that I will revive politics by creating a new party with the ability to govern, I became the first leader of the New Frontier Party.[182]

Not long after the NFP was launched, Ozawa turned on his long-term ally, former Kōmeitō Secretary-General Ichikawa. As soon as Ozawa found out that public criticism of Sōka Gakkai was growing stronger after the July 1995 Upper House election, he attempted to get rid of Ichikawa, his partner in the so-called 'Ichi-Ichi duo'. The focus of the upcoming Diet session was going to be reform of the Religious Corporations Law (*Shūkyō Hōjinhō*), so it was inconvenient from Ozawa's point of view that the former Kōmei group would be the focus of criticism. That is why Ozawa wanted Ichikawa to resign from his position as chairman of the NFP's Policy Affairs Research Council, and Kanzaki Takenori, also from the Kōmei group, to resign as chairman of the Lower House Steering Committee. Of course, in the past Ozawa had dumped Hata in the same way for the Ichi-Ichi duo. As a result, Ichikawa transferred his loyalty from Ozawa to Hata, joining the growing number of party members estranged from him, including Hosokawa.[183]

When Ozawa himself became NFP president in December 1995, people started to leave the party because of discord with him. The internal rows over Ozawa's leadership was a direct cause of the breakup of the party.[184] In October 1996, when the first Lower House election was held under the new leadership, the NFP lost, winning only 156 seats to the LDP's 239. After the election, the party continued to be plagued by defections, including Hata who left to form the Sun Party in December 1996 and Hosokawa who left in June 1997. These were both men whom Ozawa had installed as prime minister at different times. By December 1997, so many had left the NFP that Ozawa had little choice but to announce its dissolution. He had tried to 'manage things with…an attitude of "shut up and listen to me", but everyone became fed up and good quality people left one by one'.[185]

Ozawa's brief explanation for the break-up was that he had received a request from Kōmeitō members to carry out a split in the party smoothly so that they could contest the 1998 Upper House election by themselves and he had complied with that request.[186] He did not elaborate on why the Kōmeitō members had requested the split in the first place. In view of the impending election, Ozawa could not tolerate this defection and so decided to dissolve the party. The NFP split three ways into pro-Ozawa, anti-Ozawa and former Kōmeitō groups.

Given Ozawa's reputation, when the LP formed a coalition with the LDP in November 1998 the negotiations were led by Chief Cabinet Secretary Nonaka, who drew up the policy agreement between the two parties with Ozawa. As Nonaka himself put it, 'even if [we] have to prostrate ourselves before the monster [Ozawa], we have to manage the twisted Diet'.[187] Other key figures in the LDP fiercely opposed the coalition, including the YKK group – Koizumi, Yamasaki Taku and Katō Kōichi. Later there were secret talks between Obuchi and Ozawa at the Kantei in early March 2000. Ozawa said, 'I'd like to ask you to dissolve the LDP. After I dissolve the Liberal Party too, we can get together and produce a major conservative coalition. If you cannot, we will withdraw from the LDP-Liberal coalition'.[188] Obuchi later recounted that 'Icchan [Ichirō] again spoke nonsense. The LDP was formed in 1955, after the merger of the Liberal Party and the Japan Democratic Party. Considering the efforts that seniors have made, I cannot dissolve the LDP and destroy it'.[189] On 1 April 2000 Obuchi and Ozawa had secret talks for about 20 minutes. In the meeting Ozawa is said to have demanded the ouster of Nonaka, telling Obuchi that Nonaka was trying to drive a wedge between him and his followers by urging them to leave their boss and the LP and rejoin the LDP. Ozawa also asked to rejoin the LDP in the hope of regaining power in the ruling party. Obuchi refused Ozawa's requests and decided to let him leave the ruling coalition.[190] After the talks, Obuchi announced the dissolution of the alliance with the LP. That night, around 11pm, he had a stroke. He died six weeks later.

Kaifu also relates the story of the destruction of the coalition, which the LP left in April 2000. As he recalled:

> after a year had passed since the coalition was formed (in 2000), Ozawa, yet again, suggested leaving it…Whilst thinking to myself, 'oh no, not again', I tried to persuade him, 'don't do it this time'. But Ozawa's conclusion was that 'if we don't, the other party will override us'…When Prime Minister Obuchi collapsed and passed away immediately after the party leaders' meeting with Ozawa…there were murmurs that 'Ozawa killed him'. In any case, that was the last time I worked with him. It is simply exhausting getting involved with that 'destroyer'…Perhaps it is karma, or maybe even some kind of illness, that he has such an extreme disposition.[191]

For Ozawa, destruction was a means to increase his presence and influence.[192] This certainly played out in the Kan and Noda administrations of 2010–12, when Ozawa attempted to bring both governments down in a noisy political farce, the Kan administration with a motion of no-confidence and the Noda government with his departure from DPJ ranks.[193]

Genuine reformer or power-hungry politician?

At the heart of the Ozawa enigma is a debate about ends and means. What has been the end to which Ozawa's machinations and manoeuvrings have been put? Has power been the means and reform the end? Has Ozawa pursued power primarily in order to drive a programme of reform? Alternatively, has reform merely been a policy tool that Ozawa has used from time to time in order to justify his ambition to take power?[194] In short, does Ozawa value power for its own sake?

In the end, 'explaining Ozawa' boils down to a debate about his 'supreme objective' or 'ultimate goal'. His admirers are unanimous that his endless political scheming is all for a purpose – that he is the greatest reformer of Japanese politics and acts from a sense of conviction. Former LDP politician Yamaguchi Toshio, for example, portrayed him as a conviction-driven idealist.[195] Another defender of Ozawa against his many critics, Watanabe Kensuke, wrote, 'For Ozawa, administrations are only a means for realising his political principles'.[196] Similarly, Oka and Hughes, whilst conceding that 'Ozawa is certainly a political animal',[197] argued that 'it is politics with a purpose'.[198] Such observations suggest that Ozawa did not pursue power for its own sake but in order to achieve reform in line with his own vision.[199]

Certainly Ozawa would claim that his fundamental ambition was 'reforming Japan's system of politics'. He said that if he 'needed to choose, I would always choose reforms. Rather than wait to die without doing anything, I would always choose to open the gates and sally out'.[200] He made this clear in numerous interviews with scholars and others, describing himself as a reformer by upbringing[201] and 'anti-establishment' like his father,[202] and claiming that his 'own goal is pure and simple, the reform of politics'.[203] By anti-establishment he meant being 'anti' the existing power structure, authority and order, in other words, being opposed to the LDP's political ideas and escaping from bureaucratic rule.[204] Ozawa described the origins of his reformist ideas as follows:

> When I ran for election for the first time, I viewed politics through my father. My father had strong antipathy towards the establishment, probably because he was extremely poor. As such, he did not associate with financial circles…I strongly exhibit similar tendencies too. It has been more than 20 years since I entered the world of politics, but I have barely associated with economic circles during that time, although I started to come into contact with them more frequently from around the time I became secretary-general. I tend to criticise the establishment. I had been seeing that aspect of my father since I was in my late teens, so I developed a strong feeling that I did not want to bow down to the establishment.[205]

Ozawa's anti-establishmentarianism could also be traced back to his roots in Tohoku, where he shared in the 'anti-centre, anti-power, anti-establishment nature…dormant in the hearts of the people of Tohoku'.[206] Ozawa advocated the introduction of single-seat constituencies in his first election campaign in 1969 and in every campaign after that.[207] He then began to propel reforms forward as LDP secretary-general[208] and when Keiseikai split in 1992, he argued that he needed to gain power so that he could mount his revolution from within.[209]

However, should Ozawa's description of himself and those of his allies and former employees be accepted uncritically? Many view the portrayal of 'Ozawa the reformer' with a great deal of scepticism, if not cynicism. During the early 1990s in particular, when Ozawa, tainted by the Kanemaru Sagawa Kyūbin scandal, rose from the ashes of the Keiseikai to project a shining image of himself as a reformer, he was arguably trying to divert attention from possible prosecution. Certainly the banner of reform brilliantly served Ozawa's political purposes at the time.

In reality, Ozawa's push for reform was sporadic, often surfacing when it was most advantageous to his political advancement and frequently providing a convenient policy rationale for destructive political behaviour. In this conception, Ozawa's reform goals were not actually ends but in fact the means to bolster his political fortunes. He took up the cause of reform when it suited his political purposes.

Focusing on Ozawa's *modus operandi* – the way in which he conducted himself as a politician and his political methods – as opposed to his stated goals – in short, what he did rather than what he said – reveals more about his true political nature because it illuminates what his fundamental political values, beliefs, intentions and priorities are (his *honne*), rather than merely his rhetoric or *tatemae*. This focus reveals a politician with a voracious appetite for power who will stop at nothing to achieve his own political supremacy whilst managing cleverly to cloak naked power seeking in the language of reform. It meant that Ozawa's politics ran on two separate tracks: the public policy track and the private politicking track. These represented Ozawa's two faces: the public 'reform' face and the private power-seeking face. Brandishing reform credentials and ambitions made Ozawa sound credible and respectable as a politician; it could be also used to justify particular political acts. After his experiences in 1993 – the true turning point in his political career – when Ozawa emerged victorious by turning the cause of political reform greatly to his political advantage, he consistently resorted to the rhetoric of reform to justify his actions and to galvanise support amongst his followers and the wider electorate. With the passage of time, however, his rhetoric notwithstanding, Ozawa's push for reform diminished, as did his credibility as a reformer. His desire for power became more apparent as the main driver of his actions and political choices – to which his period in the DPJ attests.

In any administration of which he was a part, Ozawa consistently chose to operate as the principal power broker rather than the principal policy entrepreneur. When he was finally in a position to advance his quest for greater structural reform of the political system in the DPJ government launched in 2009, he chose not to be a formal participant in the government executive. As it turned out, this choice directly conflicted with his goal of buttressing cabinet power over policymaking, to which he could have made a great contribution. If he had genuinely believed in institutionalising his own political structural reforms, he would have actively sought the prime ministership or positions in the government executive whose leadership powers, particularly vis-à-vis the bureaucracy, he so avidly sought to aggrandise in his political reform plans. Instead, Ozawa assumed the position of secretary-general with alacrity, controlling the numbers, the positions and the money in the party and, as it turned out, key government spending policies that could be used for politically strategic distributive purposes.

Acting as secretary-general was, in fact, Ozawa's preferred role in government. He routinely occupied this position as the power behind the throne in various administrations. Tanaka once explicitly advised him to aim to be secretary-general if he wanted to be a politician.[210] Oka also recounts a conversation that Ozawa had with Nakasone, who, when made LDP secretary-general in 1972, was gleeful that 'officials came to him with all the information they supplied to the Prime Minister, often *before* they briefed the Prime Minister'.[211] This lesson was not lost on Ozawa.

According to Oka, Ozawa deliberately selected the secretary-general's position in the Hatoyama government because it put him in a position to implement his long-held ideas and policies.[212] The irony of such an alleged ambition (and Oka's argument) is that the kind of political reforms that Ozawa had originally advocated would have eliminated the secretary-general's position as one with influence over government policy by centralising policymaking power in the prime minister and cabinet, not in the party, still less in its secretary-general. No equivalent position of ruling party secretary-general exists in Westminster parliamentary cabinet systems – Ozawa's model for Japan. Ozawa sought a position that was premised on the old pre-reform system of the LDP, one that actually gained even more power after electoral reform with government funding of political parties (funding that was distributed by the secretary-general) alongside the enhanced powers of the party executive over electoral endorsements. Furthermore, with Ozawa's centralisation of the reception of petitions through the secretary-general's office, he beefed-up the power of the office in a deliberate move to make the position of secretary-general even more influential as a figure not just in the party but in the government itself. Edano, when appointed to the position of DPJ secretary-general in June 2010, declared, 'We will change it [the system of accepting petitions single-handedly by the secretary-general] to a fair system'.[213]

While Ozawa's imprint on the Hatoyama administration was absolutely clear-cut with respect to government spending programmes, it was other DPJ politicians, such as Edano and Sengoku, who stepped up to the plate on political reforms. If Ozawa had remained a proactive reformer in the Hatoyama government he would have aligned himself with these reformers and acted in ways that helped to institutionalise operational features of the reformed political structures along Westminster lines. This would have meant less power to the party as a policy and budget-making entity, and more power to the prime minister and cabinet, including the new ministerial committees and the new National Strategy Unit as the precursor to the National Strategy Bureau. Ozawa would have chosen to play a prominent role in these 'new' political structures. He would not have undercut the political reforms to which he had contributed so much by buttressing his own individual policymaking power as DPJ secretary-general. Even Ozawa's abolition of the PRC, which could be considered an important political structural reform, was undertaken so that power over party policy with implications for special interests and for electoral strategy could be concentrated in his own hands and would not have to be shared with either policy specialists in the party or with ordinary backbenchers seeking to gain policy expertise.

Similarly, Ozawa's main goal was said to be the creation of a two-party system,[214] yet time and again he chose a course that directly conflicted with this goal. He demolished the NFP, a party that had great potential as a mainstream conservative alternative to the LDP. Even his core objective of smashing the LDP was betrayed by periodic approaches to the party. Having promised to destroy the old system and build a new one in 1993–94, he was back in the fold four years later when the LP signed the coalition agreement with the LDP in 1998. Again, less than a decade later, in 2007, Ozawa was actively pursuing the option of a 'grand coalition' with the LDP. Even in 2011 Ozawa toyed with the same idea in order to get rid of the Kan government. Indeed, during both the Kan and Noda administrations, Ozawa acted as a wrecking ball inside the DPJ, destroying it as a major alternative ruling party.[215] Moreover, such destructive action inside the party ruined any chance of its operating as a cohesive legislative unit along Westminster lines.[216] Such a record only made sense in terms of personal power seeking rather than a steadfast plan to restructure Japan's party system along bipartisan lines.

Ozawa's own actions thus sabotaged developments that would have consolidated political reforms that he himself helped to engineer, such as centralising policymaking power in the cabinet, creating a two-party system and consolidating the DPJ as a Westminster-style alternative ruling party. Ozawa failed to obey the new rules and observe the new reform principles that he had a large part in setting. He treated these instrumentally as subordinate goals and, if necessary, as expendable. Given an opportunity to pursue his own power-seeking interests at the cost of compromising reforms, Ozawa consistently chose power over principle. He might have sought political system change, but he had not changed as a politician. His main goal was consistently to wield supreme power, not to achieve structural reform of either the political system or the economy. While certainly advocating, formulating and assisting in the implementation of key political reforms, particularly with respect to entrenching the general principle of greater power to politicians at the expense of bureaucrats in order to strengthen political leadership, and proselytising the virtues of single-member districts and two majority parties vying for power on the basis of competing programmes, Ozawa was personally concerned most with the pursuit of power. Aggrandising his position at the centre of Japanese politics is the ambition that makes the most consistent sense of his behaviour, methods and practices. In short, power maximising rather than reform maximising has been his true end goal. Even Ozawa's former secretary Ishikawa acknowledged that Max Weber's description of a political 'boss' was an apt way to characterise Ozawa: '[He] seeks power alone, power as a source of money, but also *power for power's sake*.'[217]

Certainly Ozawa's obsession with power also made sense of his preoccupation with winning: winning elections, winning positions of power for himself and ensuring his preferred candidates won in elections including for the party leadership. Indeed, according to many observers and fellow politicians, Ozawa's preference was for dictatorial or hegemonic power – nothing less than running the ruling party and the entire government. He was in his element when in a position of supreme power, controlling administrations and key policies. 'Reform' provided not only a convenient rationale for anything he wanted to do in politics, a notion that he could manipulate for tactical advantage and a useful mantra that he could reiterate to disguise his real objectives, but also, if implemented, it could provide a further means of augmenting his power in government. There is little convincing evidence that Ozawa valued reform for its own sake even as an ancillary goal. Insofar as he genuinely promoted reform, it was always instrumental to his pursuit of power.

Reprising the Tanaka model of old politics

The model of old politics that Ozawa reprised was essentially the Tanaka model. It prevailed in Japan in the 1970s and lingered on in some respects until Koizumi arrived in office in 2001 and attempted to root it out by 'destroying the LDP', ignoring the factions and offering a different type of leadership based largely on direct policy appeals to non-aligned voters, particularly in urban areas. Ozawa was Tanaka's most prominent disciple, protégé and 'favourite' (*hizokko*),[218] and a true heir to his style of politics.[219]

As a freshman politician, Ozawa learnt the basics under Tanaka, who was an executive of the Satō faction.[220] As Ozawa relates:

> I was elected for the first time when I was 27 years of age in 1969. I became an Upper House Diet member and knocked on Tanaka Kakuei's door. Tanaka was already a big executive in Satō (Eisaku)'s faction; being only a rookie Diet member, I would have appeared like a child to him. I was, however, treated by him really well for some reason...Since then, I have been trained in the fundamentals of politics by Tanaka. I think that I am who I am now because I was nurtured by such an outstanding politician as Tanaka Kakuei.[221]

Tanaka had strong feelings for Ozawa because of his likeness to his own dead son, Masanori, who was born in the same year as Ozawa but who died when he was three.[222]

At Tanaka's death Ozawa said: 'Tanaka not only taught me the ABC's of politics from the time I was first elected to the national legislature but also was concerned about me like a real father'.[223] When attending every session of Tanaka's trial for bribery,[224] Ozawa would wait until the end of the hearing in order to meet Tanaka's eyes and bow deeply.[225] Ozawa explained that he was motivated by 'sentiment...The man in power of the day, who took care of me, was made to sit on…a bench all day long and I couldn't bear it if he was there alone with nobody around'.²²⁶ When Ozawa was 'asked whether Tanaka's political techniques and the way he made money, which were revealed in the trials, came in handy, Ozawa said, "There was no need [for the information]. *Oyaji* had shown me everything that he was doing, so I understood them very well'.²²⁷ Ozawa also clearly anticipated the day when he might too be in the dock, saying, 'As a politician, I was thinking: "if I were put in the same situation in court, how should I be?…What would I do if I were him?" I was listening to the trial thinking these kinds of things all the way through'.²²⁸ Ozawa continued staunchly to defend Tanaka ever after, saying that 'he had been unfairly singled out. "I'm not saying 'Tanaka no oyaji' was perfect…it wasn't only Tanaka-san who was doing that kind of thing…Everyone – citizens, politicians and bureaucrats – used to do that," Mr. Ozawa said, calling Mr. Tanaka a "scapegoat"'.²²⁹ During the Hatoyama administration, Ozawa had a visit to Tanaka's tombstone televised, indicating to the public that he still held Tanaka in the highest esteem.

Ozawa's *modus operandi* echoed Tanaka's in several key areas: in his autocratic and dictatorial political style, which was modelled on Tanaka's method of factional management; in his excessive reliance on the public works construction industry as a source of votes and political funding; in his grand design for reform that doubled as a public works plan; in his pursuit of government and party control based on the 'the power of numbers'; in his stepping into Tanaka's shoes as the 'father' of money politics; in his faithful adherence to Tanaka's basic electioneering principles; and in his attempts to act as kingmaker in the DPJ.

In the factional dictator's footsteps

After the inauguration of the DPJ administration the media soon reported high levels of public distrust and dislike of Ozawa because of concerns that 'he could become a dictatorial ruler, just as his mentor Tanaka was'.²³⁰ His autocratic leadership style in the DPJ was a carbon copy of his factional management style.²³¹ His iron-fisted rule was attributed to the fact that he grew up in a pure factional culture.²³² As Itō Atsuo elaborated:

> In the past, factions in the LDP were top-down fighting groups, organisations with strict hierarchical relationships in which members must obey the leader. Ozawa imported this culture of factions into the DPJ management. Any objections or protest against Ozawa were considered outrageous. This is why democracy has been lost from the DPJ.²³³

The Tanaka faction, in particular, was run along strict hierarchical lines. Members of the faction exhibited loyalty so absolute that it was called Tanaka's 'army' (*gundan*). A line of command ran from top to bottom, with the entire organisation moving at Tanaka's behest.²³⁴ Kaifu was able to witness Tanaka's absolute control firsthand:

In the Tanaka faction, there was what was called the five clauses, and people followed openly these almost gang-like rules, where white will become black if the leader says it is black. 'If you don't like it, leave!' That was how it was. However, everybody knew very well that if they were to leave, they would get shot down, and so everybody held their tongue. Doesn't this sound rather familiar? Yes, it is very similar to the way Ozawa Ichirō deals with things. He followed only these sorts of traits of Tanaka.[235]

Ozawa behaved like Tanaka as the supreme commander of his 'corps' of faction members, expecting strong loyalty from his followers and issuing advisories, words of encouragement and commands in a way that was not evident in other DPJ groups. Ozawa also dispensed patronage to members in the same way that Tanaka had done. Members were under heavy pressure to do what Ozawa said because failure to obey could result in a withdrawal of favours and good will. Ozawa's political relationships were relationships of reciprocal exchange, built on the dispensation of patronage and reciprocal obligation rather than on the nurturing of personal ties and genuinely shared policy beliefs (see Table 1.1).

The essential similarities between the Tanaka and Ozawa factions were captured in terminology such as 'Heisei's Tanaka army' (*Heisei no Tanaka gundan*).[236] The Ozawa faction was a *gundan* because of the high levels of discipline and loyalty amongst its 'troops'. It was the only group in the DPJ that could boast levels of unity and solidarity that approximated the Tanaka faction, giving it similar machine-like characteristics. In fact, at its peak of reputedly around 150–170 members, the Ozawa group was actually larger than the Tanaka *gundan*, which at its largest numbered 141 people.

Like Tanaka, Ozawa liked to demonstrate power to his followers in order to underpin his position of command. The tradition of holding New Year parties was one such way in which Ozawa could display his commanding presence. Directly following Tanaka's practice of impressive New Year parties at the Mejiro Palace (Tanaka's home in Mejiro), Ozawa gathered together 166 Diet members at the beginning of 2010, displaying the full extent of his power.[237]

Importantly, just as in the Tanaka faction, 'loyalty to the faction was prioritised over loyalty to the party…[so] it was inevitable for the faction to become "a party within the party"',[238] and even an 'opposition party within the ruling party' (*tōnai yatō*) (see Table 1.1). As Ozawa's constant political machinations in the DPJ under the Kan and Noda administrations showed, his faction was essentially at his disposal in terms of being able to be moved as a bloc in inter- or intra-party manoeuvrings and in his attempts to secure his position, dominate the party and force his political will on successive prime ministers.[239]

Only in terms of the 'quality' of its members was the Ozawa faction not considered to be on a par with Tanaka's *gundan*. 'Quality' here mainly refers to the professional standing of its members. Tanaka's faction had more influential members, many of them with extensive political experience, while Ozawa's had members with less experience and was somewhat unreliable. Ozawa recognised this but all he could do was add more members.[240] His was a 'very lightweight army'.²⁴¹ In fact, most of Ozawa's most loyal supporters were first-term Diet members who were elected with his direct help and who thought that regime change was achieved because of Ozawa's power. They supported him because of his decisiveness and 'power to implement'.²⁴²

Perhaps the best example of Ozawa's political machine or *gundan* in operation was the campaign it mounted to elect him as DPJ president (and prime minister) in September 2010. The base of the Ozawa camp was the ANA Intercontinental Hotel in Roppongi, Tokyo. It reserved all the meeting rooms on the sixth floor, and young Diet members and secretaries mounted a telephone offensive. Their method of calling and the order in which they called people were meticulously managed. They had been well trained by Ozawa in the art of canvassing, pressuring support groups such as the postmasters, truckers, private sector trade union organisations, and soliciting support from other Diet members.²⁴³ As Gotō put it, 'The Ozawa camp piled the pressure on the management of Diet members' *kōenkai* and on their support groups to make sure they would back Ozawa. This approach demonstrated the "Tanaka army corps method" [*Tanaka gundan hōshiki*], which Ozawa mastered through personal experience during the LDP'.²⁴⁴ Ozawa turned the leadership campaign into a mini general election, with his cohorts also out in the streets campaigning on his behalf. It was the Ozawa political machine at work. The myth of the invincibility of Ozawa's *Tanaka gundan hōshiki* was only dispelled when Ozawa was defeated in the election. The Tanaka army corps method did not prove successful in the end.²⁴⁵

Capturing the construction kingdom

Ozawa also modelled himself on Tanaka in the way in which he converted government-funded public works into a tradable political commodity. Tanaka 'was the founder of general contractor-based politics'²⁴⁶ and the original architect of the so-called 'public works state' (*doboku kokka*). The concessions (*riken*) relating to construction were the most important amongst a spectrum of interests that Tanaka brought together for the purpose of winning elections, 'sucking up' political funds from companies and organisations, and allocating quotas of votes for them to deliver.²⁴⁷

Within the LDP, Tanaka also established the *zoku giin* structure and became a 'construction *zoku* without parallel',²⁴⁸ ensuring that his own faction dominated the membership of the construction tribe (*kensetsu zoku*).²⁴⁹ The *kensetsu zoku* formed an iron triangle with construction ministry bureaucrats and construction companies. It was forged by Tanaka's enormous political strength. When Kanemaru and Takeshita took over the faction from the ailing Tanaka, both wooed voters and the construction industry with pork-barrel projects. They 'had a virtual lock on deciding disbursement of the large national public works budget'.²⁵⁰ The Takeshita-Kanemaru faction also took over control of the MOC from the Tanaka faction,²⁵¹ thus strengthening the construction iron triangle.²⁵² Kanemaru himself became the Don of the construction tribe.²⁵³

Ozawa was 'the direct descendent of the Tanaka-Kanemaru line',[254] stepping into Kanemaru's shoes as construction kingpin.[255] In fact, his direct personal connections to construction contractors went back to the days of his father, Saeki, who was once appointed as minister of construction.[256] His father was related by marriage to the former Vice-President of Kajima Corporation Watanabe Kisaburō, as their wives were sisters.[257] Ozawa then married Fukuda Kazuko, whose family owned Fukuda Gumi, a powerful construction company in Niigata, which was a major financial backer of Tanaka. It was Tanaka himself who introduced Kazuko to Ozawa and told him to marry her. The marriage fused construction company money with the LDP's predilection for public works. Ozawa reportedly said that he did not care whom he was marrying if the marriage were fixed by Tanaka.[258] Construction was, therefore, in both Ozawa's DNA and kinship.

Like Tanaka, Ozawa was also very skilled at political exploitation of industries that were desperate to obtain public works.[259] He put his feet on the career ladder as a *kensetsu zoku* by serving for one year as parliamentary vice-minister of construction in the Fukuda cabinet in 1976–77, immediately followed by the post of director of the Lower House Construction Committee for two years from 1978 to 1980, enabling him to establish good connections with construction bureaucrats. A former senior MOC bureaucrat recounted that when Ozawa became parliamentary vice-minister, one of his superiors said to him, 'Ozawa Ichirō *sensei* is still young, but Tanaka Kakuei *sensei* favours him and he is Tanaka *sensei*'s favourite disciple. He is young but he is important, so look out for him with the utmost care'.[260] MOC bureaucrats considered him in a class of his own, with senior executives in the ministry sensitive to his mood and eager to treat him well.[261] During the 1980s, there was even something called the 'Ozawa School' (Ozawa Gakkō) in the MOC, which consisted of the administrative vice-minister, chief engineer, minister's secretariat counsellor, bureau chiefs and Ozawa.[262] Takahashi Yoshinobu later revealed that Ozawa's 'influence over general contractors really started to strengthen when he was appointed LDP secretary-general (in August 1989) and seized effective power over the allocation of public works. From around this time, many general contractors and people connected to the construction ministry started to frequent Ozawa's office'.[263]

In the early 1990s, with Kanemaru's support, Ozawa became chairman of the National Land and Construction Research Association (Kokudo Kensetsu Kenkyūkai), which had been established by Kanemaru and was made up of LDP *kensetsu zoku* members. While it 'was a "study group" on the surface, in actuality it had significant power over the distribution of public works amongst general contractors'.[264] According to Takahashi, the association was also part of the 'Ozawa School'.[265] Nonaka described the typical way in which the school functioned:

> Every year, towards the end of the year when the budget was being formulated, politicians gathered in the administrative vice-minister's office with their local specialty products and alcohol and drank with the administrative vice-minister [and other top MOC officials]…while listening to hourly updates on the budget. Ozawa was the one who came late at night and sat

down on the highest seat. You couldn't join the 'Ozawa School' unless you were approved by Ozawa. I was only able to join the 'Ozawa School' together with Election Committee Chairman Koga and others after having been parliamentary vice-minister of construction...The (Nishimatsu) case was a continuation of the tradition of the 'Ozawa School'.[266]

Through his leadership of the group, Ozawa was able to exercise influence over the MOC, the construction *zoku* and *zenekon*, as well as over the allocation of budgetary funds for public works ordered by the government right up until the time he left the LDP. When he formed the RP, leading members of the National Land and Construction Research Association moved with him. Even after the general election of 1993, when Ozawa became the power broker in the non-LDP coalition administration, he continued to be the 'Don of *kensetsu zoku* members'.[267]

It is impossible to know how Ozawa compares with Tanaka in terms of the scale of funds collected from construction companies, but it is clear that the amounts were considerable and his connections with this pork-barrel interest were comparable to Tanaka's. Many construction contractors in Ozawa's home prefecture of Iwate pointed to the yawning gap between the image that Ozawa liked to project as a reformer, and the reality of his deep and intimate connections to the public works construction industry:

> 'What Ozawa says and does are completely different. He talks about noble things like "reform" and "change", but in his hometown he is doing the same things as Kakuei Tanaka'. Ozawa mobilises the construction industry in elections, approves of expanding public works and is constantly shadowed by suspicion of collusion in relation to the distribution of public works – in the local construction contractors' eyes, Ozawa is a 'pork-barrel' politician just like his mentor Tanaka Kakuei.[268]

How the Ozawa office successfully conducted the triple elections in Iwate in 1995 – gubernatorial, municipal (Morioka City) and Upper House – showed him repeatedly using Tanaka's electoral techniques.[269] Ozawa 'built his own version of the "Etsuzankai Kingdom"[270] in Iwate – the "Ozawa Kingdom"'.[271]

The structural similarities even extended to key links in the chain of influence such as bid rigging. The system that operated in Japan in the 1990s and subsequently was essentially established by Tanaka. The selection of the companies that would undertake huge public works projects was undertaken through bid rigging amongst the major *zenekon*. In Tanaka's time, this organisation was called the Management Roundtable Conference (Keiei Kondankai). While it involved the Dons of bid riggers such as key executives from Kajima Construction and Tobishima Construction (Tobishima Kensetsu), Tanaka was the kingpin who managed it.[272] He siphoned off *jōnōkin*, which were several per cent of the tendered price, from the *zenekon* who got the public works contracts. The system also operated amongst small and medium-sized regional construction companies. This was the kind of set-up that Ozawa continued to run in Iwate Prefecture.[273]

A grand design for remodelling the nation

Like Tanaka, Ozawa also endeavoured to make a grand design for developing nationwide infrastructure serve his political interests, particularly in raising money from construction companies. Tanaka became prime minister by presenting a plan for *Building a New Japan: A Plan for Remodelling the Japanese Archipelago* (using a bulldozer)[274] in 1972,[275] which increased investment in construction to almost one quarter of gross national product (GNP).[276] Ishikawa described it as 'Japan's first manifesto'.[277] The plan was justified in terms of bringing Japan's infrastructure into the modern age, but it rationalised large-scale public works projects across the country, which helped to secure the LDP's electoral fortunes (and Tanaka's own personal political fortunes). Tanaka made sure that his own constituency in Niigata was liberally bestowed with construction projects, particularly rail and road networks linking remote Niigata to Tokyo.[278]

The Tanaka 'reconstruction' model was copied in *Blueprint*. Ozawa outlined a plan to reverse Tokyo's urban concentration and promote regional decentralisation involving massive public investment in new Shinkansen lines, more and better airports, more expressways, proper sewage facilities and the construction of a new capital.[279] In terms of funding, Ozawa suggested the raising of a total of ¥200 trillion for public investment to provide employment for regional residents including the provision of rural community sewerage works worth ¥22 trillion. The ¥200 trillion was equivalent to 40 per cent of gross domestic product (GDP).[280] Ozawa justified the expenditure by stating, 'Regional areas will provide opportunities for young people burning with enthusiasm, which will then in turn lead to stimulating regional areas. If this happens, the various problems that rural areas currently face will be resolved'.[281]

The power of numbers

The power of numbers is reputedly in Ozawa's genes, inherited from Tanaka.[282] He was consistently a strong believer in the principle that 'numbers are power' (see Table 1.1).[283] The theory that numbers equate with power holds that the largest faction controls the ruling party, which controls the government, ergo, the largest faction controls the government in the mode of 'a one-faction-dominant structure'.[284]

Tanaka set out to build the biggest faction in the LDP, called the Mokuyō Kurabu, or Thursday Club, with Ozawa as secretariat chief. Expanding his faction was Tanaka's 'highest priority'.[285] The numbers would guarantee the biggest share of the spoils in any new government and more cabinet seats than any other faction, whoever the prime minister was.[286] When Tanaka was asked:

> about the source of his kingmaker-like power in an interview with *Newsweek* magazine published in May 1981, he answered, 'The policymaker in Japan is the LDP. So it is only natural that the one who has leadership of the LDP makes the decisions on politics, based on the principles of democracy. The

prime minister is merely a representative agent whose job is to implement policies'...What made Tanaka into a superpower who even treats the prime minister as his representative? In an interview published with *Shūkan Asahi* in June 1981, Tanaka clearly explains that it was the power of numbers.[287]

This meant that Tanaka controlled not only personnel affairs in the cabinet and party but also decisions on all important policies and budget distribution.[288]

Ozawa 'developed as a factional politician in this environment'.[289] Indeed, the reason why he fought with Obuchi over the post of chairman when the Keiseikai split was because he was 'trying to seize the Keiseikai's "numbers"'.[290] Like Tanaka, he remained focused on numerical strength as the key to power[291] and his biggest asset remained 'his expert command of the "logic of Nagata-chō numbers" devised by Tanaka'.[292] This resulted in parliamentary democracy on the surface but the secret behind it was a dual power structure, a hidden power that controlled the official power structure but which could not be removed.[293] As the shadow shogun's direct pupil, Ozawa remained the source of this dual power structure problem in Japanese politics for many years.[294] No one except for Tanaka 'wielded absolute power based on the dual power structure as openly as Ozawa'.[295] He successfully recreated such a power structure in the administrations of Prime Ministers Kaifu, Hosokawa and Hatoyama.

Following the 'father of money-power politics'[296]

Ozawa, in the Tanaka mould, showed how the logic of Nagata-chō numbers and money politics were inextricably linked in 'the power of money theory: "politics is numbers", "numbers are power" and "power is money"'.[297] Ruling by numbers made the ability to raise large quantities of funds mandatory, and here both Tanaka and Ozawa excelled. When describing Tanaka's *modus operandi*, Kaifu observed, 'The source of the "Tanaka Kakuei-style power" of politicians such as Takeshita Noboru, Kanemaru Shin, "the master" of the Upper House Aoki Mikio, and Ozawa Ichirō lies here – they had an abundance of money, were surprisingly generous with that money and were extremely strong in elections'.[298] In fact, it was reputedly Ozawa who 'raised and distributed the massive amounts of largess that oiled the [Tanaka] system'.[299] Ozawa displayed even 'wilier control of money than Kakuei'.[300]

Ozawa's money-raising skills were the reason for his meteoric rise in the LDP. Satō compared his upwards trajectory in LDP ranks in the 1980s to Hashimoto Ryūtarō's lacklustre record. Both these politicians began their political careers at more or less the same level, but Ozawa rose to prominence much more rapidly. By securing the post of secretary-general and with complete back-up from Kanemaru as chairman of the Keiseikai, Ozawa was able to gain access to party coffers and use these funds freely to secure victory in the 1990 Lower House election, centralise the flow of factional funds into party headquarters and expand the number of his followers. As a result, 'money and power became concentrated in Ozawa'.[301] Hashimoto, in contrast, was secretary-general in the Uno Sōsuke administration but resigned his position after only a month, when the LDP was defeated in the 1989 Upper House election. As Satō points out, 'There was no "Kanemaru" supporting Hashimoto. Here is the huge difference between those two'.[302] The relationship between Ozawa and Hashimoto remained very rivalrous and was known as the 'Ichi-Ryū confrontation'.[303] When Hashimoto later stood for the presidency of the LDP, a scandal involving a Ginza hostess was leaked to the media. The rumour reputedly came from someone in the Ozawa camp.[304]

In 1993, when Ozawa needed to expand his power base by increasing the number of his followers in the RP, he simply adopted the Tanaka method of factional management by relying on money to maintain his group.[305] Toshikawa despaired at the time: 'The task of completely eliminating the domination of money politics...will take a long time. It will never be completed as long as the script for political action is written by power broker Ichiro Ozawa of the Japan Renewal Party, the man who was set to follow in the footsteps of Takeshita and Kanemaru'.[306] However, Ozawa defended Kanemaru's behaviour in relation to accepting political donations and was strongly opposed to his resigning from the Diet.[307] He admitted to being guided and taken care of by Kanemaru, who was 'a very good mentor and a benefactor'.[308] Kaifu, on the other hand, condemned Kanemaru and when he became head of the NFP, he resolved to keep Ozawa on a short leash with respect to fundraising:

> As I was about to work together with Secretary-General Ozawa once again, I firmly kept in my mind to strictly monitor his aggressive fund-collecting as party leader. So, taking the electoral funds endorsed by the party for example, we only gave around ¥1 million to ¥3 million, and we could not and did not provide him with any surprisingly large amounts of money.[309]

When the Hatoyama-Ozawa duo were officially number one and two in the first nine months of the DPJ's 2009–10 administration, Ozawa's conduct prompted negative comments about the striking parallels with LDP precedents and Tanaka's behaviour. Matsumura observed that Ozawa had built 'an effective political machine by making the most use of the art of patronage...[and] established one of the largest financial war chests of any political party, using tactics reminiscent of Tanaka'.[310] In the same way, Ozawa built a huge factional war chest in order to solidify leadership over his group and strengthen its unity. Kan also viewed his personal conflict with Ozawa during 2010–11 as very much a clash of political methods and principles. He alluded to the fact that his (i.e. Kan's) roots lay 'in opposition to the political machine epitomized by the late former Prime Minister Kakuei Tanaka [with] Ozawa...a Tanaka protégé'.[311]

Like Tanaka, Ozawa was also beset by corruption scandals that thwarted his political ambitions and undermined his standing amongst the public. As Kuji put it, 'The shadow of doubt [about their involvement in corruption and criminality] was always hovering over these two and Kanemaru'.[312] Ōkubo's arrest prompted Yamazaki to observe that Ozawa was the same as Tanaka and Kanemaru in using money to obtain power and in their weak points originating from 'this money-making process'.³¹³

Despite winning a verdict of 'innocent', Ozawa's fate was indelibly influenced by the outcome of his trial just as Tanaka's was. In fact, his own trial and that of his secretaries were like a political death by a thousand cuts. They discredited his money-oriented political style, tainted what was left of his political career and forever discredited him as a possible leader of Japan.

Tanaka-style campaigning

Faction building was not only interwoven with money politics, it was also intimately connected to electoral strategy. It was once said of Tanaka, 'His unusual grasp of electoral strategy and his willingness to expend considerable personal energy to advance the electoral chances and careers of would-be followers further reinforced his strength within the factional system'.³¹⁴ At election time, his 'aid proved invaluable for his faction members. He provided funds, advice, and help in organising *kōenkai*…with members designated in nearly every village and town in a candidate's constituency, *kōenkai* became tightly managed political machines able to count on traditional webs of social obligations to reap votes'.³¹⁵ In short, Tanaka's electoral and factional strategies were closely interlinked.

Central to the myth of Ozawa's electoral genius were also the techniques that Tanaka taught him.³¹⁶ The focus was on grassroots election campaigning, 'visiting 30,000 houses individually, making 50,000 street speeches and walking around (and talking) until the blisters on your feet are broken'.³¹⁷ Ozawa justified this approach in terms of elections being the origin of democracy. When the media cynically criticised his enthusiasm for elections as 'just about Kakuei's theory that numbers give rise to power',³¹⁸ Ozawa did not deny it but instead said:

> Grassroots elections are actually about listening to the people's voices. We push into the crowd of ordinary people and listen to each and every one of their voices. Their voices become policies and we realise them as politicians. That is the basis of democracy. [You think that] once we have the numbers that's the end? That's just a bad joke. We go around and listen to the people in elections.³¹⁹

Ozawa described another dimension of Tanaka's teachings about election campaigning, calling it the *kawakami* (upstream strategy):

> Tanaka, whose advice was always detailed and clear, said to me, 'Start the election campaign from upstream'. In other words, the campaign needs to start with grassroots door-to-door election campaigns, particularly from agricultural areas with smaller populations. The cities where people are gathered can be done later. Use your feet to visit people one by one without relying on organisational support. That was what he taught…I too tell new candidates about this teaching by Tanaka, to 'start election campaigns from

upstream'. I also advise them, 'Meet lots of voters. Don't be scared, and just jump right into the middle of them. It will become a valuable asset in the future. New candidates have to visit people door-to door, and also do "street speeches" in stations and busy streets every day. If you do not want to do it, then you should not become a politician'.[320]

One of Ozawa's close aides also reported, 'Kaku-san said, "There are voters that live even in the deepest of the snowy mountains. [Candidates need to] go to every nook and cranny and into alleyways to make speeches and shake hands. Start upstream and move downstream. This is the basics of elections", and put it into practice himself. Ozawa is doing the same exact thing now'.[321]

Former secretary Ishikawa agreed that 'Ozawa is well known for his "upstream tactic". [In elections] he starts by securing votes in rural areas in the initial stages, and advances to the urban areas in the final stages. This tactic is said to be passed on from Kakuei Tanaka, and it has been successful especially in regional districts'.[322] In preparing the DPJ for victory in 2009, Ozawa lectured young DPJ politicians about the virtues of street preaching. He simply said: 'Make speeches on the street 50 times a day. Go into the back of the back of alleyways and shake hands with as many voters as possible.'[323]

That was not all. Tanaka advised Ozawa on how to recruit, fund and support candidates in elections who owed their loyalty to him personally. It was in line with this teaching that Ozawa allocated his 'army of secretaries' who were professionals at elections to provide back-up to individual candidates.[324] He was the only faction leader apart from Tanaka and Takeshita at the peak of their factional powers who could get away with injecting their secretaries into the campaigns of other politicians.[325] A Diet member close to Ozawa explained this particular tactic in the 2010 Upper House election: 'Mr. Ozawa's view is that it is his duty to have first-time candidates elected and foster them. He has sent a considerable number of secretaries to their constituencies and has received information from them'.[326] For example, Ozawa sent his secretary as adviser to the election campaign of a new candidate for the Kyoto prefectural seat, Kawakami Mitsue, a former student of the Ozawa Ichirō *seiji juku*. She had just freshly resigned as Diet representative for the PR constituency of Kinki, a seat that she won in the 2009 Lower House election. Ozawa advised her to carry out a door-to-door election campaign and to give stump speeches on street corners and shake hands with passers-by 50 times a day.[327] Many of the staff members in the Kawakami camp were also pro-Ozawa Diet members and their secretaries.[328]

However, Toshikawa condemned the Tanaka-Ozawa style of politics where 'they build boss-henchmen relationships by helping their followers win elections'.[329] Because Ozawa was involved in his personally selected candidates' success in the elections, these candidates became 'Ozawa-believers' when they were elected.[330] It was almost a religious experience – 'practising "teachings" such as "making 50 speeches on the street" and "selling yourself rather than policies" by communicating with voters and ultimately being elected'.[331] On top of this was, of course, money in the form of party subsidies, which Ozawa did so much to establish and which strengthened his powers even more.[332] Using these techniques and resources, Ozawa was able to maximise the size of his factional grouping and then use it as the primary instrument of his influence in the party and in government.[333] He was also able to perpetuate the myth that he excelled at winning elections, something that was absolutely integral to his faction-building method. His electoral record over time was in fact mixed, but the great victories for the DPJ in 2007 and 2009 convinced most in the DPJ that 'elections needed to be handled by Ozawa'.[334] Hatoyama certainly credited Ozawa with the 2009 election victory and immediately handed the position of secretary-general to him as a reward.

Kingmakers

Another aspect of the Tanaka *modus operandi* to which Ozawa aspired was the ability to act as kingmaker – to form governments and control key posts, particularly those of ruling party president and prime minister, and ruling party secretary-general (the keeper of the spoils), even if he were on the 'outer' in the party or ejected from all official positions within it (see Table 1.1). Tanaka showed an exceptional ability to control key appointments and developments in Japanese politics even when he no longer held office or was part of the ruling LDP. After he resigned as prime minister in December 1974, he continued to build his faction, which regained strength with the help of abundant funding. Within four years the faction 'had become so large that no man could become party president without Tanaka's assent. No longer king, Tanaka had become king-maker'.[335] As the 'shadow shogun of Mejiro', Tanaka thus set up a system in the LDP whereby 'the person with the biggest power base became the kingmaker, not the prime minister'.[336] He 'used his faction's numbers to accomplish behind the scenes what he couldn't do up front'.[337] His power remained 'so long as the Tanaka faction itself stayed united and loyal to him',[338] although Ozawa opposed the maintenance of Tanaka's latent influence within the LDP after he was arrested in the Lockheed scandal.[339]

Many years later, when forced to resign as DPJ secretary-general in June 2010, Ozawa attempted to continue reigning over the DPJ in the same role as 'kingmaker'.[340] He searched around for a candidate to run against Kan as president of the DPJ. He asked Tanaka Makiko to stand, offering her the support of 200 of his own followers, politicians in the DPJ who would vote according to his orders. Makiko declined the offer.

It was for the August 2011 DPJ presidential election, however, that Ozawa reserved his most serious attempt to act as kingmaker.[341] Despite having been suspended from the party, he mobilised his group behind Kaieda Banri. As early as June 2011, Ozawa invited to his house about 20 close associates from the Lower House, asking them to preserve their unity because of the importance of the group maintaining its solidarity in choosing the next party leader and prime minister. According to one of those who attended, Ozawa said, 'What's important is whom we choose as our next leader. We have to work as one'.[342] Just before the election, he told a gathering of his supporters, 'This is our chance to show everyone how strong we are'.[343] Indeed, the courting of Ozawa and his group by almost every candidate in the leadership election demonstrated the extent to which his 'bloc vote' was considered a vital ingredient in any potential victory.[344]

In both Ozawa's and Tanaka's cases, their personal political power was essentially grounded in their large factions, regardless of their formal role in the government and in the party (see Table 1.1). Even if the leader were discredited by scandal, the group carried on, allowing the leader to continue to exercise political influence from behind the scenes. If Ozawa was unable do something himself, he could operate through his 'loyal henchmen'.[345] In this way, Ozawa, like Tanaka, was always 'at the fulcrum of the seesaw of Japan's politics. The power relations between his supporters and those who opposed him moved the see-saw up and down, shaping the political scene'.[346]

Not surprisingly, whether in government or out of it, whether inside the ruling party or outside it, Ozawa remained for many decades a key figure in political developments in Japan. His fellow politicians did not have the luxury of being able to ignore his presence or his potential to shape or disrupt the political scene. He was important because of his political resources: the politicians he could influence, the votes he could control, the funds he could gather and the connections he could mobilise.

Conclusion

Over the course of his political career, Ozawa's dictatorial personality, manner and ways became legendary, as did strident criticism of his behaviour as a politician. As Watanabe put it, Ozawa became a 'despised legend' because he was 'high-handed, arbitrary, selfish and a destroyer'.[347] Certainly, these aspects of Ozawa's conduct played out in full public view in the Hatoyama administration. Without occupying a high post in the government itself, Ozawa wielded decisive influence over the entire spectrum of government, Diet and party affairs, including policies, Diet management, elections and party funding, as well as appointments to government and party posts – all requiring his approval. His influence certainly extended far beyond the formal powers and duties of his office as DPJ secretary-general. Despite being part of a new government and one of the primary architects of so-called 'regime change', Ozawa exercised controlling power from behind the scenes from his customary position as 'shadow shogun'. His preference for dictating political developments from 'an apparent supporting role'[348] had not changed. He had learned years before from Tanaka's example how important power broking and backroom politics were.[349]

Moreover, Ozawa's personal leadership style and political relationships were little different from those he maintained in the 'old' LDP. More specifically, they replicated key aspects of the Tanaka model of politics, particularly the authoritarian rule that Ozawa imposed on his own faction and his attempts to extend his political control more broadly to the party, including acting as kingmaker based on his leadership of the largest intra-party faction. His political methods also showed striking parallels to Tanaka's in other respects, such as his incorporation of public works into a grand reform plan, his use of government-subsidised public works to generate political funds from the construction industry, and his liberal distribution of funds and electoral assistance to followers and new recruits in order to maximise the size of his faction as the primary instrument of his power. Like Tanaka, Ozawa was a quintessential 'money power politician', demonstrating the interconnectedness of money and numbers as the basis of his political power and the foundation of the 'dual power structure' through which he could control governments without even holding an official position in it.

Accumulating political funds and building the biggest faction in order to run parties and governments represented the quintessence of the Tanaka model and the political culture that he forged, which Ozawa helped to perpetuate, and which continued to hold sway in the LDP for another two decades until electoral reform eroded some of its key pillars and Koizumi put it under the blowtorch. As a relic of the Tanaka model, Ozawa thus remained a political anachronism, a hangover from an earlier era and a player of old politics in what was essentially the new landscape of Japanese politics. Ozawa failed to appreciate that in this new political environment, as Koizumi showed, a politician could build public popularity and widespread support within a party by successfully engaging with the media, which challenged Ozawa's theory of 'numbers and money = power' based on an old factional mindset.

When determining Ozawa's primary political motivation, shallow power-seeking goals and the quest for hegemonic influence consistently made the most sense of his political behaviour and methods. Ozawa certainly cloaked his ambition in the rhetoric of reform. However, whatever his policy goals – whether structural reform of the political system or merely routine policy choices – the role that he actually chose to play in successive administrations and the formal positions in governments that he chose to hold, were not those of a policy entrepreneur. For a senior Japanese politician with more than four decades' experience in the highest echelons of Japanese politics, his lack of ministerial (and prime ministerial) experience was indicative. It suggested that his deepest motivation was not to act out deeply held reform convictions but to wield political power – something he was able to do by creating a dual power structure in several administrations in which he figured as a prominent figure in the party, not in the government. More often than not, Ozawa opted for the position of party secretary-general, where he could exercise control over key political resources and thus hold sway over fellow party members, using this as a base from which to extend his influence over entire governments.

As time passed, Ozawa appeared to lose much of his reform zeal. In the early 1990s he put on a much more convincing demonstration as a reformer than he did in the Hatoyama administration and later. In fact, the early 1990s were the only time when he preached and helped to implement a systematic and wide-ranging reform agenda. Not only was *Ozawa-ism* (published in 2006) a pale shadow of *Blueprint*, but Ozawa's most significant contributions to political system reform were also made in the early 1990s. This made the Ozawa of that period much more of a 'new' politician than he was in later years. Subsequently, when given the opportunity to consolidate earlier reforms, particularly during the Hatoyama administration, he failed to do so by acting in ways that directly undermined his earlier contributions to reform.[350] As a result, Ozawa's reform legacy is mixed: big on ambition, but much smaller on delivery. Although reform in his earlier days was instrumental to his political ambition to wield supreme power, his later behaviour suggested that only ambition to acquire power remained. He appeared to revert to old politics pure and simple, with his behaviour increasingly taking on the appearance of an end game: one geared to his political survival. While Ozawa's ascendancy in Japanese politics was marked by political dominance and dictatorial behaviour, on the political slide he adopted the behaviour of a typical spoiler, putting self-interest ahead of the wider party, government and national interest, thus seeking to bring down the existing political structure around his ears. This propensity was in full view under the Kan and Noda administrations of 2010–12.

Notes

1. This term also has connotations of 'political strongman', 'big wheel', big gun' and 'power behind the throne'.
2. Martin and Yoshida, 'Ozawa Set to be DPJ Secretary General', www.japantimes.co.jp/cgi-bin/nn20090904a1.html.
3. Gotō, '"Ozawa fūji"', diamond.jp/articles/-/9433.
4. 'Yūsei hōan', www.nikkei.com/news/editorial/article/g=96958A96889DE2EAE2E7 E2EAE4E2E0E7E2E7E0E2E3E28297EAE2E2E2;n=96948D819A938D96E38D8D 8D8D8D.
5. Tanaka, 'Shinseiken', diamond.jp/articles/-/5774.
6. Ibid.
7. Yamazaki, 'Ozawa Ichirō-shi to kenryoku', diamond.jp/articles/-/4929.
8. He used the words 'Ore wa kite inai' in Japanese, which literally means 'I haven't heard about that'. Reinterpreted in daily parlance, it can mean that 'I have not been consulted prior to the decision', i.e. there has been no *nemawashi*, so I do not accept it. This is explained in Satō, 'Shinteikoku shugi', p. 115.
9. See George Mulgan, 'No Interests', www.eastasiaforum.org/2009/09/20/no-interests-no-connections-and-no-expertise-the-man-in-charge-of-japanese-agriculture/.
10. Sugiyama, 'Saidai no atsuryoku dantai', business.nikkeibp.co.jp/article/topics/20091210/211447/.
11. Ibid.
12. Ibid.
13. Akasaka, '"Posuto Hatoyama"', gekkan.bunshun.jp/articles/-/216; Yamazaki, 'Ozawa Ichirō-shi to kenryoku', diamond.jp/articles/-/4929. Sengoku and Hirano also apologised to the newly appointed members who had to give up their positions in the GRU.
14. Yamazaki, 'Ozawa Ichirō-shi to kenryoku', diamond.jp/articles/-/4929.
15. Ibid.
16. See also below.
17. Yamazaki, 'Ozawa Ichirō-shi to kenryoku', diamond.jp/articles/-/4929. See also below.
18. Ibid.
19. 'Kan shin taisei', in *Nihon Keizai Shinbun*, p. 3.

20 Yamazaki, 'Ozawa Ichirō-shi to kenryoku', diamond.jp/articles/-/4929. See also below.
21 Ibid.
22 'Ozawa Ichirō-shi e no kenryoku ichigenka', diamond.jp/articles/-/5735. See also below.
23 Iinuma, 'Referendum on Ozawa', p. 8.
24 'Japan Can't Seem to Shake Off Old Ghost', e.nikkei.com/e/ac/20100222/TNW/Nni20100222OP7DIARY.htm.
25 Abiru, 'Minshutō', p. 45.
26 'Iron Fist', www.yomiuri.co.jp/dy/editorial/20100322TDY02307.htm.
27 Nikaido, 'Like Ally Ozawa', ajw.asahi.com/article//behind_news/AJ201109089673.
28 'Dictator Ozawa', www.pluto.dti.ne.jp/mor97512/EN158.HTML. See also below.
29 Matsuda, *Kakuei ni Narenakatta Otoko*, p. 196.
30 Itō, 'Gisō kenkin', p. 115.
31 Hongo, 'Ozawa's Sway', www.japantimes.co.jp/text/nn20100128f1.html.
32 'Opposition Rides Ozawa', www.japantimes.co.jp/text/nn201002024.html.
33 Ubukata said, 'after receiving the people's opinion that he should be indicted, his first step should be to resign as secretary-general'. *NHK News 7*, 28 April 2010. According to another source, he said, 'If [Ozawa] is unable to obtain public understanding [of his explanation on the campaign funding scandal], he should leave the post – that is a majority [opinion] within the party'. Toshikawa and Katz, 'Flailing', p. 2.
34 Ibid.
35 Ibid.
36 Ibid.
37 'Seikai saihen', www.fsight.jp/article/5599.
38 'DPJ Fights', e.nikkei.com/e/ac/TNKS/Nni20100315D12HH383.htm.
39 'Seikai saihen', www.fsight.jp/article/5599.
40 'Sentaku Magazine', www.japantimes.co.jp/cgi-bin/eo20100419a1.html.
41 Itō, 'Gisō kenkin', p. 115. See also Chapter 6.
42 Tsujihiro, 'Kan Sōri', diamond.jp/articles/-/9386.
43 '"Minna no Tō wa Ozawa san iranai"', in *Asahi Shinbun*, p. 4.
44 Yamazaki, 'Ozawa Ichirō-shi e no kenryoku ichigenka', diamond.jp/articles/-/5735.
45 Tazaki, Yamaguchi and Azumi, 'Ozawa Ichirō wa Nihon o dō shiyō to iu no ka', p. 137.
46 Matsuda, *Kakuei ni Narenakatta Otoko*, p. 116.
47 Ibid., p. 8.
48 Suganuma, 'Ozawa Ichirō kanjichō jidai', p. 31.
49 Kuji, *Ozawa Ichirō – Sono 'Kyōfu Shihai'*, p. 39.
50 Watanabe, *Ano Hito*, p. 37.
51 Oka, *Policy Entrepreneurship*, p. 59.
52 Hirano, *Ozawa Ichirō to no nijūnen*, p. 26.
53 Iinuma, 'Referendum on Ozawa', p. 9.
54 Kuji, *Ozawa Ichirō – Sono 'Kyōfu Shihai'*, p. 39.
55 Yamaguchi, 'Ozawa Ichirō no kenkyū', p. 146.
56 'The Tumultuous Life of Ichiro Ozawa', ajw.asahi.com/article/behind_news/politics/AJ201204260030.
57 Tahara, '"Fukō" na seijika', www.nikkeibp.co.jp/article/column/20120426/307058/.
58 Ibid. See also below.
59 Ibid.
60 See Chapter 6.
61 'The Tumultuous Life of Ichiro Ozawa', ajw.asahi.com/article/behind_news/politics/AJ201204260030.

62 McCarthy, 'Japan's Shadow Shogun', www.independent.co.uk/news/world/japans-shadow-shogun-nurses-grievance-in-silence-ichiro-ozawa-right-is-the-man-behind-the-government-but-hes-not-talking-to-journalists-terry-mccarthy-reports-from-tokyo-1466282.html.
63 Watanabe, *Ano Hito*, p. 215.
64 Quoted in Iinuma, 'Referendum on Ozawa', p. 9.
65 Ōtake, 'Seiji kaikaku', p. 26.
66 Yakushiji, 'Kako no hatsugen', astand.asahi.com/magazine/wrpolitics/2012072300010.html. See also below.
67 Ishikawa, *Zōkingake*, p. 50.
68 'Nail in Kingpin', e.nikkei.com/e/ac/TNKS/Nni20100623D23HH994.htm.
69 McCarthy, 'Japan's Shadow Shogun', www.independent.co.uk/news/world/japans-shadow-shogun-nurses-grievance-in-silence-ichiro-ozawa-right-is-the-man-behind-the-government-but-hes-not-talking-to-journalists-terry-mccarthy-reports-from-tokyo-1466282.html.
70 This comment was directed at the *Asahi Shinbun*. Ozawa's exact words were: 'It made me think that the *Asahi Shinbun* is gutter press or they practise black journalism' (meaning journalism that deals with scandalous and shady information for the purpose of gaining profit by blackmailing the figure in question). Yakushiji, 'Kako no hatsugen', astand.asahi.com/magazine/wrpolitics/2012072300010.html. Ozawa's comment followed the newspaper's headlining of his comment, 'It doesn't matter which woman you sleep with', which he made in an elevator in the Diet building in late April 1994 in response to a reporter who asked about the JSP's opposition to the unified parliamentary group (*kaiha*) called 'Kaishin' that Ozawa was trying to set up just before the inauguration of the Hata cabinet. Ozawa refused to be interviewed by the *Asahi Shinbun* for six months following the incident. Ibid.
71 Schlesinger, *Shadow Shoguns*, p. 275.
72 Hashimoto, 'Minshutō zen daihyō', p. 376.
73 Schlesinger, *Shadow Shoguns*, p. 274.
74 Watanabe puts this down to Ozawa's disillusionment with the way question time was conducted in the Diet. *Ozawa Ichirō Kirawareru Densetsu*, pp. 261–64.
75 See also below.
76 See also below.
77 Ōtake, 'Seiji kaikaku', p. 18.
78 Shinoda, 'Ozawa Ichirō as an Actor', p. 56.
79 Otake, 'Forces for Political Reform', p. 283.
80 Kaifu, *Seiji to Kane*, p. 102. However, Kaifu also wrote, 'Ozawa actually followed my orders surprisingly obediently [saying]…"In the end, it is your decision, so that is fine. I understand, we will do it that way"…[F]or me, his superior, he was a convenient and reliable subordinate'. Ibid., pp. 101–2.
81 Quoted in ibid., p. 101. Ozawa denied ever making this comment to Kaifu. Ozawa is also reported to have said something similar about former Prime Minister Nakasone. According to Matsuda, 'when Tanaka Kakuei was exercising his power as a shadow *shōgun* and the Tanaka faction was supporting Nakasone Yasuhiro in the LDP leadership election in November 1982, Ozawa said, "We chose Nakasone with the intention to seize not only the party but also the cabinet. We prefer a light and empty *mikoshi* because we can handle it as we want"'. *Kakuei ni Narenakatta Otoko*, p. 85.
82 Satō, *Ozawa Ichirō no Himitsu*, p. 229.
83 McCarthy, 'Puppet-master', www.independent.co.uk/news/world/puppetmaster-in-a-hall-of-mirrors-ichiro-ozawa-is-the-man-of-steel-behind-japans-next-premier-writes-terry-mccarthy-1459438.html.
84 Kumon, 'From the Editor', p. 2.
85 Matsuda, *Kakuei ni Narenakatta Otoko*, p. 139.
86 Ibid., p. 139.

87 Kaifu, *Seiji to Kane*, p. 162.
88 Schlesinger, *Shadow Shoguns*, p. 272.
89 Kuji, *Ozawa Ichirō – Sono 'Kyōfu Shihai'*, p. 39. Hosokawa himself did not necessarily agree with the depiction of Ozawa as the real power behind the throne in his administration, perhaps because it undervalued his own role and achievements. He wrote, 'I did not have at all the feeling the government was a dual power structure'. *Naishōroku*, p. 519.
90 Terry McCarthy, 'Puppet-master', www.independent.co.uk/news/world/puppetmaster-in-a-hall-of-mirrors-ichiro-ozawa-is-the-man-of-steel-behind-japans-next-premier-writes-terry-mccarthy-1459438.html.
91 Shinoda, 'Ozawa Ichirō as an Actor', p. 51.
92 Hosokawa, *Naishōroku*, p. 24.
93 Shinoda, 'Ozawa Ichirō as an Actor', p. 51.
94 Ibid.
95 Wright, *Japan's Fiscal Crisis*, p. 202.
96 Shinoda, 'Ozawa Ichirō as an Actor', p. 54.
97 Ibid., p. 56.
98 Ibid., p. 56.
99 Kuji, *Ozawa Ichirō – Sono 'Kyōfu Shihai'*, p. 209.
100 Shinoda, 'Ozawa Ichirō as an Actor', p. 60, quoting Murayama, *Murayama Tomiichi ga Kataru*, p. 31.
101 Watanabe, *Ano Hito*, p. 11.
102 Kuji, *Ozawa Ichirō – Sono 'Kyōfu Shihai'*, pp. 208–9.
103 Ibid.
104 Ibid., p. 209.
105 Watanabe, *Ozawa Ichirō Kirawareru Densetsu*, p. 248.
106 Iinuma, 'Referendum on Ozawa', p. 8.
107 Endō, *Shōhi Sareru Kenryokusha*, p. 63, quoting from Ozawa's *Nihon Kaizō Keikaku*. See also Ōtake, 'Seiji kaikaku', p. 27.
108 Tazaki, Yamaguchi and Azumi, 'Ozawa Ichirō wa Nihon o dō shiyō to iu no ka', p. 43.
109 Watanabe, *Seiji Kaikaku to Kenpō Kaisei*, p. 44.
110 Ibid.
111 Ibid., pp. 45, 46.
112 Yakushiji, 'Kako no hatsugen', astand.asahi.com/magazine/wrpolitics/20120723 00010.html.
113 Ibid., quoting from a 15 October 1994 *Asahi Shinbun* interview with Ozawa.
114 See also Curtis, *The Logic of Japanese Politics*, p. 122.
115 Quoted in Gaunder, *Political Reform*, p. 103.
116 Quoted in Kuji, *Ozawa Ichirō – Sono 'Kyōfu Shihai'*, p. 208.
117 Mori, 'Kano Determined to Make a Difference', ajw.asahi.com/article/behind_news/AJ201108247690.
118 Quoted in 'Ozawa shintōwa Shū San 50 nin de', www.nikkeibp.co.jp/article/column/20120703/314579/.
119 'Gabanansu', in *Mainichi Shinbun*, p. 1.
120 Mikuriya, 'The DPJ's Uncharted Journey', www.japanechoweb.jp/diplomacy-politics/jew0216/4.
121 Abiru, 'Minshutō', p. 45.
122 Yamazaki, '"Gaman no dekinai otoko"', diamond.jp/articles/-/4879.
123 Abiru, 'Minshutō', p. 45.
124 Quoted in Shinohara, 'The Grand Coalition', www.japanechoweb.jp/diplomacy-politics/jew0602/3.
125 Kobayashi, 'Shōhizei', diamond.jp/articles/-/8730.
126 Matsuda, *Ozawa Ichirō, Kyoshoku no Shihaisha*, p. 233.
127 Ibid., p. 231.

128 Kuji, *Ozawa Ichirō – Sono 'Kyōfu Shihai'*, p. 208.
129 Endō, *Shōhi Sareru Kenryokusha*, p. 62.
130 Quoted in Kuji, *Ozawa Ichirō – Sono 'Kyōfu Shihai'*, p. 218.
131 Yamazaki, '"Gaman no dekinai otoko"', diamond.jp/articles/-/4879.
132 Watanabe, *Ozawa Ichirō Kirawareru Densetsu*, p. 53. See also below.
133 Quoted in Kuji, *Ozawa Ichirō – Sono 'Kyōfu Shihai'*, p. 210.
134 Iinuma, 'Referendum on Ozawa', p. 9.
135 Ōtake, 'Seiji kaikaku', pp. 26, 27.
136 Takahashi, 'Ozawa moto hisho', p. 132. See also below.
137 Kaieda, *Boku ga Ozawa (Seiji) o Kirai*, pp. 17–18, 53.
138 Itō, *Seitō Hōkai*, p. 59.
139 Yamaguchi, 'Ozawa Ichirō no kenkyū', p. 145.
140 Ōshima and Ōnishi, 'Sokkin Koike Yuriko daigishi', p. 153.
141 Matsuda, quoting a veteran executive from Mizusawa City in *Ozawa Ichirō, Kyoshoku no Shihaisha*, p. 218.
142 Quoted in ibid., p. 231.
143 Yamaguchi, 'Ozawa Ichirō no kenkyū', p. 145.
144 Itō, *Seitō Hōkai*, p. 59.
145 Endō notes how Ozawa 'disappears during important situations'. *Shōhi Sareru Kenryokusha*, p. 62. Kuji also criticises Ozawa for 'dropping out of sight when he faces an inconvenient situation and wants to avoid responsibility'. *Ozawa Ichirō – Sono 'Kyōfu Shihai'*, p. 205. Watanabe writes that 'Ozawa always disappeared from the centre stage of politics whenever he became embroiled in political scandals. He never used to hold press conferences and was criticised for disappearing without a trace'. *Ozawa Ichirō Kirawareru Densetsu*, p. 80. In his earlier book, Watanabe comments that Ozawa 'went "missing" for two weeks over the Kanemaru problem [in 1992] when he was examining measures for dealing with the prosecution and conducting careful information analysis and discussions with his team of Diet members and legal specialists'. *Ano Hito*, p. 67.
146 See, for example, Hosokawa, *Naishōroku*, p. 230–31.
147 Ibid., p. 238.
148 Kuji, *Ozawa Ichirō – Sono 'Kyōfu Shihai'*, p. 28.
149 Matsuda, *Ozawa Ichirō, Kyoshoku no Shihaisha*, p. 231.
150 Tahara, 'Kenbōjussū, www.nikkeibp.co.jp/article/column/20120627/314051/.
151 Kaieda, *Boku ga Ozawa (Seiji) o Kirai*, p. 94.
152 Satō, 'Ozawa shin jiyū shugi no haiboku', astand.asah4i.com/magazine/wrpolitics/2011083000002.html?iref=webronza.
153 Quoted in Matsuda, *Ozawa Ichirō, Kyoshoku no Shihaisha*, p. 126.
154 Matsuda, *Ozawa Ichirō, Kyoshoku no Shihaisha*, p. 231.
155 Ibid., pp. 125–26.
156 Tachibana, 'Ososugita shūen', p. 102.
157 Kuji, *Ozawa Ichirō – Sono 'Kyōfu Shihai'*, p. 211.
158 Ibid. See also below.
159 Toshikawa, 'Kan versus Ozawa', p. 3.
160 Kamikubo, 'Seijika no "kessa"', diamond.jp/articles/-/9298.
161 Itō, 'Dare mo shiranai', p. 141.
162 Tahara, '"Fukō" na seijika', www.nikkeibp.co.jp/article/column/20120426/307058/.
163 Kamikubo, 'Seijika no "kessa"', diamond.jp/articles/-/9298.
164 Kaieda, *Boku ga Ozawa (Seiji) o Kirai*, p. 83.
165 See also Angel, 'Pork, People, Procedure, or Policy?', pp. 2–3. Gaunder, *Political Reform*, p. 104. Others argue that the Socialists broke away because Ozawa was at the time attempting to form a new party without consulting them. See Stockwin, 'Party Politics', p. 100.
166 Watanabe, *Ozawa Ichirō Kirawareru Densetsu*, p. 225.

167 Satō, *Ozawa Ichirō no Himitsu*, p. 232.
168 Angel, 'Pork, People, Procedure, or Policy?' p. 4.
169 Kaieda, *Boku ga Ozawa (Seiji) o Kirai*, p. 87.
170 Ibid.
171 Ibid., p. 86.
172 Ibid., p. 86.
173 Scheiner argues that Ozawa was willing to antagonise the JSP because he believed that it would never link up with the LDP and more LDP defectors would join the coalition. *Democracy Without Competition*, p. 222.
174 Quoted in Watanabe, *Ozawa Ichirō Kirawareru Densetsu*, p. 13.
175 Kaieda, *Boku ga Ozawa (Seiji) o Kirai*, p. 91. See also Angel, 'Pork, People, Procedure, or Policy?' p. 3. He refers to the LDP and JSP's mutual abhorrence and fear of the renegade Ozawa (p. 3).
176 Kaieda, *Boku ga Ozawa (Seiji) o Kirai*, p. 120.
177 Ibid., p. 121.
178 Ibid.
179 Ibid., p. 122.
180 Ibid., p. 95.
181 Ibid.
182 Kaifu, *Seiji to Kane*, pp. 166–67.
183 Kaieda, *Boku ga Ozawa Seiji o Kirai*, pp. 132–33.
184 Martin and Yoshida, 'Ozawa Set to be DPJ Secretary General', www.japantimes.co.jp/cgi-bin/nn20090904a1.html.
185 Kaifu, *Seiji to Kane*, pp. 168–69.
186 Ōshima and Ōnishi, 'Sokkin Koike Yuriko daigishi', p. 151.
187 Uesugi, 'Nejire mo mata min'i', diamond.jp/articles/-/8759.
188 Matsuda, *Kakuei ni Narenakatta Otoko*, p. 149.
189 Ibid.
190 Tada, 'Ichiro Ozawa Now Isolated', www.japantimes.co.jp/cgi-bin/eo20000428.html.
191 Kaifu, *Seiji to Kane*, pp. 173–74.
192 'Panel Discussion on Noda's New Cabinet', 2 September 2011.
193 See Chapter 6.
194 As Oka puts it, 'Is Ozawa Ichiro a genuine reformer...Or is he a power broker who cloaks himself in the garments of reform while he pursues naked power?' *Policy Entrepreneurship*, p. xii. See also Gaunder, 'Reform Leadership', p. 185.
195 Yamaguchi, 'An Insider's View', p. 29.
196 Watanabe, *Ozawa Ichirō Kirawareru Densetsu*, p. 20.
197 Oka and Hughes, 'Ozawa as We Knew Him', p. 10.
198 Ibid.
199 Other defenders include Etō, 'Why I Back Ozawa Ichirō', pp. 18–23, and Otake, 'Forces for Political Reform', pp. 269–94.
200 Quoted in Watanabe, *Ano Hito*, p. 110.
201 Etō, 'Why I Back Ozawa Ichirō', p. 20. Ozawa's father devoted much of his political career to the cause of single-seat constituencies. Oka, *Policy Entrepreneurship*, p. 13.
202 Ozawa said, 'Anti-establishment is probably in my blood as a result of influence from my father'. Quoted in Watanabe, *Ozawa Ichirō Kirawareru Densetsu*, p. 37.
203 Ozawa, 'My Commitment to Political Reform', p. 10.
204 Watanabe, *Ozawa Ichirō Kirawareru Densetsu*, p. 37.
205 Quoted in Watanabe, *Ano Hito*, p. 107.
206 Watanabe, *Ozawa Ichirō Kirawareru Densetsu*, p. 37.
207 Oka, *Policy Entrepreneurship*, p. 71.
208 Ibid., p. 24.
209 Ozawa, 'My Commitment to Political Reform', p. 10.

210 Oka, *Policy Entrepreneurship*, p. 72.
211 Ibid., fn. 9, p. 167.
212 Ibid., p. 3.
213 'Kan shin taisei', in *Nihon Keizai Shinbun*, p. 3.
214 See, for example, Oka, *Policy Entrepreneurship*, p. 80.
215 See Chapter 6.
216 Spirling, 'Party Cohesion'.
217 Ishikawa, *Akutō*, p. 200, emphasis added.
218 Kabashima and Steel, *Changing Politics in Japan*, p. 131.
219 As Angel wrote, 'If Kakuei Tanaka, the personification of evil for Japan's political reformers, has a living heir, he is Ichiro Ozawa'. 'Pork, People, Procedure, or Policy?' p. 3.
220 Kaieda, *Boku ga Ozawa Seiji o Kirai*, p. 53.
221 Ozawa, *Ozawashugi*, pp. 19–20.
222 Watanabe, *Ano Hito*, p. 137.
223 Hunziker and Kamimura, *Kakuei Tanaka*, www.rcrinc.com/tanaka/ch5-4.html.
224 Every Wednesday morning from 10am, Ozawa in the company of Tanaka's secretary, Hayasaki Shigezō, would attend court to observe the proceedings. Matsuda, *Kakuei ni Narenakatta Otoko*, p. 75. There were 191 court sessions altogether running from 1977 to 1983. See Schlesinger, 'Flashback', blogs.wsj.com/japanrealtime/2011/09/30/flashback-ozawa-in-court/. This is despite Ozawa's history of betraying Tanaka who was deeply shocked by Ozawa's participation in the Sōseikai, which was a *coup d'état* that took place in the Tanaka faction in February 1985 aiming at taking it over in order to make Takeshita prime minister, and which precipitated Tanaka's stroke and retirement from political activities. Matsuda, *Kakuei ni Narenakatta Otoko*, pp. 71, 72, 79, 80, 81, 82. Ozawa later referred to the fierce opposition from Tanaka when he formed the Sōseikai, saying, 'Even though I was yelled at [by Tanaka], I went to Mejiro everyday and repeated, "Please understand". I must have had a sense of trust that he would eventually forgive me'. Quoted in Watanabe, *Ano Hito*, p. 138.
225 Schlesinger, 'Flashback', blogs.wsj.com/japanrealtime/2011/09/30/flashback-ozawa-in-court/.
226 As quoted by Schlesinger, from Watanabe, *Ano Hito* (p. 158), in 'Flashback', blogs.wsj.com/japanrealtime/2011/09/30/flashback-ozawa-in-court/.
227 Watanabe, *Ano Hito*, p. 138.
228 As quoted by Schlesinger in 'Flashback', blogs.wsj.com/japanrealtime/2011/09/30/flashback-ozawa-in-court/.
229 As quoted by Schlesinger, in ibid.
230 Ishizuka, 'Japan Can't Seem to Shake Off Old Ghost', e.nikkei.com/e/ac/20100222/TNW/Nni20100222OP7DIARY.htm.
231 Itō, '"Seiji kaikaku no kishu"', tukamoto-office.seesaa.net/article/141084654.html.
232 Tachibana, 'Ososugita shūen', p. 108.
233 '"Seiji kaikaku no kishu"', tukamoto-office.seesaa.net/article/141084654.html.
234 Tachibana, 'Ososugita shūen', p. 108.
235 Kaifu, *Seiji to Kane*, p. 57.
236 Itō, 'Dare mo shiranai', p. 138.
237 The figure attending has also been put at 165. See Chapter 6.
238 Iseri, '"Seitō" Hōkai', p. 57.
239 See Chapter 6.
240 Toshikawa Takao, quoted in Sekai, 'Ozawa vs. kensatsu', p. 59.
241 Toshikawa, 'Ozawa Not Out of the Woods', p. 5.
242 *NHK News 7*, 6 September 2010.
243 Gotō, '"Ozawa fūji"', diamond.jp/articles/-/9433.
244 Ibid.
245 Ibid.

246 'Saiaku!' blog.goo.ne.jp/handa3douzo/e/829ba12a41604bec9e2ba2a7a2add57b.
247 Kuji, *Ozawa Ichirō – Sono 'Kyōfu Shihai'*, p. 25.
248 Mizuguchi, 'Political Reform', p. 248.
249 Stockwin reports that more than two thirds of the members of the construction tribe belonged to the Tanaka faction. Stockwin, *Dictionary*, p. 336. In fact, as Kuji reports, 'The Tanaka faction was a conglomerate of *zoku giin* members. The group consisted of *kensetsu zoku* [construction tribe], *unyu zoku* [transportation tribe], *yūsei zoku* [postal administration tribe], *shōkō zoku* [commerce and industry tribe], *kokubō zoku* [defence tribe] etc. and these *zoku giin* members were stationed everywhere'. Kuji, *Ozawa Ichirō – Sono 'Kyōfu Shihai'*, pp. 24–25.
250 Mizuguchi, 'Political Reform', p. 248.
251 Satō, *Ozawa Ichirō no Himitsu*, p. 217.
252 Toshikawa, 'Kanemaru Scandal', p. 16.
253 Woodall describes him as the '"don of all dons" in the public works arena'. *Japan Under Construction*, p. 89.
254 Kuji and Yokota, *Seiji ga Yugameru Kōkyō Jigyō*, p. 19.
255 Satō, *Ozawa Ichirō no Himitsu*, p. 71.
256 Matsuda, *Kakuei ni Narenakatta Otoko*, p. 163.
257 Ibid., p. 174.
258 Yamaguchi, 'Ozawa Ichirō no kenkyū', p. 147. See also Chapter 6.
259 Kabashima, *Doken Tengoku Nippon*, p. 77.
260 Matsuda, *Ozawa Ichirō, Kyoshoku no Shihaisha*, p. 39.
261 Ibid.
262 Matsuda, *Kakuei ni Narenakatta Otoko*, p. 118.
263 Takahashi, 'Ozawa moto hisho', p. 130.
264 'Ozawa-shi wa kensetsu zoku giin no don', in *Shinbun Akahata*, p. 15.
265 Takahashi, 'Ozawa moto hisho', p. 130.
266 Matsuda, quoting Nonaka from a *Yomiuri Shinbun* article of 12 May 2009, in *Ozawa Ichirō, Kyoshoku no Shihaisha*, p. 243.
267 'Ozawa-shi wa kensetsu zoku giin no don', in *Shinbun Akahata*, p. 15.
268 Kuji and Yokota, *Seiji ga Yugameru Kōkyō Jigyō*, p. 13.
269 Ibid., p. 24.
270 'Etsuzankai' was the name of the Tanaka's local support organisation in Niigata.
271 Kuji, *Ozawa Ichirō – Sono 'Kyōfu Shihai'*, pp. 22–23.
272 Ibid., p. 27.
273 Ibid.
274 'Saiaku!' blog.goo.ne.jp/handa3douzo/e/829ba12a41604bec9e2ba2a7a2add57b.
275 The original title in Japanese was *Nihon Retto Kaizōron*.
276 Woodall, *Japan Under Construction*, p. 100.
277 Ishikawa, *Akutō*, p. 178.
278 Kabashima, *Doken Tengoku Nippon*, p. 74.
279 Ozawa, *Blueprint*, pp. 165–68.
280 Katz, 'Part 2: Tanaka's Protégé', p. 6.
281 Kuji and Yokota, *Seiji ga Yugameru Kōkyō*, p. 133.
282 Suzuki, *Saigo no Ozawa Ichirō*, p. 36.
283 Ishikawa, *Akutō*, p. 186.
284 Schmidt, 'The DPJ and its Factions', p. 3.
285 Mizuguchi, 'Political Reform', p. 247.
286 Oka, *Policy Entrepreneurship*, pp. 20–21.
287 Tachibana, 'Ososugita shūen', p. 95.
288 Ibid., p. 96.
289 Watanabe, *Ano Hito*, p. 195.
290 Matsuda, *Kakuei ni Narenakatta Otoko*, p. 151.

291 Yakushiji, *Whither Japanese Politics*, www.tokyofoundation.org/en/topics/politics-in-persepctive/post-ozawa-era.
292 Akasaka, 'The Making of a Non-LDP Administration', p. 8.
293 Tachibana, 'Ososugita shūen', p. 97.
294 '"Ozawa shihai"', diamond.jp/articles/-/3752.
295 Tachibana, 'Ososugita shūen', p. 101.
296 'A Magician in Japan', www.economist.com.hk/node/592427.
297 Okamoto, 'Naze "Tōkyō Kōken Kenjichō" wa Ozawa Ichirō o mamotta ka', p. 33. According to Okamoto, this logic should be called a '"fossil" of postwar politics' (ibid.).
298 Kaifu, *Seiji to Kane*, p. 58.
299 Kabashima and Steel, *Changing Politics in Japan*, p. 131.
300 Matsuda, *Kakuei ni Narenakatta Otoko*, p. 206.
301 Satō, *Ozawa Ichirō no Himitsu*, pp. 73–74.
302 Ibid., pp. 73–74.
303 Toshikawa, 'Hitsuyō na no wa "Ushiwakamaru"', gendai.ismedia.jp/articles/-/32961.
304 Satō, *Ozawa Ichirō no Himitsu*, p. 146.
305 Ibid., pp. 77, 109.
306 Toshikawa, 'Kanemaru Scandal', p. 17.
307 Ozawa, 'My Commitment to Political Reform', p. 9.
308 'Shin Kanemaru', www.nytimes.com/1996/03/29/world/shin-kanemaru-81-kingmaker-in-japan-toppled-by-corruption.html.
309 Kaifu, *Seiji to Kane*, p. 167.
310 Matsumura, 'Ozawa: Japan's Secret Shogun', www.japantimes.co.jp/cgi-bin/eo20100204a1.html.
311 'Ozawa Prepares', www.asahi.com/english/TKY201104140127.html.
312 Kuji, *Ozawa Ichirō – Sono 'Kyōfu Shihai'*, p. 26.
313 'Ozawa Ichirō-shi wa tsugi no sōridaijin ni fusawashiku nai', diamond.jp/articles/-/7032.
314 MacDougall, 'The Lockheed Scandal', p. 219.
315 Mizuguchi, 'Political Reform', p. 248.
316 Itō, 'Dare mo shiranai', p. 139.
317 Ibid.
318 Suzuki, *Saigo no Ozawa Ichirō*, p. 69.
319 Quoted in ibid., pp. 69–70.
320 Ozawa, *Ozawashugi*, pp. 20, 21, 22.
321 Suzuki, *Saigo no Ozawa Ichirō*, p. 67.
322 Ishikawa, *Akutō*, p. 122.
323 Suzuki, *Saigo no Ozawa Ichirō*, pp. 65, 66.
324 Yamazaki, 'Ozawa Ichirō-shi e no kenryoku ichigenka', diamond.jp/articles/-/5735.
325 Itō, 'Dare mo shiranai', p. 140.
326 'Yomu seiji', in *Mainichi Shinbun*, p. 1.
327 '(Seiji no genba)', in *Yomiuri Shinbun*, p. 4.
328 Yamazaki, 'Ozawa Ichirō-shi e no kenryoku ichigenka', diamond.jp/articles/-/5735.
329 Toshikawa, 'Rising and Setting Suns', p. 4.
330 Yamazaki, 'Ozawa Ichirō-shi e no kenryoku ichigenka', diamond.jp/articles/-/5735.
331 Ibid.
332 Ibid.
333 See also Chapter 6.
334 Itō, 'Dare mo shiranai', p. 139.
335 'Kakuei Tanaka', www.encyclopedia.com. See also Curtis, *The Logic of Japanese Politics*, p. 82.
336 Hara, 'Kokumin', diamond.jp/articles/-/9199.

337 Obuchi, 'In Defense of the Mainstream', p. 17.
338 Oka, *Policy Entrepreneurship*, p. 22.
339 Hoshi, 'Left Behind by the Reform Bandwagon', p. 2.
340 Matsuda and Kaneko, 'Tōnai gurūpu ga habatsu ka', p. 4.
341 See also Chapter 6.
342 'Kyūshinryoku', in *Yomiuri Shinbun*, www.yomiuri.co.jp/feature/20100806-849918/news/20110614-OYT1T00937.htm.
343 'DPJ's "Escape from Ozawa"', e.nikkei.com/e/ac/tnks/Nni20110826D2608A15.htm.
344 See also Chapter 6.
345 Yamazaki, 'Seiji fuzai',diamond.jp/articles/-/10554.
346 Toshikawa, 'Rising and Setting Suns', p. 4.
347 Watanabe, *Ozawa Ichirō Kirawareru Densetsu*, p. 248.
348 Sekiguchi, 'Japan's "Destroyer"', blogs.wsj.com/japanrealtime/2012/11/28/japans-destroyer-eyes-comeback-with-party-no-7/.
349 McCarthy, 'Japan's Shadow Shogun', www.independent.co.uk/news/world/japans-shadow-shogun-nurs...ng-to-journalists-terry-mccarthy-reports-from-tokyo-1466282.html.
350 Cf. Gaunder, *Political Reform*, p. 83, 105.

6   *Datsu* Ozawa

Ozawa's predisposition for practising old rather than new politics was clearly displayed during the Kan and Noda administrations, a period that can be characterised more broadly as *datsu* Ozawa (getting rid of Ozawa's influence). After his resignation as secretary-general in June 2010, Ozawa's situation became fraught with uncertainty. The Hatoyama government might have been in his pocket, but the new Kan administration certainly was not. The prime minister refused to cede the kind of control over party, Diet and policy affairs that Ozawa exerted during the Hatoyama administration. Kan nominated prominent anti-Ozawa politicians to important ministerial and party posts, elevating the DPJ's next generation of leaders, dubbed the 'seven magistrates'. Including Sengoku and Edano as the most prominent and influential members, these politicians exemplified the 'new' politics model much more than Ozawa did himself. They stood for a different style of politics, preferring to lead through the power of policy ideas and argument rather than through the exercise of personal and factional power. Unlike the Ozawa group, which was fixated on appointments to top positions in the party, on elections and on political manoeuvring to gain power, the Maehara-Edano group (Ryōunkai) and Noda's faction (Kaseikai) emphasised policies. An anti-Ozawa stance also became a unifying factor for these and Kan's group.

The appointments of Sengoku as chief cabinet secretary and Edano as DPJ secretary-general particularly irked the Ozawa camp and it festered as an issue, becoming an underlying cause of the clash between Kan and Ozawa in the subsequent party leadership race.[1] Edano made a point of declaring, 'I want to be regarded as a new type of secretary-general rather than [Ozawa's] successor'.[2] The new administration was aiming to promote greater transparency in party management, which had been closed under Ozawa's control.[3]

Kan also appointed Noda as minister of finance and new member of the cabinet. Both Noda and Edano had been denied more senior posts in the Hatoyama administration because of their criticism of Ozawa. Other appointments also gave the 'impression of *datsu* Ozawa'[4] including Maehara as minister of land, infrastructure and transport, and Okada as minister of foreign affairs. Soon after Kan became prime minister he said, 'All the Cabinets that depended on Ozawa, such as Hosokawa, Hata, Obuchi and Hatoyama, have had short life spans. I will never bow my head to him'.[5] Indeed, Kan 'embarked on an anti-Ozawa crusade'.[6]

The new administration also resurrected the PRC, thus reviving the tradition of active policy discussions within the party whilst ostensibly maintaining the principle of unifying policymaking under cabinet leadership. The revival of the PRC was considered symbolic of the new Kan-led DPJ because of Ozawa's previous monopolisation of all party policy activities during the Hatoyama administration. The politician who had most persistently called for the PRC's revival despite Ozawa's disapproval was appointed to chair it – Genba Kōichirō. The Kan administration was hoping to assuage the discontent of DPJ backbenchers who had objected to their exclusion from policymaking. It was yet another attempt to take back power from Ozawa.

In response, Ozawa manoeuvred in ways that helped to fracture and destroy the DPJ as a major ruling party, and with it, the embryonic two-party system that he had so assiduously proclaimed to be his true end goal. His objective was to bring down his political enemies within the DPJ leadership, which meant first the Kan administration and then the Noda administration. The fruitless confrontation of Ozawa vs. anti-Ozawa, which continued the political pathology first seen two decades previously in the LDP, not only placed Ozawa at the centre of the political stage[7] but also became a key, if not the key factor in the decline and fall of the DPJ as a major alternative ruling party. Because he could not bend the DPJ leadership to his will, Ozawa eroded the parliamentary party from the inside, undermining its capacity to govern by mounting hostile campaigns against party executives and government leaders, constantly distracting them from the myriad tasks of governing. Just as in the old LDP days, when forced into an anti-mainstream faction, he sought to divide the party in an attempt to rule. Merely containing and constraining Ozawa proved to be almost a full-time job for both the Kan and Noda governments, but they were only minimally and sporadically successful in overcoming his 'sabotage from within'. In this campaign, Ozawa relied almost exclusively on the principal instrument of his power – his faction – elevating its role to that of *tōnai yatō*.

The September 2010 leadership battle

Even on the 'outer' as he was when Prime Minister Kan expressed a wish for him to 'be quiet for a while' after his resignation in June 2010, Ozawa had the Kan government under siege with his threat to stand for the party leadership in mid-September. He met Hatoyama on 25 August and reportedly demanded that Kan's *datsu* Ozawa stance be retracted, including the dismissal of various members of Kan's administration, as a condition for his not running in the leadership race.[8] In fact, he pushed for the total removal of the 'anti-Ozawa' group, including Sengoku, Edano, PRC Chairman Genba and Chairman of the Election Campaign Committee Azumi Jun. These positions were all important in terms of their influence over party policies, resources and election strategy. Ozawa particularly objected to Sengoku, who had become a key figure in the Hatoyama administration as minister for government revitalisation, civil service reform and national strategy, whom he could not control.

Despite Hatoyama's request that Kan treat Ozawa properly, Kan refused Ozawa's call for 'whole party unity' (*kyotō itchi taisei*) as the price of his not contesting the party presidential election, and declined to make any backroom deals on personnel appointments. 'Whole party unity' was code for allowing Ozawa back in, enabling him as the most powerful faction boss to nominate his followers to important positions and to retain *de facto* power over the party and government (see Table 1.1). Such an arrangement would perpetuate the division of power at the heart of government that had characterised the Hatoyama administration. Kan took the principled stance that if he engaged in any backroom deals with Ozawa, 'the politician, Kan Naoto, will die'.[9]

In the light of Hatoyama's failed mediation, Ozawa made up his mind to run in the leadership election, justifying his decision in terms of Kan's refusal to consider the 'whole party unity approach' and the need to overcome the national crisis in the wake of the earthquake and tsunami.[10] His supporters were urging him to run because of their own reduced prospects under Kan's 'getting rid of Ozawa line' (*datsu Ozawa rosen*), while Ozawa himself was worried that he would lose supporters to the Kan camp if his faction lost election funding.[11]

Kan did waver on the Ozawa issue nearer to the election, announcing that he would reverse his *datsu Ozawa* stance and return to the 'troika' (Kan-Hatoyama-Ozawa) system of party unity.[12] In fact, Ozawa wanted the 'troika-plus-one system' where authority would be shared by Kan, Ozawa, Hatoyama and Koshiishi, who was head of the DPJ's Upper House caucus. Both Kan and Hatoyama were willing to accept this option in the hope of averting a party rift. However, what Kan had in mind for the shared leadership idea was like a 'council of advisers' to which he would go to for advice, but which would not hold real power. Ozawa, on the other hand, thought that the 'three-plus-one system' would operate like a supreme leaders' council, which would have veto power over party management, policy matters and financial issues. When he also demanded posts for his followers in exchange for not running in the presidential race, Kan refused.[13] Hatoyama attempted to head off the inevitable division by again trying to persuade Kan to offer Ozawa at least the deputy prime ministership or a key party post, but Kan resisted, saying that 'the place to decide such matters is "not behind closed doors"'.[14]

Having declared himself a contestant in the presidential race, Ozawa and Kan gave a joint press conference. Kan was the first to go on the attack, saying, 'I want Mr. Ozawa to explain properly to the people what kind of prime minister he is going to be…I can't imagine him sitting in the budget committee for a long time'.[15] Ozawa replied, 'I will fulfil my role sincerely in my own way',[16] suggesting that there were no rules of political conduct that would stand in the way of his behaving according to the dictates of his personality. Kan then raised the 'politics and money' issue and referred to his own transparency when it came to his political funding.[17] He added, 'if Ozawa wants to become leader and prime minister…then he will need to give a good explanation [of his role in the scandal that led him to resign as secretary-general]'.[18] To this, Ozawa responded, 'I've been subjected to compulsory investigation by the public prosecutors but they didn't find anything. People talk about having to explain to the Diet, but the Diet does not have a right to conduct compulsory investigations. I've explained this many times'.[19]

Ozawa's fundamental reason for contesting the leadership was because he found himself in the intolerable situation of being relegated to the political periphery, which prevented him from assuming his customary role as the leading power broker and veto player. He calculated that he could call on strength in numbers – his 150-strong faction, plus the group led by Hatoyama, which was the second largest in the DPJ and which had around 60 members, to bring the total to 210. This gave him a good chance of winning the leadership ballot. He might also draw some support from the 30-strong members of the former DSP and SDP groups in the party.[20]

However, despite Ozawa's theoretical strength in numbers, Kan won the election. Speculation ensued that Kan's victory was due to the intense dislike of Ozawa amongst many DPJ Diet members, rather than to any great faith in Kan's abilities as prime minister. At least one first-term Diet member was quoted as saying that his decision to vote for Kan was based on the fact that this would enable DPJ junior politicians such as himself to discuss and debate policy more freely and actively under Kan than they would under Ozawa.[21] The comment was a reference to Ozawa's refusal to permit first-term Diet members to take part in the GRU screening because in his opinion they were not ready for it, and because he wanted them to focus on their electorates and on thanking their supporters.[22] Others in the parliamentary party doubted that Ozawa had the calibre to be prime minister, given that he had only served as a minister once and only for six months, and knowing that he would prefer to be in the position of kingmaker, enabling him to manage the prime minister from behind the scenes. Media commentators generally agreed that it was dislike of Ozawa that had unified the anti-Ozawa forces, 'the feeling that "I really hate that guy"'.[23]

Even in defeat, Ozawa continued to appeal for party unity and, on these grounds, requested that Kan give the positions of chief cabinet secretary and secretary-general to his faction. Kan, however, refused. Although Ozawa said at a meeting of his supporters, 'Together with you all, as one rank and filer, I will do all I can to make the DPJ-led government successful',[24] there were doubts about whether this was truly Ozawa's intention. In fact, his subsequent behaviour made it clear that he had no intention of being 'just an another DPJ Diet member'. He presented Kan with two major issues of Diet management: dealing with both 'opposition parties outside the ruling party' (*tōgai yatō*) and a *tōnai yatō*.[25]

One of the questions facing Ozawa at this time was whether he would lead his supporters out of the DPJ. Because of Ozawa's record of using party labels as mere flags of convenience, the option of forming a new party was not completely out of the question. At the time, however, Ozawa realised that this was likely to be a journey into the political wilderness. In 1993, when he broke with the LDP, he had used electoral reform as the clarion call not only to galvanise his own supporters but also the electorate, a new party and a new coalition government. There was nothing equivalent in 2010, no call for reform that would resonate with the voters, legitimise Ozawa's break-up of the DPJ and provide a foundation for a new party. Moreover, there were no other parties or elements within parties that would seriously consider joining with an Ozawa breakaway group. Linking up with his old party – the LDP – was hardly a credible option given the aversion of practically its entire parliamentary membership, and particularly its leaders and ex-leaders, to Ozawa personally. The New Kōmeitō also had a strong allergy to Ozawa because of his dictatorial ways and questionable record on money politics.[26]

In addition to the lack of issues to galvanise cross-party and public support, and the absence of obvious allies outside the DPJ, there was Ozawa's dubious record of *kinken seiji*. Because he was still under a 'money-politics' cloud, the prospect of solid voting support for a new Ozawa-led party was low. Compelled by political realities to remain in the DPJ, Ozawa thus turned to undermining the Kan administration in a bid to create another more congenial to his interests – one in which he could regain power over the party, over policy and over the government more generally.

Kan's bid for unity

Kan and Ozawa met to discuss personnel matters the day after the party presidential election but the meeting was very short, lasting only ten minutes. The prime minister had decided to appoint Okada as the new secretary-general and Edano as chief cabinet secretary, which merely underlined Kan's intention to maintain his *datsu* Ozawa line. Another who had kept his distance from Ozawa – Genba – was reappointed DPJ policy chief, while Hachiro Yoshio, a Kan supporter, replaced Tarutoko as chairman of the DPJ's Diet Affairs Committee.[27]

Kan's gesture towards party unity was to offer the post of deputy party president to both Ozawa and Koshiishi, who declined. These would have been nominal positions without power in the party. However, Kan did say that he would ask Ozawa to serve the party in a number of different ways. He was also reported to be thinking of offering Ozawa a senior party post relating to election affairs.[28]

In the end, Kan modified his '*datsu* Ozawa' stance to some extent by incorporating the Ozawa faction into his administration, appointing senior members to important but not key posts. Two Ozawa supporters were selected as ministers: Kaieda as minister of state for economic and fiscal policy and Ōhata Akihiro as METI minister. Kan also appointed ten pro-Ozawa politicians as deputy ministers and parliamentary secretaries in order to try to heal the internal party rift and as a positive gesture to party unity. For example, the head of Isshinkai, Suzuki Katsumasa, was given the post of parliamentary secretary of internal affairs and communications. The deputy head of Isshinkai, Matsuki Kenkō, a close aide of Ozawa's, was appointed parliamentary secretary of agriculture, forestry and fisheries. Ozawa's closest aide, Hidaka Takeshi, became parliamentary secretary of environment. Others were Azuma Shōzō, who was chosen as deputy minister of the Cabinet Office and Tsutsui Nobutaka who was appointed senior vice-minister of agriculture, forestry and fisheries. Kan's objective was to give some of Ozawa's closest supporters a stake in his administration and, in this way, try to bridge the divide between pro- and anti-Ozawa forces.

However, Kan's so-called 'unified party structure' was more rhetorical than real. In particular, he was not prepared to budge on the position of secretary-general, the keeper of the party's power and purse. Moreover, although Ozawa was effectively relegated to the outer reaches of the party, this did not mean that he had laid down his political weapons and accepted defeat as final in the sense of surrendering to Kan's ascendancy. His post-election behaviour could only be described as the beginning of a campaign of 'psychological warfare' against Kan.[29]

Sabotaging the Kan administration

Using the TPP issue

Kan very quickly came to regret his strategy of allowing so many of Ozawa's supporters into positions where they could undermine his government's policies. Japan's possible participation in the TPP became one of the most prominent issues on which they chose to fight him. Amongst the 'saboteurs' were METI Minister Ōhata, who was *de facto* leader of the Hatoyama group and a former socialist representing a semi-rural constituency in Ibaraki. Given his ministerial position, he was a vital player in advancing Japan's trade policy and would normally, as trade minister, be expected to adopt a strong pro-trade, pro-market position. However, Ōhata displayed only muted enthusiasm for Japan joining the TPP, which was one of Kan's pet policy projects, saying that this was neither a foregone conclusion nor a top priority for the government.[30]

In addition, Senior MAFF Vice-Minister Tsutsui, from rural Niigata, another politician from the same socialist stable as Ōhata, proclaimed that he believed in 'cultivating [domestic] agriculture', meaning he prioritised domestic food self-sufficiency over opening Japan's agricultural market. The appointment of Ozawa henchman and Isshinkai executive Matsuki as parliamentary secretary of agriculture, forestry and fisheries proved equally problematic. Top of the list of Matsuki's policy proposals was the idea that a system should be constructed in which domestic agriculture could play two key roles: supplying food and preserving the environment, which were also strongly suggestive of an anti-liberalisation stance. Despite his position in the government, Matsuki joined the group of DPJ Diet members opposing Japan joining the TPP (the 'study group to oppose the TPP'), as did former Prime Minister Hatoyama (who was adviser to the group) and leader of the PNP, Kamei Shizuka. A total of 110 politicians – the majority of whom belonged to the Ozawa faction – attended the first meeting of the study group on 21 October 2010. It was organised by Matsuki and MAFF Minister in Kan's first cabinet, Yamada Masahiko, who was very close to Ozawa. It was widely viewed as a gathering of Ozawa loyalists who wanted to show their dissatisfaction with the Kan administration. Ozawa himself made no attempt to curb the activities of his followers in the study group, even though their views, in theory, conflicted with his own. Their anti-TPP campaign continued relentlessly through the end of 2010 and into 2011.

Ozawa as the axis of internal party conflict

The division in the parliamentary party along pro- and anti-Ozawa lines became even more pronounced over time. Ozawa became the central 'axis of conflict' within the party – to the point where people were asking why he bothered to stay. The situation was reminiscent of the state of affairs in the LDP just before Ozawa's defection in 1993.

By late 2010 Ozawa was openly raising the question of replacing the prime minister as Kan's management of the government faltered. The more transparently weak and unpopular the prime minister became, the more Ozawa campaigned behind the scenes to destabilise his administration. He could not undertake official activities to unseat the prime minister because he was now subject to the mandatory indictment process following the No. 5 Committee's recommendation on 4 October, so he used his followers to undertake various acts of sabotage of the administration.

Ozawa did not have it all his own way, however. Prime Minister Kan mounted a campaign to get rid of Ozawa by everything short of actually terminating his membership of the party. He focused on Ozawa's Achilles heel when procedures for Ozawa's mandatory indictment began, distancing his administration from the issue and demanding accountability from Ozawa. What followed was a series of manoeuvrings by both the Kan and Ozawa camps around the issue of Ozawa's appearing before the Lower House Deliberative Council on Political Ethics. Attendance at the council was normally on a voluntary basis and its resolutions had no binding power. The opposition parties were demanding that Ozawa go even further and present himself to the Diet to give sworn testimony, a much more serious step than questioning by the political ethics council where giving vague and untrue answers was not illegal. If false testimony were made in testimony to the Diet, the member in question would face perjury charges.[31]

1 To appear or not to appear

For the Kan side, Ozawa's fronting up to the council was important to demonstrate that the administration was distancing itself from money politics. Ozawa responded by saying that he would appear before the Diet if it summoned him to answer allegations about his political finances.[32] He agreed to go along with whatever the Diet decided on the issue of his responsibility to explain himself to the public. This could include either sworn testimony to the Diet or appearing at the political ethics council. However, this was the calm before the storm. Ozawa's position hardened following the No. 5 Committee's recommendation in October that he be mandatorily indicted. He quickly adopted the argument, 'Since I will be giving an explanation in court, which is a much more rigorous venue than the political ethics council, there is no need to explain in the Diet'.[33]

Ozawa went even further in early December by canvassing a number of tactics to bring the Kan government down. One was to collect signatures requesting a plenary meeting of DPJ Diet members in both houses. Such a meeting could demand the resignation of the party leader.[34] Another pressure tactic was to engineer the mass resignation of the Ozawa group's senior vice-ministers and parliamentary secretaries. Ozawa then went to the Kantei to tell Kan directly that he would not attend the political ethics council. They had a heated exchange with Ozawa declaring that he would not attend even if the council voted to summon him. He presented a written document to Kan, which stated that the political ethics council represented part of the Diet's autonomous function and should not, therefore, interfere with the judicial arm of government. He was to repeat this separation of powers argument when asked to testify before the Diet after his own trial began on 6 October 2011. However, as Okada and others pointed out, fulfilling legal responsibilities (in court) and political responsibilities (to explain to the Diet and public) were two quite different matters. Ozawa's attitude was clearly high-handed as there had been few cases in the past where a Diet member had persistently refused to follow a request from party executives to testify before the council. Kan hinted at reprisals including a recommendation for Ozawa to leave the party.

Ozawa expressed concern to other Diet members about Kan's tough approach, raising the possibility of the prime minister agreeing to the opposition's call to summon him before the Diet as a sworn witness or pressuring him to leave the party. He accused Okada and Sengoku of conspiring to force him out of the party. The prime minister and Ozawa had another meeting on 25 December but no agreement was reached. Observers commented later on the obvious tension at the meeting. Kan did look Ozawa in the eye, gave him only a slight bow and ended up not mentioning Ozawa testifying to the council.[35] It looked as though Kan did not have the courage to expel Ozawa from the party and was alarmed by the Ozawa group's threats that the DPJ would collapse if Ozawa were expelled.[36]

The next day, in response to Kan's repeated demands and the day after the DPJ executive agreed to vote to summon Ozawa to appear before the council, Ozawa suddenly changed his mind. His declaration to give unsworn testimony to the council was generally received positively. Kan stated that the fact that Ozawa had made a decision to attend was a big step forward.[37] Ozawa attributed his decision to pressure from Rengō Chairman Koga Nobuaki for the DPJ to stay united, and to feeling bad for being the cause of such a public stir.[38]

However, Ozawa's apparent compliance merely moved the bone of contention to the timing of his appearance. He made it conditional on the success of Diet deliberations on the budget. His obduracy in the face of pressure from the DPJ executive and anti-Ozawa members of the party inevitably led to calls for his expulsion from the DPJ. The hard-liners in the party were quite confident that not many DPJ members would leave with him if he were given his marching orders. Moreover, getting rid of Ozawa would boost the administration's popular standing.

By year's end, the Kan executive was requesting Ozawa to leave the party voluntarily as well as to attend a hearing of the political ethics council, while the LDP, New Kōmeitō and Your Party (YP) positioned themselves to summon Ozawa to the Diet as a sworn witness. Even if they did not get their wish, they were still happy to see quarrels continue within the DPJ. As for the administration, it still had the option of acceding to the opposition parties' request for Ozawa to give sworn testimony. The usual obstacle, however, was opposition from Ozawa's supporters.[39]

In the New Year, Prime Minister Kan publicly reinforced his posture of eliminating Ozawa's political influence. He declared that 2011 would be the 'year of settling the Ozawa issue'[40] and drawing a firm line against money politics. At the New Year's Day party at the Kantei, Kan openly attacked Ozawa, saying:

> He will soon be forcibly indicted, so his political activities will become extremely limited. Politically, he is gradually vanishing...I recently read Hosokawa's and Kaifu's books. What they both had in common as prime ministers was that their administrations were led astray and eventually collapsed and became completely mutilated as a result of Ozawa's manipulation. In the end, they were both disgusted and held a grudge against Ozawa and that was all that was left.[41]

When asked at the New Year press conference what Ozawa should do if he were subject to compulsory indictment, Kan said: Ozawa 'must clarify his course of action as a politician. And if he needs to focus on his court case, he should do that'.[42] When pressed further about whether concentrating on the trial meant resigning as a Diet member, Kan did not deny the proposition. He even said: 'It is desirable for Mr. Ozawa to consider this and to make a decision on his resignation.'[43]

It was initially thought that the party would issue a formal recommendation for Ozawa to resign and if he refused, the prime minister would take the step of expelling him. However, because Ozawa's case was unprecedented in that he was subject to compulsory indictment after the prosecutors themselves had dropped the case against him, Okada persuaded Kan not to go as far as expelling him, but to stop at suspending Ozawa's membership. It was not the loss of Ozawa himself that Okada feared; it was the prospect of a serious split in the party if a large number of Ozawa's acolytes left with him.

Ozawa met with Koshiishi and Hatoyama in early January and agreed to attend the political ethics council without conditions, declaring that he would comply with any Diet decision concerning his appearance 'at any time'.[44] However, what followed was another game of cat and mouse, this time between Ozawa and Chairman of the Political Ethics Deliberation Council Doi Ryūichi (who was close to Prime Minister Kan) over exactly when Ozawa would appear before the council. Ozawa continued with inconsistent positions on the timing of his appearance. Both Kan and Okada intended to have the council vote to require Ozawa to appear before it if he refused to do so voluntarily. However, opposition from pro-Ozawa Diet members on the council forced abandonment of the plan.

In a meeting of ruling and opposition party secretaries-general and Diet Affairs Committee chairmen in late January, Okada explained how he had failed to persuade Ozawa to give unsworn testimony to the political ethics council. He also disclosed why the DPJ was reluctant to go to the next step – agreeing to summon Ozawa to give sworn testimony to the Diet. It was, according to Okada, because 'sworn testimony is grave'.[45] Summoning a sworn witness could be done with the unanimous agreement of the board of directors (*rijikai*) of the Budget Committee with the penalty for refusing to attend up to a year in prison or a maximum ¥100,000 fine. However, some Budget Committee directors were DPJ politicians close to Ozawa. Recommending that Ozawa withdraw from the DPJ was also hard to achieve. Issuing a recommendation to resign from the party required a decision by the DPJ's Standing Officers Council. Many of its 33 members were close to Ozawa, such as Supreme Adviser Hata Tsutomu and DPJ Vice-President Yamaoka, which made such a recommendation impossible. Moreover, even if such a recommendation were issued, Ozawa would not leave.[46]

The other possibility – Ozawa breaking away and forming a new party – also seemed remote. Ozawa gauged that not many of his supporters would follow him out of the party, so it was preferable for him to stay in the DPJ for the time being and continue to lead a *tōnai yatō*. This way everything that Kan wanted to do would be rejected and he would not be able to achieve anything. In short, he would be crushed not by opposition from the LDP and New Kōmeitō but by opposition from within his own party.[47]

The first moves in this direction were taken by Ozawa and his coterie of supporters in early 2011. At the point when the question of how the DPJ would punish Ozawa had reached a critical stage, he began holding meetings with a small group of supporters to affirm their intention to get rid of Kan. This group in turn began meeting with neutral DPJ members (neither pro- nor anti-Ozawa), as well as considering the option of deputy ministers and parliamentary secretaries close to Ozawa resigning from their positions. These tactics constantly raised the twin spectres of disunity and confusion in the party. At a meeting of the DPJ on 12 January, Kan was roundly derided by Ozawa affiliates who were in a 'get Kan' mood. They jeered the prime minister, subjecting him to questions and comments such as:

> 'why don't you implement the manifesto?', 'local elections are coming up and there are people who don't want to stand for the DPJ'…'the TPP and consumption tax issues – the way you brought them out is too sudden so please deal with them in a better fashion', 'the fact that Okada doesn't think that the party is divided – this needs to be reconsidered, and do you think of Ozawa as an enemy or a friend – if you could please answer that question clearly', 'the secretary-general has said that it is not internal conflict, but public opinion thinks otherwise and we have to take their opinion seriously and do our job.'[48]

Kan said, 'I wanted to aim for clean and open politics in the leadership election, so that was the promise that I made to everyone and that promise was accepted and so with that understanding, I'd like to keep on going. I'm one of the people that wishes for a unified party the most'.[49] However, in his second cabinet, formally anointed two days later, the prime minister continued his *datsu Ozawa rosen*, and the make-up of the cabinet showed it. Kan, Edano and Sengoku from the government side and Okada from the party side remained the core of the administration's management. These four and Azumi, who was appointed chairman of the Diet Affairs Committee and senior vice-minister of defence, were all known for their critical attitude towards Ozawa.

The appointment of new members to the Standing Officers Council on 19 January was also weighted in favour of those who were anti-Ozawa. These appointments were considered significant because the council had the power to determine the punishment of DPJ Diet members. The scenario in the Kan executive's mind was punishing Ozawa after his mandatory indictment if he refused to offer an explanation to the Diet.[50]

2 Ozawa's mandatory indictment

When the court-appointed lawyers mandatorily indicted Ozawa on 31 January, reactions were relatively calm because the decision had been expected. Thereafter, the debate in the party shifted from Ozawa's appearance before the political ethics council to the nature of his punishment because of the indictment. Some DPJ Diet members claimed that this needed to be decided as a party, while others said that punishment was not necessary owing to the principle of innocent until proven guilty.[51] So the party still remained divided.

For his part, Ozawa insisted that he would not leave the party and aimed to do his work as a Diet member while dealing with his trial. He told reporters that he had no intention of resigning his Diet seat or leaving the DPJ. His followers were confident that because the party leadership had not been able to force Ozawa to attend the political ethics council, they would not be able to punish him either.

Kan meanwhile claimed over and over again that the government had to end the 'politics and money' problem once and for all. He talked to Ozawa at the Kantei, asking him to explain to the Diet and to leave the party voluntarily until his trial was over. Ozawa replied that his position on attending the political ethics council had not changed and that he had no intention of leaving the party. Kan, in response said, 'it has become necessary for a punishment as a party. The decision is to be made by the party'.[52]

Kan was hoping to punish Ozawa in order to 'cut him off completely' (*Ozawa kiri*),[53] thereby promoting discussions with the opposition on issues such as raising the consumption tax as well as stabilising his administration. Some in the LDP executive were prepared to work with the government if it dismissed Ozawa. Because the pro-Ozawa group was opposed to Kan's high-priority policy issues, such as the TPP, raising the consumption tax and comprehensive social security reform,[54] Kan also saw Ozawa as a direct obstacle to the success of his policy initiatives, so *Ozawa kiri* was a strategy not only to buoy his administration but also to promote particular policies.[55] However, the strategy was a double-edged sword given that accelerating moves to sever ties with Ozawa would risk arousing severe opposition from within the party. If Ozawa ended up leaving, it would weaken the foundations of the Kan regime even if only a limited number of people left with him.[56]

3 Attack and counterattack

Dispute then began in the DPJ about what the appropriate punishment for Ozawa should be, if any. The executive led by Kan and Okada thought to urge Ozawa to leave the party as punishment for his indictment. Those opposed to Ozawa in the wider party were also talking about his voluntary resignation, rather than his expulsion. Kan was one of the hard-liners, however, going as far as wanting Ozawa to resign from the Diet, but Okada did not support this, saying a Diet member was chosen by voters.[57] In the end, there was general agreement that taking some form of disciplinary action was the only way to settle the issue, with most of the executive agreeing to the lesser punishment of suspending Ozawa's party membership because, 'We have no choice but to consider the "two-thirds majority" [in the House of Representatives]'.[58]

Ozawa's position was that he would fight the trials but not resign from the DPJ. His refusal to go voluntarily was Okada's cue to consider suspending him from the party, referring the issue to the party executive committee in mid-February. Of the committee, 80 per cent were in favour of punitive action against Ozawa.[59] At the committee meeting, Okada suggested a plan to suspend Ozawa's membership until the judgment of the court was decided, allowing the suspension to be lifted if he were found innocent.[60] The committee decided to propose this course of action to the Standing Officers Council, which was due to make the formal decision after asking the party's Political Ethics Committee, which was chaired by the DPJ's supreme adviser Watanabe Kōzō, to rule on the appropriateness of the punishment.[61] In the January round of appointments to the ethics committee, Ozawa supporters had been replaced with those who distanced themselves from him.

The prospect of hostile action by the DPJ executive prompted equally hostile retaliation from Ozawa's political allies, with 16 of them applying to Secretary-General Okada to leave the DPJ-led parliamentary group (Minshutō *kaiha*) in the Lower House and to form a new floor group called the 'the group to take responsibility for political change by the DPJ'.[62] Of the 16, 14 were members of Hokushinkai, the group of first-term Lower House Diet members who were part of the larger Ozawa group. They wanted to throw down a direct challenge to the Kan administration over its treatment of Ozawa. Despite public claims that they opposed the Kan government because it had abandoned the DPJ's manifesto and its promises to the people,[63] their primary motivation was political rather than policy-related. They had several objectives in playing a game of chicken with the Kan administration: to make its Diet management strategy completely unworkable, to protest against the party's punishment of Ozawa and to put pressure on Kan to resign as prime minister.

Leverage for the group was handily supplied by the Kan administration's precarious numbers in the Diet, particularly its lack of a majority in the Upper House and the fact that it fell short of a two-thirds majority in the Lower House by a small margin, which allowed the 16 rebels to use their threat of not voting with the government as a political weapon. Using this leverage was all part of Ozawa's strategy of making it as difficult as possible for the Kan administration to govern. The DPJ in the Upper House was already led by anti-Kan politicians close to Ozawa, with Koshiishi and Nishioka, a former LP henchman, poised to assist Ozawa's strategy of undermining the Kan administration's legislative strategy and countering the pro-Kan DPJ Lower House executive.

Leader of the group of 16, Watanabe Kōichirō from the Tokyo PR bloc who had known Ozawa for many years, said that the group would decide whether or not to support the budget-related bills after they had scrutinised their contents. One member said, 'If the party leadership punishes former leader Ozawa, we will not leave the party but we will not cooperate with the party in managing Diet affairs'.[64] Watanabe called for the prime minister's resignation, declaring 'the Kan administration has no legitimacy'.[65] He claimed that the group would be 'the true DPJ'.[66] Kan's response was to say, 'we're trying hard to implement the manifesto that was established while Ozawa was the party leader, but...there are some things that are not possible to implement'.[67]

Watanabe denied that the actions of the gang of 16 had been masterminded by Ozawa. Nevertheless, the group's action suggested that their primary allegiance was to Ozawa, not to the DPJ, in line with Ozawa's prescription of 'faction first'. Certainly, in the view of the protagonists, their actions were made easier by the fact that they saw themselves as followers of Ozawa rather than as members of the DPJ. All but second-termers Watanabe and Toyoda Juntarō had been recruited by Ozawa, who was in charge of the DPJ's election strategy in 2009 and who inserted them as candidates into the party list in the PR blocs. They had no special attachment to the DPJ, seeing themselves as Ozawa's candidates and as politicians who owed their seats to Ozawa.

Though Ozawa himself denied any advance knowledge of the group of 16's request to leave the DPJ's Lower House caucus, the group had in fact met with him secretly beforehand to inform him of their intentions. He told them that 'Kan is a failure. The DPJ is also a failure'.[68] He also revealed that the whole idea of a group of his followers leaving the DPJ's Diet caucus (without leaving the DPJ itself) had been suggested to him by Hirano Sadao, who was well versed in Diet rules. When Ozawa met up with Hirano in late 2010, Hirano suggested to Ozawa that resigning from the DPJ's floor group was the only way to replace Kan without anyone leaving the DPJ.[69] He also raised the possibility of alliances with Osaka Governor Hashimoto Tōru and Nagoya Mayor Kawamura Takashi, suggestions that were later contemplated by Ozawa. One member of the group also affirmed that they were prepared to leave the party,[70] including possibly collaborating with the regional Genzei Nippon (Tax Cuts Japan) party led by Kawamura, who was close to Ozawa and who also had connections to Matsuki, one of Ozawa's main lieutenants. There were even moves behind the scenes for

Kawamura, who had been in touch with Ozawa, to form a new party that would welcome the 16 Diet members.[71] Ozawa was supportive of making contact with a range of political parties, observing that, 'The trend over the next 10 years will be grand coalitions and regional alliances'.[72] Ozawa actually met with Kawamura, saying that he had been with the DPJ for a long time, but the essence of the DPJ (cutting taxes, as opposed to the LDP's tax increases) was now out of order, so he could understand why the group of 16 did what they did.[73] He also told Kawamura that changing the national system was necessary to carry out reforms and that they should work together.[74] Although not everyone in the Kawamura camp was happy about the idea of their leader cosying up to Ozawa because of the taint of scandal surrounding him, Kawamura himself seemed unaffected by such concerns, saying that he would extend cooperation for the sake of the nation on the condition tax cuts would be promoted.[75]

The prime minister offered a harsh response to the group of 16's action, condemning their move as 'absolutely incomprehensible'.[76] Okada's response was to call Kawamura 'the enemy'.[77] He cited Diet regulations that did not permit members of a party unilaterally to leave parliamentary groups. The regulations required that when Diet members applied to form a new parliamentary caucus, the head of their old group – that is, Okada – would have to approve and then officially report it to the Lower House speaker in a written document. Because Okada would not approve the move, the required written document would not be submitted and therefore the Lower House could not accept the application to form a new parliamentary group.[78] Hence the action failed, formally speaking. The Standing Officers Council suspended Watanabe's party membership for six months and withdrew his party allowance to distinguish him from the others in the group. The council issued reprimands to the remaining 15 members.

A few days after the internal revolt by the gang of 16, the DPJ Standing Officers Council voted on 22 February to suspend Ozawa's membership until the verdict at his trial was finalised. The party ethics committee also approved the punishment. Okada explained the council's decision in terms of Ozawa's refusal to comply with calls to testify to the Lower House Deliberative Council on Political Ethics. Kan also sought understanding for the punishment, explaining that he had asked Ozawa to leave voluntarily but he had refused.[79] Under suspension all party posts had to be relinquished, politicians could not stand as candidates for party executive positions or attend party meetings and hence they lost their voting rights, could not run in elections as official DPJ candidates and could not be chairman of the DPJ constituency branch, although they still had to pay their party dues and follow party restrictions such as agreements or disagreements regarding bills.[80] So a suspended member had to vote with the party in the Diet but was cut off from electoral endorsement and party funds.

The suspension meant that Ozawa could not stand for party president or vote in the next party presidential election and would face the next general election without the benefit of the DPJ's financial backing or endorsement if the election were held within his period of suspension. It also meant that Ozawa lost his position as head of the DPJ's Iwate (4) branch, effectively halting the supply of political funds from the party branch. Another potential impact arose indirectly in terms of Ozawa's relations with his followers. Lack of power and position in the party inevitably meant cutbacks in the flow of Ozawa's patronage, which had negative repercussions for his supporters in terms of their own political prospects, ultimately undermining their loyalty to Ozawa and the overall solidarity of his group given its fundamental grounding in patron-client relations.

Ozawa blasted the suspension, describing it as 'unwarranted', 'unprecedented' and 'unjust',[81] and asserting that there was 'no rational reason why I should be (singled out)'.[82] It was 'unjust' because party rules stipulated that a suspension could last no longer than six months and yet the party had suspended his membership until the outcome of his trial, which was more than a year away.[83] He was thrown back on to his group as his main political weapon against the Kan administration and on to reinforcing their confrontational tactics.

To protest against the party's punishment of Ozawa and to weaken Kan's grip on the leadership, Matsuki resigned his position as parliamentary secretary of agriculture, forestry and fisheries. He justified it by declaring his opposition to the Kan administration's review of the 2009 DPJ election manifesto and its position in favour of participating in the TPP.[84] Those close to Kan were very critical of Matsuki's 'betrayal', because as parliamentary secretary, he was supposed to support the prime minister.[85]

The group of 16 also protested against Ozawa's punishment by absenting themselves from the Lower House plenary session's vote on the fiscal 2011 budget on 1 March. This action did not materially affect the passage of the bill through the house but it did call the administration's leadership into question. On the same day as the Lower House budget vote, Ozawa filed an eight-page complaint with the Standing Officers Council against the party leadership's decision to suspend his party membership.

Although the group of 16's boycott of the budget vote had no impact on the passage of the budget itself, the DPJ leadership indicated the need to penalise them in some way. Their concern had shifted to the passage of the budget-related bills, which required a majority in both houses. The DPJ's strategy of seeking to secure a two-thirds majority necessary for a possible override, which was dependent on the cooperation of the SDP, was neutralised without the support of all DPJ Lower House members.

Not all members of the Ozawa group supported a possible boycott. Some voiced disquiet that they would be seen by the public as taking the budget-related bills hostage. It was significant that those who had absented themselves from the Lower House budget vote were from PR constituencies, while those who were from single-seat districts were concerned that their local constituents might view such a move as a dereliction of their duty as ruling party Diet members. Their plan was to stay in the party, vote for the budget-related bills and then run one of their own representatives in the DPJ presidential election should Kan resign.[86] Moreover, the not-so-veiled counter-threat from the DPJ executive was to pull DPJ endorsement from anyone who failed to vote with the party in the Diet. The prime minister also warned that he might call a snap election in the face of threats from Ozawa's disciples not to vote for government bills. When Kan started hinting at the possibility of dissolving the Lower House, those in the group of 16 without a solid support base began to look uneasy.

At a press conference, Ozawa declared that the group's boycott of the budget vote was action taken on their own account, but he expressed his tolerance for such behaviour.[87] He told one of the rebels, 'This is the first shot'.[88] His words raised the question whether he was planning a scenario where he would leave the DPJ to fight a general election as head of a new political grouping. Although his ideal scenario was to topple the Kan administration, he called on his followers to prepare for a dissolution of the Lower House and a general election. In the meantime, he was analysing the situation in each constituency from Hokkaido to Okinawa.[89]

Ozawa's manoeuvrings were seen as an attempt to build solidarity in his group in order to support a possible realignment of political forces, including the creation of some kind of grand coalition of like-minded politicians.[90] Clearly taking hold in his mind was the possibility of establishing a new party, which would begin with the formation of a new bloc of DPJ defectors in the Diet. This group would be in a position to take over from the DPJ should it lose government.

In the meantime, manoeuvring for a 'post-Kan phase' continued, with Ozawa's most prominent public aide Yamaoka planning to inaugurate a policy group called 'the group to restore principles and policy for the change of government and to protect the livelihoods of the people', with more than 80 DPJ Diet politicians as members.[91] The *raison d'être* of the group, according to Yamaoka, was to adopt a confrontational stance vis-à-vis the Kan administration over the issue of implementing the DPJ's manifesto, which the government was planning to review.[92] Failing to honour the manifesto gave Ozawa a policy issue around which to mobilise his followers and provided a policy front for their political machinations within the party and their disruptive and rebellious activities in the Diet. Ozawa's attachment to the original 2009 manifesto was also due to its past success as a proven vote winner in the election, with its big-spending appeals to broad categories of non-aligned voters combined with *baramaki* handouts to special interests such as farmers, and fiscal constraint limited to cuts in 'wasteful expenditure'. The DPJ's attempt to meet this goal in 2009–10, however, had fallen well short of expectations and the commitments it had made, a process to which Ozawa himself contributed little if anything.

4 Post-disaster plotting against the Kan administration

After a brief hiatus in the DPJ's internal bickering in the wake of the 11 March triple disaster of earthquake, tsunami and nuclear reactor failure, Ozawa and his followers subsequently used the events and the poor showing of the DPJ in the nationwide local elections in April to undermine the Kan administration further. Far from rallying around the Kan government at a time of national crisis, Ozawa actively sabotaged attempts to build a consensus in the party on how to deal with the disaster. Indeed, he used the crisis as grounds for a renewed offensive against Kan, seeing an opportunity to turn the disaster to his own political advantage.

When the DPJ's losses in the April local elections were still fresh in Diet members' minds, Ozawa gathered about 20 of his close followers at his home in Fukazawa, Tokyo. The meeting ended Ozawa's one month-long absence from the political scene.[93] He was emboldened by the DPJ's poor showing in the local elections, which was the trigger for a renewed effort to overthrow the Kan administration. Ozawa addressed the gathering, advocating support for a no-confidence motion in the government. He was hoping to re-enact his success back in 1993, which had completely turned the political situation around.[94] Ozawa said, 'if 80 people from the DPJ agree, a no-confidence motion can be passed'.[95] His group was confident that it could collect the required number of votes, stepping up its efforts to woo others to join with them. Ozawa meanwhile sought to reassure possible allies inside the DPJ that he did not plan to break up the party, by saying that he had no intention of defecting.

By the end of May Ozawa was openly declaring that he was prepared to take on Kan for what he saw as 'the government's mishandling of the continuing nuclear-energy crisis'.[96] He argued, 'the prime minister should step down to pave the way for a new political era in Japan'.[97] However, whether any new political era was possible given Ozawa's intentions merely to restore his power was debateable. His real goal was to engineer a political situation in which he could exert a controlling influence on the government. This might be from behind the scenes under a new DPJ leader or as the leader of a possible new coalition outside the DPJ. In the best of all worlds, Ozawa would have preferred to realise his classic scenario in which he orchestrated a political realignment by breaking up the DPJ and forming a new party with a group of his supporters in tow, thus exploiting the weakened Kan administration. Ozawa would then try to marry up his group of supporters with other parties or defectors from other parties. One option was enticing LDP defectors to join with him, thus splitting both the LDP and the DPJ, and forming a new political grouping. He was quoted as saying that 'he could work with a government led by Sadakazu Tanigaki'.[98]

Engineering such a political realignment, however, depended on whether and to what extent those in other parties would be prepared to defect and join a new Ozawa party. For many Diet members he was damaged goods, a spent force and a political pariah. Even if he were acquitted at his trial, his future would continue to be dogged by his past money-politics scandals, and so he would likely operate in the shadow of the law and the courts, which would reduce his popular appeal.

Another key issue was how many of his devotees would be willing to abandon the DPJ to form the core of a new, smaller party. Some Ozawa faction members would follow him out of loyalty, but many who put their political careers first would make the strategic decision that it would be unwise to leave with Ozawa unless he could guarantee their re-election and promise them a bright future. Only those with nothing to lose – representatives of the PR blocs in the Lower House with little chance of securing DPJ endorsement in the next election and virtually no chance of winning even if they did because of their low placement on the party list – would possibly consider such a move. The other side of this coin for Ozawa was that those Lower House politicians more inclined to leave with him – the Ozawa-dependent rookies recruited, trained, funded and personally endorsed by him when he was DPJ secretary-general – were the most electorally vulnerable and so would be unlikely to survive a Lower House election. He would be leading a party of the unelectable.

Evidence that only a small number of DPJ politicians would leave with Ozawa was the limited number of regular attendees at Isshinkai meetings, which were held almost every day after the intra-party conflict had intensified.[99] Ozawa appeared to retain the fervent support of a core group of 20–30 acolytes who remained staunchly loyal, but even adding Hokushinkai members on to this number would not mean that the Ozawa faction was large. Moreover, not all Isshinkai and Hokushinkai members would leave with him.[100] It was likely that the majority of his followers would remain in the ruling party. Calculating the numbers that Ozawa could possibly call up revealed the shortcomings of any defection strategy.

For Ozawa, another important consideration was the political funding for which a new party would be eligible – where numbers were again important. The question was whether without access to rich DPJ coffers he would have sufficient funds to entice his followers to leave with him and to fight any subsequent election campaign. If the new party aspired to anything more than minor party status, the Ozawa group would have to put up candidates to run against the LDP and DPJ in most districts. The cost would be at least ¥1 billion, which was a large sum of money at a time when Ozawa was rumoured to be short of funds.[101]

Ozawa's past record as a political destroyer and the kind of old politics he typified would also count against him. Prospective members of a new Ozawa party would need to factor into their calculations whether they would be able to build a political future within a traditional leader-follower paradigm, rather than in a party of collective decision makers, which was internally democratic and offered opportunities for advancement based on ability.

Adding all these factors together, Ozawa and his supporters faced huge disincentives to abandon the DPJ, no matter how much they hated those in the party leading the administration. Not surprisingly, Ozawa continued to deny any intention of breaking away. Political reality compelled him to remain where he was, not because of any particular attachment to the DPJ, or because he really believed in the importance of consolidating a two-party system, but because his own prospects outside the party were so meagre. He was simply not in a position to reprise the role he played in 1993 as the key architect of major party realignment.

Under the circumstances, Ozawa's only option was engineering a change in the power structure within the DPJ whilst remaining within it. This made sense of his proposed no-confidence motion in the cabinet, the resignations from sub-ministerial positions by senior members of his faction and the threatened sabotage of the government's legislative programme by his followers. In fact, all of Ozawa's machinations after losing the DPJ leadership election in September 2010 suggested that he was planning a comeback *in the DPJ*: staying in the party, getting rid of Kan and his cabinet, and establishing an administration more amenable to his manipulation in the short term and more predisposed towards making him leader in the medium term. He saw his future in terms of an acquittal at his trial and possibly running again for the party leadership.

The Kan administration's weakness was grist to Ozawa's mill, providing him with hope that he could possibly engineer its downfall. The last thing Ozawa and his group wanted was for Kan to dissolve the Diet and call a general election given the electoral vulnerability of many of his followers. They were counting on the fact that this would be an act of desperation on Kan's part. Because the Tohoku disaster and nuclear power accident restricted Kan's power to dissolve the Diet, the Ozawa faction felt it could act without fear of facing the electorate. It was this reasoning that led to their prospective support for the motion of no confidence presented to the Lower House plenary session in June.[102]

5 The failed vote of no confidence in the Kan cabinet

When it became clear that the opposition parties led by the LDP and New Kōmeitō were considering submitting a motion of no confidence in the Kan cabinet, Hatoyama and Koshiishi initially counselled restraint, urging Ozawa not to try to mount a coup against Kan using this option.[103]

Although Ozawa had only limited pipelines to the LDP centring on former Secretary-General Koga Makoto, he had an ally in PNP leader Kamei Shizuka, who also had his eye on a post-Kan scenario. Ozawa's supporters were mulling over the possibility of forcing Kan to resign and then holding out with a temporary government in which Kamei would be prime minister. Koga also met with Kamei to discuss party realignment.

On the 27 May, the LDP and New Kōmeitō resolved jointly to submit a no-confidence motion against Kan for his unsatisfactory conduct in dealing with the disaster. Ozawa also publicly expressed the view that the sooner Kan was replaced the better,[104] although he preferred Kan to resign voluntarily. He had been buoyed by the numbers that had attended his 69th birthday party on 24 May – around 160.

On 1 June, three of the opposition parties – the LDP, New Kōmeitō and the Sunrise Party of Japan – submitted a motion of no confidence in the cabinet. It was due to be voted on in the Lower House plenary session on the afternoon of 2 June. Those who led the submission in the LDP were Ozawa's ally Koga Makoto and former Prime Minister Mori Yoshirō, whom Ozawa saw as part of a scenario whereby he would 'use his links with older politicians in the LDP to create a grand coalition as a framework to secure his return to power'.[105] With just the three parties' support, the motion would not have passed, but there were strong indications of defections from the DPJ side. Ozawa announced his intention to vote in favour of the motion, which he was confident would be successful.[106] Hatoyama also announced that he would support the motion after a meeting with Kan. Former MIAC Minister Haraguchi followed with a statement of his support. The tension mounted significantly in the party with these declarations.

Kan declared that he was ready to dole out strict punishments to those members of the party who voted in favour of the resolution, including throwing them out of the party. Okada also stated that support for an opposition party vote of no confidence in the cabinet could be countenanced only on the condition that the DPJ Lower House Diet members left the party. One senior DPJ official recommended that all the rebels should be given the axe, making it easier for the government to revise the manifesto.[107]

The crucial question, however, was how many members of the party Ozawa could mobilise in favour of the motion. Those strongly in favour included the gang of 16 who had earlier broken from the DPJ's Lower House caucus on the budget vote, as well as those Ozawa-allied deputy ministers and parliamentary secretaries who had submitted their resignations at the Kantei on the same day.[108] If 50 Ozawa followers supported the motion, that still left it short of about 30 votes so the Ozawa group put a lot of pressure on the Hatoyama group of 40 or so Lower House Diet members, which it viewed as a potential source of support. Hatoyama, however, continued to vacillate until almost the last minute. Another meeting with the prime minister prompted him finally to opt in favour of rejecting the motion on the condition that Kan resigned. He told Kan 'to step down soon after a basic disaster reconstruction law is passed and the compilation of the second supplementary budget for fiscal 2011 is in sight'.[109] Kan also referred to a memorandum that he had exchanged with Hatoyama, which mentioned the reconstruction law and the second supplementary budget.

Before the vote on 2 June Prime Minister Kan declared to a meeting of DPJ Lower House members that he would resign at the point when the Tohoku earthquake and tsunami disaster were resolved to a certain level. With this announcement, the tension in the party suddenly fell away. Kan's declaration had pulled the rug out from underneath the opposition parties and rebel factions, and the attempt to overthrow the Kan administration collapsed.[110]

It was following Kan's remarks that Hatoyama told the meeting that he would oppose the no-confidence motion. The Ozawa group then decided that members were to vote on the basis of their own independent decision.[111] The reality was that Kan's offer to resign had completely turned the tables on the Ozawa group, prompting one of Ozawa's supporters to observe, 'It is the end. This is the complete destruction of the motion of no confidence. It is incredible that [he] was trapped by such an easy strategy'.[112]

The no-confidence motion was lost by a substantial margin of 293 to 152 for a total of 445 votes cast in the 480-seat chamber, with most of the DPJ and the PNP voting against it. Only two members of the DPJ voted for the motion – Matsuki and Yokokume Katsuhito, who had recently expressed his intention to leave the DPJ and had already tendered his resignation from the DPJ prior to the no-confidence vote – with 15 absent or abstaining. Ozawa was one of those absent. Two other members of the Ozawa group also put in a non-appearance. They were reputedly sick and had medical certificates explaining their absence. A total 12 others abstained. A number of senior party members and Ozawa loyalists made a last-minute effort to dissuade Matsuki, who had announced his intention to vote for the no-confidence motion, to change his mind, but he would not be dissuaded.

The LDP would not have been able to contemplate such a no-confidence motion had it not been for the Ozawa group within the DPJ and its apparent willingness to destabilise the Kan administration even at the risk of sparking severe intra-party conflict. Ozawa's role in the crisis was pivotal for that reason. The move had all the hallmarks of a cynical grab for power by both sides – for Ozawa to regain power in the party and for the LDP to regain power over government. Policy differences were thrown out the window. Politics, not principle, was driving a temporary alliance of convenience.

As it turned out, the LDP misjudged the numbers that they thought Ozawa could and would mobilise in favour of such a motion. Not enough members of the Ozawa faction were prepared to leave the DPJ. Their goal was really to force Kan's resignation.[113] This was extreme anti-mainstream factional behaviour reminiscent of the worst excesses of the LDP. Ozawa's actions only made sense in terms of a power play. He wanted to get rid of Kan because of their mutual animosity, and resurrect his influence in the party and on the administration from outside the cabinet whilst keeping the DPJ as the ruling party.[114]

Whether the no-confidence motion succeeded or failed, Ozawa calculated that it would be to his advantage. If the motion were lost, it would still undermine the government. The Kan administration was already governing from a shaky position and this would make it even shakier. The action might also be risk-free in terms of any likely punishment dished out to the rebels. If Kan followed through with his threat to expel those who voted for the motion, it would further endanger the DPJ's two-thirds majority in the Lower House. On the other hand, if Kan left a group of rebellious politicians within the party, they could continue to threaten his Diet management strategy. If the no-confidence motion succeeded, the prime minister and cabinet would be given two choices: either resign, or dissolve the Diet and call a snap election within ten days.[115] Whatever Kan chose, it would mean the end of him and his cabinet. This would ensure a change of administration, which might be more to Ozawa's liking.

The main risk was that the no-confidence motion would allow Kan the option of dissolving the Diet and calling a general election. Ozawa was counting on Kan not doing this for several reasons: the difficulty of holding a general election given the significant dislocation in the disaster-stricken areas; the fact that it would destroy Kan's government; and the very poor prospects facing the DPJ in the poll. In fact, it was the March disaster that really opened up the opportunity to pass the vote of no confidence more or less with impunity given that it was highly unlikely that Kan would dissolve the Diet in those circumstances.

As soon as the Diet vote was taken differences emerged between Kan and Hatoyama over the interpretation of their agreed memorandum. The gap between their respective understandings was evident in the fact that at the meeting of DPJ Lower House members, the prime minister never actually used the word 'resign' when describing his intentions. Nor did he specify exactly when he would leave office and he did not use the word 'resign' in the memo itself.

Hatoyama had saved the Kan government, which was not his intention, which had been to secure a promise from Kan to leave office. Hatoyama and his supporters then decided to collaborate with Ozawa to plan their next move, including gathering the signatures necessary to call a general meeting of all DPJ Diet members in order to demand that the leadership of the government and party resign. The LDP also planned a censure motion against Kan in the Upper House which Ozawa's supporters were hopeful would drive the prime minister out.[116]

The threat of holding a plenary session of DPJ members in both houses to force Kan to resign was one that the Ozawa group had canvassed from time to time. What had consistently ruled it out was the need for the signatures of one third of the party's Diet membership, which the Ozawa group was unable to secure. Moreover, as existing party regulations made it impossible to vote to depose the party president, a three-step process was necessary: obtain the required numbers to hold the meeting; change the party regulations to add provisions allowing the removal of the party's president; and then take a vote to dismiss Kan. Each step of the way the anti-Kan DPJ Diet members would have to muster the necessary numbers, which was by no means assured. Moreover, even if he were dumped as DPJ president, Kan might not necessarily resign as prime minister. That would require a separate Diet vote. The difficulties attached to this option explained why the Ozawa group had jumped at the opportunity to undermine Kan by threatening to join the vote of no confidence in his government in June.

What these various manoeuvres also demonstrated was that Ozawa did not have the numbers to get rid of Kan, underlining just how powerless he was to effect either a change of government or a realignment of political forces. Although he could make Kan's political life difficult, he could not remove him from office.

Ozawa's punishment for his abstention from the Diet vote on the no-confidence motion was suspension of his party membership for three months. While choreographing the potential revolt within the DPJ, he avoided expulsion. As his membership was already suspended, this imposed no additional punishment on him. In fact, the party effectively avoided further punishment of Ozawa by handing out this sentence. It was the equivalent of serving a prison term concurrently with another for a different offence.

As for the other 14 members of the DPJ who had also abstained from the vote, seven including Tanaka Makiko received the same punishment as Ozawa in having their party membership suspended for three months. This deprived them of the right to vote in any DPJ presidential election held during that period. The five first-term Diet members in the group of abstainers received only severe reprimands and were permitted to vote in a presidential election. Two other DPJ Lower House members were not punished because of their doctors' certificates. The two DPJ members who voted for the motion – Matsuki and Yokokume – were expelled from the DPJ. Because there were only two involved, decisive action presented no problem for the DPJ executive.

In the aftermath of the failed no-confidence vote the conflict between Kan and Ozawa deepened. The issue of upholding the DPJ's 2009 election manifesto, particularly 'putting people's lives first', became the mantra that Ozawa and his storm troopers adopted in sustaining their anti-Kan campaign. They argued that many of Kan's policies had gone against the party's 2009 pledges to wrest control of policymaking from the powerful bureaucracy, cut wasteful spending and put more cash into people's pockets.

Failing to honour the manifesto's promises was an easy and politically convenient weapon with which to attack Kan and his administration. At its heart was a simplistic view that defied logic and the changed circumstances in which Japan found itself, including public acceptance of the need to modify the DPJ's spending promises in the light of the triple disaster. There were already many parts of the manifesto that had been changed and adjusted over time, so it was an oversimplified argument to talk about maintaining or not maintaining it. Ozawa's professed attachment to it could be explained by the fact that it contained all of his populist big-spending promises, which in turn encapsulated his elections-first approach. This mindset infected his entire group and reinforced the clear lines of division between it and the rest of the parliamentary party. It inevitably gave rise to a fundamental structural division within the party between the policy-first standpoint of the DPJ leadership and the politics- or elections-first approach of Ozawa and his group.

Tactics of the DPJ leadership on the anti-Ozawa side included forming a possible alliance with the opposition in order to gain advantage over the Ozawa camp, with Sengoku and Okada making various approaches to key members of the LDP. The Kan administration went outside the DPJ to secure the LDP's and New Kōmeitō's cooperation in passing the budget-related bills, for example. Such a 'temporary coalition of convenience' provided a strategy for the government to outflank opposition from within the DPJ, enabling it to pass legislation without the benefit of votes from Ozawa supporters if necessary. As Kobayashi observed, 'The DPJ can justify the grand coalition by saying it wants to "break away from the remnants of old-fashioned politics"'.[117]

Replacing Kan

One of the main reasons why Ozawa and his followers remained in the DPJ was the hope of replacing Kan in the DPJ presidential election that would take place after his resignation. Ozawa's ambition was to act as kingmaker, fielding a candidate through whom he could wield power. This was vital in ultimately paving the way for his own return to high office. On the other hand, for Prime Minister Kan, this was exactly the scenario that had made him so reluctant to resign, given his fear of a revival of Ozawa's influence.[118]

In the short term, the pro- and anti-Ozawa pathology in the party shifted to the choice of DPJ leader. It was symptomatic of Ozawa's weakened position that there was no obvious contender from the Ozawa camp, but there was a long list of potential candidates to choose from if Ozawa were to act as kingmaker. The list included former Foreign Minister Maehara, Finance Minister Noda, Chief Cabinet Secretary Edano, Deputy Chief Cabinet Secretary Sengoku, DPJ Secretary-General Okada, State Minister in Charge of National Policy Genba, MAFF

Minister Kano Michihiko, METI Minister Kaieda, former Environment Minister Ozawa Sakihito, and the previous candidate for the post in June 2010, Tarutoko. It was generally thought that neither the Ozawa nor Hatoyama factions would field their own candidate, but would cooperate to hold sway as the largest bloc of votes within the DPJ. The question was how unified the groups would be in trying to choose Kan's successor. Because both had failed to act in a uniform manner in the no-confidence vote, Ozawa and Hatoyama's powers of cohesion within their respective groups appeared to have weakened. According to one report, both blocs had been shedding numbers and key members.[119]

In mid-June, Ozawa held a succession of meetings with his followers in an attempt to restore his unifying force.[120] At a June meeting when Ozawa brought together 20 first-term Lower House members at his home in Tokyo, he underlined the importance of group solidarity in choosing the next leader. He made the same argument at an August meeting, saying, 'Let us take a careful appraisal of the candidates...When the time comes, what will be important is unity'.[121] The number Ozawa could muster for the leadership ballot was said to be about 120–140, which still made it the largest bloc of votes in the DPJ. Its size suggested that it might have the casting vote in the leadership election, or at the very least, could offer crucial support for the victor. Indeed, the question of whom Ozawa would support became the most prominent issue in the party in the lead-up to the election. Ozawa himself, of course, could not vote because his membership was suspended and he would, therefore, be entirely absent from the proceedings. Nevertheless, the fact that he was attracting the most attention in the election once again underlined the Ozawa-centred power structure within the party.[122]

Ideally Ozawa wanted to place himself in a better position in the next government than he had been in the Kan administration. His aim was to make some sort of comeback with support from his own and Hatoyama's group by acting together to determine the outcome of the leadership election. He believed that he would be found innocent at his trial and this would form the basis of another bid for power. Close aide, Hirano Sadao, reported in early August that Ozawa had hinted that he was willing to run again for the party's leadership once his criminal trial was over. When Hirano had earlier suggested that he run for the prime ministership to succeed Kan while concurrently battling his court case, Ozawa replied, 'I can't do that. The prime minister is in a position that can interfere with the judiciary...Should I be allowed to do it, it must be done after the trial is over and done with. I can't cede my ground on it. That's my creed, philosophy as a human being'.[123]

By late August, there were five firm nominations for party president: Noda, Maehara, Kaieda, Kano and former MLIT Minister Mabuchi Sumio; several other politicians indicated that they were intending to run, or were exploring the option, or were considered possibilities: Ozawa Sakihito, Tarutoko and Akamatsu. What characterised the race from the start was the number of candidates and would-be prime ministers beating a path to Ozawa's door, thinking that his support was indispensable.[124] Questions about how to deal with Ozawa became the focus of a press conference with the five candidates on 27 August. YP leader

Watanabe Yoshimi offered the scathing comment, 'Talks are all about whether to pay tribute to Ozawa or break away from him. Their struggles have never gotten out of that low level'.[125] Because none of the competing camps could reach the victory line with just their own votes, all coveted the votes of the Ozawa faction and also those of Hatoyama's faction. The fact that all of them were prepared to make contact with Ozawa or his associates, or actively to seek his support, merely drew attention to Ozawa's customary role as kingmaker.[126]

Having been the first to put his name forward in the very early stages in the hunt for a Kan replacement, Finance Minister Noda met with a close associate of Ozawa's in early June, just after Kan announced that he would resign on an unspecified date in the future. Noda also met with Koshiishi at the beginning of August.[127] In a lecture presented on 18 August Noda declared, 'The driving force of the change of the government in 1993 was Mr. Ozawa. He is still in the center of the political world. He is a rare person'.[128] Superficially, Ozawa and Noda did not have much in common when it came to their declared policy positions: Ozawa was opposed to increasing the consumption tax but Noda in his 'Visions for an Administration' published in *Bungei Shunju* on 10 August expressed a strong determination to hike the consumption tax to 10 per cent by the mid-2010s.[129] More immediately, Noda expressed his support for raising taxes for post-quake reconstruction as well as an early decision on the TPP,[130] to which the Ozawa group was also opposed. In earlier days, Noda did not get along particularly well with Ozawa given their previous rivalry for the DPJ leadership in 2008 and the allegations of dubious tactics used by the Ozawa group to pressure Noda into withdrawing his bid.[131] Nevertheless, Noda was said to be 'ready to bury the hatchet with Ozawa'.[132] He even flip-flopped on his policy commitments, saying in a meeting with Hatoyama, 'People say that I'm committed to the idea of raising taxes and forming a grand coalition (with opposition parties). But I'm not'.[133]

Others seeking to secure Ozawa's backing were Kaieda, Ozawa Sakihito, Mabuchi and Kano. METI Minister Kaieda visited Ozawa's office and sought his endorsement directly, although he buttered up key Ozawa allies first. It was widely believed in Kaieda's camp that he could not win the leadership election without Ozawa's support and so he was prepared to advocate a 'pro-Ozawa' attitude,[134] including revising his suspension. When former Environment Minister Ozawa met with Ozawa, he expressed his desire to receive Ozawa's 'instructions'.[135] Mabuchi also met Ozawa twice, making the right noises about opposing the consumption tax and Kan's confrontational attitude towards Ozawa.[136] He was also in favour of issuing bonds for reconstruction purposes, as was Kano who was an early prospect for support from the Ozawa group and who said at a meeting of younger Diet members that 'We should not exclude any colleagues in the party'.[137]

Maehara, who announced his decision to run very late in the piece, was said to have curried favour with Koshiishi earlier in 2011.[138] Maehara said he would be flexible in dealing with issues relating to the manifesto and highlighted the need for party unity – both statements signalling a certain softening of his anti-Ozawa line. He declared a 'unified party' approach when he announced his candidacy, making it clear that he would not disregard Ozawa's supporters. He wanted to avoid a direct confrontation with Ozawa while at the same time not wishing to appear as someone who would cave into Ozawa's demands.[139] Some members of the Ozawa group expressed support for Maehara because he offered the best prospect of reviving the DPJ's fortunes. Even Maehara's closest ally, Sengoku, previously in the forefront of the anti-Ozawa forces and seen as the biggest obstacle to cooperation between Maehara and Ozawa, met secretly with Ozawa and requested his cooperation in unifying the party.[140] Ozawa, however, was not in a conciliatory mood, saying 'I have always wanted to proceed through party unity, but all of you worked to remove me from the picture'.[141] According to Isshinkai chairman, Suzuki Katsumasa, 'Ozawa was prepared to support Maehara provided he did not appoint an anti-Ozawa politician as secretary-general, rather than insisting on the party lifting his suspension'.[142] On another issue close to Ozawa's heart – opposition to any tax increases – Maehara sat on the fence because of the sluggish state of the economy, while calling for more use of private funds.[143]

Complicating any thawing of Maehara's relationship with Ozawa, however, was the fact that his bid for the leadership was said to have been prompted by concern that the intra-party group led by Ozawa would dominate the party. In short, fear of Ozawa's power was the key to his bid.[144] One of Maehara's aides:

> quoted him as saying if an Ozawa-backed candidate wins the DPJ election and the post of the party's secretary general is assumed by someone loyal to Ozawa, Maehara and his group members would be at a serious disadvantage. If this were to happen, the rights of fielding DPJ candidates in Diet elections as well as the party's fund management would be put under control of the Ozawa group.[145]

Maehara also rejected the option of lifting Ozawa's suspension and was the only candidate taking a clearly negative stand on this.

Tax increases, Diet strategy – the possibility of forming a grand coalition with the main opposition parties – and the question of lifting the suspension on Ozawa's DPJ membership became the three big issues in the leadership race. They were all essentially dictated by the Ozawa agenda. Kaieda, Mabuchi and Kano were anti-coalition, while Maehara was keen and Noda was 'open to the idea'.[146] Those closest to Ozawa were firmest on the issue of reinstating Ozawa's DPJ membership – Kaieda, Mabuchi and Ozawa Sakihito. Kaieda took the strongest pro-Ozawa stance. He was so eager for Ozawa's support that he even flip-flopped on the TPP, switching from support to opposition. In fact, on a range of policy matters, Ozawa and Hatoyama began exerting control over Kaieda's policies in advance of the election. He completely capitulated not only in terms of opposing the TPP and not increasing the consumption tax and forming a coalition with the opposition, but also in terms of adopting a cautious stance on decommissioning all nuclear power plants across the nation and implementing a policy of unbridled infrastructure spending. Such a spending spree would be funded by construction and interest-free bonds in lieu of tax increases, which was Ozawa's policy. Kaieda was not entirely happy with all aspects of his Ozawa-directed policy agenda, however, muttering to his aides that his newly adopted policy positions on the TPP and nuclear power plants were 'not my policies'.[147]

In spite of Kaieda accepting the Ozawa script, Ozawa waited until just before the election – Friday 26 August, with the election to be held on Monday 29 – to reveal the name of his preferred candidate – Kaeida. He was reportedly uncertain about whom to back until the last minute. Kaieda was neither Ozawa's first choice nor his best choice. He declared, 'If I can't have the best choice, I will at least have the better one'.[148] He complained that 'I am really tired [of supporting Kaieda]. It would be much easier for me to stand in the election by myself'.[149] It was only in the end, at a loss for a better candidate to back, that Ozawa settled for Kaieda, as a candidate from the Hatoyama group, over Kano and Haraguchi, although he still equivocated, questioning whether Kaieda could attract sufficient votes.[150]

In the best of all possible worlds, Ozawa's goal was to replace Kan with a front man prime minister so he could drive political developments from behind the scenes. If he were influential in the selection of the new leader, he could call in the favour in terms of choosing new ministers and party executives from the Ozawa camp through whom he could exercise clout over the new administration. The selection process for party leader was tailor-made for Ozawa to ride back to power and recover his influence in the party and government, and in particular, to meet his demand for the position of DPJ secretary-general.[151] He had made the appointment of someone close to him to this position a condition of his group's support.[152] Ozawa's support would, therefore, come at the cost of ceding control over the party as well as over policy measures distributing political largesse, which would require Ozawa's stamp of approval under the kind of dictatorial regime that he had imposed during the Hatoyama administration. Any puppet government such as this might pay a high price in terms of loss of public support as well as poor prospects for cooperation with opposition parties.

The contenders who approached Ozawa, however, seemed to be willing to pay the price of sidling up to him for support. While Kan had refused to compromise on his principle of keeping Ozawa firmly at arm's length and fought to maintain a so-called Ozawa-free administration (*Ozawa nuki seiken*), he had also paid a price. He had to contend with endless sabotage by Ozawa and his followers, who acted as Ozawa proxies in both the Diet and the party. If Ozawa lost out again under a new leader, the prospect was that he would continue his strategy of making life difficult, if not impossible, for the incumbent, just as he had done with Kan. This lesson was not lost on the contenders for the leadership.

Noda's unexpected victory

Ozawa took charge of building a majority for Kaieda, saying to the young Diet members that he had personally trained, 'please regard this situation as you would if the person who is standing for election were me'.[153] He encamped in a hotel suite and phoned party members asking for their support.[154] At a meeting of his group, which was also attended by Kaeida, Ozawa said, 'Let's work together in aiming towards Prime Minister Banri Kaieda'.[155] He told his supporters, 'This is our chance to show everyone how strong we are'.[156]

As a result of Ozawa's full-on campaign, the belief that Kaieda was 'Ozawa's puppet' spread in the party and made it more difficult for him to gain support amongst other members.[157] In the eyes of many, Ozawa's backing was a liability rather than an asset. Anyone elected with Ozawa in a kingmaker role would produce a *de facto* Ozawa administration, hence a vote for Kaieda was really a vote for Ozawa's return to power.

Ozawa understood Kaieda's weaknesses as a candidate and reportedly influenced some members of his group to engage in tactical voting in the election. One theory was that he was trying to avoid a run-off between Kaieda and Maehara, whom he suspected would win because of his greater appeal to the wider electorate and to DPJ Diet members for that reason. This strategic calculation led him to throw some support behind Noda in the first round, which rocketed him into second place, and which produced, in Ozawa's mind, a preferred run-off between two more equal candidates – Kaieda and Noda.[158] According to another version of this theory, a secret deal was done between Ozawa and Noda at a meeting prior to the leadership election. Noda reportedly promised to name Koshiishi as secretary-general, and in return, Ozawa promised to direct as many as ten votes his way in the first round, rather than to Kaieda, his preferred candidate.[159]

As for the actual vote, Noda finished second in the first round, with Kaieda winning the most votes (143). Noda then won the runoff by picking up most of the votes of the other three candidates who had left the field – Maehara, Kano and, to a lesser extent, Mabuchi. In fact, between the first and second rounds, Noda jumped from 102 votes to 215 votes – more than double, while Kaieda only won 177 votes. Noda secured what appeared to be a strong anti-Ozawa vote.[160] Once more, the DPJ had turned against the shadow shogun. Kaieda's 'Ozawaism' appeared to cost him victory despite the Ozawa camp's promises of posts such as minister, deputy minister and parliamentary secretary to mid-level Upper House members if they voted for Kaieda. They were the only group to make such promises, which aroused opposition from some DPJ-ers who made comments such as, 'It is like looking at the LDP leadership election in the old days'.[161]

The number of votes won by Kaieda suggested that Ozawa-controlled politics from behind the scenes had come to an end.[162] This was Ozawa's fourth consecutive defeat – when he supported Tarutoko for the DPJ leadership in June 2010; when he himself was defeated for the same job in September 2010; when attempting to overthrow the Kan cabinet in the no-confidence motion in June 2011; and finally Kaieda's election loss – all primarily as a result of the aversion to him within the party.

According to politicians close to Ozawa, solidarity amongst the members of the Ozawa group had weakened, with some members confused over whom to support in the leadership election.[163] Even the first-term Diet members who formed the bulk of the membership appeared to have gained more independence.

Although they still relied to some extent on Ozawa for funds, favours and advice, and eschewed any outright confrontation with their 'master', their votes were not automatically at his disposal.[164] The Ozawa group had already looked unstable over the no-confidence vote and most estimates of the number in his group put it at under 100 and certainly fewer than the 150 reputedly in the Ozawa faction during the Hatoyama administration.

Whatever the number of intra-party votes Ozawa could mobilise, the Ozawa group itself remained the largest single faction within the DPJ. Although it might not have been able to deliver a positive result in the leadership election, it could still potentially wreak destruction on the DPJ by engaging in disruptive acts and destabilising both the party and the administration as it had done under Prime Minister Kan.

With a view to maintaining his power within the party, Ozawa considered integrating the members of his three loosely connected intra-party groups (Isshinkai, Hokushinkai and the Upper House Ozawa group) into one bloc in order to form a united front for the DPJ's presidential election in 2012.[165] Ozawa said, 'I would like the groups to come together and study from scratch on making policy recommendations. I will come to the fore myself'.[166] He seemed to have judged that his group would not be able to maintain unity unless he put himself forward as leader. He wanted to change his group into an organisation with the same degree of unity as the old factions in the LDP in order to confront Noda as the DPJ's new leader with an eye to the next leadership election.[167] Under this scenario, his three former secretaries would be found innocent, he would be acquitted at his own trial around April 2012, and then he would emerge victorious in the September 2012 DPJ leadership contest. He was quoted as saying, 'When the false charge is cleared, and if I have public expectations on my shoulders at the time, I will run for the DPJ presidential election'.[168]

Noda the conciliator

Noda was initially more conciliatory towards Ozawa than Kan, eschewing Kan's policy of sidelining Ozawa, which had proven so divisive. The DPJ was effectively two parties depending on which view of Ozawa its Diet member politicians held. Healing this rift would not be easy because of Ozawa's propensity to cause trouble for governments that he could not control. As a new breed of politician, just like his predecessor, Noda in his outlook and *modus operandi* could not have been more different from Ozawa. If his administration came under Ozawa's influence, it would be called a 'dual control' (*nijū shihai*) set-up just like Hatoyama's, whereas if Noda attempted to become Ozawa-free, the split in the party would deepen.[169] Avoiding both these possibilities made the task of dealing with Ozawa a delicate balancing act.

Ozawa affirmed that he wanted to support Noda, but it depended on what arrangements he made on personnel affairs.[170] Whether a secret deal had been made beforehand or not, Noda ostensibly took Ozawa's interests into consideration and appointed Koshiishi as DPJ secretary-general. This was an act of conciliation directly designed to placate Ozawa, which Noda clearly understood was the price of party unity. Koshiishi was about the only person with whom Ozawa would be satisfied in that role, particularly as it was impossible to appoint Ozawa himself, given the suspension of his party privileges. Noda had earlier said that the secretary-general's position would be the key to determining whether his administration could establish a unified party structure.[171] Noda also calculated that Koshiishi's appointment would be a plus in dealing with the twisted Diet. Koshiishi thus covered the two biggest potential political problems facing Noda's administration. The major downside was that appointing Koshiishi to the position of DPJ secretary-general would allow Ozawa indirectly to influence the distribution of party funds and personnel decisions.[172]

As another olive branch to the Ozawa camp, Noda appointed Hirano Hirofumi (Hatoyama's man) to the position of chairman of the Diet Affairs Committee.[173] Hirano had been vocal in his criticism of Kan's leadership. Noda then balanced out his party appointments by putting Maehara into the position of chairman of the re-established and strengthened DPJ PRC, which Ozawa had abolished. The position of acting PRC chairman was given to Sengoku, with a view, it was said, to the PRC ultimately crushing the Ozawa group.[174]

Meanwhile, Koshiishi became a key player in the appointment of deputy ministers and parliamentary secretaries, fielding requests from Ozawa's group, although not necessarily agreeing with all of them.[175] Noda also allowed Ozawa's men effectively to colonise the secretary-general's office with his appointments to the posts of deputy secretaries-general. He selected one of Ozawa's key lieutenants, Suzuki Katsumasa, as senior deputy secretary-general in charge of Diet affairs and No. 2 in the secretary-general's office. Noda also chose Ozawa's former secretary Hidaka as one of the six deputy secretaries-general. In fact, Hidaka had already served in this post when Ozawa was secretary-general in the Hatoyama administration. Koshiishi delegated to Hidaka the tasks of devising election campaign strategies and allocating party funds and endorsement. Hidaka was also put in charge of distributing government patronage, with the secretary-general's office once more the sole conduit for petitions to the ruling party presented by lobby groups, including prefectural and municipal governments. These were all functions that Ozawa had jealously appropriated to himself and his office when secretary-general of the DPJ in the Hatoyama administration.

To the government side, Noda appointed key Ozawa ally Yamaoka as chairman of the National Public Safety Commission and minister of state for consumer affairs and food safety, and another Ozawa supporter, Ichikawa Yasuo, as minister of defence, both gestures to intra-party harmony. In general, Ozawa expressed great satisfaction with Noda's choice of cabinet members and party executives, calling it 'well-balanced'.[176]

Nevertheless, several important questions faced the Noda administration in dealing with Ozawa. The first was whether Koshiishi would channel party funds, personnel appointments and electoral endorsements in response to Ozawa's orders. The second was the extent to which Ozawa would be permitted to influence the distribution of government largesse given that Koshiishi's office quickly became the target of special interest group requests.[177] The third was how well Koshiishi could undertake management of the party with the two opposing camps of pro- and anti-Ozawa.[178] The fourth was whether Ozawa would be able to influence party policy with Maehara in charge, and whether Maehara's appointment would, in theory, clip Ozawa's wings in this respect. Maehara would likely resist Ozawa's interference in the party's policy affairs.

The final question concerned the suspension of Ozawa's party privileges, which had been a big topic in the election. Koshiishi declared before the election that 'whoever becomes leader has to revise Ozawa's suspension and get him to cooperate, otherwise there is no future for the DPJ'.[179] However, the conviction of Ozawa's three secretaries in September 2011 and Ozawa's own trial, which began in October 2011, put this beyond reach. Both events served to reduce Ozawa's influence further, even before the outcome of his own trial, by making him unacceptable for any high posts, which undermined the loyalty of his followers. One of the key issues for them was Ozawa's lack of direct control over party funding because he held no party executive posts. Moreover, amongst the DPJ members who had voted for Noda, the view was strong that they should not revise Ozawa's punishment. Noda himself was non-committal.

Reverting to form

It did not take long for serious divisions between the Ozawa group and the Noda administration to surface. Difficulties were initially created between Ozawa and Noda by the poor performance of Ozawa affiliates as ministers. Indeed, the two Ozawa allies chosen by Noda for his cabinet – Yamaoka and Ichikawa – were the two worst-performing ministers, with Yamaoka also tinged by allegations of corruption. Like Ozawa, Yamaoka had accepted political donations from multimedia marketing businesses whilst repeatedly justifying pyramid schemes himself and giving support to an alleged pyramid investment scheme. He was, therefore, and as the opposition parties argued, 'not fit to be the minister in charge of protecting consumers from scams'.[180] Hirano Hirofumi, Hatoyama's right-hand man and supporter of Ozawa, was another poor performer in his job as chairman of the DPJ's Diet Affairs Committee.

The departure of Yamaoka and Ichikawa from Noda's cabinet in the mid-January reshuffle, as well as Okada's appointment to the position of deputy prime minister was interpreted as a clear move away from prioritising intra-party harmony, given that Okada had been a central figure in Kan's *datsu Ozawa rosen*. Noda made a pointed reference to Ozawa's possible reaction by saying, 'A politician shouldn't be so narrow-minded as to refuse extending cooperation simply because a certain person assumes a certain post'.[181] Nevertheless, in the interests of balance, Noda did select Ozawa's supporter and chairman of his Upper House group Mokuyōkai, Tanaka Naoki, who had no particular expertise in defence matters, as minister of defence.[182]

More serious than these personnel issues were the policy disputes between Ozawa and the Noda executive. These increasingly became a disguised power struggle just as under the Kan administration. The policies in question were the proposals to negotiate Japan's entry into the TPP and to raise the consumption tax to 10 per cent by 2015. On the TPP, Ozawa condemned the way in which the Noda government was handling the issue, rather than whether or not Japan should join the TPP, given his own professed support for the principle of free trade. This was the same approach that he had adopted under the Kan administration. He criticised the speed and alacrity with which the Noda administration was pursuing the TPP option without first putting safety nets in place. Furthermore, for political reasons, he tacitly encouraged his group to play a key role in the intra-DPJ, anti-TPP lobby, which was spearheading internal party opposition to the Noda administration's trade policy. Despite not participating in the anti-TPP group himself and not signing the JA-sponsored Diet members' petition against the TPP, he advised, 'You can get members from my group to participate in gathering signatures'.[183]

In the end, Ozawa's anti-administration stance came down to opposition to the single dominant issue of the consumption tax increase on which Ozawa and his group picked a very serious fight with the prime minister. Ozawa unleashed a fierce campaign to block Noda's attempt to accomplish what he elevated to his signature policy goal. While framed as a policy dispute it was, however, primarily a political rather than a policy battle. In choosing to wage war with the Noda administration over the consumption tax, Ozawa aimed to topple it on an issue that he calculated would gain him popular support. His 'principled' opposition disguised a more self-serving political strategy.

In early December, Ozawa held an informal meeting with members of Hokushinkai, propounding what was to become one of his main arguments against the consumption tax rise: that because the government's administrative and fiscal reforms had been inadequate, it could not secure the necessary understanding of the people for a hike in the consumption tax. He then began holding policy study meetings of his group twice a week in order to galvanise opposition to the consumption tax rise.

By late December, the intentions of a group of junior DPJ members to bolt from the party became widely known. Almost all the defectors were close to Ozawa, including Isshinkai's Uchiyama Akira who had been a leading light in Ozawa's campaigns against the Kan administration, while some, including Watanabe Kōichirō, had also been participants in the 'gang of 16' who had applied to leave the DPJ's parliamentary group in February 2011.

Ozawa did not necessarily approve of their action because of the implications for numbers in his own group. He repeatedly urged them to stay in the DPJ, saying the timing was not right, but his attempts at persuasion were to no avail. The defections were interpreted as a sign of Ozawa's weakening hold over his faction[184] and growing dissatisfaction amongst its members that he was no longer able to secure a majority of supporters within the party. This meant that even if Ozawa made a bid for the DPJ presidency in the election due in September 2012, he would not emerge victorious.[185] Without his factional numbers, he was like an emperor without his clothes.

In order to try to keep the defectors under his influence, Ozawa consulted with Matsuki and Suzuki Muneo, his former ally in the DPJ, now the leader of New Party Daichi.[186] However, on 28 December, Suzuki registered a new party initially called the New Party Daichi-True Democratic Party (Shintō Daichi-Shinminshutō), which later became the New Party Daichi-True Democrats (Shintō Daichi-Shinminshu) and which absorbed some DPJ defectors.[187] Altogether, 11 DPJ Diet members left the party, with nine of these forming the New Party Kizuna (Shintō Kizuna) on 30 December.[188]

Other members of Ozawa's group were attracted to the idea of joining up with Hashimoto's Osaka Restoration Association (Ōsaka Ishin no Kai). Immediately after Hashimoto's successful election in November 2011, when he switched from Osaka prefectural governor to Osaka City mayor, the first place he visited was Ozawa's office in the Diet where he held open the prospect of possibly aligning with the Ozawa group in Eastern Japan.[189] He reportedly said, ' Mr. Ozawa is amazing. He has a very good understanding of power'.[190] The members of Ozawa's group were entranced at the prospect of linking up with Hashimoto, wanting to leave the DPJ as soon as possible. Ozawa was somewhat disconcerted by their pleas and had to calm them down reasoning, 'Don't be rash. If we are unified we can seize the initiative…The [Osaka] Restoration [Association] doesn't have any seats in the Diet. If we keep together they will come to us'.[191]

It was at that point that Ozawa decided to work seriously on creating a new 'supra-party group' or 'proto-Ozawa party' in lieu of unifying Isshinkai, Hokushinkai and the group of Ozawa-affiliated members in the Upper House into one big faction. The first meeting of the new intra-party group, Shinseiken, on 21 December attracted 106 members. Calling it a 'study group' and retaining the existing framework of Ozawa's three factional groups was undertaken in order to lessen fears in the DPJ that an integrated Ozawa group could spur conflict in the party.[192] Ozawa was named chairman. Initial preparations to launch the group went back to August, when Kaieda lost his bid for the DPJ leadership.[193] Its formation could also be attributed to Ozawa's idea to 'break out' of the loose group mode of the DPJ and unify his various groups into one new policy group, which could make policy recommendations to the Noda government. As a figure close to Ozawa explained, 'If more than 100 people move together as a group, Noda's executives will not be able to ignore them in terms of policies or in Diet deliberations. If it becomes necessary, they can form a "new party". That is how they are trying to stir things up'.[194] This was essentially parroting Ozawa's old line that he had used at the breakup of the NFP: 'There is nothing to worry about if 100 people are united'.[195]

Officially, the Shinseiken was supra-partisan (chōtōha). Its 106 members were made up of 95 Ozawa group members in addition to 11 DPJ defectors who had moved to other minor parties – New Party Kizuna, Shintō Daichi-Shinminshu and Genzei Nippon led by Nagoya Mayor Kawamura. In reality, however, the Shinseiken was the 'party' of the Ozawa faction in the DPJ. It was organised for the purpose of strengthening unity amongst Ozawa's followers and heading off moves by some in his faction to leave the DPJ. It also enabled Ozawa to hedge his bets when facing an uncertain political future, including the possibility of leaving the DPJ himself and taking his supporters in tow under a new party umbrella.

With 100+ members, Shinseiken affiliates were hoping to attract greater numbers to their cause. Many of its executives were key politicians who had made life extremely difficult for former Prime Minister Kan and were now deploying the same tactics against Prime Minister Noda. Its secretary-general was Azuma, one of the five pro-Ozawa DPJ Diet members holding sub-cabinet positions in the Kan administration who had resigned just before the no-confidence motion in June 2011 in order to put more pressure on Kan. The head of its secretariat was Isshinkai leader Suzuki. Another fervent Ozawa supporter, Kawauchi Hiroshi, was one of its two 'observers' and perhaps the most vocal challenger of Noda's consumption tax hike proposal within the Ozawa group. Advisers included Yamaoka and Haraguchi, who aspired to be prime minister with Ozawa's support. The possibility was raised of PNP ex-leader Kamei also throwing in his lot with the group. In addition, Ozawa and Hatoyama agreed to form a strong partnership between Shinseiken and the Hatoyama group in the DPJ. Non-Ozawa group members who attended Shinseiken's inaugural meeting were mainly from the Hatoyama group.

Shinseiken's eight sectional committees on policy themes such as state governance, crisis management and the tax system were an attempt to arm itself with theoretical backing on these policies.[196] It argued strongly for increasing government spending on social welfare and economic stimulus measures, promoting fiscal and administrative decentralisation, and preventing any consumption tax increases. As Ozawa told the group, 'We will be able to find more fund sources (other than a tax hike)'.[197] With its populist slogan ('putting people's lives first') and policy package, the group's members were hoping that it would gain support from the public.

On 3 February, Ozawa and Hatoyama met and agreed to oppose the consumption tax increase being proposed by Noda. Regarding the possibility of his leaving the DPJ, Ozawa asked, 'Which canary has forgotten his song?',[198] implying that it was Noda, not he, who had cast aside the manifesto promises of the DPJ, thus underlining his intention to remain in the DPJ and enact the 2009 manifesto. Although he did not dismiss the need for a consumption tax increase at a later date, he argued that the government needed to cut administrative waste first through administrative and other reforms.[199] He also denounced Noda for over-emphasising a consumption tax hike whilst paying insufficient attention to social security reform.[200] Raising the consumption tax was also a breach of trust because the Noda government had not overhauled Japan's governance system as it had promised in its 2009 election manifesto.[201]

Although Ozawa admitted that he had advocated a 10 per cent consumption tax 20 years previously, he emphasised the need first to change the nation's administrative system through decentralisation. He explained that the government had sufficient funding sources for the time being as long as it carried out real reforms, by using, for example, the more than ¥30 trillion in funds categorised as subsidies, policy expenses and expenses for public works.[202]

Ozawa was motivated by pressing political considerations in pursuing his campaign against the consumption tax increase. First, he wanted to highlight his own prominence in the party at a time when he was fighting his court case and his party membership suspension was still in effect. Fighting on the tax front enabled him 'to exert his presence'.[203]

Second, battling the government over such a prominent policy issue provided a cause around which Ozawa could rally his troops. His unifying force had been diminishing because of his continuing suspension and lack of access to party funds, which reduced his ability to dispense financial patronage. Younger members were publicly expressing their dissatisfaction with the 'reversal of largesse' that now required them to pay membership fees for the group's ordinary meetings, and the fact that Ozawa was no longer readily distributing money to members.[204] The lack of customary privileges that Ozawa faction members had previously enjoyed when Ozawa had his hands on the levers of patronage also undercut their willingness to fall into line with his policy positions and act under his orders. In short, Ozawa's group was in danger of gradual disintegration and he desperately needed something around which to galvanise its members.

Third, Noda's proposed consumption tax rise threw down a direct challenge to Ozawa's 'elections-first' principle. He feared that if an election were called, the DPJ would suffer a crushing defeat. Ozawa was also aware that his own group faced impending annihilation in an election and a consumption tax increase would simply set the seal on their collective demise. In particular, it would sound the death knell for first-term Diet members with their rather feeble electoral support bases, who made up the majority of his followers. This presented Ozawa with the prospect of a massive reduction in the size of his faction and therefore a substantial decline in his influence. He acknowledged, 'If we face an election the group will be stamped out'.[205]

At Shinseiken meetings, Ozawa reiterated many of his arguments against the consumption tax rise, particularly the need for changing the governing structure first, and eliminating waste, all missions on which the DPJ scored very low. He also pronounced on matters pertaining to the bureaucracy, declaring an anti-*amakudari* stance and continuing his battle with the CLB by saying 'People think of the Cabinet Legislation Bureau as the "guardian of the law", but this is not true. Their job is to write laws and texts that comply with the government's intention, and I think that as a result they have produced various things that are legally and ideologically wrong. It is the legislative body's job to correct these'.[206]

Because Ozawa greatly feared the prospect of a general election being held on the issue of a consumption tax rise, he continued to position himself and his followers to best advantage in facing such an election. This included the option of realigning political forces prior to the actual poll. He kept his door wide open for overtures from Hashimoto, regarding him as potentially offering the possibility of a political alliance that would offer an alternative and more positive political future than staying in the DPJ. However, while Ozawa desperately wanted Hashimoto because he would be of great political use, from Hashimoto's point of view, Ozawa was fine to associate with but scary to join forces with fully.[207]

Ozawa's immediate objective was to cause a commotion in the party, using the prospect of a new Ozawa party as a threat, then regain the initiative after being found not guilty in his court case at the end of April. The reality was that he faced the crumbling foundations of his power. He had only two cards: threatening to defect from the DPJ with his group and sponsoring a no-confidence motion. However, both risked a Lower House election the outcome of which many in his group considered 'unbearable'.[208] Ozawa understood this. It was in his interests to unseat the Noda cabinet but not the DPJ government, just as with the Kan administration. He did not deny the possibility of running in the next DPJ leadership election, saying, 'I am willing to fulfil any role if it is heaven's will. I want to offer my last service'.[209] However, in order to maximise his chances in the election, he had to prevent the vote on the consumption tax hike bill from taking place.[210]

Noda went ahead and submitted his consumption tax proposal to prior examination (*jizen shinsa*) by the DPJ in an attempt to reach a consensus amongst party members in favour of his plan, but the intra-party debate just provided a platform for Ozawa's supporters to use ever-more extreme tactics to try to block the proposal. They were both verbally and physically confrontational in party debates on the issue. Ozawa also made a point of meeting with his group almost daily in order to maintain their solidarity. He outlined a plan for group members holding party posts and executive positions in the government to resign, the same tactic that he had used against Kan.

In the end, Noda's patience ran out. Initially conciliatory towards Ozawa, he reached the point when he had had enough. Ozawa and his allies were proving the biggest obstacle to his efforts to achieve the consumption tax increase. According to one report, Noda really disliked Ozawa, with one associate saying that merely using a word beginning with the letter 'o' was 'enough to put the prime minister in a bad mood'.[211] Noda began to consider the possibility of completely cutting ties with Ozawa as the price of a successful enactment of the consumption tax legislation. He held secret talks with LDP leader Tanigaki to counter Ozawa's moves.[212] This marked the beginning of another round of psychological warfare – this time involving Ozawa, Noda and Tanigaki, with Noda playing the dissolution card to try to keep Ozawa and his supporters in check while he searched for ways to cooperate with Tanigaki.[213]

Ozawa's acquittal in his trial on 26 April reinvigorated his campaign against Noda. This was the moment when the Shinseiken launched their all-out campaign to overthrow the cabinet.[214] The LDP was secretly placing their hopes on Ozawa intensifying strife within the DPJ over the consumption tax hike, thus opening up a path to a Lower House dissolution and a general election, which it wanted.[215] Former Prime Minister Asō Tarō made a critical comment at a meeting of his faction, saying, 'The [structure where] people behind the scenes have more influence than the executives on stage is exactly the same as the old politics that the DPJ has been criticising'.[216] Leader of the Sunrise Party of Japan (Tachiagare Nippon) said, 'Ozawa has been exercising influence for the past few decades not only on his party but also over Japanese politics as a whole, but those days are over'.[217]

The immediate issue concerning Ozawa was the reinstatement of his membership from where he could aim to return to the position of either secretary-general or president. Koshiishi began moves to lift Ozawa's suspension in the party executives' meeting on 7 May and in the Standing Officers Council on 8 May, which lifted the suspension. The timing was significant, given that the deadline for the appeal of the Ozawa verdict was 10 May. Koshiishi was determined to have Ozawa firmly back in the fold prior to this decision, particularly if it went against him.

On 9 May, the designated lawyers made their decision to appeal and not surprisingly some in the party complained that the decision to lift Ozawa's suspension had been taken too early. Nevertheless, the decision by the party executive had been taken and they were not intending to revisit it. At the same time, the appeal immediately placed constraints on Ozawa's political activities, reducing his prospects for running in the September leadership election. Ozawa's plan for a comeback was dashed, which left him with few options.[218] Some commentators wrote him off, while others thought this might be premature.[219] A surprising number of Ozawa followers (96) attended a Shinseiken meeting the day after the appeal. Some, however, complained that they were pressured to attend.

Those close to Ozawa reported that he was not that discouraged[220] because it was unlikely that an innocent verdict would be overturned.[221] He was determined not to alter his political course no matter how his court case concluded, which was why the appeal did not shake up the core members of the Ozawa group as much as expected. Their plan of action had already been decided.[222] Both Ozawa and his group were prepared to accept second best to Ozawa himself, making another bid for the DPJ leadership, namely, replacing Noda with someone who, at the very least, would allow Ozawa to exert influence over the allocation of important positions and party funds. According to an Ozawa follower, the group's priority was to recruit someone who 'could become the face of the election, someone who does not see Ozawa as an enemy and someone we can trust'.[223] The name Hosono Gōshi surfaced in this context. He was regarded as potentially an outstanding young prime minister with useful experience as a cabinet member. The fact that he was even younger than Osaka City Mayor Hashimoto Tōru would be his selling point. Hashimoto had distanced himself from Ozawa after the designated lawyers appealed the verdict in May. Ozawa attended a party hosted by Governor of Aichi prefecture, Ōmura Hideaki, on 14 May, saying, 'Let us work together and tackle the great reforms', but Hashimoto did not attend the party in person and only sent a congratulatory telegram.[224] Ozawa was also somewhat resentful that Hashimoto had appropriated the idea of changing the governing structure of the country, making it his selling point.[225] At a press conference on 18 May, Governor of Tokyo Ishihara Shintarō expressed his intention to invite Hashimoto as a lecturer to his new *seiji juku*, but in regard to Ōmura said, 'If he's going to associate with Ozawa, I have no intention of working with such a person'.[226] Ishihara was known truly to dislike Ozawa, telling those close to him that he had an instinctive dislike of him. On a TV programme he commented, 'It's ridiculous that Mr. Ozawa has influence over the party'.[227]

The ambitions of the Ozawa faction continued to be shaped by the fact that 'the power of numbers' was still working in its favour insofar as it remained the largest group in the DPJ. However, as before, the Ozawa group did not have the numbers to ensure victory for their nominated candidate, although they could certainly contribute either to the victory or defeat of other candidates if they acted as a coherent, united force. As Gotō commented,

> I think there are a lot of Diet members who associate Ozawa with a dirty image and think 'Even if I can work with him in regard to the consumption tax, I cannot work with him in larger frameworks like the leadership election'. The number of Ozawa-children has already dropped significantly…A sentiment close to hatred amongst those of kin has developed between pro-Ozawa and anti-Ozawa party members. Ozawa always says 'I am the DPJ' and provokes those around him, but people around him think, 'Why is he the original when he joined later?'[228]

Ozawa's travails were compounded by an unfortunate personal scandal in which a mid-June issue of the weekly magazine *Shūkan Bunshun* reprinted an 11-page letter reportedly from Ozawa's ex-wife, who denounced him for deserting his followers in Iwate after the March 2011 disaster. According to the letter, in the wake of the tsunami and nuclear meltdown, Ozawa abandoned his followers in his home constituency, who had been hit hard, and went to western Japan. He had 'run away' with his secretaries out of fear of spreading radiation contamination from the damaged Fukushima nuclear plant. Given Ozawa's own criticisms of Kan's handling of the disaster, his actions, if his wife's allegations were to be believed, represented the height of hypocrisy.

Nevertheless, the possibility remained that Ozawa could still undermine his own party and the Noda administration should he, once again, pressure his followers to vote against the government in the Diet on the consumption tax hike bills, or should he choose the 'destruction' (or realignment) option by leaving the party and taking a large group of followers with him. It was perhaps for this and other reasons, such as flattering Ozawa's vanity as a prominent personage in the party, that Noda in the full glare of media publicity decided to hold two meetings with Ozawa to ask for his cooperation in passing the consumption tax bills.[229] Ozawa refused to change his position, however, so Noda moved directly to approaching the LDP instead, outflanking any move that Ozawa might make. Tanigaki said, 'I'd like to see whether Noda will part ways with Ozawa even if this means splitting the party. The fundamental cause of the politics of indecision is that there are two heads – Ozawa and Noda – and the party doesn't know which way to go'.[230] Around mid-June it was revealed that Noda and Tanigaki held two telephone conferences. A grand coalition between the DPJ and LDP was reputedly agreed in secret between Noda and Tanigaki as part of their final agreement on submitting the bills to raise the consumption tax. Such a move would resolve the twisted Diet and also neutralise Ozawa's continuing influence in the DPJ, if indeed he still remained within it. Such a grand coalition would also cut off any threatening third parties such as Hashimoto's Osaka Restoration Association.

Ozawa later condemned the decision to form a three-party agreement (with the New Kōmeitō) to increase the consumption tax as 'collusion' (*dangō*).[231] It precipitated his move to leave the DPJ. He calculated that if the consumption tax bills were passed, the election could at least be fought along the lines of pro- and anti-increase parties. He told one of his close allies, 'We will be able to fight in the next election on a platform of opposition to the consumption tax hike and breaking away from nuclear power. We will win the election'.[232]

On 20 June, Ozawa assembled members of his group and issued orders for preparations to be made for forming a new party. The following day at a meeting of his Lower House group, he asked members to vote against the consumption tax legislation, describing it as 'a blasphemy and betrayal of the people'.[233] After the meeting, Ozawa met with each member individually in a separate room and said, 'I want you to act with me',[234] asking them to sign a letter of resignation from the party. Ozawa kept hold of these resignations for future use.[235] About 50 members reputedly signed the letters, which had been prepared by senior members of the group. Ozawa repeatedly used the words 'final battle' to his close aides.[236] He delivered an ultimatum via Koshiishi: if the DPJ could not keep its promise to the people (and not raise the consumption tax), he and his group would leave the party.[237] The response from one of Noda's close allies was defiant: 'Even if they leave, we don't care.'[238]

Given that the political tide had so profoundly turned against Ozawa in the party, with the majority of DPJ Diet members supporting the Noda tax hike, Ozawa realised that his campaign against it and Noda had failed. Moreover, with Noda successfully lining up political allies in the opposition LDP and New Kōmeitō, Ozawa knew he had to make good his threats and jump ship or reveal his lack of power and loss of prospects in the party. Noda's coup in gaining the support of the LDP and New Kōmeitō for the tax hike had taken Ozawa by surprise. He had calculated that the DPJ moderates would never stand for Noda ditching the DPJ's key campaign pledge to offer a minimum guaranteed monthly pension as the price of opposition support for his consumption tax legislation.[239]

Nevertheless, Ozawa figured that three key elements were working in his favour. First, as in 1993 when he took a group of followers out of the LDP, he had found an issue around which he could unify his group and on which he could organise a new party as well as galvanise the electorate. It would enable him to mount a populist campaign based on the DPJ's original manifesto and its pledge to protect the lives of the people.

Second, Ozawa believed that he had newfound leverage in the Diet. This was not to threaten the government's two-thirds majority as his group had tried to do in early 2011 over the Kan administration's budget-related bills, but to undermine the DPJ's majority in the Lower House. Because of defections and departures over the intervening months, it would need only 53 DPJ defectors to accomplish such a manoeuvre.[240]

Third, Ozawa calculated that given the strong likelihood that the DPJ would lose the next election anyway, he was better off leading a new party in opposition rather than remaining in the DPJ, where he faced the antipathy of many of its members (and certainly most of its executives). Breaking away from the DPJ at least offered the chance of being able to engineer the political situation to his advantage in whatever new political landscape emerged in the aftermath of the DPJ's electoral defeat.

In the interim, Ozawa and his group unleashed a full-scale offensive both inside and outside the DPJ against the consumption tax increase. Even though Ozawa's party membership had been reinstated, he did not attend official party meetings to discuss the consumption tax but scripted his group's opposition tactics from behind the scenes. Members of his group were the loudest and most vociferous at party meetings on the tax. Ozawa also competed with the Noda executive for the allegiance of party members, particularly those taking an uncommitted, neutral position on raising the consumption tax. He was aiming to lure a minimum of 53 defectors, claiming that at least 60 would vote against the legislation, while the prime minister and other DPJ leaders were making frantic efforts to dissuade those loyal to Ozawa from leaving. This was a high-stakes game entailing big political risks for Ozawa. Although political realignment on the basis of a pro-tax hike vs. anti-tax hike stance was theoretically possible, for personal, political and policy-related reasons, it was highly unlikely that a substantial number from any other party or political group would be prepared to join forces with an Ozawa-led breakaway faction. No progress had been made on cooperating with Hashimoto in Osaka, for example.

Moreover, Ozawa's disruptive activities within the ruling party were generally poorly received by voters, many of whom, whilst objecting to the consumption tax rise, were also opposed to the political drama that Ozawa had unleashed within the DPJ in order to block Noda's policy agenda. The media and other commentators found Ozawa's anti-tax arguments unconvincing as well as criticising him for consistently arguing for the principle of strong political leadership whilst being responsible for creating a structure where he had become the root cause of the 'politics of indecision'.[241] The polls revealed a public that had grown weary of Ozawa's disproportionate influence in politics, with only 26 per cent wanting him to continue to wield this influence, which was less than half wanting the opposite (64 per cent).[242] They were also sceptical about Ozawa's motives, thinking that while Ozawa was openly pursuing an anti-consumption tax cause, what he was really wanting to do was grab back political power. As one veteran DPJ politician (probably Watanabe Kōzō) remarked, 'For Ozawa, policies and principles are nothing more than tools for coming to power'.[243]

Conclusion

Ozawa spent the entire period of the Kan administration in retaliatory mode because he found Kan's *datsu* Ozawa stance intolerable. He hated being excluded from the centre of power and so he waged war against the leadership of his own party. Ozawa's 'divide and destroy' strategy was directly responsible for the internecine political bickering that plagued the Kan administration. It ensured that despite being 'on the outer' in the party and government, politics still revolved around Ozawa. At best he hobbled the administration's policy and legislative programme; at worst – at a time of national emergency – he exhibited a level of self-absorption that deserved a high degree of censure. His actions against the Kan administration were those of a spoiler who thought only of his political self-interest. He demonstrated little inclination to cooperate with the party leadership on any issue, refusing to recognise their authority, thus considering himself above the obligations of other DPJ backbenchers. He was certainly far from the self-styled 'foot soldier' that he claimed to be. On the contrary, his behaviour revealed an overweening sense of entitlement to power. Clearly he did not care about the party unless he was leading it. Despite his repeated claims that he did not intend to leave the DPJ, and his assertion when running for the DPJ leadership in April 2006 that 'I decided that this would be my last party and that I would bury my bones in this party',[244] he had no compunction about doing his absolute best to shred it when it would not bend to his will. He was a polarising figure who contributed mightily to the state of disarray in the government, to the dysfunctionality in Japanese politics generally and to the destabilisation of successive DPJ administrations. In all these respects, Ozawa was merely reverting to form. He was directly behind the perennial power struggles that had characterised every regime in which he had ever been a part – no matter what party hat he wore. In the Kan and Noda administrations, it became a battle for supremacy in which there turned out to be no winners.

As for Ozawa's much-proclaimed goal of establishing a two-party system, in undermining successive DPJ administrations, he managed to destroy the best prospect in decades for a major alternative ruling party to emerge and consolidate its position vis-à-vis the LDP. Although the DPJ proved too big for Ozawa personally to break up, his constant cat-and-mouse games with the party leadership and his sabotage of key elements of its legislative programmes had the effect of reversing what progress there had been towards the establishment of a two-party system. His extreme anti-mainstream factional behaviour was a tactic to bring down the government of the day and an extraordinary reversal for a politician who was so apparently convinced of the virtues of a strong two-party system. It suggested that Ozawa was a malign and unpredictable force who would resort to Machiavellian plotting and scheming in order to engineer a political outcome favourable to his interests – even at the price of undermining progress towards his own stated structural reform goal.

Ozawa's behaviour was a powerful example to his followers of an almost total disregard for party interests and for party unity, despite appeals to the concept of 'whole party unity' – which amounted to little more than Ozawa's term for allowing him back into a position of power. His own actions and those that he encouraged in his followers served to devalue party affiliation and encourage the formation of breakaway groups within the ruling party. The Ozawa group accused Kan, Noda and other DPJ executives of being the source of disunity, confusion and chaos in the party, when in fact, it was they who were the primary cause and catalyst of the perennial chaos and confusion, acting if not at Ozawa's behest, then certainly with his encouragement, tacit or otherwise. He manipulated his faction from behind the scenes, behaving like a master controller, continually scripting members' words and actions, mobilising them through constant meetings where they were indoctrinated into the Ozawa line and generally orchestrating sabotage of the ruling party from the inside.

For much of the Kan and Noda administrations, Ozawa was a rogue politician leading an intra-party revolt. He engineered several high-stakes games including a vote of no confidence, as well as threats and actions to withhold individual votes on government legislation, and to withdraw his group from the DPJ altogether, thus splitting the party. In these respects, his conduct represented quintessential old politics where political loyalties were primarily personal and faction-based rather than party-based, where the need for unity on policy set by the cabinet was not accepted and where there was endless jockeying for personal political advantage, potentially at the party's expense. In this model, personal and factional loyalty trumped party loyalty, party discipline counted for little and policy commonalities were almost irrelevant, except as an instrument of political opportunism.

Although effectively ousted from power, Ozawa remained the fulcrum around which Japanese politics continued to revolve, given his capacity for disputation and fracture. The personal loyalties of his group's members were counterbalanced by his sullied reputation amongst many of those who encountered him in the political world. Ozawa thus continued to evoke either great devotion or tremendous antipathy. He was an enormously divisive figure who was either loved or loathed, hero or villain, hence the split in the DPJ between pro- and anti-Ozawa forces, making it even more difficult for the ruling party and government to operate as a unified whole. On too many occasions, the DPJ was riven with infighting between the Ozawa-led cohort and the rest, which seriously undermined its capacity to govern.

Because the pursuit of supreme power was Ozawa's *raison d'être*, political realignment remained permanently on his agenda if he calculated that such a course of action would be to his advantage. In the meantime, he slowly built up a record of failure in his attempts to take back power. Having already lost followers because of his mandatory indictment, Ozawa's trial also set him apart from the rest of the political world. Some supporters asked, 'is such a person a suitable leader for the party?' His refusal to give clear explanations – to the Diet and at press conferences – and his changing accounts of crucial details of where he sourced his funds, all led to the conclusion, whether endorsed by the outcome of the trial or not, that he was guilty of violating the PFCL. Certainly, this was the verdict in the court of public opinion, which had negative implications for the electoral viability of any Ozawa-led party. While the trial dragged on, it served to threaten Ozawa's political standing and further underlined his pariah status as someone whom not only the media but also his own party leadership were asking to 'remove himself from the political scene'.[245]

Moreover, the longer Ozawa's party suspension lasted and he was unable to hold executive office and tap into party funds, the more his influence over his own group diminished because of his shrinking patronage. Ozawa's prospects for a successful run at the DPJ leadership in September 2012 also depended on the outcome of his trial. When declared innocent, the question remained whether he would be successful in obtaining the backing not only of DPJ Diet members but also of the wider party membership and supporters as well as local assemblymen who would vote in the DPJ leadership election. After all, he had lost out in the same race in September 2010 and it was difficult to think that his popularity had increased compared with two years previously. This ambition was finally closed off when the designated lawyers acting as prosecutors decided to appeal the verdict at his trial.

Ozawa's weakened position was also reflected in the noticeably diminished position of his group in the DPJ. Under the Noda administration, members were initially not quite so eager to engage in destructive acts and push their weight around, having gained concessions from Noda over key appointments to party executive posts. However, by December 2011, the relationship between Ozawa and Noda began to sour. Ozawa and his group campaigned in an increasingly open and hostile fashion against the two signature policies of the Noda administration: the TPP and the consumption tax rise. For Ozawa, this was more about policy opportunism than policy principle, given his previous support for both a consumption tax rise and free trade. His habitual resort to the populist language of 'acting on behalf of the people' from whom he took his authority to act became a tired refrain that lacked credibility.

It could be argued that a rupture between Ozawa and the DPJ might, in the end, be a positive development for the DPJ, given his destructive potential in situations where he could not control the levers of power. There was clearly only a very troubled future for the DPJ with him in it. Even in a position where he could not lead given his money-politics travails, he did not want anyone else to take over if it meant that he, Ozawa, was stripped of power within the party, and so the DPJ habitually became a two-headed monster.

Notes

1 Harada, 'Sukōpu: Kyotō ashibumi', p. 2. See also below.
2 'Kan shin taisei', in *Nihon Keizai Shinbun*, p. 3.
3 'Sukōpu: Ozawa rosen no shūsei kasoku', in *Tōkyō Shinbun*, p. 2.
4 Yamazaki, 'Kan Shinshushō', diamond.jp/articles/-/8377.
5 'Ozawa Moves', www.asahi.com/english/TKY201108130261.html.
6 Ito and Fukue, 'Picks Mirror more Pragmatic Tack', www.japantimes.co.jp/news/2012/01/14/national/picks-mirror-more-pragmatic-tack-bid-to-exert-leadership/#.UYn_ueDtIqY.
7 Watanabe, *Ozawa Ichirō Kirawareru Densetsu*, p. 42.
8 'Minshu daihyōsen', in *Tōkyō Shinbun*, p. 1.
9 Kamikubo, 'Seijika no "kessa"', diamond.jp/articles/-/9298.
10 'Ozawa-shi ga Minshutōdaihyōsen ni shutsuba hyōmei', www.asahi.com/politics/update/0826/TKY201008260089.html?ref=reca.

11 Kamikubo, 'Kan naikaku', diamond.jp/articles/-/13585.
12 Uesugi, '"Densho bato"', diamond.jp/articles/-/9254.
13 'Twists and Turns', *Daily Yomiuri*, www.yomiuri.co.jp/dy/national/T100901006367.htm.
14 'Editorial: After Messy Start, DPJ Race Must Come Down to Policy', e.nikkei.com/e/ac/tnks/Nni20100831D3ZJFF05.htm.
15 *NHK News 7*, 1 September 2010.
16 Ibid.
17 Ibid.
18 Ibid.
19 Ibid.
20 Ito, 'Ozawa to Challenge Kan', www.japantimes.co.jp/cgi-bin/nn20100827a1.html.
21 Takahara, 'Rookies Hold Crucial DPJ Votes', search.japantimes.co.jp/cgi-bin/nn20100910f1.html.
22 Ibid.
23 Uesugi, '"Densho bato"', diamond.jp/articles/-/9254.
24 'Kan Wins', e.nikkei.com/e/ac/TNKS/Nni20100914D14NY736.htm.
25 Gotō, '"Ozawa fūji"', diamond.jp/articles/-/9433.
26 'Playing Ends Off the Middle', www.japantimes.co.jp/cgi-bin/eo20100419a1.html.
27 'In Shifting Away from Ozawa, Kan Invites DPJ Discord', e.nikkei.com/e/ac/tnks/Nni20100917D16JFA14.htm.
28 Martin and Ito, 'Kan Cruises to Victory', www.japantimes.co.jp/cgi-bin/nn20100915a1.html.
29 Kishi, '"Kan Ozawa"', diamond.jp/articles/-/9267.
30 'TPP: Sanka wareru Minshu', mainichi.jp/select/biz/news/20101027ddm001020007000c.html.
31 'Ozawa Sworn Testimony Sought', www.yomiuri.co.jp/dy/national/T101222004894.htm.
32 'Ozawa to File Suit', e.nikkei.com/e/ac/tnks/Nni20101014D14JF923.htm.
33 'Ozawa-shi, Shikkōbu ni fuman', in *Yomiuri Shinbun*, p. 4.
34 See also below.
35 'Kan seiken', mainichi.jp/select/seiji/news/20101226k0000e010017000c.html.
36 'Nagata-chō gekishin sukūpu', gendai.ismedia.jp/articles/-/1760.
37 *NHK News 7*, 28 December 2010.
38 Ito and Takahara, 'Ozawa Agrees to Give Unsworn Testimony', www.japantimes.cojp/cgi-bin/nn20101229a1.html.
39 Yamazaki, 'Kan shushō', diamond.jp/articles/-/10983.
40 '(Jijikokkoku) Tenbō naki Ozawa giri', in *Asahi Shinbun*, p. 2.
41 Akasaka, 'Sengoku ga nagashita namida', gekkan.bunshun.jp/articles/-/230.
42 'Kan Shushō: "Ozawa shi-shintai, mizukara handan o"', mainichi.jp/select/seiji/news/20110104k0000e010036000c.html.
43 'Ozawa kiri sengen', *Asahi Shinbun*, p. 1.
44 'Ozawa and the Diet', www.houseofjapan.com/local/ozawa-and-the-diet.
45 Takahara and Fukue, 'Opposition Issues Ozawa Terms', www.japantimes.co.jp/text/nn20110128a8.html.
46 'Kan seiken', mainichi.jp/select/seiji/news/20101226k0000e010017000c.html.
47 Tahara, 'Ozawa ha no "tōnai yatō"', www.nikkeibp.co.jp/article/column/20101214/254639/?rt=nocnt.
48 *NHK News 7*, 12 January 2011.
49 Ibid.
50 '(Jijikokkoku) Tenbō naki Ozawa giri', *Asahi Shinbun*, p. 2.
51 *NHK News 7*, 31 January 2011.
52 *NHK News 7*, 10 February 2011.
53 Yamazaki, 'Kan Shinshushōno keizai seisaku', diamond.jp/articles/-/8377.

54 '(Jijikokkoku) Tenbō naki Ozawa giri', *Asahi Shinbun*, p. 2.
55 Ibid.
56 Akasaka, '"Ozawa kiri"', gekkan.bunshun.jp/articles/-/229.
57 Akasaka, 'Sengoku ga nagashita namida', gekkan.bunshun.jp/articles/-/230.
58 '(Gekitotsu 2011) Kyō kinkyū yakuinkai', *Sankei Shinbun*, p. 5.
59 'Sukōpu: Ozawa-shi shobun', in *Tōkyō Shinbun*, p. 2.
60 *NHK News 7*, 15 February 2011.
61 The ethics committee was the party organ that advises the council.
62 'Minshu bunretsu bukumi', in *Yomiuri Shinbun*, p. 1.
63 Toshikawa, 'Kan Gone by June', p. 3.
64 'Ozawa-kei no ichibu', in *Yomiuri Shinbun*, p. 1.
65 'Minshu bunretsu bukumi', in *Yomiuri Shinbun*, p. 1.
66 Koh, 'Ozawa's "Children"', blogs.wsj.com/japanrealtime/2011/02/17/ozawas-children-semi-revolt-trouble-for-kan/.
67 *NHK News 7*, 21 February 2011.
68 'Kan Hangs By a Thread', www.houseofjapan.com/local/kan-hangs-by-a-thread.
69 'Kaiha ridatsu todoke', in *Asahi Shinbun*, p. 4.
70 'Ozawa Rebels Put Kan in Pinch', e.nikkei.com/e/ac/TNKS/Nni20110217D17JFF02.htm.
71 Toshikawa, 'Kan Gone by June', p. 3.
72 *NHK News 7*, 18 February 2011.
73 Ibid.
74 'Ozawa-shi ga yotte kuru ninki no chiiki seitō', *Asahi Shinbun*, p. 4.
75 Ibid.
76 'Ozawa Rebels put Kan in Pinch', e.nikkei.com/e/ac/TNKS/Nni20110217D17JFF02.htm.
77 Sekiguchi, 'Sukōpu: Ikioizuku han-shikkōbugawa', p. 2.
78 'Punish Ozawa at your Peril', www.japantimes.co.jp/cgi-bin/nn20110218a1.html.
79 'Ozawa Minshu moto daihyō: Shobun kettei', in *Mainichi Shinbun*, p. 2.
80 *NHK News 7*, 15 February 2011.
81 Takahara and Fukue, 'DPJ Suspends Ozawa', www.japantimes.co.jp/cgi-bin/nn20110223a1.html.
82 Ibid.
83 Ozawa's suspension was to last 15 months.
84 'Minshu Ozawa-kei no Matsuki seimukan ga jii hyōmei', in *Asahi Shinbun*, p. 1.
85 Sekiguchi, 'Sukōpu: Ikioizuku han-shikkōbugawa', p. 2.
86 'Kan Hangs By a Thread', www.houseofjapan.com/local/kan-hangs-by-a-thread.
87 '16 nin honkaigi kesseki "hitotsu no kangaekata"', in *Mainichi Shinbun*, p. 5.
88 Kuramae, 'Tōkaku jiki saguru Ozawa-shi', p. 4.
89 'Ozawa Seeks Support', www.asahi.com/english/TKY201103110181.html.
90 Ibid.
91 Sekiguchi, 'Sukōpu: Minshu giren hossoku rasshu', p. 2.
92 Ibid.
93 It also took a month for Ozawa to post words of sympathy for disaster victims on his own personal website. His few short paragraphs offered no constructive suggestions as to how to deal with the crisis. It took him another eight months to visit some of the worst-affected areas in his own prefecture. See also below.
94 '"Kan nuki renritsu"', gekkan.bunshun.jp/articles/-/241.
95 Ibid.
96 Hayashi and Sekiguchi, 'WSJ: Ozawa Challenges Kan', e.nikkei.com/e/ac/tnks/Nni20110527D27JF067.htm.
97 Ibid.
98 'Ozawa Prepares', www.asahi.com/english/TKY201104140127.html.
99 Toshikawa, 'Etsunen', www.insideline.co.jp/column/column.html.

100 Ibid.
101 Ibid. See also Chapter 7.
102 Kamikubo, 'Kan naikaku', diamond.jp/articles/-/13585.
103 Katz, 'Don't "Let the Games Begin"', p. 1.
104 Hayashi and Sekiguchi, 'WSJ: Ozawa Challenges Kan', e.nikkei.com/e/ac/tnks/Nni20110527D27JF067.htm.
105 Nonoyama, '"Dairenritsu"', www.fsight.jp/article/10556.
106 'Noda seiken', in *Sankei Shinbun*, p. 1.
107 'DPJ Rift Widens', e.nikkei.com/e/ac/tnks/Nni20110531D30JFA10.htm.
108 'Vote-grabbing', e.nikkei.com/e/ac/tnks/Nni20110602D01JFA11.htm.
109 'Kan Survives No-confidence Vote', www.yomiuri.co.jp/dy/national/T110602005835.htm.
110 Miyazaki, 'Kore o "chabangeki" to yobazu shite nan to yobu ka?', diamond.jp/articles/-/12550.
111 Hara, 'Kono kuni', diamond.jp/articles/-/12568.
112 Uesugi, 'Fushinninan hiketsu!', diamond.jp/articles/-/12553.
113 'Kan naikaku', diamond.jp/articles/-/13585.
114 'Kono kuni', diamond.jp/articles/-/12568.
115 In the four no-confidence motions that had passed under Japan's post-war constitution, the prime minister in all cases dissolved the Lower House and called an election instead of resigning.
116 'Timing of Kan's Exit', e.nikkei.com/e/tnks/Nni20110602D02JFA17.htm.
117 Quoted in Takahara, 'Even Tougher Year May Lie Ahead', www.japantimes.co.jp/cgi-bin/nn20110101f2.html.
118 'Point of View', ajw.asahi.com/article/0311disaster/fukushima/AJ201108045264.
119 'Minshutō: Kobato "ridatsu"', mainichi.jp/select/seiji/news/20110615ddm005010150000c.html.
120 'Kyūshinryoku kaifuku?', www.yomiuri.co.jp/feature/20100806-849918/news/20110614-OYT1T00937.htm.
121 'Ozawa Moves to Regain Influence', www.asahi.com/english/TKY201108130261.html.
122 Akasaka, 'Ozawa Ichirō mata mo ya yaburetari', gekkan.bunshun.jp/articles/-/249.
123 'Ozawa Signals Veiled Willingness', www.thefreelibrary.com/Ozawa+signals+veiled+willingness+to+vie+for+leadership+after+trial.-a0263726562.
124 'Ozawa Moves to Regain Influence', www.asahi.com/english/TKY201108130261.html.
125 Minami, 'Policy Debate', www.asahi.com/english/TKY201108270283.html.
126 Akasaka, 'Ozawa Ichirō mata mo ya yaburetari', gekkan.bunshun.jp/articles/-/249.
127 Katz, 'Barons Anoint Noda', p. 3.
128 'Ozawa Remains Kingmaker', www.asahi.com/english/TKY201108220263.html.
129 'Post-Kan DPJ', www.yomiuri.co.jp/dy/national/T110810005847htm.
130 'Maehara Against Reconstruction Tax Hike', e.nikkei.com/e/ac/TNKS/Nni20110814D14JF786.htm?NS-query=DPJ%20leadership%20election.
131 Nonoyama, '"Kessen mokuzen"', www.fsight.jp/article/4487.
132 Myoraku, 'Noda, with Eye on Future', ajw.asahi.com/article/behind_news/AJ201108257650.
133 'Who's Who of DPJ Leaders', www.asahi.com/english/TKY201108200153.html.
134 'Kaku kōho', www.yomiuri.co.jp/feature/20100806-849918/news/20110828-OYT1T00342.htm.
135 'Who's Who of DPJ Leaders', www.asahi.com/english/TKY201108200153.html.
136 'Ozawa Moves to Regain Influence', www.asahi.com/english/TKY201108130261.html.
137 Ibid.
138 'Tsugi no sōri Maehara', gendai.ismedia.jp/articles/-/2109.

139 'Maehara's Tightrope Strategy', ajw.asahi.com/article//behind_news/AJ201108257452.
140 Tanaka, 'Maehara-shi no daihyōsen shutsuba', diamond.jp/articles/-/13707.
141 'Maehara's Tightrope Strategy', ajw.asahi.com/article//behind_news/AJ201108257452.
142 Akasaka, 'Ozawa Ichirō mata mo ya yaburetari', gekkan.bunshun.jp/articles/-/249.
143 'Candidates' Positions', e.nikkei.com/e/ac/tnks/Nni20110827D27JF053.htm.
144 Azuma and Ito, 'Fear of Ozawa's Power', www.yomiuri.co.jp/dy/national/T110823006082.htm.
145 Ibid.
146 'Candidates' Positions', e.nikkei.com/e/ac/tnks/Nni20110827D27JF053.htm.
147 'Anti-Ozawa Vote', ajw.asahi.com/article/behind_news/AJ201108308360.
148 Akasaka, 'Ozawa Ichirō mata mo ya yaburetari', gekkan.bunshun.jp/articles/-/249.
149 Ibid.
150 'DPJ's "Escape from Ozawa"', e.nikkei.com/e/ac/tnks/Nni20110826D2608A15.htm.
151 'Maehara's Tightrope Strategy', ajw.asahi.com/article//behind_news/AJ201108257452.
152 'Japan's New Prime Minister', ajw.asahi.com/article/behind_news/politics/AJ20110830833.
153 Akasaka, 'Ozawa Ichirō mata mo ya yaburetari', gekkan.bunshun.jp/articles/-/249.
154 Ibid.
155 'Kingpin Ozawa', e.nikkei.com/e/ac/tnks/Nni20110826D26JF936.htm.
156 'DPJ's "Escape from Ozawa"', e.nikkei.com/e/ac/tnks/Nni20110826D2608A15.htm.
157 'Ozawa G', www.yomiuri.co.jp/feature/20100806-849918/news/20110830-OYT1T00020.htm.
158 Wallace, 'The Japanese PM Run-off', sigma1.wordpress.com/2011/08/29/the-japanese-pm-race-run-off-and-the-weekends-media-through-a-rumsfeldian-lens/.
159 Katz, 'Why Noda?', p. 1. For other theories, see also Cucek, 'Ichiro Ozawa's Last Battle', shisaku.blogspot.com/2011/08/ozawa-ichiros-last-battle-as-democrat.html, and Akasaka, 'Ozawa Ichirō mata mo ya yaburetari', gekkan.bunshun.jp/articles/-/249.
160 'Anti-Ozawa Vote', ajw.asahi.com/article/behind_news/AJ201108308360.
161 'Ozawa G', www.yomiuri.co.jp/feature/20100806-849918/news/20110830-OYT1T00020.htm.
162 'Noda shin seiken', www.asahi.com/business/news/reuters/RTR201108290081.html?ref=reca.
163 'Ozawa Consolidating Supporters', www.asahi.com/english/TKY201108310224.html.
164 Wallace, 'The Japanese PM Run-off', sigma1.wordpress.com/2011/08/29/the-japanese-pm-race-run-off-and-the-weekends-media-through-a-rumsfeldian-lens/.
165 See also the discussion on the Shinseiken below.
166 'Ozawa moto daihyō', www.yomiuri.co.jp/politics/news/20110830-OYT1T00152.htm?from=main2.
167 Ibid.
168 'Guilty Verdicts', ajw.asahi.com/article/behind_news/politics/AJ2011092712240.
169 'Kan seiken no jyūgokagetsu', www.chugoku-np.co.jp/Syasetu/Sh201108270068.html.
170 'Noda Set', findarticles.com/p/articles/mi_m0XPQ/is_2011_Sept_6/ai_n58103785/.
171 'Analysis/Noda's Party Personnel', www.asahi.com/english/TKY201108310232.html.
172 Ibid.
173 Ibid.

174 Suzuki, *Saigo no Ozawa Ichirō*, p. 137.
175 'Noda Maintains Cautious Stance', www.yomiuri.co.jp/dy/national/T11090800 5715.htm.
176 'Ozawa: Noda's Cabinet Lineup "Well-balanced"', ajw.asahi.com/article/behind_news/AJ201109059158.
177 'Noda Maintains Cautious Stance', www.yomiuri.co.jp/dy/nationa/T11090800 5715.htm.
178 Gotō, 'Noda shin seiken ga funade', diamond.jp/articles/-/13874.
179 *NHK News 7*, 30 August 2011.
180 'Ichikawa, Yamaoka Face Ax', www.japantimes.co.jp/text/nn20120108a1.html. However, Yamaoka argued that the opposition parties were blaming him for a problem that occurred before he became minister, namely his repeated comments justifying pyramid schemes.
181 'Noda's Party Unity Hopes Dim', www.yomiuri.co.jp/dy/national/T120114003873.htm.
182 Tanaka reputedly called himself a 'quasi-member' of the Ozawa group, and did not join Shinseikai when it was formed. He preferred to be known as aligned with Koshiishi. 'Noda's Party Unity Hopes Dim', www.yomiuri.co.jp/dy/national/T120114003873.htm.
183 Ichimura, 'Ozawa Ichirō ga TPP ni hantai shinai wake', business.nikkeibp.co.jp/article/topics/20111109/223726/.
184 Ito and Fukue, 'Picks Mirror more Pragmatic Tack', www.japantimes.co.jp/news/2012/01/14/national/picks-mirror-more-pragmatic-tack-bid-to-exert-leadership/#.UYn_ueDtIqY.
185 Yoshino, 'Ozawa Seeks to Reclaim Political Power', ajw.asahi.com/article/behind_news/AJ201201110049.
186 Suzuki had been discharged from prison on parole on 6 December after serving one year of a prison sentence for taking bribes, failing to report political donations and perjury.
187 These were Matsuki and Ishikawa Tomohiro from the Lower House, and Upper House members Yokomine Yoshirō and Hirayama Makoto, an Independent who belonged to the DPJ parliamentary group. The rush to form the party by year's end was due to the legal requirement for political parties to be registered by 1 January in order to receive government subsidies. Suzuki himself remained unable to run for office for five years after the completion of the prison sentence, namely 2017.
188 Having been established prior to 1 January 2012, New Party Kizuna, with its nine members, was eligible for just over ¥200 million in subsidies. 'Update1: 9 DPJ Lawmakers Submit Resignation', findarticles.com/p/articles/mi_m0XPQ/is_2012_Jan_2/ai_n58518929/. Uchiyama became head of New Party Kizuna.
189 Akasaka, 'Hashimoto Tōru', gekkan.bunshun.jp/articles/-/304.
190 '"Ozawa Ichirō" Minshutō moto daihyō', in *Liberal Time*, p. 11.
191 Akasaka, 'Hashimoto Tōru ga nerau "shushō no za"', gekkan.bunshun.jp/articles/-/304.
192 '3 Pro-Ozawa Groups', www.yomiuri.co.jp/dy/national/T111222004981.htm.
193 Ibid.
194 'Daihyōsen', in *Nikkan Gendai*, p. 424.
195 Ishikawa, 'Sōsa dankai', p. 455.
196 '"Tenka tori miete kita"', sankei.jp.msn.com/politics/news/120426/stt1204261433 0016-n1.htm.
197 Imahori and Yamamoto, 'Shōhi zōzei hōan', sankei.jp.msn.com/politics/news/120210/plc12021002040001-n1.htm.
198 'Uta o wasureta kanaria wa dochira', www.yomiuri.co.jp/politics/news/20120203-OYT1T01231.htm.
199 'Ozawa to Oppose Noda's Bills', www.japantimes.co.jp/text/nn20120205a2.html.
200 Ibid.

201 'Ozawa Says to Oppose Bills', e.nikkei.com/e/ac/TNKS/Nni20120204D04JF528. htm?NS-query=Ichiro%20Ozawa.
202 Atarashii Seisaku Kenkyūkai (Giji Yōshi), shinseiken.jp/pdf/120209.pdf.
203 Imahori and Yamamoto, 'Shōhi zōzei hōan', sankei.jp.msn.com/politics/news/120210/plc12021002040001-n1.htm.
204 Akasaka, 'Hashimoto Tōru ga nerau "shushō no za"', gekkan.bunshun.jp/articles/-/304.
205 Ibid.
206 Atarashii Seisaku Kenkyūkai (Giji Yōshi), shinseiken.jp/pdf/120322.pdf.
207 Gotō, Hara and Obi, 'Seiji koramunisuto Gotō Kenji', diamond.jp/articles/-/18112.
208 Akasaka, 'Hashimoto Tōru ga nerau "shushō no za"', gekkan.bunshun.jp/articles/-/304.
209 'Ozawa-shi "Noda oroshi" e', sankei.jp.msn.com/politics/news/120426/stt12042611120008-n1.htm.
210 Ibid.
211 Toshikawa, 'Timing of the Next Election', p. 5.
212 Sakai, 'Minshutō ni "nō saido" nashi', sankei.jp.msn.com/politics/news/120426/plc12042623540015-n1.htm.
213 Ito, 'Political Showdown', www.japantimes.co.jp/text/nn20120427a2.html.
214 Sakai, 'Minshutō ni "nō saido" nashi', sankei.jp.msn.com/politics/news/120426/plc12042623540015-n1.htm.
215 'Jimin "Kowashiya" ni kitai', sankei.jp.msn.com/politics/news/120426/stt12042623520019-n1.htm.
216 Ibid.
217 *NHK News 7*, 27 April 2012.
218 'Noda Shushō ni nokosareta saigo no "sentaku"', gekkan.bunshun.jp/articles/-/377.
219 'Fukken ni hisaku ari', gendai.net/articles/view/syakai/136509.
220 Ibid.
221 *NHK News 7*, 10 May 2012.
222 'Fukken ni hisaku ari', gendai.net/articles/view/syakai/136509.
223 'Fukken o habamareta Ozawa-shi', shukan.bunshun.jp/articles/-/1307
224 'Noda Shushō ni nokosareta saigo no "sentaku"', gekkan.bunshun.jp/articles/-/377.
225 *NHK News 7*, 12 May 2012.
226 'Noda Shushō ni nokosareta saigo no "sentaku"', gekkan.bunshun.jp/articles/-/377.
227 Imahori, '"Ishihara shintō"', p. 1.
228 Gotō, Hara and Obi, 'Seiji koramunisuto Gotō Kenji', diamond.jp/articles/-/18112.
229 Suzuki argues that Noda's intention was 'to damage Ozawa's image, while Ozawa was simply going to reassert his opposition'. *Saigo no Ozawa Ichirō*, pp. 181–83.
230 *NHK News 7*, 28 May 2012.
231 Suzuki, *Saigo no Ozawa Ichirō*, p. 26.
232 'Yotō kahansūware ni genjitsumi', in *Asahi Shinbun*, p. 3.
233 'Ozawa moto daihyō – mujun darake no zōzei hantai', www.asahi.com/paper/editorial20120619.html.
234 'Minshu no bunretsu fukahi', in *Asahi Shinbun*, p. 1.
235 Ibid.
236 'Ozawa Ichirō koppu', gekkan.bunshun.jp/articles/-/397.
237 'Ozawa shintō', gendai.net/articles/view/syakai/137323.
238 'Minshu no bunretsu fukahi', in *Asahi Shinbun*, 22 June 2012, p. 1.
239 'Miscalculation Knocks Ozawa', e.nikkei.com/e/ac/TNKS/Nni20120626D2606A18.htm?NS-query=Ichiro%20Ozawa.
240 This was calculated as follows: there were 289 DPJ seats in the Lower House out of a total of 480 (minus the speaker who did not vote). If members of the PNP were included, the government's tally rose to 292, meaning that if 53 members were to vote against the government's legislation, the ruling party would end up with 239 seats and lose its majority.

241 'Ozawa shintō wa Shū San 50 nin de "kaizu naki kōkai" e', www.nikkeibp.co.jp/article/column/20120703/314579/.
242 'Criticism of Ozawa', e.nikkei.com/e/ac/tnks/Nni20120624D2406F03.htm.
243 Quoted in 'From 10% to 3%', e.nikkei.com/e/ac/tnks/Nni20120711D1107A16.htm.
244 Watanabe, *Ozawa Ichirō Kirawareru Densetsu*, p. 265.
245 'Editorial: Time to Dump "Ozawa Politics"', e.nikkei.com/e/ac/tnks/Nni20101005D05HH087.htm.

7 Ozawa *redux*?

The vote on the consumption tax hike took place in the Lower House on 26 June 2012. When Ozawa stood before the ballot box and cast a blue vote indicating that he opposed the tax (along with 57 other Diet members including 46 members of his own group), a cheer went up amongst the opposition parties and some members of the DPJ. As he left the Lower House assembly hall, Ozawa smiled and muttered 'Good', as if to prepare himself for the new chapter in his political life that would inevitably follow.

Although the DPJ anti-consumption tax rebels within his own group fell well short of the numbers Ozawa had been able to mobilise in his glory days in the DPJ, it still represented a large number for an internal revolt of party members against their own government. One Ozawa acolyte declared, 'The Ozawa group will now be a proper opposition party'.[1] Ozawa met with 43 members from the Lower House and 14 from the Upper House, telling them, 'We were able to show that we acted with unity. This will be viewed on television by many voters all over the country. The people will undoubtedly give us even more support'.[2]

Thereafter, Ozawa maintained an aggressive attitude, refusing to compromise with Koshiishi's offers to amend the bill during deliberations in the Upper House. His demand was 'withdraw the bill from the Upper House, otherwise I'll leave the party'.[3] In setting such impossible conditions for the Noda administration to meet, it was clear that Ozawa was paving the way for his own departure. Despite Koshiishi's best efforts to reach a compromise, Ozawa finally made good on his threat to leave the DPJ on 2 July, declaring, 'The DPJ under Prime Minister Noda is no longer the DPJ that achieved regime change. I left the DPJ in order to build a politics where the people have a choice, with an eye to forming a new party'.[4]

Many in the Ozawa group, however, had doubts about whether they wanted to leave the DPJ. Their calculations were influenced by the position in which they found themselves in their own constituencies as well as lack of public support for a prospective Ozawa new party and his legal travails. One 'confided that he would not leave the party "because there is no future in leaving the party with Mr. Ozawa, who is not popular with the people"'.[5] At a Shinseiken meeting on 28 June, 61 Lower House and 20 Upper House members turned up, but in the end, a group of only 49 (initially 50) DPJ members led by Ozawa submitted their resignations to the DPJ.

Ozawa formed the PLF on 11 July with 37 Lower House members and 12 Upper House members. His rationalisation was the need to 'go beyond the DPJ framework and appeal directly to the people'.[6] The DPJ executive then formally expelled Ozawa and 36 other Lower House Diet members who had voted against the consumption tax and submitted letters of resignation. In particular, Noda demanded harsh punishment for Ozawa while holding out the prospect of a party with greater internal unity without Ozawa's fractious faction. At its inauguration, the PLF's numbers made it the third largest party in the Lower House and the fourth largest in the Upper House.

Reprising history?

Given the dead end in which he found himself, Ozawa chose the least worst option by getting out of the DPJ. It was clear that he had lost to Noda in the internal power struggle within the party, with the consumption tax merely defining the battleground rather than the real issue at stake, which was power sharing with Ozawa. The risk of leaving the DPJ was that it might prove to be a journey into the political wilderness, but it gave Ozawa the best chance of reviving his fortunes in the short term and the possibility of generating better prospects in the next general election. It put Ozawa on political life support for the time being.

In reality, by abandoning the DPJ and forming a new party with a group of his supporters, Ozawa was hoping to reprise his political triumph of 1993. After all, each time he had 'destroyed' or left a party, his band of followers had numbered 40–50, but their ranks had later swelled to much higher figures through opportunistic mergers and realignments.

There were certainly some parallels with the events of 1993. First, Ozawa picked an issue that he knew had some traction with the electorate. In opposing the consumption tax rise, he calculated that he had found a populist cause that would later underpin his electoral success. He proposed that the new political party should focus on administrative and fiscal reforms first rather than raising the consumption tax rate, while promoting increased public works investment to escape deflation. He also took up the popular anti-nuclear cause, with his new party adopting a policy of abolishing all nuclear power plants in Japan within ten years and drastically revising the nation's energy policy. At the same time, he retained his anti-TPP stance whilst supporting FTAs that would benefit Japan.

On the basis of his 'anti-consumption tax hike and anti-nuclear power' stance, he once again labelled his followers and himself as 'reformists' (*kaikakuha*), and those who remained in the DPJ as 'Old Guard' (*shukyūha*).[7] Not only did he condemn the DPJ-LDP-New Kōmeitō agreement that resulted in the successful passage of the consumption tax legislation through the Lower House as an 'illicit alliance',[8] but he also criticised the DPJ, LDP and New Kōmeitō as 'nuclear power capitalists'.[9] This was despite his own close relationship with TEPCO over the years, originally crafted by Tanaka, and his failure to attribute any blame to TEPCO over the accident at the Fukushima Daiichi nuclear power plant.[10] Moreover, he had earlier tried to bury Kan's policy of 'abandoning nuclear power', and hardly spoke about getting rid of nuclear power and how nuclear energy policies should be implemented for 16 months after the disaster.[11] His newfound anti-nuclear stance seemed merely to illustrate the 'opportunistic desperation'[12] underpinning his new party's policies.

Second, Ozawa was hoping that a sufficient number of followers would depart with him so they could reduce the ruling DPJ-PNP coalition to a minority government (this required at least 54 DPJ Diet members to leave the party), or at least aspire to the passage of a no-confidence vote in the Noda cabinet. Even if they fell short of the required number to act on their own to bring down the cabinet in a no-confidence vote (which needed at least 51 Lower House members), they could possibly envisage having sufficient numbers to realise their threat by linking up with minor party allies – the New Party Kizuna (9), New Party Daichi/True Democrats (3) and Tax Cuts Japan (1). If joined by other opposition parties such as the SDP, or possibly even the LDP and New Kōmeitō and a few other DPJ defectors, or others such as Kamei Shizuka, the no-confidence vote would be successful, precipitating a dissolution of the house and a general election.

Third, having brought down the DPJ government, the Ozawa breakaway group could hope to team up with coalition partners to form a new government. Ozawa wanted to join forces with any party that he could, regardless of whether they were major or minor 'third-pole' parties, with 'something like an "anti-tax hike national front" in mind'.[13] He also raised the possibility of presenting an alternative to both the major parties (the DPJ and LDP) by establishing a loose coalition of opposition and regional parties modelled on the 'Olive Tree' coalition in Italy in the 1990s. The obvious choices were again the New Party Kizuna exclusively made up of ex-DPJ-ers and the New Party Daichi/True Democrats, which had two former DPJ Lower House Diet members, and Tax Cuts Japan with one. Some of these minor party Diet representatives in the Lower House had earlier been members of Ozawa's new 'party in waiting', the Shinseiken. Besides Tax Cuts Japan, another regional party in Nagoya, the 'Aichi is Top of Japan' party led by Aichi Governor Ōmura, was a possible coalition partner if it successfully elected candidates to the Lower House in the next general election. Nor had Ozawa given up the idea of possibly linking up with Osaka Mayor Hashimoto. If there were no clear winner in the next Lower House election, he was even hoping that his new party might 'hold the casting vote'.[14]

However, this whole scenario fell short in a number of respects. Fewer followers left the DPJ with Ozawa than anticipated, despite his efforts to maintain the unity of his group in the months leading up to his departure. In fact, the Ozawa group split into three: those who voted against the legislation to raise the consumption tax and resigned from the DPJ; those who voted against the legislation but remained in the party; and those who supported the legislation (a considerable number) and also stayed put.[15] In the end, while 57 Lower House members voted against the consumption tax legislation, with 20 fewer Lower House members actually resigning from the DPJ to join Ozawa, the new Ozawa party single-handedly had the numbers neither successfully to pass a vote of no confidence in the DPJ, nor to deprive it of its Lower House majority.[16]

It was also on the coalition hurdle that Ozawa's best-case scenario fell down. When he left the LDP in 1993, it was after a solid year of preparations, during which time he secured the loyalty of fellow LDP defectors and established pipelines behind the scenes to other political players such as the JSP, DSP, Kōmeitō and Rengō. This time there was no possibility of any major LDP figures joining forces with him. LDP leaders such as Ishiba Shigeru, Hayashi Yoshimasa and Abe Shinzō were plotting to bring down Tanigaki but had absolutely no intention of joining hands with Ozawa.[17] Nor was there any scope for Ozawa to drive a wedge between the DPJ and the LDP/New Kōmeitō, because they had reached agreement over legislation to raise the consumption tax. So apart from the SDP, which canvassed the possibility of allying itself with Ozawa, no established party, or none with any serious electoral prospects, had any desire to form a coalition with Ozawa's new group. Tokyo Governor Ishihara said that 'nobody expected anything of Ozawa's new party'[18] and that he 'wouldn't be caught dead linking up with him'.[19] He described Ozawa's political manoeuvring 'as "self-serving"…"There is nothing principled about it"'.[20] Key personnel in Hashimoto's new regional party, the Osaka Ishin no Kai, which was potentially a major third force in national politics, were also negative about a possible alliance with Ozawa.[21] As Kawakami put it, 'no one wants to join hands with poison'.[22] Ozawa even had problems getting Suzuki Muneo's New Party Daichi/True Democrats to form a unified parliamentary group with his prospective new party.

Ozawa's new party also had other serious deficiencies: lack of 'quality' members and funding. Despite Ozawa's grandiose claim that it 'would be responsible for the future of the Japanese people',[23] his troupe now consisted of only a few loyal senior lieutenants and a small tribe of junior followers labouring under the impression that Ozawa, the legendary fundraiser and electoral wizard, would ensure their re-election.[24] Ozawa appointed himself election committee chairman and was chosen as party leader (with Yamaoka as deputy leader). Azuma was made secretary-general and Yamaoka deputy secretary-general. Suzuki Katsumasa became Diet Affairs Committee chairman. Around 70 per cent of the party's members were first-term Diet members.

Ozawa was also desperate to acquire some of the DPJ's party subsidies, which amounted to ¥16.5 billion in 2012.[25] Ozawa met with Koshiishi and asked him to split the party, calculating that this would deliver ¥4 billion into party coffers.[26] This would be a 'peaceful divorce'[27] or 'divorce by consent', rather than a secession by the Ozawa-led group, which would deprive it of DPJ funding.[28] Despite Ozawa's requests to Koshiishi, Noda showed about as much sympathy towards Ozawa on this score as Ozawa himself had demonstrated towards his former political ally and later DPJ Diet member, Hata Tsutomu, when Ozawa refused to distribute the party subsidies from the dissolution of the NFP in 1997. In short, he flatly refused.

Ozawa's new party would, therefore, receive no subsidies in 2012 and, in 2013, would be provided with an amount based on the number of Diet members it had on 1 January and its share of votes in the most recent national election. In order to generate the funds to form the new party and fight an election, Ozawa sold real estate assets belonging to Rikuzankai (an apartment unit in Tokyo), having also transferred money held by the DPJ Iwate (4) chapter to Rikuzankai around the time he left the DPJ. Part of that money was party subsidies received from DPJ headquarters. He combined these funds with donations from political groups and private individuals to make ¥300 million, which he loaned to the PLF via Rikuzankai.[29] Because this was still not enough to form a new party and fight an election, the PLF then borrowed a total of ¥800 million from Reform Forum 21 and the Reform People's Council, thus dipping into his 'treasured funds' left over after the RP and LP were dissolved. The total transferred was ¥1.89 billion.[30]

Ozawa's departure from the DPJ may not have been such a good move in other respects. In 1993 there was an electorate hungry for political reform in the wake of a succession of 'money-politics' scandals. Ozawa was able to convert this political groundswell for reform into votes for the RP in the 1993 election. This time the political dynamics were very different. Expectations of a new Ozawa party amongst the vast majority were very low. Public opposition to the consumption tax hike, as indicated by opinion polls, did not translate into support for Ozawa's party. Moreover, he was carrying the legal baggage of his unresolved court case, which was under appeal. Within a few weeks of its launch, the PLF's approval rating was a mere 1 per cent.

Ozawa's break with the ruling party also cost him key allies such as Hatoyama, who drew the line at leaving the party, which was, after all, partly his creation. Similarly, Koshiishi, Ozawa's long-term ally, wanted to avoid a split in the DPJ at all costs and did everything in his power to keep Ozawa in the party. After Ozawa left, however, Koshiishi put all his efforts into uniting the DPJ and retaining the support of Prime Minister Noda.

The new Ozawa party's policies

Despite its diminutive size, Ozawa had grandiose ambitions for the PLF. Its fundamental principles, taken directly from Shinseiken, were 'independence (meaning self-reliance) and coexistence' (*jiritsu to kyōsei*). Ozawa himself reiterated, 'The idea is that true reforms will not be possible without destroying the old establishment and creating a new set-up'.[31]

At the celebration to mark his new party's opening, Ozawa laid out his goal of expanding support for the party in order to defeat the DPJ. He criticised it for betraying the Japanese people on the promise of more generous social security outlays and for shelving reform of pensions and aged care in order to gain the support of opposition parties to the consumption tax hike.

When boiled down, the PLF's policy manifesto amounted to three key selling points: anti-nuclear power, anti-tax hike and decentralisation of power, each delivered in short catchphrases followed by an exclamation mark: 'Protect lives: towards zero nuclear power!'; 'Abolish the consumption tax rise that directly affects the people's livelihoods!'; 'Local matters will be decided by local people: [build] a society with local areas as key players!'[32] Alongside these basic policies with their keywords – 'lives', 'livelihoods' and 'local regeneration' – was a political commitment to keep promises to the people, in a clear contrast to what he regarded as the DPJ's failure in this respect.

Instead of raising the consumption tax, the PLF promised to secure funding sources by abolishing special accounts and government-related corporations and by completely banning *amakudari* by bureaucrats. It also promised to revive the economy by implementing proactive monetary and fiscal policies.[33] Establishing a 'society where local areas are the key players' encompassed Ozawa's pet theme of decentralisation and regional sovereignty. It meant transferring powers and funding sources to local governments.[34] This would lead to the stimulation of regional economies and shaking free of deflation.[35]

The platform thus contained updated and simplified versions of earlier policy lines, amounting to an admixture of populism and increased public spending combined with administrative reform. However, many voters interpreted the party's anti-consumption tax and anti-nuclear policies as simply Ozawa adopting politically expedient policies in an attempt to maximise popular support in a short time, particularly for the first-term Diet members in the PLF's ranks, whose electoral foundations were the shakiest. Arch-foe Maehara commented, 'He must take the Japanese people for fools if he thinks all he needs to win an election is to declare himself opposed to taxes and nuclear power'.[36] Former LDP Prime Minister Asō Tarō's acerbic comment was that 'a more appropriate name for Ozawa's new party would be "Put Elections First"'.[37] LDP politician Koike Yuriko, a former confidante of Ozawa from NFP and LP days, said, 'It's déjà vu. I feel like I just accidentally turned on an old videotape…He is focused not on the future of Japan but on what is happening now and how to win the next election'.[38]

The declaration that the party would stick to the DPJ's original hand-out (*baramaki*) policies also lacked credibility in view of its reluctance to raise taxes.[39] Moreover, Ozawa's commitment to putting the people's lives first could be questioned by his infrequent visits to the disaster-stricken areas in Iwate and neighbouring prefectures. One resident living in temporary housing remarked, 'Mr. Ozawa has never had a moment's thought for people in the disaster area. When it comes down to it, he's just concerned with his own affairs. He has nothing to do with us'.[40] Nonaka criticised Ozawa's policy flip-flops over the years and the self-serving nature of his anti-tax hike and anti-nuclear policies, saying, 'Ozawa has no credibility anymore and has used up his political capital. The era of Mr. Ichiro Ozawa has come to an end'.[41]

As for the TPP, many in the PLF were enthusiastic about opposing it. Party executives proposed including opposition to the TPP as a basic policy, but Ozawa decided to abandon this idea for purely political reasons. Ozawa was still hoping that his party could be one of the poles around which small parties, some of whom supported the TPP such as Your Party, could coalesce.

Manoeuvring from the other side of politics

The new Ozawa party added their names to the joint motion of no confidence against the Noda cabinet and censure motion against the prime minister, which seven opposition parties other than the LDP and New Kōmeitō submitted on 7 August to protest against the DPJ-LDP-New Kōmeitō agreement to raise the consumption tax. A similar motion was submitted to the Upper House by seven opposition caucuses, including the PLF, on 29 August.

Ozawa also touched on the possibility of submitting a no-confidence motion against the cabinet in the autumn session of the Diet. With this objective in mind, he began engaging in political manoeuvring amongst potential DPJ defectors as well as other small and mid-sized 'third-pole' parties. Ozawa thought that a general election would provide an opportunity for the PLF and other opposition parties to show their differences from the DPJ and LDP.[42] Ozawa sent out feelers to New Party Kizuna, which later merged with the PLF, bringing its total Diet membership to 57, and to New Party Daichi/True Democrats, which offered its cooperation but declined to merge. Ozawa also communicated with YP's Watanabe but Noda dissolved the Lower House unexpectedly early so as not to allow sufficient time for third-pole parties to coalesce.[43] In the end, Ozawa tried to establish a policy umbrella under which third-pole parties could unite: anti-nuclear power generation.[44] As for the remaining DPJ members, it was clear that many had had enough of Ozawa and rejected joining forces with him.[45]

The December 2012 Lower House election

Ozawa dissolved the PLF in late November 2012, teaming up with the newly formed Tomorrow Party of Japan, or TPJ (Nihon Mirai no Tō), led by Shiga governor Kada Yukiko. The merger of the PLF with the TPJ appeared to be at Ozawa's instigation. He had approached the 'squeaky clean' Kada behind the scenes to lead a new party under the banner of a nuclear-free Japan. Kada was initially reluctant to agree but was persuaded to do so by Yamada Masahiko. In fact, Yamada and Ozawa had been working quietly behind the scenes to create the new Kada party.[46] Ozawa even dissolved his own party to put more pressure on Kada.[47] He admitted that while not very well acquainted with Kada, the members of his party were fully in support of joining forces with her.

While accepting Ozawa's invitation to form the new party, Kada still had reservations about whether it would bear too much of the imprint of Ozawa's party if it were seen to be the product of an amalgamation of her new grouping with only the PLF. Yamada assured her, however, that he, Kamei and Nagoya Mayor Kawamura would also join. As the three of them were also quite strong characters, the new party would be 'less Ozawa-centric'.[48]

With the union of the PLF and TPJ, the new Nuclear-Free Party, which was jointly led by Yamada and Kawamura with Kamei as secretary-general, as well as three Lower House members of the new Green Wind Party, or GWP (Midori no Kaze) and one defector from the SDP also agreed to join. The Nuclear-Free Party had originally formed in November as an amalgamation of two new mini-parties: the Anti-TPP, Anti-Nuclear Power, Consumption Tax Hike Freeze Realisation Party, or Anti-TPP for short, which was led by Yamada, and which later joined forces with Kawamura's Tax Cuts Japan to form the Party to Achieve Tax

Cuts, Oppose the TPP and Abandon Nuclear Power Plants, or Nuclear-Free Party. They all shared a desire to end reliance on nuclear power, to freeze participation in the TPP and to suspend the consumption-tax hike.

At the time of its inauguration, the TPJ was the third-largest force in the Diet, with 61 affiliated politicians. Its most important policies were 'graduating from nuclear power', for which it set a clear goal of within ten years, opposition to the consumption tax rise and granting ¥312,000 per year for each child until they graduated from junior high school. The pledge on the child allowance as well as the creation of a unified pension programme incorporating a minimum pension benefit system resembled the same policies that were originally incorporated into the DPJ's 2009 manifesto and clearly reflected Ozawa's own policy priorities. Other policies included political, administrative and fiscal reform such as wholesale revision of the special account budget as well as regional sovereignty reform, abolition of the medical insurance system for people aged 75 and over, maintaining the individual household income compensation scheme for farmers and opposing participation in the TPP negotiations although actively promoting FTAs, etc.[49] These policies underscored the extent to which Ozawa was trying to return to the starting point of the DPJ and its winning election formula. In another familiar theme, Kada emphasised 'political leadership'[50] and declared that she 'wanted to borrow Ozawa's power and influence to help weaken the bureaucracy'.[51] She also mentioned one of Ozawa's favourite philosophical concepts – coexistence – as the 'keyword' for the party.[52] In her view, 'Unlike "old forces" [*kyūseiryoku*] that are trying to advance "politics as usual" [*kyūtaiizen taru seiji*], we want to create politics in Japan where we build peace of mind for the future.'[53]

Despite the grandiose language and the leadership of Kada, who called it a 'true' third pole, the TPJ was really the Ozawa party in a new guise, his seventh since leaving the LDP. Its policies reflected Ozawa's obsession with those in the DPJ's last manifesto, which intersected with Kada's own views. This did not prevent the DPJ and other parties pointing out that the TPJ would not be able to find funding sources for their promises and would just repeat the same mistakes as the DPJ had made.[54]

The timing of the merger and the manner in which it arose inevitably raised the question of whether Ozawa was behind the TPJ as a new 'front' party 'just for the election'.[55] The LDP's vice-president declared, 'Ozawa has been surviving so far by deceiving people and forming new parties when his reputation worsened. Isn't this party just Ozawa's means of survival?'[56] As more of the story behind the TPJ's formation was revealed, it became clear that Ozawa had indeed planned the TPJ's inauguration and persuaded Kada to lead it. He rightly saw the new party as having potentially greater electoral appeal than his own PLF, which was too patently an Ozawa party. In making Kada the face of the party, Ozawa could retreat to his favoured position of 'leading from behind', rather than being the face of the party himself. This led some observers to quip that Ozawa's presence in the party would inevitably result in the usual '"dual power structure" in which Ozawa pulled the strings and Kada acted as a figurehead'.[57]

By not appointing Ozawa to an important position and by offering assurances that she would make sure that Ozawa's power would not strengthen in the TPJ, Kada sought to avoid criticism of 'being controlled by him'.[58]

Try as she might, however, it was impossible for Kada to convince the public and other politicians that her new party was not 'Ozawa's new party in reality'.[59] In Nagata-chō it was considered to be 'nothing but Ozawa's new party'[60] with Kada merely a 'cloak'.[61] Ozawa acolytes dominated its parliamentary membership, with a former Ozawa secretary and other close aides also on the membership list.[62] Key Ozawa allies were given important posts in the party, including Mori Yūko, who was made deputy party head, while former PLF members who were close to Ozawa took on the tasks of managing the party's financial affairs, including for the election, and clerical work at its headquarters. In addition, right from the start, people in the TPJ started to use the term 'Ozawa group'.[63]

Although Ozawa was holding out hope that some kind of 'third-pole alliance' would form around the TPJ centring on opposition to the consumption tax hike and nuclear power, this ambition was not realised despite his decision to join the anti-nuclear power gathering held in front of the Diet building. Moreover, Ozawa's presence proved an electoral deadweight in the December 2012 Lower House election, which turned into a rout for the Ozawa group. The TPJ supported 121 candidates in all, but they won not a single seat in the Kinki region, including Osaka, where they supported seven former Diet members.[64] Ozawa and Kamei were the only TPJ members to win their single-member district seats, which could be attributed to their longstanding personal support bases. TPJ candidates could not even win in Ozawa's own prefecture, despite his all-out support, which reinforced the impression that voters were deserting Ozawa in his local area.[65] Ozawa himself suffered a decline of 17.1 per cent in voting support in Iwate (4), falling to 45.5 per cent of the total number of votes,[66] indicating that his electoral foundation was eroding. Several key Ozawa stalwarts also lost their seats, including Yamada, Yamaoka and Azuma, leaving him with a tiny rump of a party, no talent and few prospects. It was significant that Ozawa did not even show up at the tally centre in a Tokyo Hotel on the night of the election. Unlike in the general elections after he formed the RP and LP in 1993 and 1998, he was not able to gain the people's endorsement for his destructive actions and increase the membership of his new party. His political resurrections in the past had given the lie to those who argued that Ozawa was finished. In 2012, however, there was to be no miraculous recovery.

Post-election blues

Immediately after the election, Ozawa quickly discarded Kada because she was of no more use to him. The criticism of the TPJ – that the Ozawa-Kada union was an alliance of pure electoral convenience – was borne out. Divisions in the TPJ also emerged between the Ozawa group and those in the party who were close to Kada, particularly over appointments to important party posts. In trying to resolve the conflict, Kada tried fruitlessly to contact Ozawa, who had done his usual disappearing trick. Kada was trying to promote a power-sharing arrangement between the two groups with Ozawa appointed as adviser to the party but not to an important party post. Ozawa's supporters, however, insisted that Ozawa be appointed as party co-leader. On 28 December, just over a month after the new party was formed, Ozawa and Kada decided to part ways. According to one of Kada's aides, Ozawa wanted to get rid of Kada as soon as possible before the end of 2012 in order to secure public funding for his new party for 2013.[67]

The PLP was then established in January 2013 with the remnants of Ozawa's followers, consisting of a total of 15 Diet members (seven survivors of the December 2012 election including Ozawa himself, and eight in the Upper House). Mori Yūko was selected as deputy leader. Once again, the party's philosophy was based on the concepts of 'independence and coexistence'. Ozawa's objectives remained to 'overthrow the centralised administrative framework, establish a "society in which regional areas are the leading players and realise politics that puts the people's lives first"'.[68]

The PLP's manifesto for the July 2013 Upper House election contained remnants of old DPJ policy lines informed by social democratic principles such as support for the development and revival of small- and medium-sized businesses; providing a child allowance of approximately ¥312,000 per annum per child until the end of middle school; promoting agriculture, forestry and fisheries, food self-sufficiency and food security; reducing highway tolls; unifying the pension system; and enhancing medical and care systems.[69] On the key issue of the consumption tax, the PLP promised to freeze the tax rise and examine a system whereby the government would return the current consumption tax to the people as points.[70] The party also opposed restarting nuclear power plants and expanding existing power plants. It made a commitment to abolishing nuclear power operations by 2022 at the latest and cancelling the entire nuclear fuel cycle including the high-speed breeder reactor (Monju). The party also opposed revising the constitution, although it supported laying out the basis for SDF participation in peacekeeping operations.

Other proposals included Ozawa's idea of an employment safety net[71] as well as longstanding Ozawa policy preferences for administrative reforms that would raise alternative sources of government funding to the consumption tax hike and stamp out wasteful spending by providing unified grants to be freely used by local government bodies. Ozawa's anti-bureaucratic stance was also evident in the proposal to ban *amakudari*, which the DPJ had advocated in the 2009 general election, whilst a hint of pork barrelling survived in the promise to accelerate reconstruction from the Great East Japan Earthquake.[72] Other proposals reflected Ozawa's opposition to Abenomics, such as blocking the relaxation of regulations on dismissals, reducing electricity charges and opposing the TPP (although not economic partnerships that were in the national interest).[73] Despite some commonalities between Abenomics and Ozawa's own preference for big spending on public works as a growth strategy, Ozawa argued that it only benefited financial circles and the rich under the Koizumi-style 'law of the jungle', while ordinary people suffered higher prices for oil, electricity and food.[74]

When Ozawa joined other party leaders to present the essence of his party's policies at the Japan National Press Club prior to the 2013 Upper House election, he was hesitant, uncharacteristically diffident and stumbled over his words. Unlike all the other leaders who were confident and articulate, he ended up reading part of his presentation. As for what his own party stood for, he mouthed empty populist phrases such as 'politics exists for the people and exists to protect the people's livelihoods'. He reiterated his party's slogan: 'we will protect lives, livelihoods and the regions.'[75]

Ozawa's only electoral strategy was to try to galvanise the other opposition parties into some sort of cooperation. Despite obvious policy differences that clearly mattered not a jot to Ozawa, he argued very strongly for the need to rally all the opposition parties to join together to stand against the LDP electoral juggernaut, with the DPJ as flag bearer. With respect to a possible partnership with Ozawa, Koshiishi expressed cautious support. However, hardly any DPJ Diet members agreed because of the risk of triggering yet another split in the DPJ. Nevertheless, Ozawa did not give up the idea of cooperating with the DPJ, with all PLP Upper House members having voted for the new leader Kaieda as prime minister the previous December.

At the same time, Ozawa admitted publicly that he was 'viewed with prejudice by others'.[76] In the end, the failure of the opposition parties to cooperate reduced the PLP's status to that of just another third party, suggesting that Ozawa was finally a 'spent force', a description that had often been used prematurely in the past to describe sudden, dramatic losses in his political power. None of the 14 PLP candidates contesting seats in the Upper House election was successful, which amounted to a crushing defeat. Some, such as Yamaoka and Azuma, were refugees from the Lower House, having lost their seats in the 2012 election. They failed again. Ozawa was particularly disappointed at losing acting party leader Mori in Niigata Prefecture.

Perhaps most significantly of all, Ozawa could not even swing the election of Sekine Toshinobu in his home prefecture of Iwate, despite directly assisting his campaign and visiting the prefecture several times. It suggested that he could no longer rely on old methods of gaining support, such as pressuring the construction industry to deliver votes and provide campaign assistance, and so was forced to adopt a more open campaigning style alongside other candidates. That he did not realise how far out of touch he had become with voters registered in his obvious surprise at the election result.

When LDP Chief Cabinet Secretary Suga Yoshihide visited Iwate in order to campaign for the LDP candidate, he told the gathered crowd, 'Iwate Prefecture has long been controlled by a certain somebody. A candidate not supported by that somebody should represent you in the Diet…The opportunity has come at last'.[77] Ozawa's failure to visit Iwate's coastal communities for ten months after the tsunami disaster worked against him. It suggested that Ozawa took the support from voters in his home prefecture for granted because he thought he could bank on the usual companies and groups delivering a 'hard' vote for him and the candidates whom he supported. His miscalculation underscored how uninformed he was about the changes taking place at the electoral grassroots in the former 'Ozawa Kingdom', and how anachronistic he and his methods had become. Sekine's failure finally signalled the loss of Ozawa's grip on his home prefecture after consecutive Upper House elections won by his candidates since 1993.

In the national PR electorate, the PLP and its six party list candidates (including Yamaoka and Azuma) won only 943,836 votes, or 1.77 per cent of the total number of votes cast.[78] This compared with the 5.2 million votes that he was able to garner in the 1998 Upper House elections as the leader of the newly formed LP.[79] With fewer than 1 million votes cast for the party nationally and without a single victory in the prefectural constituencies, the PLP suffered a crushing defeat.[80] These results finally put to rest Ozawa's reputation as the 'God of elections', and perhaps even the Ozawa legend itself.[81] The party's extremely poor showing left only two members in the Upper House who had been elected in 2010 as members of the DPJ. Together with the seven politicians in the Lower House, the total for the entire party amounted to only nine Diet members, a minor party at most, and marking a sharp decline in its Diet position prior to the 2012 and 2013 elections when it was the third largest party in the house.

In the case of both the TPJ and the PLP, Ozawa had clearly led a party of the unelectable. In fact, voters dealt very harshly with all those politicians who had played an undermining, counter-productive and ultimately destructive role in the DPJ administration, particularly Ozawa's henchmen and acolytes. Even those who had migrated to other parties such as Matsuki and Yamada Masahiko were dealt with harshly by voters. The PLP's poor electoral showing meant that it was due to be paid only ¥787.87 million in public subsidies in 2013, a paltry sum compared to the LDP's ¥15.5858 billion.[82] When MIAC later distributed ¥8 billion in government subsidies to eight political parties for the July–September quarter, the PLP received just under ¥190 million compared with ¥3.9 billion for the LDP.[83]

With his party's poor election record in the Lower and Upper House elections, and with such a small number of Diet seats, it was inevitable that Ozawa would lose the ability to attract future candidates to any Ozawa party. He had finally become a political irrelevance, heralding the inevitable end of his political life.

Soldiering on

The PLP's miniscule Diet presence – only nine Diet members including two Upper House members – prevented it from asking questions in the Budget Committee. Ozawa himself rarely attended the Diet, with Secretary-General Suzuki acting as PLP spokesperson in the Diet and other inter-party policy meetings on issues such as constitutional and electoral reform, and the Fukushima nuclear disaster. The PLP's website, however, continued to clarify Ozawa's and the party's official position on a range of policies, including the Abe administration's Special Secrets Protection Law (*Tokutei Himitsu Hogohō*), which, in line with Ozawa's familiar anti-bureaucratic stance, was described as 'risking giving bureaucrats full power to rule the people and turning the country into a totalitarian state'.[84] The PLP also pushed for fundamental reform of the electoral system in order to achieve equality in the value of votes and criticised the government's economic policies for widening the social divide and the consumption tax hike for dragging down consumption. Ozawa remained opposed to the TPP on the grounds that it was an extension of the US structural talks and an attempt to apply American rules to Japan, and criticised the abolition of the income compensation scheme for farmers, which he had been pivotal in introducing.

His hoped-for scenario remained regime change in the next Lower House election as a result of proper cooperation amongst the opposition parties. Just prior to the 2013 Upper House election, he had argued strongly that despite the DPJ's palpable failures, the Japanese public still wanted a strong major party alternative and counter-force to the LDP. He railed against the one-party domination of politics and argued that politics without competition would inevitably become corrupt. Koshiishi, in his new position as Upper House vice-president, remained sympathetic to Ozawa and continued to communicate with him, showing support for the idea of an opposition alliance in the house. Ozawa was invited to the DPJ's 2014 annual convention, while he attended the new Unity Party's (Yui no Tō) inauguration ceremony.

However, the problem for parties contemplating cooperation with Ozawa was whether the high price of his cooperation was worth paying. Given his infamous reputation as a dictatorial politician who would not only control his own party but would attempt to control all others that came within his grasp, his powers of attraction were considerably diminished.

Conclusion

The dismissal of the appeal in Ozawa's legal case and his effective creation of the TPJ with Kada as leader in order to contest the 2012 election seemed to suggest that Ozawa had one more political fight in him and was not the political has-been that commentators were suggesting that he had become.[85] After all, he had been declared 'politically dead' many times before and yet had displayed Lazarus-like powers to rise up once more to the forefront of Japanese politics.

On the other hand, given Ozawa's more recent record of behaviour in the DPJ, his influence within political parties was widely regarded as negative and destructive, which limited his appeal to potential collaborators as well as to voters. The election results in 2012 and 2013 unequivocally demonstrated that the public had firmly rejected his style of politics. Ozawa had switched from being a political asset to a political liability with little or no popular following. Not even his projected image as a reformer could redeem him, with his pronouncements on reform sounding tired and lacking credibility. They merely served to underline his status as a relic from a bygone era.

Certainly in the short term, Ozawa's departure from the DPJ following a long, slow erosion of his political influence and control over his group as well as the results of two general elections were a precursor to his being consigned to the political periphery. Given his new straightened circumstances with few members in the Diet and with much diminished financial resources, it was difficult to be optimistic about his prospects. He seemed to have completely lost political momentum, a process that began with his departure from the DPJ, when the media stopped talking about him. Ozawa spent 20 years defecting from, creating and destroying a succession of political parties and coalitions. His had been a history of gyrating political fortunes. Yet it appeared as if his political peregrinations had finally reached a dead end.[86] He had effectively rendered himself almost a political irrelevance.

The question remains how stable and powerful a vehicle for Ozawa's personal ambition the PLP proves to be in the medium term, and what kind of political alliances he will be able forge that will enable him to exert influence over political developments in the future. Certainly it is doubtful whether Ozawa has abandoned his behind-the-scenes scheming. However, the Japanese public appear to have grown weary of the kind of old-school politics that he represents. Moreover, in comparison with the past, he seems a much-diminished political dinosaur mired in a previous age. To the many politicians who are wary of associating or cooperating with him, he has become a political pariah who belongs on the sidelines where he can do no harm. The Ozawa myth, which has incorporated his larger-than-life image, seems to have inexorably eroded. While Ozawa may hunger after his glory days, these have gone forever. A process of political realignment represents his only hope for the future as the leader of a very small minority party. Advancing from this point on the periphery of Japanese politics would take all of Ozawa's skills and resources.

Notes

1 'Noda seiken, kuzureru ashimoto', in *Asahi Shinbun*, p. 2.
2 Ibid.
3 Tahara, 'Ozawa Ichirō-shi wa gyaku ni oikomare', www.nikkeibp.co.jp/article/column/20120704/314829/.
4 'Ozawa shintō', www.nikkeibp.co.jp/article/column/20120703/314579/.
5 'Yotō kahansūware ni genjitsumi', in *Asahi Shinbun*, p. 3.
6 'Ozawa-shi ra ritō fukahi', in *Asahi Shinbun*, p. 1.
7 'Ozawa Ichirō koppu', gekkan.bunshun.jp/articles/-/397.
8 Emura, '"Popyurizumu"', astand.asahi.com/magazine/wrpolitics/2012071300008.html?iref=webronza.
9 'Ozawa Ichirō koppu', gekkan.bunshun.jp/articles/-/397.
10 According to Hirano, Ozawa 'had been critical of nuclear power since early times'. *Shinsetsu!*, p. 221.
11 Emura, '"Popyurizumu"', astand.asahi.com/magazine/wrpolitics/2012071300008.html?iref=webronza.
12 Toshikawa, 'Timing of the Next Election', p. 5.
13 Obi and Itō, 'Seiji anarisuto Itō Atsuo', diamond.jp/articles/-/22766.
14 Ibid.
15 'Kuzureta nidai seitō sei', digital.asahi.com/articles/TKY201207020574.html?ref=comkiji_txt_end.
16 'Ritō menbā kara futari datsuraku', gendai.net/articles/view/syakai/137356.
17 'Ozawa Ichirō koppu', gekkan.bunshun.jp/articles/-/397.
18 'Ozawa has Hard Road Ahead', www.yomiuri.co.jp/dy/national/T120701002319.htm.

19 Ibid.
20 'Ozawa Trying Shock and Awe', e.nikkei.com/e/ac/tnks/Nni20120622D2206A01.htm.
21 'Ozawa has Hard Road Ahead', www.yomiuri.co.jp/dy/national/T120701002319.htm.
22 Professor Kawakami Kazuhisa of Meiji Gakuin University quoted in 'Noda's Goal Won', www.japantimes.co.jp/cgi-bin/nn20120627a1.html.
23 *NHK News 7*, 4 July 2012.
24 Hosoya, 'What Really Comes First', www.nippon.com/en/column/g00051/.
25 Cucek, 'Public Funding', shisaku.blogspot.com.au/2012/04/party-by-numbers.html.
26 Toshikawa, 'Timing of the Next Election', p. 5. Tahara calculated that a party of around 50 members would need about ¥1 billion in electoral funds. 'Ozawa Ichirō-shi wa gyaku ni oikomare', www.nikkeibp.co.jp/article/column/20120704/314829/.
27 'Ozawa Ichirō koppu', gekkan.bunshun.jp/articles/-/397.
28 Tahara, 'Ozawa Ichirō-shi wa gyaku ni oikomare', www.nikkeibp.co.jp/article/column/20120704/314829/.
29 'Ozawa Ichirō-shi, shikinguri ni kuryo', sankei.jp.msn.com/politics/news/131130/stt13113008430004-n1.htm.
30 Ibid. See also below.
31 '(Intabyū) Shōhizei to seikai saihen', in *Asahi Shinbun*, p. 17.
32 Kokumin no Seikatsu ga Daiichi, *Seisaku*, web.archive.org/web/20121024102944/http://www.seikatsu1.jp/policy.html.
33 Ibid.
34 Ibid.
35 Ibid.
36 Hosoya, 'What Really Comes First', www.nippon.com/en/column/g00051/.
37 Ibid.
38 Ito, 'Heavyweight', www.japantimes.co.jp/text/nn20120712a1.html#.T__GaGNn785.
39 Tanaka, 'Yakushin no kanōsei', diamond.jp/articles/-/21106.
40 Hosoya, 'What Really Comes First', www.nippon.com/en/column/g00051/ quoting from the *Sankei Shinbun*, 3 July 2012.
41 Nonaka Naoto from Gakushuin University, quoted in Ito, 'Heavyweight', www.japantimes.co.jp/text/nn20120712a1.html#.T__GaGNn785.
42 Suzuki, *Saigo no Ozawa Ichirō*, pp. 215–16.
43 Ibid., pp. 226–28.
44 Ibid., pp. 235–37.
45 Abiru, 'Minshutō', p. 45.
46 Ikeguchi and Kiyonaga, 'Japan's Ex-DPJ Head's Exact Role', www.asianewsnet.net/news-39566.html.
47 Ibid.
48 Ibid.
49 Kobayashi, '"Nihon Mirai no Tō"', astand.asahi.com/magazine/wrpolitics/2012113000006.html?page=1.
50 Ibid.
51 Johnson, 'Kada Party', www.japantimes.co.jp/text/nn20121201a4.html.
52 Hirano, *Shinsetsu!*, p. 219.
53 *NHK News 7*, 2 December 2012.
54 Ibid.
55 'Mirai kōtai', in *Yomiuri Shinbun*, p. 2.
56 *NHK News 7*, 27 November 2012.
57 Ikeguchi and Kiyonaga, 'Japan's Ex-DPJ Head's Exact Role', www.asianewsnet.net/news-39566.html.
58 'Mirai, "sotsu genpatsu" todokazu', in *Asahi Shinbun*, p. 3.

59 'Mirai, nijū kenryoku uchikeshi ni yakki', www.jiji.com/jc/zc?k=201211/20121128 00938.
60 'Nagata-chō kīman', www.zakzak.co.jp/society/politics/news/20121201/plt12120114 46002-n1.htm.
61 *NHK News 7*, 27 November 2012.
62 'Mirai, nijū kenryoku uchikeshi ni yakki', www.jiji.com/jc/zc?k=201211/201211 2800938.
63 '"Mirai" no seisaku', *Asahi Shinbun*, p. 4.
64 'Kasunda mirai', in *Yomiuri Shinbun*, p. 18.
65 Nakajima, 'Mirai', p. 2.
66 'Ishin hirei ni sukuwareta', in *Yomiuri Shinbun*, p. 18.
67 'Kada, Ozawa Split Up', ajw.asahi.com/article/behind_news/politics/AJ20121229 0065.
68 Futami, 'Naze, imadoki Ozawa Ichirō ka', www.the-journal.jp/contents/futami/2012/11/post_44.html.
69 Seikatsu no tō, 'Seikatsu no tō dai 23 kai Sangiin giin senkyo 2013', www.seikatsu1.jp/political_policy.
70 *NHK News 7*, 4 June 2013.
71 Seikatsu no tō, 'Seikatsu no tō dai 23 kai Sangiin giin senkyo 2013', www.seikatsu1.jp/political_policy.
72 Ibid.
73 Ibid.
74 'Ozawa Ichirō ga katatta yatō saihen', gendai.net/articles/view/syakai/143144.
75 *NHK News 7*, 4 July 2013.
76 Matsuda, 'Tokushū waido', mainichi.jp/feature/news/20130410dde012010084000c.html.
77 'Iwate Hopefuls', www.japantimes.co.jp/news/2013/07/18/national/iwate-hopefuls-locked-in-close-race/#.UgWZGuDtIqZ.
78 'Hireiku', www.asahi.com/senkyo/senkyo2013/kaihyo/C01.html.
79 Toshikawa, '100 man byō', gendai.ismedia.jp/articles/-/36539.
80 Ibid.
81 Ibid.
82 'Seitō kōfukin, Jimin 3.5% zō, San'insen uke' in *Nihon Keizai Shinbun*, p. 4.
83 Ibid.
84 'Tokutei himitsu hogo hōan', www.seikatsu1.jp/activity/declaration/20131127ozawa-danwa.html.
85 Sekiguchi, 'Japan's "Destroyer"', blogs.wsj.com/japanrealtime/2012/11/28/japans-destroyer-eyes-comeback-with-party-no-7/.
86 Yakushiji, *Whither Japanese Politics*, www.tokyofoundation.org/en/topics/politics-in-perspective/post-ozawa-era.

8 Conclusion
Ozawa, visionary or villain?

In many respects, Ozawa has been a visionary in his endeavour to alter key institutional aspects of the Japanese political system: its party system, its electoral system and its policymaking system. He has been unique amongst Japanese law makers in having a grand design for how the political system should work and in demonstrating a concern for its future direction.

Besides his contributions to political system change, Ozawa also has wider significance as the pivot around which Japanese politics has revolved for a number of decades. As YP leader Watanabe Yoshimi once said, 'Whether one likes or dislikes Mr. Ozawa Ichirō, he has been the biggest issue in Japanese politics for over 20 years'.[1] At the very least, Ozawa has been one of Japan's most visible and vigorous politicians in the modern era,[2] a force to be reckoned with whether inside the ruling party or outside it. Part of his political prowess has been reflected in his ability to present himself as a larger-than-life figure.[3]

Undoubtedly one of the primary reasons for Ozawa's longstanding prominence has been his deployment of key instruments of political power centring on the acquisition and distribution of political funds and the amassing of a large group of loyalists amongst Diet members who backed his political ambitions. These assets were certainly decisive in extending Ozawa's political life, despite the vicissitudes of mandatory indictment and prosecution, his resignations as DPJ leader, secretary-general and member, the attacks of his own party executive and numerous backbenchers, and his failure to occupy the highest office in the land or decisively to influence the choice of the candidate to this position in more recent times.

Ozawa was able to draw on his own political funds and resources gathered as payback for the delivery of patronage to his clients in the construction industry. For decades, Ozawa exploited government-funded public works for private political gain. In the hope of winning public works contracts, construction companies were recruited and mobilised by the Ozawa office as electoral agents. They provided him and his favoured candidates with key electoral resources such as votes, funds and campaign assistance. The Isawa Dam in Iwate Prefecture stands as a monument to this style of construction-based politics centring on *doken senkyo* and *zenekon senkyo*.

Yet another important reason for Ozawa's enduring pre-eminence lay in the deft political skills that he cultivated and deployed to his political advantage over many years. The first of these was his legendary strength in elections, reflecting his understanding of what were effective electoral strategies, including the politically strategic distribution of state largesse to special interests and large social groups, and his ability to engineer the electoral success of large numbers of personally recruited candidates. The DPJ's victories in 2007 and 2009, for example, can largely be attributed to Ozawa, as can the individual victories of many 'new' faces that entered the Diet in these elections. In contrast, the DPJ's lacklustre performance in the 2010 Upper House election was partly due to Ozawa's absence from the party's election team.[4]

Another valuable political skill was Ozawa's flair for building administrations[5] and effecting 'regime change'. This was evident in 1993 with the creation of the Hosokawa administration, and again in 2009 with the formation of the Hatoyama administration. Perhaps the Hosokawa administration was his singular accomplishment in this respect. It required the gathering together of many political parties – eight in all. It is doubtful whether any other Diet member in national politics at that time could have brought off such a feat.

Finally, Ozawa consistently demonstrated genuine political leadership in addition to the 'confected' loyalties that he engendered in his followership through the distribution of patronage. Part of his powers of attraction was the respect he inspired in his followers because of his 'never say die' attitude and the possession of something akin to 'charisma'.[6] Time after time he demonstrated a phoenix-like capacity to rise from the political ashes when many had predicted his impending demise. This is notwithstanding his dictatorial ways, his Titanic ego, his desire for total control over parties and governments, his record of alienating those closest to him, and his penchant for treating both political allies and enemies with lack of due regard and respect.

Despite Ozawa's undeniable political talents and the mountain of commentary on him by both friends and foes, uncovering the 'real' Ozawa remains problematic. Viewed through the prism of old and new politics, he can be regarded as a front-room advocate of political reform, yet he perpetuated old politics through his political practices, including the way he behaved in parties, his attitude towards factions, and his behaviour as a fundraiser and policymaker. He preferred the role of backroom fixer who orchestrated deals from behind the scenes – the quintessential example of an old-style Japanese politician or shadow shogun.

These characteristics of Ozawa as a politician have lined up with another paired set of attributes: idealist and realist. He has been an idealist in his pursuit of political reforms whilst remaining a master of realpolitik in his willingness to do deals with anyone who would serve his political ends. While continually mouthing the rhetoric of reform, he acted according to a strategic power-seeking calculus that was the absolute antithesis of reform. In short, there was an enduring and fundamental disconnect between what Ozawa said and what he did. Ozawa has thus been Janus-faced: reformer and reactionary, conservative and socialist, an advocate of 'clean' politics while a practitioner of 'dirty' politics. Some might call this flexibility; others might describe it as contradictory, hypocritical and self-serving.

In the end, one must make a considered judgement about where the balance lies. A full and detailed account of Ozawa's political activities and behaviour, as attempted in this book, reaches the conclusion that while Ozawa preached new politics, he consistently practised old politics. In short, he did not practise what he preached. When it comes to having a vision for political reform, Ozawa's advocacy has never been in doubt, just his political conduct; not his goals, just his methods. The 'real' Ozawa is revealed by what he does, not what he says. In the end, the power-hungry Machiavellian Ozawa wins out over the principled Ozawa. The dominant Ozawa 'way' is not overt but covert, not open but opaque, not high- but low-profile, not clean but tainted with scandal. For Ozawa, the goal of maintaining and expanding his power has consistently overridden all others. All too often, reform has been a means, not an end in itself.

Having helped to achieve unprecedented regime change in 1993 and a similar reordering of the political world in 2009, it should have been Ozawa's continuing desire as a political reformer to entrench a healthy, functioning two-party system and a cabinet-centred government in line with the script that he himself had written. In both cases, Ozawa ignored his own script to try to maintain his own untrammelled power. He continued to operate outside the new rules he was instrumental in setting as if they did not apply to him. Although he vigorously pursued political system change, he himself did not change as a politician.

Ozawa's machinations to secure and maintain his power in the ruling party, and the constant threat of political destabilisation and realignment that he presented, profoundly undermined not only the Kan and Noda administrations but also the evolutionary process towards a two-party system in Japan. Despite his later attacks on the DPJ for violating the party's 2009 manifesto, Ozawa's manifest lack of respect for party loyalty and policy allegiance – his own and which he engendered in his followers – merely reflected his treatment of political parties over the decades – as instruments of personal power seeking rather than as formal organisations motivated by shared policy principles and a common ideology. It was difficult to reconcile this stance with Ozawa's stated goal of creating a stable two-party system where competition between the main ruling and opposition parties would be based on policy differences in a stable bipartisan system of party politics – ostensibly his main rationale for electoral reform.

So while Ozawa was an important figure in shaping the evolution of the party system in the sense of moving it from the rule of a single, dominant party through a series of coalition governments to the beginning of a two-party system, his actions threatened the consolidation of this system. His impact on the DPJ was both profound and deleterious. Although the party rebuffed all of Ozawa's attempts to bend it to his will, unlike previous parties that he had led, its resistance came at the tremendous cost of chronic instability bordering on political stasis and frequent loss of policy momentum, including further progress towards political reform. Ozawa thus turned out to be a corrosive force in the evolution of the two-party system in Japan.

Likewise, factions remained vital players for Ozawa in intra-party power plays. The DPJ groupings did not replicate exactly the LDP factions in their heyday:

there was no strict seniority principle in appointments to cabinet; the groups were not as tightly organised; and they existed mainly for elections to the leadership of the party. However, Ozawa's faction was different from all the rest in key respects. It was strictly hierarchical and consisted of a boss-leader and band of followers who displayed high levels of personal loyalty to Ozawa and dependence on his patronage. Because of these characteristics, Ozawa's 'group' could be deployed for much more than simply the DPJ's leadership election. At Ozawa's behest it was mobilised for a whole range of other purposes – for action against the party and government executive, in policy disputes and in Diet legislative processes as well as in maintaining the ever-present threat of defection. It is ironic that despite Ozawa's key goal of modernising Japan's party system, the way he led his own faction – with its heavy emphasis on money and obedience – was antithetical to the very notion of a modern political party. These aspects of Japanese politics remained salient under the DPJ, supposedly the party of 'regime change', principally because of Ozawa's influence.

Ozawa thus prevented the DPJ from further structural reform of Japanese politics by contributing to the preservation of old political institutions, organisations, groups, relationships, behaviours and norms. As much as anybody, he was responsible for the DPJ's failure to entrench new systems of politics and policymaking despite initially setting out to do so.[7]

Ozawa's record in relation to money politics was no better – perhaps worse. The balance of evidence suggests that he remained immersed in the kind of 'money-power politics' that some of the reforms he advocated were supposed to tackle. His constant scandals, legal imbroglios and connections with public works construction companies continued to bring his own reputation into disrepute, as well as casting a cloud over the conduct of Japanese politics as a whole. In fact, in so many ways, Ozawa's *modus operandi* was reminiscent of the bad old ways of LDP politics, which ultimately disqualified him as a reformer. Itō Atsuo, one of Ozawa's main critics who had worked on his staff in the past, argued that Ozawa was 'a self-contradictory figure. He has the head of a reformer, but from the neck down he is still an old, LDP-like factional politician'.[8] He may have been instrumental in getting rid of two LDP governments – in 1993 and in 2009 – but he ensured that Japanese politics never left LDP politics behind. Ozawa's style of politics was essentially based on the Tanaka model, with its key features of money politics, pork barrelling, power broking and factional supremacy. It was the prevalent model in Japan from the 1970s until Koizumi arrived in office in 2001 and tried to root it out by 'destroying the LDP', undermining the factions and offering a different type of personalised policy leadership based largely on direct appeals to unaffiliated urban voters.

Ozawa thus remained an historical anachronism, an unreconstructed figure like a shadow from the past, a throwback to an earlier era who embodied many of the pathologies of old politics. This made him a key agent of path dependence in Japanese politics. He may have 'reinvented himself several times'[9] but the essential core of his political being did not change. He merely added new layers to change the appearance of his politics but not the actual substance. The 'real'

Ozawa remained locked in the old politics paradigm, the personification of a previous political era.

Ozawa was called many bad things during his long and deep engagement in Japanese politics – by the media, by other politicians, by his former wife and erstwhile supporters, and not least by ordinary Japanese citizens, who were not slow to express their dislike for him openly. Ishikawa, Ozawa's loyal secretary, listed some of the epithets used to describe him: 'high-handed', 'dictator', 'tyrant', 'devil' and 'destroyer', to name a few.[10] Ishikawa also bemoaned the fact that when Kan was trying to defeat Ozawa by criticising his politics and money issues, the media also bashed Ozawa as a 'symbol of old politics' as well.[11]

This image was not just confected by Kan or by the media, however. It was one that Ozawa himself projected and exemplified. The spectre of Ozawa as an old-style politician continued to haunt him, harming his public persona and making Japanese voters impatient that so much energy of the country's politicians was being dissipated in unproductive power plays at the centre of which Ozawa habitually stood.

The DPJ was supposed to move Japanese politics further along the Ozawa-inspired continuum towards new politics. In 2009 it won by rejecting the LDP's politics and governance style. Although the DPJ could differentiate itself ideologically from the LDP in terms of a simple centre-left versus centre-right divide, it also wanted to stand for a new type of politics. In the end, however, it was Ozawa who effectively prevented the DPJ from attaining this goal. He was the main actor bringing LDP-like qualities back in, tarnishing the DPJ's image and raising the question whether the DPJ was in fact an LDP clone.[12]

Moreover, Ozawa practised the kind of old politics where the energies and efforts of Diet politicians were concentrated not on competing policies and competing political visions but on power struggles amongst politicians – the style of politics for which power becomes an end in itself. It is the kind of politics that is vicious, inward-looking and hard to understand for those outside Nagata-chō, and which increasingly degrades the politics of the country,[13] resulting in public apathy and disillusionment.

The September 2010 leadership contest between Ozawa and Kan was, therefore, about a lot more than the policies of the two contestants. It was also about what kind of politics Japan should have in the future. The DPJ faced a choice between two leaders from the same party who represented radically different ideals of how politics should be conducted. The subsequent intra-party war that ensued was due, at its core, to Ozawa's refusal to accept any diminution of his power as a result of his loss in that election. His loyalty to the DPJ always remained in question when he could not bend it to his will. Indeed, he pursued an all-out strategy of sabotaging the Kan administration in an attempt to ensure not only his political survival but also the perpetuation of his political predominance. He acted as a spoiler, doing all he could to bring down the Kan government. His contribution was nothing other than retrograde – for the DPJ and for Japan as well as for the Kan administration. His behaviour during the Noda administration continued along the same track. Two defiant DPJ prime ministers – Kan and Noda – thus paid a high price for Ozawa's overweening desire for political control.

One might argue that Ozawa was all along practising old politics in order to create new politics, that he wanted to restore his power in order to bring about reform. However, as the years have gone by, much of Ozawa's fervour for reform seems to have dissipated. Ironically, Ozawa in the early 1990s appeared to be much more of a new politician than Ozawa in the 2010s. Over time, his reform goals faded more into the background, leaving his old political methods and ambitions more exposed, despite the grandiose rhetoric to which he habitually resorted and the more vaguely articulated reform goals to which he alluded. Certainly, a concrete reform agenda became more and more difficult to discern, although Ozawa claimed to have written a sequel to *Blueprint*. In his 2010 campaign for the DPJ leadership, for example, the only vision of political reform that Ozawa offered was 'leadership of politicians over the bureaucracy', which he reiterated as leader of the PLF in the 2012 Lower House election campaign. This was a far cry from the comprehensive and far-reaching agenda for institutional reform that he proclaimed in earlier years. From his writings, he clearly envisaged a traditional Westminster cabinet-centred policymaking system in which the cabinet decided collectively and the party and bureaucracy followed. This path ensured the supremacy of elected politicians over bureaucrats, but Ozawa's behaviour in the DPJ did more than anybody else to undermine developments leading towards such a cabinet-centred policymaking system. Even his supporters questioned his accomplishments as a reformer, arguing that while Ozawa advocated reform, he had a long way to go before he could be called 'reformist'.[14]

In other respects also, Ozawa appears to have lost some of his finely honed political skills. One of his greatest strengths has always been his ability to formulate clear goals, whether relating to elections, politics or policies, and to devise clear strategies about how to achieve them, to which he would then apply his full power. However, in later years, his goal-driven behaviour increasingly came down to a narrowly focused, self-interested objective – using his power to retain and expand his power – a self-serving agenda geared to his political survival. In the endless machinations to which he lent himself in the DPJ, it became more difficult to discern any coherent and consistent policy goals beyond sticking to the DPJ's original manifesto and populist appeals such as the 2009 election mantra of 'putting the people's lives first', which he transposed into the title of his new party.

Moreover, because policies were always tools – for political action, for winning elections, for gaining personal political advantage, for implementing party realignment plans, and for galvanising his troops for and against particular administrations – not deeply held beliefs or convictions, Ozawa changed them quixotically according to his strategic calculations at the time. For this reason, Ozawa's policy convictions often seemed quite superficial. He might have advanced policy justifications for his behaviour but they were not the real reason why he chose a particular course of action, just a pretext.

Given the way that Ozawa discarded both policies and people, the question is whether he believed in anyone or anything.[15] His words and actions seemed to 'reflect...an enormous "emptiness" in the middle of his heart'.[16] One commentator resorted to the philosopher Nietzsche: 'Of him who surrenders himself to events there remains less and less. Great politicians can thus become completely empty men and yet once have been rich and full.'[17] In this way, Ozawa could be regarded as a mere shell of his former self.

Ozawa may still harbour some ambitions for political system change, but given that his own methods and practices consistently undermined many of the reforms that he had previously advocated, his role ultimately proved destructive, not creative, for the party of regime change in Japan and for the process of political structural reform as a whole. To the DPJ, Ozawa was both a blessing and a curse. He built it into a majority party with his electoral genius and yet he helped to bring it down with his scandals and other types of self-aggrandising behaviour.

If Ozawa had remained in the DPJ and put himself forward as a candidate for the party leadership in September 2012, this contest would have been about determining what kind of party the DPJ wanted to be and indeed the future direction of Japanese politics. An Ozawa victory would certainly have presented an entirely new challenge for Ozawa himself and a novel political situation for the Japanese public. Throughout his long career, which began in 1969, Ozawa had never led a government from the front. It was always from behind and usually from the position of party secretary-general – in the Kaifu, Hosokawa and Hatoyama administrations, for example.

As it turned out, Ozawa left the DPJ with the hope that he might again be a catalyst for realigning party politics. He was certainly open to the possibility of amalgamating with other political groupings. At the same time, however, Ozawa's departure from the DPJ looked as if it might herald the beginning of the end of his political career. His old political style undermined public support, to which the poor performance of his two new parties in the 2012 and 2013 elections attested. It was clear that voters had unequivocally rejected Ozawa's brand of politics. Similarly, his ability to attract new followers was considerably truncated, given his poor political prospects. These two political factors were mutually reinforcing. Declining popularity led to a lessening of his powers of attraction, which weakened his power further. Ozawa's legendary ability to change Japanese politics had collapsed. As Kuji once predicted, 'Ozawa is not popular. Once he loses money, power and posts, it will be the end of him'.[18]

Although it is impossible to foretell accurately whether Ozawa will stage yet another dramatic revival on Japan's political stage, given the circumstances in which he currently finds himself, his return is highly improbable. Despite his legendary powers for making comebacks, the omens are not auspicious. He has simply run out of time and supporters, and his pariah status has alienated any prospective new party allies, who do not want their own political image to be tarnished by associating with him. He has become politically redundant, a political outcast consigned to the periphery of the political arena, which no longer 'spins on the Ozawa axis'. Japanese politics has moved on from the Ozawa era. It is just a question of whether his inevitable political demise is a long drawn-out affair or a quick political death.

Ozawa's ultimate departure from politics will leave a mixed and uncertain legacy. Whatever this is, it is clear that no other politician will directly inherit it. His style of politics is widely spurned by other politicians, the public and the media. Other Diet members have no incentive to follow the Ozawa model. Nor has he groomed a successor as Tanaka and Kanemaru did. Ozawa inherited their mantle, but because he has been so jealous of his own power, so dictatorial and unable to brook any rival within his own group, he has no heir-apparent. While still in the DPJ, Ozawa jealously guarded his candidate selection know-how. Moreover, his faction was held together by his personal patronage, which made him irreplaceable. No other politician could step into his shoes in terms of money power. At the same time, the Ozawa 'way' was associated with money-politics scandals, which had unfavourable legal consequences.

The succession issue puts Ozawa in a bind. On the one hand, lack of an obvious heir remains a source of weakness in his party because members have no secure prospects. If Ozawa cannot maintain his forceful presence, whether due to ill health, or because of scandal or for some other reason including electoral failure, then he risks shedding followers, whether they are members of his faction or political party. Ozawa needs leadership positions or the prospect of positions to attract followers. Consigned to the opposition with an uncertain future presents a dismal outlook. In these circumstances, both Ozawa and his party will fizzle out and Japanese politics will move on without him. On the other hand, even if a suitable successor were to be found, the new leader, in order to build his own identity and control, would inevitably bring the curtain down on the Ozawa era. In this event, Ozawa risks being cast aside and made redundant.

In whatever manner Ozawa's political demise occurs, his particular style of politics will be extinguished with his departure from the political scene. In short, when he goes, the Ozawa 'model' will cease to exist. At some point in the future, Ozawa's long and meandering political journey will end and he will disappear from the political scene permanently, rather than just temporarily in order to plot a triumphant return, which has long been his practice. Whether this will mean that the new politics along the lines that Ozawa originally envisaged will flourish remains an open question. One thing is certain: Ozawa's exit from public life, whether a sudden or a gradual process, will be a turning point in the history of Japanese politics.

Notes

1 '"Minna no Tō wa Ozawa san iranai"', in *Asahi Shinbun*, p. 4.
2 Samuels, *Machiavelli's Children*, p. 326.
3 Sano, 'Commentary', www.asahi.com/english/TKY201009020394.html.
4 Tahara, '"Fukō" na seijika', www.nikkeibp.co.jp/article/column/20120426/307058/.
5 Ibid.
6 Some critics argue that Ozawa 'lacks the personal magnetism and charisma of past LDP bigwigs, such as former Prime Ministers Kakuei Tanaka, Takeo Fukuda and Masayoshi Ohira'. Sano, 'Commentary', www.asahi.com/english/TKY201009020394.html.

7 Mikuriya, 'Mō "Yami-shōkun" wa umarenai', p. 95.
8 '"Seiji kaikaku no kishu"', tukamoto-office.seesaa.net/article/141084654.html. Itō was quoted as saying something very similar on the TV programme 'Super Morning', when he said, 'Ozawa has the head of a reformer, but from the neck down, he is just an old LDP politician'. Itō, 'Hatsugen', ja.wikipedia.org/wiki/伊藤敦夫.
9 Samuels, *Machiavelli's Children*, p. 326.
10 Ishikawa, *Akutō*, p. 162.
11 Ibid., p. 208.
12 Oba, 'DPJ Members', e.nikkei.com/e/ac/20090720/TNW/Nni20090720FP7DPJ02.htm.
13 Hara, 'Kokumin no akireta shisen', diamond.jp/articles/-/9199.
14 Watanabe, *Ozawa Ichirō Kirawareru Densetsu*, p. 52.
15 Abiru, 'Minshutō', p. 45.
16 Ibid.
17 Nietzsche (R.J. Hollingdale trans.), *Human*, p. 284, quoted in Abiru, 'Minshutō', p. 45.
18 Kuji, *Ozawa Ichirō – Sono 'Kyōfu Shihai' no Jittai*, p. 207.

Bibliography

Abiru Rui, 'Seiji shikin shūshi hōkokusho o mite kangaeta koto, wakaranai koto', *Kuni o urei, ware to waga mi o amayakasu no ki*, 16 September 2007, abirur.iza.ne.jp/blog/day/20070916/.
Abiru Rui, 'Minshutō "A kyū senpan" hōtei (2) "Kūkyo na zangai" no kashita Ozawa Ichirō', *Shūkan Bunshun*, Vol. 55, No. 22, 6 June 2013, 44–45.
Adelstein, Jake, 'The Last Yakuza', *World Policy Journal*, Vol. 27, No. 2, June 2010, 68–69.
Akasaka Tarō, 'The Making of a Non-LDP Administration', *Japan Echo*, Vol. 20, No. 4, Winter 1993, 8–13.
Akasaka Tarō, '"Posuto Hatoyama", Ozawa no hara no uchi', *Bungei Shunjū*, 14 January 2010, gekkan.bunshun.jp/articles/-/216.
Akasaka Tarō, '"Ozawa kiri" to "dairenritsu sōdō" no yukue', *Bungei Shunjū*, 11 January 2011, gekkan.bunshun.jp/articles/-/229.
Akasaka Tarō, 'Sengoku ga nagashita namida to Ozawa no kaminadonomi', *Bungei Shunjū*, 10 February 2011, gekkan.bunshun.jp/articles/-/230.
Akasaka Tarō, 'Ozawa Ichirō mata mo ya yaburetari', *Bungei Shunjū*, 12 September 2011, gekkan.bunshun.jp/articles/-/249.
Akasaka Tarō, 'Hashimoto Tōru ga nerau "shushō no za"', *Bungei Shunjū*, 12 March 2012, gekkan.bunshun.jp/articles/-/304.
Aldrich, John H., *Why Parties? The Origin and Transformation of Political Parties in America*, Chicago, IL: University of Chicago Press, 1995.
Andō Takeshi, 'Seisō no hate no "okizari Nippon"', *Nikkei Business Online*, 2 July 2012, business.nikkeibp.co.jp/article/topics/20120628/233886/?rt=nocnt.
Angel, Robert, *Pork, People, Procedure, or Policy? What Will Reconfigure Japan's Political Party System?* Paper prepared for the Southern Japan Seminar, Panama City Beach, Florida, 8 October 1994.
Aozora no Shakaigaku, 'Saiaku! Ozawa Ichirō no taizai! (4) Zenekon seiji no teiō!' 12 November 2012, blog.goo.ne.jp/handa3douzo/e/829ba12a41604bec9e2ba2a7a2add57b.
Asahi Japan Watch, 'Ozawa: Noda's Cabinet Lineup "Well-balanced"', 5 September 2011, ajw.asahi.com/article/behind_news/AJ201109059158.
Asahi Japan Watch, 'Guilty Verdicts Could Dash Ozawa's Comeback Strategy', 27 September 2011, ajw.asahi.com/article/behind_news/politics/AJ2011092712240.
Asahi Shinbun, 'DPJ Ozawa Promises National Post Office Chiefs to Have Postal Reform Bill Enacted in Current Diet Session', 24 May 2010, 1.
Asahi Shinbun, '(Jijikokukoku) Kan karā, Shushō fukken', 9 June 2010, 2.
Asahi Shinbun, 'Minshu Ozawa-shi "ippeisotsu toshite biryoku tsukusu" Edano Kanjichō to kaidan', 10 June 2010, 1.

Bibliography

Asahi Shinbun, 'Kokka Senryaku Kyoku kōsō o dannen o kakuage sezu teigen kikan ni', 16 July 2010, 1.
Asahi Shinbun, 'Minshu daihyōsen, Ozawa-shi ga shutsuba hyōmē', 26 August 2010, 1.
Asahi Shinbun, '"Shushō no shishitsu" zessen', 2 September 2010, 1.
Asahi Shinbun, '"Minna no Tō wa Ozawa san iranai"', 3 September 2010, 4.
Asahi Shinbun, 'Editorial: Decentralization Debate', 7 September 2010, doshusei.wordpress.com/2010/09/07/editorialdecentralisationdebat/.
Asahi Shinbun, '(Shasetsu) Chiiki shuken ronsō', 7 September 2010, shasetsu.ps.land.to/index.cgi/event/475/.
Asahi Shinbun, 'Ozawa kiri sengen', 5 January 2011, 1.
Asahi Shinbun, '(Jijikokkoku) Tenbō naki Ozawa giri', 1 February 2011, 2.
Asahi Shinbun, 'Kaiha ridatsu todoke', 19 February 2011, 4.
Asahi Shinbun, 'Ozawa-shi ga yotte kuru ninki no chiiki seitō', 24 February 2011, 4.
Asahi Shinbun, 'Minshu Ozawa-kei no Matsuki seimukan ga jii hyōmei', 24 February 2011, 1.
Asahi Shinbun, 'Point of View/Yoshibumi Wakamiya: Kan Should Step Down and Return to Being a Guerrilla Lawmaker', 4 August 2011, ajw.asahi.com/article/0311disaster/fukushima/AJ201108045264.
Asahi Shinbun, 'Zōzei kaisan nara seikai saihen', 23 February 2012, 1.
Asahi Shinbun, '(Intabyū) Shōhizei to seikai saihen', 24 February 2012, 17.
Asahi Shinbun, 'The Tumultuous Life of Ichiro Ozawa', 26 April 2012, ajw.asahi.com/article/behind_news/politics/AJ201204260030.
Asahi Shinbun, 'Ozawa-shi, shōhizei zōzei hōan ni aratamete hantai shimesu', 12 May 2012, www.asahi.com/politics/update/0512/TKY201205120364.html.
Asahi Shinbun, 'Ozawa moto daihyō – mujun darake no zōzei hantai', 19 June 2012, www.asahi.com/paper/editorial20120619.html.
Asahi Shinbun, 'Yotō kahansūware ni genjitsumi', 22 June 2012, 3.
Asahi Shinbun, 'Minshu no bunretsu fukahi', 22 June 2012, 1.
Asahi Shinbun, 'Noda seiken, kuzureru ashimoto', 27 June 2012, 2.
Asahi Shinbun, 'Ozawa-shi ra ritō fukahi', 29 June 2012, 1.
Asahi Shinbun, 'Kuzureta nidai seitō sei', 3 July 2012, digital.asahi.com/articles/TKY201207020574.html?ref=comkiji_txt_end.
Asahi Shinbun, '"Mirai" no seisaku, Ozawa shoku', 30 November 2012, 4.
Asahi Shinbun, 'Mirai, "sotsu genpatsu" todokazu', 17 December 2012, 3.
Asahi Shinbun, 'Kada, Ozawa Split Up Anti-nuclear Tomorrow Party of Japan', 29 December 2012, ajw.asahi.com/article/behind_news/politics/AJ201212290065.
Asahi Shinbun, 'Hireiku, Kaihyō sokuhō, 2013 Saninsen', 2013, www.asahi.com/senkyo/senkyo2013/kaihyo/C01.html.
Asahi.com, 'Editorial: Incoherent Road Policy', 12 March 2010, www.asahi.com/english/TKY201003110392.html.
Asahi.com, 'Editorial: Six Months of Hatoyama', 16 March 2010, www.asahi.com/english/TKY201003160331.html.
Asahi.com, 'Kokudō yosan, tōketsu wa 4 rosen domari', 26 March 2010, www.asahi.com/politics/update/0326/TKY201003260514.html?ref=any.
Asahi.com, 'Editorial: Flip-flop on Highway Tolls', 23 April 2010, www.asahi.com/english/TKY201004230358.html.
Asahi.com, 'Yūsei kaikaku hōan no konkokkai seiritsu', 24 May 2010, www.asahi.com/politics/update/0523/TKY201005230332.html?ref=any.
Asahi.com, 'Ozawa-shi ga Minshutō daihyōsen ni shutsuba hyōmei', 26 August 2010, www.asahi.com/politics/update/0826/TKY201008260089.html?ref=reca.

Asahi.com, 'Ozawa Seeks Support for Political Realignment Ambitions', 12 March 2011, www.asahi.com/english/TKY201103110181.html.
Asahi.com, 'Ozawa Prepares for Move to Oust Kan', 15 April 2011, www.asahi.com/english/TY201104140127.html.
Asahi.com, 'Ozawa Moves to Regain Influence in DPJ Election', 14 August 2011, www.asahi.com/english/TKY201108130261.html.
Asahi.com, 'Who's Who of DPJ Leaders May Run for Party President', 21 August 2011, www.asahi.com/english/TKY201108200153.html.
Asahi.com, 'Ozawa Remains Kingmaker in DPJ Leadership Race', 23 August 2011, www.asahi.com/english/TKY201108220263.html.
Asahi.com, 'Maehara's Tightrope Strategy for Gaining Ozawa's Support', 26 August 2011, ajw.asahi.com/article//behind_news/AJ201108257452.
Asahi.com, 'Noda shin seiken, hikitsuzuki tōnai yūwa to yoyatō renkei ga kadai', 29 August 2011, www.asahi.com/business/news/reuters/RTR201108290081.html?ref=reca.
Asahi.com, 'Anti-Ozawa Vote Key to Noda's Victory', 31 August 2011, ajw.asahi.com/article/behind_news/AJ201108308360.
Asahi.com, 'Japan's New Prime Minister Faces a Dark Horizon', 31 August 2011, ajw.asahi.com/article/behind_news/politics/AJ20110830833.
Asahi.com, 'Analysis/Noda's Party Personnel Picks Reflect Need for Unity, Balance', 1 September 2011, www.asahi.com/english/TKY201108310232.html.
Asahi.com, 'Ozawa Consolidating Supporters for Next DPJ Election', 1 September 2011, www.asahi.com/english/TKY201108310224.html.
Asahi.com, 'Editorial: Ozawa Still Refusing to Give an Explanation', 8 October 2011, www.asahi.com/english/TKY201110070305.html.
Asia News Network, 'Ozawa Must Take Responsibility', 2 February 2011, www.asianews.net/home/news.php?sec=3&id=17181.
Asiaone News, 'Ozawa Aims to Regain Clout after Election', 6 June 2010, www.asiaone.com/News/Latest+News/Asia/Story/A1Story20100606-220500.html.
Atarashii Seisaku Kenkyūkai (Giji Yōshi), 9 February 2012, shinseiken.jp/pdf/120209.pdf.
Atarashii Seisaku Kenkyūkai (Giji Yōshi), 22 March 2012, shinseiken.jp/pdf/120322.pdf.
Atarashii Seisaku Kenkyūkai, 'Shinseiken "Rippōfu no arikata" bunkakai chūkan hōkoku gaiyō', 7 June 2012, shinseiken.jp/pdf/rippougaiyou.pdf.
Atarashii Seisaku Kenkyūkai, 'Keiki taisaku chūkan torimatome', 6 September 2012, shinseiken.jp/pdf/keikityuukan.pdf.
Atarashii Seisaku Kenkyūkai, '"Kuni no tōchi" benkyōkai chūkan hōkoku', n.d., shinseiken.jp/pdf/kunityuukan.pdf.
Azuma Takeo and Ito Yutaka, 'Fear of Ozawa's Power Key to Maehara's Bid', *Daily Yomiuri* online, 24 August 2011, www.yomiuri.co.jp/dy/national/T110823006082.htm.
Blechinger-Talcott, Verena, 'Shifting Incentives for Political Leadership', in Marie Soderberg and Patricia A. Nelson (eds) *Japan's Politics and Economy: Perspectives on Change*, London and New York: Routledge, 2009.
Bowen, Roger W., *Japan's Dysfunctional Democracy: The Liberal Democratic Party and Structural Corruption*, New York and London: M.E. Sharpe, 2003.
BPnet, 'Ozawa shintō wa Shū San 50 nin de "kaizu naki kōkai" e', 3 July 2012, www.nikkeibp.co.jp/article/column/20120703/314579/.
Bungei Shunjū, 'Wareware wa naze kaikaku o mezasu ka', Vol. 70, No. 13, December 1992, 136–149.
Bungei Shunjū, '"Kan nuki renritsu" shuyakutachi no dōshōimu', 11 May 2011, gekkan.bunshun.jp/articles/-/241.

Bungei Shunjū, 'Noda to Ozawa ga idomu "Roshian rūretto"', 10 April 2012, gekkan.bunshun.jp/articles/-/332.

Bungei Shunjū, 'Noda Shushō ni nokosareta saigo no "sentaku"', 8 June 2012, gekkan.bunshun.jp/articles/-/377.

Bungei Shunjū, 'Ozawa Ichirō koppu no naka no "sensō"', 10 July 2012, gekkan.bunshun.jp/articles/-/397.

Christensen, Raymond V., 'Electoral Reform in Japan: How it was Enacted and Changes it May Bring', *Asian Survey*, Vol. 34, No. 7, July 1994, 589–605.

Chūgoku Shinbun, 'Kan seiken no jyūgokagetsu', 27 August 2011, www.chugoku-np.co.jp/Syasetu/Sh201108270068.html.

Cucek, Michael, 'The Dark Side of the Moon', *Shisaku*, 8 February 2010, shisaku.blogspot.com/2010/02/dark-side-of-moon.html.

Cucek, Michael, 'Comment on "Japanese Leadership Fails at Post-disaster Reconstruction Test"', 22 August 2011, www.eastasiaforum.org/2011/08/14/japanese-leadership-fails-at-post-disaster-reconstuction-test/#more-20887.

Cucek, Michael, 'Ichiro Ozawa's Last Battle as a Democrat?' *Shisaku*, 24 August 2011, shisaku.blogspot.com/2011/08/ozawa-ichiros-last-battle-as-democrat.html.

Cucek, Michael, 'Public Funding of Elections', *Shisaku*, 11 April 2012, shisaku.blogspot.com.au/2012/04/party-by-numbers.html.

Curtis, Gerald, *The Logic of Japanese Politics: Leaders, Institutions, and the Limits of Change*, New York: Columbia University Press, 1999.

Daily Yomiuri, 'Iron Fist Suppresses Free Speech Within DPJ', 22 March 2010, www.yomiuri.co.jp/dy/editorial/20100322TDY02307.htm.

Daily Yomiuri, 'Twists and Turns on Ozawa's Path to Candidacy', 2 September 2010, www.yomiuri.co.jp/dy/national/T100901006367.htm.

Daily Yomiuri, 'Ozawa's Power Built on Cash, Report Shows', 2 December 2010, www.yomiuri.co.jp/dy/national/T101201005616.htm.

Daily Yomiuri, 'Ozawa Sworn Testimony Sought', 23 December 2010, www.yomiuri.co.jp/dy/national/T101222004894.htm.

Daily Yomiuri, 'Kan Survives No-confidence Vote', 3 June 2011, www.yomiuri.co.jp/dy/national/T110602005835.htm.

Daily Yomiuri, 'Post-Kan DPJ Preparations Gathering Pace', 11 August 2011, www.yomiuri.co.jp/dy/national/T110810005847htm.

Daily Yomiuri, 'Noda Maintains Cautious Stance', 8 September 2011, www.yomiuri.co.jp/dy/national/T110908005715.htm.

Daily Yomiuri, 'Ex-Ozawa Aides Found Guilty/Decisions on All 3 Certain to Affect Former DPJ Head's Trial', 27 September 2011, www.yomiuri.co.jp/dy/national/T110926005647.htm.

Daily Yomiuri, 'Ozawa Pleads Not Guilty', 7 October 2011, www.yomiuri.co.jp/dy/national/T111006005170.htm.

Daily Yomiuri, 'Ozawa's Remarks Inconsistent', 7 October 2011, www.yomiuri.co.jp/dy/nation/T111006005909.htm.

Daily Yomiuri, 'PM Indicates Intention to Join TPP Talks', 10 October 2011, www.yomiuri.co.jp/dy/nationa/T111009003175.htm.

Daily Yomiuri, '3 Pro-Ozawa Groups Rally the Forces', 23 December 2011, www.yomiuri.co.jp/dy/national/T111222004981.htm.

Daily Yomiuri, 'Noda's Party Unity Hopes Dim', 15 January 2012, www.yomiuri.co.jp/dy/national/T120114003873.htm.

Daily Yomiuri, 'Ozawa Prosecution Mulls Appeal', 29 April 2012, 1.

Daily Yomiuri, 'Ozawa has Hard Road Ahead', 2 July 2012, www.yomiuri.co.jp/dy/national/T120701002319.htm.

Diamond, 'Seiji anarisuto Itō Atsuo ga konmei kiwameru seiji o kiru!' *Diamond Online*, No. 19, 14 June 2011, diamond.jp/articles/-/12698.

Diamond, 'Seiji koramunisuto Gotō Kenji, aratana seikyoku o kiru! "Noda seiken wa konmei no 'onnen seiji' o fusshoku dekiru ka"', *Diamond Online*, No. 35, 9 September 2011, diamond.jp/articles/-/13959.

The Economist, 'A Magician in Japan: Will the "Koizumi Revolution" Catch or Fizzle?' 26 April 2001, www.economist.com.hk/node/592427.

The Economist, 'Bad Blood: A Change of Finance Minister Shows Who Wields Power in Japan's Ruling Party', 6 January 2010, www.economist.com/world/asia/displayStory.cfm?story_id=15210046.

The Economist, 'Japan's Leadership Challenge – The Dark Side: Ichiro Ozawa has Troubling Connections. Yet Some in Japan Cast him as a Saviour', 9 September 2010, www.economist.con/node/16992215?story_id=16992215.

The Economist, 'Japan's Ichiro Ozawa: A Shadow of a Shogun', 30 June 2012, www.economist.com/node/21557788.

Emura Junichirō, '"Popyurizumu" "anchi" to shite no Ozawa shintō no seisaku', *Webronza*, 14 July 2012, astand.asahi.com/magazine/wrpolitics/2012071300008.html?iref=webronza.

Endō Kōichi, *Shōhi Sareru Kenryokusha: Ozawa Ichirō kara Koizumi Junichirō e*, Tokyo: Chūō Kōron Shinsha, 2001.

Endō Noriko, 'TPP wa kiki de wa naku kōki', *Diamond Online*, No. 125, 15 November 2010, diamond.jp/articles/-/10068.

Etō Jun, 'Why I Back Ozawa Ichirō', *Japan Echo*, Vol. 20, No. 1, Spring 1993, 18–23.

Foreign Press Center, Japan, 'Inauguration of the Aso Cabinet and the Political Situation from Now On', 29 September 2008, www.at.emb-japan.go.jp/English/japanbriefarchive.htm.

Foresight, 'Hatoyama seiken o torikakomu nijū sanjū no "fuan"', 15 December 2009, www.fsight.jp/article/5332.

Foresight, 'Seikai saihen fukumi de, Seikyoku wa gogatsu "saidai no yamaba" e', 16 April 2010, www.fsight.jp/article/5599.

47News, 'Kenkin jittai, kaimei e, Zenekon shiten kanbu ra chōshu', 12 March 2009, www.47news.jp/CN/200903/CN2009031201000914.html.

Fudesaka Hideyo, 'Kenryoku tōsō to seikyoku dake no otoko – Ozawa Ichirō', *Japan Business Press*, 27 August 2012, jbpress.ismedia.jp/articles/-/35958.

Fudesaka Hideyo, 'Seijika toshite no meimyaku wa mohaya tsukita Ozawa Ichirō', *Japan Business Press*, 10 September 2012, jbpress.ismedia.jp/articles/-/36052.

Futami Nobuaki, 'Naze, imadoki Ozawa Ichirō ka', *The Journal*, 10 November 2012, www.the-journal.jp/contents/futami/2012/11/post_44.html.

Futami Nobuaki, 'Ozawa "Seikatsu no Tō" wa dai nikyoku ni nareru ka', *The Journal*, 31 January 2013, www.the-journal.jp/contents/futami/2013/01/post_46.html.

Gaunder, Alisa, 'Reform Leadership in the United States and Japan: A Comparison of John McCain and Ozawa Ichirō', *Leadership*, Vol. 3, No. 2, May 2007, 173–190.

Gaunder, Alisa, *Political Reform in Japan: Leadership Looming Large*, London and New York: Routledge, 2007.

Gendai Bijinesu, 'Nagata-chō gekishin sukūpu: Tsugi wa Maehara ka Okada', 20 December 2010, gendai.ismedia.jp/articles/-/1760.

Gendai.net, 'Fukken ni hisaku ari, Ozawa gurūpu ga yōi suru kakushidama', 11 May 2012, gendai.net/articles/view/syakai/136509.

Gendai.net, 'Ozawa shintō yoyū no shūake enki', 30 June 2012, gendai.net/articles/view/news/137323.

Gendai.net, 'Ozawa Ichirō ga katatta yatō saihen 3-nen shinario', 27 June 2013, gendai.net/articles/view/syakai/143144.

George Mulgan, Aurelia, *Japan's Failed Revolution: Koizumi and the Politics of Economic Reform*, Canberra: ANU E-Press, 2002.

George Mulgan, Aurelia, 'No Interests, No Connections and No Expertise: The Man in Charge of Japanese Agriculture', *East Asia Forum*, 20 September 2009, www.eastasiaforum.org/2009/09/20/no-interests-no-connections-and-no-expertise-the-man-in-charge-of-japanese-agriculture/.

George Mulgan, Aurelia, 'The Perils of Japanese Politics', *Japan Forum*, Vol. 21, No. 2, September 2009, 183–208.

Goromaru Kenichi, '(Minshutō kenkyū 4) "Chokusetsu kyūfu"', *Asahi Shinbun*, 8 September 2009, 4.

Gotō Kenji, '"Ozawa fūji" o nerau Kan shushō no kyōmi bukai jinmyaku', *Diamond Online*, No. 116, 17 September 2010, diamond.jp/articles/-/9433.

Gotō Kenji, 'Noda shin seiken ga funade: Hayaku mo kusuburu onnen no hidane', *Diamond Online*, No. 135, 5 September 2011, diamond.jp/articles/-/13874.

Gotō Kenji, Hara Eijirō and Obi Takuya, 'Seiji koramunisuto Gotō Kenji ga "posuto 4.26 seikyoku" o kiru!' *Diamond Online*, No. 263, 7 May 2012, diamond.jp/articles/-/18112.

Hanaoka Nobuaki, *'Ozawa Shintō' wa Nani o Mezasu ka?! Nihon ga Jōcho Seiji to Ketsubetsu Suru Hi*, Tokyo: Sando Ke Shuppankyoku, 1994.

Hara Eijirō, 'Kokumin no akireta shisen sura rikai dekinai tei reberu', *Diamond Online*, No. 77, 27 August 2010, diamond.jp/articles/-/9199.

Hara Eijirō, 'Kono kuni no seiji wa naze kaku mo rekka shita no ka', *Diamond Online*, No. 17, 6 June 2011, diamond.jp/articles/-/12568.

Harada Satoru, 'Sukōpu: Kyōtō ashibumi, Jitsuryokusha angya', *Tōkyō Shinbun*, 16 September 2010, 2.

Hashimoto Gorō, 'Minshutō zen daihyō Ozawa Ichirō o meguru nazo', *Nikkan Gendai*, 27 April 2012, 374–379.

Hatena Diary, 13 November 2010, d.hatena.ne.jp/kojitaken/20101113/1289625937.

Hayano Tōru, *Ozawa Ichirō Tanken*, Tokyo: Asahi Shinbunsha, 1995.

Hayashi Yuka, 'Long, Hot Summer for Kan, Ozawa and DPJ', *JapanRealTime*, 24 August 2010, blogs.wsj.com/japanrealtime/2010/08/24/long-hot-summer-for-kan-ozawa-and-dpj/.

Hayashi Yuka and Sekiguchi Toko, 'WSJ: Ozawa Challenges Kan Over Nuclear Crisis', *Nikkei.com*, 27 May 2011, e.nikkei.com/e/ac/tnks/Nni20110527D27JF067htm.

Herzog, Peter J., *Japan's Pseudo-Democracy*, Kent: Curzon Press, 1993.

Hirano Sadao, *Ozawa Ichirō to no Nijūnen: 'Seikai Saihen' Butaiura*, Tokyo: Purejidentosha, 1996.

Hirano Sadao, *Shinsetsu! Ozawa Ichirō Bōsatsu Jiken – Nihon no Kīki wa Sukueru ka*, Tokyo: Bijinesusha, 2013.

Hirata Ikuo, 'DPJ Must Take Care Not to Let "Kindness" Stifle Self-help Spirit', *Nikkei Weekly*, 2 November 2009, e.nikkei.com/e/ac/20091102/TNW/Nni20091102OP2KIND1.htm.

Hongo Jun, 'Ozawa's Sway Over DPJ Remains Absolute', *Japan Times*, 28 January 2010, www.japantimes.co.jp/text/nn20100128f1.html.

Hoshi Hiroshi, 'Left Behind by the Reform Bandwagon: Ozawa's Political Strategy', *AJISS-Commentary*, No. 88, 9 April 2010, www.jiia.or.jp/en_commentary/pdf/AJISS-Commentary88.pdf.

Hosokawa Morihiro, *Naishōroku: Hosokawa Morihiro Sōridaijin Nikki*, Tokyo: Nihon Keizai Shinbun Shuppansha, 2010.
Hosoya Yuichi, 'What Really Comes First for Ozawa Ichirō?' *Nippon.com*, 18 July 2012, www.nippon.com/en/column/g00051/.
House of Japan, 'Ozawa and the Diet', 24 January 2011, www.houseofjapan.com/local/ozawa-and-the-diet.
Hunziker, Steven and Kamimura Ikuro, *Kakuei Tanaka: A Political Biography of Modern Japan*, n.d., www.rcrinc.com/tanaka/ch5-4.html.
Ichimura Takafumi, 'Ozawa Ichirō ga TPP ni hantai shinai wake', *Nikkei Business Online*, 10 November 2011, business.nikkeibp.co.jp/article/topics/20111109/223726/.
Ichinokuchi Haruhito, 'Minshutō no "Nōkyō Tubusi" ga kasoku suru', *Foresight*, 1 November 2009, www.fsight.jp/article/5241.
Iinuma Yoshisuke, 'Referendum on Ozawa: The Monthly Magazines Examine the Shadow Shogun', *The Oriental Economist Report*, Vol. 78, No. 4, April 2010, 8–9.
Iinuma Yoshisuke, 'Behind the Gridlock: Why Japan Seems Ungovernable', *The Oriental Economist Report*, Vol. 79, No. 3, March 2011, 5–6.
Ikeguchi Jiro and Kiyonaga Yoshihiro, 'Japan's Ex-DPJ Head's Exact Role Not Yet Clear', *Yomiuri Shinbun*, 29 November 2012, www.asianewsnet.net/news-39566.html.
Ikushima Akihiro, 'Sukōpu: Shikkōbu hihan', *Tōkyō Shinbun*, 2 July 2010, 2.
Imahori Morimichi, '"Ishihara shintō" futatabi ugoita', *Sankei Shinbun*, 21 May 2012, 1.
Imahori Morimichi and Yamamoto Takeshi, 'Shōhi zōzei hōan', *MSN Sankei News*, 10 February 2012, sankei.jp.msn.com/politics/news/120210/plc12021002040001-n1.htm.
Ise Akifumi, *Ozawa Ichirō no Wanryoku Pointo Yomi*, Tokyo: Asuka Shuppansha, 1994.
Iseri Hirofumi, '"Seitō" hōkai genshō o okoshita Jimintō', *Sekai*, No. 799, December 2009, 53–62.
Ishihara Nobuo, *Kan Kaku Aru Beshi*, Tokyo: Shogakukan, 1998.
Ishikawa Kazuo, 'Seifu yotō no seisaku kettei shisutemu "kakushō seisaku kaigi" shinsetsu', 19 September 2009, blog.canpan.info/ishikawa/archive/471.
Ishikawa Tomohiro, *Akutō Ozawa Ichirō ni Tsukaete*, Tokyo: Asahi Shinbun Shuppan, 2011.
Ishikawa Tomohiro, *Zōkingake: Ozawa Ichirō to iu Shiren*, Tokyo: Shinchōsha, 2012.
Ishikawa Tomohiro, 'Sōsa dankai no kyōjutsu chōsho ga kotogotoku shōko fusaiyō ni nari Ozawa-shi no muzai ga nōkō ni', in 'Ozawa Ichirō saiban hōdō: Seiki no bōryaku no zenryaku o shōhō', *Nikkan Gendai*, 27 April 2012, 453–455.
Ishizuka Masahiko, 'Japan Can't Seem to Shake Off Old Ghost of Money Politics', *Nikkei Weekly*, 22 February 2010, e.nikkei.com/e/ac/20100222/TNW/Nni20100222OP7DIARY.htm.
Isoyama Tomoyuki, 'Can the DPJ Government Recover?' *Nikkei Business Online*, 14 June 2010, business.nikkeibp.co.jp/article/eng/20100614/214930/.
iStockAnalyst, '"Ōkubo "Ordered Nishimatsu Fund Switch"', 20 March 2009, www.istockanalyst.com/article/viewiStockNews/articleid/3135483.
Itagaki Hidenori, *Heisei Dōran: Ozawa Ichirō no Yabō*, Tokyo: Dieichishi, 1993.
Itō Atsuo, *Seitō Hōkai: Nagata-chō no Ushinawareta Jūnen*, Tokyo: Shinchōsha, 2003.
Itō Atsuo, 'Dare mo shiranai Minshutō kenkyū: Ozawa chirudoren hyakunin de "Tanaka ha" fukkatsu, Seitō o tsukaisute ni shite kita otoko ga futatabi daihabatsu o tsukuriageru', *Bungei Shunjū*, Vol. 87, No. 11, September 2009, 138–144.
Itō Atsuo, 'Gisō kenkin no tenmatsu to Ozawa no soko shirenu senryaku (Sono 2)', *Chūō Kōron*, 13 January 2010.
Itō Atsuo, '"Seiji kaikaku no kishu" ga yami shōgun ni naru hi', *Chūō Kōron*, Vol. 125, No. 3, March 2010, 100–103, tukamoto-office.seesaa.net/article/141084654.html.

Itō Atsuo, 'Hatoyama • Ozawa jinin! Sore de mo Ozawa rosen shikanai Minshutō no danmatsuma', *Chūō Kōron*, Vol. 125, No. 7, July 2010, 58–63.

Itō Atsuo, 'Hatsugen', n.d., ja.wikipedia.org/wiki/伊藤敦夫.

Ito Masami, 'Ozawa Challenges Abe on Office Outlays', *Japan Times*, 30 January 2007, www.japantimes.co.jp/cgi-bin/nn20070130a.html.

Ito Masami, 'LDP Basks in First Solid Performance in Years', *Japan Times*, 12 July 2010, www.japantimes.co.jp/text/nn20100712a9.html.

Ito Masami, 'Ozawa to Challenge Kan for DPJ Helm', *Japan Times*, 27 August 2010, www.japantimes.co.jp/cgi-bin/nn20100827a1.html.

Ito Masami, 'Political Showdown, and Possibly Poll, Loom', *Japan Times*, 27 April 2012, www.japantimes.co.jp/text/nn20120427a2.html.

Ito Masami, 'Heavyweight Already in Election-survival Mode', *Japan Times*, 12 July 2012, www.japantimes.co.jp/text/nn20120712a1.html#.T__GaGNn785.

Ito Masami, 'Ozawa Vows New Party Will Dethrone Noda's DPJ', *Japan Times*, 2 August 2012, www.japantimes.co.jp/news/2012/08/02/national/ozawa-vows-new-party-will-dethrone-nodas-dpj/#.UX3U7ODtIqY.

Ito Masami and Fukue Natsuko, 'Picks Mirror more Pragmatic Tack, Bid to Exert Leadership', *Japan Times*, 14 January 2012, www.japantimes.co.jp/news/2012/01/14/national/picks-mirror-more-pragmatic-tack-bid-to-exert-leadership/#.UYn_ueDtIqY.

Jackson, Paul, 'What's Taking Ozawa So Long?' *The Diplomat*, 13 December 2010, the-diplomat.com/tokyo-notes/2010/12/13/whats-taking-ozawa-so-long/.

Japan Brief, 'Prime Minister Kan to Remain in Post After Winning Reelection as DPJ President', 17 September 2010, www.at.emb-japan.go.jp/English/japanbriefarchive.htm.

Japan Press Weekly, 'DPJ is Urged to Investigate Fund-raising for Ozawa', 16 December 2009, www.japan-press.co.jp/modules/news/index.php?id=562.

Japan Times, 'Ozawa Followers Form DPJ Faction', 23 January 2004, www.japantimes.co.jp/cgi-bin/nn20040123a5.html.

Japan Times, 'Ozawa Tied to Nishimatsu Cash', 6 March 2009, www.japantimes.co.jp/cgi-bin/nn20090620a1.html.

Japan Times, 'Dam Bidders said Needed Ozawa's OK', 15 January 2010, www.japantimes.co.jp/text/nn20100115a1.html.

Japan Times, 'Opposition Rides Ozawa, Hatoyama Over Scandals', 2 February 2010, www.japantimes.co.jp/text/nn201002024.html.

Japan Times, 'Sentaku Magazine: Playing Ends Off the Middle', 19 April 2010, www.japantimes.co.jp/cgi-bin/eo20100419a1.html.

Japan Times, 'Playing Ends Off the Middle', 19 April 2010, www.japantimes.co.jp/cgi-bin/eo20100419a1.html.

Japan Times, 'Battle Heats Up Between Rival Kan, Ozawa Camps', 28 August 2010, www.japantimes.co.jp/cgi-bin/nn20100828a2.html.

Japan Times, 'Ozawa, Kan Both Vow Local Power', 10 September 2010, www.japantimes.co.jp/cgi-bin/nn20100910a4.html.

Japan Times, 'Prosecutors Forced My Confession', 18 January 2011, www.japantimes.co.jp/text/nn20110118a3.html.

Japan Times, 'DPJ Execs to Go Easy on Ozawa', 3 February 2011, www.japantimes.co.jp/cgi-bin/nn20110203a6.html.

Japan Times, 'Editorial: Trial of Mr. Ozawa's Aides', 11 February 2011, www.japantimes.co.jp/cgi-bin/ed20110211a1.html.

Japan Times, 'Punish Ozawa at Your Peril', 18 February 2011, www.japantimes.co.jp/cgi-bin/nn20110218a1.html.

Japan Times, 'Ichikawa, Yamaoka Face Ax in Reshuffle', 8 January 2012, www.japantimes.co.jp/text/nn20120108a1.html.
Japan Times, 'Ozawa to Oppose Noda's Bills to Hike Sales Tax', 5 February 2012, www.japantimes.co.jp/text/nn20120205a2.html.
Japan Times, 'Noda's Goal Won but Divided DPJ Still Threatens Turmoil', 27 June 2012, www.japantimes.co.jp/cgi-bin/nn20120627a1.html.
Japan Times, 'Iwate Hopefuls Locked in Close Race', 18 July 2013, www.japantimes.co.jp/news/2013/07/18/national/iwate-hopefuls-locked-in-close-race/#.UgWZGuDtIqZ.
Japan Times, 'Ozawa Top Fund Raiser in 2012', 7 December 2013, www.japantimes.co.jp/news/2013/12/07/national/ozawa-top-fund-raiser-in-2012/#.UqQ8reKls-8.
Japan Today, 'Ozawa Top Recipient of Political Funds for Second Year in a Row', 8 December 2011, www.japantoday.com/category/politics/view/ozawa-top-recipient-of-political-funds-for-second-year-in-row.
Jiji.com, '[Zukai, shakai] Rikuzankai jiken', 25 November 2011, www.jiji.com/jc/graphics?p=ve_pol_ozawa-rikuzankai20111125j-02-w290.
Jiji.com, 'Mirai, nijū kenryoku uchikeshi ni yakki', 28 November 2012, www.jiji.com/jc/zc?k=201211/2012112800938.
Johnson, Chalmers, 'Structural Corruption, and the Advent of Machine Politics in Japan', *Journal of Japanese Studies*, Vol. 12, No. 1, Winter 1986, 1–28.
Johnson, Eric, 'Kada Party Seen Banking on Ozawa', *Japan Times*, 1 December 2012, www.japantimes.co.jp/text/nn20121201a4.html.
The Journal, 'Minshutō daihyō senkyo to wa nani ka?' 31 August 2010, www.the-journal.jp/contents/kokkai/mb/post_230.html.
Kabashima Hideyoshi, *Doken Tengoku Nippon*, Tokyo: Nippon Hyōronsha, 1997.
Kabashima Ikuo and Steel, Gill, *Changing Politics in Japan*, Ithaca, NY: Stanford University Press, 2010.
Kaieda Banri, *Boku ga Ozawa (Seiji) o Kirai na Honto no Wake*, Tokyo: Niki Shuppan, 1996.
Kaifu Toshiki, *Seiji to Kane: Kaifu Toshiki Kaikoroku* (author trans.), Tokyo: Shinchōsha, 2010.
Kamikubo Masato, '"Ozawa shihai" no shiteki no mato hazure', *Diamond Online*, No. 38, 8 December 2009, diamond.jp/articles/-/3752.
Kamikubo Masato, 'Saninsen ga kagi o nigiru', *Diamond Online*, No. 43, 16 February 2010, diamond.jp/articles/-/7423.
Kamikubo Masato, 'Seijika no "kessa" ga medatsu Minshutō daihyōsen', *Diamond Online*, No. 57, 7 September 2010, diamond.jp/articles/-/9298.
Kamikubo Masato, 'Kan naikaku de hakarazu mo shimesareta', *Diamond Online*, No. 16, 17 August 2011, diamond.jp/articles/-/13585.
Kamiya Setsuko, 'Ozawa Sticks to Innocence Plea as Court Case Begins', *Japan Times*, 7 October 2011, www.japantimes.co.jp/cgi-bin/nn20111007a1.html.
Kamiya Setsuko and Ito Masami, 'Onus on Aides as Ozawa 'Can't Recall" Fund Details', *Japan Times*, 12 January 2012, www.japantimes.co.jp/text/nn20120112a4.html.
Kaneki Akinori, 'Ozawa Ichirō wa, tenmei ga tsukutta kichō na Nihon seiji no "yūseiran" de aru! (zen)', *Net IB News*, 9 July 2013, www.data-max.co.jp/2013/07/09/post_16454_kmk_1.html.
Kaneki Akinori, 'Ozawa Ichirō wa, tenmei ga tsukutta kichō na Nihon seiji no "yūseiran" de aru! (go)', *Net IB News*, 11 July 2013, www.data-max.co.jp/2013/07/11/post_16454_kmk_1.html.
Kaneko Keiichi and Isogai Hidetoshi, '(Minshutō kenkyū 3): Ōendan wa "ippiki ōkami" tachi, Seisaku rinen ni eikyō ataeru', *Asahi Shinbun*, 5 September 2009, 4.
Kase Kenichi, Tanaka Satoko and Sawaaki Hikita, 'Ozawa ryū zenekon senkyojutsu, meibo 15 manninbun ya kōkendo ranku', *Asahi.com*, 1 February 2010, www.asahi.com/seikenkotai2009/TKY201001310346.html.

Katz, Richard, 'Janus-faced DPJ: One Face to the Future, Another to the Past', *The Oriental Economist Report*, Vol. 78, No. 2, February 2010, 1–2.

Katz, Richard, 'Ozawa: Creator and Destroyer: The "Shiva" of Japanese Politics', *The Oriental Economist Report*, Vol. 78, No. 2, February 2010, 8–9, 10.

Katz, Richard, 'Part 2: Tanaka's Protégé, Ichiro Ozawa, the "Shiva" of Japanese Politics', *The Oriental Economist Report Alert*, 2 February 2010, 4.

Katz, Richard, 'Part 3: Creator and Destroyer, Ichiro Ozawa, The "Shiva" of Japanese Politics', *The Oriental Economist Report Alert*, 3 February 2010, 2.

Katz, Richard, 'Ozawa: The Shiva of Japanese Politics, Creator and Destroyer', *East Asia Forum*, 18 February 2010, www.eastasiaforum.org/2010/02/18/ozawa-the-shiva-of-japanese-politics-creator-and-destroyer/.

Katz, Richard, 'LDP Drops in PR Vote Share from 2007, but Gains in Rural Seats; Kan Likely Out Soon; Possible Early LH Vote', *The Oriental Economist Report Alert*, 12 July 2010, 3.

Katz, Richard, 'What's at Stake? Battle for Soul of DPJ', *The Oriental Economist Report*, Vol. 78, No. 9, September 2010, 1–2.

Katz, Richard, 'Don't "Let the Games Begin": Voters Frustrated with Renewal of Political Circus', *The Oriental Economist Report*, Vol. 79, No. 5, May 2011, 1–2.

Katz, Richard, 'Kan: A Very Lame Duck: Sengoku Seeks "Grand Coalition"', *The Oriental Economist Report*, Vol. 79, No. 6, June 2011, 1–2.

Katz, Richard, 'Why Noda? Biggest Challenge: To Overcome LDP Obstructionism', *The Oriental Economist Report*, Vol. 79, No. 9, September 2011, 1–2.

Katz, Richard, 'Barons Anoint Noda: Behind the Curtain', *The Oriental Economist Report*, Vol. 79, No. 9, September 2011, 3–4.

Katz, Richard, 'It's Leadership, Stupid!: Noda Falling on DPJ's Sword Over Consumption Tax', *The Oriental Economist*, Vol. 29, No. 12, December 2011, 1–2.

Katz, Richard and Toshikawa Takao, 'Yukio, We Hardly Knew Ya: Can Kan De-claw Ozawa?' *The Oriental Economist Report*, Vol. 78, No. 6, June 2010, 1–3.

Kikuchi Hisashi, *Ozawa Ichirō no Seiji Bōryaku: Seikai no Ura no Ura ga Wakaru Hon*, Tokyo: Yamate Shobō Shinsha, 1991.

Kishi Hiroyuki, '"Kan Ozawa" no nitaku to iu higeki', *Diamond Online*, No. 104, 3 September 2010, diamond.jp/articles/-/9267.

Klein, Axel, 'Ozawa's "seiji juku"', *SSJ-Forum*, 5 September 2010, ssj.iss.u-tokyo.ac.jp/archives/2010/09/ssj_6334_ozawas.html.

Kobayashi Masaya, '"Nihon Mirai no Tō" wa kibō no hoshi tari eru ka', *Webronza*, 3 December 2012, astand.asahi.com/magazine/wrpolitics/2012113000006.html?page=1.

Kobayashi Yoshiaki, 'Shōhizei de mo Futenma de mo nai Minshutō haiboku no shinsō akutā no henka kara sēji no henka e', *Diamond Online*, No. 6, 13 July 2010, diamond.jp/articles/-/8730.

Koh Yoree, 'Ozawa's "Children" in Semi-revolt: Trouble for Kan', *Japan Real Time*, 17 February 2011, blogs.wsj.com/japanrealtime/2011/02/17/ozawas-children-semi-revolt-trouble-for-kan/.

Kohno Masaru, *Japan's Postwar Party Politics*, Princeton, NJ: Princeton University Press, 1997.

Kōno Masaru, '93 nen no seiji hendō – mō hitotsu no kaishaku', in *Reviasan* [Leviathan], Tokyo: Bokutakusha, 1995, 17.

Krauss, Ellis S. and Pekkanen, Robert J., *The Rise and Fall of Japan's LDP: Political Party Organizations as Historical Institutions*, Ithaca, NY and London: Cornell University Press, 2010.

Kuji Tsutomu, *Ozawa Ichirō – Sono 'Kyōfu Shihai' no Jittai* (author trans.), Tokyo: Marujusha, 1996.
Kuji Tsutomu and Yokota Hajime, *Seiji ga Yugameru Kōkyō Jigyō – Ozawa Ichirō Zenekon Seiji no Kōzō* (author trans.), Tokyo: Ryokufū Shuppan, 1996.
Kumon Shumpei, 'From the Editor', *Japan Echo*, Vol. 20, No. 4, Winter 1993, 2–5.
Kuramae Katsuhisa, 'Tōkaku jiki saguru Ozawa-shi', *Asahi Shinbun*, 2 March 2011, 4.
Kyodo News, 'Secretary of DPJ Leader Ozawa Arrested Over Illegal Donations', 3 March 2009, home.kyodo.co.jp/modules/fatStory/index.php?storyid=426508.
Kyodo News, 'Ozawa's Secretary Pleads Not Guilty in Nishimatsu Funds Scandal', 18 December 2009, www.thefreelibrary.com/2ND+LD%3A+Ozawa's+secretary+pleads+not+guilty+in+Nishimatsu+funds…-a0215718562.
Kyodo News, 'Ozawa Signals Veiled Willingness to Vie for Leadership after Trial', 8 August 2011, www.thefreelibrary.com/Ozawa+signals+veiled+willingness+to+vie+for+leadership+after+trial.-a0263726562.
Kyodo News, 'Noda Set to be Named Japan's Next Prime Minister', 30 August 2011, findarticles.com/p/articles/mi_m0XPQ/is_2011_Sept_6/ai_n58103785/.
Kyodo News, 'Ozawa Earns Biggest Amount of Political Funds for 2nd Straight Year', 7 December 2011, findarticles.com/p/articles/mi_m0XPQ/is_2011_Dec_12/ai_n58504083/.
Kyodo News, 'Update1: 9 DPJ Lawmakers Submit Resignation in Protest at Noda's Policies', 28 December 2011, findarticles.com/p/articles/mi_m0XPQ/is_2012_Jan_2/ai_n58518929/.
Kyodo News, 'Ozawa Denies Role in Funds Scandal', 10 January 2012, injectionmoldes.blogspot.com.au/2012/01/ozawa-denies-role-in-funds-scandal-says.html.
Liberal Time, 'Seiji shudō o tate ni iyō na "kōtetsu jinji" renpatsu', *Liberal Time*, Vol. 10, No. 3, March 2010, 10–13.
Liberal Time, '"Hisho yūzai" "shikin busoku" de kasoku suru Ozawa Ichirō banare', *Liberal Time*, Vol. 11, No. 12, December 2011, img.fujisan.co.jp/digital/actibook/2489/1301276354/710414/_SWF_Window.html?uid=16392643&pwd=297573316939000&bid=710414.
Liberal Time, '"Ozawa Ichirō" Minshutō moto daihyō to no renkei wa kitai usu', *Liberal Time*, 12 January 2012, 11.
Lijphart, Arendt, *Democracies*, New Haven, CT: Yale University Press, 1984.
MacDougall, Terry, 'The Lockheed Scandal and the High Costs of Politics in Japan', in Andrei S. Markovits and Mark Silverstein, *The Politics of Scandal: Power and Process in Liberal Democracies*, New York: Holmes and Meier, 1988.
Mainichi Daily News, 'Confusion Over Highway Tolls the Latest Drama of Bungling Hatoyama Gov't', 26 April 2010, mdn.mainichi.jp/perspectives/news/20100426p2a00m0na002000c.html.
Mainichi Daily News, 'Ozawa Bears Heavy Responsibility for Conviction of Aides Over Funding Scandal', 4 October 2011, mdn.mainichi.jp/perspectives/news/20110927p2a00m0na007000c.html.
Mainichi Shinbun, 'Gabanansu kuni o ugokasu dai 1 bu sei to kan 8, Ozawa-shi ni futatsu no kao', 10 January 2010, 1.
Mainichi Shinbun, 'Shasetsu: "Kashotsuke" shiryō', 17 February 2010, mainichi.jp/select/opinion/editorial/news/20100217k0000m070123000c.html.
Mainichi Shinbun, 'Yomu seiji: 10 saninsen rupo Nagano (sono 1)', 1 July 2010, 1.
Mainichi Shinbun, 'Ozawa Minshu zen kanjichō futatabi shikkōbu hihan "tadashii koto wo shuchō suru"', 1 July 2010, 5.
Mainichi Shinbun, 'Minshutō daihyōsen: Shushō "datsu Ozawa" o keizoku', 26 August 2010, 1.
Mainichi Shinbun, 'Minshutō daihyōsen: soshikigatame hageshiku', 10 September 2010, 2.

Mainichi Shinbun, 'Kan seiken: Fukuro kōji, Ozawa-shi mondai to yatō renkei', 26 December 2010, mainichi.jp/select/seiji/news/20101226k0000e010017000c.html.

Mainichi Shinbun, 'Kan Shushō: "Ozawa shi-shintai, mizukara handan o, nentō kaiken"', 4 January 2011, mainichi.jp/select/seiji/news/20110104k0000e010036000c.html.

Mainichi Shinbun, 'Ozawa Minshu moto daihyō: Shobun kettei', 23 February 2011, 2.

Mainichi Shinbun, '16 nin honkaigi kesseki "hitotsu no kangaekata" Ozawa moto daihyō', 4 March 2011, 5.

Mainichi Shinbun, 'Minshutō: Kobato "ridatsu" aitsugu gurūpu no kyūshinryoku teika fushinninan sōdō', 15 June 2011, mainichi.jp/select/seiji/news/20110615ddm005010150000c.html.

Mainichi Shinbun, 'TPP: Sanka wareru Minshu', 27 October 2011, mainichi.jp/select/biz/news/20101027ddm001020007000c.html.

Makabe Akio, 'Ichi keizai gakusha kara mita "Ozawa seikyoku" no okame hachimoku', *Diamond Online*, No. 234, 3 July 2012, diamond.jp/articles/-/20960.

Mamiya Jun, 'The Iron Triangle and Corruption in the Construction Industry', *Tokyo Business Today*, Vol. 61, November 1993, 10–13.

Martin, Alex, 'Ozawa Girds for Major Diet Reform', *Japan Times*, 7 January 2010, www.japantimes.co.jp/cgi-bin/nn20100107f1.html.

Martin, Alex and Ito Masami, 'Kan Cruises to Victory in DPJ Election', *Japan Times*, 15 September 2010, www.japantimes.co.jp/cgi-bin/nn20100915a1.html.

Martin, Alex and Takahara Kanako, 'Kan, Ozawa Kick Off DPJ Poll Race', *Japan Times*, 2 September 2010, www.japantimes.co.jp/cgi-bin/nn20100902a1.html.

Martin, Alex and Yoshida Reiji, 'Ozawa Set to be DPJ Secretary General', *Japan Times*, 4 September 2009, www.japantimes.co.jp/cgi-bin/nn20090904a1.html.

Matsuda Kenya, *Ozawa Ichirō Kyoshoku no Shihaisha* (author trans.), Tokyo: Kōdansha, 2009.

Matsuda Kenya, 'Zenekon marugakae senkyo ga kizuita "Ozawa shinwa" to iu kyozō', *Gendai Business*, 26 February 2010, gendai.ismedia.jp/articles/-/268.

Matsuda Kenya, *Kakuei ni narenakatta Otoko: Ozawa Ichirō Zen Kenkyū* (author trans.), Tokyo: Kōdansha, 2011.

Matsuda Kyōhei and Kaneko Keiichi, 'Tōnai gurūpu ga habatsu ka', *Asahi Shinbun*, 3 September 2009, 4.

Matsuda Takakazu (interviewer) and Kobayashi Yoshiaki (ed.), 'Tokushū waido: Saninsen e, dō deru Ozawa Ichirō-shi', *Mainichi Shinbun*, 10 April 2013, mainichi.jp/feature/news/20130410dde012010084000c.html.

Matsumura Masahiro, 'Ozawa: Japan's Secret Shogun', *Japan Times*, 4 February 2010, www.japantimes.co.jp/cgi-bin/eo20100204a1.html.

McCall Rosenbluth, Frances and Thies, Michael F., *Japan Transformed: Political Change and Economic Restructuring*, Princeton, NJ and Oxford: Princeton University Press, 2010.

McCarthy, Terry, 'Puppet-master in a Hall of Mirrors', *The Independent*, 6 August 1993, www.independent.co.uk/news/world/puppetmaster-in-a-hall-of-mirrors-ichiro-ozawa-is-the-man-of-steel-behind-japans-next-premier-writes-terry-mccarthy-1459438.html.

McCarthy, Terry, 'Japan's Shadow Shogun Nurses Grievance in Silence', *The Independent*, 9 December 1993, www.independent.co.uk/news/world/japans-shadow-shogun-nurses-grievance-in-silence-ichiro-ozawa-right-is-the-man-behind-the-government-but-hes-not-talking-to-journalists-terry-mccarthy-reports-from-tokyo-1466282.html.

Mikuriya Takashi, 'Mō "yami shōkun" wa umarenai: Rekishiteki ni mite mo shōmi kigen ga kireta Ozawa Ichirō', *Chūō Koron*, Vol. 125, No. 3, March 2010, 86–95.

Mikuriya Takashi, 'The DPJ's Uncharted Journey', *JapanEchoWeb*, No. 2, August–September 2010, www.japanechoweb.jp/diplomacy-politics/jew0216/4.

Minami Akira, 'Policy Debate Takes a Back Seat in DPJ Race', *Asahi.com*, 28 August 2011, www.asahi.com/english/TKY201108270283.html.
Ministry of Internal Affairs and Communications, 'Seiji shikin kanren', 30 November 2011, www.soumu.go.jp/senkyo/seiji_s/kanpo/shikin/h22_yoshi_111130.html.
Minshutō, 'Seifu yotō no seisaku kettei shisutemu "kakushō seisaku kaigi" o aratamete setsumei', 12 October 2009, www.dpj.or.jp/article/17082/政府 与党の政策決定システム「各省政策会議」を改めて説明%E3%80%80小沢幹事長、輿石幹事長職務代行.
Mitchell, Richard H., *Political Bribery in Japan*, Honolulu: University of Hawai'i Press, 1996.
Miyazaki Tomoyuki, 'Kore o "chabangeki" to yobazu shite nan to yobu ka?' *Diamond Online*, No. 282, 3 June 2011, diamond.jp/articles/-/12550.
Mizuguchi Hiroshi, 'Political Reform: Much Ado About Nothing?' *Japan Quarterly*, Vol. 40, No. 3, July 1993, 246–257.
Mori Mayumi, 'Kano Determined to Make a Difference', *Asahi Shinbun*, 24 August 2011, ajw.asahi.com/article/behind_news/AJ201108247690.
Mori McElwain, Kenneth and Reed, Steven R., 'Japanese Politics in the Koizumi Era: Temporary Anomaly or a Paradigm Shift?' in Steven R. Reed, Kenneth Mori McElwain and Shimizu Kay (eds) *Political Change in Japan: Electoral Behavior, Party Realignment, and the Koizumi Reforms*, Stanford, CA: Walter H. Shorenstein Asia-Pacific Research Center, 2009, 281–292.
Morita Minoru Unravels Japan, 'Dictator Ozawa mustn't Entangle Govt. in his Personal Battle', 27 January 2010, www.pluto.dti.ne.jp/mor97512/EN158.HTML.
MSN Sankei News, '[Ozawa hikoku ronkoku kyūkei (1)] "Jijitsu de nakereba, muzai ni sureba tariru"', 9 March 2012, sankei.jp.msn.com/affairs/news/120309/trl12030913060004-n3.htm.
MSN Sankei News, '"Tenka tori miete kita"', 26 April 2012, sankei.jp.msn.com/politics/news/120426/stt12042614330016-n1.htm.
MSN Sankei News, 'Jimin "kowashiya" ni kitai', 26 April 2012, sankei.jp.msn.com/politics/news/120426/stt12042623520019-n1.htm.
MSN Sankei News, 'Ozawa-shi "Noda oroshi" e', 26 April 2012, sankei.jp.msn.com/politics/news/120426/stt12042611120008-n2.htm.
MSN Sankei News, 'Ozawa-shi, saido kaidan shite mo gōi wa konnan', 30 May 2012, sankei.jp.msn.com/politics/news/120530/plc12053013420011-n1.htm.
Murayama Tomiichi, *Murayama Tomiichi ga Kataru 'Tenmei' no 561-Nichi*, Tokyo: K.K. Best Sellers, 1996.
Myoraku Asako, 'Noda, with Eye on Future, Ready to Bury Hatchet with Ozawa', *Asahi Shinbun*, 25 August 2011, ajw.asahi.com/article/behind_news/AJ201108257650.
n.a., *Ise Akifumi*, Tokyo: Asuka Shuppansha, 1994.
n.a., 'Kakuei Tanaka', in *Encyclopedia of World Biography*, 2004, www.encyclopedia.com.
n.a., *The Democratic Party of Japan, DPJ Manifesto for the 2005 House of Representatives Election: Nippon Sasshin: Toward a Change of Government*, 30 August 2005, www.dpj.or.jp/english/manifesto5/pdf/manifesto_05.pdf.
n.a., *Manifesto, The Democratic Party of Japan's Platform for Government*, 2007, www.dpj.or.jp/english/manifesto/DPJManifesto2007.pdf.
n.a., 'Ichiro Ozawa, President, the Democratic Party of Japan', in *Manifesto, The Democratic Party of Japan's Platform for Government*, 2007, 2, www.dpj.or.jp/english/manifesto/DPJManifesto2007.pdf.
n.a., 'Reducing the Number of Diet Members by more than 10 Percent', in *Manifesto, The Democratic Party of Japan's Platform for Government*, 2007, 54, www.dpj.or.jp/english/manifesto/DPJManifesto2007.pdf.

n.a., 'Political History 2. Toward the Era of a Two-party System', in *Manifesto, The Democratic Party of Japan's Platform for Government*, 2007, www.dpj.or.jp/english/manifesto/DPJManifesto2007.pdf.

n.a., *2009 Change of Government, The Democratic Party of Japan's Platform for Government*, 2009, www.dpj.or.jp/english/manifesto/manifesto2009.pdf.

n.a., 'Five Policies', in *2009 Change of Government, The Democratic Party of Japan's Platform for Government*, 2009, 4, www.dpj.or.jp/english/manifesto/manifesto2009.pdf.

n.a., 'Employment and the Economy', in *2009 Change of Government, The Democratic Party of Japan's Platform for Government*, 2009, 16, www.dpj.or.jp/english/manifesto/manifesto2009.pdf.

n.a., 'The Vision of Government in a Hatoyama Administration', in *2009 Change of Government, The Democratic Party of Japan's Platform for Government*, 2009, www.dpj.or.jp/english/manifesto/manifesto2009.pdf.

n.a., 'Ozawa-shi, moto hisho, gyōsha...shinjitsu o kataru no wa dare?' 22 May 2010, www.iza.ne.jp/news/newsarticle/event/crime/394062/.

n.a., '[Yuragu "Ozawa Ōkoku"] (Jō) Kensetsu gyōsha mo "kokoro" banare', 28 June 2010, www.iza.ne.jp/news/newsarticle/politics/politicsit/409335/.

n.a., 'Yamazaki Kensetsu, Ozawa-shi gawa ni kenkin nisenmanen chō', 18 July 2010, www.iza.ne.jp/news/newsarticle/event/crime/417103/.

n.a., 'Seiken kōtai de mezashita koto wa nan datta no ka – Kenpō no kihon rinen ni tsuite', 28 February 2012, shinseiken.jp/pdf/H240228.pdf.

n.a., 'Seiken kōtai de mezashita koto to wa nan datta no ka – Hijō jitai ni okeru kiki kanri to anzen hoshō – kenpō 9 jō o megutte', 13 March 2012, shinseiken.jp/pdf/H240313.pdf.

n.a., 'Tokutei himitsu hogo hōan no Shūgiin kyōkō saiketsu o ukete', 27 November 2013, www.seikatsu1.jp/activity/declaration/20131127ozawa-danwa.html.

n.a., 'Nentō shokan Seikatsu no Tō daihyō Ozawa Ichirō', 8 January 2014, www.seikatsu1.jp/activity/declaration/20140108ozawa-danwa.html.

Nagata Tarō, 'Ozawa saiban "ten no koe to shinsai fukkō"', *Nōsei Undō Jānaru*, No. 101, February 2012, 14.

Nakajima Kazuya, 'Mirai "Ozawa kakushi" urame', *Mainichi Shinbun*, 17 December 2012, 2.

Nakano Koichi, 'Panel Discussion on Noda's New Cabinet by Nakano of Sophia University & Nishikawa of Meiji Uni', *Foreign Correspondents' Club of Japan*, 2 September 2011.

Negishi Takurō, 'Ozawa-shi no kōsoshin', *Asahi Shinbun Digital*, 26 September 2012, digital.asahi.com/articles/TKY201209260180.html?ref=comkiji_txt_end_kjid_TKY201209260180.

Newsweek, 'Waiting in the Wings, The DPJ is Poised to Win Control of Japan, but its Agenda is Far from Clear', 28 March 2009, www.newsweek.com/2009/03/27/waiting-in-the-wings.html.

NHK, 'Ozawa Cautious about Cooperation with Noda', 29 August 2011.

Niconico Live, 'Ozawa Ichirō x Kareru van Worufuren kōkai tōronkai & kisha kaiken', 28 July 2011, live.nicovideo.jp/watch/lv57454701.

Nietzsche, Friedrich, *Human, All Too Human: A Book for Free Spirits* (trans. R.J. Hollingdale), Cambridge: Cambridge University Press, 1996.

Nihon Keizai Shinbun, 'Ozawa-shi, Taiketsu shoku zenmen ni', 12 April 2006, 2.

Nihon Keizai Shinbun, 'Karendā naki Hatoyama Kantei (Kazamidori)', 2 January 2010, 2.

Nihon Keizai Shinbun, 'Yūsei hōan no sessoku shingi wa kakon o nokosu', 25 May 2010, www.nikkei.com/news/editorial/article/g=96958A96889DE2EAE2E7E2EAE4E2E0E7E2E7E0E2E3E28297EAE2E2E2;n=96948D819A938D96E38D8D8D8D8D.

Nihon Keizai Shinbun, 'Kan shin taisei, jinji katamaru', 8 June 2010, 3.

Nihon Keizai Shinbun, 'Futenma zei zaisei, Ōkina sa – Kan shushō, Nichibei gōi junshu uttae (Minshutō daihyōsen)', 2 September 2010, 3.
Nihon Keizai Shinbun, 'Seitō kōfukin, Jimin 3.5% zō, San'insen uke', 18 September 2013, 4.
Nikaido Isamu, 'Like Ally Ozawa, New DPJ Secretary-general Keeps Tight Lid on Info', *Asahi Japan Watch*, 8 September 2011, ajw.asahi.com/article//behind_news/AJ201109089673.
Nikkan Gendai, 'Koizumi 5 nenkan no akusei o hanzai ni toenai no ka', 13 April 2006, web. archive.org/web/20060413172124/http://www.gendai.net/.
Nikkan Gendai, 'Seiken kōtai senkyo o mokuzen ni shite iru kono jiki ni yatō dai ittō tōshu no dai ichi hisho taiho ni ura wa aru no ka', 27 April 2012, 36–41.
Nikkan Gendai, 'Nān mo nakatta kakushidama, "Kensatsu wa daishittai" no daigasshō ga okoru zo, Ozawa hisho o kyogi kisai dake de taiho, kiso', in 'Ozawa Ichirō saiban hōdō: Seiki no bōryaku no zenryaku o shōhō', 27 April 2012, 57–59.
Nikkan Gendai, 'Mizutani moto kaichō ni "gishō" no kako, Mizukara no jikkei kaihi no tame, kōhan de uso', in 'Ozawa Ichirō saiban hōdō: Seiki no bōryaku no zenryaku o shōhō', 27 April 2012, 120–122.
Nikkan Gendai, 'Seiki no bōryaku: Ozawa jiken zen uchimaku 5, Kontei kara kuzuresatta kensatsu no "uragane kenkin shinario"', in 'Ozawa Ichirō saiban hōdō: seiki no bōryaku no zenryaku o shōhō', 27 April 2012, 266–268.
Nikkan Gendai, 'Daihyōsen, Ozawa gurūpu kyōi no kessokuryoku', in 'Ozawa Ichirō saiban hōdō: Seiki no bōryaku no zenryaku o shōhō', 27 April 2012, 423–424.
Nikkan Gendai, 'Ozawa Ichirō shinshun intabyū, Noda seiken no dekata shidai de "ari to arayuru sentakushi ga aru"', in 'Ozawa Ichirō saiban hōdō: Seiki no bōryaku no zenryaku o shōhō', 27 April 2012, 425–430.
Nikkan Gendai, 'Ritō menbā kara futari datsuraku, dakara dōshita?' 3 July 2012, gendai.net/articles/view/syakai/137356.
Nikkei Weekly, 'Ozawa Emerges as King of Cash', 12 October 2009, e.nikkei.com/e/ac/20091012/TNW/Nni20091012IS9FUND2.htm.
Nikkei Weekly, 'DPJ Betrays Campaign Pledges', 21 December 2009, www.nni.nikkei.co.jp/e/ac/20091221/TNW/Nni20091221FR9BUDG1.htm.
Nikkei Weekly, 'Pulling Strings, Wielding Power', 28 December 2009–4 January 2010, www.nni.nikkei.co.jp/e/ac/20091228/TNW/Nni20091228FR0CHARG.htm.
Nikkei Weekly, 'Small Parties Boast Outsize Influence in Coalition', 28 December 2009–4 January 2010, www.nni.nikkei.co.jp/e/ac/20091228/TNW/Nni20091228FR0CHARG.htm.
Nikkei Weekly, 'Kan's Story MOF Start', 11 January 2010, e.nikkei.com/e/ac/20100111/TNW/Nni20100111FR1FMINS.htm.
Nikkei Weekly, 'Parties Brace for Hot Summer', 11 January 2010, e.nikkei.com/e/ac/20100111/TNW/Nni20100125GY1POL00.htm.
Nikkei Weekly, 'Ozawa Submits to Questioning', 25 January 2010, e.nikkei.com/e/ac/20100125/TNW/Nni20100125FP30ZAWA.htm.
Nikkei Weekly, 'When There's Doubt, Politicians have Duty to Provide Answers', 1 February 2010, e.nikkei.com/e/ac/20100201/TNW/Nni20100201OP4SUSPI.htm.
Nikkei Weekly, 'DPJ Pinned by Own Electioneering', 17 May 2010, e.nikkei.com/e/ac/TNW/Nni20100517FP9KARU3.htm.
Nikkei Weekly, 'Hasty Policy Implementation Looks Like Vote-buying', 17 May 2010, e.nikkei.com/e/ac/20100517/TNW/Nni20100517FP9KARU2.htm.
Nikkei Weekly, 'DPJ Election Debate Chills Growth Hopes', 13 September 2010, e.nikkei.com/e/ac/TNW/Nni20100913OP6EDIT1.htm.

Nikkei.com, 'DPJ's Ozawa Warns Against Scaling Back Campaign Promises', 12 December 2004, e.nikkei.com/e/ac/tnks/Nni20100412D12JFN02.htm.
Nikkei.com, 'Public Works Budget Looking Like Political Tool Again', 12 February 2010, www.nni.nikkei.co.jp/e/ac/tnks/Nni20100211D11JFA07.htm.
Nikkei.com, 'Public Support for Hatoyama Govt Edges Down to 43%', 1 March 2010, e.nikkei.com/e/ac/TNKS/Nni20100228D28JFF01.htm.
Nikkei.com, 'Ozawa, Chamber of Commerce Chief Discuss Growth Strategies', 12 March 2010, e.nikkei.com/e/ac/TNKS/Nni20100311D11JFA20.htm.
Nikkei.com, 'DPJ Fights to Retain Old Identity as Ozawa Tightens Grip', 16 March 2010, e.nikkei.com/e/ac/TNKS/Nni20100315D12HH383.htm.
Nikkei.com, 'Govt Cuts Just 4 of 200 Road Projects Under FY10 Budget', 27 March 2010, e.nikkei.com/e/fr/tnks/Nni20100326D26JFA17.htm.
Nikkei.com, 'Govt Eyes Lowering New Expressway Tariff After Enactment of Law', 22 April 2010, e.nikkei.com/e/ac/TNKS/Nni20100423D22JFA26.htm.
Nikkei.com, 'Ozawa's Argument on Highway Ops "Contradictory": Maehara', 23 April 2010, e.nikkei.com/e/ac/TNKS/Nni20100423D23SS861.htm.
Nikkei.com, 'Sandwiched Hatoyama Puts Off Final Word on Toll Plan', 23 April 2010, e.nikkei.com/e/ac/TNKS/Nni20100422SS769.htm.
Nikkei.com, 'Prosecutors Question Ozawa's Ex-aide Over Case Against Ozawa', 17 May 2010, e.nikkei.com/e/ac/TNKS/Nni20100517D17JF678.htm.
Nikkei.com, '"Nokyo" Losing Say in Agripolicy', 24 May 2010, e.nikkei.com/e/ac/20100524/TNW/Nni20100524FT0FARM1.htm.
Nikkei.com, 'Nail in Kingpin Ozawa's Political Coffin Nigh?' 23 June 2010, e.nikkei.com/e/ac/TNKS/Nni20100623D23HH994.htm.
Nikkei.com, 'Editorial: After Messy Start, DPJ Race Must Come Down to Policy', 31 August 2010, e.nikkei.com/e/ac/tnks/Nni20100831D3ZJFF05.htm.
Nikkei.com, 'Kan Wins DPJ Leadership Battle', 14 September 2010, e.nikkei.com/e/ac/TNKS/Nni20100914D14NY736.htm.
Nikkei.com, 'In Shifting Away from Ozawa, Kan Invites DPJ Discord', 17 September 2010, e.nikkei.com/e/ac/tnks/Nni20100917D16JFA14.htm.
Nikkei.com, 'Editorial: Time to Dump "Ozawa Politics"', 5 October 2010, e.nikkei.com/e/ac/tnks/Nni20101005D05HH087.htm.
Nikkei.com, 'Ozawa to File Suit Against Inquest Panel Decision for Indictment', 14 October 2010, e.nikkei.com/e/ac/tnks/Nni20101014D14JF923.htm.
Nikkei.com, 'Kan Faces Bumps on Road to Trade Pacts', 20 October 2010, e.nikkei.com/e/ac/TNKS/Nni20101020D19JFA25.htm.
Nikkei.com, 'Ozawa's Indictment Signals End of an Era', 1 February 2011, e.nikkei.com/e/ac/tnks/Nni20110201D01HH528.htm.
Nikkei.com, '3 Ex-Ozawa Aides Plead Not Guilty to False Fund Reporting', 7 February 2011, e.nikkei.com/e/ac/tnks/Nni20110207D07JF092.htm.
Nikkei.com, 'Ozawa Rebels Put Kan in Pinch', 18 February 2011, e.nikkei.com/e/ac/TNKS/Nni20110217D17JFF02.htm.
Nikkei.com, 'DPJ Rift Widens as Ozawa Threatens to Go Rogue', 31 May 2011, e.nikkei.com/e/ac/tnks/Nni20110531D30JFA10.htm.
Nikkei.com, 'Vote-grabbing Heats Up Ahead of Confidence Test', 2 June 2011, e.nikkei.com/e/ac/tnks/Nni20110602D01JFA11.htm.
Nikkei.com, 'Timing of Kan's Exit a New Flash Point in DPJ', 3 June 2011, e.nikkei.com/e/tnks/Nni20110602D02JFA17.htm.

Nikkei.com, 'Maehara Against Reconstruction Tax Hike', 14 August 2011, e.nikkei.com/e/ac/TNKS/Nni20110814D14JF786.htm?NS-query=DPJ%20leadership%20election.

Nikkei.com, 'DPJ's "Escape from Ozawa", Part III', 26 August 2011, e.nikkei.com/e/ac/tnks/Nni20110826D2608A15.htm.

Nikkei.com, 'Kingpin Ozawa Backs Trade Minister Kaieda in Party Leadership Race', 26 August 2011, e.nikkei.com/e/ac/tnks/Nni20110826D26JF936.htm.

Nikkei.com, 'Candidates Positions on Key Issues in DPJ Leadership Race', 27 August 2011, e.nikkei.com/e/ac/tnks/Nni20110827D27JF053.htm.

Nikkei.com, 'Ozawa Says to Oppose Bills on Sales Tax Hike Promoted by Noda', 4 February 2012, e.nikkei.com/e/ac/TNKS/Nni20120204D04JF528.htm?NS-query=Ichiro%20Ozawa.

Nikkei.com, 'Ozawa Trying Shock and Awe Against Noda', 23 June 2012, e.nikkei.com/e/ac/tnks/Nni20120622D2206A01.htm.

Nikkei.com, 'Criticism of Ozawa Not Translating to Support for Noda', 25 June 2012, e.nikkei.com/e/ac/tnks/Nni20120624D2406F03.htm.

Nikkei.com, 'Miscalulation Knocks Ozawa "the Destroyer" Off Stride', 27 June 2012, e.nikkei.com/e/ac/TNKS/Nni20120626D2606A18.htm?NS-query=Ichiro%20Ozawa.

Nikkei.com, 'From 10% to 3%: Ozawa's Sales Tax Shuffle', 12 July 2012, e.nikkei.com/e/ac/tnks/Nni20120711D1107A16.htm.

Nikkei.com, 'Ozawa Vows to Abolish All Nuclear Power Plants within 10 Years', 1 August 2012, e.nikkei.com/e/ac/tnks/Nni20120801D01JF925.htm.

Nishibe Susumu, 'Tanaka Kakuei, Product of Japanese Democracy', *Japan Echo*, Vol. X, No. 2, Summer 1983, 67–68.

Nishida Mutsumi, 'Embattled Parties Face Off', *Nikkei Weekly*, 13 July 2009, e.nikkei.com/e/ac/20090713/TNW/Nni20090713FP6NISID.htm.

Nishikawa Shinichi, 'Panel Discussion on Noda's New Cabinet by Nakano of Sophia University & Nishikawa of Meiji Uni', *Foreign Correspondents' Club of Japan*, 2 September 2011.

Nonoyama Eiichi, '"Kessen mokuzen" de towareru Minshutō "seiken dasshu" no honkido', *Foresight*, 1 October 2008, www.fsight.jp/article/4487.

Nonoyama Eiichi, 'Seiji kaikaku no kagi o nigiru tōei "netto kenkin" jijō', *Foresight*, 1 June 2009, www.fsight.jp/article/4959.

Nonoyama Eiichi, 'Sōsenkyogo "Ozawa ha" wa Minshutō o nigiru', *Foresight*, 1 August 2009, www.fsight.jp/article/5091.

Nonoyama Eiichi, '"Ozawa kanjichō vs kensatsu" no daini raundo wa "kashika hōan"', *Foresight*, 1 March 2010, www.fsight.jp/article/5513.

Nonoyama Eiichi, '"Atta jijitsu ga taisetsu" na Ozawa • Akiya kaidan no hamon', *Foresight*, 1 April 2010, www.fsight.jp/article/5598.

Nonoyama Eiichi, '"Bunretsu senkyo" ni kakaru Ozawa-shi no "kugatsu fukken"', *Foresight*, 11 June 2010, www.fsight.jp/article/5617.

Nonoyama Eiichi, 'Ozawa-shi shutsuba to "daimedia no don" o musubu ten to sen', *Foresight*, 10 September 2010, www.fsight.jp/article/5740.

Nonoyama Eiichi, '"Dairenritsu" "jiki shushō" o meguru hyakka sōmei', *Foresight*, 10 June 2011, www.fsight.jp/article/10556.

Nōsei Undō Jānaru, 'Yamada Toshio giin kokkai nikki', *Nōsei Undō Jānaru*, No. 90, April 2010, 8–9.

Oba Shunsuke, 'DPJ Members Already Bickering', *Nikkei Weekly*, 20 July 2009, e.nikkei.com/e/ac/20090720/TNW/Nni20090720FP7DPJ02.htm.

Obi Takuya and Itō Atsuo, 'Seiji anarisuto Itō Atsuo, kōchaku seiji o kiru!' *Diamond Online*, No. 290, 8 August 2012, diamond.jp/articles/-/22766.

Obuchi Keizō, 'In Defense of the Mainstream', *Japan Echo*, Vol. 20, No. 1, Spring 1993, 13–17.
Oda Hajime, *Ozawa Ichirō Zenjinzō*, Tokyo: Gyōken Shuppankyoku, 1992.
Oh Takeshi, 'Jimin no ashimoto ni makareta nōgyō yosan no "gekiyaku"', *Foresight*, 19 January 2010, www.fsight.jp/article/5446.
Oka Takashi, *Policy Entrepreneurship and Elections in Japan: A Political Biography of Ozawa Ichiro*, London and New York: Routledge, 2011.
Oka Takashi and Hughes, Llewelyn, 'Ozawa as we Knew Him: Reflections from Two Former Aides', *The Oriental Economist Report*, Vol. 78, No. 2, 2010, 6–7, 10.
Okamoto Junichi, 'Shitō! "Nihon no Don" vs Tokusō kensatsu', *Shinchō 45*, Vol. 29, No. 2, February 2010, 28–33.
Okamoto Junichi, 'Naze "Tōkyō Kōken Kenjichō" wa Ozawa Ichirō o mamotta ka', *Shinchō 45*, Vol. 29, No. 3, March 2010, 28–33.
Okuno Shūji, *Ozawa Ichirō Hasha no Rirekisho*, Tokyo: Dēta Hausu, 1994.
Osawa Juro, 'Japan's Kan Takes on Rival in Debates', *Wall Street Journal*, 5 September 2010, online.wsj.com/article/SB10001424052748703417104575473480826754628.html.
Ōshima Tatsuo and Ōnishi Motoharu, 'Sokkin Koike Yuriko daigishi ga kataru Ozawa Jiyūtō', *Shūkan Asahi*, Vol. 103, No. 2, 16 January 1998, 151–153.
Otake Hideo, 'Forces for Political Reform: The Liberal Democratic Party's Young Reformers and Ozawa Ichirō', *Journal of Japanese Studies*, Vol. 22, No. 2, Summer 1996, 269–294.
Ōtake Hideo, 'Seiji kaikaku o mezashita futatsu no seiji seiryoku – Jimintō wakate kaikakuha to Ozawa gurūpu', in Ōtake Hideo (ed.) *Seikai Saihen no Kīnkyū: Shin Senkyo Seido ni yoru Sōsenkyo*, Tokyo: Yūhikaku, 1997, 3–33.
Ozawa Ichirō, 'Seiji kaikaku yaraneba sōsenkyo ga yarenai', in Matsushita Seikei Juku no Kai (ed.) *2010-nen Kasumigaseki Monogatari*, 2nd edn, 1991, 180–190.
Ozawa Ichirō, 'My Commitment to Political Reform', *Japan Echo*, Vol. 20, No. 1, Spring 1993, 8–10.
Ozawa Ichirō, *Blueprint for a New Japan: The Rethinking of a Nation*, Tokyo: Kodansha International, 1994.
Ozawa Ichirō, *Ozawashugi* (author trans.), Tokyo: Shūeisha, 2006.
Page, Scott, 'Path Dependence', *Quarterly Journal of Political Science*, Vol. 1, No. 1, 2006, 87–115.
PanOrient News, 'Ichiro Ozawa Headed for Indictment', 4 October 2011, www.panorientnews.com/en/news.php?k=476.
Park Cheol Hee, 'Bloodless Revolution: How the DPJ's Win Will Change Japan', *Global Asia, A Journal of the East Asia Foundation*, Vol. 4, No. 4, Winter 2010, www.globalasia.org/l.php?c=e247.
Pollack, Andrew, 'Shin Kanemaru, 81, Kingmaker in Japan Toppled by Corruption', *The New York Times*, 29 March 1996, www.nytimes.com/1996/03/29/world/shin-kanemaru-81-kingmaker-in-japan-toppled-by-corruption.html.
Prime Minister of Japan and his Cabinet, *Policy Speech by Prime Minister Naoto Kan at the 174th Session of the Diet*, 11 June 2010, www.kantei.go.jp/foreign/kan/statement/201006/11syosin_e.html.
Reed, Steven R., 'Realignment between the 1996 and 2000 Elections', in Steven R. Reed (ed.) *Japanese Electoral Politics: Creating a New Party System*, London and New York: RoutledgeCurzon, 2003.
Reed, Steven R., Mori McElwain, Kenneth and Shimizu Kay, 'Preface', in Steven R. Reed, Kenneth Mori McElwain and Shimizu Kay (eds) *Political Change in Japan: Electoral Behavior, Party Realignment, and the Koizumi Reforms*, Stanford, CA: Walter H. Shorenstein Asia-Pacific Research Center, 2009, vii–xii.

Reed, Steven R. and Scheiner, Ethan, 'Electoral Incentives and Policy Preferences: Mixed Motives behind Party Defections in Japan', *British Journal of Political Science*, Vol. 33, No. 3, 2003, 469–490.

Reed, Steven R. and Shimizu Kay, 'An Overview of Postwar Japanese Politics', in Steven R. Reed, Kenneth Mori McElwain and Shimizu Kay (eds) *Political Change in Japan: Electoral Behavior, Party Realignment, and the Koizumi Reforms*, Stanford, CA: Walter H. Shorenstein Asia-Pacific Research Center, 2009, 5–26.

Saito Jun, 'Pork-barrel Politics and Partisan Realignment in Japan', in Steven R. Reed, Kenneth Mori McElwain and Shimizu Kay (eds) *Political Change in Japan: Electoral Behavior, Party Realignment, and the Koizumi Reforms*, Stanford, CA: Walter H. Shorenstein Asia-Pacific Research Center, 2009, 67–86.

Sakai Hiroshi, 'Minshutō ni "nō saido" nashi', *MSN Sankei News*, 26 April 2012, sankei.jp. msn.com/politics/news/120426/plc12042623540015-n1.htm.

Sakai Takayuki and Hisada Hiroshi, 'Minshutō daihyōsen: Ozawa-shi shuchō "ikkatsu kōfukin"', *Mainichi Shinbun*, 7 September 2010, mainichi.jp/select/seiji/news/20100907ddm008010143000c.html.

Samuels, Richard J., *Machiavelli's Children: Leaders & their Legacies in Italy & Japan*, Ithaca, NY and London: Cornell University Press, 2003.

Samuels, Richard J., 'Politics, Security Policy, and Japan's Cabinet Legislation Bureau: Who Elected these Guys, Anyway?' *JPRI Working Paper*, No. 99, March 2004, www.jpri.org/publications/workingpapers/wp99.html.

Sankei Shinbun, '"Minshutō kaibō" Daiichibu: Seiken no katachi (1) Ayausa rotei "Ozawa shushō"', 2 March 2009, sankei.jp.msn.com/politics/situation/090302/stt090302000 8000-n1.htm.

Sankei Shinbun, 'Yūsei kyōkō toppa jisezu', 25 May 2010, 3.

Sankei Shinbun, '(Seiron): Keiō daigaku kyōju Takenaka Heizō, Yūsei "kaiaku" de kokumin futan nen 2 chō en', 9 June 2010, 7.

Sankei Shinbun, 'Ozawa-shi ritō kankoku mo', 21 December 2010, 1.

Sankei Shinbun, '(Gekitotsu 2011) Kyō kinkyū yakuinkai', 3 February 2011, 5.

Sankei Shinbun, '"Ozawa-shi gawa ni uragane 1 oku en haratta"', 27 April 2011, sankei.jp. msn.com/affairs/news/110427/trl11042711260003-n1.htm.

Sankei Shinbun, 'Ozawa Ichirō-shi, shikinguri ni kuryo', 30 November 2011, sankei.jp.msn. com/politics/news/131130/stt13113008430004-n1.htm.

Sankei Shinbun, 'Noda seiken, Hōkai no ashioto shōhizei zōzei hanpatsu', 28 December 2011, 1.

Sano Shinichi, 'Commentary: Duel Should Expose True Side of Overrated Ozawa', *Asahi Shinbun*, 3 September 2010, www.asahi.com/english/TKY201009020394.html.

Satō Junichi, *Ozawa Ichirō no Himitsu* (author trans.), Tokyo: Dēta Hausu, 1993.

Satō Masaru, 'Satō Masaru no shin teikoku shugi no jidai (13) Ishikawa giiin ga boku ni katatta koto', *Chūō Kōron*, Vol. 125, No. 3, March 2010, 112–123.

Satō Masaru, 'Ozawa shin jiyū shugi no haiboku', *Webronza*, 30 August 2011, astand. asahi.com/magazine/wrpolitics/2011083000002.html?iref=webronza.

Satō Shō, 'Izumo no Ozawa "ame to muchi"', *Aera*, 31 May 2010, web.archive.org/web/20100609015014/http://seiji.yahoo.co.jp/column/article/detail/20100531-01-0101.html.

Scheiner, Ethan, *Democracy Without Competition in Japan: Opposition Failure in a One-Party Dominant State*, Cambridge: Cambridge University Press, 2006.

Schlesinger, Jacob M., *Shadow Shoguns: The Rise and Fall of Japan's Postwar Political Machine*, Stanford, CA: Stanford University Press, 1999.

Schlesinger, Jacob M., 'Flashback: Ozawa in Court', *JapanRealTime*, 30 September 2011, blogs.wsj.com/japanrealtime/2011/09/30/flashback-ozawa-in-court/.
Schmidt, Carmen, 'The DPJ and its Factions: Benefit or Threat?' *Hitotsubashi Journal of Social Studies*, Vol. 43, 2011, 1–21.
Scott, James C., 'Patron-client Politics and Political Change in Southeast Asia', *American Political Science Review*, Vol. 66, No. 1, March 1972, 91–113.
Seikatsu no tō, 'Seikatsu no tō dai 23 kai Sangiin giin senkyo 2013, Seisaku wa kore da!' n.d., www.seikatsu1.jp/political_policy.
Seisaku, 'Kokumin no Seikatsu ga Daiichi', n.d., web.archive.org/web/20121024102944/http://www.seikatsu1.jp/policy.html.
Sekai, 'Ozawa vs kensatsu: "Kenryoku tōsō" o, Minshushugi e, Satō Masaru X Toshikawa Takao', *Sekai*, No. 802, March2010, 54–63.
Sekiguchi Katsumi, 'Sukōpu: Ikioizuku han-shikkōbugawa, Minshu no kiretsu hirogaru', *Tōkyō Shinbun*, 25 February 2011, 2.
Sekiguchi Katsumi, 'Sukōpu: Minshu giren hossoku rasshu', *Tōkyō Shinbun*, 10 March 2011, 2.
Sekiguchi Toko, 'Japan's "Destroyer" Eyes Comeback with Party No. 7', *Japan Real Time*, 28 November 2012, blogs.wsj.com/japanrealtime/2012/11/28/japans-destroyer-eyes-comeback-with-party-no-7/.
Sharp, Andy, 'Ozawa-Kan Leadership Finale', *The Diplomat*, 13 September 2010, the-diplomat.com/tokyo-notes/2010/09/13/ozawa-kan-leadership-finale/.
Shepsle, Kenneth A., 'Rational Choice Institutionalism', in R.A.W. Rhodes, Sarah A. Binder and Bert A. Rockman (eds) *The Oxford Handbook of Political Institutions*, Oxford: Oxford University Press, 2006, 23–38.
Shima Yasuhiko, Kamisawa Hiroyuki and Mitsuhashi Asako, 'Ozawa Kanjichō, kensatsu to no taiketsu tsuzuku', *Asahi Shinbun*, 9 February 2010, www.asahi.com/special/ozawa_sikin/TKY201002060200.html.
Shimizu Isaya, 'Ozawa Looks to British Example', *Nikkei.com*, 12 October 2009, e.nikkei.com/e/ac/20091012/TNW/NNi10091012FP9OZAWA.htm.
Shimizu Masato, 'Friendship, Self-interest Drive "7 magistrates + 1"', *Nikkei Weekly*, 20 July 2009, e.nikkei.com/e/ac/20090720/TNW/Nni20090720FP7DPJ01.htm.
Shinbun Akahata, 'Ozawa-shi wa kensetsu zoku giin no don', 13 October 1993, 15.
Shinbun Akahata, 'LDP and DPJ Must Come Clean about Acceptance of Illegal Donations', 13 March 2009, www.japan-press.co.jp/2009/2614/scandal_3.html.
Shinbun Akahata, 'Ozawa-shi kanren seiji dantai', 1 January 2010, www.jcp.or.jp/akahata/aik09/2010-01-01/2010010123_01_1.html.
Shinbun Akahata, 'Zenekon senkyo Ozawa ryū', 7 February 2010, nitiban.blog.ocn.ne.jp/blog/ozawa_gigoku.pdf.
Shinoda Tomohito, 'Truth Behind LDP's Loss', *Washington-Japan Journal*, Vol. II, No. 3, Fall 1993, www.iuj.ac.jp/faculty/tshinoda/ldploss.html.
Shinoda Tomohito, 'Ozawa Ichirō as an Actor in Foreign Policy-making', *Japan Forum*, Vol. 16, No. 1, 2004, 37–62.
Shinohara Fumiya, 'The Grand Coalition and Qualifications of a Prime Minister', *Japan Echo*, No. 6, June–July 2011, www.japanechoweb.jp/diplomacy-politics/jew0602/3.
Shūgiin [House of Representatives], 'Kokkai kaikaku e no torikumi', n.d., www.shugiin.go.jp/itdb_annai.nsf/html/statics/ugoki/h11ugoki/h11/h11kaika.htm?OpenDocument.
Shūkan Bunshun, 'Fukken o habamareta Ozawa-shi ga daihyōsen de katsugu mikoshi no namae', 17 May 2012, shukan.bunshun.jp/articles/-/1307.
Shūkan Gendai, 'Tsugi no sōri Maehara Seiji to iu otoko', 26 February 2011, gendai.ismedia.jp/articles/-/2109.

Shūkan Shinchō, 'Hitsuyō na no wa hasso no tankan da', *Shūkan Shinchō*, Vol. 43, No. 2, 15 January 1998, 134–138.
Spirling, Arthur, 'Party Cohesion in Westminster Systems: Inducements, Replacement and Discipline in the House of Commons, 1836–1910', Seminar paper, ANU College of Arts and Social Sciences, 11 March 2014.
Stockwin, J.A.A., *Dictionary of the Modern Politics of Japan*, London and New York: Taylor & Francis, 2003.
Stockwin, J.A.A., 'Party Politics in Japan', in Inoguchi Takashi and Jain Purnendra (eds) *Japanese Politics Today: From Karaoke to Kabuki Democracy*, New York: Palgrave Macmillan, 2011, 89–108.
Sudō Takashi and Takeshima Kazuto, 'Minshutō daihyōsen: Tettei hikaku Kan vs Ozawa/2', *Mainichi Shinbun*, 3 September 2010, 3, web.archive.org/web/20100906142028/http://mainichi.jp/select/seiji/minshudaihyousen/hikaku/news/20100903org00m010016000c.html.
Suganuma Eiichirō (ed.), 'Ozawa Ichirō kanjichō jidai no subete o hanasō', *Shūkan Asahi*, Vol. 96, No. 25, 21 June 1991, 28–31.
Sugiyama Toshiyuki, 'Saidai no atsuryoku dantai "Ozawa Kanjichō shitsu"', *Nikkei Business Online*, 10 December 2009, business.nikkeibp.co.jp/article/topics/20091210/211447/.
Suzuki Tetsuo, *Saigo no Ozawa Ichirō – Dare mo Kakenakatta 'Gōwan' no Sugao*, Tokyo: Ōkura Shuppan, 2013.
Tachibana Takashi, 'Ososugita shūen', *Bungei Shunjū*, Vol. 71, No. 8, August 1993, 94–111.
Tada Minoru, 'Ichiro Ozawa Now Isolated', *Japan Times*, 28 April 2000, www.japantimes.co.jp/cgi-bin/eo20000428.html.
Tahara Sōichirō, 'Ozawa ha no "tōnai yatō" de Minshu wa tsubusareru no ka', *BPnet*, 15 December 2010, www.nikkeibp.co.jp/article/column/20101214/254639/?rt=nocnt.
Tahara Sōichirō, '"Fukō" na seijika, Ozawa Ichirō-shi wa muzai de kō ugoku', *BPnet*, 27 April 2012, www.nikkeibp.co.jp/article/column/20120426/307058/.
Tahara Sōichirō, 'Kenbōjussū o megurasu Ozawa Ichirō no "kenryoku kōsōshi"', *BPnet*, 28 June 2012, www.nikkeibp.co.jp/article/column/20120627/314051/.
Tahara Sōichirō, 'Ozawa Ichirō-shi wa gyaku ni oikomare, ritō sezaru o enakatta', *BPnet*, 5 July 2012, www.nikkeibp.co.jp/article/column/20120704/314829/.
Takahara Kanako, 'Rookies Hold Crucial DPJ Votes', *Japan Times*, 10 September 2010, search.japantimes.co.jp/cgi-bin/nn20100910f1.html.
Takahara Kanako, 'Even Tougher Year May Lie Ahead for Kan', *Japan Times*, 1 January 2011, www.japantimes.co.jp/cgi-bin/nn20110101f2.html.
Takahara Kanako and Fukue Natsuko, 'Opposition Issues Ozawa Terms', *Japan Times*, 28 January 2011, www.japantimes.co.jp/text/nn20110128a8.html.
Takahara Kanako and Fukue Natsuko, 'DPJ Suspends Ozawa', *Japan Times*, 23 February 2011, www.japantimes.co.jp/cgi-bin/nn20110223a1.html.
Takahashi Yoshinobu, 'Ozawa moto hisho ga jitsumei kokuhatsu! "Watashi wa damu kōji 'ten no koe' o kiita!"', *Shūkan Shinchō*, Vol. 55, No. 14, 8 April 2010, 130–132.
Takayasu Kensuke, 'Kokka Senryaku Kyoku wa nani o subeki ka?' *Sekai*, No. 799, December 2009, 140–147.
Takenaka Harutaka, 'Introducing Junior Ministers and Reforming the Diet in Japan', *Asian Survey*, Vol. 42, No. 6, 2002, 928–939.
Tanaka Kakuei, *Nihon Retto Kaizōron*, Tokyo: Simul Press, 1973.
Tanaka Naoki, 'New Two-party System in the Bud', *Nikkei Weekly*, 28 December 2009, e.nikkei.com/e/ac/20091228/TNW/Nni20091228OP0TANAK.htm.

316   Bibliography

Tanaka Naoki, 'Japan Politics Seeks New Character', *Nikkei Weekly*, 25 January 2010, e.nikkei.com/e/ac/20100125/TNW/Nni20100125OP3TANAK.htm.
Tanaka Shūsei, 'Shinseiken wa "Ozawa kataguruma seiken"!?' *Diamond Online*, No. 2, 10 September 2009, diamond.jp/articles/-/5774.
Tanaka Shūsei, 'Naze meikaku na seisaku nakushite seiken seitō ni nareta no ka', *Diamond Online*, No. 73, 3 March 2011, diamond.jp/articles/-/11355.
Tanaka Shūsei, 'Maehara-shi no daihyōsen shutsuba, "datsu Ozawa'i wa?' *Diamond Online*, No. 97, 25 August 2011, diamond.jp/articles/-/13707.
Tanaka Shūsei, 'Noda shushō wa Hosokawa moto shushō no "gyōkaku yūsen no chūkoku" ni shitagau beki da', *Diamond Online*, No. 102, 22 September 2011, diamond.jp/articles/-/14110.
Tanaka Shūsei, 'Yakushin no kanōsei hikui "Ozawa shintō" sae kyōi ni', *Diamond Online*, No. 140, 5 July 2012, diamond.jp/articles/-/21106.
Tanaka Yoshitsugu, 'Seijiteki jiken no seijiteki kōso', *The Journal*, 9 May 2012, www.the-journal.jp/contents/kokkai/2012/05/post_299.html.
Tazaki Shirō, 'Yamaguchi Jirō and Azumi Jun, 'Ozawa Ichirō wa Nihon o dō shiyō to iu no ka', *Shinchō 45*, Vol. 29, No. 2, February 2010, 34–46.
Tōkyō Shinbun, 'Ozawa kanjichō, Kanryō no iinkai tōben "kinshi"', 2 October 2009, 2.
Tōkyō Shinbun, 'Ozawa-shi no shibu, 7400 man mikisai', 1 December 2010, 1.
Tōkyō Shinbun, 'Sukōpu: Ozawa-shi shobun', 8 February 2011, 2.
Tōkyō Shinbun, 'Sukōpu: Ozawa rosen no shūsei kasoku', 8 June 2011, 2.
Tōkyō Shinbun, 'Minshu daihyōsen, Ozawa-shi ra 9 nin wa tōhyōken nashi', 21 August 2011, www.tokyo-np.co.jp/article/politics/news/CK2011082102000022.html.
Toshikawa Takao, 'Kanemaru Scandal Rips the Lid of LDP Money Politics', *Tokyo Business Today*, Vol. 61, October 1993, 14–17.
Toshikawa Takao, 'Ozawa Not Out of the Woods: Rumors of Deal with Prosecutors', *The Oriental Economist Report*, Vol. 78, No. 2, February 2010, 4–5.
Toshikawa Takao, 'Chickens Roosting: DPJ Loss in Nagasaki Due to Ozawa Scandal', *The Oriental Economist Report*, Vol. 78, No. 3, March 2010, 3–4.
Toshikawa Takao, 'Not-so-merry Month of May: Decision Time for Hatoyama, Ozawa', *The Oriental Economist Report*, Vol. 78, No. 5, May 2010, 4–5.
Toshikawa Takao, 'Master in his Own House? Ozawa Waiting to Pounce on Kan', *The Oriental Economist Report*, Vol. 78, No. 7, July 2010, 3–4.
Toshikawa Takao, 'Kan Versus Ozawa: DPJ Infighting', *The Oriental Economist Report*, Vol. 78, No. 8, August 2010, 3–4.
Toshikawa Takao, 'Showdown at DPJ Corral: Kan vs. Ozawa', *The Oriental Economist Report*, Vol. 78, No. 9, September 2010, 3–5.
Toshikawa Takao, 'Rising and Setting Suns: Ozawa Down, Sengoku Up', *The Oriental Economist Report*, Vol. 78, No. 11, November 2010, 4–5.
Toshikawa Takao, 'Etsunen suru Kan vs Ozawa no "saishū sensō"', *Tokyo Insideline*, 28 December 2010, www.insideline.co.jp/column/column.html.
Toshikawa Takao, 'Kan Gone by June: Budget Impasse, Difficulty of Election Gambit', *The Oriental Economist Report*, Vol. 79, No. 3, March 2011, 3–4.
Toshikawa Takao, 'Barons Annoint [sic.] Noda: Behind the Curtain', *The Oriental Economist Report*, Vol. 79, No. 9, September 2011, 3–4.
Toshikawa Takao, 'Noda's Leadership Style: Delay as a Mode of Governance', *The Oriental Economist Report*, Vol. 79, No. 12, December 2011, 3–4.
Toshikawa Takao, 'Taxes uber alles: Noda Faces Down Ozawa; Hopes for Deal with LDP', *The Oriental Economist Report*, Vol. 80, No. 4, April 2012, 1–3.

Toshikawa Takao, 'Twilight of the Former God: Ozawa Era Ending with a Whimper', *The Oriental Economist Report*, Vol. 80, No. 6, June 2012, 3–4.
Toshikawa Takao, 'Hitsuyō na no wa "Ushiwakamaru" to 14 nin no Shūgiin giin', *Gendai Business*, 7 July 2012, gendai.ismedia.jp/articles/-/32961.
Toshikawa Takao, 'Timing of the Next Election: What will Noda Do Next?' *The Oriental Economist Report*, Vol. 80, No. 8, August 2012, 4–5.
Toshikawa Takao, '100 man byō mo erarezu seiji seimei o tatareta Ozawa Ichirō ni wa Tanaka Kakuei ya Tokonami Takejirō no bannen no sugata ga kasanaru', *Gendai Business*, 27 July 2013, gendai.ismedia.jp/articles/-/36539.
Toshikawa Takao and Katz, Richard, 'Flailing, DPJ-led Coalition Could Lose Upper House Majority in July', *The Oriental Economist Report*, Vol. 79, No. 4, April 2010, 1–3.
Tsujihiro Masafumi, 'Kan Sōri ga jikaku subeki Minshutō seiken no kekkan wa nani ka', *Diamond Online*, No. 112, 15 September 2010, diamond.jp/articles/-/9386.
Tsutsumi Gyō, 'Ozawa Ichirō no "Nihon haijakku" o soshi seyo', *Liberal Time*, Vol. 10, No. 3, March 2010, img.fujisan.co.jp/digital/actibook/2489/1301276354/320545/_SWF_Window.html?uid=16129246&pwd=297050528975611&bid=320545.
Uchida Kenzō, '"Ozawa Ichirō" to wa nan datta no ka: Kaikaku no kishu, mata no na o dokusaisha ga gojūgonen taisei o hōkai sasete haya sannen', *Bungei Shunjū*, Vol. 74, No. 15, December 1996, 118–126.
Uesugi Takashi, 'Ozawa kanjichō ni yoru chinjō ipponka ga', *Diamond Online*, No. 103, 26 November 2009, diamond.jp/articles/-/1963.
Uesugi Takashi, 'Nejire mo mata min'i', *Diamond Online*, No. 134, 15 July 2010, diamond.jp/articles/-/8759.
Uesugi Takashi, 'Densho bato zen shushō no chaban ni gen shushō ga furimawasarete daihyōsen shosen wa Ozawa shi ga yūri ni', *Diamond Online*, No. 140, 2 September 2010, diamond.jp/articles/-/9254.
Uesugi Takashi, 'Fushinninan hiketsu!' *Diamond Online*, No. 177, 3 June 2011, diamond.jp/articles/-/12553.
Uno Shigeki, 'Ozawa Ichirō-shi ni miru "seijika no rīdāshippu"', *Foresight*, 22 October 2012, www.fsight.jp/article/11884.
van Wolferen, Karel, *Dare ga Ozawa Ichirō o Korosu no ka: Kakusakusha Naki*, Tokyo: Kadokawa Shoten, 2011.
Wakatabe Masazumi, 'Kan Zaimu Daijin wa honki ka?' *Voice*, 10 February 2010, shuchi.php.co.jp/article/792.
Wallace, Corey, 'The Japanese PM Run-off and the Weekend's Media through a Rumsfeldian Lens', 29 August 2011, sigma1.wordpress.com/2011/08/29/the-japanese-pm-race-run-off-and-the-weekends-media-through-a-rumsfeldian-lens/.
Wang, Justin Shouming, *Ozawa's Children: Money, Numbers and Power in the DPJ*, graduate thesis, Faculty of Arts and Social Sciences, National University of Singapore, 2012.
Watanabe Kensuke, *Ano Hito: Hitotsu no Ozawa Ichirō Ron* (author trans.), Tokyo: Asuka Shinsha, 1992.
Watanabe Kensuke, *Ozawa Ichirō Kirawareru Densetsu* (author trans.), Tokyo: Shōgakukan, 2009.
Watanabe Osamu, *Seiji Kaikaku to Kenpō Kaisei: Nakasone Yasuhiro kara Ozawa Ichirō e*, Tokyo: Aoki Shoten, 1994.
Watanabe Tetsuya and Fujita Nao, 'Kokkai kaikaku kanren hōan o yotō teishutsu', *Asahi.com*, 15 May 2010, www.asahi.com/seikenkotai2009/TKY201005140634.html.
Winkler, Chris, 'About Hatoyama, Ozawa', *SSJ-Forum*, 5 September 2011, ssj.iss.u-tokyo.ac.jp/archives/2011/09/ssj_6837_fwd_re.html.

Woodall, Brian, *Japan Under Construction: Corruption, Politics, and Public Works*, Berkeley, CA: University of California Press, 1996.

Wright, Maurice, *Japan's Fiscal Crisis: The Ministry of Finance and the Politics of Public Spending, 1975–2000*, New York: Oxford University Press, 2002.

Yakushiji Katsuyuki, 'Kako no hatsugen ni miru Ozawa Ichirō-shi (jō) – "Nihongata konsensasu shakai" no hitei', *Webronza*, 20 July 2010, astand.asahi.com/magazine/wrpolitics/2012071900005.html?iref=webronza.

Yakushiji Katsuyuki, 'Kako no hatsugen ni miru Ozawa Ichirō-shi (ge) – kenryoku dasshu ga jiko mokutekika shita seijika', *Webronza*, 25 July 2010, astand.asahi.com/magazine/wrpolitics/2012072300010.html.

Yakushiji Katsuyuki, *Whither Japanese Politics in the Post-Ozawa Era?* The Tokyo Foundation, 9 August 2012, www.tokyofoundation.org/en/topics/politics-in-persepctive/post-ozawa-era.

Yamagishi Issei, 'Ozawa-shi kabau Shamin Fukushima-shi', *Asahi Shinbun*, 11 May 2012, www.asahi.com/politics/update/0511/TKY201205110140.html.

Yamaguchi Jirō, 'The Failings and Potential of the DPJ Administration', *Japan Echo Web*, No. 1, June–July 2010, www.japanechoweb.jp/diplomacy-politics/jew0110/5.

Yamaguchi Toshio, 'An Insider's View of Ozawa Ichirō', *Japan Echo*, Vol. 20, No. 4, Winter 1993, 25–29.

Yamaguchi Toshio, 'Ozawa Ichirō no kenkyū: Shoseiron to sutemi no hakairyoku', *Bungei Shunjū*, Vol. 71, No. 10, 1993, 144–149.

Yamashita Kazuhito, 'TPP seikyoku ga maneki kanenai Ozawa ha no kaitai', *Webronza*, 13 December 2010, astand.asahi.com/magazine/wrbusiness/2010121300015.html?iref=webronza.

Yamazaki Hajime, '"Gaman no dekinai otoko" Ozawa Ichirō-shi wa keieisha nara daishikkaku', *Diamond Online*, No. 4, 8 November 2007, diamond.jp/articles/-/4879.

Yamazaki Hajime, 'Ozawa Ichirō-shi wa tsugi no soridaijin ni fusawashiku nai', *Diamond Online*, No. 73, 25 March 2009, diamond.jp/articles/-/7032.

Yamazaki Hajime, 'Ozawa Ichirō-shi e no kenryoku ichigenka', *Diamond Online*, No. 104, 4 November 2009, diamond.jp/articles/-/5735.

Yamazaki Hajime, 'Ozawa Ichirō-shi to kenryoku no rebarejji', *Diamond Online*, No. 111, 23 December 2009, diamond.jp/articles/-/4929.

Yamazaki Hajime, 'Kan shinshushō no keizai seisaku', *Diamond Online*, No. 133, 9 June 2010, diamond.jp/articles/-/8377.

Yamazaki Hajime, 'Tatakae, daihyōsen! Ima sara "toroika" de mo arumai', *Diamond Online*, No. 145, 1 September 2010, diamond.jp/articles/-/9238.

Yamazaki Hajime, 'Seiji fuzai wa Nihon no tsuyomi no araware mo shirenai', *Diamond Online*, No. 161, 22 December 2010, diamond.jp/articles/-/10554.

Yamazaki Hajime, 'Kan shushō wa sude ni "tsunde iru" no de wa nai ka', *Diamond Online*, No. 166, 2 February 2011, diamond.jp/articles/-/10983.

Yasumoto Mariko, 'Ozawa Reaches Goal: Clout to Grow', *Japan Times*, 31 August 2009, www.japantimes.co.jp/text/nn20090831b7.html.

Yomiuri Online, 'Kaku kōho, seisaku no sabetsuka ni fushin', 28 August 2011, www.yomiuri.co.jp/feature/20100806-849918/news/20110828-OYT1T00342.htm.

Yomiuri Online, 'Ozawa G, mōretsu na tasūha kōsaku', 30 August 2011, www.yomiuri.co.jp/feature/20100806-849918/news/20110830-OYT1T00020.htm.

Yomiuri Online, 'Ozawa moto daihyō, gurūpu tōgō no ikō', 30 August 2011, www.yomiuri.co.jp/politics/news/20110830-OYT1T00152.htm?from=main2.

Yomiuri Shinbun, '(Seiji no genba) Gekisenku o yuku (12), Shōbu wa "saigo no 1 giseki"', 6 July 2010, 4.

Yomiuri Shinbun, '"Nodo kara te ga deru hodo hoshii" Rikuzankai bunpaikin', 30 November 2010, www.yomiuri.co.jp/politics/news/20101130-OYT1T01191.htm?from=top.
Yomiuri Shinbun, 'Ozawa-shi, shikkōbu ni fuman', 12 December 2010, 4.
Yomiuri Shinbun, 'Ozawa-kei no ichibu, Kaiha ridatsu mo, Shūin hirei jūsūnin, Shikkōbu ni hanki', 17 February 2011, 1.
Yomiuri Shinbun, 'Minshu bunretsu bukumi', 18 February 2011, 1.
Yomiuri Shinbun, 'Kyūshinryoku kaifuku? Daihyōsen ni sonae?' 15 June 2011, www.yomiuri.co.jp/feature/20100806-849918/news/20110614-OYT1T00937.htm.
Yomiuri Shinbun, 'Uta o wasureta kanaria wa dochira', 4 February 2012, www.yomiuri.co.jp/politics/news/20120203-OYT1T01231.htm.
Yomiuri Shinbun, 'Kasunda mirai, Kada daihyō "kettō jikan sukunaku"', 17 December 2012, 18.
Yomiuri Shinbun, 'Mirai kōtai maibotsu o kenen', 17 December 2012, 2.
Yomiuri Shinbun, 'Ishin hirei ni sukuwareta', 18 December 2012, 18.
Yosano Kaoru, 'Shintō kessei e hara wa kukutta – Nihon keizai o sukuu "suteishi" ni naru – Tanigaki Sōsai ni wa shitsubō shita. Watashi ga ketsudan o kudasu toki ga kita', *Bungei Shunjū*, Vol. 88, No. 5, April 2010, 134–143.
Yoshida Shinichi and Yamamoto Shūji, 'Giin o umidasu kosuto', in Sasaki Takeshi, Yoshida Shinichi, Taniguchi Masaki and Yamamoto Shūji (eds), *Daigishi to Kane: Seiji Shikin Zenkoku Chōsa Hōkoku*, Tokyo: Asahi Shimbunsha, 1999, 11–37.
Yoshino Norihisa, 'Ozawa Seeks to Reclaim Political Power, but Doubts Remain', *Asahi Japan Watch*, 11 January 2012, ajw.asahi.com/article/behind_news/AJ201201110049.
Yuka Hayashi and Toko Sekiguchi, 'Transcript of Interview with Ichiro Ozawa', *Wall Street Journal*, 27 May 2011, online.wsj.com/article/SB10001424052702304066504576348263512336934.html.
Zakzak, 'Nagata-chō kīman no futokoro jijō', 1 December 2012, www.zakzak.co.jp/society/politics/news/20121201/plt1212011446002-n1.htm.

Index

Abe Shinzō 16, 25, 76, 273
Aichi is Top of Japan Party 272
Akamatsu Hirotaka 74, 153, 175, 243
Akiya Einosuke 154
All-Japan Trucking Association (*Zennihon Torakku Kyōkai*) 150, 154, 160
Anti-TPP Party 276
Aoki Mikio 203
Asō Tarō 16, 113, 255, 275
Azuma Shōzō 225, 253, 273, 278, 280, 281
Azumi Jun 135, 160, 221, 230

Conservative Party (*Hoshutō*) 90

Daizen Fumio 109
Deguchi Chōshitsu 92
Democratic Party of Japan (DPJ) *see* Ozawa Ichirō
Democratic Socialist Party (DSP) (Minshatō) 74, 182, 189, 223, 273
Doi Ryūchi 228
Doi Takako 190

Edano Yukio 71, 83, 161, 178, 194, 220, 221, 224, 230, 242

Food and Agriculture Revitalisation Council (*Shokuyō to Nōgyō Kasseika Kyōgikai*) 153
Fudesaka Hideyo 15, 138
Fukuda Kazuko 200
Fukuda Takeo 175, 200
Fukuda Yasuo 16, 65, 184–85, 200
Fukushima Mizuho 143–44, 150
Fujii Hirohisa 81, 83, 145, 148–49, 187
Fujiki Shinya 153
Funada Hajime 189
Futami Nobuaki 131

Genba Kōichirō 221, 224, 242
Government Revitalisation Unit (GRU) (*Gyōsei Sasshin Kaigi*) 153, 175, 223
Green Wind Party (GWP) (*Midori no Kaze*) 276

Hachiro Yoshio 224
Haraguchi Kazuhiro 73, 238, 246, 253
Haranaka Katsuyuki 160
Hashimoto Ryūtarō 203–4
Hashimoto Tōru 40, 232, 252, 254, 256, 258, 259, 272, 273
Hata Tsutomu 15, 16, 20, 47, 59, 62, 63, 74, 80, 132, 185, 187, 189, 190, 220, 229, 273; Hata faction 15, 16, 60, 61
Hatoyama Yukio 60, 65, 73, 74, 75, 110, 143–44, 148–49, 150, 154, 207, 221–23, 225, 228, 238, 239, 240–41, 243, 244, 245, 253, 274; Hatoyama administration 40, 81, 110, 130, 132, 137–40, 143–51, 152, 156, 163, 165, 166, 174–81, 186, 19, 203, 209, 220, 221–22, 246, 248, 287, 292; *see also* Ozawa Ichirō
Hidaka Takeshi 90, 224, 249
Hiraiwa Gaishi 44, 78
Hirano Hirofumi 175, 249, 250
Hirano Sadao 13, 18, 47, 74, 232, 243
Hosokawa Morihiro 16, 21, 42, 44, 61, 62, 181–82, 186, 187, 188, 203, 220, 228, 292; Hosokawa administration 29, 41, 62, 78, 79, 91, 131, 141, 180, 182, 186, 287
Hosono Gōshi 153, 183, 256
Hayashi Yoshimasa 273

Ichikawa Yasuo 249, 250
Ichikawa Yūichi 16, 187, 190
Ikeda Hayato 175

Ikeda Mitsutomo 98–100, 102, 104, 105, 106
Inoue Takashi 84
Ishiba Shigeru 273
Ishihara Nobuteru 109
Ishihara Shintarō 256, 273
Ishikawa Tomohiro 30, 42, 90, 98–101, 102, 104, 105, 106, 107, 111, 195, 202, 206, 290
Itō Atsuo 22, 60, 76, 80, 177, 177, 186, 289
Itō Shōichirō 92

Japan Agriculture (JA) 44, 45, 153, 154, 251
Japan Association of Corporate Executives (JACE) (*Keizai Dōyūkai*) 154
Japan Chamber of Commerce and Industry (*Nihon Shōkō Kaigisho*) 154
Japan Communist Party (JCP) 15, 94, 138
Japan Dental Association (*Nihon Shika Ishikai*) 74, 154
Japan Medical Association (JMA) (*Nihon Ishikai*) 154, 160
Japan New Party (JNP) (*Nihon Shintō*) 16, 63, 182, 188, 189
Japan Socialist Party (JSP) (*Nihon Shakaitō*) 16, 19–20, 21, 44, 63, 74, 182, 188–90
Japanese Trade Union Confederation (*Rengō*) 16, 74, 155, 159, 227, 273

Kada Yukiko 276–79, 282
Kadowaki Kazutsugu 92
Kaieda Banri 42, 71, 73, 74, 131–32, 166, 207, 224, 242, 243, 244, 245–47, 252, 280
Kaifu Toshiki 14, 17, 178, 189, 190, 191, 197–98, 203, 204, 228; Kaifu administration 18, 29, 181, 292
Kajiyama Seiroku 59, 61, 187
Kamei Shizuka 63, 150–51, 154, 225, 238, 253, 272, 276, 277
Kan Naoto 33, 45, 65, 68, 71, 72, 73, 74–75, 76, 83–84, 95, 110–11, 130, 140, 145, 150, 155–60, 165, 175, 176, 177–78, 179, 185, 188, 204, 290; Kan administration 130, 155, 156, 160, 162, 164, 165, 187, 191, 195, 198, 210, 220–46
Kan Nobuko 75
Kanazawa Kei 97
Kanemaru Shin 46, 58, 59, 60, 79, 95, 96, 101, 175, 176, 183, 187, 192, 199–200, 203–4, 293

Kano Michihiko 184, 243, 244, 245, 245, 247
Kanzaki Takenori 190
Katō Kōichi 186, 191
Kawakami Mitsue 160, 206
Kawakami Yoshihiro 147
Kawamura Hisashi 104–5
Kawamura Takashi 232, 233, 252, 276
Kawauchi Hiroshi 253
Keidanren 38, 44, 154
Kobayashi Kōki 71
Koga Nobuaki 74, 227, 238
Koike Yuriko 186, 187, 275
Koizumi Junichirō 2, 15, 36, 69, 129, 130, 135–37, 149, 150, 156, 164, 165, 191, 196, 209, 289; Koizumi administration 34, 128, 135, 163
Komiyama Yōko 83, 136
Kōno Yōhei 62
Koshiishi Azuma 74, 222, 224, 228, 231, 238, 244, 247, 248–50, 256, 258, 270, 273, 274, 280, 281
Kudō Kentarō 86, 87
Kunisawa Mikio 97, 98

Liberal Democratic Party (LDP) 3, 4, 17–23, 22, 26, 27, 33, 63, 74, 76, 91, 93, 113, 133, 137, 139, 143, 144, 145, 186, 189, 199, 202, 228, 238, 240, 242, 255, 257–59, 275, 281; 2012 election 1, 10; *see also* Ozawa Ichirō
Lockheed scandal 101, 111, 207

Mabuchi Sumio 243, 244, 245, 247
Maehara Seiji 146, 149–50, 187, 220, 242, 244–45, 247, 249, 250, 275
Masuda Hiroya 87, 90, 158
Matsuki Kenkō 74, 224, 225, 232, 233, 239–40, 241, 252, 281
Matsuoka Toshikatsu 25
Ministry of Agriculture, Forestry and Fisheries (MAFF) 44, 133, 147–48, 153, 156, 175, 184, 225, 243
Ministry of Construction (MOC) 84, 87, 88, 90, 199–201
Ministry of Economy, Trade and Industry (METI) 113, 225, 243, 244
Ministry of Finance (MOF) 41, 131, 144, 159, 182
Ministry of Foreign Affairs (MOFA) 37, 41, 144
Ministry of Health and Welfare (MHW) 182

Ministry of Internal Affairs and Communications (MIAC) 72, 73, 238, 281
Ministry of Land, Infrastructure and Transport (MLIT) 146, 147, 243
Mitsui Wakio 74
Mitsuzuka Hiroshi 59, 60
Miyazawa Kiichi 15, 20, 58, 59–62
Mizutani Isao 99
Mochizuki Shigeru 88, 89, 92
Monden Eiji 153
Mori Yoshirō 238
Mori Yūko 278, 279, 280
Motegi Toshimitsu 109
Murakoshi Hirotami 177
Murayama Tomiichi 182, 188, 189

Nakamura Shirō 61
Nakanishi Eiichirō 160
Nakasone Yasuhiro 179, 194
Nambu Akihiro 148
Natano Shigeto 83
National Association of Commissioned Postmasters (*Zenkoku Tokutei Yubinkyokuchōkai* or *Zentoku*) 74, 154, 160
National Central Union of Agricultural Cooperatives (*Zenkoku Nōgyō Kyōdō Kumiai Chuōkai* or *JA-Zenchū*) 153; *see also* Japan Agriculture (JA)
National Federation of Farmers' Agricultural Policy Campaign Organisations (*Zenkoku Nōgyōsha Nōsei Undō Soshiki Renmei* or *Zenkoku Nōseiren*) 153
National Strategy Unit (NSU) (*Kokka Senryaku Shitsu*) 144, 145, 194
New Kōmeitō (*Kōmeitō*) 16, 21, 66, 131, 154, 177, 182, 187, 188, 189, 190, 224, 228, 229, 238, 242, 258, 271, 272, 273, 276
New Party Daichi-True Democratic Party (*Shintō Daichi-Shinminshutō*)/New Party Daichi-True Democrats (*Shintō Daichi-Shinminshu*) 252, 272, 273, 276
New Party Harbinger (NPH) (*Shintō Sakigake*) 21, 41, 63, 64, 188–89
New Party Kizuna (*Shintō Kizuna*) 252, 272, 176
new politics 1, 3–4, 5–8, 9–10; *see also* Ozawa Ichirō
Nikai Toshihiro 113
Nishioka Takeo 74, 83, 231
Noda Yoshihiko 40, 66, 76, 130, 161–62, 165, 187, 220, 242, 243, 244–48, 273; Noda administration 130, 155, 160,
162, 164, 165, 191, 195, 198, 210, 220, 221; *see also* Ozawa Ichirō
Noda Takeshi 83
Nonaka Hiromu 78, 148, 178, 187, 191, 200, 275
Nonoyama Eiichi, 142
Nuclear-Free Party 276–77

Obuchi Keizō 26, 35, 36, 43, 58, 59, 60, 65, 78, 175, 187, 191, 203, 220
Ōhata Akihiro 224, 225
Okada Katsuya 72, 132, 137, 187, 224, 227, 228, 229, 230, 231, 233, 242, 250
Okamura Tadashi 154
Okazaki Akifumi 97
Ōkubo Takanori 25, 77, 95–101, 104, 105, 106, 138, 204
Okuda Keiwa 189
old politics 1, 3–4, 5–8, 9–10, 66, 109, 110, 111; *see also* Ozawa Ichirō, Tanaka Kakuei
Ōmura Hideaki 256, 272
Ōshima Tadamori 140
Ōta Kazumi 136
Ozawa Ichirō: and 1983 Lower House election 84; and 1990 Lower House election 76, 203; and 1993 Lower House election 61, 78, 85–86; and 1996 Lower House election 89, 131; and 1998 Upper House election 89; and 2000 Lower house election 90; and 2004 Upper House election 68; and 2005 Lower House election 68, 133; and 2007 Upper House election 16, 68, 133, 135, 136, 207, 287; and 2009 Lower House election 16–17, 65, 67, 68–69, 72, 75, 76, 95, 109–10, 148, 155, 206, 207, 287; and 2010 Upper House election 69, 71, 110, 130, 138, 146, 149, 150, 151, 153, 155, 160, 164, 177, 206, 287; and 2012 Lower House election 276–81, 291, 292; and 2013 Upper House election 279–81, 282, 292; and agricultural policy 132–34, 147–48, 156–57, 162–63; *Blueprint for a New Japan* 12–13, 14, 18, 24, 26, 28, 35, 41, 43, 46, 47, 62, 70, 129, 132, 135, 137, 139, 143, 144, 151, 163, 179, 202, 209, 291; and bureaucracy 2, 8, 13, 14, 28–35, 36, 47, 134, 140–41, 159, 176, 195, 254, 279, 291; and construction companies 3, 77–79, 84–109, 113, 133, 142, 148, 157–58, 164, 199–202, 209, 286, 289; and

consumption tax 41–43, 66, 69, 131–32, 156, 159, 160–62, 164, 165, 166, 188, 230, 251, 253–55, 257, 262, 270–78, 279; and decentralisation 8, 38–40, 158, 162, 274; and Democratic Party of Japan (DPJ) 10, 12, 16–17, 22–23, 25, 28, 31–35, 39, 44–45, 63, 65–66, 67–75,76, 92, 95–97, 100, 106, 109–11, 112, 129, 130, 132, 133, 134, 135–44; 144–66, 174–81, 184–85, 191, 193–94, 204–5, 206–8, 220–62, 270–76, 277, 280, 281, 282–83, 287–93; and economic policy 2, 8, 40–45, 129–66; and election finances 68–69, 70–72, 76–79; and election manifestos 29, 38, 40, 43, 45, 132, 133, 134; 2007 DPJ manifesto: 20, 21, 25, 36, 44, 130, 132, 133–34, 136, 151–53; 2009 DPJ manifesto: 21, 25, 28, 31, 39, 43, 45, 66, 84, 130, 134, 138, 145, 151–53, 155, 158, 185, 232, 235, 241–42, 253, 258, 288; and electoral reform 2, 5, 13, 14, 17–23, 24, 26, 47–48, 61, 62, 70–71, 111–12, 193, 282; enigma of 3–4, 192–96, 209–10, 287–88; and factions 3, 6, 13, 67–75, 112, 197–99, 202–3, 287, 288–89; and Kan administration 220–46, 251, 255, 259–61, 271–72, 288, 290–91; and Liberal Democratic Party (LDP) 2, 12, 13–17, 18, 20–21, 23, 29, 35–36, 43, 47–48, 58–66, 77, 78, 79–81, 82, 8785, 87, 88, 89, 109, 112, 129, 130, 133, 134, 134, 136, 146, 147, 148, 149, 151–54, 156, 159, 164, 176, 177, 178, 181, 182, 184, 185, 188, 191, 192, 195, 201, 204, 207, 208–9, 221, 223–24, 226, 229, 230, 236, 271, 272, 276, 277, 280, 288, 289; and Liberal Party (LP) (*Jiyūtō*) 21, 26, 28, 29, 35, 41, 43, 45, 47–48, 63–65, 68, 72, 79–83, 90, 96, 100, 107, 112, 129, 133, 163, 180, 185–88, 187, 188, 190, 191, 232, 237, 274, 275, 278, 281; and money politics 3, 6, 13, 23–25, 75–111, 112–13, 203–5, 209, 226, 227, 236, 274, 289, 293; and neo-liberalism 2, 43–45, 129, 130, 135–36, 156, 163, 164; and New Frontier Party (NFP) (*Shinshintō*) 21–22, 24, 28, 29–30, 35, 38, 41, 42, 43, 63–65, 79–80, 81, 82–83, 87, 89, 91, 96, 107, 112, 131, 184, 186–88, 189, 190–91, 195, 204, 252, 275; and new policies and new politics 1, 3–4, 5–10, 12–48, 287, 290–91, 293; and Noda administration 248–62, 270–71, 272, 275–76, 288, 290–91; and nuclear policy 258, 271–72, 274–79, 281; and old politics 1, 3–4, 5–10, 58–114, 210, 283, 287–91; Ozawa faction 67–75, 197–99, 202–8, 221–48, 251–59, 261, 289, 293; *Ozawashugi* 13, 15, 19, 20, 28, 31, 33, 44, 46, 47, 137, 184; and party subsidies 2, 6, 13–14, 24, 79–84, 109, 206–7, 237, 273–74; and party system 2, 5, 6, 13–26, 62–70, 195, 288; and People's Life First (PLF) (*Kokumin no Seikatsu ga Daiichi*) 66, 112, 271–76, 277, 291; and People's Life Party (PLP) (*Seikatsu no Tō*) 66, 112, 279–83; and pensions 41, 132, 136, 137, 152, 155, 156, 161; personality 64, 185–88, 191; and political leadership 3, 7, 13, 25–26, 27–28, 47, 188–91, 195, 197–99, 207–8, 221–24; prosecution of 103–9, 111, 113, 205, 222–23, 226–28, 231–32, 238, 248, 250, 255–56, 262, 282; and Public Prosecutors Office (PPO) 93, 96–98, 101–3, 106, 108, 113; and public works 146–50, 151, 156–57, 164, 199–202, 209, 279, 286; and regime change 13, 14–17, 26, 185, 208, 288–89; and relation of party and cabinet 27–29, 32, 137–44, 174–78, 288, 291; and Renewal Party (RP) 16, 35, 61, 63–64, 80, 81, 86, 88, 96, 132, 139, 149, 182, 186, 187, 189, 201, 204, 274, 278; role in Hatoyama administration 137–55, 165, 174–81, 174–81, 184–85, 193–95, 203, 204, 249; secretaries prosecuted 95–101, 104, 105–6, 205, 250; and Shinseiken 35, 37–38, 40, 66, 162, 252–55, 270, 272, 274; and social policy 2, 41, 45–47, 156; and Tomorrow Party of Japan (TPJ) (*Nihon Mirai no Tō*) 66, 276–79, 281, 282; and Trans-Pacific Strategic Economic Partnership (TPP) 45, 155, 162, 164, 225–26, 230, 244, 245–46, 251, 262, 271, 275, 279, 282; and *yakuza* 95; *see also* consumption tax etc.; Ozawa faction; and fund-raising 76–79, 84–95; money politics; and institutional reform 26–40; new policies; and international policy 14, 37, 46, 162–63;

Ozawa Saeki 17

Ozawa Sakihito 243, 244, 245

People's New Party (PNP) (*Kokumin Shintō*) 17, 151, 154, 225, 239, 253, 272
Political Funds Control law (PFCL) 25, 78, 79, 82, 95–96, 98, 100–109.
Public Prosecutors Office (PPO) 93, 95–103, 104–5, 106, 108

Recruit scandal 14, 60, 78, 101
Rengō *see* Japanese Trade Union Confederation

Sagawa Kyūbin scandal 58–61, 78, 101, 192
Satō Eisaku 175, 196, 203
Satō Taisuke 83
Sekine Toshinobu 280–81
Sengoku Yoshito 150, 166, 175, 194, 220, 221, 227, 230, 242, 245, 249
Shii Kazuo 95
Social Democratic Party (SDP) (*Shamintō*) 17, 143, 150, 151, 223, 272, 273, 276
Sōka Gakkai 63, 78, 154, 188, 189, 190
Special Investigation Department (SID) 93, 98; *see also* Public Prosecutors Office (PPO)
Suga Yoshihide 280
Sugiyama Toshiyuki 175
Sun Party (SP) (*Taiyōtō*) 80
Sunrise Party of Japan (*Tachiagare Nippon*) 148, 238, 255
Suzuki Katsumasa 74, 224, 245, 249, 253, 273, 281
Suzuki Muneo 252, 273

Takagi Tsuyoshi 155
Takahashi Yoshinobu 85, 86, 88, 90, 91, 97, 101, 142, 164–65, 185, 200
Takashima Yoshimitsu 177
Takemura Masayoshi 41, 186
Takeshita Noboru 14, 41, 44, 46, 60, 101, 131, 179, 203; Takeshita faction (*Keiseikai*) 15, 17, 58–59, 61, 64, 78, 168, 178, 181, 182, 185–86, 187, 192, 199, 203–4
Tamura Kōtarō 146
Tanaka Kakuei 3, 4, 13, 15, 46, 60, 101, 111, 175, 182, 187, 194, 196–209, 289, 293; Tanaka faction 15, 16, 111, 168, 196–99, 202–3, 205–8
Tanaka Makiko 34, 72, 73, 241
Tanaka Naoki 72, 250
Tanigaki Sadakazu 139, 177, 236, 255, 257, 273
Tasso Takuya 89, 90
Tarutoko Shinji 73, 224, 243, 247
Tax Cuts Japan Party (*Genzei Nippon*) 232, 272
Toyoda Juntarō 232
Tsuge Yoshifumi 74
Tsutsui Nobutaka 225

Ubukata Yukio 177
Uchiyama Akira 251
Unity Party (*Yui no Tō*) 282
Uno Sōsuke 204

Watanabe Hideo 187
Watanabe Hiroyasu 78
Watanabe Kensuke 189, 192
Watanabe Kisaburō 200
Watanabe Kōichirō 251
Watanabe Kōzō 139, 150, 231, 259
Watanabe Michio 59, 60
Watanabe Yoshimi 178, 244, 276, 286
Weber, Max 195

Xi Jinping 144

Yamada Masahiko 153, 156, 225, 276, 278, 281
Yamagishi Akira 16
Yamaguchi Toshio 192
Yamahana Sadao 16
Yamaoka Kenji 83, 229, 235, 249, 250, 253, 273, 278, 280, 281
Yamasaki Taku 191
Yokokume Katsuhito 239, 241
Yokomichi Takahiro 74
Yonezawa Takashi 24, 83
Yosano Kaoru 148
Your Party (YP) (*Minna no Tō*) 178, 228, 243–44, 275, 276, 286
Yoshida Shigeru 47